INTERNATIONAL
HANDBOOK
OF
EDUCATIONAL REFORM

INTERNATIONAL
HANDBOOK
OF
EDUCATIONAL REFORM

Edited by
Peter W. Cookson, Jr.,
Alan R. Sadovnik,
and Susan F. Semel

GREENWOOD PRESS
New York • Westport, Connecticut • London

Library of Congress Cataloging-in-Publication Data

International handbook of educational reform / edited by Peter W.
   Cookson, Jr., Alan R. Sadovnik, and Susan F. Semel.
      p. cm.
   Includes bibliographical references and index.
   ISBN 0–313–27277–8 (alk. paper)
      1. Educational change—Case studies.   I. Cookson, Peter W.
   II. Sadovnik, Alan R.   III. Semel, Susan F.
   LA135.I58   1992
   370—dc20   91–30586

British Library Cataloguing in Publication Data is available.

Library of Congress Catalog Card Number: 91–30586
ISBN: 0–313–27277–8

First published in 1992

Greenwood Press, 88 Post Road West, Westport, CT 06881
An imprint of Greenwood Publishing Group, Inc.

Printed in the United States of America

The paper used in this book complies with the
Permanent Paper Standard issued by the National
Information Standards Organization (Z39.48–1984).

10 9 8 7 6 5 4 3 2 1

CONTENTS

PREFACE

International educational reform is an important topic. During the 1980s there were significant educational reform movements in a number of countries. Some of these movements resulted in educational change, others did not. The purpose of this handbook is to provide an overview of some of these reforms and changes in twenty-seven countries. It is not meant to be exhaustive as one handbook cannot cover all of the important countries and reforms. It is, however, meant to be representative, as we attempted to select countries from different geographic regions, with different levels of development, and with different political and economic systems.

There are countries that have been omitted that we would have liked to include. Space limitations made this impossible. Although we ordinarily would not mention a particular chapter that is omitted, there is one whose absence leaves us properly open to criticism and therefore we must mention it. Part III originally was supposed to include chapters on race, class, and gender. The chapter on race, however, was not completed, leaving the section on comparative issues in stratification somewhat incomplete. We believe strongly that inequalities based on race are critical and regret the absence of such a chapter. We apologize in advance for its omission and refer readers to the appropriate sections of many chapters for separate discussions of race.

This handbook illustrates the complexity of international educational reform and the significant educational movements and reforms of the past decade. Time, however, does not stand still for scholarship and historical events have caught up with and, in some instances, passed the discussions in the book. This is especially true in Eastern Europe, the Soviet Union, and South Africa, where monumental political upheavals and changes are occurring as this book goes to press. Hopefully, we will be able to publish a second edition, which will update necessary sections of the book. Nonetheless, we believe the handbook provides an outstanding resource for students and scholars of educational reform.

ACKNOWLEDGMENTS

An international handbook is an immense undertaking. This volume could not have been completed if it were not for the assistance of a number of colleagues and support staff.

This handbook grew out of a symposium on International Educational Reform presented at the American Educational Research Association Annual Meeting, in San Francisco, March 1989. The presenters were Peter W. Cookson, Jr., Denis Lawton, Alan R. Sadovnik, Susan F. Semel, and James J. Shields. The symposium generated a great deal of discussion and interest and, immediately following the meetings, Greenwood Press asked the three of us to edit this handbook.

The selection of authors for an international handbook is a difficult and important process. Philip Altbach, Mark Ginsburg, Ivor Goodson, Sidney Grant, Andreas Kazamias, Gail Kelly, and Denis Lawton provided assistance in the selection of authors for the handbook and gave generously of their time and expertise in putting us in touch with authors. Fortuitously, the theme of the Comparative and International Education Society Annual Meeting in Anaheim, March 1990, was International Education Reform. At this meeting we were able to hear a number of papers that fit nicely into the handbook and they appear here in revised form. The Comparative and International Education Society has provided an important forum for our work and for discussions with scholars from around the world about educational reform.

A number of colleagues provided valuable insights about drafts of chapters or papers presented at the American Education Research Association, Comparative and International Education Society, and the American Sociological Association. These include William Cummings, Kevin Dougherty, Barbara Falsey, Kumiko Fujimura-Fanselow, John Meyer, Francisco Ramirez, James J. Shields, and Geoffrey Walford.

We would like to thank all of the contributing authors who responded quickly
to our telephone calls, faxes, and letters for information and additions. Without
their timely responses, this book would not have met the deadlines.

The editorial team at Greenwood Press provided professional assistance and
guidance throughout. George Butler, the acquisitions editor, made valuable comments on the entire manuscript and thoughtful editorial advice. Penny Sippel,
the production editor, provided thoughtful comments and helped us to complete
the book within the time schedule.

Last, but certainly not least, we received exceptional secretarial and research
support from a number of people at Adelphi University. Elizabeth Hendry and
Janet Murphy provided outstanding secretarial support. Elizabeth Hendry also
provided essential computer support. Her knowledge of word processing and
how to convert discs into WordPerfect was vital to the completion of this book.
The Faculty Computer Lab and the following: Martha Meyer, Brian Helman,
and Danielle Daum, at Adelphi University provided technical assistance. Linda
Bunting, a graduate assistant in 1989–1990, provided assistance in research and
word processing. Eva Roca provided invaluable assistance on the chapters on
Latin American Countries. Carla Hernandez, a graduate assistant in 1990–1992,
was the glue that held this project together. She provided research, editorial,
proofreading and word processing assistance, and helped maintain a sense of
order amidst what often seemed like chaos. She worked calmly under the pressure
of deadlines and prepared the tables, endnotes, and reference sections for the
final manuscript, which often meant reformatting discs into WordPerfect. Linda
DeVries, a graduate assistant in 1991–1992, also provided editorial support.

During the completion of this handbook, Gail Kelly died. She was a leader
in the field of comparative and international education and feminist scholarship.
Her chapter on gender and higher education in this volume combines her long
interest in both areas and is an important contribution to understanding gender
inequality in an international context. We dedicated this book to her memory
and hope it contributes to the field, comparative and international education,
that she did so much to nurture and help develop.

INTERNATIONAL
HANDBOOK
OF
EDUCATIONAL REFORM

1

INTRODUCTION

Peter W. Cookson, Jr., Alan R. Sadovnik, and Susan F. Semel

The 1980s were years of intense international debate about the goals and structures of educational systems. During this period a series of reform efforts were made in a number of countries. The purpose of this handbook is to provide a sociological, historical, political, philosophical, economic, and international context for understanding these reform efforts and to present a comparative analysis of both the ''rhetoric'' of reform and the substantive changes in education. Aside from the last two chapters which deal with issues of inequality, each chapter in this handbook focuses on one country and explores a number of common themes. These themes include the relationship between level of economic development and educational reform, the historical context of educational reform, educational expansion, literacy movements, achievement levels, curriculum reform, pedagogic reform, equity and excellence, minority groups and women, the relationship between public and private education, the role of the state, and effective school programs.

The countries included in this handbook are meant to be representative, not definitive of patterns of educational reform. We adopted two basic strategies in selecting countries to be included. Our first criterion was to select countries that represented educational reform globally. The educational reforms in these countries are significant in their own right and give us a sense of educational reform movements throughout the world. Our second criterion was to include countries that were significant in terms of either population or power (usually both). We felt that a handbook that did not include these countries would be deficient in terms of its usefulness to scholars and the public at large. As the reader will see, we have listed these countries alphabetically, rather than by region or by political or economic orientation. After a great deal of thought, we recognized that alphabetization precluded value judgments about regionality, politics, and economics.

The authors of these chapters are truly international. In many cases, we have asked scholars in individual countries to write chapters about the reform movements within their national boundaries. In other cases, we have asked recognized international authorities to write about educational reform in a particular country of their expertise. Many of the authors in the handbook are recognized comparativists, and others are beginning their careers. We feel that this mixture has given the work a sense of vitality as well as scholarship. We have also included a special section entitled "Comparative Issues in Stratification." We believe that this section is rather unique and provides the reader with critical insights on how the issues of race, caste, class, and gender shape educational reform and, in turn, are shaped by educational reform movements.

Because this volume is a handbook and a resource for scholars, policymakers, and the public, we have not attempted to synthesize these chapters into an introductory essay. This would be a prodigious task of questionable value. However, this introduction does include a few thoughts about the nature of international educational reform and the intellectual and policy challenges that various reforms present. We should also mention that the very word "reform" is not neutral. What do we mean by reform, especially in the context of different societies and cultures? Are all educational changes progressive, or are some changes, in fact, retrogressive? Who decides whether or not a reform represents progress? In the section below, we reflect on these issues and on some of the methodological issues that confront comparativists when they examine international educational reform.

INTERNATIONAL EDUCATIONAL REFORM:
COMPLEXITIES, PERCEPTIONS, AND REALITIES

In the epilogue to J. B. Bury's (1955[1932]:351), *The Idea of Progress*, the author discusses the "illusion of finality." By this he means that human beings seem to have a strong inclination to imagine a time and a place when history will stand still. Utopian thought pervades much of our thinking about this life and the next. Those of us who take an interest in educational reform from a historical point of view know that there is no finality and that all reform movements are historically contextualized and grow out of major sociological, political, intellectual, and economic currents. In a world that is increasingly interdependent, these currents have a way of sweeping over national boundaries. It is not by chance that educational reform has been at the forefront of national agendas in the last decade. The pace of technological, political, and economic change has been so rapid that we can speak with some certainty of a new era, sometimes referred to as postindustrial society. Whether or not this label completely or accurately captures all the important changes that are taking place in the world today, it does give us a sense of how rapidly events are moving throughout the world.

Explaining educational reform is complex because schools are embedded in society and are themselves complex forms of social interaction. Sociologist Margaret S. Archer (1979:3) has written, "to understand the nature of education at any time we need to know not only who won the struggle for control, but also how: not merely who lost, but also how badly they lost." Archer suggests that education can never be successfully treated as a laboratory experiment. Analytically, we may ask: Who gets it? What happens to them during it? Where do they go after it? Thus, broadly speaking, education can be viewed in terms of inputs, processes, and outputs. Questions about educational reform are, by their nature, resistant to simple answers. According to Archer (1979:1–2), these questions "embrace problems about educational opportunity, selection and discrimination, about the management and transmission of knowledge and values, and about social placement, stratification and mobility." Reform issues ask us to reflect on the effects of society upon education and on the consequences of education for society.

Today, as different nations grapple with the many changes that confront them, they often look to education as a panacea for their problems. But education, in and of itself, cannot resolve cultural and structural contradictions that give rise to social tension and dislocation. Many thoughtful observers recognize that the "crisis in world education" seems to be chronic and that some may have lost their sense of idealism concerning the efficacy of education to solve major social problems. Philip H. Coombs (1985:13–14) has written that "The aura of euphoria that had surrounded all things educational in the earlier Age of Innocence had by now been transmuted into a Crisis of Confidence." Coombs suggests that education alone cannot reform society. We also know, however, that, without educational reform, most societies will flounder, especially if they wish to participate in the world market. Describing and analyzing the relationship between the world market and national educational systems, however, is far from simple.

It is evident that when one talks about educational reform, the cultural, religious, historical, political, and economic context of each country must be taken into consideration. Moreover, these same factors can be operating simultaneously and divergently within each region of each country, as well as within each town and city. The micro-politics of competing cultures and values remind us that sweeping generalities can mask a great deal of variation.

Yet, there is a need to develop an embracing analytic framework for understanding the huge educational changes that are taking place globally because, without such a framework, we can make little sense of what educational change means in terms of policy and classroom life. While this is an enormous topic, we would like to touch on two areas of analytic concern: one substantive and one methodological. Our first concern is to identify the underlying issues driving educational reform during the 1980s and into the 1990s. We take as our unit of analysis the world system. Following Charles C. Ragin's (1987) distinction between observational units and explanatory units, we recognize that nation-states are still basic units of observation, but we suggest that the transnational linkages between states represent the explanatory units of analysis. This observation leads us to the methodological problem of how to study educational reform movements in the context of the larger social changes which have made our globe increasingly interlinked, interactive, vulnerable, and volatile. Do we rely on the traditional national case study approach, or do we develop sophisticated types of variable analyses that will allow us to compare change within the context of a world system? Following Emile Durkheim's formulation that society precedes education, we suggest that the appropriate analysis for the study of international educational reform should begin at the societal level Not only is education embedded in society and culture, but it also includes the family, youth organizations, mass media, peer groups, sport, tourism, cultural institutions, films, theaters, museums, and medical and social services. Analyses of educational reforms that overlook the many informal educative experiences to which individuals and groups are exposed are likely to overemphasize the importance of formal pedagogy.

POSTEDUCATIONAL EXPANSION REALITY SHOCK

In this context we must wonder, has education failed to achieve its goals, or have we expected too much from education? Clearly, the educational sector in virtually every country has expanded enormously. The works of Ramirez and Boli-Bennett (1982) and others have amply demonstrated the expansion of education, particularly in the post–World War II period. A number of studies examine the purposes and motivations of those who have promoted education as the primary mechanism for economic and political development. In reviewing the literature in this area, we see that there are at least four major theories about educational expansion and reform. The *evolutionary or neo-evolutionary theory* of educational reform emphasizes the linear evolution of society and suggests that somehow educational reform and social progress are naturally and positively correlated. *Modernization theory* begins with the postulate that modern societies are rational and that education is a major force in creating what has been called the export society. This theory suggests that change and reform should lead to high student participation rates and a standard curriculum that will meet the needs of developing societies. *Dependency theory* hypothesizes that educational expansion and reform are, in fact, a form of neocolonialism that allows core countries to remain culturally and economically dominant over periphery countries, without having to resort to overt military occupation. The latent function of educational reform is to create a "lumpenbourgeoisie" that will represent the interests of the core countries in the periphery countries. The *Marxist theory* on international educational change is that reform movements that originate with the capitalist class will not liberate subordinate groups. True educational reform, from a Marxist perspective, must aim at creating critical consciousness and help to mobilize the subordinate classes to bring about structural changes.

Reviewing these four major theoretical explanations of educational expansion and reform, we sense that, while each of these theories can explain elements of the reform movements after World War II, none of them offers us a satisfactory explanation of why educational expansion has generated a world crisis in education. It is still not entirely clear that the link between education and economic development, political socialization and participation in the world system, is linear or unidirectional. The educational crises of the 1980s, whether perceived or real, arose, in our opinion, not so much because education had failed to produce the desired outcomes, but because the educational tail cannot wag the social dog. Wherever we look, we see policymakers arguing that educational reform will revitalize their economy and society. This argument, we believe, while reassuring in its message, has little evidence to support it. We suggest that an examination of the relationship between the state and the individual is a good place to begin in explaining international educational reform movements.

Ramirez and Boli-Bennett (1982) have argued that educational institutionalization and the expansion of education can be explained by the dialectic between the ideologies of state expansion and individualism. The synthesis, if you will, of this dialectic is the growth of citizenship. Thus, schools are thought to be places where individuals become citizens. Continuing with this line of reasoning, we might hypothesize that, as long as the world was divided into nation-states, the concept of national citizenship was a unifying ideology that justified educational expansion. Years of education has become a proximate measure of a nation-state's capacity to create loyal citizens. The content of that educational experience was of secondary importance. Collins' (1979) concept of the credential society might well be applied to the global society. Thus, education has become a form of negotiable, credentialized cultural capital that is only tangentially related to actual economic development. Educational cultural capital has gained favor in the international status marketplace and has allowed personnel transfers from core countries to periphery countries and vice versa.

What may have occurred in the 1980s, we hypothesize, is that the international value of educational credentials may have been deflated in terms of their comparative social and cultural worth. That is, the international exchange rate for educational credentials declined, relative to their previous worth. This occurred for two reasons. First, the fact that education is so weakly linked to outcomes undermines the ideology that the greater the educational attainment, the higher the productivity. Second, as more and more people attend school, the cultural capital value of primary and secondary schooling declines. In order to remain competitive at the level of cultural capital acquisition, more groups attempt to achieve even higher levels of education. This inflated educational marketplace leads to a crisis of credentialism. Moreover, because the state has invested so much in creating the credential scramble, a crisis in credentialism becomes a crisis in citizenship. Thus, throughout the 1980s, we saw state after state attempting to reassert its control over the credentializing process. We hypothesize that a major motivation for educational reform may have less to do with international competition than with the maintenance of social relationships within each country and within the world system.

This crisis in citizenship has been accelerated by a massive transformation in the world economic system. To say that there has been a great growth in the service sector of the world economy is something of an understatement. What the new technologies have done is transform not only the kinds of businesses that are created and maintained, but also the kinds of products that are consumed. The explosion of information on a worldwide basis has made the nineteenth-century concept of the nation-state increasingly anachronistic.

As the nation-state has, in a sense, become weakened within the world system, the multinational corporation has grown stronger. As the multinationals have penetrated the world economy, they have brought with them an ideology of consumership that competes with the ideology of citizenship. Becoming a world-class consumer may have more salience in individuals' lives than loyal citizenship. Thus, educational systems controlled by the nation-state become increasingly obsolete. The secular belief in education that swept the globe after World War II may have run its course. The total educational system may, in time, transform our concept of education and restructure how schools interface with other social institutions. We suggest that understanding educational reform in a world perspective might well begin with an analysis of societal changes and the linkages between these macro-changes and the educational sector.

For some time now, many scholars have been suggesting that the unit of analysis in comparative education ought to be the world system rather than the nation-state. While we are in sympathy with much of this line of reasoning, we believe that case study methods are still important because they contextualize our understanding of the relationship between culture and education and keep us theoretically and empirically grounded. Case studies alone, however, make it difficult to establish causation in explaining educational reform movements. The issue of causation in comparative studies is one that has sparked a great deal of debate within the field (Ragin, 1987). This debate will not be settled quickly or easily, but we hope that the sophisticated case studies presented in this volume provide a basis for the discussion and illumination.

Clearly, these observations are meant to be suggestive and to stimulate thinking about the causes and consequences of educational reform movements. The strength of this handbook is that it allows readers the opportunity to compare reform movements among many different countries and, thus, utilize a truly comparative form of analysis. The chapters in this handbook represent a rich mine of knowledge that can be extremely useful to scholars and policymakers as they attempt to make sense out of the complexity of the real world of educational reform.

REFERENCES

Archer, Margaret S. 1979. *Social Origins of Educational Systems*. London: Sage Publications.

Bury, J. D. 1955 [1932]. *The Idea of Progress: An Inquiry into Its Growth and Origin*. New York: Dover.

Collins, Randall. 1979. *The Credential Society*. New York: Academic Press.

Coombs, Philip H. 1985. *The World Crisis in Education: The View from the Eighties*. New York: Oxford University Press.

Ragin, Charles C. 1987. *The Comparative Method: Moving Beyond Qualitative and Quantitative Strategies*. Berkeley: University of California Press.

Ramirez, Francisco O., and John Boli-Bennett. 1982. "Global Patterns of Educational Institutionalization." In *Comparative Education*, ed. P. G. Altbach, R. F. Arnove, and G. P. Kelly. New York: Macmillan, pp. 15–36.

Part I

Educational Reform in the 1980s: National Case Studies

2

ARGENTINA

Ana Muñoz-Sandoval

Argentina has been ruled for long periods by de facto governments. In the past fifty years, de facto governments have spent more time in power than have democratic governments. The myriad of adjustments to unpredictable political changes, caused by de facto governments, affects not only the economy but also the stability of the social structure. Some of those changes are discussed here to the extent that they affect the educational realm.

Political changes have brought periods of success, failure, contradiction, and rapid change that often conflict with existing educational philosophy and practice. For example, in the last two decades, Argentina has become economically depressed, which has had pronounced effects on the current educational system. A new monetary system has been implemented in an attempt to salvage the decaying economy. Thus far, this move has resulted in little improvement. Furthermore, major funds were diverted to finance the recent war with England, a war that resulted in a defeat for Argentina. Prior to this short war, there were violations of human rights that added to the psychological turmoil from which the country is slowly recovering under a new democratic government. All these factors have taken a toll on Argentinian education. The impact of these forces will not be clear for decades to come.

This chapter focuses on the interrelated factors affecting Argentinian education. As in other countries, the impact of these factors is a complex matter since education, in turn, affects society as a whole. Table 2.1 presents a historical summary of the major reforms, proponents, and events that have impacted Argentinian education since 1796.

This overview discusses topics that not only are controversial but also are based on conflicting literature, making analysis difficult. All the information

Table 2.1
Argentina: Educational Historical Perspective

Successful School Reforms Laws\Acts	School Reforms That Were Not Successful	Other Proponents\Events That Influenced The Education Field
1796. "Manifiesto de la casa de Tucumán."		1796. Manuel Belgrano elitist view of education.
1853. Argentinian Constitution.		
		1862.Bartolomé Mitre\President
1868-1874. Domingo Faustino Sarmiento. President and Educator.		1862-1886. Mitre\Avellaneda, higher education program.
a) education for all		1878. Law 934. Free, public,
b) preparation for work		and private education.
c) technological education		1878. Nicolas Avellaneda\Pres.
		School census. 1/3 of
1882. "Primer Congreso Pedagógico."		437 schools were private.
		1880.Roca & Alsina\Land Grants
1884. Law 1420.		Roca\President "Administration
Division of Church & State Uniformity in curriculum,		and Peace."
and also Law 1597, which regulates the university.		1883. 94% of the students claimed to be of Argentinian origin.(Socialization process)
1890. Positivistic Period Large funds allocated for education.		1893. Victor Mercante writes La crisis de la pubertad.
	1916* Carlos Saavedra Lamas Proposed a new school level.	Interest in the preadolescent period and the psychological development.
	1918* Cordoba Reform. Political, social and educational changes.	1916/1922-1928/1930. Irygoyen. Large increment of education- al all levels. The literacy rate went from 20% to 4%.
	1922* Middle class look for reforms in the	
1945-1955. Juan Domingo Perón\President.	political changes.	
Build many schools for vocationaonal training.	1956** Low school budget.	
1947. Law 10.047, Provisi-ons for private education.	1968-1983** Dark period in education. Started	
1983-1989. Raúl Alfonsín\ President. Eliminated	new school buildings.	
entrance exams to make the system more meritocratic.		
1988."Congreso Pedagógico"		

* Cirigliano sees these as education failures.   ** Not a school reform.

reviewed for this chapter was available in Spanish. Certain meaning is always lost in a translation, and even the best translation has possibilities for further interpretation.

EDUCATION IN ARGENTINA FROM 1800 TO 1960

Argentina gained independence from Spain in 1810. Even before the earliest days of freedom, the people had a sense of national identity that influenced the first education proclamation. The Manifiesto de la casa de Tucumán was initiated fourteen years before the Declaration of Independence of 1810. One of the important issues proclaimed in this manifesto was that education would be free from the Spaniards' influence for all generations to come. To some extent, this proclamation was in protest to the educational plans promoted by the Spaniards, of whom one representative was Manuel Belgrano, prior to the 1796 manifesto. In spite of his elitist view of education, Manuel Begrano, a spokesman of what the Spaniards represented, went on to become one of the leaders of this new nation.

The Argentinian Constitution was amended in 1853 and provided a solid foundation for the educational system. Among its many provisions, the Constitution stated that education would be free and that each of the provinces would be responsible for providing education for their population (Braslavsky, 1989: 59). Because of the economic wealth of the time, the government also provided adequate financial allocations for the field of education. It is at this point in history that the country established its roots of prosperity with a constitutional foundation that has served for over a hundred years.

Many individuals helped establish the educational policies that even today continue to serve as the foundation for school reforms. One of these visionaries, exemplary for his dedication and political influence, was Domingo Faustino Sarmiento. Today, he is known as the Father of Argentinian Education because of his awareness of the need for school reforms. This concern began when he was a young school teacher and increased while he was a governor in the province of San Juan. In 1849, while in political exile in Chile, he wrote *Educación Popular*, a book that inspired education not only in Argentina, but in most of Latin America as well. For the visionary Sarmiento, education had to be universal, free, and available for all, regardless of beliefs, religion, or ethnic background. He espoused these issues two years preceding his 1862 presidential term.

In order to train teachers for the educational system, Sarmiento brought American educators into Argentina. To improve the way of life in this foundling nation, he encouraged European immigration. Settlement by immigrants, according to Sarmiento, was the only way to eradicate the vast country's desolation. Over a quarter million immigrants entered Argentinian soil during his presidential term, bringing with them a vast array of diverse ideas. This large immigrant population had considerable influence on the existing population of less than 2 million. The Father of Education believed that bringing Europeans would make the nation more prosperous and that it would benefit from the wide array of ideas. Sarmiento improved education in general, something that will be ingrained forever in Argentinian society.

Sarmiento saw teaching as an inspiration for the future, and he chose women for this ennobling task, an occupation that has remained a low-paying job. However, over a hundred years ago, women had few opportunities for professional employment. These educational improvements, from the education of teachers to universal education for all (see Table 2.1), were achieved during his two presidential terms, and others were implemented after his second term.

Not all educational changes began during Sarmiento's presidential terms. In fact, it was during the term of Sarmiento's predecessor, Bartolome Mitre, that the universal education movement was introduced in Argentina. Mitre was pressured by the Argentinian people to establish a form of education that would address the needs of the population. In speeches after his presidential term ended, Mitre gave evidence of his elitist views: he admitted that his motivation for making education more widely available was solely the result of societal pressures. Without this public pressure, then, we could assume that education before Sarmiento would have continued to be offered to a small minority, maintaining the status quo. Sarmiento later united with President Avellaneda to create a model for the university level. This model has been the basis for tertiary education, even when it has served only a small minority, and it was provided for those who were from the upper echelons of society.

Less than two decades later, Sarmiento's goal of universal education was becoming a reality, for the country was now educating larger numbers of students regardless of ethnic background. Furthermore, all the newly arrived immigrants were also required to attend school. Unfortunately, schoolchildren, regardless of where they were born, claimed nationality based on their parents' country of origin. Therefore, the school system soon had to serve a different function: to help unite a country formed by diverse enclaves of immigrants. An effort was made through the school system to encourage students to recognize a single national identity. This effort necessitated studies in the areas of language, history, and origin of this newly formed nation. The school thus served as a strong connection between language and nationality, as evidenced by the 1883 census in which 94 percent of the student body now claimed its nationality to be Argentinean, demonstrating the school's potential as a socializing power. This socialization program extended to the teachers as well. Teacher training was implemented at this time, and the first priority was mainstreaming. Culture and language training were provided for most of the teachers who were from abroad, and the Spanish language for instruction was frequently minimal. Cultural identity was an important goal to be accomplished by all those participating in the realm of education.

By the time the Industrial Revolution was felt in Argentina, the trend of educational pragmatism was in full force in the industrialized nation. It is due to this influence that the Argentinian society found itself in need of educational reform; the educational system had to be adjusted to the new more practical demands of the time. Around this time, the universities, having failed to address the need for training in technology, were closed in order to revise their curricula. Training in the field of technology was necessary to compete with other countries that were already active in the Industrial Revolution. The Industrial Revolution itself and the closing of the universities did not cause a detrimental economic impact, for the country continued to have an economy based on agricultural export. Because of the economic affluence of the time, the education model continued to be conservative.

Some political leaders of the time were opposed to the idea of free universal education. Some strongly argued that education should not be the obligation of the state; moreover, they stated, it should not be left completely to outsiders or to the few in power, and it should be provided mainly by the family. The prime argument was that if responsibilities were relegated to the state in the future, the people would expect to receive even more. Part of this reasoning included the idea that taking money from some and providing services for others was not just.

Because of the rapidly growing number of schools, a school census was taken in 1878; it revealed that the country had 437 schools, one-third of which were private Catholic schools. This large number of private schools shows the great influence of the Catholic Church in Argentina, a stronghold that continues to the present day, in spite of reforms that clearly have addressed the separation of church and state.

Another trend toward a more pragmatic approach to education was given impetus by certain pressures in the government. Under Nicolas Avellaneda, Law 934 was passed in 1878, making three types of education available: (1) free, (2) public, and (3) private. Even though universal education had already been established, this new law provided wider choices for education. It was a great step forward in educational attainment, since up to this period 80 percent of potential students either had never attended an educational system, having learned the basics at home, or, because of economic necessities had never completed their education. This large number of nonparticipating students was far from Sarmiento's dream of universal education.

Another proponent of education who contributed to educational reform was President Julio Roca. He held office for two six-year terms starting in 1880, and was therefore in power long enough to be able to make major educational goals a reality. Under Roca, the visionaries of the time, Sarmiento, Urquiza, and Avellaneda, among others, saw education as the most indispensable tool for creating and developing the state. In their opinion, to become a united nation the country needed to achieve cultural uniformity and that could be attained by widespread education which would influence politics, economics, and culture. Their quest for their educational goals continued, and in 1882 the same group joined efforts with others in developing plans for two important educational events: El Congreso Pedagógico (the Pedagogical Congress), and El Consejo Nacional de Educación (the National Council for Education). The Pedagogical

Congress and the promulgation of provincial educational laws were the two most important factors in designing an institutional model for public education that was accepted by the people (Braslavsky and Krawczyk, 1988: 10). In the Pedagogical Congress, not only the most distinguished Argentinian educators gathered to plan the future of education, but also educators from Brazil, Paraguay, Uruguay, Costa Rica, El Salvador, Nicaragua, and the United States. The goal was to expand and improve the educational system while maintaining a level of quality, in order to make the country prosperous within a democratic framework (Bravo 1984: 53). Once again, this visionary pedagogical movement was conceived with the idea that education was a necessity for national unity and public participation, and the concern was to make the country into a great nation economically, politically and culturally—a country that would be able to compete with the other nations of the world. The Pedagogical Congress also established that the efficient functioning of the school had to be conducted by professionals trained by the "normal" schools (Braslavsky and Krawczyk, 1988: 12), and that religious teaching had to be delivered outside the classroom (which became a law two years later as part of educational Law 1420).

Law 1420, enacted in 1884, was Argentina's most successful reform in the field of education. It made primary education obligatory and free (organized by grades and nonreligious) to all those between the ages of six and fourteen. It is the only law at the national level that complements the constitutional principles. Law 1420 also established the separation of church and state. The educational visionaries who participated in these influential decisions introduced a separate law for the university level: Law 1597 was to regulate higher education.

During President Roca's successful term, his political views on "Administration and Peace" extended to the educational arena. Educator and researcher Gustavo Cirigliano has commented that during Roca's presidential term the administrative structure of education became established but Roca failed to outline a law for secondary education. This omission continues to the present (Cirigliano 1964: 15). Rights from land grants influenced society even today, for these grants created an elite class of landowners who continue to have astronghold on the economy.

During the positivist era, 1890–1920, efforts were made to follow John Dewey's educational philosophy of equalization and full human development. Pragmatism was in the air, and plans were developed to incorporate such programs into the curricula. Another positive factor that enabled changes to occur was the availability of funds. During this period Argentina spent over 16.4 percent of its budget on education. This was a large budget, perhaps one of the largest ever spent in Argentina, and it was influenced by a similar European trend of generous spending in the field of education.

The 1890–1920 period was a thriving educational period. Although at times ideological goals were not clearly spelled out, it was nevertheless a period of creative thought with implications for education. It was during this time, for example, that Victor Mercante wrote *La crisis de la pubertad* [The crisis of puberty] in which he proposed a more pragmatic form of education. According to his philosophy, the psychophysiological changes of preadolescence could be facilitated by a different type of education—one that involved creativity and activity. Mercante proposed practical training in the technical field to complement classroom instruction during the last two years of primary school, thus creating a new level of education. Experts of the time believed that this new level of education was necessary because puberty is not a period characterized by intellectual preoccupation. Moreover, a student's training had to be in an occupation that could have applications to the student's economic future. This philosophy showed that the development of the individual with some scientific knowledge was very much in the mind of these educational proponents. Carlos Saavedra Lamas, during his term as a cabinet minister, attempted to put Mercante's philosophy into practice, but this effort did not take root, even though the pilot projects were a success. Saavedra Lamas's project was proposed in order to offset the high dropout rate for students in the fourth grade, which reached a level of about 50 percent (Cirigliano, 1973: 81).

At this time, other philosophers wrote educational theories, but it is Mercante's work that would later influence and serve as the basis for the 1918 Cordoba Reform, a reform that became well known around the world. Some philosophers have compared Mercante's ideas to Law 1420, because of their avant garde nature. The difference between the two lies in the fact that the Cordoba Reform was promulgated for the university level, whereas the Saavedra Lamas project was directed toward the high school level. Similar projects to the one Saavedra Lamas proposed in 1916 have been suggested once more and were discussed in terms of educational changes during the 1960s and 1970s, and once again in 1988.

During the presidency of Hipolito Yrigoyen (1916–1922 and 1928–1939), formal education progressed even further. A wide range of educational programs, reforms, and construction of school buildings were made possible during Yrigoyen's years in office. During his terms enrollment doubled at the secondary and tertiary levels, and the illiteracy rate declined from 20 to 40 percent (Bagiani, 1990: 51). This was a significantly high literacy rate.[1] No other presidential period up to that date, or even up to now, could claim this successful rate of literacy. In addition, higher education was improved, becoming a more liberal system than the previous one. National expenditures in education increased, a trend that would be reversed with the de facto governments that followed Yrigoyen's. (Since Yrigoyen's overthrow, no other elected president has completed two terms in office.) It was during this period that Carlos Saavedra Lamas designed the project to add a new level of instruction in the last two years of primary school, which, as already mentioned, failed because Argentina's educational system continued to cater primarily to the needs of an agrarian society. Saavedra Lamas, as well as other educators, categorized the educational structure as nondemocratic, because the curriculum was based solely on the needs of those who would continue on to secondary and tertiary education.

The Law of 1922 was passed following the reforms of 1916 and 1918. It was at this time that the middle class began looking for changes in the political structure. Educator Cirigliano is very critical of these three major reforms, which he sees as failures (Cirigliano, 1964: 34). Even though the goals of the proposed reforms were sound, they failed in their implementation, moving the educational system backward. In spite of this implementation failure, impact from two reforms was felt; during 1900 and 1920, primary schools had the largest enrollment increase in the history of education in Argentina (Wiñar, 1974, found in Braslavsky and Krawczyk, 1988: 14). By 1931 more than seven out of ten children of school age were attending primary school.

Primary education again showed positive growth under Juan Domingo Perón (1946–1955). Under Perón's military regime, a pragmatic program was implemented, perhaps influenced by the strong opposition to the status quo. The participation of working-class members in the presidential cabinet, an uncommon occurrence in prior government, may have unleashed opposition to the status quo. This integration was extended to different sectors of the society, causing a ripple effect in education. From 1945 to 1955, Perón's military government gave new recognition to the needs of the lower class, a policy which, combined with the national wealth, resulted in an expansion in social services. Another positive expansion was in industry: Perón initiated school programs in which students spent half a day in class and half a day learning a trade or occupational skill in a factory. These factories, which needed labor, were often built in proximity to a school, and the majority of participants were members of the lower classes, including a large number from the rural areas, and dropouts who had not completed the fourth grade. Recruitment extended to other working groups over the age of eighteen, older individuals, and those with special needs. Different kinds of programs were developed to teach basic or remedial education. Those recruited into these programs, regardless of age, were assisted educationally as well as economically.[2] The curriculum was based on the National Technical Programs, but before Perón's term ended these programs were recognized as part of the educational system. David Wiñar, among others, considers this type of school as a concept for the future. After Perón's overthrow, these programs became less important.

Perón was a strong leader, implementing changes in all social aspects and giving the blue-collar workers prosperity and recognition, something no other president in the previous fifty years had done. Perón's financial resources came from the grain and cattle sold to countries involved in World War II.[3] The money from the Banco Central was mismanaged and gone forever by the time of Perón's downfall, leaving behind a large working class that expected benefits from resources that were no longer there. Perón created a mirage of prosperity which was gone by the time he returned from exile in Spain; his third presidential term ended with his death and the overthrow of his second wife, María Estela Martínez de Perón, in 1976.

EDUCATION SINCE 1960

In Argentina, whenever the government changes hands, previously implemented programs are discarded. Political shifts have in many cases limited the possibilities of success. This lack of continuity has been characteristic for over fifty years, for no elected president has completed two terms and most of the governing has been done by de facto governments. This discontinuity has produced economic limitations that affect the society as a whole, which in turn are reflected in the field of education.

Although the earlier reforms at the beginning of the century were profound in their long-term views, they were not without controversy. These early reforms have influenced education not only in Argentina but in other countries in Latin America and Europe as well. For example, France has adopted many aspects of the Cordoba Reform of 1918. This reform, started by students in the Cordoba province of Argentina, sought to improve the low professional standards of university educators. It is interesting that such an avant-garde movement began at the oldest university in Argentina, which was created in 1613.

In contrast to Perón's wealthy display during his regime, which lasted until 1955, is the period from 1966 to 1976 which some educators see as the dark period in education, owing to the government's low expenditure and participation in education.[4] The following two events, even though they are not primarily school reforms, have nevertheless had an effect on the school system. In 1968, as a result of the predominance of unemployed teachers, a new educational requirement materialized. From that date on, teachers were required to attend a university in order to receive proper credentials. Prior to this ruling, teachers attended only the "normal" school, which consisted of six years after the completion of primary school. This prolonged period of studies and the expenses involved in higher education resulted in a shortage of available teachers. Consequently, the system had to employ teachers who were not properly trained in education, offering less educational expertise to the student.

Authoritarian education programs were implemented during the de facto governments from 1976 to 1983, starting in March 1976. Those involved in education were under strict orders from the Education Ministry to restore order and authority to a highly chaotic society (Filmus and Frigerio, 1988: 13). Furthermore, the prohibition from the authoritarian government extended to the interaction among participants in the educational system, including the community, school administration, and teachers. Parental participation was limited to paying the school's fees, occasionally helping with the celebration of a national holiday, and attending to a student's disciplinary problems. This enforced noninteraction among parties led to the isolation of these groups, allowing the development of a more hierarchical system. By keeping each group isolated, the military found it easier to exercise power.

Curricular and extracurricular activities also became more limited during this period. Laws and prohibitions were extended to the material used in the classroom. According to testimony taken from some of the teachers, if the books found on a provided list were those allowed to be in the classroom, then it was assumed that the books not included must be prohibited (Braslavsky, 1985; Filmus and Braslavsky 1988: 18). Another rule established uniform examinations throughout the country. This was a new and conflicting phenomenon because each province could, to a great extent, adjust the prescribed curricula to fit their own needs. Deviations of any kind from these rules were forbidden, and in cases of resistance the sanction consisted of coercion and threat.

The transition to a democracy started with a newly elected democratic government in 1983; this striving for freedom has remained constant for seven years. At the time the current government came into power, the society had clear goals for the country's educational future: the state helped to fulfill the wishes of the people. Free interaction among those involved was part of the government's plan; parents, school personnel, and students became involved. The country's youth had been active in projects while awaiting governmental changes, and by 1983 they were ready to express their goals. Education in the transition to democracy[5] brought a reversal in philosophy from the previous system, and changes have now become evident in education. The present philosophy seems to reflect an intertwining of old and new policies, creating a new set of views. Instead of discarding previous successful implementation, even though it may be left by the de facto government, the idea is to add to the established policies, thereby making the system more efficient. Since 1983, for example, the people have demanded the reimplementation of the "lost order" at the high school level to curtail behavioral classroom problems.[6] This combination of the old and the new is bound to make a difference. Modifications incorporated in this fashion will give the educational arena a stability seldom known in the Argentinian educational system (Braslavsky, 1989: 104).

This period also has brought long-awaited changes desired by groups that had suffered discrimination. Low socioeconomic groups did not have the means to prepare for the educational entrance examination, cutting them off from furthering their education. This entrance examination consisted of achievement material that required special preparation, which most of the schools failed to provide. In order to make the system more meritocratic, President Raúl Alfonsín eliminated entrance exams, thus ending a conservative weeding-out process that had existed for over a century. Since 1983, entrance to a desired high school has been based on drawing names from all participants. Therefore, all students have an equal chance, eliminating the previous nonmeritocratic system. However, some universities may still administer their own subject exams, but this is not the same as the previous entrance exam.

Because of this large increase in the number of students now eligible to attend school, adjustments had to be made. Not only did the government create new buildings, but in places where large populations existed the community got involved in remodeling buildings to meet the new educational needs. Parental involvement extended not only to improving buildings, but also to the curricula and to implementation. These significant changes were occurring at all levels: the people, the government, the educational system, and the society. Apparently, even more important was their relationship to each other after an enforced non-participatory rule.

Another major initiative in the field of education that stemmed from the constitutional government elected in 1983 was the call to convene the Segundo Congreso Pedagógico Nacional (Second National Pedagogical Convention). This second congress was proposed in commemoration of the centennial of the first Congreso Pedagógico held in 1882. In this second convention, which was based on the first Convention, all the people participated, and because of the complexities of preparation, decision, and the selection of representatives the convention was not held until 1988. In this assembly, 299 delegates participated.

These two conventions bear certain differences. The most relevant is that in the second congress the invitation was extended to those at least fifteen years of age or older in addition to teachers, other educators and government officials. The invitation was also extended to all social organizations, including those in the political arena (Braslavsky and Krawczyk, 1988: 48), and in spite of the protest of some groups, even the previous de facto government participated.

It is difficult to isolate specific points from a project of this magnitude, but certain events that add a new dimension should be mentioned. One is the Catholic Church's participation, a subject that resulted in a book: *Educación y Proyecto de Vida* [Education and life project]. This work illustrates the church's historical participation in Argentina's education and its renewed attempt to take a strong position in the field, which directly affects private education. Another important event associated with the second congress was that the people from the rural areas of Jujuy Province participated. In order to break the isolation barriers created by speaking other languages (in this case their native language), these groups requested education in the Spanish language as well as in a foreign language, surprising the educators and representatives to the Segundo Congreso Pedagógico (Braslavsky and Krawczyk, 1988: 53). Another proposed reform in the second congress was the establishment of a new educational level covering those who were not continuing into secondary school, thereby providing a tool for those who spend limited years in the system. These proposed educational changes were very similar to those proposed by Saavedra Lamas in 1916. Also discussed in the second congress were economic limitations and their effects on education; these limitations had the characteristics of a crisis, which was an unknown factor in 1884.

With its uncompleted analysis of all proposals, the congress took on an aura of unfinished business. Up to 1989, 8,975 proposals had been scrutinized, leaving many more to be compiled and analyzed. This is a gigantic project, especially when we consider that many more are only fragments of difficult reading material and others are too general for the purpose of the specific solutions needed for the decades to come. However, some materials was prioritized, such as the twenty-four judicial reports and one report from the National Assembly.

Even with all the shortcomings that a conference of this caliber holds, the magnitude of the congress in the educational arena is perhaps even more profound than the one held in 1882. The purpose of the 1882 congress was to form an educational program; the 1988 congress, held over one hundred years later, served to introduce reforms into the educational system. This freedom to produce and to participate has no precedent when compared to the attitudes and impositions of the previous government. For the last half century educational reforms had been de facto, produced in the upper echelons of the bureaucracy rather than by consultation and consensus. The return to democracy has permitted innovation and educational changes (Braslavsky and Krawczyk, 1988: 184). Changes of this magnitude had not been instituted in the last hundred years.

EDUCATIONAL LEVELS

Argentina has four levels of education: pre-primary, primary, secondary, and tertiary. However, not all the levels were introduced at the same time, and not all of them are obligatory, as in the case of preschool. Included in these levels are rural and private education, the one because it is strongly discriminatory as a direct result of the physical and linguistic isolation of this group, and the other because it contributes directly to those who are able to afford the school fees.

Rural Education

Groups that receive less from the system are those in the rural areas of Argentina. As a norm, people in these regions participate less in education, and the causes, for all practical purposes, seem justifiable. Many of the provinces are physically isolated because almost half of the country's total population is concentrated in metropolitan Buenos Aires. Moreover, this large population concentration (according to Borsotti, in 1977, 81 percent) has made the system highly centralized, leaving those in rural areas (19 percent) with very little power.[7] Consequently, the majority of services and educational institutions are concentrated in urban areas. Education in the isolated provinces can leave as much as two-thirds of the population without the level of literacy necessary for full participation in the society. This duality between urban and rural areas can be observed in the low educational attainment of the isolated provinces. For example, between 1970 and 1980 the percentage of those who did not complete primary school between the ages fifteen and nineteen was over 40 percent (see Table 2.2), depending on the province's economy.

Educational attainment improved during the 1980s in a few provinces. Catamarca and Salta made the biggest improvement. Not included in Table 2.2,

Table 2.2
Educational Attainment of 15 to 19 Year Olds Who Did Not Complete the
Primary Level, 1970 and 1980

	Percentage not attending school	
Provinces	1970	1980
La Pampa	29,6	19,5
San Juan	30,8	18,2
La Rioja	33,2	22,6
Chubut	38,9	25,2
Tucumán	39,6	22,5
Río Negro	40,0	29,6
Entre Ríos	41,3	24,5
Catamarca	43,0	24,7
Neuquén	44,5	31,0
Jujuy	45,8	28,6
Salta	46,9	26,5
Formosa	48,1	34,1
Corrientes	48,2	37,2
Chaco	49,5	36,7
Santiago del Estero	49,7	36,2
Misiones	55,1	39,0

Modified from table 10. In Tedesco, Braslavsky, and Carcioffi (1987:129).

Capital Federal in greater Buenos Aires has the lowest percentage: it went from
a low 11 percent to 5.4 percent. This discrepancy shows the difference between
urban and rural educational attainment, a problem that keeps growing as more
people continue to move to urban areas.[8]

In order to ameliorate this discrepancy, in the period between 1976 and 1982
a new program went into effect. This program, called Expansión y Mejoramiento
de la Educación (EMER), has created 380 new school buildings and has expanded
the 500 existent buildings. This was made possible by a budget of $100 million,
of which 50 percent will be financed by the Banco Internacional de Desarrollo
(Tedesco, Braslavsky, and Carcioffi, 1987: 131–132). Up to 1987, no evaluation
of this program had been done.

Preschool Level

Preschool is not obligatory in Argentina, but it has shown more rapidly increasing enrollments over the last ten years than any other level (Krawczyk,
Malajovich, and Vior, 1985: 13). The majority of the schools at this level are
private, and most of those attending this level come from the upper class. Most
of the revenues for this level of education, even at the private level, are provided
by each of the provincial states. The successful educational centers at this level
are those that have adopted the preschool-religious model directly (Tedesco,
Braslavsky, and Carcioffi, 1987: 38), since the private education models were

established prior to this enrollment increase. As the preschool level continues to grow, a lack of properly trained teachers becomes evident.[9]

Researchers in the developed nations have pointed out the advantages of preschool, especially in programs like Head Start, which was developed in the United States in the 1960s in order to provide educational remediation for those with limited incomes. According to Tedesco et al. (1987: 36), no comparable research of this nature has been done in Argentina to determine whether those who have attended preschool have greater socialization and developmental skills.

In Argentina, those in the poorer sectors are at two particular disadvantages. First, the chances of attending preschool are limited; second, even when the opportunity to attend preschool exists, the curriculum provides less cognitive material. One may argue that attending school with a poor curriculum is better than not attending any school, and that even a school with a high emphasis on the socialization process is better preparation than coming into primary school without the skills learned at this level.

By 1986, 8,015 functioning preschools were officially registered in Argentina (Braslavsky, 1989: 80). This figure represents an increase of 670 schools since 1973, but it is far from adequate to accommodate all students between the ages of four and five.

Primary Level

The primary is the most important educational level, for it deals with the formation of the younger individual. Consequently, it is the only obligatory level for all children in Argentina between the ages of six and fourteen. Through the years, the upper age limit has varied from fourteen to sixteen. Recently, some have proposed that the age limit of required education should be at the fourth grade, or age twelve, whichever comes first. Politically, this is the most decisive level since it pertains to the majority of children in the country. It is also at this level that success and failure in attaining a level of literacy occurs, and depending on the period of attendance, different levels of literacy are achieved. Without basic literacy skills, the individual cannot become a successful member of society. The decision of who will continue on to secondary and higher education also becomes crucial at this level. The National Constitution of 1853 specified that primary education was the responsibility of the provincial government. The Lainez law of 1905 made a provision for those provinces that were unable to provide education for the entire population: the national government created public schools in order to provide education in provinces that lacked proper resources (Braslavsky and Krawczyk, 1988: 14). This expansion was extremely important because it was strongly needed to consolidate the national state. All the national schools created after 1905 became part of the provincial government in 1978. Since then each province has been economically responsible for its schools.

In 1985 Argentina had 20,700 primary schools. Of those, 200 still depended on the national state, 17,801 on the provincial governments, and 2,226 were private (Braslavsky and Krawczyk, 1988: 24). Almost 5 million children attended the primary level, a number that is bound to increase under the democratic government, as will the number of teachers. As the census of 1980 shows, 244,217 children were not attending school, and most of these come from the poor provinces. We can assume that many of those children not attending school in 1980 have now been incorporated into the school system by the democratic government, but no recent figures have been reported, and none will be available until the next national census, which will take place in 1990.

In 1983 there were twenty-six school curricula in Argentina—those of the twenty-four provinces, one for the municipality of Buenos Aires, and one for the few national primary schools. These curricula share certain differences and commonalities (Braslavsky, 1989: 92), and each school can modify its curriculum according to need.

A uniform curriculum was introduced under the military regime that started in 1976. However, this new curriculum limited the learning process. The curriculum prescribed in books for the first grade of primary school contained only thirteen letters: a, d, e, i, l, m, p, n, o, t, u, s, y. The letter s was included to be used in plurals; the letter y, which means "and," was included to be used as the conjunction and in the first person: "yo" (see Braslavsky, 1989: 95). These thirteen letters limited the learning of vocabulary and created a world that was not familiar to the student. The same method was applied to the reading and writing exercises. Vocabulary familiar to the student, such as "leche, yo, desayuno" (milk, I, breakfast), could not be included in the reading and writing because it was not in the letters prescribed. Consequently, the contrived material found in the school reading and in the material to be learned in class consisted of *only* the prescribed letters, making the vocabulary foreign to the student's everyday life. This process extended up to the third grade. This type of education became stranger to the student than the one prescribed under the elitist view, and can be seen as a negative school reform. Since 1983, a new curriculum has been proposed for this level of education because the country continues to use the curriculum established during the de facto period of 1976 to 1982, which is extremely limited. Throughout the years of the democratic period, education has become a more widely used tool for many more students. Certain reforms that affected the primary level were decisive in the attainment of secondary education, and these are discussed below.

Secondary Level

The major weeding out of students occurs at the primary level; only about 50 percent of those starting primary level ever get to the secondary level (Cirigliano, 1973: 81). What is important in the attainment of the primary level becomes an even greater factor at the secondary level. The parents' education and expectations are very important in the student's attainment of the secondary level, as is encouragement from the parents. Until 1983, even though parents from the lower class saw the advantages of a high school diploma, they were not able to afford the private tutoring that the high school entrance exam required. Over the years this entrance examination had been the greatest impediment to entering high school. In the past, those able to attend were those who were able to pay for a year of private tutoring, and not necessarily those who really wished to attend. For those wanting to attend, if their parents could not "buy" into the system,[10] there was no way for the student to begin to prepare for this major transition. For those planning to attend high school, the beginning of the last year of primary school is the point at which the long-term commitment must have already taken place. Such a commitment concerns not only the students but also the parents, because they are the ones who pay for this major decision. This "initiation" process can be an expensive one. Some parents go out of their way to pay for private tutoring, and in large families the youngest benefits from the money brought in by older siblings already in the workforce. In many families the birth order determines the chances for further education.

In order to make education at this level more meritocratic, the democratic government of 1983 eliminated the high school entrance exam. As noted earlier, selection to the desired schools was done by a lottery system. This system was instituted in order to give all students an equal chance. Another measure was the elimination of the uniform at the high school level.[11] For years this uniform had been white; private schools have now adopted different colors, as have some technical schools, where a uniform may be required for vocational training.

Another measure designed to make the system more meritocratic was the implementation of a different grading system in order to make it more generalized than the previous scale, which was one to ten. In 1988 a new scale was added, divided into four levels. This concept was wider, and it followed the scale of reaching the educational objectives, failing, and two levels in between. Interaction among educational participants was encouraged in order to improve the present nonmeritocratic educational system. The result of this wide socialization was the organization of student centers, a process that began in large numbers. Previously, student centers had been prohibited, a ban that dated from the 1930s, with short periods when it was lifted.

This new sense of freedom created unforeseen conflicts at this level of education which manifested itself in behavioral problems. As a coping strategy for this new phenomena and to indicate their discontent, teachers engaged in large-scale absenteeism. It was their way of protesting the students' new behavior; previously behavior had been strictly controlled under the military.

Tertiary Level

Argentina has forty-nine universities, twenty-two of which are private, twenty-six national, and one is provincial (La Rioja Province). The tertiary level of education is divided into university and nonuniversity. The national institutions of higher education are free to everyone.

One can assume that those who receive education from kindergarten on are usually those who enter the tertiary level. Furthermore, those who have had the advantage of attending better institutions throughout the three prior levels are rewarded with better possibilities for entering the tertiary level. This process of selection does not seem very different than that which governs the transition from primary to secondary level, and the same factors that discriminate in these prior levels are also present at this level.

The university reforms under Mitre/Avellaneda were implemented for a society that was an agrarian-cattle exporter. Consequently, Argentina inherited an educational system whose objectives were geared toward satisfying the needs of the people involved in exports, landownership, and administration—in other words, the upper echelons of the society.

Those attending the tertiary level comprise less than 10 percent of the total who begin the first grade in the school system. Of those reaching this level, the number of females and males becomes equal, although women continue to go into education in great numbers, which is considered to be a nonuniversity track and continues to be poorly paid. Educational programs for teacher training mushroomed during 1973 on, creating a large body of available educators. Under the military, large allocations of resources were available to prepare teachers. Regardless of political ideology, women continue to join the teaching forces by attending the tertiary level, which is not considered a university track. Others not considered for a university track are those who come from technical high schools. Not until recently have they been able to attend a system of higher education, segregating those from a limited economic background as well as women. During the de facto government of 1978, many students from limited income backgrounds were qualified to attend the tertiary level.

When the democratic government came to power in 1983, these limiting constraints were lifted and many more attended at the university level, an increase of more than twice the original number between 1983 and 1986. This was influenced by the first political measures of implementing the "ingreso irrestricto a las universidades nacionales" (Braslavsky, Cunha, Filgueiro and Leméz, 1989: 83) [nonrestrictive admissions to the national universities], which is comparable to open admissions (though some universities may have the right to administer an achievement exam in their area).

Furthermore, from 1983 to 1987, the tertiary level of education was the only level of education that had reached the process of institutional reorganization (Braslavsky, 1989: 67). This reorganization consisted in breaking away from the 1966 dictates in which personnel other than those involved in academia could participate in the university environment. During the next military period, 1976–1983, many nonacademic university employees were hired; university professionals could not be hired owing to their political ideologies. Positions obtained under the de facto government have been eliminated under the new democratic

Table 2.3
Private Education: Student Enrollment, 1963 and 1983

School level	1963	1983
Preschool		
Total number	109,359	602,226
Private	35,638	190,836
Primary		
Total number	3,097,240	4,511,122
Private	371,067	799,487
Secondary		
Total number	688,711	1,466,424
Private	199,965	443,849
Tertiary		
Total	208,551	580,626
Private	14,812	141,431

Modified from Krawczyk, Malajovich, Vior (1985:11).

government, reaching an institutional reorganization needed for a more efficient educational organization.

Private Education

Private education since 1947 has extended the buying power of those with the advantage of participating. Under the Perón regime from 1945 to 1955 private education became highly subsidized. This trend has continued under subsequent military regimes, which has not helped educate the poor sector of the population. (For greater detail on this issue, see Braslavsky, 1986: 50–53.) In the last twenty-five years privatization has increased at all levels, except at the primary level (see Table 2.3). Salaries for teachers in private schools became subsidized under Law 13,047, enacted in 1947, and have been maintained by other military governments.

It was under the elected government of Frondizi that the creation of private universities was proposed, giving autonomy to those private institutions that had previously belonged to the state. Thus, other nonmilitary participants have influenced the privatization of educational institutions. Interestingly, those that benefit from this process are already in strong economic positions. The common worker, who pays taxes, not only contributes to national and state education, but also subsidizes the private system, the same one that their offspring will not be able to participate in.

EDUCATIONAL ATTAINMENT AND LIMITATIONS

The reasons why students do not complete their education are complex and often difficult to isolate. Not all students benefit from education that lacks practical applications, since it has no relevance to future needs. In fact, the traditional form of education caused the largest dropout rate in Argentina in the first century after its independence. Almost 80 percent of those attending abandoned the educational system, although some researchers do not believe that dropping out of school is synonymous with failing; failing is only one of the ways it is manifested (Laino and Guerra, 1989: 62).

Student success or failure can be determined first by socioeconomic level and second by school environment. In addition, student and parental aspirations can influence what the student achieves through the formal Argentinian educational system. Argentina's educational system in general limits entrance to those who belong to certain groups. In order to present a brief view of who benefits and who is discriminated against in education, some different aspects are discussed separately.

School Retention

Even though the state does not approve of retention in the first year of primary school, great numbers of students are held back at this level. This phenomenon seldom occurs in schools located in the more affluent economic neighborhoods, and it never happens in private institutions. Retention figures for the first grade indicate that, of the total numbers of students who start the first year, 25 percent are kept back for a year. If one also takes into account those who drop out of the system during this period, the figure is almost 40 percent. The factors that determine the dropout rates seem to be fundamentally socioeconomic. The Argentinian school system, therefore, is not successful for those who go through the first grade. More than one-third of those entering the system, or 37.7 percent do not go into the second grade (Cirigliano, 1969: 24–25). Furthermore, 56 percent of those who start do not complete the sixth grade (Cirigliano, 1973: 39). These are alarming rates for a developing nation and illustrate that the Argentinian educational system is strongly segmented (Braslavsky, 1985: 49).

Limitations: Buildings and Hours Attended per Day

Other factors that influence educational attainment in Argentina are the quality of the buildings where classes are held, the number of students per classroom, and the number of hours attended per day. The quality of the educational institution depends largely on the neighborhood where the student lives. Because of the lack of physical space in certain sectors, the hours attended per day can vary; while some students are able to attend only two hours per day, others may attend the entire day. The schools where the larger number of students take classes are overcrowded, and the rural to urban shift has added to the present overcrowded conditions. However, some students from affluent areas participate in all their extracurricular activities in the same school, spending up to eight hours in the same school building. Because of segregation, those born in certain circles, either economic or social, traditionally tended to remain in the same circle, as it was almost impossible to infiltrate institutions on higher economic levels. This limitation has changed with the drawing system instituted by the democratic government in 1983.

In an effort to minimize the discrimination process, the democratic government created additional high schools between 1983 and 1986, and the number increased from 4,915 to 5,638 buildings. This 723-school increment was larger than that of a decade earlier—404 schools (Braslavsky, 1989: 82). Attempts have also been made to serve other education groups in the last decade. A number of institutions have been developed to cater to those who have not finished high school. These high schools operate at night in order to accommodate those in the work force. Presently, there are 190 centers for adult education at the high school level, and of those, almost 100 are located in metropolitan Buenos Aires.

Literacy Rates

Over the last several decades, Argentina has been losing its status as an educationally privileged country, compared to other Latin American countries (Braslavsky, 1989: 79). In 1980, with a population of less than 25 million, over 1 million were illiterate (1,264,650), and over 6 million (6,711,634) fifteen years of age or older did not complete enough years of schooling. Perhaps this last group includes some of those who may be functionally literate but are unable to successfully participate in society. This goes hand in hand with the limited chances certain people have for participating in society, as described earlier under Rural Education.

In order to improve the literacy rate, the national government planned to create 17,500 centers by the end of 1986. The plans were not only to teach these people to read and write, but also to train them for some kind of occupation. Thus far, this campaign to eradicate illiteracy has produced 1,118 centers with 136,000 students and 8,300 teachers (Braslavsky, 1989: 80)

Limitations in Funding

Those who make decisions about funding issues are usually driven by the political ideology of the time, which is not static. Seemingly, decision makers try to ignore the educational implications that their choice of funding may bring for the poor, as even these decisions become the social determinants for future generations. Furthermore, most decisions are centralized, benefiting the cities with larger populations, since the rural communities do not have the political sophistication required to exert pressures (which may be due to their political isolation). As Borsotti has stated, it seems doubtful whether these classes have a clear idea of goals and the possible means of achieving them (Borsotti, 1984: 62). On the other hand, they have been denied the opportunity to participate, because when given the opportunity, as in the case of the convocation for the Second Pedagogical Congress, they will voice their opinions. For example, the indigenous people from Jujuy knew exactly what they needed in order to succeed and partake in society.

The military government has provided generously for the private education sector, and it has been done in spite of the fact that almost 80 percent of all educational enrollment, at different levels, takes place in the public education system (Braslavsky, 1989: 88). Then it becomes clear that the rationale behind the massive allocations for private education is as follows: those with better economic means will prefer the private system, even though the public system has provided quality education for over a hundred years. So far, most of the people have preferred the public system, but this may be changing since parents and educators, in the last few years, have gathered together in order to create private schools. It is hard to pinpoint if this shift has occurred because the public schools were not meeting the demands of education or because of the funding provided to private education. What is not yet clear is whether this new view may, in the long run, destroy a sound public system that has educated students for over a century.

How Family Income Affects Educational Attainment

Some of the components that influence educational outcomes are location, economics, family structure, parents' education, numbers of siblings, birth order, motivation, aspirations, teacher's expectations, as well as the politics of the time and school attendance. Another component is the parents' socioeconomic background, which affects their offspring's level of educational attainment. This becomes apparent from the first day a student steps into school. The human capital brought to class becomes evident from kindergarten on, as it is here that educational segmentation begins, even when those from poor socioeconomic background usually do not participate at this level in the same number as those from the upper classes. For the poor, school is a foreign environment, and their ignorance becomes evident. Lack of the expected cultural traits needed in education does not help effect the transition to the first grade, nor does it contribute to their educational progress later on. (For further material on this subject, refer to Braslavsky, 1985: 58.)

Lacking the proper human capital in the educational environment is a limitation, and the poor continue to be at disadvantage to compete in the educational arena. For some, this is the case even after seven years of compliance with the primary school system. Because of their low socioeconomic background, they already have received much less from the educational system. Until recently, most of these have been students who will select the same type of schools that female students have been attending. This is the case even when female students have received better grades and have completed primary education in larger numbers. Furthermore, by the end of their last year in high school, many of the economically disadvantaged students are already working, even though the working age, by law, is sixteen. Although these students see schooling as a preferred activity to working, their chances for completing high school are not very high.

Other factors contribute to school failure among the poor; their tendency to have more siblings, for example, limits their school success. For economic reasons, some students have chores around the house or work outside the home. A student's work influences the time spent on homework, which in turn has an effect on the learning process. The outcome of their school success often depends on the amount of time they spend working, which may reflect negatively on their school work. Failure stemming from family economic constraint is becoming more widespread in the poor sectors, due to the declining economy and the devaluation of the salaries. This factor further limits the educational opportunities of the economically disadvantaged. Another factor that limits the completion of school is moving from one school to another. Many causes are involved here, such as moving from one city to another, changes in the family structure, and loss of jobs. Two other reasons for school failure are low parental education and lack of parental interest in the children's future education; both have a negative influence on the attainment of education, showing that family expectation and economics affect the educational attainment of the next generation.

Family Aspirations

Parental contributions and interest, as well as expectations, can have great influence on the outcome of the student's educational attainment, which in turn is influenced by socioeconomic factors. This influence becomes apparent from the kindergarten on, but becomes more decisive at the transition to high school and higher education. Upper class parents view the completion of a high school education as their offspring's choice and are willing to let their children choose the school they wish to attend (Braslavsky, 1985: 74). They appear to be more casual about what a high school certificate provides, perhaps because of the assurance their parental model provides. They have the assurance that the school their children are attending has a better curriculum, which will apply directly to the next levels of education, and they will be better prepared to take the required entrance exam. In most instances the students will not need to take the entrance exam because they have good grades. They will also attend the most desirable and prestigious schools, leaving those from poor sectors to prepare and carry the burden of a more limited preparation.

Lower socioeconomic parents who want their offspring to succeed would prefer an occupation in liberal arts or business, which in many instances requires tertiary education. If nothing else, and in large numbers, parents in this group see a diploma, certificate, or another degree as an indispensable tool for a white-collar job and a better way of life.[12]

Curriculum Irrelevant to the Needs of the Society

The majority of the population in the nineteenth century accepted school as an organization that served to provide the necessary tools for individuals to become functioning members of the society. The school of this period gave children of different ethnic backgrounds the possibility of education and social-ization which could facilitate mainstreaming into the larger society.

How the school administration interprets the curriculum and how it applies to a certain school depends on the goals of the particular school. In some schools, more importance is given to the achievement section of the curriculum, while for others the primary emphasis is on the social interaction of the student body. The same curricular design is adopted by the private schools, although most seem to select curricula that are directed to the field of achievement. In con-cordance with their curricular policies, some schools adjust their curriculum to fit the needs of the population attending a particular school, influenced by their criteria and the expectation raised by the parents. Some primary schools adjust their programs of study to future needs for the transition into the secondary level, facilitating the transition from one level to the next, but this happens only in a few primary schools that are located in the affluent neighborhoods. Although curricular freedom was curtailed during the military period from 1976 to 1983, the Argentinian school system has had some freedom over the years.

Discrimination by the School System

Because of the social differences and segmentation of the school system, some primary schools located in less affluent areas do not teach during the last year of classes. Teachers take into account that those who will continue their education will be paying for their learning. Once more, it becomes apparent that the educational system seems to cater to those who may continue their education.

Lacking economic resources for paying private tutoring has made educational segmentation and discrimination more profound, further limiting those who can-not afford private tutoring. As late as 1982, between 50 and 96 percent of the students, depending on the school, were paying their way in order to prepare for entry into secondary school. Although some high schools do not require an entrance exam, they impose their own requirements, which in most instances consist of higher grades that the poor can seldom obtain. In this instance, the poor carry a double burden by not continuing to the next level, which also means not learning in the last year of primary school. Argentina has developed an unnamed tracking system based on socioeconomic background without regard for an individual's ability. Not only does the school system fail to collaborate in the success of the student's education, but also if the parents do not cooperate in a joint effort with the school the victim becomes the culprit. In the end it is the student who is blamed for the lack of effort in succeeding in the education offered (Tedesco, 1984: 41). In this instance, it seems that it is the system that has failed the student, and not the other way around. In order to curtail discrimination based on socioeconomic background, the democratic elected government of Raúl Alfonsín passed a law prohibiting entrance exams in 1983.

Teacher Expectations

Another important contributor to educational attainment is the teacher's expectation. How successful students are in the process of learning is based in great part on teacher expectation, which has been termed self-fulfilling prophecy in the United States (Apple, found in Braslavsky, 1985: 41).[13]

The pressures by the de facto administration have resulted in a period of compliance and obedience in which classroom learning became second in priority. Because of lack of communication with other entities, the feeling has been one of isolation—isolation extended not only to the classroom, but also to institutions used by the school such as parks, museums, and athletic centers.

Over the last century Argentina has produced a great number of trained teachers. According to Cirigliano, the ratio of students to teacher is about twenty-two to one (1973: 39). (This ratio does not exist in the regular classroom, because most of these teachers are unemployed, since the system produces more teachers than can be employed.) Before 1983, many earned money through private tutoring, preparing students for their entrance exams. The expectations of working at home have changed for many teachers. The elimination of the entrance exams by the new democratic government may mean no income for those who used to work at home. Often those employed are no better off, for their salaries are meager and it is not unusual for a paycheck to be months overdue.

Teachers' Lack of Training about Individual Difference

In the past, if students did not adjust to the educational system, they were added to the list of those who did not make it through the school system. Hence, those with special needs were put in special institutions designed for their needs. This situation was a result of the political-educational belief that considers the problem to be of medical-pedagogic scope. This has changed as a result of the research collected during the 1960s and 1970s.

Because of this research, the General Assembly of the United Nations declared the year 1981 to be the year of the disabled.[14] This proposal was made in recognition of the special education needs of the disabled, which led to the incorporation of these individuals into the educational system. Even during the military regime, this positive aspect in education was retained, and certain programs for the handicapped and those students with special needs were instituted in the 1970s. The special education enrollment increased during those years to over 14 percent annually. Groups with special needs now attend school in larger numbers, and enrollment numbers continue to grow; by 1982 it had increased to 17.6 percent. (Tedesco, Braslavsky, and Carcioffi, 1987: 134 and Table 31).

CONCLUSION

Carlos Menem was democratically elected the new president of Argentina in 1989. Because of the country's increasing problems, he took office five months early. Many believe that his predecessor, Raúl Alfonsín, did all he could to help his country politically and economically. The fact that his efforts failed represents the effect of serious underlying problems, regardless of political ideology. The depth of the problems faced by Argentina will not be easily resolved by the array of unanswered questions, of which the most pressing are:

1. How is Argentina going to provide the advantages that many have come to expect but the economy cannot deliver?
2. How is the educational system going to cope with the increasing number of students now eligible to enter different levels of education?
3. Can the country afford to budget remedial education for those who are poorly prepared?
4. Are present schools willing to lower their educational standards in order to accommodate incoming students with an inferior preparation?
5. What will be the source for educational monies in a declining economy?
6. What are the implications to society when many more children below the age of fourteen are entering the workforce?
7. Is the country headed in the right direction educationally?

These seven questions are the most crucial ones to be solved by the Argentinian democratic government, but solutions won't be easily reached, since the country is no longer one of the ten richest nations in the world. Since the 1970s it has experienced a growing foreign debt (which was nonexistent a few decades ago). In fact, "Argentina has suffered triple digit annual inflation in 15 of the past 16 years. Last year, inflation soared to 4.924 percent."[15]

Until recently, Argentina's students were considered children from a developing nation because of the wealth of the society. The existence of a few minors who worked was not noticeable, or it was even ignored because of their small numbers—in spite of the fact that it was denounced to the official authorities. This situation has now changed, with children working in large numbers, much as they do in other Latin American countries (CENEP, 1984, found in Braslavsky, 1985: 52). Based on resent economic reports, we can speculate that present economic limitations will slow the development of needed educational programs. Alfonsín's elimination of entrance exams may have produced new problems that have not yet become apparent. Argentina, a country with sound educational foundations, can no longer claim to have the highest literacy rate in Latin America. Furthermore, without the participation of large educated masses, the country will face unforeseen social problems.

The idea of holding the Second Pedagogical Congress was a tremendous step in the right direction, for which it has a long agenda of educational improvements. This shows that the educational system is going back to the foundations, even if those foundations were not the most meritocratic and the educational philosophies not the most broad. The foundations were good enough to educate 90 percent of its population, even if it was only for a short period of time. With this congress, education seems to be coming full circle. As discussed in this chapter, the first congress was convened in order to create an educational system, and the second to reform and amend the present educational system. This wide interest from educators and the people suggests the awareness of needed educational reforms. Some of the participants in the Second Pedagogical Congress knew that recently 600 teachers had disappeared; 5 to 10 million books had been burned or destroyed by the military (De Lella and Krotsch, 1989: 37). The longest teacher strike in Argentina's history occurred in 1988. Perhaps this second congress served to ameliorate past events, resulting from the de facto mandates, a time that can be considered the nonenlightenment period in Argentinian education.

The increase in the number of schools, teachers, and buildings after 1983 represents a great hope for the educational system under the democratic government. Another step was the creation of 17,500 adult schools in 1986. In addition, the implementation of the EMER program (Expansión y mejoramiento de la Educación Rural) which was created under the de facto government, continues educating those in the provinces.

The new prospects seem hopeful, but it is the economic situation that may thwart the best intentions for improvement. Without a sound economic structure, the money will not filter down to education, because education is not an isolated phenomenon but is interrelated to the society in general. The country can make it if it continues to improve the educational attainment of its young, a fight that started even before the nation was freed from the Spaniards in 1810.

Educational proponents have always been concerned with improving education. The future educational philosophy should be drawn from some contemporary educators' ideas which produce a certain déjà-vu of past educators' philosophies: to improve educational services, to reduce cost, to extend granting to many more people, to surpass budgetary limitations, to reach places and levels where it is not possible to get with conventional methods, searching for contemporary technology (Tedesco, 1988: 75).

The revival of past educational concerns that were discussed in the Second Pedagogical Congress suggests that Argentina is beginning to flourish in the educational realm.

NOTES

1. The literature does not provide figures on how this attainment was counted, but it is a breakthrough.

2. David L. Wiñar (1970). There was a scale of payment depending on the participant's level of apprenticeship.

3. Eduardo Angeloz (1989: 57). "Se puede," si ganamos en confiabilidad. *Argentina ¿Tiene salida?*. He quotes General Perón, saying that the Banco Central had so much wealth that it was not even possible to walk through the hallways.

4. Cecilia Braslavsky (1988 and 1985) describes the different political period and its effects on education; see: *Respuesta a la crisis educativa* and *Educación en la transición a la democracia*.

5. For greater detail on this topic, see Cecilia Braslavsky (1989), *Educación en la transición a la democracia*, and Braslavsky and Nora Krawczyk (1988).

6. See Braslavsky (1985, p. 29).

7. For further discussion on this issue and differences on rural versus urban, please refer to Borsotti (1984) and Tedesco, Braslavsky, and Carcioffi (1987: 47).

8. According to recent demographic studies, in Latin America as much as 70 percent of the population lives in urban areas. See *Excelsior*, July 12, 1990, pp. 1, 11.

9. The preschool level has been documented by researchers (Braslavsky, 1985: 57, and Tedesco, Braslavsky, and Carcioffi, 1987: 39). This is because this level of education is a relatively new introduction to the school system and many provinces have not completely developed their curricula, while others are in the research stages. For this last point, see Kantor in Mino, Lorena, Clara, and Dávila (1989: 107).

10. For a detailed discussion of discrimination at this level of education, see Cecilia Braslavsky (1985) and Filmus and Braslavsky (1988).

11. Throughout the years a uniform in England has been a means of equalizing class differences. There is no mention of what idea was behind the elimination at the high school but not the primary level.

12. See Braslavsky (1985).

13. Other educators have also developed theories about the nature of self-fulfilling prophecy—for example, Rosenthal and Jacobson (found in Tedesco, 1984: 40).

14. For a discussion in special education, "¿Hay una pedagogia especial?" (Is there special pedagogy), refer to the work of Berta Perelstein de Braslavsky (1984).

15. "Argentina Will Resume Interest Payments to Banks," *Los Angeles Times*, July 7, 1990, D3, p. 73.

REFERENCES

Angeloz, Eduardo, 1989. " 'Se puede,' si ganamos en confiabilidad." *Argentina ¿Tiene salida?* Buenos Aires: Clarin Aguilar.
Bagiani, Hugo E. 1990. "Variantes socio-educativas argentinas (1880–1930)." *Propuesta Educativa*. Facultad Latinoamericana de Ciencias Sociales. FLACSO 2:49–53.
Borsotti, Carlos A. 1984. *Sociedad rural, educación y escuela en América Latina*. Serie educación y sociedad. Buenos Aires: KAPELUZ–UNESCO–CEPAL–PNUD.
Braslavsky, Berta Perelstein de. 1984. "¿Hay una pedagogía especial?" *Revista argentina de educación* 4: 27–44.
Braslavsky, Cecilia. 1985. *La discriminación educativa en Argentina*. Buenos Aires: Colección FLACSO.
———. 1986. "Responsabilidad del estado y la sociedad." *Revista Argentina de educación* 7:41–61.

Braslavsky, Cecilia, Luis Antonio Cunha, Carlos Filgueiro and Rodolfo Leméz. 1989. "Evolución de los sistemas educativos en los procesos de transición a la democracia y el caso argentino." *Educación en la transición a la democracia.* Santiago, Chile: UNESCO/OREALC, p. 11–109.

Braslavsky, Cecilia and Nora Krawczyk. 1988. *La escuela pública.* Buenos Aires: Cuadernos FLACSO.

Bravo, Hector Félix. 1965. *Sarmiento, pedagogo social.* Buenos Aires: Editorial universitaria de Buenos Aires.

————. 1984. "Homenaje al Congreso Pedagógico de 1882." *Revista argentina de educación* 4:51–58.

Cirigliano, Gustavo F. J. 1964. *Educación y futuro.* Buenos Aires: Editorial Columbia.

————. 1969. *Educación y política. El paradojal sistem de la educación argentina.* Buenos Aires. Libreria del colegio.

————. 1973. *El proyecto argentino. De la educación política.* Buenos Aires: Editorial Pleamar.

De Lella, Cayetano, and Carlos Pedro Krotsch, eds. 1989. *Congreso Pedagogico Nacional, evaluación y perspectivas.* Buenos Aires: Editorial Sudamericana. Instituto de estudios y acción social.

Filmus, Daniel, and Cecilia Braslavsky. 1988. *Ultimo año del colegio secundario y descriminación educativa.* Buenos Aires: Cuadernos FLACSO, p. 73.

Filmus, Daniel, and Graciela Frigerio. 1988. *Educación, autoritarismo y democracia.* Buenos Aires: Cuadernos FLACSO. Miño y Dávila, eds.

Kantor, Debora. 1989. "Acerca de la autoridad docente en el jardin de infantes." *Propuesta educativa.* Miño y Dávila, eds. Facultad Latino americana de Ciencias Sociales. FLACSO, 1:107–10.

Kaufman, Ana Maria. 1989. Educación para y en la democracia. *Argentina ¿Tiene salida?* Buenos Aires: Clarin Aguilar.

Krawczyk, Malajovich and Vior. 1985. "Aportes para una demistification." *Revista Argentina de Educación.* 6:7–17.

Laino, Dora, and Patricia Guerra. 1989. "Fracaso escolar." *Revista argentina de educación* 12:61–73.

Puigross, Adriana. 1990. "Sistema educativo. Estado y sociedad civil en la reestructuración del capitalismo dependiente. El caso argentino." *Propuesta Educativa.* Facultad Latinoamericana de Ciencias Sociales. FLACSO 2:40–48.

Tedesco, Juan Carlos. 1970. *Educación y sociedad en la Argentina (1880–1900).* Buenos Aires: Ediciones Pannedille.

————. 1984. "Capacitación de educadores para áreas marginales." *Revista argentina de educación* 4:25–51.

Tedesco, Juan Carlos. 1988. "Hacia la renovación democrática de la educación." *Respuesta a la Crisis Educativa.* Compiladores C. Braslavsky y Daniel Filmus. Buenos Aires: Cántaro, FLACSO-CLACSO, pp. 183–201.

————, Cecilia Braslavsky, and Ricardo Carcioffi. 1987. *El proyecto educativo autoritario. Argentina 1976–1982.* Buenos Aires: FLACSO, Miño y Dávila, Editores.

García Vázquez, Enrique. 1989. *La Argentina: Cuarenta años de inflación.* Buenos Aires: El Ateneo.

Wiñar, David L. 1970. *Poder político y educacion. El peronismo y la Comisión Nacional de aprendizaje y orientación profesional.* Buenos Aires: Instituto Di Tella, Documento de trabajo.

3

AUSTRALIA

Richard Teese

Few decades in the history of Australian education could rival the 1980s for the flurry of reform activity that touched every state and territory. Higher education, technical education, and secondary education all experienced major changes either in organization or in programs, or in both. Educational conflict was often acute and drawn out. It promises to continue into the 1990s as new arrangements are tested and as the environment that has influenced so much activity evolves. Given the breadth and complexity of change—and indeed the ambiguity inherent in some of the most important reforms—it is useful to focus on one particular arena rather than attempting to catalogue activity over all sectors. In Australia secondary education has undoubtedly been the most important domain of reform. Changes have been most bitterly fought at this level. The need for reform as well as the impediments to change have here been most obvious. (For a useful review, see DEYA, 1983.)

By way of introduction, the organization of secondary education in Australia and the context of change during the 1970s and early 1980s are reviewed in the first part of our discussion. The major reform effort undertaken in the state of Victoria is then examined in depth. Arguably, it is in Victoria that the transformation of secondary education has gone furthest and that the aims and problems of reform can be displayed most clearly.

ORGANIZATION OF SECONDARY EDUCATION IN AUSTRALIA

Most children in Australian secondary education attend public high schools which offer six years of instruction, usually begun at the age of twelve. Some states and territories (and some nongovernment systems) provide junior and senior high schools, a model that has been influential. In general, the Australian public high school is organized to serve a district and in principle every child in that district. But several states maintain a few establishments that are selective at intake and that recruit across the state as a whole. Public schools are administered by central rather than local authorities.

Traditionally, the program offered by public high schools has been "academic preparatory," that is, serving mainly to matriculate students to university or to present them for public examinations administered by universities and recognized by major institutional employers for recruitment. After World War II commercial and vocational streams were introduced to accommodate rising numbers of students and as part of a restructuring of provision which often saw the phasing out of separate vocational or technical schools in favor of "comprehensive" provision in high schools. Formal grouping or "streaming" (tracking) practices accompanied this diversification of programs. However, from the end of the 1960s these practices tended to be abandoned, at least in some states, as public examinations for students completing lower levels of schooling were ended and as curriculum control at these levels increasingly passed to the schools themselves. Today programs at senior level continue to be set and examined by curriculum and assessment authorities representing higher education as well as schools. They have taken the place once occupied by universities (see McGaw and Hannan, 1985). A major feature of Australian secondary education is a large and influential private sector, representing 30 percent of enrollments.

THE CONTEXT OF REFORM

One basic problem dominated the concerns of official inquiries into Australian secondary education in the 1980s and of government efforts at reform: the failure of schools to accommodate the needs of the whole school-age population. Although a mass system of public high schools had been built after World War II, their narrow academic curriculum had meant high dropout rates and marked social and gender inequalities in attainment. In 1980 three out of every four boys and more than two-thirds of girls entering public secondary schools in Australia left before the final year (Year 12) (DEET, 1989: 38). Schools in working-class areas generally recorded lower completion rates (DEET, 1987; Teese, 1987: 89–93; Teese, 1989a: 250–257). By contrast, private non-Catholic schools had very high completion rates, were more successful at Year 12 examinations, and their students were disproportionately represented in university intakes (Anderson and Vervoorn, 1983; Deet, 1989; Teese, 1989b). Despite high levels of youth unemployment during the 1970s, school completion rates stagnated or actually fell.

Efforts to reform the senior secondary curriculum in Victoria met with little progress during the postwar years. Public schools grew to become the largest sector, but control over the curriculum rested with the universities, and private schools exercised as much formal power and more influence than the mass district high schools. However, in the mid–1970s some schools developed alternative Year 12 programs, while colleges of technical and further education (TAFE) and the working-class technical schools that had once been their junior departments began to offer bridging courses into tertiary studies. Both developments were of great importance because they pioneered new approaches to curriculum and because they proved to be the main refuge for young people when further severe recession in 1982 saw the teenage labor market collapse. (For alternative courses, see Batten, 1989; Freeman, 1987; Hannan, 1985: 63–71; Reid, 1981).

The development of alternative Year 12 courses, the key role which these played in absorbing the many new students staying on at school after 1982, and the proliferation of credentials representing the same formal level of schooling compelled a major public review of the secondary school curriculum. In June 1983 the Labor government in Victoria commissioned a ministerial committee to review education and training provision for all teenagers (other than those in apprenticeships or in higher education). Chaired by the distinguished educationalist, Jean Blackburn, this committee issued a *Discussion Paper* in May 1984 and its final *Report* in March 1985 (MEV, 1984, 1985).

THE BLACKBURN REVIEW OF POSTCOMPULSORY SCHOOLING

In its first report, the ministerial review committee recognized that the project of democratizing secondary education in Victoria could go no further under the weight of institutional restraints. "Victoria is now at a turning point. . . . The efforts made over the last two decades to transform a stage of provision originally designed for a minority into one in which the majority of the age group could purposefully participate have reached the boundaries of what is possible within the existing framework" (MEV, 1984: 3). There were major structural impediments to the progress of democratic reform. Public secondary education was split between high schools and technical schools; colleges of technical and further education (TAFE) competed with secondary schools; establishments supplying six years of secondary education to local communities were generally too small to achieve curriculum breadth and were organizationally unsuitable for older teenagers; the influence of higher education selection needs was excessive; and responsibility for curriculum was divided between various government and independent statutory authorities. The framework of educational provision was diversified and complex, and it lacked any overall coordination. Taking account of all types of educational activity (other than apprenticeships), more than half of the young people entering secondary school continued to Year 12 level in 1982 (MEV, 1984: 3). But the scope for accommodating a higher proportion was limited.

The failure to integrate the development of secondary education during the years of postwar expansion and to achieve a coordinated and balanced system of curriculum control had led to serious deficiencies and weaknesses in the nature of provision and in the educational activity of different population groups. The senior curriculum in public high schools was narrowly focused on higher education, leading, on the one hand, to early and excessive specialization for those groups that could cope with course demands and, on the other hand, to high dropout rates among those young people who could not cope. Curriculum offerings, though quite varied across the system as a whole, were badly segmented by institutional divisions (above all, school and TAFE), and real choice was "partly illusory." The overriding influence of higher education selection meant that streams of study accredited by the state curriculum authority, but not recognized by universities, were devalued (MEV, 1984: 25, 29). The proportion of young people completing school, though underestimated by some commentators—especially in connection with public high schools—was still "unacceptably low" (MEV, 1984: 14). There were major social inequalities in the chances of completing school and in access to different streams within the curriculum (though the committee did not comment on this aspect and may have had no direct evidence about it). Alternative courses that had been developed "often lacked coherent purposes, and, having second class status, have constituted a form of streaming reactive to the academic mode rather than challenging it" (MEV, 1984: 25). Finally, diversification had led to a confusing proliferation of credentials (MEV, 1984: 30–31).

Through its *Discussion Paper*, the activities of its working groups, and its final *Report* (March 1985), the ministerial review committee produced a range of far-reaching recommendations for the future development of secondary education in Victoria. Many of its proposals were directed at the organizational framework. High and technical schools were to be amalgamated, thus ending seventy years of class division. Senior secondary colleges (or at least senior campuses of schools amalgamated into complexes) were to offer program breadth and a mature environment. TAFE colleges were to be excluded from offering preparatory courses, but their technical and vocational subjects were to be coordinated with school curricula. A single credential—the Victorian Certificate of Education—was to replace all existing credentials and was to be taken over the final two years of school as an integrated, semesterized program. There was to be one agency controlling all curriculum and assessment matters at the upper secondary level—the Victorian Curriculum and Assessment Board. A policy of expanding higher education was to be pursued with the federal government (the main funding body for universities and colleges of advanced education, for which tuition fees had been abolished in 1974). This was aimed at ensuring that higher education places would be available for at least half of all Year 12 students. Funds were also to be sought to encourage universities to diversify their methods of selection and to provide suitable services to support a broader range of students (MEV, 1985: 65).

Besides these proposals aimed at changing the organizational framework, the review committee made recommendations for the reform of the curriculum itself. The new certificate was to bring all students together through some compulsory common studies; it was to ensure breadth by obliging science students to take at least some arts or humanities subjects and, conversely, humanities students at least some mathematics, science, or technology units. Specialized preparation suitable for university purposes was also built into the two-year structure of the new certificate. Other recommendations were directed at breaking down the division between theoretical and applied work and developing whole programs oriented toward broad classes of occupations. Basing itself on the experience of school-based innovations, such as the School Year 12 and Tertiary Entrance Certificate, the Blackburn committee also endorsed practices such as student contracts for work requirements, an emphasis on personal responsibility, and student evaluation of courses, instructional methods, and assessment. It also recommended that 50 percent of assessment in all subjects be school-based as distinct from externally examined. To ensure breadth and commonality in the learning experiences of young people, it was also proposed that all students should study "work in society." This proposal reflected the Blackburn committee's concern that the concept of general education had hitherto excluded "the history and experience of significant sectors of the population" (MEV, 1984: 25).

How important were these proposed reforms? The recommendations on school organization were not novel or original ideas. Amalgamation of high and technical schools had been attempted unsuccessfully as far back as the 1920s and was again rebuffed in 1960. The exclusion of TAFE colleges from offering preparatory courses was a logical extension of merging technical schools and high schools; and the senior colleges or senior campuses proposal was modeled on existing institutions in Tasmania, the Australian Capital Territory, and the Catholic system in Victoria. However, taken together these recommendations would have led to the creation of the organizational platform necessary for the fundamental reforms being proposed for the curriculum. Schools offering a diversity of courses and an environment in which students could take personal responsibility for their work were essential to overcome the joint problems of narrow specialization focused on exams and student alienation. The establishment of a single certificate, incorporating a diversity of paths and with a large component of school-based assessment, reasserted the claim of *all* students to a respected program and credentials and laid down the challenge to universities to relate positively to the whole age group, not simply their traditional clientele.

But the committee's recommendations on curriculum were by far the most important. The requirements of breadth and commonality in the new certificate demanded a cultural participation from students whatever their background, which contrasted markedly with the examinations culture of the old Higher School Certificate. Controversial as the proposed study of "work in society" proved to be, it did seek to challenge the view fostered by the regime of external examinations that a young person should renounce the study of social institutions and practices from the moment when intellectual maturity and personal responsibility most favored and recommended it. As to the requirement of academic breadth, hadn't this been actively promoted by the headmasters of private schools in days not so remote when their establishments faced much less competition at the exams and when cultural broadening was deemed essential for success at university? (See the views expressed in MU, 1962: 58.)

To provide a professional orientation to applied and general (nonspecialist) studies in mathematics, sciences, and technology was another extremely important proposal. For it aimed at securing positive recognition of a variety of studies in these fields, thus making them meaningful and accessible to a diversity of groups in striking contrast to the canonical uniformity and remoteness of preparatory mathematics and physical sciences as prescribed under the old regime. The curriculum proposals also sought to converse the principles of academic self-management, program integration, evaluation, and descriptive reporting which had governed earlier innovations, notably STC.

On assessment, teachers and teachers unions saw the proposals of the Blackburn committee as too limited and even retrograde. The review committee had failed to recommend the abolition of external examinations. Their removal had been the direction in which the Victorian Institute of Secondary Education (VISE)—the statutory curriculum authority in charge of Year 12 courses—had been moving since 1981 (VISE, 1984a: 11; VISE, 1984b). Second, the Blackburn committee's own working party on credentials rejected a role for external exams (MEV, 1985: II, 67). Instead, it proposed statewide consensus moderation of school-assessed work. The Blackburn committee went against this advice by retaining exams. Its chairperson, Jean Blackburn, later defended this decision as regrettable but necessary, "given the restrictions on entering higher education and the widespread community disquiet about abolishing external exams and the fears that abolition would favour schools with better connections with people in higher education" (*The Age*, September 19, 1985).

Despite this fundamental weakness, the Blackburn reform proposals were of great importance. They focused on curriculum breadth, developed a framework for integrating the general and technical courses that had sprung up around the old Higher School Certificate (HSC), and laid the organizational basis for the new curriculum. A common credential was to be available to all young people through a variety of challenging and valued pathways that were balanced and that in key areas were shared. If external examinations remained, the committee at least tried to orient curriculum design toward personal responsibility for work, toward independence in learning, and away from the examinations regime loathed and feared by many students.

DEVELOPING THE NEW CURRICULUM

In May 1985 the Victorian government accepted all the major recommendations of the Blackburn report, beginning with the target of achieving a participation rate in upper secondary schooling of 70 percent by 1995. Consultative processes were set in train to resolve controversial issues and to establish mechanisms for implementing the reforms. Established in 1986, the new Victorian Curriculum and Assessment Board (VCAB) was charged, in effect, with the complete transformation of the senior secondary curriculum in the state. A brief review of the developmental tasks carried out by VCAB between 1986 and 1990 will highlight the distinctive features of the new curriculum as well as the magnitude and significance of this historic undertaking.

To describe the senior secondary curriculum in Victoria in the mid–1980s would have required a listing of over 2,000 accredited units of study connected with rival certificates, taught in different or sometimes the same establishments, assessed in fundamentally different ways, administered by three different authorities, and accredited by thirteen different agencies (VISE, 1986: 11). Curriculum planners had to integrate all this activity into one certificate. This did not mean simply classifying, grouping, and rationalizing various components into a few major strands of study. For the problem was how to conserve the strengths of sometimes radically opposed curricula (for example, the most fully prescriptive as against student-negotiated programs), while at the same time tackling their weaknesses and not accepting variety for its own sake.

The integration of the curriculum had to occur under three basic constraints. The school population was diverse, but fluid, and could not and should not be accommodated in fixed curriculum tracks. Schools needed substantial autonomy in curriculum if the whole range of the population was to be respected and futures were not to be prejudged. But diversity of school activity needed to be limited. Work in one school should not be so radically different from work in another that students were challenged less in one, offered less, and at a state level credited with less. Autonomy should not operate to validate inequality by allowing cultural arbitrariness in curriculum content to operate at the local level rather than more overtly through central prescriptions.

These three general constraints explain one of the key features of the new VCE. In place of fixed syllabi, the curriculum planners employed by VCAB produced "study designs"—frameworks of goals, concepts, and tasks, with supporting materials and examples. Schools were given the role of generating specific courses of study conforming to these frameworks. Over the developmental phase of the VCE (1986–1990), study designs were completed for a total of forty-four studies, involving 200 semester-length units for Years 11 and 12. These studies range across the arts, business, humanities, mathematics, science, and technology. The study designs, while prepared by curriculum writers, were negotiated with teachers and academics, modified, and eventually given a trial in schools.

The VCE study designs, besides making schools central to course development, also laid great stress on personal responsibility for school work, on fostering independence as well as cooperative study methods, and on assessing for a variety of skills in student learning and reporting of work. This curriculum-based approach to assessment, reflected in a breadth of techniques, including the use of investigative or research projects, was aimed at reversing the tendency for final examinations to dictate shallow learning strategies and to weaken both the intrinsic and functional value of the senior secondary curriculum for higher studies. Research had shown, for example, that under the HSC regulations no obvious relationship operated between "deep" approaches to learning (high student interest, search for connections, wide reading) and examinations performance. This was despite the fact that selection to higher education was based on HSC results as supposed predictors of future success. Some students chose the most strategically valuable subjects (those with high honors yields) without any personal interest in them and without adopting approaches to learning which would be expected at university. "School contexts where intense emphasis is placed on formal academic achievement are associated with a tendency towards minimalist, reproductive, and uncompromisingly competitive approaches to learning" (Ramsden, Martin, and Bowden, 1987: 49, i).

Evaluation of "phase one" studies (English, mathematics, and Australian Studies) implemented in pilot schools during 1989 indicated that VCE work requirements, though creating new pressures for students and teachers, were well received and regarded positively. For example, in the case of Australian Studies, there was "widespread agreement among teachers that independent learning skills, organization skills and personal development were all fostered in students." Higher levels of student interest were reported. However, some students did not accept the legitimacy of the new Australian Studies course. They resented its compulsory and intrusive nature: "academically able students who saw their futures as 'secure professionals' questioned the relevance of the course. . . . 'I'm going to be a vet [veterinary surgeon] so I don't need to know about unemployment' " (Northfield et al., 1989: 44). Teachers found the new framework stimulating and productive, though more demanding.

Just as it was important to achieve a curriculum orientation in assessment practice, there also had to be a balance in methodologies which suited the various roles that the new certificate was expected to play. If schools were to enjoy substantial autonomy in generating programs consistent with central guidelines, teachers also had to have a major input into assessment, and this had to extend across all VCE studies, avoiding a hierarchy of prestige. But counterbalancing this, there needed to be common tasks that really did ensure that comparable expectations and demands were made of all students and in all studies. Under the new VCE, these are known as common assessment tasks (CATs). They include traditional examinations, folios of work, oral and aural tests, practical tasks (e.g., in physics or in industrial design), and essays. Some CATs are externally set and marked, but others are school-assessed, with samples being re-marked externally by verification panels. This provision means that in fact more external assessment exists under the new VCE than under the old HSC system. The new assessment procedures were given a trial during 1989 and 1990 and were evaluated independently. The report of the evaluation team endorsed the common assessment tasks as introducing "a range of assessment methodologies which better accommodate the range of objectives of the curriculum than do external examinations alone" (VCAB, 1990). Simulations of higher education selection were also conducted using results from the CATs. These showed that the new assessment practices could satisfactorily meet the selection needs of tertiary institutions. Moreover, much fuller information of a qualitative kind would be available to all users of the new certificate, thanks to the range of assessment practice itself and the detailed reporting of tasks and student attainments.

CONCLUSION

By 1992 all young people enrolling in senior secondary schools in Victoria will be studying the Victorian Certificate of Education. They will be able to choose from a wide variety of studies and to construct programs that reflect their occupational aspirations as well as their personal interests. They will be expected to take personal responsibility for their work requirements and will need to develop learning strategies of long-term value rather than short-term gain. In contrast to the old HSC, specialist preparation will have to be balanced by generalist work in the arts, humanities, sciences, mathematics, or technology as also by the common subjects of English and Australian Studies. While there will be local differences in the content of each of the forty-four studies, they will be sufficiently similar in design and in assessment tasks to mean that across the state young people will have access to the same programs, will be challenged in basically similar ways, and will be awarded a comparable certificate.

The history of reform in Victoria shows that innovations taken on the margins of the system can spread through it, thanks to the diversity of *administrative authority* which exists within a functionally integrated network of institutions. Some high schools were able to opt out of the university-controlled curriculum, while still offering generalist courses acceptable to colleges and universities (Hannan, 1985: 63–71). TAFE colleges and technical schools were able to offer generalist courses and, at least until the mid–1980s, escaped the reach of the central curriculum authority. But the very fact that the tendency for secondary education to split into sectors with radically different approaches to curriculum and assessment has been arrested on terms at least provisionally acceptable to university authorities should alert us to the ambiguity of reform. The retention of some external exams, the increase in the real level of external assessment, the reintegration of public secondary schools into one system, and the exclusion of TAFE colleges from offering general courses have all consolidated the framework of secondary education. This consolidation is not inherently progressive (Hannan, 1985: 62). It may just as well prove conservative in its effects by restoring a common basis on which students can be evaluated and compared, but over which schools themselves do not exercise sufficient control. The more integrated and centralized the system of secondary education, the more exposed to the demands of higher education institutions. If these do not share in the objectives of schools but exercise their legal autonomy to impose selective entry standards, the reform of secondary education will be undermined.

POSTSCRIPT

On June 7, 1990, the University of Melbourne made known to a seminar for secondary teachers that it proposed to reject twenty-seven of the forty-four VCE studies for selection purposes. Only the most traditional studies would be retained.

REFERENCES

Anderson, D. S., and A. E. Vervoorn. 1983. *Access to Privilege: Patterns of Participation in Australian Post-Secondary Education.* Canberra; Australian National University Press.

Batten, Margaret. 1989. *Year 12: Students' Expectations and Experiences.* Melbourne: Australian Council for Educational Research.

DEET. 1987. *Completing Secondary School in Australia: A Socio-Economic and Regional Analysis.* Canberra: Commonwealth Department of Employment, Education and Training.

————. 1989. *Retention and Participation in Australian Schools: 1988 Update.* Canberra: Commonwealth Department of Employment, Education and Training.

DEYA. 1983. *Youth Policies, Programs and Issues: An Australian Background Paper.* Commonwealth Department of Education and Youth Affairs. Canberra: Australian Government Publishing Service.

Freeman, Meredith. 1987. *One for All: Designing a Universal, Comprehensive and Challenging Senior Curriculum,* Canberra: Curriculum Development Centre.

Hannan, Bill. 1985. *Democratic Curriculum. Essays on Schooling and Society,* Sydney: Allen and Unwin.

McGaw, Barry, and Bill Hannan. 1985. *Certification in Upper Secondary Education.* Canberra: Curriculum Development Centre.

Melbourne University. 1962. *Schools and Universities Conference 1962,* Carlton: University of Melbourne.

MEV. 1984. *Discussion Paper.* Ministerial Review of Postcompulsory Schooling. Melbourne: Ministry of Education.

————. 1985. *Report.* Ministerial Review of Postcompulsory Schooling. Melbourne: Ministry of Education.

Northfield, Jeff, et al. 1989. *Responding to the Challenge. An Evaluation of the VCE Pilot Programs.* Melbourne: VCAB.

Ramsden, Paul, Elaine Martin, and John Bowden. 1987. "Approaches to Studying in Different School Environments." *Research Working Paper 87.12.* Melbourne: Centre for the Study of Higher Education, University of Melbourne.

Reid, Paul, 1981. *The STC Book.* Melbourne: STC Group.

Teese, Richard. 1987. "Regional Differences in High and Technical School Demand in Melbourne, 1951–1985." *Australian Geographical Studies* 25:84–101.

————. 1989a. "Gender and Class in the Transformation of the Public High School in Melbourne, 1946–85." *History of Education Quarterly* 29:237–259.

————. 1989b. "Australian Private Schools, Specialization and Curriculum Conservation." *British Journal of Educational Studies* 37:235–252.

VCAB. 1990. *Board Report*, No. 43. Melbourne: Victorian Curriculum and Assessment Board.

VISE. 1984a. *Towards a Revised Policy for Curriculum and Assessment in the Victorian HSC Program: A Paper for Discussion*. Melbourne: Victorian Institute of Secondary Education.

————. 1984b. *Senior Studies Options—Reality or Myth*. Prepared by Ray Taylor. Melbourne: Victorian Institute of Secondary Education.

————. 1986. *Viewprints*, No. 6. Melbourne: Victorian Institute of Secondary Education.

4

BRAZIL

Robert Cowen and Maria Figueiredo

This chapter concentrates on the reform of education in Brazil during the last twenty-five years, but it also identifies long-term historical forces and factors that have framed Brazilian education up to and including the 1950s. It is against these historical forces and factors that the contemporary situation can be more sensitively evaluated.

The social origins of the Brazilian educational system have a number of specific characteristics, including a tradition of French cultural, political, and institutional influence. Much later this influence combined with an increasing American influence, which in turn produced a variety of strenuous local reactions by Brazilians. The relatively late development of public education is noticeable whether at the elementary or at the higher educational levels, in comparison with countries in Europe, and with Argentina within the Latin American context. Moreover, the development of the schooling system was marked by significant inequalities, for example, in regional provision, and often reflected in straight-forward ways, the socioeconomic stratification of Brazilian society. These characteristics dominated the initial origins of the educational system in Brazil, especially in combination with the role of the Catholic Church, and the ideological assumptions of local and national political elites. These forces have continued to affect, and to some extent frame, contemporary educational reform dilemmas.

THE FRAMING OF CONTEMPORARY REFORMS

Among the earliest influences on the creation of schooling in Brazil was the work of the Jesuits (de Azevedo, 1950; Lima, 1974; Ribeiro, 1965). They provided schooling mainly for a Portuguese clientele, with some provision for the local Indians, in the process affecting local Indian traditions in an effort to save Indian souls. Their work involved the collection of Indians into plantations, both for the purpose of making the missionary effort economically self-sufficient and, of course, of transmitting the Catholic faith. The expulsion of the Jesuits in 1879, as they increasingly came into conflict with the Portuguese state, was followed by an effort to "modernize" education, following the ideas of the Marquis of Pombal. Pombal made an effort to establish a national administrative system for running education, under the influence of the ideals of the French Enlightenment.

As was so often the case in Brazil, political events produced considerable consequences for the emerging school system. After 1808, with the flight of the Portuguese Royal House to Brazil, the influence of France increased after the Napoleonic period (de Moura Castro, 1983; Schwartzman, 1979). The French first began to send cultural missions to Brazil between 1816 and 1840, and some of the modernization of the public sector, which had been visible in France, was copied in Brazil. For example, in a flurry of activity around 1810, the Royal Military Academy, the Naval Academy, and the Royal Press were established. Following the model of the Grandes Écoles in France, schools in areas like agriculture, engineering, surgery, and chemistry were created in Bahia which was the capital of Brazil at this time, and also in Rio and Ouro Preto by the 1830s. The long-term effects of this pattern of institution building included the creation of a problem that had subsequently to be dealt with: the existence, not of a university system, but of a large number of specialist and "isolated" faculties. In addition to this flurry of institution building, the emerging Brazilian middle classes, which as a mark of distinction would typically speak French if they were lawyers or senior bureaucrats or military officers, became interested in the positivist ideas of Auguste Comte; ideas reflected in the motto on the Brazilian national flag ("Order and Progress"). This theme of positivism, and the sense that history can be not only understood but also controlled by sociological laws, reemerges at various points in Brazilian history, most notably with the considerable confidence of the 1964 military elite which based its ideas about the modernization of Brazil on Western social science theory (Burns, 1980; Schooyans, 1973).

It should not be assumed that these French influences, from ideas and from institutional transfer, added up to the creation of a schooling system throughout Brazil. In fact, they were obstacles to the wide diffusion of schooling within Brazil. For example, in the northeast, landowners of large properties sometimes made provision for some kind of schooling on their land; but this fitted uneasily with the continued existence of socioeconomic repression and, indeed, slavery (until 1888). Thus, although the middle classes in urban areas began to gain access to education, including education in church schools, the development of something that might be called a Brazilian educational system was delayed until the period between the world wars. It is in the interwar period that the creation of the first university in Brazil can be dated; and it was gradual industrialization that began to create the need for schools in the cities (Cunha, 1980; Schwartzman, 1979), to prepare persons for the new range of emerging occupations, and partly to permit Brazilians to catch up with the (relatively low) level of education that immigrants from Europe were bringing with them.

The majority of this European immigration was concentrated around Sao Paulo, Rio, and the southeast of the country, which in the late nineteenth and early twentieth centuries was industrializing. Thus, it was this area of Brazil that had the jobs and to which immigrants came. There were two kinds of immigrants: those from Europe, particularly Italians and Germans; and Brazilians who themselves migrated from other sections of Brazil, most particularly the agricultural northeast (Burns, 1980; Junior, 1976). This theme of regional inequality and internal migration continues to affect how Brazilian education is provided, especially in the large cities such as Sao Paulo and Rio, and now with shifts in the population pattern, even cities such as Belo Horizonte. A complex system of federal, state, and municipal financing makes providing equal education very difficult to implement. The influx of rural immigrants places a special strain on the urban schooling systems, particularly in terms of the provision of teachers, the eradication of illiteracy, and the retention of children in schools and, of course, the financing of education, which the parents of poor children can rarely afford.

Early patterns of socioeconomic stratification, which overlap somewhat with the migration and regional issues, have continued to plague Brazilian education (Carone, 1970; Cunha, 1977; Fausto, 1977; Nagle, 1974). In the late nineteenth and twentieth centuries, Brazil's aristocratic and upper middle-class families tended to seek for their children a European education, especially a French one. At the other end of the social stratification system, a very large number of children received no formal schooling whatsoever, particularly children of indigenous Indians who often lived in isolated communities until well into the late twentieth century, and other Brazilians who were encapsulated by rural and impoverished urban environments. Even where a system of schooling began to grow in the cities, for the emerging working and middle classes, it was an education system that made sharp distinctions between public and private education, the provision of education for boys and education for girls, and which confirmed status distinctions through curriculum differentiation. The prestigious parts of the education system, under the influence of French notions of cultivation, tended to replicate social stratification in cultural form by stressing the literary, access to foreign language, an understanding of history: appropriate characteristics of future elite members. In contrast, knowledge of technique and technology was increasingly associated with the schooling of members of the emerging lower middle class (Cunha, 1980). However, this dichotomous replication of social stratification in knowledge forms was modified by the idea of a "scientific community" in Brazil, an idea introduced through the French institutional transfer in the early part of the nineteenth century. This concern with scientific studies has retained a foothold, especially in the areas of medicine, and biotechnology. Nevertheless, it is also true that there is a private fee-paying sector of education, to which the middle classes will try to send their children, parallel with a public sector of education, which is rather poorly financed, and which the majority of the population attend if they attend school at all (Cunha, 1980; Freitag, 1979; de Oliveira Romanelli, 1978; Warde, 1977).

What gives particular life and dynamic to these long-term patterns is the shifts in Brazilian society in the twentieth century in terms of the pressures for industrialization and urbanization, disputes about the role of the Catholic Church in education, the rise of positivist and progressive ideas, and the rather dramatic shifts in national politics since the 1920s (Cury, 1978).

1920–1963

Industrialization began to affect the Brazilian economy in the early part of the twentieth century (Furtado, 1972; Ianni, 1963; Junior, 1976; Pereira, 1987). Between 1907 and 1920 the number of industrial workers doubled, but the main formation of the Brazilian economy remained agricultural and dependent on the extractive industries of the primary sector until after World War II. Thus, the demand for education, and especially an education appropriate for running a modern system of industrial technology, did not increase at a rapid rate until the early 1940s. Many members of the middle classes who had received an education typically went back into the servicing of educational institutions, or into state employment.

From the early part of the century, a slow alteration in class formation was occurring in Brazil. The working classes in urban areas began to experiment with unions and slowly moved into conflict with the agricultural oligarchies of the northeast and, for that matter, some parts of the south. Thus, there was an intersection between the movement to industrialization and an alteration of the social class base of politics. This ultimately led to a struggle for control of the state, which became particularly visible in the 1930s. In particular, following the policies of industrialization aimed at import substitution, the urban middle classes were strengthened in numbers and political formation, and an organized working-class movement began to emerge. By the 1930s there was a revolutionary movement, which culminated in a nationalist dictatorship and the closing of Congress in 1937. The leader of Brazil who emerged was Getulio Vargas (Skidmore, 1967).

In parallel with these industrial changes and political foment, educationalists began to define the nature of an educational system appropriate to the new state, including the idea of making provisions for the education of the majority of the people. Under the influence of the ideas of John Dewey, educationists began to debate the nature of a suitable pedagogical style for an expanded system of education. These ideas took shape in the form of the Pioneer's Manifesto (de Azevedo, 1932), *Manifesto dos Pioneiros*, in 1932. Progressive efforts at reform did not change the content of secondary education, which remained literary rather than scientific; oriented toward the civil service rather than toward technical studies and applied sciences; and marked by little serious attention to vocational and technical education. Although the enrollment in academic secondary schools increased, the majority of such schools were private (e.g., 70 percent of enrollment in secondary academic schools was in the private sector in 1938) and the provision of apprenticeship schemes and higher technical schools grew slowly.

Efforts to reform the school system continued after 1942 because it was becoming increasingly obvious that a modern, well-trained labor force was not being produced (Chargas, 1978). But these efforts were relatively unsuccessful. It was not until the postwar period and American intervention that major shifts in the nature and style of the schooling system occurred (Cury, 1978; de Mello, 1978; de Oliveira Romanelli, 1978).

In the immediate postwar period President Vargas served a second term from 1950 to 1954); President Getulio Kubitschek came to power between 1955 and held office until 1960. It was in this period that Brazil went through a considerable expansion of industry, within the framework of an ideology known as *desenvolvimentismo* (Evans, 1979; de Oliveira, 1981; Skidmore, 1967). The consequences for education were considerable.

The major intention was to build up a strong industrial national economy, under the slogan "50 Years in 5," by government planning and financial assistance from overseas. In particular, foreign influence was exerted on technical education and on elementary education. Part of the pressures on the government at the time included the desire to reorganize the whole education system through legislation: indeed, the first national education law (*Diretrizes e Bases da Educacao*) was passed in 1961. The main thrust of the reform was to try to democratize the school system, by unifying the separate institutions at the secondary level, such as industrial, commercial, agricultural, and academic schools (De Barros, 1980; de Oliveira Romanelli, 1978). Despite these efforts, the secondary school system was not unified, did not expand rapidly enough during the 1950s and 1960s, and enrollment dropped in relation to the demographic expansion of the age group (Nunes, 1980; de Oliveira Romanelli, 1978).

Thus, educational reform in Brazil between 1920 and 1960 was influenced by the slow movement from industrialization in terms of import substitution to industrialization as the basis of a strong national economy. Various education reform efforts were made, because of the demands by new social classes, an emerging industrial oligarchy, which, at least in the southern states, began to match some of the power of the agricultural oligarchy, and the populist expectations of both the Vargas and Kubitschek regimes. However, the continued existence of separate forms of secondary education posed a problem, and efforts to reunite institutions of secondary education were not completely successful. Thereafter Law 5692/1971 created a new structure for primary and secondary education based on the model of the "integrated school" (Figueiredo, 1981). In addition, vocational and technical education remains a special problem in terms of what kind of vocational or technical education should be provided, on what scale of provision, and which foreign models should be adopted within Brazil.

In the end, these tensions between populist demands, emerging industrial elites, and the middle classes produced, amidst the crisis of development problems, the military takeover of 1964, which established the reform debate on a completely different footing.

1964–1978

The period just before the coup was characterized by workers' strikes, a decline in the rate of economic growth, an increase in inflation, the nationalization of foreign enterprises, and discussions of agrarian reform. The political fabric of the society was, in the view of the military, under threat, and it was the coup which in the view of the military would reestablish political stability (Figueiredo, 1987).

One of the major consequences of the 1964 coup in Brazil was educational reform. The period after 1964 was dominated by a theory of development which anticipated Brazil rapidly becoming a developed society; income per capita was expected to double, and growth rates in economic terms to be in the order of 8 percent. The proposition and the underpinnings of this plan (which was the first national plan of economic and social development outlined in 1972) was that political stability would be crucial to such development and that international aid would be extremely useful (Burns, 1980; Cardoso, 1977; Pereira, 1972; Schneider, 1971).

The role of education would be central. The education system was conceptualized as a source of human capital, and state planning would ensure the effectiveness of development plans (Arapiraca, 1982; Figueiredo, 1986; Freitag, 1979; de Oliveira Romanelli, 1978). Brazil moved closer to the United States and accepted the fact that U.S. influence on modernization would be considerable. The intention was to tie the Brazilian economy into the international capitalist system of production. Nationalization of foreign enterprises and notions of a collectivist economy were rejected. The consequences of the coup included a further concentration of income in the hands of those in the industrial sector of the economy. Development policies became export oriented, and real wages fell. In addition, an increase in regional inequalities occurred, as well as an increase in external debt and the penetration of the economy by foreign capital.

Politically, the interpretation of the national interest was seen in terms of the cold war—the Brazilian government had no doubt about its anticommunist stance—and a geopolitical concept of a continental America (Silva, 1967). This particular political view, formulated in the Superior War College as early as 1949, located Brazil firmly within the Western bloc, dependent on the United States for its commercial relationships, its economic development, and its progress (Figueiredo, 1987).

Particular consequences, from these political and economic views, followed for higher education. A major Education Reform Act was passed in 1968, and several detailed analyses have been offered of this reform in terms of the part played by advice and experts from USAID (Figueiredo, 1986). As early as 1964, American experts had begun to formulate principles for the reform of higher education. Three main aims were proposed: the reorganization of the higher education system; the creation of systems of graduate education and research; and the need to train teachers and administrators for secondary and primary schools (Figueiredo, 1986).

The intention was that the higher education system would become more efficient, would be better organized, and would have a revised content. It was decided that higher education courses should take place in universities and not in "isolated" institutions. The Federal Council of Education in Brazil was requested to identify educational districts, within which existing institutions of higher education could be consolidated. Again, following the principle of centralization, councils were established at the national level to keep teaching and research under review and to deal with course coordination and rationalization. In addition, there was a requirement that departmental structures be established within universities.

The knowledge transmitted by the university system was organized into graduate, undergraduate, and extension levels. The credit system was introduced. The curriculum followed the compulsory and elective principles of the American system. The university entrance examination was reorganized and standardized (Figueiredo, 1986; Haar, 1977).

This initial wave of reform was supplemented by subsequent national development plans. In those plans, the explicit view of the relationship between national development and the formation of human capital was sustained, as was the degree of planning from the center. The multiplication of central agencies, normally referred to in acronyms, indicates the wish to guide, to coordinate, and to influence from Brasilia (Figueiredo, 1986). These agencies were staffed by planners, many of whom had received training in the United States, along with considerable advice from the United States and international agency personnel.

Alongside this energy and effort at reform, it should also be noted that physical repression of dissent by the military was occurring. In a context of political struggle, among the many casualties were academic freedom and the ability of universities to run their own affairs. Most critics of the government were silenced, and some (such as Paulo Freire, Fernando Henrique Cardoso, and Celso Furtado) were forced into or chose exile until about 1979. Very considerable resentments built up against the military government, as its economic policies began to fail in the 1970s. Toward the end of the military period, there were also a large number of critics—academics, middle-class parents, students, members of the professional class—who were dissatisfied with the priorities in educational reform insisted on by the government. Much of that effort had been devoted to the higher education system, with some efforts also being made to standardize cur-

ricula, improve literacy through MOBRAL, and improve the provision of vocational-technical education. However, the standardization of curriculum had
included a compulsory vocational-preparation element, which the middle
classes were irritated by but managed to avoid; state-run literacy programs have
failed to eradicate illiteracy among adults (or in schools), and the vocational
schools and curricula were increasingly criticized as preparing young people in
inappropriate skills for nonexistent job categories. And, of course, there were
alternative visions, of a more democratic educational system, waiting to be expressed as "abertura," the gradual opening up of the political system, began to
occur.

1979–1989

The interesting characteristic of this decade, in comparison with Brazil's years
under military rule, is that there has been very little formal, national-level, effort
to change the educational system through major laws, decrees, presidential directives, or acts of Congress. In fact, only two pieces of national legislation on
education were passed in 1979–1989: law 7044/82, which abolished the compulsory nature of vocational education as prescribed in Law 5692/71; and the
Federal Council of Education Resolution No. 6/86, which altered the common
core curriculum organization for primary and secondary education. Why?

The immediate interpretative proposition to explain the differences between
the last two decades in Brazilian education and the earlier period is to suggest
that the military government in the 1960s and 1970s conceptualized its reforms
within a clear ideological framework, linked with strong geopolitical perspectives
on Brazil's place within the hemisphere, economically and politically. In contrast, in the most recent decade of Brazilian national life, the presidential leadership, which was on offer following the death of Tancredo Neves, was of the
"lame duck" sort. That is, President Sarney occupied the vice-presidency for
reasons of internal party politics in Brazil. Neves's sudden death promoted Sarney
to the presidency, but without the general political legitimacy that Neves had
earned in the hustings and without the powerful political networks that Neves
had developed over forty years in public life. Thus, it was extremely difficult
for Sarney, who in any event was confronted by major economic crises, to
conceptualize, generate, and institutionalize major reforms within the Brazilian
tradition of centralized administration in a wide range of the sectors of Brazilian
life, including education, especially as public criticism of his administration
grew rapidly, as seen in the weekly popular journals, *Isto E* and *Veja*.

Thus, in contrast to the military period, which made major efforts to reform
higher education, to establish secondary and primary education on a more systematic basis, and to initiate controversial programs in the area of vocational
education, the Sarney government has displayed little coherence in its educational
policies, lacking both political will and educational vision at the center. Politicians are not the only significant actors in the creation of education and schooling

systems. The role of Brazilian educationists and social thinkers in recent decades must also be considered.

The military period was characterized by a protest of silence against the 1968 and 1971 reforms, which were undertaken with the authoritarian style of the period of military rule. During the period of military government, the educational professionals, particularly those in universities, were united by their dislike, or at best minimal tolerance, of the military regime (Selcher, 1986).

The consequences of the "abertura" in the period following 1979 were that a stimulating but acrimonious debate developed at the university level. The late 1970s and early 1980s were marked by an extensive flow of publications in the social sciences, with a mainly Marxist framework. In education a great many books and articles heavily criticized the 1968 (higher education) and 1971 (primary and secondary education) reforms, within the same theoretical and intellectual framework (Berger, 1972; Cunha, 1980; Fernandes, 1975; Freitag, 1979; Nosella, 1986).

Academics from the left have reached a consensus about how to interpret the reforms: both have been charged with serving the hidden aims of the authoritarian regime and its political ideology of development and social control. Education and schools, they have charged, had been shaped by the interests of capitalism. The critique was especially strong on the theme of the fragmentation of the university, and the destruction of university autonomy and academic freedom. For example, it was pointed out that universities were deprived of decision-making power over curriculum, syllabi, evaluation, accreditation, and entrance examinations, and could not determine the number of students and staff, or decide matters related to the teaching career.

The other characteristic of this debate has been that the radicals have tended not only to disagree with conservative educationalists, especially those they associated with the previous regime, but have disputed among themselves about the nature of the radical solutions that might be adopted in Brazilian education. Therefore, what the professional community has lacked is a common voice, or a consensus on the major areas of reform which are currently needed in Brazil. As a corollary, the problem has been that no three or four issues have been singled out by debate as being at the center of the current educational problems of Brazil.

Nevertheless, it is becoming increasingly clear to politicians that universalization of primary education is the first and most urgent reform requirement of Brazilian education. This idea, that elementary education is important, is a reversal of the recent history of Brazilian educational reform. Since the 1940s the main lines of development of Brazilian education have been in the area of the improvement of secondary and higher education. This concern with higher education predates the military regime. The establishment of institutions such as Instituto Nacional de Estudos Pedagógicos—INEP (National Institute for Educational Research), Coordenaçao de Aperfeiçoamento de Pessoal de Ensino Superior—CAPES (Agency for Higher Education Staff Improvement), and Conselho Nacional de Pesquisa e Desenvolvimento Cientifico—CNPq (National Council for Scientific Research and Development) are indications of the Brazilian government's concern to develop a well-trained and talented elite in a number of sectors of Brazilian life, such as politics, business, law, and within a variety of technocratic professions. The contemporary shift of concern to primary education, then, reverses this historic tendency (Soares, 1989). In one sense, what we are seeing is the entry of Brazilian education into the nineteenth century. That is, somewhat as France in 1833, England in 1870, and Prussia began to perceive the significance of a good basic elementary education system, so too, Brazil has approached this perspective. It will be recalled that the movements to provide a good basic elementary education in France, Prussia and England were primarily political: a concern for political and social stability, and, in the case of Prussian education, a concern for the moral regeneration of the nation after the defeats inflicted on Prussia by Napoleon. Later, in Europe, there developed a major concern with the ways in which the education and schooling system might service the new kind of society emerging under the impact of the Industrial Revolution. Thus, by 1910 there was widespread concern, in Australia, Canada, Britain, France, and Germany, for the provision of vocational and technical education to produce the semiskilled and skilled personnel needed to service an industrial economic system.

Interestingly, then, this sequence of educational reform has been reversed in Brazil. First there emerged a concern for vocational and technical education among the conservative political elite, a concern for what the Brazilians called professionalization, before a concern for elementary education. Although primary education is compulsory and free for eight years by law, until recently the Brazilian government has shown little political commitment to the universalization of primary education.

In fact, the number of teenagers (up to fifteen years of age) who completed eight years of schooling in the 1970s and 1980s increased from 30 to 42 percent. However, this group came from the middle class and from some sectors of salaried workers' groups that had offered political support to the regime. Only with the Calmon Amendment (1984) has there been a national awareness of the need to allocate more resources to education, though in law, there is no guarantee that a substantial percentage of the education budget will go to elementary education.

These "politics of nonreform" in Brazilian education must be linked with social class stratification in Brazil. In the last forty years Brazil and its educational system have been very much at the service of the Brazilian middle class, especially the urban middle classes. Thus, in the last forty years we have seen a considerable growth in prestigious private schools and a massive expansion of the higher education system (Figueiredo, 1986). This higher education system, notably the Federal Universities with their free tuition and good teachers, has been stocked with children of middle-class families. Other persons, often of poorer economic background, have indeed taken up places in the higher education system, but they have done so in the more expensive private university system, which has not always been staffed by the most able teachers (Cowen and Figueiredo-Cowen, 1989).

Thus, what may be emerging in Brazil now is a shift in the provision of educational resources in terms of social class. A strengthening of public elementary education means a de facto willingness to divert state money to the general population. The monopoly on the political framing of the educational service by the middle class is being reviewed under the dictates of electoral pressure and electoral popularity. Here it might be worth noting that the opposition in the recent presidential elections, particularly opposition of candidates as represented by Brizola and Lula, had mobilized trade union members, semiskilled and unskilled working laborers, at the hustings. Any new concessions by President Collor de Mello would be very interesting political adaptations from an administration that was seen as an alternative to a left-wing government, and a much needed response to the obvious weaknesses in Brazilian economic performance created by the lack of an educated, highly motivated, and efficient labor force at factory and field level.

But somewhat as in Britain, the politics of educational reform run deeper than a change in political figureheads. Considerable political mobilization is occurring in Brazil today. The first significant change is associated with the transition to democracy and the "New Republic." Under Figueiredo, the last military president, many academics, politicians, and artists who had been in exile since 1964 returned to Brazil and resumed their (at first, nonpolitical) activities. This was the case, for example, of Paulo Freire, Darcy Ribeiro, Celso Furtado, Fernando Henrique Cardoso, Leonel Brizola, Miguel Arraes, and Luiz Carlos Prestes. Second, a very important political momentum, called *diretas ja* (direct elections now), emerged in the mid–1980s. This movement gained national dimensions. Hopes for democratization, including reforms of a different nature, with societal participation, and cutting down inflation, which had reached very high levels during the period of the military regime were widespread. Freedom of speech became no longer forbidden, and critiques of governmental policies (publications, seminars, discussion in academic circles) slowly reemerged. Leading social theoreticians and academics, including a good proportion of educationalists, made efforts to gain access to political life. For example, Cardoso became a senator and later was one of the candidates for the Sao Paulo government; Darcy Ribeiro was elected vice-governor of Rio; Celso Furtado was appointed minister of culture. Thirdly, in 1982, in the first free elections since 1964 for governors and mayors in the main states and largest cities, the opposition party Partido do Movimento Democrático Brasileiro, PMDB—(Brazilian Democratic Movement Party)—gained tremendous political space. The state and municipal secretaries of education were headed by or had as main advisers educationists with leftist tendencies. Thus, public awareness of a different ideology was being created among different social strata.

These changes in political climate, together with the political context (despite the disappointments of the Sarney period) have led to educational changes, and piecemeal and partial educational innovation. Thus, although at the federal level, there has been a lack of coherence of vision and of coherent and programmatic educational reform, at the local level, there are partial and sectoral alterations in educational provision.

Space has been found, for example, for new initiatives in education in Sao Paulo, Rio, and Minas Gerais. A striking experience has been the attempt to implement full-time primary and secondary schools in Rio and Assis, Sao Paulo (Paro et al., 1988). The Rio experience, the Integrated Centers of Public Education (CIEPs), was conceptualized and implemented by Ribeiro (Ribeiro, 1986). The CIEPs permit children, especially those from low-income families, to stay in school for the whole day. There they have classes, tutorials, four meals, cultural activities, medical and dental assistance, textbooks, and uniforms. The CIEP proposal is based on Gramsci's concept of hegemony and education: the aim is to develop the intellectual progress of the masses, and it is argued that by enabling the masses to be part of an intellectual-moral bloc, a critical consciousness in their ability to transform reality can be achieved. Thus, CIEPs are meant to be used as a radical instrument for political and educational change.

Concurrently, there is a stress on the in-service training of teachers. A Training Pedagogical Consultancy Team, implemented in each CIEP, is in charge of advising on the construction of pedagogical practices inside each school. This permits a rethinking of the political role of the school from the point of view of content, methodology, and administration. Seven principles orient the training programs (which are of two kinds—intensive, lasting ten days, or continuous): (1) the political goal, that is, the engagement of teachers in relation to pupils; (2) democratic and participative management; (3) consideration of the clientele's culture, taking into account social and economic differences; (4) selection, by relevance to the educational practice, of curriculum content; (5) the unification of content and methods; (6) interdisciplinary; and (7) the evaluation system— to evaluate not what the pupil does not know but what he or she has managed to add to his/her previous knowledge and practice.

Of course, the CIEP experience is still very recent. Even though the pedagogical and social principles are widely recognized as the solution for those children in most need, there are and have been a number of difficulties. First, the number of schools must increase; Leonel Brizola's government target was to build 500 CIEPs by 1986, but only 100 were fully implemented. (Brizola was a harsh opponent of Sarney, which made it very difficult to obtain federal resources.) Second, the next state government did not fully commit itself to a plan of expansion. Third, the CIEP is a revolutionary experience within the Brazilian educational tradition. It needs to be analyzed critically, and an interest in critical appraisal is already visible in the research done by the staff in the Carlos Chagas Foundation (Paro et al., 1988). In may be that the new Collor government will take up the CIEP experience and expand it in different parts of

Brazil. The issue was raised in the second phase of Collor's presidential campaign.

A different educational change, also important and also local, was attempted in Minas Gerais: a ground-up educational innovation. When Tancredo Neves was elected governor in 1983, two academics were in charge of the Secretariat of Education: Secretary Otavio Elisio, from the Faculty of Engineering, and Superintendent Neidson Rodriques, from the School of Education. They planned the Minera Conference of Education as a participatory reform. Discussions took place inside schools all over the state. Then the debate moved to the municipal level, culminating in a written document. This document was discussed in the Regional Divisions of Education. The outcomes were then discussed in a major state conference, and the proceedings (as directives for education in Minas Gerais) went back to the schools for approval or amendments. The secretary then formulated the Mineiro Plan of Education, based on the amended proceedings. Some of the new practices implemented (and later borrowed by the great majority of Brazilian states, including Sao Paulo and Rio) include the reformulation of literacy policies through the creation of a basic cycle of literacy (the first two years of primary education); the creation of governing bodies inside the schools: and a general assembly of teachers, pupils, administrators, and parents which will create committees with autonomy to decide matters such as timetables, programs, evaluations, optional disciplines, and the recommendation of names for head-teachers (until recently a highly political issue).

Practices that are not institutionalized through federal laws may not live long. The current governor of Minas Gerais has tried to abolish some of the policies. Thus, despite the courage and the imagination of these local examples of educational change, there remains a strong tradition in Brazil for carrying out reform from the center. Within this tradition, it is important to sketch briefly the social processes and educational implications of the new debate that preceded the Brazilian Constitution.

A major political and social event of the last decade was the debate about and the drawing up of a new Constitution. Discussions took place in a variety of associations and trade unions, and among students and educationists. For example, the 1986 National Conference of Education, held in Goiania, was completely devoted to this issue. Everyone, stimulated by the wave of political democracy, wanted to contribute to suggestions to be offered to Congress. The Constitution in its particular references to education was seen as a major opportunity to conceptualize and generate educational reform.

The chance that this process of Constitution-writing offered must be understood in terms of traditional reform processes in Brazilian history, in which political and educational reforms have taken place at the level of the national political elites, thus denying mass participation. In this case, while special subcommittees were being set up in Congress for different areas in relation to the Constitution (e.g., the Sub-Committee for Education), a large group made up of representatives from national organizations involved directly or indirectly with the educational problem—for example, the National Association of Higher Education Teachers (ANDES), the National Association of Students (UNE), the Brazilian Society of Researchers and Scientists (SBPC), the National Trade Union (CUT)—organized themselves to put forward their claims. Four main principles were advocated: (1) the right to free education at all levels; (2) the allocation to education of at least 13 percent of the monies raised from income tax and at least 25 percent of the state and municipal budget to education; (3) the spending of public money only in state schools, with no public resources allocated to private education; and (4) the democratization of education in terms of access, permanence and administration.

The National Association for Postgraduate Studies in Education (ANPEd) had been a very active participant in the debate over new directions on education. During its Eleventh Annual Conference in 1988, thirty-two general principles were presented as suggestions for the new legislation on education. The major themes of these principles were redefinitions of the role of the state, established in terms of duties; curriculum policies (and the concept of work and education); and management and systems of power and control.

In terms of the duties of the state, ANPEd argued that special attention should be given to preschool education: it is a right of the child, a duty of the state, and a choice of the family. The responsibility of the state for creating conditions that permit compulsory access to basic education was also emphasized. Stress was also placed on adult education: young and adult workers who did not attend school at the appropriate age should be guaranteed access to various kinds of education. They must also have a particular working week with no reduction in wages. The state must also guarantee the right to trade union affiliation for staff at all levels of education.

In terms of curriculum policies, ANPEd stressed decentralization of the curriculum for preschool education at state and municipal levels. It accepted a national common basic curriculum for primary and secondary education, provided that regional and local differences were respected as well as the special conditions of the urban and rural working class. It argued that the relationship between work and education should be understood in the light of theories of polytechnical education. This principle was to be adopted and implemented at the second level of basic education and should include an emphasis on knowledge of the foundations of Brazil's social structure and state policies; mastery of the foundations of different techniques used in modern production; and knowledge of the production process and its relations with society.

At the university level, ANPEd reasserted claims for academic freedom (i.e., pedagogical and scientific autonomy). This freedom refers particularly to curricula of courses and evaluation, which here is conceptualized as an instrument for policy formulation aimed at quality development of the institution.

ANPEd's views on the management of educational institutions included a stress on democracy in management at all levels of education and effective participation of all social classes, especially the working class. Democratic management was also identified with both the establishment of a teaching career at the national level and salary equivalences at each of the three governmental levels: federal, state, and municipal. In terms of finance, complete autonomy was demanded. University budgets should be decided and distributed inside the institution. The same policy of noninterference by the state should be adopted in relation to the appointment of high-level administrators (elections are advocated) and to the management of staff.

Interlocking here, in these perhaps idealistic proposals by an important pressure group, are three issues that run through Brazilian educational history and Brazilian efforts at educational reform. The first deals with the principle of public money being allocated to public (state) institutions. This debate is not new in Brazil; it revived, to a certain extent, the debate on public and private education that dominated the 1930s, especially the constitutional debate of 1934. The Pioneers of Education (the New School Movement, led by Anisio Teixeira, Dewey's follower) heavily influenced the discussion on the 1961 educational reform while it had been debated at length in Congress. Today, the liberal educationists advocate the same issue; public resources should be spent on state schools. But the power of the church has remained and is now being shared by private, nonreligious groups. Their private primary and secondary schools have a middle-class clientele that still acts as a powerful pressure group. As a result of the private lobby group, the Congress assumed an ambivalent position on this issue.

The second issue is related to the principles of university autonomy and academic freedom. Not only have these principles have been claimed by the academic community since the creation of the Brazilian university, but they were also a major claim in the Cordoba Manifesto of 1918, widespread in Latin America. They are still not fully implemented.

What continues to exist is the perennial Brazilian gap between the vision of order and progress, and reality; and the Brazilian positivist faith in the power of law. Even with a new Constitution, "the passage from an authoritarian order to an open and democratic one does not take place by simple magic" (Iglesias, 1985)—and neither does the transition from an authoritarian education system to an open and democratic one. Educational reform in Brazil has begun again as a process, but it remains as it has done so throughout Brazilian history, as terribly dependent on the oscillations of politics and political change.

REFERENCES

Arapiraca, Jose de Oliveira. 1982. *A USAID e a educacao brasileira*. Sao Paulo: Cortez.

de Azevedo, Fernando. 1932. *Manifesto dos Pioneiros de Educacao Nova*. Rio.

———. 1950. *Brazilian Culture*. Trans. William Rix Crawford. New York: Macmillan Co.

Berger, Manfredo. 1972. *Educacao e Dependencia*. 2d ed. Rio: Difel.

Burns, E. 1980. *A history of Brazil*. New York: Columbia University Press.

Cardoso, Fernando Henrique. 1977. *O modelo politico brasileiro*. Sao Paulo: Difel.

Carone, Edgar. 1970. *A Republica Velha*. Sao Paulo: Difusao Europeia do Livro.

Castro, Claudio de Moura. 1983. "The Impact of European and American Influences on Brazilian Higher Education." *European Journal of Education* 18 (4): 367–375.

Chargas, Valnir. 1978. *O Ensino de Primeiro e Segundo Graus: Antes, Agora e Depois?* Sao Paulo: Ed. Saraiva.

Cowen, Robert, and Maria Figueiredo-Cowen. 1989. "Educational Excellence: The Case of Brazil." *Higher Education Policy* 2 (3): 14–17.

Cunha, Luiz Antonio. 1977. *Educacao e Desenvolvimento Social no Brasil*. 2d ed. Rio: Liv. Francisco Alves.

———. 1980. *A universidade tempora. O ensino superior da colonia a era de Vargas*. Rio: Civilizacao Brasileira.

Cury, Carlos Roberto Jamil. 1978. *Ideologia e educacao brasileira*. Sao Paulo: Cortez e Moraes.

De Barros, Roque Spencer M. 1980. *Diretrizes e Bases da Educacao*. Sao Paulo: Pioneira.

Evans, Peter. 1979. *Dependent Development: The Alliance of Multinational, State and Local Capital in Brazil*. Princeton, N.J.: Princeton University Press.

Fausto, Boris. 1977. *Historia Geral da Civilizaçao Brasileira*. Rio: Difel.

Fernandes, Florestan. 1975. *Universidade Brasileira: reforma ou revolucao*. Sao Paulo: Alfa-Omega.

Figueiredo, Maria C. M. 1981. "Curriculum Issues in Brazil: Traditions, Policies and Problems." *Compare* 11, 1: 89–98.

———. 1986. "Academic Freedom and Autonomy in the Modern Brazilian University– A Comparative Analysis." Unpublished Ph.D. thesis, University of London.

———. 1987. "Politics and Higher Education in Brazil: 1964–1986." *International Journal of Educational Development* 7, 3: 173–181.

Freitag, Barbara. 1979. *Educacao, Estado e Sociedade*. 3d ed. Sao Paulo.

Furtado, Celso. 1972. *Analise do modelo brasileiro*. 3d ed. Rio: Civilizacao Brasileira.

Haar, J. 1977. *The Politics of Higher Education in Brazil*. New York: Praeger.

Ianni, Octavio. 1963. *Industrializacao e Desenvolvimento Social no Brasil*. Rio: Civilizacao Brasileira.

Iglesias, Francisco. 1985. *Constituentes e Constituicoes Brasileiras*. Sao Paulo: Braziliense.

Junior, Caio Prado. 1976. *Historia Economica do Brasil*. Sao Paulo: Brasiliense.

Lima, Lauro de Oliveira. 1974. *Estorias da Educaçao no Brasil: de Pombal a Passarinho*. Rio: Ed. Civilizacao Brasileira.

de Mello, Guiomar Namo. 1978. *Escola Nova, Tecnicismo e Educacao Compensatoria*. Sao Paulo: Loyola.

Nagle, Jorge. 1974. *Educacao e Sociedade na Primeira Republica*. Sao Paulo: Ed. da Universidade de Sao Paulo.

Nosella, Paolo. 1986. "Educacao Tradicional e Educacao Moderna." *Educacao e Sociedade*, no. 23.

Nunes, Clarice. 1980. *Escola e dependencia, o ensino secundario e a manutencao da ordem*. Rio: Achiamé.

de Oliveira, Francisco. 1981. *A Economia Brasileira: Critica a Razao Dualista*. Petropolis: Vozes.

Paro, Victor Henrique, et al., 1988. *Escola de Tempo Integral: Desafio para o Ensino Publico*. Sao Paulo: Cortez.

Pereira, Luiz Carlos Bresser. 1972. *Desenvolvimento e Crise no Brasil*. Sao Paulo: Braziliense.

————. 1987. *Economica Brasileira*. Sao Paulo: Braziliense.

Ribeiro, Darcy. 1965. *A universidade necessaria*. 3d ed. Rio: Paz e Terra.

————. 1986. *O livro des CIEPs*. Rio: Bloch.

Romanelli, Otaiza de Oliveira. 1978. *Historia de Educacao no Brasil* (1930/1973). Rio: Vozes.

Schneider, Ronald M. 1971. *The Political System of Brazil: Emergence of a "Modernizing" Authoritarian Regime, 1964–1970*. New York.

Schooyans, M. 1973. *Destin du Bresil: La Technocratie Militaire et son Ideologie*. Gembloux: Duculot.

Schwartzman, Simon. 1979. *Formacao de comunidade cientifica no Brasil*. Sao Paulo: Ed. Nacional.

Selcher, Wayne A., ed. 1986. *Political Liberalisation in Brazil*. London: Westview Press.

Silva, Golbery do Conto e. 1967. *Geopolitica do Brasil*. Rio: Jose Olympio.

Skidmore, T. E. 1967. *Politics in Brazil*. New York: Oxford University Press.

Soares, Magda Becker. 1989. *Alfabetizacao no Brasil: o estado do contecimento*. Brasilia: INEP.

Stepan, A. 1971. *The Military in Politics: Changing Patterns in Brazil*. Princeton, N.J.: Princeton University Press.

Warde, Miriam Jorge. 1977. *Educacao e Estrutura Social*. Sao Paulo: Cortez e Moraes.

5

CANADA

Dennis Thiessen

National reviews of educational reform often cast their nets quite broadly in search of fundamental themes, issues, and directions. The typical analysis focuses on the content of reforms, with more recent portrayals also addressing the reform process. Inevitably, given the centralization of most educational systems, the reports rely on policy statements, resource documents, and studies produced or sponsored by the departments of education. Consequently, the view most represented in the literature is one of mandated and large-scale reform. Rarely are national accounts portrayed from the ground floor through the experiences of teachers. The teachers' place in educational reform depends on the parameters set by power, geography, and diversity, and the teachers' ability to work within and, where necessary, to alter how these themes affect their professional lives. More extensive and in-depth studies of teachers, their perspectives, their situation, and their practices, have questioned traditional assumptions about the place of teachers in educational reform.

In most mandated changes in the 1980s, teachers were in the position of the educationally reformed, targets of agendas predominantly determined by departments of education. Repeated difficulties with implementation slowly shifted attention to the schools as the primary units of reform and to teachers as the key agents in the reform process. The traditional view of teachers as the objects of reform persisted but in tension with an emerging view of teachers as educational reformers.

A growing number of studies of teachers, their perspectives, their circumstances, and their practices, have questioned the traditional assumptions of teachers as the recipients of educational reform. In their complex world, teachers are portrayed as reformers in their own classrooms. They initiate many changes within the professional and social realities of the workplace. They cope with the demands of mandated reforms, adapting and sometimes, where necessary, postponing and resisting the prescribed practices. This chapter compares the two contrasting "places" of teachers in educational reform in the 1980s and anticipates the 1990s as a decade in which creating conditions that enable teachers to elaborate and extend their present capacity as educational reformers will become the priority.

To understand and evaluate the place of teachers in educational reform requires both insights into their particular experiences and appreciation of the wider organizational societal structures that frame their work. In subsequent sections, this chapter introduces the provincial character of the education system and the pervading themes of power (patterns of governance), geography (constraints of distance), and diversity (sensitivity to linguistic and cultural pluralism) that permeate Canadian society and induction. After a review of the major reforms in the 1980s, the text then addresses the "place" of teachers as either reformed or reformers. The final section projects into the 1990s with recommendations which re-form the reforming realities of Canadian teachers.

A NOTE ON SOURCES

In preparation for this chapter, I used the following guidelines to determine the selection of sources:

- Multiple Perspectives: to convey many points of view of key stakeholders in educational reform.
- Published and Unpublished, Formal and Informal: to represent information in different forms, for different audiences, and for different purposes.
- Canadian Studies of and by Teachers: to offer empirical accounts of teachers' actions, thoughts, and perspectives in reform.

To compare perspectives, I requested information and comments from the departments of education, teachers' federations, and a sample of school boards from across Canada. With the exception of school boards (40 percent response), over 80 percent of the groups sent documents and letters or contacted me by telephone.

Relevant documents were also located in Canadian educational journals, newsletters, and newspapers. Through the Canadian Education Index, Canadiana, and collections at the libraries of Canadian Education Association and the Ontario Institute for Studies in Education, I also uncovered numerous references that were either unpublished or not widely circulated.

Canadian studies of and by teachers increased significantly during the 1980s. They were not easily accessible, were widely dispersed, and were inconsistently listed in bibliographical sources. Some reports by Canadians studied non-Canadian teachers; some studies of Canadian teachers were conducted by non-

Canadian researchers; some inquiries by Canadian researchers of Canadian teachers applied frameworks and methods developed in other countries to gather and make sense of the data. I relied primarily on those studies that were done by Canadian researchers with Canadian teachers, especially when supported by departments of education, teachers' federations, and universities. Valuable research from school boards was not included.

The sources on educational reform in Canada and the place of teachers in the process, though growing rapidly in the 1980s, are in a relatively uncoordinated state. The information is often submerged in wider reports and discussion about either educational change or teaching. Circulation is frequently restricted. When located, the references are more attentive to local and provincial matters. The chapter then should be read as a first run, a synthesis of Canadian-only sources that deserves further analysis in future reviews.

THE CANADIAN EDUCATION SYSTEM

Canada does not have a national education system.[1] Under the Constitution Act of 1982 (formerly the British North America Act of 1867), education is the responsibility of the provinces. The involvement of the federal government is restricted primarily to provision of educational services to particular sectors (native groups, armed forces, penitentiaries), to funding of educational services to the two northern territories (Yukon and Northwest territories), and to financial support for educational programs of national priority (for example, bilingualism, multiculturalism, occupational and apprenticeship training). Other agencies maintain a national consciousness about education (for example, the Council of Ministers of Education, the Canadian Education Association, the Association Canadienne D'Éducation de Langue Français) through dissemination and persuasion (Canadian Education Association, 1984; Connelly, Crocker, and Cass, 1985). The authority to initiate, administer, and evaluate educational reform, however, stays within provincial borders.

School or education acts in each province outline the governance, organization, and regulations of the system. Education policy is the responsibility of the minister of education, whereas the implementation of policy flows through the department (or ministry) of education to school boards (*commissions scolaires* in Quebec), which are under the control of elected (appointed by the provincial and/or municipal governments in a few areas) trustees. The Department of Education supervises and evaluates school programs, establishes courses of study, approves resources (textbooks, audiovisual materials, computer software), defines duties for particular roles (trustees, educational officials, principals, teachers), determines rules to guide the operation of school boards, and provides financial support. School boards have jurisdiction over most staffing matters, program implementation, funding through local property assessment, and the management of the school system. Locally, further delegation of duties and responsibilities to schools may occur but at the discretion of the school board and according to the limitations declared by provincial authorities. Educational reform follows and works within this provincially based, permissive hierarchy.

In several provinces, both public (nonsectarian) and separate or denominational (often Roman Catholic) schools receive tax support. Most provinces have publicly funded programs for five year olds. From this age, elementary school extends to ages eleven to thirteen, while secondary school begins for twelve to fourteen year olds' and continues with programs for those to the age of eighteen. Students in Quebec complete secondary school by Grade 11 (sixteen year olds) but follow this with an intermediate level of two or three years at a collège d'enseignement général et professional (CEGEP). Elementary schools concentrate on interdisciplinary and basic learning in language, computation, science, social studies, and the arts (physical, expressive, practical). Secondary schools offer a range of subjects, some compulsory and some optional, in clusters or levels to enable students to prepare for the workplace or postsecondary education. Periodic reviews of these substantive and structural dimensions of schools often precipitate reforms.

Without a national department of education or educational policy, the Canadian education system appears pragmatic, less political than some countries (OECD, 1976: 19), and responsive to local and provincial needs. Beneath this aura of technical efficiency lies a set of complex and pervasive themes, which are national in scope, enduring, and problematic to educational reform.

PERVADING THEMES IN CANADIAN SOCIETY AND EDUCATION

Canada repeatedly addresses questions of *power* (control, centralization, and participation), *geography* (distance, distribution, and dialogue), and *diversity* (language, culture, and equality).[2] These themes persist over time, location, and circumstance, implicitly setting the parameters for any social and political agenda. Education, as an integral part of the social organization of Canadian society, both embodies and confronts the themes in efforts to sustain and reform its programs and practices. The following outline introduces three elements in each theme and the expression of these elements in Canadian society and education in the 1980s.

Power: Control, Centralization, and Participation

Canada's political system operates within the principle of federalism. Constitutional provisions for the division of authority at the national, provincial, and municipal levels specify separate and shared responsibilities. Jurisdictional disputes are primarily arguments about the location and not the existence of centralization. Hierarchical structures predominate. Control over policies, structures, and broad strategies remains in the hands of elected political bodies variously situated in terms of accountability and accessibility and with an administrative organization to support the implementation of their work. To participate more directly in decisions that affect their lives, Canadians need more local opportunities to shape key areas. But any realignment of fundamental powers may inhibit the ability of provincial and federal governments to influence wider segments of Canadian society.

A parallel division of authority occurs among the provincial departments of education, school boards, and schools. At the school board level, lines of accountability are complicated further by disagreements between trustees and senior administrators over the scope and direction of their respective responsibilities. Nonetheless, the conflict is still over which centralizing body should be in control. Educators in each level differ on the bounds of their zones of decision making (Lortie, 1969) and on the degree to which one zone should frame and be framed by the other zones.

Geography: Distance, Distribution, and Dialogue

With an area of 9,976,185 square kilometers, Canada is the second largest country in the world. Its comparatively small population of over 26 million people is unevenly distributed across ten provinces and two territories (for example: Ontario, 9.5 million, Prince Edward Island, 130,000, Northwest Territories, 53,000) and are concentrated in urban areas (30 percent live in Vancouver, Toronto, and Montreal) and within 200 kilometers of the border with the United States. Improved transportation and communication technologies lessen but do not overcome the reality and perception of distance. When so far apart, it continues to be difficult for Canadians to feel they are part of any dialogue about national interests.

Though not on the same scale, similar concerns about distance and distribution prevail in school boards and within the provincial organization of education. Urban school boards cope with the density of population (the 39 largest school boards cover 19,000 to 103,000 students), country school boards deal with fewer students but larger areas, and remote schools and school boards combat their isolation. Opportunities for dialogue among educators and between educators and other stakeholders at both local and provincial levels face the challenges of accessibility, time, and space.

Diversity: Language, Culture, and Equality

The third pervading theme in Canadian society is the nature of and response to linguistic and cultural diversity. Canada supports a policy of multiculturalism within a bilingual framework. Multiculturalism recognizes the contribution and place of ethnic groups in the development of the nation, while bilingualism endorses the importance of language in the duality of the "two founding peoples," Canadians from French and British descent. Yet cultural pluralism lives in tension with linguistic duality. Canadians struggle with the extent to which they can and should maintain a balance between their bilingual heritage and cultural mosaic. They search for equitable solutions that both respect the divisions within society and bridge the divide.

The diversity in Canadian society finds its way into every level of the education system. Provincial departments of education establish goals consistent with the federal policies of bilingualism and multiculturalism. School boards translate the goals and policies into such programs as English and French-as-a-Second Language, French immersion, heritage language, and intercultural and global education. In addition to linguistic and cultural diversity, educators also work with differences in gender, ability, socioeconomic circumstances, and community attitudes and traditions. The "diversity of diversities" threatens the previously unquestioned unity of purpose in the education system. Providing equal opportunities or, more ambitiously, equal outcomes, though unifying, may act against an equitable response to personal, social, and cultural differences.

Summary

The social themes of power, geography, and diversity pervade the Canadian education system in parallel but not necessarily corresponding forms. Hierarchical traditions in governance persist in tension with bottom-up or shared decision making. Physical and psychological separation between and within levels perpetrate loose and sometimes fragmented connections among educators. Demands for instructional and programmatic responses to the needs of an increasingly diverse student population intensify. Teachers live under these enduring and evolving conditions and with an accelerating call for reforms in their practices.

EDUCATIONAL REFORMS: NATIONAL TRENDS IN THE 1980s

Educational communities cannot escape the pervading themes in Canadian society. Consequently, reforms in the 1980s also addressed shifts in power (standards, performance, and shared responsibility), geography (opportunity, accessibility, and interaction), and diversity (program, responsiveness, and community), albeit in ways unique to the contextual realities of each province, school board, and school. Table 5.1 illustrates the range of major reforms associated with the three societal themes.[3] The following sections analyze the elements in each theme and comment on the current state of the reforms in the educational system.

Power: Standards, Performance, and Shared Responsibility

The structure and specificity of the reforms (see Table 5.1A) clarified and, to some extent, redistributed expectations for all levels of the educational system.

Table 5.1
Major Educational Reforms in the 1980s

A. Students, Performance, and Shared Responsibility

- Movement toward the core curriculum: Expanded notion of the "basics" at both elementary and secondary levels. In addition to communication and computational skills, the curriculum should help students develop their creative and critical thinking, computer literacy, and capacity to make responsible decisions.

- Prescription in program: In secondary schools, increased compulsory courses and graduation requirements. Curriculum guidelines became more detailed and directive about content, resources, teaching and learning strategies, and organization.

- Focus on evaluation: Present at all levels, including systematic provincial testing, program reviews, performance appraisal, development of benchmarks, and projects to improve student evaluation practices.

- Involvement of a wider range of stakeholders: On both advisory and decision-making bodies, parents, teachers' federations, and other relevant interest groups provided greater input and direction to the formation of policies.

- Reexamination of the financial basis for supporting elementary and secondary education: Funding formulas are under review. The proposals center on the redistribution of fiscal responsibility and the equitable allocation of resources given the disparities within each province.

B. Opportunity, Accessibility, and Interaction

- Technological development in communication: In addition to instructional applications, computers used to develop networks for sharing materials, managing records, and exchanging information.

- Delivery of distance education programs: Diversified approaches to correspondence education, independent learning, and "packaged" (videotapes, audiotapes, computer software, printed material) courses, especially for students and teachers in remote or isolated areas.

- Decentralization of school support units: Various service structures, storefront offices, centers of excellence, and research and development projects located in smaller towns and cities in key regions of the province.

- Linkages with the "public": Improved and increased contact with all segments of the community. The public received information, responded to surveys or requests for aid, volunteered, or participated in programs such as cooperative education.

- Restructure of staff roles: In conjunction with changes in such areas as special education, teacher education, and program services, teachers worked more closely with paraprofessionals, resource staff (for example, special education teachers and consultants, speech therapists, psychologists), librarians, mentors, peer coaches, and school administrators.

Table 5.1 (continued)

C. Program, Responsiveness, and Community

• Accommodation of groups with specific learning requirements: Organized services for students with physical or learning disabilities and with exceptional talents or gifted abilities.

• Inclusion of younger and older students: Attended to the needs of early childhood education (for example, introduction of junior kindergarten programs) and to the demands of adults for further options to continue their education (for example, adult learning centers and training programs).

• Improvement of transitional strategies: Through more intensive guidance and intervention, schools assisted students in their movements into school, from kindergarten to Grade 1, from elementary to secondary school, and into either the workplace or postsecondary education.

• Preservation of linguistic and cultural traditions: Strengthened efforts to offer services in both French and English where numbers warrant. French-immersion programs increased, as did heritage language options. Initiatives developed to respond to the particular needs of native students.

• Agency of social change: Continued to respond to problems in society with resources, units, or awareness programs in such areas as child abuse, AIDS, drugs, gender, environment, prejudice, literacy, and global understanding.

School boards and schools received more responsibility for managing the process of reform, while departments of education concentrated on the definition, regulation, and review of reform. Furthermore, all levels became more open to outside influence, seeking input and involvement from a wider range of stakeholders. Although tasks and operational decisions were more decentralized, accountability was not. Lines of authority were more clearly drawn throughout the system and ultimately linked to the departments of education. As designers and watchdogs of the standards, the departments of education retained control over establishing the priorities, framework, and criteria for what happens in schools. School boards and schools affected these directions but toiled more in their designated roles as translators and implementors of the provincial agenda.

Geography: Opportunity, Accessibility, and Interaction

Educational reforms (see Table 5.1B) in the 1980s also confronted the problems of physical and psychological distance for students and teachers. If people could not get to education, then education had to go to the people. Technological development enabled secondary school students to enroll in programs not offered locally, teachers to receive information about the latest resources and innovations, and interested citizens to inquire about the changing opportunities in the educational system. Overcoming distance with technological convenience was difficult to achieve on a wide scale.

For teachers, isolation was more a consequence of organizational tradition than physical separation. Increasingly, the reforms opened classroom doors and brought teachers closer to colleagues, administrators, parents, and community members. Greater contact provided a network of support and an opportunity to build mutual understanding. Teachers did not have to work alone or without assistance.

The reforms stimulated more routes for cross physical and psychological distances. Students and teachers had more chances to learn, to communicate, and to be part of a wider educational community. Proximity and availability, however, were not sufficient conditions to ensure sustained interaction.

Diversity: Program, Responsiveness, and Community

Some reforms were programmatic responses to the pluralistic clientele in schools (see Table 5.1C). Within the common goal of promoting fully functioning citizens in Canadian society, educational policies also differentiated programs to provide for students who varied in language, culture, religion, gender, location, ability, career aspiration, and economic circumstance. Accommodating the many differences in society was part of the growing social obligation felt throughout the educational system. Strained by an already overloaded curriculum, some schools struggled to adopt these reforms. The status and support of new programs generally reflected the local conditions and presence of diversity. Programs that genuinely responded to diversity clashed with the desire for common goals and a sense of community.

Summary

The reforms swelled and intensified an already crowded and complicated agenda. Familiar tensions emerged within and across reforms. Standardization confronted differentiation. Provincial control of key decisions clashed with local autonomy. Organizational efficiency collided with collegial necessity. Attempts to shrink the educational world (reforms of geography) both sharpened and, to some degree, exacerbated the tensions between power and diversity. Teachers lived in the midst of these conflicts, trying to make sense of the shifting landscape, order, and direction of reform.

TEACHERS' "PLACE" IN EDUCATIONAL REFORM

Teachers stand at the chalkface of reform. Their actions and the impact of their actions on student learning are the reference points for defining, implementing, and evaluating educational change. Historically, teachers have been *educationally reformed*, the final stop of a "pass-it-on" process set in motion by provincially mandated reforms. Was this their place in the 1980s? Or are they *educational reformers*, the arbiters and architects of meaningful changes in classrooms and schools?

The Educationally Reformed

Officially, teachers have no place in educational reform. In most provincial education or school acts, the Department of Education has the authority to initiate changes. School boards, schools, and, in some cases, directors of instruction and principals are responsible for the implementation of policy. The duties of teachers include such areas as competent instruction (Alberta, 1988), order and discipline (New Brunswick, 1983), or program design, supervision, and assessment (British Columbia, 1989). If remaining effective in the classroom is equivalent to following provincial regulations, then teachers are implicated in reform especially when changes in curriculum policies occur. Otherwise, they have no formal license to significantly deviate from approved programs and procedures.

The reforms listed in Table 5.1 were designed to change how teachers worked with their students, other teachers, and in their organizations. In the classrooms, teachers were to expand the applications of computers, individualize programs, and stimulate creative and critical thought. Their daily strategies would accommodate the spectrum of needs, in particular for those whose exceptionalities, social and cultural circumstances, or religious affiliations demand special care. While mindful of basic requirements in skills and knowledge for each level, grade, or subject, their programs would also extend into the community, address social concerns, and prepare students for successful transitions to the next phase of their schooling.

Changing organizational patterns created situations where teachers would work with greater support from professionals, colleagues with special training, and outside resources. Closer links to both administrative structures and parent and community groups would improve communication and accountability. Teachers would then open their classroom doors and admit those who help, seek information about, and scrutinize what they do.

The only official option of teachers was to adopt these reforms as replacements for and improvements on their current practices. Such changes cast teachers as the targets and students as the beneficiaries of reform. As the objects of reform, teachers were expected to follow mandated changes.

Outside the statutes, however, teachers were acknowledged as more than the recipients and messengers of provincial changes in policy. A growing consciousness about the complexity of implementation (Fullan, 1982) resulted in numerous provincial support documents and locally developed models and procedures, each of which gave considerably more involvement to teachers in the reform process. Approaches were rational, linear, and structured. They specified steps and timelines, organized resources, and clarified roles and responsibilities. Teachers were the "core of any improvement effort" (Saskatchewan Education, 1985: 43), the "final curriculum decision-makers and primary facilitators of learning'' (Ontario Ministry of Education, 1988: 8), and the "key agents of implementation'' (Taylor and Werner, 1989: 8). Accordingly, teachers became part of provincial writing teams, piloted and assessed proposed changes, and assisted in local and regional strategies (British Columbia Ministry of Education, 1982; Prince Edward Island, Department of Education, n.d.). Furthermore, the deliberate shift of more resources and authority to schools (Coleman, 1984, 1987) gave teachers the opportunity to influence the entry and application of reforms in their workplace. Only through participation in all segments of the reform process would teachers build the sense of commitment and ownership necessary to implement change. Teachers were construed not only as endpoints and conduits of reform (Clandinin and Connelly, forthcoming) but also as aids and catalysts in the reform process.

Participation came in particular forms, however. Teachers had the opportunity to provide input to new developments, support implementation, and react to the implications of reforms for their classrooms. Although a few were more active (for example, on writing teams), the conditions that surrounded their involvement limited their influence. Except in implementation, teachers had no special status in the reform process. The voices of other stakeholders were also sought, especially during review and development activities. Furthermore, the increased specification of roles coupled with the greater concerns about accountability strengthened the control of departments of education in such matters as standards, program requirements, and evaluation. With centralization reinforced, the shifts to more school-based responsibility in reform were more acknowledgments of where most change strategies should occur than a transfer of authority of teachers. Wide-scale participation was minimal; official recognition for the place of teachers in reform was still nonexistent.

Summary

Teachers continued as the objects of reform, albeit moving targets who talk back, especially when changes are off the mark. But their activity was without much influence on what comes their way, why, how it arrives, or who sends it.

The following assumptions perpetuated the place of teachers as the educationally reformed and the place of departments of education and their agents, school boards, as the comptrollers of reform.

• Teachers are fundamentally alike, have similar views, work under comparable circumstances, and react in predictable ways.

• In the classroom, teachers establish and sustain relatively uncomplicated routines and traditions. Theirs is a world of order, stability, and continuity.

• Teacher-initiated changes are primarily modifications of existing practices. Limitations of time, resources, and opportunity restrict the extent to which teachers pursue significant adaptations and redirections.

• Major reforms require a level of authority and support that is beyond the capacity of most teachers.

• Departments of education have the resources, structure, and obligation to determine major reforms and to regulate their applications. School boards have the organization and responsibility to manage and assist teachers in their efforts to implement reforms.

In the 1980s few questioned the importance of teachers in reform, but many doubt that significant changes would occur without the direction and intervention of departments of education and school boards. Whether teachers became educationally reformed in ways that benefit their students then depended on the efficiency, consistency, and accountability of the system set up by the department of education.

EDUCATIONAL REFORMERS

"Place" has another meaning for teachers as educational reformers. The teachers' place refers to the location, to the home of reform in classrooms and schools. In their place, teachers initiate, control, and where necessary, transform what happens. In the course of their interactions with students, teachers regularly reform their practices.

Teachers are the source for this view. The nature of their perspectives and practices are told through surveys (Dow and Whitehead, 1981; King, Warren, and Peart, 1988; Pensegrau, 1984; Tuinman and Brayne, 1988), naturalistic or focus group interviews (Flanders, 1983; Flanders and Wilson, 1990; Thiessen, 1985, 1989; Werner, 1988), case studies (Anderson, 1989; Cole, 1986; Kilbourn, 1986, 1990; Maguire, 1989; Olson and Eaton, 1987; Reicken and Grimmet, 1989; Russell, Munby, Spafford, and Johnston, 1988; Young, 1985, 1990), narratives (Clandinin, 1986; Connelly and Clandinin, 1988; Elbaz, 1983), collaborative autobiographies (Butt and Raymond, 1989; Butt, Raymond, and Yamagishi, 1988), phenomenological or hermeneutic inquiries (Boyce, 1983; Darroch and Silvers, 1982; Van Manen, N.D., 1988, 1990), action research (Carson and Couture, 1988), and vignettes, stories and critiques by teachers themselves (Church, 1989; Frankcombe, Grieve, Watson, and Werner, 1983; Leavitt, 1989; Peel Board of Education, 1989–1990; Townsend, 1989). These accounts represent the experiences of teachers in four areas: working conditions, social realities, involvement in decision making, and classroom practices. The life of teachers as educational reformers unfolded within the four areas of experience.

Working Conditions

By the mid–1980s, declining enrollments had reduced the full-time elementary and secondary school teaching population to 256,000. There were slightly more female than male teachers. On average, teachers were over forty years of age and most held at least one postsecondary degree. Their combined years of experience and academic qualifications placed many teachers at maximum salary, on a scale that made them the highest paid teachers in the world (CEA Newsletter, 1989).

The student-teacher ratio was 16 and the median class size was 24, with a range from under 10 to over 40 in each classroom depending on the age, composition, subject, and exigencies of local settings. Despite few changes during the decade, class size became a symbol of deteriorating working conditions. Teachers felt pressed to do more with the same number of students and few favorable adjustments in time and resources to support their efforts. They had more programs to implement, more records to keep, more people to inform, more demands of the school, school board, and department of education to meet, and greater student diversity to address. With few changes in time for planning, consultation, or deliberation, money, and support personnel, teachers perceived a widening gap between expectations and those conditions that would enable them to respond to the growing need to individualize and personalize instruction.

Teachers then had difficulty with reforms from outside because the changes invariably required a very different workplace for successful implementation. The priority of individualized and differentiated curriculum, for example, required classrooms with fewer students and more access to paraprofessional assistance. Without some sensitivity to the implications of the reform for conditions of work, teachers were limited in their capacity to act as reformers of these changes. Conversely, rarely were working conditions obstacles when teachers understood what was feasible, which conditions were alterable, and how the change would proceed given the present situation in their classrooms, schools, and community. Their ability to reform depended on their knowledge of and influence over their working conditions.

Social Realities

For many teachers, the working conditions determined their social patterns in schools. They spent most of their time in classrooms working with students. Their contacts with other teachers were often restricted to procedural matters, organizational meetings, or brief exchanges during breaks. Other conversations arose as part of the emerging network of in-school resource people responsible for coordinating programs for students with special needs. More extended discussions and relationships with peers developed in groups informally bound by a common interest or in formal teams arranged by administrators and focused on a particular reform. Despite renewed efforts in school improvement, instructional supervision, and teacher evaluation, the communication with vice principals and principals concentrated on the efficient operation of schools. Opportunities for professional dialogue then were restricted to fleeting interactions in an overloaded day. Student-teacher interactions dominated their social experience.

Teachers valued professional talk (regardless of its infrequency) for its instrumental utility with mandated reforms and for its collegial development with school-based reforms. In mandated reforms, teachers looked for other teachers who could illustrate and demonstrate the expected changes and suggest various transitions and uses for their classrooms. In school-based reforms, teachers were less concerned with instruction and immediate application. They had a better understanding of the rationale for the reform and relied on increased dialogue with their peers to build collegiality during the shared experience of reform.

Involvement in Decision Making

In many areas, teachers did not have much voice and choice. King, Warren, and Peart (1988: 21) observed:

Teachers work within the confines of curriculum established by government and a tradition of responding to the expectations of the public. Much of how they instruct, inform, counsel and discipline students is determined before they set foot in their classrooms by legislation, the organization of the schools and the education system, current philosophies of public education, pressure from parents and the public to achieve specific goals and the students' attitudes and plans.

Individually, teachers had control over the selection of materials, methods, and student evaluation strategies. They had some license in classroom management and some autonomy to examine alternative points of view. Yet, except for some influence through their federations, teachers sustained little collective clout in decisions about school programs and organization at a local level or in decisions about policy, goals and directions, and accountability at a provincial level. Once outside the classroom door, teachers had a diminished role in decisions that directly affected their practice.

Reforms not of their making were difficult for teachers to own. Ownership was not simply a product of participation, persuasion, or eventual identification. Who decides what to change, when, how, and why mattered. Ownership was also about power over the content and form (Goodson, forthcoming) of their practices. Except for those reforms that were either relatively unproblematic to implement or immediately applicable to their classrooms, teachers were reluctant to take possession of a change that denied them a controlling share in the process.

Involvement and ownership were not issues in reforms begun by teachers. Conflicts emerged when their reforms clashed with mandated reforms. If teachers ignored, coopted, or opposed mandated reforms, they were labeled reactionaries or resistors. In fact, they were protectors of their own reforms and conscientious objectors of incompatible reforms imposed by others.

Classroom Practices

Teachers, through interactions with students, constructed subcultures in their classrooms. Each classroom evolved its own rhythms, spatial character, and operational norms. It was a complex and dynamic environment shaped by both forces outside classrooms and actions by teachers.

In the kaleidoscope of classroom situations, teachers engaged in polysynchronous acts balancing the need for order, control, and certainty with the demands of adaptation, redirection, and creativity. They periodically disrupted routines searching for working relationships with students that better matched the cultural uniqueness of the classroom and the narrative unities (Connelly and Clandinin, 1988) of students and themselves. Their practices became working hypotheses, pragmatic tests of their perspectives in the fluctuating world of their classrooms.

The problem of mandated reforms was their entrance into a place that was already reforming. They arrived as intrusions with the potential to "contaminate the environment created by the teacher" (Boyce, 1983: 469). Teachers had to assess the possibility of conflict between their perspectives and the orientation of the reform. Once they worked through their own resistance to the change, they had to explore its personal (Is it compatible with the teachers' values?) and practical (How is it done? Can they do it?) worth for their classrooms. In this series of interpretive acts, teachers translated the change in ways that made sense for their circumstances. Werner (1988: 107) captures the ongoingness of this process:

The task may be initiated by a group called the developers and then further extended by teachers. Rather than assuming that they complete the innovation, developers at some point turn their work over to teachers who continue developing and modifying it. There may be agreement initially concerning its interpretation, but the ways in which the different parties continue to define what it is in their classrooms will reflect the various perspectives and contexts from which they individually work, with the result that the program may be in more or less constant change. What may have been apparent common sense at one time may become diverging views later on as redefining occurs. The meaning of the original project becomes changed over the course of experiencing its realization, and so innovations undergo modification or are discarded over time.

Deviations were more than unavoidable errors in the early phases, regrettable byproducts of experimentation, or epiphenomena. They were ongoing translations and transformations as innovations got closer to the personal and contextual realities of teachers.

Inside classrooms, teachers were reformers by trade. Their moves had the appearance of instrumental responses to immediate concerns, but, over time, their actions often were either accommodations to the subtle rhythms and balance of the classroom subculture or incremental adjustments in a broader story of reform. Through careful and persistent examination of their classroom experiences, teachers reformed their practices.

Summary

As educational reformers in the 1980s, the teachers' "place" was to arbitrate and design what happens in their classrooms. Teachers regularly renovated their place. They understood the present social conventions and working conditions within their school and the ways to influence these conventions and conditions to effect change. They were busy reflecting on classroom life, trying out alternative strategies, evaluating the consequences of their actions, and introducing new possibilities. Into these cycles of internal reform entered mandated changes. Teachers confronted these impositions and sustained their role of reformers if they were able to negotiate working conditions implicated by the change, had access to informed peers, could refuse unwarranted innovations, and received time to interrogate and struggle with the proposed redirection of their practices.

Underlying the place of teachers as educational reformers were the following assumptions:

- Teachers vary in biography, perspective, and personal and social circumstances.
- Classrooms are dynamic, complex, interactive, and self-contained environments in which teachers and students create their own cultural identity.
- Teacher-initiated changes are part of the ongoing reforms in classrooms. The practices of teachers are acts of reform.
- Though sometimes directed and defined by sources outside the school, reforms are constructed and reconstructed from within the classroom.
- Teachers reform their practices through inquiry.

Whether mandated by the Department of Education or developed by teachers, reforms contend with the conditions, control, and context of teachers' work. When the site of reform was the teachers' place, teachers were in a position to keep reforms in their sights. But to act as effective reformers, teachers needed their diversity, individual and collective judgments, and ongoing search for meaning and justified practices both accepted and valued.

ANTICIPATING THE 1990s: RE-FORMING THE NATURE OF REFORM

The pervading themes of power, geography, and diversity maintained the place of teachers as the educationally reformed throughout the 1980s. Major decisions about reform were made by the Department of Education and according to the perceived needs and will of society. Change strategies focused on closer links between departments of education, school boards, and schools, and between all levels of education and key stakeholders, on more specific directions and more intensive support mechanisms, and on clearer regulations and expectations. Teachers were more visible during the reform process, but primarily in the service of the centralized agenda. As the 1990s began, the perpetual struggle with reform, however, was forcing a reexamination of the traditional position of teachers as consumers of reform.

For departments of education, there was little reason to hand over the mantle of reform to teachers. Arguments that portrayed teachers as reformers came from teachers' federations (Canadian Teachers' Federation, 1989) and university researchers, each of whom relied on anecdotes or studies of a few selected and exceptional teachers to make their case. Evidence of a few innovative teachers did not persuade policymakers that widespread innovation was the norm in the classroom. The prevailing position was that teachers rarely initiated significant changes; most made adjustments to reestablish business as usual. Still a puzzle, however, was the struggle of implementation. Large-scale, mandated reforms only trickled into some classrooms. If the classroom is the place where reforms must come alive, then the nature of reform and the teachers' place in the process will have to be re-formed. The 1990s will be a decade in which teachers as educational reformers will experiment with different forms of engagement in educational change. To re-form reform in ways that center the process in the teachers' world will require changes in the traditional educational responses to the pervading themes in Canadian society. Some of these changes started in the 1980s and will continue into the twenty-first century. The recommendations outlined below are organized by the themes of power, geography, and diversity. They are an agenda for re-forming reform and building from the image of teachers as educational reformers which emerged in the 1980s.

Power

1. In education or school acts, formally recognize teachers as educational reformers.
2. Involve many stakeholders in some, and every teacher in all, decisions about reform.

Without official inclusion in provincial statutes, teachers will not have a decisive voice in reform. The typical portrayal of teachers in terms of duties or responsibilities should also stipulate their rights. Consequently, in addition to stating the duties of teachers as educational reformers, the acts should specify their rights of consultation, support, and veto in the reform process.

Unlike teachers, not every stakeholder is directly affected by each reform decision. In a system of mutual constraints and influence, teachers have the only voice that needs to be heard regularly. Where possible, every teacher should participate; representative strategies should be the exception and not the rule. Their importance should evolve from their individual and collective part in deliberations with stakeholders who have a vested and shared interest in each decision. Teachers should develop an interdependent base from which to shape the nature of reform.

Geography

3. Restructure the workday to enable teachers to reform their practices collectively.
4. Extend the use of communication networks to help teachers initiate, elaborate, and evaluate their reforms.

Teachers who work both alone and in concert with other teachers develop more informed and justified reforms for their classrooms. The school day should afford opportunities that permit teachers to escape the psychological and physical isolation imposed by traditions which insist that they spend their time primarily in classrooms with their students. Their workday should provide time for professional talk, to compare notes, to consider innovations from outside developers, to review and exchange ideas and resources, to observe and critique each other's practices, to create and experiment with alternative approaches, and to build a community of reformers.

With the aid of ongoing technological advances, teachers should be able to identify and interact with reformers in distant schools, school boards, or departments of education. Improvements in video and audio transmission should make face-to-face encounters feasible and practical for teachers regardless of their location. The possibilities of joint decision making, mutual support, and collaborative reform should be available on a large scale.

Diversity

5. Increase the capacity of teachers as reformers by reducing the size of their classes.
6. Acknowledge and support personal and contextual variability in reform.

Teachers are well aware of the diversity of both their students and the programs developed to address the varied aspirations, interests, and rights of students. Responding to a wide range of needs is a fundamental principle for teachers, but to live by the standard of individualized and personalized instruction will require a significant reduction in class size. Altered workdays, improved networks, empowered roles, or formal recognition as reformers will not result in significant classroom changes unless teachers have fewer students with whom to work in more intense, meaningful, and productive partnerships.

The diversity of students and programs is also characteristic of teachers. Theirs is a world of personal and contextual variability. Reforms, especially those from outside, will continue to fail if they either ignore the perspectives of teachers and the uniqueness of their classrooms or overwhelm these differences with *one-*

size-fits-all proclamations. Teachers should take hold of reforms and determine personally, educationally, and socially justified adaptations for their classroom. The resulting diversity should display the richness of reforms orchestrated by teachers and should serve as a catalyst for further innovation.

CONCLUSION

Will the 1990s become a period of re-forming reform? The recommendations of geography are possible now and likely will intensify interactions among teachers and between teachers and other stakeholders inside and outside the educational system. Restructuring their interactions will depend less on technological feasibility and more on the perceived social and professional importance of these contacts for ongoing classroom reforms.

Increased pressure to meet the needs of a more diverse student population will bring the issue of class size to a crisis point. Resolutions will vary from reductions in class size for certain segments (for example, in Ontario legislation requires smaller classes for children in their first three years of school), to specialization in fewer areas especially for elementary school teachers, to strategic placements of paraprofessionals to assist with differentiated program delivery. It will be more difficult to sustain support for diversity in teacher perspective and classroom culture. Acknowledging classroom diversity in reform will clash with the traditional distribution of power.

Shifts in power will be the most complex theme to re-form. Recognizing teachers as the primary educational reformers will compel the reconstruction of hierarchical working relationships. The authority of departments of education will come more from their ability to work closely with teachers, to understand diversity among programs, teachers, and students, and to seek information that addresses mutual concerns and facilitates productive debate. Some comments from teacher federations suggest that this form of partnership will take some time to create. Reacting to the government's handling of destreaming in the early years of secondary school, Jim Head, president of the Ontario School Teachers' Federation, stated:

What teachers would like to see is an honest ongoing effort by government to involve them in the process of reform, with an eye to improving on what is already a fine school system, rather than the approach taken by successive governments—radical upheaval of the system every 5 to 10 years, characterized by top-down decision making, inadequate resources for effective implementation of whatever the plan, and little true evaluation of the system's real strengths and weaknesses at any one time.

In a similar vein, Elsie McMurphy, president of the British Columbia Teachers' Federation, during a speech at their 1989 general meeting, called on teachers to press for a lead role in reform as "self-directing partners in implementing change" and to dispel the government's lingering view of teachers as "reactive dependents" (p. 11).

An awakening to and reconceptualization of teachers as educational reformers will require much more than accepting studies that portray the practices of teachers as acts of reform. As reformers, teachers will occupy a politically different place, one that relies on their reciprocal connections with key stakeholders for their influence and importance. Meaningful reforms, if their roots begin and build from the will and capabilities of teachers, will make the struggle inevitable and worthwhile.

NOTES

1. Numerous references provide general overviews to education in Canada (Blair, 1988; Canadian Education Association, 1984; Connelly, Crocker, and Kass, 1985; Statistics Canada 1989a, 1989b; Sova, 1990).

2. Various observers refer to power, geography, and diversity in their examination of education in Canadian society. Easton (1988) and Wilkinson (1986) assess the financing of education, whereas Ghosh and Ray (1987), Kach, Mazurek, Patterson, and DeFaveri (1986), Stevenson and Wilson (1988), and Wotherspoon (1987) critique the social and political relationship between education and society.

3. The Council of Ministers (1981, 1984, 1986, 1988, 1989) provides regular reviews of educational reforms in Canada. The Canadian Educational Association publishes a newsletter nine times yearly, outlining major initiatives at the local, provincial, and national levels. Common (1981), Henchey (1989), and Wideen (1988) also comment on recent trends in educational change.

REFERENCES

Alberta Education. 1988. *The Practice Review of Teachers Regulation*. Edmonton, Alberta: Council on Alberta Teaching Standards.
———. 1989. *School Act*. Edmonton, Alberta.
Anderson, S. 1989. "The Management and Implementation of Multiple Changes in Curriculum and Instruction." Unpublished doctoral dissertation, Ontario Institute for Studies in Education. Toronto, Ontario.
Aoki, T. 1984. "Towards a Reconceptualization of Curriculum Implementation." In *Alternative Perspectives on School Improvement*, ed. D. Hopkins, and M. Wideen. London: Falmer Press.
———, K. Jacknicke, and D. Franks, eds. 1986. *Understanding Curriculum as Lived: Curriculum Canada VII*. Vancouver, British Columbia: Centre for the Study of Curriculum and Interaction, University of British Columbia.
Blair, R. 1988. "Canada." In *The Encyclopedia of Comparative Education and National Systems of Education*, ed. T. Postlethwaite. New York: Pergamon Press.
Boag, N. 1980. "Teacher Perception of Curricular Change." Unpublished doctoral dissertation, University of Alberta, Edmonton, Alberta.
Borman, S. 1984. "Improving Teacher Practice: A Case Study of School-based Curriculum." Unpublished master's thesis, Simon Fraser University, Burnaby, British Columbia.
Boyce, E. 1983. "An Ethnography of Teacher-Staff Perspectives." Unpublished doctoral dissertation, University of Alberta, Edmonton, Alberta.

British Columbia Ministry of Education. 1982. *Guidelines for Program Implementation*. Victoria, British Columbia.

————. 1989. *School Act*. Victoria, British Columbia.

Butt, L. 1986. *Curriculum Implementation: A Needs Assessment of the Western Ontario Region*. London: Ontario Ministry of Education, Western Region.

Butt, R., J. Olson, and J. Daignault, eds. 1983. *Insiders' Realities, Outsiders' Dreams: Prospects for Curriculum Change. Curriculum Canada IV*. Vancouver, British Columbia: Centre for the Study of Curriculum and Interaction, University of British Columbia.

————, and D. Raymond. 1989. "Studying the Nature and Development of Teachers' Knowledge Using Collaborative Autobiography." *International Journal of Education* 13(4): 403–418.

————, D. Raymond, and R. Ray. 1988. "Biographical and Contextual Influences on an Ordinary Teacher's Thoughts and Action." In *Teacher Thinking and Professional Action*, ed. J. Lowyk, C. Clarke, and R. Halkes. Lisse, Holland: Swets and Zeitlinger.

————, D. Raymond, and L. Yamagishi. 1988. "Autobiographical Praxis: Studying the Formation of Teachers' Knowledge." *Journal of Curriculum Theorizing* 7(4): 87–164.

Canadian Education Association. 1984. *An Overview of Canadian Education*. Toronto, Ontario.

————. 1989. "Good Pay." *Newsletter* 403(3).

Canadian Teachers' Federation. 1988. *Teaching in Canada 1988*. Ottawa, Ontario.

————. 1989. *Innovations in Teaching Resumes of the Hilroy Fellowship Program*. Ottawa, Ontario.

Carson, T. 1983. "Conversations with Participants about Curriculum Implementation." Paper presented at a meeting of the American Educational Research Association. Montreal, Quebec.

————. 1985. *Curriculum Implementation as School Improvement: What are the Possibilities for Praxis?* Occasional Paper No. 36. Edmonton, Alberta: Department of Secondary Education, University of Alberta.

————. 1986. "Curriculum Implementation as a Problem of Human Action." In *Curriculum as Lived. Curriculum Canada VII*, ed. T. Aoki, K. Jacknicke, and D. Frank. Vancouver, British Columbia: Centre for the Study of Curriculum and Instruction, University of British Columbia.

————, and J. C. Couture, eds. 1988. *Collaborative Action Research: Experiences and Reflections*. Improvement of Instruction Series, Monograph Number 18. Edmonton, Alberta: Alberta Teachers' Association.

Centrale de l'Enseignement du Québec. 1984. *Restaurer l'école publique*. Montreal, Quebec: Mémoire au Conseil Supérieur de l'Éducation.

Chung, C. 1985. "Perceptions and Preferences of Teachers for the Distribution of Decision-making." Unpublished doctoral dissertation, University of Alberta, Edmonton, Alberta.

Church, S. 1989. *From Teacher to Teacher: Opening Our Doors*. Armdale, Nova Scotia: Halifax-County-Bedford School Board.

Clandinin, D. 1986. *Classroom Practice: Teacher Images in Action*. London: Falmer Press.

————, and F. M. Connelly. (Forthcoming). "Teacher as Curriculum Maker." In *Hand-*

book of Research on Curriculum, ed. P. Jackson. Washington, D.C.: American Educational Research Association. (Draft copy.)

Cole, A. 1986. "Teachers' Spontaneous Adaptations: A Mutual Interpretation." Unpublished doctoral dissertation, University of Toronto, Toronto, Ontario.

Coleman, P. 1984. "Improving Schools by School-based Management." McGill Journal of Education 19(1): 25–42.

———. 1987. "Implementing School Based Decision Making." Canadian Administrator 26(7): 1–11.

Common, D. 1981. "Two Decades of Curriculum Innovation and So Little Change." Education Canada 21(3): 42–47.

Connelly, F. M., and D. J. Clandinin. 1985. "Personal Practical Knowledge and the Modes of Knowing: Relevance for Teaching and Learning." In Learning and Teaching the Ways of Knowing, ed. E. Eisner. Eighty-Fourth Yearbook of the National Society for the Study of Education. Chicago: University of Chicago Press.

———, and D. J. Clandinin. 1988. Teachers as Curriculum Planners: Narratives of Experience. New York: Teachers College Press.

———, R. Crocker, and H. Kass. 1985. Policies, Practices, and Perceptions. Vol. 1. Toronto, Ontario: OISE Press.

Connors, B. 1986. "Inservice: A Re-search." In Curriculum as Lived. Curriculum Canada VII, ed. T. Aoki, K. Jacknicke, and D. Frank. Vancouver, British Columbia: Centre for the Study of Curriculum and Instruction, University of British Columbia.

Conseil Supérieur de l'Éducation. 1984. The Conditions of Teaching. Quebec City, Quebec: Ministry of Education.

———. 1988. Rapport annuel 1987–1988 sur l'état et les besoins de l'éducation. Quebec City, Quebec: Government du Quebec.

Council of Ministers. 1981. Education in Canada. Report to the 38th Session, International Conference on Education, Geneva.

———. 1984. Education in Canada 1981–1983. Report to the 39th Session, International Conference on Education, Geneva.

———. 1986. Education in Canada 1984–1986. Report to the 40th Session, International Conference on Education, Geneva.

———. 1988. Recent Trends in Curriculum Reform at the Elementary and Secondary Levels in Canada. Report presented to the OECD's Centre for Educational Research and Innovation. Toronto, Ontario.

———. 1989. Education in Canada 1986–1988. Report to the 41st Session, International Conference on Education, Geneva.

Crocker, R. 1983. "The Functional Paradigms of Teachers." Canadian Journal of Education 8: 350–361.

———. 1989. Towards an Achieving Society. (Final report of the Task Force on Mathematics and Science Education). St. John's, Newfoundland: Province of Newfoundland and Labrador.

Darroch, V., and R. Silvers, eds. 1982. Interpretive Human Studies: An Introduction to Phenomenological Research. Washington, D.C.: University Press of America.

Dickson, W. 1989. Growth and Improvement: Expectations for CBE Mission Fulfillment. Calgary, Alberta: Calgary Board of Education.

Dow, I., and R. Whitehead. 1981. *New Perspectives on Curriculum Implementation*. Toronto, Ontario: Ontario Public School Teachers' Federation.

Easton, S. 1988. *Education in Canada: An Analysis of Elementary, Secondary, and Vocational Schooling*. Vancouver, British Columbia: Fraser Institute.

Egan, K. 1986. *Teaching as Story Telling: An Alternative Approach to Teaching and Curriculum in the Elementary School*. London, Ontario: Althouse Press, Faculty of Education, University of Western Ontario.

Elbaz, F. 1983. *Teacher Thinking: A Study of Practical Knowledge*. London: Croom Helm.

Erickson, G. 1987. "Constructivist Epistemology and the Professional Development of Teachers." Paper presented at a meeting of the American Educational Research Association Symposium on Educational Implications of Personal and Social Construction of Knowledge. Washington, D.C.

Federation of Women Teachers' Association of Ontario. 1989. *Professionalism*. Toronto, Ontario.

Flanders, T. 1983. "Teacher Realities, Needs and Professional Development." In *Insiders' Realities, Outsiders' Dreams: Prospects for Curriculum Change. Curriculum Canada IV*. ed. R. Butt, J. Olson, and J. Daignault. Vancouver: Centre for the Study of Curriculum and Instruction, University of British Columbia.

———, and D. Wilson. 1990. *Teaching Comes of Age: Responding to the Challenges of Change*. A Report for the Task Force on Teaching Conditions and Professional Practices. Vancouver, British Columbia: British Columbia Teachers' Federation.

Frankcombe, B., T. Grieve, R. Watson, and W. Werner, eds. 1983. *Program Implementation Experiences: Cases from British Columbia*. Vancouver, British Columbia: Program Implementation Services, British Columbia Ministry of Education and Centre for Study of Curriculum and Instruction, University of British Columbia.

Friesen, J., R. Carson, and F. Johnson. 1983. *The Teacher's Voice: A Study of Teacher Participation in Educational Decision-making in Three Alberta Communities*. New York: University Press of America.

Fullan, M. 1982. *The Meaning of Educational Change*. Toronto: OISE Press.

———. 1985. "Change Processes and Strategies at the Local Level." *The Elementary School Journal* 85(3): 391–421.

———, S. Anderson, and E. Newman. 1987. *Support Systems for Implementing Curriculum in School Boards*. Report to Ontario Ministry of Education. Toronto, Ontario: OISE Press.

———, and F. M. Connelly. 1987. *Teacher Education in Ontario: Current Practice and Options for the Future*. Toronto, Ontario: Ontario Ministry of Education.

———, and P. Park. 1981. *Curriculum Implementation: A Resource Booklet*. Toronto, Ontario: Ministry of Education.

———, and A. Pomfret. 1977. "Research on Curriculum and Instruction Implementation." *Review of Educational Research* 47(1): 335–397.

Gaskell, T. 1983. "Staff Renewal/Curriculum Improvement." Unpublished doctoral dissertation, University of Tennessee, Knoxville.

Ghosh, R., and D. Ray, eds. 1987. *Social Change and Education in Canada*. Toronto, Ontario: Harcourt Brace Jovanovich.

Goodson, I. (forthcoming). *Subjects and Schooling*. London: Routledge.

Graham, E. 1983. "Multiple Realities in a Social Studies Classroom." Unpublished doctoral dissertation. University of Alberta, Edmonton, Alberta.

Grants, L. 1987. "Mainstreaming Learning Disabled Students at the Junior High Level: A Study of Teachers Attitudes and the Variables Which Affect Attitudes." Unpublished master's thesis, University of British Columbia, Vancouver, British Columbia.

Greene, M. 1984. "The Professional Development Activities of Southern Alberta Teachers." Unpublished doctoral dissertation, Indiana University, Bloomington, Indiana.

Grimmett, P. 1987. "The Role of District Supervisors in the Implementation of Peer Coaching." *Journal of Curriculum and Supervision* 3(1): 3–28.

Hannay, L., and N. Chism. 1988. "The Potential of Teacher Transfer in Fostering Professional Development." *Journal of Curriculum and Supervision* 3(2): 122–135.

Hargreaves, A. (1989a). "Curriculum Policy and the Culture of Teaching." In *Reinterpreting Curriculum Research: Images and Arguments*, ed. G. Milburn, I. Goodson, and R. Clark. London, Ontario: Althouse Press and London, England: Falmer Press.

———. 1989b. *Elementary Teachers' Use of Preparation Time: Project Report*. Toronto, Ontario: Ontario Institute for Studies in Education.

Haysom, J. 1987. "How Do Teachers Evaluate Their Lessons?" in *Classroom Action Research Network, Bulletin No. 8. Action Research in Development*, ed. B. Somekh, A. Norman, B. Shannon, and G. Abbott. Cambridge: Cambridge Institute of Education.

Head, J. 1990. "Let Teachers in on Education Reform. Letter to the Editor." *The Toronto Star*, April 2, p. A18.

Henchey, N. 1989. "The Evaluation of Educational Reforms: A Canadian Perspective." Paper presented to a workshop on the Evaluation of Education Reforms, sponsored by Unesco and the Max Planck Institute, Berlin, Germany.

Hiebert, B. 1985. *Stress and Teachers: The Canadian Scene*. Toronto, Ontario: Canadian Education Association.

Highley, W. 1984. "Middle Aged Teachers: Perceptions of Their Careers." Unpublished doctoral dissertation, University of Alberta, Edmonton, Alberta.

Hood, R. 1986. "A Study of Decision-making Procedures Related to School Tasks and Teacher Participation." Unpublished master's thesis, Dalhousie University, Halifax, Nova Scotia.

Hopkinson, S. 1986. "Life in Three Multicultural Classrooms: The Notion of Intersubjectivity in Teaching and Learning." Unpublished doctoral dissertation, University of Alberta, Edmonton, Alberta.

Jacobson, E., and L. Kuehn. 1986. *In the Wake of Restraint. The Impact of Restraint on Education in B.C.* Vancouver, British Columbia: British Columbia Teachers' Federation.

Jeffrey, G. 1989. "Teacher Effectiveness in Nova Scotia." *Journal of Education* 400: 6–11.

John, H., W. Andrews, and T. Rogers, eds. 1982. *Canadian Research in Education: A State of the Art Review*. Ottawa, Ontario: Social Studies and Humanities Research Council.

Canada   93

Kach, N., K. Mazurek, R. Patterson, and I. DeFaveri. 1986. *Essays in Canadian Education*. Calgary, Alberta: Detselig Enterprises Ltd.

Kilbourn, B. 1986. "Situational Analysis of Teaching in Clinical Supervision." In *Learning about Teaching Through Clinical Supervision*, ed. J. Smyth. London: Croom Helm.

————. 1990. *Constructive Feedback: Learning the Art*. Toronto: OISE Press.

King, A., W. Warren, and M. Peart. 1988. *The Teaching Experience: A Profile of Ontario Secondary School Teachers*. Toronto, Ontario: Ontario Secondary School Teachers' Federation.

Koplin, R. 1988. "Professional Growth: One Teacher's View." *Research Forum* 2: 6–8.

Lam, Y. 1983. "Determinants of Teacher Professionalism." *Alberta Journal of Educational Research* 29(3): 168–179.

Leavitt, M., ed. 1989. *Teaching All the Children: Stories from the Classroom*. Fredericton, New Brunswick: New Brunswick Department of Education.

Leithwood, K. ed. 1982. *Studies in Curriculum Decision Making*. Toronto, Ontario: OISE Press.

————, ed. 1986. *Planned Educational Change*. Toronto, Ontario: OISE Press.

————, M. Fullan, and G. Heald-Taylor. 1987. *Ontario's School Improvement Project*. Report to the Ontario Ministry of Education. Toronto, Ontario: OISE Press.

Lortie, D. 1969. "The Balance of Control and Autonomy in Elementary School Teaching." In *The Semi-Professions and Their Organization*, ed. A. Etzioni. New York: Free Press.

Losier-Cool, R. 1985. "La réforme en éducation. Et la réponse est!...Mais quelle est la question?" *Nouvelles* 16(13): 1–12.

MacKinnon, A. 1987. "Detecting Reflection in Action among Preservice Elementary Science Teachers." *Teachers and Teacher Education* 3(2): 135–145.

Maguire, M. 1989. "Understanding and Implementing a Whole-Language Program in Quebec." *The Elementary School Journal* 90(2): 143–159.

Manitoba Education. 1988. *High School Education: Challenges and Changes*. Winnipeg, Manitoba.

Manitoba Teachers' Society. 1989. *Policy Handbook*. Winnipeg, Manitoba.

McAlpine, L. 1985. "The Educator-as-Evaluator: Facilitating Professional Development." Unpublished doctoral dissertation, Ontario Institute for Studies in Education, Toronto, Ontario.

McGiffin, G. 1983. "Coaching for Application: A School-Based Staff Development Project." Unpublished doctoral dissertation, University of Massachusetts, Boston.

McMurphy, Elsie. 1989. *President Elsie McMurphy's Speech to the BCTF Annual General Meeting*. Mimeograph: Vancouver, British Columbia: British Columbia Teachers' Federation.

Miller, J. 1986. *A Study of In-service Practices and Teachers' Views on Potential Roles for an Inservice Development Centre*. Saskatoon, Saskatchewan: Saskatchewan Teachers' Federation.

————, and W. Seller. 1985. *Curriculum Perspectives and Practice*. New York: Longman.

Mohan, E. 1982. *An Overview of Inservice Education and Training of Teachers in the Provinces of Canada*. Toronto, Ontario: Council of Ministers.

Mullaley, J. 1986. "Teachers' Perceptions of Change." Unpublished doctoral dissertation, Ontario Institute for Studies in Education, Toronto, Ontario.

Munby, H. 1986. "Metaphor in the Thinking of Teachers: An Exploratory Study." *Journal of Curriculum Studies* 18: 197–209.

Neil, A. 1985. "How the Experience of Inservice Teacher Education Can Be Made Worthwhile." Unpublished doctoral dissertation, University of Alberta, Edmonton, Alberta.

New Brunswick Department of Education. 1987. *Schools Act*. Fredericton, New Brunswick.

Nova Scotia Department of Education. 1988. *Public School Programs 1988–89, 1989–90*. Halifax, Nova Scotia.

Oberg, A. 1986. "Using Construct Theory as a Basis for Research into Teacher Professional Development." *Journal of Curriculum Studies* 19(1): 55–65.

————. 1987. "The Ground of Professional Practice." In *Teacher Thinking and Professional Practice*, ed. J. Lowyck, C. Clark, and R. Halkes. Lisse, Holland: Swets and Zeitlinger.

Olson, J. 1980. "Teacher Constructs and Curriculum Change." *Journal of Curriculum Studies* 12(1): 1–11.

————. 1985. "Changing Our Ideas about Change." *Canadian Journal of Education* 10(3): 294–308.

————, and S. Eaton. 1987. "Curriculum Change and the Classroom Order." In *Exploring Teachers' Thinking*, ed. J. Calderhead. London: Cassell.

Ontario Ministry of Education. 1985. *Professional Development Practices*. Provincial Review Report, No. 6. Toronto, Ontario.

————. 1988. *Curriculum Management*. Toronto, Ontario.

Ontario Secondary School Teachers' Federation. 1989. *The Challenges: The Directions*. Toronto, Ontario.

Organization for Economic Co-operation and Development. 1976. *Reviews of National Policies for Education: Canada*. Paris.

Pansegrau, M. 1984. "Teachers' Perspectives on Inservice Education." *Alberta Journal of Educational Research* 30(4): 239–258.

Park, P., and M. Fullan. 1986. *Issues of Professional Development: Ontario Curriculum 1986*. Toronto, Ontario: Ontario Teachers' Federation.

Peel Board of Education (1989–1990). *Let's Talk. (Project Newsletter for Talk: A Medium for Learning and Change.)* Mississauga, Ontario.

Pike, M. 1981. "Structures of Curriculum Change as Experienced by Teachers." Unpublished master's thesis, University of British Columbia, Vancouver, British Columbia.

Prince Edward Island Department of Education. (n.d.) *Role of Pilot Teachers*. Mimeograph.

Province of British Columbia. 1988. *A Legacy for Learners*. The report of the Royal Commission on Education. Vancouver, British Columbia.

Raymond, D. 1984. "Interpreting Curriculum Change: Teachers' Practical Knowledge as Revealed in Group Planning." *McGill Journal of Education* 19(3): 228–241.

Reicken, T., and P. Grimmett. 1989. "Teaching, Practicality, and Conformity: Issues Relating to Practitioner Use of an Innovation." Paper presented at a meeting of the Canadian Society for the Study of Education, University of Laval, Quebec City, Quebec.

Ruddy, S. 1983. "Burnout in the Teaching Profession: An Exploratory Study." Unpublished master's thesis, University of Calgary, Calgary, Alberta.

Russell, T., and P. Johnson. 1988. "Teachers Learning from Experiences of Teaching: Analysis Based on Metaphor and Reflection." Paper presented at a meeting of the American Educational Research Association, New Orleans.

Russell, T., H. Munby, C. Spafford, and P. Johnson. 1988. "Learning the Professional Knowledge of Teaching: Metaphors, Puzzles, and the Theory-Practice Relationship." In *Reflection in Teacher Education*, ed. P. Grimmett, and G. Erickson. Vancouver, British Columbia, and New York: Pacific Press, and Teachers College Press.

Saskatchewan Education. 1984a. *Curriculum and Instruction Review 1: What They Said: Educational Views of Saskatchewan People*. Regina, Saskatchewan.

―――. 1984b. *Curriculum and Instruction Review 2: Saskatchewan Education: Its Programs and Policies*. Regina, Saskatchewan.

―――. 1984c. *Curriculum and Instruction Review 3: Saskatchewan Children: Their Lives and Needs*. Regina, Saskatchewan.

―――. 1984d. *Directions: The Final Report*. Regina, Saskatchewan.

―――. 1985a. *Curriculum and Instructional Review 4: Toward the Year 2000: Future Directions in Curriculum and Instruction*. Regina, Saskatchewan.

―――. 1985b. *Curriculum and Instruction Review 5: School Improvement: Building a More Effective Learning Environment*. Regina, Saskatchewan.

―――. 1988. *Understanding the Common Essential Learnings: A Handbook for Teachers*. Regina, Saskatchewan.

Saskatchewan Teachers' Federation. 1983. *Inservice Education: Discussion Paper and Policy Proposal*. Saskatoon, Saskatchewan.

Seven Oaks School Division No. 10 n.d. *Functions of Teachers*. Mimeograph.

Sinclair, L. 1990. "Good Teachers, Good Conditions: Bargaining for Quality Education." *Teacher* 2(5): 1–3.

Sova, G., ed. 1990. *1990 Corpus Almanac and Canadian Sourcebook*. 25th Annual Edition. Don Mills, Ontario: Corpus Information Services.

Statistics Canada. 1989a. *Canada Year Book 1990*. Ottawa, Ontario.

―――. 1989b. *Education in Canada: A Statistical Review for 1987–1988*. Ottawa, Ontario.

Stevenson, H., and J. D. Wilson, eds. 1988. *Quality in Canadian Public Education*. London: Falmer Press.

Taylor, A., and W. Werner. 1989. *School District Planning of Curriculum Implementation*. Victoria, British Columbia: Educational Program Implementation Branch, British Columbia Ministry of Education.

Thiessen, D. 1985. *More than Marks: What Teachers Say about Student Evaluation*. Toronto: Ontario Public School Teachers Federation.

―――. 1989a. "Curriculum Change Constructs and Orientations." Unpublished doctoral dissertation, University of Sussex, Brighton, England.

―――. 1989b. "Teachers and Their Curriculum-Change Orientations." In *Reinterpreting Curriculum Research: Images and Arguments*, ed. G. Milburn, I. Goodson, and R. Clark. London: Falmer Press and Althouse Press.

―――. 1990. "Classroom-based Teacher Development." In *Understanding Teacher Development*, ed. A. Hargreaves and M. Fullan. London: Cassell.

Tomkins, G. 1986. *A Common Countenance: Stability and Change in the Canadian Curriculum.* Scarborough, Ontario: Prentice-Hall.

Townsend, R., ed. 1989. "Tales from the School." *Contexts of Policy Action* 1(1): 1–24.

Tuinman, J., and R. Brayne. 1988. *The On-Site Personnel Who Facilitate Learning.* Commissioned Papers: Vol. 4, British Columbia Royal Commission on Education. Victoria, British Columbia: British Columbia Ministry of Education.

Van Manen, M. 1988. *The Tact of Teaching: Human Science Monograph.* Edmonton, Alberta: Faculty of Education, University of Alberta.

———. 1990. *Researching Lived Experience: Human Science for an Action Sensitive Pedagogy.* London: Althouse Press.

———, ed. n.d. *Texts of Teaching.* Edmonton, Alberta: Human Science Research Project, Faculty of Education, University of Alberta.

Werner, W. 1980. "Implementation: The Role of Belief." In *Implementation Viewpoints*, ed. L. Daniels and I. Wright. Vancouver, British Columbia: Centre for the Study of Curriculum and Instruction, University of British Columbia.

———. 1981. "An Interpretive Approach to Curriculum Implementation." In *Curriculum Research and Development and Critical Student Outcomes*, ed. K. Leithwood and A. Hughes. Curriculum Canada, 3rd ed. Vancouver, British Columbia: Centre for the Study of Curriculum and Instruction, University of British Columbia.

———. 1988. "Program Implementation and Experienced Time." *Alberta Journal of Educational Research* 34(2): 90–108.

Whitney, T. 1983. "Social Reality in a Grade Four Class: A Case Study." Unpublished master's thesis, University of Alberta, Edmonton, Alberta.

Wideen, M. 1988. "School Improvement in Canada." *International Journal of Qualitative Research in Education* 1(1): 21–38.

Wilkinson, B. 1986. "Elementary and Secondary Education Policy in Canada: A Survey." *Canadian Public Policy* 12(4): 535–572.

Williams, L. 1986. "Developmental Patterns of Teaching Careers." Unpublished doctoral dissertation, University of Alberta, Edmonton, Alberta.

Wotherspoon, T. 1987. "Introduction: Conflict and Crisis in Canadian Education." In *The Political Economy of Canadian Education*, ed. T. Wotherspoon. Toronto, Ontario: Methuen.

Young, J. H. 1985. "Participation in Curriculum Development: An Inquiry into the Responses of Teachers." *Curriculum Inquiry* 15(4): 387–414.

———. 1990. "Curriculum Implementation: An Organizational Perspective." *Journal of Curriculum and Supervision* 5(2): 132–149.

6

CHINA

John N. Hawkins

To discuss educational reform in China is to deliberate on a process that has been underway almost continuously since the establishment of the People's Republic in 1949. Here we must distinguish between "reform" (*gaige*) and "revolution" (*geming*) since both terms have been used to label the various educational changes that have taken place in China during the past five decades. The term *gaige* implies the alteration of existing models with a view to "correcting" (*gai*) and "removing" (*ge*) those aspects that have been deemed inefficient and lacking in quality. By contrast, *geming* uses one character from the term for reform (*ge*) but pairs it with *ming* which implies much more dramatic action, literally, "removing the will of heaven" or overthrowing completely existing models. Recent events in the past five years in Chinese education clearly fall under the rubric of reform rather than revolution (compared, for example, with the period of the Cultural Revolution when the entire educational system was called into question).

Changes in Chinese education since the mid–1980s have been in response to several of the educational reform issues facing many other developing nations. China has experienced a greatly expanded educational system during the past decade and as such has had to cope with issues related to quality and equality, investment choices both of domestic resources and those of multilateral organizations (e.g., World Bank), lack of fit between reforms and implementation, use of education for skill development on the one hand and nation building on the other, and the general problem of managing an ever more complex educational system (Rondinelli, Middleton, and Verspoor, 1990). As Chinese educational policymakers worked their way through these diverse educational challenges, they quickly recognized the limits of educational reform in terms of overall financing, uncertain political, economic, and social conditions, resistance from teachers and the educational bureaucracy, varying degrees of commitment from the government, and the general complexity involved in reforming an educational system servicing over half a billion people. As Rondinelli et al. point out (1990), coming up with new ideas has never been a problem in educational reform; making them work is another matter.

China's current reform efforts must be viewed in the context of the numerous educational reform (and revolutionary) movements launched since 1949. The very establishment of the People's Republic constituted a major educational reform as the entire system was subjected to great scrutiny by the new leaders and various parts were either removed or restructured to bring them into line with the prevailing political and economic model. Curriculum was changed, the educational cycle was reoriented, literacy campaigns were launched, the educational structure was realigned, and the administrative apparatus was further centralized. This continued down to the 1960s with variations and different emphases depending on current governmental priorities. Radical movements such as the Hundred Flowers Movement (1956), the Great Leap Forward (1958), the Socialist Education Movement (1962), and eventually the Cultural Revolution (1966) all served to push the educational system in one direction ("red") or another ("expert").[1] Under either of these rubrics could be found a variety of other educational reforms, but it is generally agreed that the politicization of Chinese education was an ongoing process during the first three decades of the People's Republic (Sautman, 1990). Thus, China has sought to strike a balance between a pragmatic approach of providing the economy and polity with skilled personnel who are at once competitive nationally and internationally, as well as loyal and patriotic citizens. These two goals have collided over the years but never as dramatically as in June 1989 when Chinese troops were called on to harshly suppress the student democracy movement. While not totally derailing the educational reforms launched since 1985, the June events have pushed the political orientation to the forefront once again amidst a continued desire to pursue a sustained modernization drive. This confusion of goals is evident in recent official pronouncements on the role of education and in the practical application of education for development strategies. Thus, the past continues to frame somewhat current educational reforms, and, as will be shown in the pages that follow, these reforms have had a dramatic impact on almost all levels of the educational enterprise.

Given the breadth of the concept of educational reform and all that it encompasses, a somewhat less ambitious goal will be attempted than to seek to analyze each major aspect of China's educational structure. Instead, five central topics will be discussed which contain within them many of the important issues of educational reform. First, China's overall educational policy (since the mid–1980s) will be examined to provide the official and unofficial context in which more specific reforms have been carried out. Second, some brief observations will be made on the issue of educational administration and cadre training (the bureaucratic glue that attempts to hold the system together). Next, the ongoing problem of educational financing and the "economics of education" will be highlighted, with a particular focus on policies arrived at during the past five years. Then the discussion will move to the formal and nonformal levels of education (precollegiate and higher education) where the major reforms have been focused. Finally, because of the critical nature of China as a rural society undergoing rapid transformation, a review of recent rural educational reforms will be conducted.

NATIONAL EDUCATIONAL POLICY

In an unprecedented meeting from October 27 to November 1, 1984, the Committee on Education, Science, and Culture of the National People's Congress met in Beijing to codify the many rules and regulations on education and thus institutionalize the educational reform movement. This was the first effort to provide a "law for education" (*jiaoyu lifa*) since the founding of the People's Republic in 1949. It was pointed out at the meeting that, although many rules and regulations have developed and evolved since 1949, they had never been recognized in a legal sense, and thus the need arose to provide some legal guidance for existing educational policies as well as various new reforms. Specifically mentioned at the meeting were issues related to compulsory education, basic education, funding, and teacher training (*RMRB* November 2, 1984).

Shortly thereafter, a fifteen-year educational development plan was announced which broadly outlined the essential characteristics of China's educational reform movement (Wu and Li, 1988). Sanctioned by the State Council, the National Commission of Education, the National Commission of Planning, and the Ministry of Labor and Personnel, the plan mandated that every province, autonomous region, and municipality (e.g., Shanghai) under the direct leadership of the central government invest two years time in forecasting for the next fifteen years. Each locale was instructed to consider local needs with national needs, combine modern methods with traditional ones, assess existing personnel needs, and generally develop local planning methods that would enable localities to conduct decentralized planning, later to be aggregated and transmitted to Beijing. The Beijing plan developed in 1984 was to be used as a model, one that coincided with the Seventh Five-Year Plan and projected personnel needs at all levels: precollegiate, vocational-technical, higher education, teacher training, as well as financing, and administration. The county (*xian*) was to be taken as the local unit of analysis, and each county office was expected to initiate plans based on local conditions and a set of guidelines sent down from the central government.

As was the case with previous efforts, the guidelines provided only very general directions (for example, "consider local conditions, raise educational quality, involve the schools, conduct teacher training, base recommendations on research"; see Wu and Li, 1988: 31). This directive did little to guide the counties, cities, municipalities, villages, or any other unit in China, but it did get the reform movement launched. By 1987 and 1988 several broad reform themes could be identified. First, then Premier Zhao Ziyang gave general assurance that "the relationship between the Party and the intellectuals had been changed fundamentally" (*RMRB*, March 6, 1987: 1). It was announced that the atmosphere surrounding educated personnel had become more harmonious and democratic, and that educators and other skilled personnel should be given "full play" to carry out new and innovative reforms where needed.[2]

The broad outlines of educational reform goals were further articulated in 1988 and most recently (following the events in Tiananmen) in 1989. Over the past decade these goals have not changed significantly; rather, they have shifted emphasis depending on which political or economic issue happens to be at the top of the national agenda. In summary, there has been general agreement that popularizing nine-year compulsory education has been a central reform goal—basic education as the foundation for further educational development. Teacher reform within this context (in terms of both higher pay and increasing quality) as well as the further development of vocational and technical education has also been stressed, with a particular emphasis on rural education and new measures to attract and retain skilled personnel to the rural sector. The further growth and quality of higher education and adult education has been generally agreed upon with some recent twists, as will be discussed below. Reforming the structure of education, both management and financial, has been a key goal characterized by substantial disagreement over the degree of centralization and decentralization. Finally, the importance of moral and political education has moved to the forefront of official debate since June 1989 (*RMRB*, June 27, 1988; Li, December 23, 1989).

These basic reform issues are not terribly different from those of previous reform periods in China. What makes them somewhat unique, however, is the context in which they have been pursued. This context is characterized by dramatic economic reform, frenzied political upheavals, and an escalating international coupling of China with the world economic system. In some respects these conditions have placed China's educational reforms at a crossroads, one road leading backward to more familiar territory for China's current leadership, and another leading toward an unknown but perhaps more challenging future. How these reforms have evolved during the past five years in selected areas will be the focus of the remainder of this chapter.

ADMINISTRATIVE AND STRUCTURAL REFORM

China's administrative structure has been evolving steadily since 1949, and somewhat like ping pong it has bounced between an emphasis on either central or local control (Hawkins, 1983). In line with the overall economic reforms launched in the mid–1980s which stressed more local responsibility and control and, as the political mood shifted toward more democratization, pronouncements were made regarding the need to strengthen educational decision making and planning powers at the provincial, autonomous region, and municipal levels while transferring management powers to the key cities and counties. This multiple layering of administration (basically a division of labor whereby central authorities plan and local authorities implement) brought local officials more into the direct management of schools under their jurisdiction. There was a period in the mid–1980s when this trend toward local authority moved more quickly than the educational bureaucracy anticipated. Schools were established without central approvals, innovative curricula developed, and a variety of degrees and certificates were issued leading to a restatement of official policy in late 1989: "As far as China's system for running schools, they mainly should be run by the state. . . . There have been some disorderly phenomena, such as indiscriminate issuance of diplomas and unauthorized establishment of schools" (Li, 1989). The direction now seems to be toward a recentralization of authority for overall management of schools, continuing to allow, however, for a significant measure of local responsibility, principally economic.

Another structural area that has come under scrutiny has been that of job assignments. For at least three decades this domain had been almost exclusively dominated by the central authorities. By 1986, with the reform of the centralized contract and assignment system, attempts were made to bring the schools and employer units into more direct contact with each other in order to rationalize supply and demand. While maintaining that this direction is still desirable, the importance of the state plan has been reemphasized. Although flexibility is being stressed, the role of the state has been reasserted. The methods of "bringing supply and demand sides together" and "allowing two-way selections" between selected schools and employer units do not mean that the state has relinquished its dominant role in job assignments. Students taking advantage of this more flexible method of seeking employment must be "guided" to seek jobs that are identified as crucial within the state plan, particularly those jobs that are located in grass-roots units, the countryside, remote and frontier areas, and hardship professions (Li, 1989). The message seems clear. The decentralized trend toward graduate placement pursued since 1986 has been qualified substantially, reasserting the role of the state. In order to avoid unemployment ("or waiting for employment") and the vagaries of supply and demand, and to be assured of a position that will be guaranteed, students have been assured that "the state will be responsible for assigning proper jobs to qualified graduates provided they submit themselves to its needs" (Li, 1989: 11).

The dilemma that China's educational officials have faced since the founding of the People's Republic over the respective roles of central and local authorities reasserted itself in 1990. The inclination to shift both authority and responsibility to local educational units (maintaining planning functions with the central Commission on Education) and to allow a somewhat free-wheeling approach to new educational enterprises has been contained. Although local educational units are to be free to exercise certain decision-making powers regarding their educational missions, it has been stressed that this must take place within the "laws and regulations of the state" (Li, 1989: 10). Since the laws and regulations of the state are not clearly defined, it appears that this educational reform will be stalled for the foreseeable future.[3] The reassertion of political control over education has spread even to the Special Economic Zones, where many assumed that administrative control of educational enterprises would remain in the hands of local educators (Hawkins and Koppel, 1990).

EDUCATIONAL FINANCE REFORM

The educational enterprise in China has been funded in a multiplicity of ways since 1949. The central authorities have always had the most to say about collection and allocation of funds for both formal and nonformal schooling. However, as the educational system expanded (in response to an ever increasing population base), it became increasingly inefficient (as well as expensive) for the central government to manage the entire education funding process. Early on, central and local authorities experimented with various ways of combining state resources with locally funded educational initiatives and with nongovernmental sources. The result was a general pattern whereby a mix of about three to one (central-local to nongovernmental) emerged in the 1980s (*RMRB*, May 26, 1984). On the whole, this model proved quite successful as government sources increased 3.34 times in 1988 compared with 1978 (Li, 1989: 12), thus ensuring the availability and steady growth of educational funds during this period of expansion. The average annual increase in educational funding in 1987 from all government sources was 15.3 percent. Twenty percent of all educational funds were spent on higher education, reflecting the continued expansion of this sector (*Zhongguo Jiaoyubao*, June 28, 1988). Critical to the success of this reform was the ideological position that education was linked to economic growth. Viewing education as a factor of production allowed the central authorities to increase allocations and link it to the broader economic reforms that were taking place (*RMRB*, November 3; November 29; December 24, 1988).

Nonetheless, the fact remained that as fast as the funding grew, the school-age cohort (as well as adult needs) grew even faster. Population growth has rapidly continued despite the one-child family, thus putting an enormous strain on the educational resource base and actually resulting in a net decrease in the percentage of public funds used for teaching. This realization forced the government to promote a funding reform scheme to be "gradually established" that would utilize several funding mechanisms. First, the state share would gradually be increased, and educational funding would be put on a priority basis. Second, industrial enterprises, nonformal enterprises, and local populations would increase their share through increased taxation and surcharges earmarked for educational purposes. Third, tuition increases would be enacted for all students beyond the compulsory level (Grade 9). Finally, a work-study program has been suggested that will be combined with an educational foundation to provide student-based aid (Li, 1989). Relying more on local sources to provide educational funding seems to be a major feature of the funding reform. This approach, combined with closer auditing of educational expenditures (recognizing a substantial inappropriate use of allocated funds), is seen as one way to affect cost-savings and to improve educational quality (*Beijing Review*, April 1989).

An aspect of the less centralized approach to funding, especially for research institutes, focused on the need for enterprises to rely less on central funds and more on generating a portion of their total budget from productive relations with industry. For example, there are over 2,000 research institutes in China, belonging to over fifty ministries. Prior to 1986, each institute received both funds and directions from the ministry level, often resulting in inefficient operation and ineffective research products. Institutes received funding regardless of the quality of their products or their usefulness in supporting industrial needs. The new funding reform now requires research institutes to forge links with industry, not only to produce more applied research products but also to subcontract to industrial units and thus relieve the burden of central funding (*RMRB*, April 30, 1987).

Educational funding reforms appear to be one area where central authorities continue to support a more decentralized and participatory environment. The recent political backlash has not been reflected in the area of educational finance. This is perhaps easy to explain if one considers the difficulty budgetary situation confronting the Beijing government (*FEER*, May 10, 1990) and the relief that is accorded by allowing schools and research institutes to be more self-supportive. The central authorities continue, however, to be increasingly concerned with the appropriateness of expenditures and with assurance that the educational output (particularly for research institutes) is linked to both industry and agriculture.

THE FORMAL, NONFORMAL STRUCTURE

China's vast educational system consists of what can be called a formal system of precollegiate education, typically nine years (but varying depending on the region). Enrolled at the primary level are almost all those in the school-age cohort; enrollment drops off substantially at the secondary level.[4] A parallel nonformal system exists, consisting of work-study programs, literacy programs, television and distance education activities, and so on. Finally, an elite, higher education track is in place catering to those few who are able to score sufficiently high on the national entrance exams to enter.

Basic Education: The Precollegiate System

The adoption by the National People's Congress (NPC) of the Law on Compulsory Education of the People's Republic of China in 1986 marked the beginning of the first major reform of China's precollegiate level of basic education since the 1950s. The intent was gradually to implement a nine-year compulsory system throughout China's cities and villages beginning with the more densely populated urban centers and spreading gradually to the interior. By 1988 it was estimated that 97 percent of school-age children were enrolled in primary schools and that 66 percent of all of China's rural counties had "popularized" primary school and were accredited to expand junior middle school education (Li, 1989).

Since 1949 China's leaders have invested considerably in the basic education sector; the fundamental infrastructure for both the urban and rural sectors is well developed. Yet, as in other areas, population growth continues to outstrip efforts to provide funds and facilities for the enormous precollegiate school-age cohort. Irregular attendance and enforcement of enrollment policies led to the 1986 reform, but with a 1.1 billion population it is one thing to pass a regulation on compulsory education and quite another to implement it. A number of acute problems have continued to plague this sector of China's education system beginning with the physical plant itself. During the past decade the central authorities have spent billings of yuan simply repairing and rebuilding existing school facilities which literally were falling down, created a hazard for the students who managed to attend them (Hawkins and Stites, 1991).

Having instituted the compulsory education reform, the central authorities have recognized the need to monitor its implementation. The State Council has thus authorized the National Commission of Education to establish an inspection department for both elementary and secondary schools. This body apparently has both political and pedagogical purposes. Politically, it has been empowered to systematically inspect and evaluate the precollegiate level to assure that government policies and regulations are being followed and that the system is developing in a manner consistent with "Chinese characteristics" (*RMRB*, January 12, 1987). It also has an evaluation component focused on the management and administration of the schools and teaching quality.

Several provinces have been singled out as the focus of an in-depth study by the National Commission to assess the effectiveness in implementing the compulsory nine-year system. The core of the study will be to determine the pace and scope of implementating the compulsory law, the widespread problem of student dropout (especially in the rural sector and among girls), the issue of teacher resources, pay and morale (all in short supply), and the general problem of underfinancing for this sector (*RMRB*, August 8, 1988). Early reports on the expansion of basic education and its success are not encouraging. There remain almost 200 million illiterates among whom are 70 million school-age youth. One million new illiterates are added to the total each year. Thirty-four percent of China's counties have not yet reached stated standards (*RMRB*, March 23, 1989). The attention being paid to implementing the compulsory education law indicates that the basic educational system is faltering and can be considered a sector that has both political problems and structural defects.

Maintaining an adequate supply of high quality and motivated teachers has been a persistent problem and one that has not yet been solved. As early as 1984, a major effort was made to increase teachers' salaries by pumping more than a billion *yuan* into the salary structure. Teacher salaries lagged behind almost all other work categories, teachers were short of housing, often living in crowded dormitories, high school graduates seldom chose teaching as a profession or preferred college track, and the entire system was suffering from a "teacher drain" (*RMRB*, December 26, 1984). Although these financial reforms have had a positive impact, it is by no means clear that the crisis in the teacher ranks is over (Li, 1989).

More recent data suggest that undergraduates select teachers' colleges because of low examination scores rather than a desire to become a teacher (or for gender considerations). The teacher education institutions themselves are a weak link in the higher education chain, typically being underfunded and lacking the facilities enjoyed by other sectors in higher education. The graduates of these institutions are similarly uninspired when it comes to entering the teaching profession.[5] As Lynn Paine (1990) points out, the state has attempted to reform the teaching profession by utilizing two avenues: regulation and allocation. Regulation has been pursued by instituting a series of certification measures, and allocation through the reward system mentioned above. The net result has been mixed, but it seems clear that teachers in the late 1980s were better paid and educated than they were a decade earlier, and are a potential force for change at the precollegiate level.

Higher Education

Perhaps no educational sector has been as dramatically influenced by both the recent economic reforms and the vicissitudes of political policy than higher education. China's university and college structure (along with the intellectuals who staff it) has consistently presented the leadership with a dilemma. On the one hand, higher education has been at the forefront of China's effort to modernize, to provide the high level of techniques and technologies needed to propel China into the modern world. On the other hand, universities and the professors and students within them have been at the vanguard of various movements to criticize the government, from the Hundred Flowers Movement of 1956 to the recent pro-democracy movement. The higher education structure has been both essential and a threat to the established order.

The centralization–decentralization issue has also been hotly debated with respect to higher education. China's leadership has been searching for a formula that will resolve the contradiction between desiring a higher educational structure that will foster economic modernization while not stretching the boundaries of political reform (Hayhoe, 1989).

The first major reform document issued on higher education since the launching of the Four Modernizations Movement in 1976 was from the Central Committee. Basically it reaffirmed an earlier (1963) "Decision on Unifying Management in Higher Education" which stressed the need for strong central control over most aspects of the higher education enterprise (Hayhoe, 1989). Nevertheless, several new features were articulated in the reform. First, the research mission of the university was formally recognized, placing it on an equal footing with teaching.

Second, intellectuals found they had entered the ranks of the working class, thus shielding them to some degree from the kind of class struggle to which they had been subjected in previous years. Third, greater authority was delegated to university presidents, allowing some flexibility with respect to university administration. Fourth, political education was deemphasized (Hayhoe, 1989).

With the disestablishment of the Ministry of Education in 1985 and the formation of the National Commission of Education, the role of the central authorities vis-à-vis higher education was rearticulated. It was flatly stated that all macro-level authority and control of higher education would reside with the National Commission. This included enforcing and implementing all regulations of all universities and colleges in China, conducting personnel forecasting and thereby determining curriculum, enrollment targets, faculty hiring needs, physical plant construction and financing, and personnel policies. Political and ideological work was also to be coordinated by the Commission, as was China's rapidly expanded program of sending students and scholars abroad (Zhang, 1988). The distinction remains between those universities under central guidance and more local colleges and tertiary institutions managed by provincial governments and municipalities, but the centrality of policy formation permeates the entire structure.

Parallel with the management decisions referred to above was a move to significantly expand higher education enrollment and institutions. A document issued from the State Council in 1983 urged the rapid expansion of higher education as one of the keys to "realizing our country's modernization" (Zhang, 1988: 987–989).[6] The floodgates were opened, and it is estimated that 100 new institutes of higher learning were established during the years 1984 and 1985, or about one every four days. By 1988 China had over 1,000 ordinary institutions of higher learning and about 4 million college students enrolled (Li, 1989). Graduate degree granting began in 1980, and by 1988 a total of 74,000 master's degrees and 1,286 doctoral degrees had been granted (*RMRB*, October 20, 1988). Both local and central educational officials began raising questions of control and quality, leading finally to the pronouncement that:

We should strictly limit the establishment of new institutes of higher learning . . . we should concentrate on readjusting and rectifying ordinary institutions of higher learning in the next few years. Institutes that are not up to the state's standards should be improved, and some should be suspended or merged with others. . . . In principle, the State Education Commission will not approve the establishment of institutes of higher learning in the future (Li, 1989: 13).

The move to consolidate and "rectify" was undoubtedly influenced as much by the pro-democracy movement as it was by the overexpansion of the system. It coincided with reports that large numbers of graduates had been "sent down" to factories, farms, and other local units to do "practical training" for one to two years. Justified in terms that were reminiscent of the Cultural Revolution ("to better understand society and raise their ability to handle practical work and increase their feelings for the working people"), it is now a regulation that any graduate who is assigned government work, broadly speaking, must spend one to two years receiving "practical training" (*RMRB*, November 8, 1989).

Higher education reform has thus been a peculiar mix of efforts to encourage more independent research, expand the system, thus allowing more access for China's huge college-age cohort and increasing local university-level administrative responsibility, while recentralizing large-scale planning and repoliticizing the universities through old-style political education and postgraduate "practical work."[7] Students, intellectuals, and university administrators seem to be in a holding pattern waiting for something to happen—waiting for the central authorities to clarify what are clearly mixed signals regarding the future of China's premier educational level.

RURAL EDUCATION: THE GREATEST CHALLENGE

The many advances made in education since 1949 have not been shared spatially. Much of the progress in universalizing primary education, expanding secondary and higher education, and instituting research programs has been focused on China's urban centers. Although much headway has been made in extending literacy to China's rural masses (and differential success has been achieved in primary education), it remains a fact that the 80 percent of China's 1 billion plus people who live in rural settings have not benefited from the investment in education, the quality of teachers, the facilities, and the expansion of opportunity that has characterized urban China.

The gap between rural and urban China in terms of education has narrowed and widened at different times during the past four decades. Large-scale political movements such as the Great Leap Forward and the establishment of the commune structure did result in increased enrollments and expanded facilities, although the instruction offered was often of poor quality. The rural reforms enacted since 1976, replacing the commune system with the production responsibility or household contract system, transferred educational authority from the commune to the township and county levels. The implications for rural educational reform were great, both positive and negative (Hawkins, 1988). More recently, a series of policies have been formulated, designed to address the continuing economic, educational, and cultural gap between China's rural areas and urban centers (*Nongcun*, 1988).

More recently, China's educational and political leaders have refocused attention on the massive educational needs of the rural sector. The rural reforms referred to above released much creative energy, resulting in rising rural income, a variety of entrepreneurial sideline activities, and increases in selected areas of rural production. However, the dismantling of the commune structure had a negative effect on large-scale agriculture, rural infrastructure projects, and the application of scientific agricultural management techniques, leading to the conclusion that progress in agriculture could only be achieved by dramatically increasing the quality of the rural workforce (He, 1988). The rural areas are reported to be disadvantaged both in terms of basic education and vocational-technical education. Past neglect is summed up by a saying: "When some leaders have a meeting about industry, it will last half a day. If they talk about agriculture, it will last as long as a cigarette. If they meet about culture, education and hygiene, it will end immediately" (Ma, 1988). Despite the principal need for agricultural-technical education, only 29 percent of students in rural areas are enrolled in such programs. A central goal for most parents is to have their children attend regular, basic education with the hopes that they will do well on the college entrance examination and basically escape to an urban occupation. The result is that literally millions of middle school graduates neither enter the universities nor are equipped for rural life (Wu Yiying, 1988). Thus, the Commission on Education has launched a research drive to find out more about rural educational needs at all levels. Flexibility seems to be the key word when discussing rural educational reforms. The compulsory nine-year rule apparently will not be binding in the rural areas where "universal education" will be pursued.[8]

Another aspect of the reform is to link the three levels of rural education (basic, vocational, and continuing) to local county development needs. The tendency of school administrators to encourage students to go on to higher education has resulted in an acute shortage of graduates prepared to enter either agriculture or local industry. Thus, the current reform movement is concentrating on increasing both the quantity and quality of primary and middle-level graduates, trained in a core of basic subjects and specialized technical skills. A major problem in implementing this reform, however, is the lack of technically skilled teachers. To address this issue, a plan has been designed to provide for both forward and backward linkages to the cities—the cities providing science and technology from their universities and colleges, and the counties and towns serving as transmission points to the rural areas. Incentive packages are being designed to encourage graduates of urban programs to work in rural areas as teachers and advisers and particularly to encourage local rural students who graduate from urban institutions to return to their region. By not assigning urban positions to graduates of technical programs at the county level, it was found that graduates tended to stay in the region, thus serving local development needs.[9]

The shift from agriculture to nonagriculture is also being encouraged through programs designed to foster small enterprises. This is being hailed as an "historic change" in the rural economy (Xiang, 1988). The central characteristics of this change are the general increases in agricultural production since 1978, the expansion of village and town enterprises (accounting for 20 percent of the total labor force in rural areas), the diversification of rural production,[10] and increases in rural vocational and technical schools designed to utilize applied technology to support both agricultural modernization and nonagricultural enterprises. The educational implications of this shift are many: rural vocational education has been elevated in the discussion of educational reform, a management training plan has been proposed to support the rise in rural commodity production, new teaching methods are being encouraged in order to bring curriculum and instruction more in line with rural developmental needs, and cooperative research links with towns and cities are being advocated (Xiang, 1988).

In short, rural education, long ignored and neglected, is moving to the front of the educational reform agenda. The rhetoric is strong, but it remains to be seen whether or not policy recommendations are being put in practice. There is some evidence that experimental projects have been initiated, and current research efforts by U.S. scholars indicate that there is an increasing emphasis on expanding training programs for the rural nonagricultural sector.[11] Major problems remain, however—the persisting desire of parents to have their children attain higher education, thus discouraging them from attending more practical and applied training programs; the generally low educational level of the rural sector; the lack of adequate curricular and instructional strategies. If these can be addressed in a positive fashion, China's rural transformation can continue to proceed as it must if the majority of the population are to share in the fruits of modernization.

CONCLUSION

It is difficult to reach any firm conclusions regarding China's educational reforms during the past decade. In some ways, the events of June 1989 forced a reassessment of the reforms both by China's educational leaders and outside observers. Indeed, it does seem that educational reform in China during this period has been characterized by a haphazard process of moving forward, and then, just as abruptly, moving back again. The effort to codify educational policies and practices by introducing legislative measures and linking "educational law" with the overall planning process seemed to be a positive step in separating the educational mission from the capriciousness of national politics. This was no sooner done, however, than politics entered the scene again as the nation pushed ahead with economic reform, but backtracked politically. The slogan "Politics in Command" is once again in use in China, especially with respect to education.

This was expressed most distinctly in the area of educational administration and management. As the economic reforms of the late 1970s proceeded, a parallel administrative reform surfaced, aligning a decentralized economic system with a similar educational management strategy. In this sense, June 1989 was indeed a major turning point as the system recentralized in several critical ways, setting back a more responsible, self-governance model for much of China's educational system. Given the complexity of China's educational enterprise, however, it appears unlikely that this trend can continue. China's educational administrators as well as faculty seem to be waiting for "something to happen" rather than to be completely demoralized. If the economic reforms are to continue (and there appear to be no strong factions in the central government or CCP supporting a return to pre–1978 policies), then a more flexible and vibrant educational system will be essential to respond to rapidly changing economic needs.

One signal that this is a reasonable assumption is the educational finance structure. Driven partly by budgetary needs (which, cynically viewed, might be one way the government shirks its duties) but also by a desire to diversify, educational finance has expanded to relieve the role of the central authorities and tap into the funding potential of local governmental and nongovernmental agencies. This enlarged financial base, involving more people and organizations, will create vested interests and a sense of ownership that may eventually translate into increasing independence and local control. This has not happened to any large degree yet, but the potential is clearly there.

The entire educational structure from the precollegiate to the collegiate level is plagued with a variety of afflictions ranging from an aging physical plant at the precollegiate level to an aging professorate in China's colleges and universities. Poor instructional quality can be found at all levels, but particularly in the basic educational system, translating in uneven enrollments, large numbers of dropouts, and declining literacy. Despite the relatively large-scale expansion of China's educational institutions, the key word these days is "quality"—how to recover it, increase it, and maintain it. The enactment of compulsory education was a progressive step, but enforcement is a distant goal. China's educational leaders rightly seem to be putting a great deal of emphasis on the formal system while not abandoning the many nonformal advances that have been made during the past four decades. One of the biggest impediments to achieving these goals, however, is the continuing population problem. Again, just when some steps forward have been attained, it seems the population growth rate pushes the system back again.

Finally, surrounding these formidable problems (and the urban centers where many of the reforms have been enacted) is the vast countryside where China's 800 million live and work. Here, as was discussed above, is where the greatest transformation is taking place as increasingly large numbers of traditional farm families leave agriculture for nonagricultural work. Thus, apart from the need to continue to provide and expand basic educational opportunities, China's educational policymakers are faced with the demand for increased and more relevant vocational-technical education, both focused on agriculture and on the expanding commodity production and service system.

Thus far, as a result of the rural economic reforms enacted since 1978, entrepreneurial activity has outstripped government planning. Private and semi-private educational and training programs have surfaced in recent years, creating new opportunities for China's rural population. Although some of these efforts have been quite successful, many have been of low quality and the government is now moving in to provide more regulation and control. Yet, there seems to be confusion in the ranks as some leaders continue to call for further reform and others for a return to more state-controlled enterprises (resembling but not replicating the commune system). Most leaders, however, agree that the "rural problem" must be solved if China's overall economic progress is to be maintained.

It is in fact this political-economic mix that seems to be in turmoil in recent years, particularly since the reaction against the democracy movement. The economic picture is blurred, and it has been the forward movement in the economy that has kept some semblance of political order. If unemployment and underemployment (both rural and urban) continue to rise, the government will have much more to deal with than striking intellectuals and students. And the rhetoric regarding the need to invest heavily in all levels of education, particularly rural, will more than likely remain just that—rhetoric. It appears that China's educational reforms are once again at a major turning point, for the moment, continuing to lurch ahead with selective political backtracking. The drive to "modernize," however, is a powerful force that the next generation of China's leaders will more than likely be swept along with.

NOTES

1. The debate regarding the importance of having an educational system emphasizing either "red" or "expert" continues to this day, although in a peculiar way. "Redness," or focusing attention on the political correctness of education, has been restated through political training classes; yet the government continues to stress the need to have high-quality technical education to train a cadre of technically competent graduates up to world standards.

2. At the same time, and somewhat prophetically, a Study Center for Youth Ideological Study (*Qingnian Sixiang Jiaoyu Yenjiu Zhongxin*) was established in Beijing to increase young people's awareness of political issues and to promote patriotic values. Administered under the direction of the Ministry of Propaganda and the Communist Youth League, this new center was an early Chinese Communist party (CCP) response to the growing student democracy movement (*RMRB*, May 20, 1987).

3. The need for more and better trained educational administrators has also been stressed as a chief aspect of administrative and structure reform. To this end, the reform movement has called for combining formal business enterprises to manage and administer the various educational levels (*RMRB*, February 20, 1987; September 16, 1989).

4. Educational statistics in China are notoriously unreliable, but general trends can be found in *World Development Report 1989*, published by the World Bank.

5. In interviews conducted by Paine (1990), one student flatly declared, "I would rather be a toilet cleaner than a high school teacher."

6. The report projected a 75 percent increase in university enrollments over the period 1983–1987, the initiation of several new "forms" of higher education (broadcast and television universities, correspondence colleges, factory-worker-run universities, rural extension colleges, and so on), and a dramatic increase in construction funds.

7. Certain universities have been targeted more for political education than others. Beijing University, the hotbed of the student movement, has had its enrollment cut back and military-style political education implemented (*U.S. News*, August 28, 1989). At

other universities, political education borders on boredom as students are forced to read the speeches of Deng Xiaoping and other party leaders (*FEER*, May 31, 1990).

8. "Universal education" refers to the accessibility of junior middle school education to those who would seek it, thus recognizing the impossibility of enforcing compulsory schooling.

9. This was just an experiment reported by He Dongchang (1988), and it is not known whether or not it has been replicated elsewhere. It does, however, speak to the seriousness of the employment and skill problems of the rural areas.

10. In 1987 the number of peasants running businesses exceeded 12 million; while the brakes have been put on this movement, it is likely to continue to expand as rural production rises (Xiang, 1988).

11. Ms. Wang Jian, a doctoral student in the comparative education program at UCLA, is working with the author on a study of this sector in Liaoning Province. A pilot study suggests that provincial officials and local authorities are allocating increasing quantities of resources to rural nonagricultural training programs.

REFERENCES

Beijing Review. 1989, April. Pp. 17–23.
Far Eastern Economic Review (FEER). 1990, May 10. p. 8.
———. 1990, May 31. P. 18.
Hawkins, John N. 1983. *Education and Social Change in the People's Republic of China*. New York: Praeger.
———. 1988. "Education and Rural Transformation." *Comparative Education Review*. 32, No. 1, pp. 266–81.
———, and Bruce Koppel. 1990. "Rural Transformation and Educational Change in Shenzhen." *Education Handbook*, ed. Irving Epstein. Westport, Conn.: Greenwood Press.
———, and Reggie Stites. 1991. "Strengthening the Future's Foundation: Elementary Education Reform in the Peoples Republic of China." *Elementary Education Review*, pp. 41–60.
Hayhoe, Ruth. 1989. *China's Universities and the Open Door*. New York: M. E. Sharpe.
He Dongchang. 1988. "Nongcun Jiaoyu Zhuyao Wei Dangdi Jianshe Fuwu." *Renmin Jiaoyu* 3.
Li Tieying. 1989. "Report on Several Educational Issues in China." *Xinhau* (Beijing).
Ma Zaixin. 1988, February 22. "Jiannande Zhuanzhe: Zhongguo Nongcun Jiaoyu Gaige Shuping." *Renmin Ribao*: 3.
Nongcun Jiaoyu Gaige Wenxian He Ziliao Xuanbian [Selected documents and materials on rural educational reform]. 1988. Beijing: Educational Science Press.
Paine, Lynn. 1990, January 27. "Teaching, Teachers, and the State in the PRC." Paper presented at the UCLA Conference on Education in Modern China.
Renmin Ribao (RMRB), November 2, 1984; May 26, 1984; January 7, 1987; January 12, 1987; February 20, 1987; March 6, 1987; April 30, 1987; June 27, 1988; August 8, 1988; October 20, 1988; November 3, 1988; November 29, 1988; December 24, 1988; March 23, 1989; September 16, 1989.
Rondinelli, Dennis A., John Middleton, and Adriaan M. Verspoor. 1990. *Planning Educational Reforms in Developing Countries: The Contingency Approach*. Durham, N.C., and London: Duke University Press.

Sautman, Barry. 1990, February 25. "Politicization, Hyperpoliticization and Depoliticization of Chinese Education: Causes, Consequences, and Prospects." Paper presented at Comparative and International Education Society Conference.

U.S. News and World Report. 1989, August 28. P. 13.

Wu Fusheng. 1988. "Woguo Nongcun Jiaoyu Gaige Ruogan Wenti." *Jiaoyu Yanjiu* 3: 16–20.

Wu Yiying, and Li Jinfeng. 1988. "Jinxing Diqu Rencai Xuqiu Yuce, Zhiding 15 nian Jiaoyu Fazhan Guiha" ["A forecast of the need for qualified personnel to develop a 15-year educational development plan"]. In *China Education Yearbook 1985–1986*, ed. Zhang Jian. Changsha: Hunan Educational Press, pp. 27–33.

Xiang Chongyang. 1988. "Nongcun Jingjide Fazhan He Nongcun Jiaoyu Gaige." *Renmin Jiaoyu* 3: 5–6.

Zhang Jian. 1988. *Zhongguo Jiaoyu Nianjian (1985–1986) [Chinese educational yearbook].* Changsha: Hunan Educational Press.

Zhongguo Jiaoyubao. 1988, June 28. Pp. 1–2.

7

COLOMBIA

Mary Ann Larsen-Pusey

As has so often happened before in Colombian history, current policymakers have resorted to a top-down model to achieve changes in the educational system. Some of these changes have been aimed at addressing quality and equity issues while reaching the primary goal of national development. The post–National Front (1974–1986) governmental reforms have included reorganizing the total educational system (public and private), expanding adult and continuing education, issuing major curricular reform legislation, restructuring the teaching profession, and institutionalizing research as an integral activity in higher education. Not only has reform been top-down, but also the upper levels of the public sector have been targeted more frequently than the primary level or the private sector. Some writers allege that educational reform in Colombia has privileged secondary and higher education at the expense of literacy and primary school education (Herrera, 1986; Lebot, 1979).

Prior to discussing current reform and the issues, however, we need to give a brief overview of Colombia's traditional educational system, point out prior reform efforts that serve as the basis of current reforms, and describe the major reform movements in Colombia during the 1980s.

THE COLOMBIAN EDUCATIONAL SYSTEM

The Colombian educational system has been and continues to be centralized, with a Ministry of Education under the direction of a minister of education appointed by the country's president. The ministry oversees public and private elementary and secondary schools, develops curricular frameworks, and assumes responsibility for teacher in-service and promotion. The postsecondary educational system, both public and private, is administered through the Instituto para el Fomento de la Educacion Superior (ICFES), established in 1968 as part of the administrative reforms of the National Front governments.

Traditionally, the educational system consisted of up to five years of primary (fewer in rural areas) and six years of secondary school, followed by professional training at the university, although a very small percentage completed all levels. According to data from ICFES, in 1974 approximately 70 percent of eligible children were enrolled in primary schools, 35 percent in secondary schools, but fewer than 6 percent finished university training (ICFES, 1975). As we will see in the next section, two different reform efforts have dealt with expanding the system, with more success being achieved at the upper levels.

From colonial days, the church has played a major role in Colombian education. Early education at all levels was entirely in the hands of the church. The struggle for a dominant role in education has been a continual one between Liberal and Conservative governments (Franco and Tunnerman, 1978; Lebot, 1979). After independence, the Liberal governments succeeded in establishing secular education, but with the Concordat of 1887 the church regained state recognition and protection of its power. Many educational institutions at every level continue to be operated by the church, and religion is part of the curriculum in secular schools.

At the primary and secondary levels, the curriculum has tended to be humanistic and philosophical, and the pedagogy memoristic (Sanin Echeverri, 1970). At the university level the education has been aimed primarily at producing professionals (Departamento Nacional de Planeacion, 1979). Teachers at the primary level received their training in normal schools operated as part of the secondary school system; secondary teachers may or may not have had pedagogical training at the university level; university teachers tended to be part-time *catedraticos* who taught part-time alongside their regular professional practice. During this century, reform efforts have dealt with various aspects of this system as will be shown in the next section.

PREVIOUS REFORM EFFORTS

In this section, we need to point out two major reform movements that have taken place during this century. The first took place under the Liberal government of Lopez Pumarejo during the 1930s, and the second began in the late 1950s and lasted through the early 1970s under various administrations more popularly known as the National Front.

Liberal Reforms of the 1930s

The major aim of the reform efforts during the 1930s was to secularize the education system at all levels and to expand the number of years of schooling in rural areas. The philosophy underlying the reforms included two basic tenets. The first was that the state should both provide and direct education rather than leave it to private initiative; the other was that education needed to be more scientific and work-related.

The resulting reforms (Law 12 of 1934, Laws 21 and 68 of 1935, and Law 35 of 1937) were far-reaching. Free and compulsory education at the primary level was legally recognized as the duty of the state; the first public secondary schools were established; the Ministry of Education was reorganized to provide oversight and direction to the educational system; teacher preparation became part of the state's responsibility; state support was provided for developing a public university with a scientific thrust; and the academic career was established.

The higher education reforms were the most significant. Although several public universities had been founded at the time of independence from Spain, the major universities were in the hands of the Catholic Church. Throughout the nineteenth century, the Conservative and Liberal parties struggled for control of the educational system. The Conservatives wanted an educational system that was scholastic, Catholic, and privately controlled; the Liberals advocated a public, secular system (Molano and Vera, 1982).

The Liberal government of Lopez Pumarejo enacted three measures that impacted higher education. Law 21 provided for teacher training in general: normal schools for training primary school teachers and the School of Education (later the Escuela Normal Superior) to train teachers for the normal schools as well as to serve as supervisors and inspectors in the educational system. Areas of study for teacher training were determined: philosophy and pedagogy; history and geography; physics and mathematics; chemistry and biology; philology and languages (Molano and Vera, 1982). Law 68 provided for strengthening and unifying the Universidad Nacional de Colombia (UNC), giving it a semblance of self-governance and autonomy, as well as for building a campus to house the up-until-then separate, isolated *facultades*. The first Faculty of Science was founded, and social sciences became part of the university curriculum (Briceno, 1988; Franco and Tunnerman, 1978; Molano and Vera, 1982; Uricoechea, 1984). Law 35 provided for the academic career at the UNC: professors were to work full time and exclusively in the university, with responsibility for research as well as teaching (Molano and Vera, 1982). Restrepo (1983) states that this reform gave a semblance of stability to the university professoriate, but notes that it only applied to public universities and primarily the UNC.

Lebot (1979) observes that the depth of these reforms has been overstated. Their effect was superficial given the lack of real commitment, especially in terms of improving the lower levels. The reform remained more of a "proposal" (Lebot: 34) on paper than an effective, systematic plan of reform.

The Reforms under the National Front

The appearance of a modern state attempting to industrialize itself, with both internal pressure and external aid, served as the basis for educational reform after World War II. After years of violent confrontation, the Liberal and Conservative parties reached a formal agreement upon the overthrow of the Rojas Pinilla dictatorship in the mid–1950s to share power during a period of sixteen years. These governments were known as the National Front. While the National Front officially began in 1962, for reform purposes it began in 1958. The objectives of the reforms of this period were to expand educational opportunity both numerically and through curricular diversification, to change the structure of secondary and higher educational institutions, and to provide a qualified professoriate for secondary and higher education. The overriding goal was to bring about national development through education (Florez, Franco, and Galviz, 1985; Moreno Narvaez, 1982; Pabon de Restrepo, Pereira, and Unda, 1986; Parra and Carvajal, 1979; Rama, 1970; Serna Gomez and Moreno Narvaez, 1985). Secondary goals were integration and modernization of the educational system.

The first reform objective, expanding educational opportunity, came about as a result of social pressure from groups other than the elite which traditionally had access to secondary and higher education. Numerical expansion occurred in two ways: by admitting larger numbers of students at existing public institutions, and by creating new public and private institutions. Curricular diversification occurred in both secondary and higher education: at the secondary level, reorganization of the educational system led to diversification in the public sector; at the university level, new undergraduate and graduate course offerings reflected the growing emphasis on both the natural and social sciences, education and teacher training, as well as new technological fields (ICFES-Colciencias, 1981; Florez et al., 1985; Restrepo, 1983).

In 1962, as part of the expansion move at the secondary level, Decree 45 changed the classical six-year secondary education program (*Bachillerato*) into two cycles: a basic one of four years followed by another of two years oriented more toward vocational skills. By 1967 the government secured the financing necessary to create a public system of diversified schools based on the U.S. comprehensive school model—the Institutos Nacionales de Ensenanza Media (INEM). Planning for the INEMs had begun in 1963 using the new secondary system legislated in Decree 45.

The INEMs were to serve as a model for secondary reform in two ways: curricular and professorial. The two cycles of four years of basic education followed by two years of technical and vocational schooling were adhered to. Full-time teachers held university degrees and were to work exclusively at the INEM. During the hours they were not directly involved in instruction, they were involved in curricular planning and development. Attempts to reform or expand existing private secondary schools met with resistance and were abandoned (Moreno Narvaez, 1982:48).

The second objective, administrative reorganization and restructuring of the educational system, occurred in 1968 with changes at the Ministry of Education and the creation of a series of decentralized agencies. Among these were ICCE (for construction of schools), ICFES (to oversee higher education), and COL-

CIENCIAS (to lend assistance for research efforts at the universities, particularly in science and technology) (Franco and Tunnerman, 1978; Moreno Narvaez, 1982). While some policymakers wanted to integrate the system, there was insufficient support for integration to take place.

Attempts were also made to change the traditional university into a modern one patterned after the North American university. In 1970 ICFES published a series of papers known as El Plan Basico (Basic Plan) which culminated a decade of work by policymakers. The Basic Plan criticized the organization and structure of the university and proposed reform actions: a national testing and admission system for secondary school graduates to be administered through ICFES, greater flexibility in the programs allowing for interinstitutional transfer by students, resolution of conflicts in the administration of the universities, reformation of teacher training, abandoning its European structure, improvement of university library facilities, development of a corps of qualified university professors, establishment of criteria for being a university professor, improved salaries for professors, and the expansion of responsibilities in the academic community to involvement in teaching, research, and service—the roles of the academician in the university in the United States.

Implementing the Basic Plan on a national scale was difficult, if not impossible. With international financial assistance, it was partially implemented in four universities: the Universidad del Valle in Cali, the Universidad Industrial de Santander in Bucaramanga, the Universidad de Antioquia in Medellin, and the UNC in Bogotá. Students and professors saw the Basic Plan as foreign intervention and as a threat to autonomy; subsequently, public universities suffered a series of student protests. Franco and Tunnerman (1978) note that between 1973 and 1976 the public sector lost nearly 40 percent of its academic time.

Moreno Narvaez (1982) concluded that the reforms aimed at modernizing higher education under the National Front failed. He attributed that failure to the reform plans themselves and to the sociopolitical circumstances of the Colombian university. According to Moreno Narvaez, the general impression gained by looking at the various documents was that there was no global vision of the problem; generalizations were atomized, disparate, and superficial. He alleges a lack of continuity in the planning, with little concern for knowing what existed, what had been done, and what remained to be done. Most of the research studies carried out were diagnostic in nature with little evaluation of the reform efforts. A policy document from the Oficina de Planeacion of the Universidad Pedagogica Nacional (1986) points out that the hostile reaction to the recommendations impeded in-depth knowledge about them. The authors further allege, as did Rama (1970) and Franco and Tunnerman (1978), that the pedagogical premises implicit in the reforms contemplated in the Basic Plan were neither sufficiently disseminated nor carefully studied. All conclude that the diagnoses in the studies underlying the Basic Plan were, and continue to be, valid.

The third objective, providing a qualified professoriate for secondary and higher education, served as the basis for a series of other reforms under the

National Front. Part of the administrative reorganization in 1968 included re-organizing the National Pedagogical University and making teacher training part of the university's mission. Education *facultades* were established at several public universities for training secondary school teachers, but the long-term goal was to create a national university system to prepare teachers for every level of the educational system and thus improve the quality of education.

In sum, the primary result of the National Front reforms was educational expansion, both in making secondary and higher education accessible to greater numbers of students and diversifying the curriculum. This expansion was to provide workers with technical and scientific training as well as humanistic and academic studies for industry. To do this, existing public institutions admitted more students, and new ones, both public and private, were created throughout the country. Statistics (Departamento Nacional de Planeacion, 1979) showed that student enrollment in higher education increased from 19.8 percent of eligible youth in 1935 to 49.2 percent in 1977.

This period also reflected a not wholly successful attempt to change the tra-ditional higher education system of semiautonomous professional schools into a university with scientific ends using a top-down change model. In addition to the larger student bodies, growth in higher education circles also included a wider range of curricular offerings and increased numbers of both full- and part-time professors. Teacher education and basic sciences became part of higher educational responsibility. More professors depended on their full-time profes-sorial assignment for their livelihood (Pelczar, 1977). In the next section, the focus shifts toward attempts to complete the reforms begun a decade earlier under the National Front.

EDUCATIONAL REFORM SINCE THE NATIONAL FRONT

The reform goal under the post–National Front governments has continued to be aimed at achieving national development through the integration and mod-ernization of the educational system. Under two different presidential adminis-trations, four major tasks were undertaken. These were the reorganization and integration of the entire educational system from the primary to the university level under President Turbay and addressing equity and quality issues within President Betancourt's development plan, Change with Equity. These included the expansion of continuing education and curriculum reform at the primary and secondary levels, the restructuring of the teaching profession, and the institu-tionalization of research and the academic career. These change efforts had roots in the reforms under the National Front described in the previous section. These four areas of reform will be discussed here, particularly the institutionalization of research and the academic career in higher education.

Reorganization and Integration of the Educational System

Between 1975 and 1978, the government nationalized the financing of secondary schools, removing responsibility from the states and municipalities. It also passed a statute regulating the teaching profession, and reorganized the primary and secondary education system into three cycles: five years of basic primary, four years of basic secondary, and two years of middle vocational education. The goals for primary and secondary education were outlined: academic and personal growth of the student, civic responsibilities and critical thinking, vocational training and motivation for continued education. The administration of public and private education as well as in-service and promotion of teachers was regulated. Responsibilities for financing public education were outlined. The groundwork for curricular reform was established by describing the characteristics of the curriculum: flexibility and integrity, balanced scope and sequence, and articulation from level to level (Diaz Osorio, 1985).

To complete the task of educational integration, the government then turned its attention to reorganizing postsecondary education. Triggering some of the provisions of the decrees were concerns manifested at various levels regarding national development and needing a different mission for higher education. The other contributing factor was the crisis of public higher education which had its roots in the reactions to the earlier reform attempts.

In 1977 the Departamento Nacional de Planeacion had presented a document to the Consejo Nacional de Rectores (National Council of University Presidents) held in Popayan (later published in *La Revista Colombiana de Educacion*, 1979:83–98). The basic argument underlying its proposal was "the need to develop research capacity as a requisite condition for cultural, scientific and technological advancement" (1979:83). It charged that the Colombian university has assumed a passive stance, with its principal role being to train people who upon graduation would be in charge of managing problems and "imported technologies which the nation had not participated whatsoever in developing" (p. 91). The Departamento also called for adding basic and applied research to the teaching functions of the professoriate and reorienting the teaching function from transmission of knowledge to stimulation of research among the students. Finally, it proposed restructuring higher education in Colombia—adding institutions providing technical training and shorter careers to the system and restructuring universities and their goals.

In 1980 the government issued a series of decrees that the president described as "culminating the integration of the Colombian educational system" (Preface Decree 80, no date). The basic legislation, Decree 80, established the mission of higher education and tied it to national development, and provided the objectives of the higher education system, noting the need to integrate it with the other basic sectors of the nation and to guarantee the quality of education at all levels by promoting scientific and pedagogical preparation of teaching and research personnel. Decree 80 also established four levels of postsecondary education: (1) Short-term professional training of two years mainly in different types of administrative and business areas; (2) technological training; (3) university training (public and private); and (4) advanced or graduate training. While recognizing the church's right under the Concordat to full control of training clerical personnel, it asserted the state's right to control the quality of all secular studies in church-related institutions.

Decree 81 reorganized ICFES and provided a legal framework for carrying out its duties, which included monitoring and regulating postsecondary education. ICFES must approve programs for both public and private institutions. The decree also made obligatory the standardized tests instituted in the Basic Plan for students finishing secondary education. Decree 82 established the legal dispositions pertaining to the UNC in much the same way that Decree 80 did for the rest of the universities. Decree 83 regulated the institutions providing short-term professional training. Decree 80 is of the most interest here and is treated in greater detail in the discussion of the institutionalization of research in higher education.

Continuing Education and Curricular Reform

In 1982 as part of the national development plan known as Change with Equity, the government turned its attention to educational opportunity and curricular reform. While educational television, literacy drives, and distance programs had existed since the 1960s, new emphasis was given to distance education in all modalities—primary, secondary, technical, and university (Zapata, 1986). Earlier, Decree 80 had authorized postsecondary institutions to provide greater access by establishing sectional sites and required them to provide continuing education as part of their service to the community. Tellez (1984) points out that, at the higher education level, private institutions have done more in establishing programs in distance and continuing education than have public ones. The public institutions have feared that such programs will reduce resources for residential programs and have questioned the quality of such programs. Yet such programs provide opportunities for providing primary and secondary teachers who have no teacher education at the university level (Restrepo, 1986).

Of greater interest is the curricular reform, Decree 1002, issued in 1984 which aimed at changing the focus of teaching in primary and secondary schools. The curricular reform established goals and objectives for the various subjects taught and studied (Diaz Osorio, 1985). It appears to be an attempt to provide a theoretical framework with philosophical bases in two camps: Piagetian developmental constructivism and Skinnerian behaviorist reductionism. The reform provided for instructional design based on behavioral objectives—an educational technology model (Diaz, 1985; Hernandez, 1984).

No other reform since the Basic Plan has caused such a furor (Diaz, 1985; Gantiva, 1986; Mockus, et al., 1983; Quiroz, 1985; Vasco, 1985; Velez, 1988). Teachers saw it as a means of disqualifying them and taking away their authority

(Mockus, 1984). In reaction, a popular bottom-up reform effort known as the pedagogical movement has appeared. This national, grass-roots organization of teachers from all levels is trying to redefine pedagogy, the role of the teacher, and the social function of the school.

Some of the critics point to the foreign origins of the framework; others criticize its emphasis on technology to the exclusion of humanism (Hernandez, 1984). Gantiva (1986:12) sums up the criticism of the curricular reform as the government having "legalized the basic goals and objectives of education without relating them to the social, cultural or academic reality of the nation." He further states that the pedagogical movement does not pretend to create a factory of teaching models, but rather to "create a new vision of life and culture—a new mentality." Velez (1988) notes that since neither parents nor students have been consulted, teachers are the only vehicle for addressing the issues underlying the curricular reform.

Restructuring the Teaching Profession

In 1979 the government issued Decree 2277 which established norms for teachers at the primary and secondary levels. It provided a national *escalafon* (salary schedule) and regulated finances, in-service and continuing education, as well as procedures for evaluation and promotion.

As part of the reorganization of the educational system, the system of normal schools was integrated into the secondary system, with pedagogical training being one of the options in the two-year vocational cycle. As part of the reorganization of higher education, new attention was paid to the role of the *facultades* of education. The quality of the professoriate and the training they give their students has been a source of debate (Catano, 1980; Chiappe and Myers, 1982; Eder de Zambrano, 1982; Gonzalez, 1983; ICFES-Colciencias, 1981; Serna Gomez, 1984; Tellez, 1986). The general feeling is that teachers, including university professors, receive little recognition and that the profession lacks prestige (Larsen-Pusey, 1988). As noted previously, teachers have reacted to this state of affairs by establishing their own movement to reassert control over their own destiny.

Institutionalizing Research and the Academic Career

A major aspect of Decree 80 has been to institutionalize research as an integral part of the academician's role in higher education. Colombian educators have debated the legitimacy and effectiveness of such change by decree. This discussion has resulted in a series of studies and essays on research in higher education (Alvarez and Falco, 1983; Catano, 1980; Chiappe and Myers, 1982; Eder de Zambrano, 1982; Gonzalez, 1983; ICFES-Colciencias, 1981; Restrepo, 1983; Uricoechea, 1984; Velez, 1988; Vidal, 1984; Vivas, 1980, 1982). Here, we will discuss the major provisions in Decree 80 related to the professoriate in universities and graduate programs.

Decree 80 defined the roles and obligations of both full-time and part-time professors. It incorporated teaching and research for full-time personnel and established a system for ranking the professoriate. It set standards for faculty promotion, including research and publications as well as degrees and professional development. Scientific research was made a central goal of university education for professors and students. Graduate programs (reserved to institutions legally recognized as universities) were established with the central objective of preparing personnel for research and scientific activities or for specialization. The decree provided for limited contracts and a once-in-a-lifetime sabbatical after seven years of service.

In his analysis of the decree as it relates to research, Restrepo (1983) discusses four central aspects:

1. It established research as a principal activity for higher education.
2. It recognized that research training should be a general attribute of the university professor.
3. It incorporated a support system for research into administrative functions and budgets.
4. It differentiated the role of research for the different levels of postsecondary education (indirectly giving privilege to public institutions over private ones in this regard).

Restrepo notes that provision was made for building the infrastructure necessary for implementing research through planning systems, libraries, statistical information, and so on, but he points out that there was considerable delay in implementing the decree. The Association of University Presidents asked for two years to comply with the article that required setting aside 2 percent of the budget for research.

A study of full-time professors of science, humanities, and social sciences in nine public universities (Larsen-Pusey, 1988) shows that in the intervening years the decree has continued to be controversial and its implementation has been only partially successful. For some universities, it meant losses of privileges already gained (unlimited tenure and sabbatical); for others, it provided stability and benefits for the professoriate. Professors are pessimistic about their ability to carry out the requirements of the decree with regard to research. Few feel they have adequate training to conduct research. This is not surprising given that only 12 percent hold doctoral degrees. Barriers reported by professors include limited financial resources and poor physical facilities, especially laboratories and libraries. They complain that bureaucratic red tape makes it difficult to secure books and equipment needed in their teaching and research endeavors. Finally, they note that, without a national data base, they find it difficult to keep current in their field or to disseminate the results of their research.

Colombian educators have expressed concern that little research is being done in the Facultades de Educacion (Cajiao, 1987; Catano, 1980, 1984; Chiappe and

Myers, 1982; Gonzalez, 1983; Pabon de Restrepo, Pereira, and Unda, 1986; Serna Gomez and Botero Jaramillo, 1983; Tellez, 1986; Vidal, 1984). The two-tiered system documented in Larsen-Pusey (1988, 1990) indicates that professors in the *facultades* of education have less training for conducting research. It also shows they have more limited resources and poorer physical facilities when compared to the four universities targeted for modernization during the National Front reform efforts. The academic preparation of professors working in the *facultades* of education tends to be a four-year undergraduate degree followed by a master's degree earned at a Colombian university; the number with doctorates is extremely limited.

ISSUES IN THE RECENT REFORMS

The underlying goal of these reforms continues to be national development, just as it was under the National Front. At the same time, the recent reforms have attempted to address other issues. Equity issues undergird the expansion of continuing and distance education as well as the integration of the educational system. Quality issues are inherent in restructuring the teaching profession, institutionalizing research and the academic career, and the curricular reform. Certainly, the role of the state in controlling private education was part of the reorganization and integration of the educational system. The problem is whether such reforms can be achieved by decree or whether they will be achieved only on paper.

More encouraging is the discussion that has surrounded these reforms and the grass-roots efforts at dealing with equity and quality issues (Zubieta and Gonzalez, 1986). The pedagogical movement has involved teachers from all levels in a common goal of redefining education, pedagogy, and curriculum. Teachers are talking about inequities in the system and how they can combat the complaints about the lack of quality in Colombian education. Colombian researchers are also beginning to examine these issues (Facundo, 1986; Velez, 1988).

Equity and quality issues continue to exist and need to be addressed. Rural sectors continue to receive less education. Velez (1988) notes that such problems as the political interests in hiring teachers, the critical financial state of the public sector, teachers' low pay, and the politicalization of their professional associations have tended to lower the effectiveness of teachers and to adversely affect the quality of education in general. Little attention has been paid to the education of minority groups (Lopez de Aguja and Hernandez, 1984) or gender issues (Colectivo de Mujeres, 1984). Rhetoric abounds, but educators are skeptical that real change can or will occur without commitment of resources (Larsen-Pusey, 1988).

CONCLUSION

This chapter has provided a historical context for reform in Colombia. Reform in three periods was top-down: the Liberal reforms of the 1930s, the National

Front reforms from the mid–1950s through the mid–1970s, and the post–National Front reforms since 1976. The early reforms tended to center on secondary and higher education; attempts to provide universal primary education were never achieved. Expansion was achieved by the modernization reforms under the National Front but at the cost of stability and quality. The recent reforms have begun to address equity and quality issues, but much remains to be done. The success of these reforms will depend, in part, on the affected parties' reception and on the commitment of resources by the government. The emergence of a grass-roots reform effort and the interest in educational research by Colombian educators are encouraging signs. The task is formidable.

REFERENCES

Briceño, Rosa. 1988. "University Reform, Social Conflict, and the Intellectuals: The Case of the National University of Colombia." Unpublished dissertation. Palo Alto: Stanford University.

Cajiao, Francisco. 1987. "La Formación de Docentes en Colombia" [Teacher training in Colombia]. Lecture given at Reunión Nacional de Facultades de Educación, March 3, 1987, at Universidad Pedagógica Nacional in Bogotá. Mimeo.

Cataño, Gonzálo. 1980. "Sociología de la Educación en Colombia" [Sociology of education in Colombia]. Revista Colombiana de Educación 5:9–30.

———. 1984. "Estudios de Posgrado en Educación: Evaluación de una Experiencia" [Graduate studies in education: evaluation of an experience]. Revista Colombiana de Educación 13:78–107.

Chiappe, Clemencia, and Robert Myers. 1982. "El Fortalecimiento de la Capacidad Investigativa en Educación en Colombia 1960–1981" [Strengthening the research capacity in education in Colombia 1960–1981]. Revista Colombiana de Educación 9:77–108.

Colectivo de Mujeres. 1984. "La Discriminación de la Mujer en la Escuela" [Discrimination against women in schools]. Revista Trimestral del Centro de Estudio e Investigación Docente (CEID) de la Federación Colombiana de Educadores, 79–84.

Decreto 80 of 1980. No date. Bucaramanga: Universidad Industrial de Santander.

Departamento Nacional de Planeación. 1979. "Consideraciones para la Reforma de la Educación Superior" [Considerations for higher education reform]. Revista Colombiana de Educación 3:83–98.

Diaz, Mario. 1985, June. "Contradicciones de una Pedagogía Retórica" [Contradictions of a rhetorical pedagogy]. Educación y Cultura 4:22–33.

Díaz, Osorio, José Jaime. 1985. "Estudio e Interpretación de la Resolución 17486 del Ministerio de Educación Nacional" [Study and interpretation of Resolution 17486 of the National Ministry of Education]. Estudios Educativos 21–22: 161–181.

Eder de Zambrano, Doris. 1982. "Estudio Sobre Facultades de Educación" [Study of the schools of education]. Bogotá: MEN. Mimeo.

Facundo, Angel. 1986, July. "Investigaciones Sobre Calidad de la Educación" [Research on the quality of education]. Educación y Cultura 8:14–16.

Flórez, R., F. A. Franco, and R. Galvis. 1985. El Saber Pedagogico del Profesor en

Medellín [Pedagogical knowledge of the professor in Medellín]. Medellín: Editorial Copiyepes.

Franco, Augusto, and Carlos Tunnerman. 1978. *La Educación Superior en Colombia* [Higher educatión in Colombia]. Bogotá: FES.

Gantiva, Jorge O. 1986, December. "Los Fines de la Educación y la Práctica Pedagógica" [Goals of education and teaching practice]. *Educación y Cultura* 10:6–12.

González, José A. 1983. *Diagnóstico de los Programas Académicos de las Licenciaturas en Educación—Biología* [Diagnosis of the academic programs of the four-year biology programs in education]. Bogotá: ICFES.

Hernández, Carlos Augusto. 1984. "La Reforma Curricular: Cientifismo y Taylorización" [Curricular reform: scientificism and Taylorization]. *Educación y Cultura* 2(September):35–42.

Herrera, Martha Cecilia. 1986. "La Educación en la Segunda República Liberal (1930–1946)" [Education in the Second Liberal Republic 1930–1946]. *Revista Colombiana de Educación* 18:84–97.

ICFES. 1975. *La Educación Superior en Colombia: Documentos Básicos para su Planeamiento* [Higher education in Colombia: basic planning documents] (Vols. 1–2). Bogotá: ICFES.

ICFES-Colciencias. 1981. "Las Ciencias Exactas y Naturales en la Universidad Colombiana" [Exact and natural sciences in the Colombian university]. *Ciencia, Tecnología y Desarrollo* 5(4):383–566.

Larsen-Pusey, Mary Ann. 1988. *Higher Education in Colombia: The Perspective of the Professoriate*. Ann Arbor, Mich.: University of Michigan.

———. 1990. "The Public University in Colombia: A Two-tiered System." Paper presented at the annual conference of the Comparative and International Education Society Conference, Anaheim, Calif.

Lebot, Ivon. 1979. *Educación e Ideología en Colombia*. [Education and ideology in Colombia]. Bogotá: Editorial La Carreta.

López de Aguja, Esperanza, and Luciano Hernández. 1984. "Hacia una Verdadera Educación Indígena" [Towards true education for the indigenous peoples]. *Revista Trimestral del Centro de Estudio e Investigación Docente (CEID) de la Federación Colombiana de Educadores*, 75–79.

Mockus, Antanus. 1984, September. "Movimiento Pedagógico y Defensa de la Calidad de la Educación Pública" [Pedagogical movement and the defense of quality in public education]. *Educación y Cultura* 2:27–34.

———, Carlos Hernandez, Berenice Guerrero, José Granes, Maria Clemencia Castro, Jorge Charum, and Carlo Federici. 1983, June. "La Reforma Curricular y el Magisterio" [Curricular reform and the teaching profession]. Paper presented at the Twelfth Congress of the Colombian Federation of Educators, Bucaramanga. Reprinted in *Educación y Cultura* 4:65–88.

Molano, Alfredo, and Cesar Vera. 1982. *Evolución de la Política Educativa Durante el Siglo XX: Primera Parte* [Evolution of educational policy during the twentieth century: part one]. Bogotá: Centro de Investigaciónes Universidad Pedagógica.

Moreno Narváez, Fabio. 1982. *La Planeación Educativa Durante la Frente Nacional: Aportes para su Análisis y su Historia* [Educational planning during the National Front: aids for analysis and history]. Bogotá: Universidad Pedagógica Nacional–Centro des Investigaciónes Universidad Pedagógica.

Pabón de Restrepo, N., C. Pereira, and P. Unda. 1986. "La Investigación en las Fa-

cultades de Educación'' [Research in the schools of education.] Paper presented
to the Reunión Técnica de Decanos de Facultades de Educación y Directores de
Departamentos de Educación o Pedagogía. Bogotá: Universidad Pedagogía.
Mimeo.
Parra Sandoval, Rodrigo, and M. Elvira Carvajal. 1979. ''La Universidad Colombiana:
De la Filosofía a la Tecnocracia Estratificada'' [The Colombian university: from
philosophy to stratified technocracy]. *Revista Colombiana de Educación* 4:131–
141.
Pelczar, Richard. 1977. ''The Latin American Professoriate: Progress and Prospects.''
Higher Education 6(2):235–254.
Quiroz, Alonso. 1985, June. ''El Decreto 1002: Una Pérdida de Identidad Cultural del
Maestro'' [Decree 1002: the teacher's loss of cultural identity]. *Educación y
Cultura* 4:58–62.
Rama, German. 1970. *El Sistema Universitario en Colombia* [The university system in
Colombia]. Bogotá: Universidad Nacional de Colombia.
Restrepo, Bernardo. 1986, April. ''La Educación a Distancia: Una Alternativa para la
Formación de Docentes'' [Distance education: An alternative for teacher prepa-
ration]. *Educación y Cultura* 7:27–31.
Restrepo, Gabriel. 1983. ''Institucionalización de la Investigación en la Universidad:
Análisis Histórico'' [Institutionalization of research in the university: historical
analysis]. *Ciencia, Tecnología y Desarrollo* 7(1–2):33–73.
Sanín Echeverri, Jaime. 1970. *La Universidad Nunca Lograda* [The university never
reached]. Bogotá: Voluntad.
Serna Gómez, Humberto. 1984. ''Formación Pedagógica de Profesores Universitarios y
Recursos para la Docencia'' [Pedagogical preparation for university professors
and resources for teaching]. In PREDE/OEA/CINDA, *Pedagogía Universitaria
en América Latina: Antecedentes y Perspectivas.* Santiago: Centro Interuniver-
sitario de Desarrollo, pp. 51–59.
———, and M. Botero Jaramillo. 1983. ''Aproximaciones a un Diagnóstico sobre las
Facultades de Educación en el País y Políticas para su Futuro Desarrollo'' [Ap-
proximating a diagnosis of the schools of education in the country and policies
for their future development]. *Educacion Superior y Desarrollo* 2(4):4–17.
———, and Fabio Moreno Narváez. 1985. *Desarrollo Científico y Humanístico de la
Universidad Colombiana* [Scientific and humanistic development of the Colombian
university]. Bogotá: ICFES.
Téllez, Gustavo. 1984, September. ''La Política Educativa y el Plan de Desarrollo''
[Educational policy and the development plan]. *Educación y Cultura* 2:49–54.
———. 1986, April. ''La Universidad Pedagógica Nacional: Proceso y Principios de
una Reforma'' [The national pedagogical university: principles and process of
reform]. *Educación y Cultura* 7:31–36.
UPN Oficina de Planeación. 1986. ''Antecedentes, Fundamentos y Desarrollos de la
Reforma Académica de la UPN'' [Antecedents, foundations, and development of
academic reform at the UPN]. Bogotá: UPN. Mimeo.
Uricoechea, Fernando. 1984. ''La Institucionalización de la Práctica Científica en Colombia'' [Institutionalization of scientific practice in Colombia]. *Ciencia, Tecnología, y Desarrollo* 8(1–4):39–55.
Vasco, Carlos. 1985, June. ''Conversación Informal sobre la Reforma Curricular'' [In-
formal conversation about the curricular reform]. *Educación y Cultura* 4:11–18.

Vélez, Eduardo. 1988. "Estudios sobre Educación y Sociedad en Colombia" [Studies on education and society in Colombia]. *Revista Colombiana de Educación* 19:80–106.

Vidal, J. 1984. "Las Facultades de Ciencias de la Educación" [The Schools of Education Science]. *Educación y Cultura Revista Trimestral del Centro de Estudio e Investigación docente (CEID) de la Federación Colombiana de Educadores. Separata Especial.*

Vivas, Jorge. 1980. "Ciencia, Tecnología y Estilos Académicos" [Science, technology and academic style]. *Revista Colombiana de Educación* 6:87–101.

———. 1982. "Marco de Referencia para el Estado Universidad-Empresa en América Latina" [A frame of reference for the university-business state in Latin America]. *Revista Colombiana de Educación* 6:45–74.

Zapata, Vladimir. 1986. "Educación no Formal: Educación Popular" [Nonformal education: mass education]. *Estudios Educativos* 24:67–97.

Zubieta, Leonor, and Olga Lucía González. 1986, July. "El maestro y la Calidad de la Educación" [The teacher and the quality of education]. *Educación y Cultura* 8:8–13.

8

CUBA

Rolland G. Paulston and
Cathy C. Kaufman

This chapter presents a chronology of the struggle for educational reform in Cuba. We chose a historical context so that the reader may better understand the relationships between those advocating reform and those opposed to reform efforts during major periods in Cuba's turbulent history.

In our research model, presented in Figure 8.1, the action dimension of reform and the sociological dimensions of power are interfaced in a manner that will facilitate the consideration of four basic questions addressed to each reform period, that is, the period of Spanish colonial rule, the period of U.S. military occupation and domination, the quasi-republican period, and the revolutionary period under Fidel Castro.

Four key questions are posed in this chapter.

1. Who controlled education and how did attempts at educational reform either facilitate or frustrate their objectives?
2. Who opposed educational reform efforts or had them imposed on them? How did the reform efforts of those in power serve to strengthen or alter the educational and political status quo, or generate sufficient conflict to challenge the existing system and foster further educational change?
3. Did reform goals aim at changing structures or values, and what factors facilitated or limited reform efforts?
4. Under what conditions did change, if any, come about, and what short- and long-term effects can be identified?

By looking at the reform experience within each time frame of the model, we will attempt to actualize the paradigmatic bias of conflict integral to most Latin

Figure 8.1
Model of Educational Reform Efforts in Cuba

Major Reform Periods	Reform Advocates	Reform Goals	Reform Opponents	Short-Term Effects	Long-Term Effects
Anti-Colonial (1879-1889)	Independence Leaders and revolutionary University Students.	Cuban independence and a Cuban University.	Spanish Colonial authorities and Church officials.	Strengthened independence movement. Students executed and martyred.	Legitimized central role of university students as leaders in political and educational reform.
U.S. Military Occupation (1898-1903) and Political/Economic Domination (1908-1933)	U.S. educational authorities and emergent professional class.	Re-orient education to the U.S. public school model -- ie, comprehensive practical, co-ed, with local control.	Cuban Nationalists and Cultural Traditionalists.	Reforms successfully put into operation under U.S. supervision with U.S. resources.	Cuban resentment at U.S. domination. Educational system reverted to Hispanic model with U.S. departure.
"Quasi-Republic" (1933-1959)	Revolutionaries (Mella)	To link university to class struggle and revolution.	Dictators, police and U.S. Commercial interests.	Repression -- revolutionary students murdered.	Created martyrs for present revolutionary regime.
	Liberals (Cordova Movement)	To reform University to lead democratic development and university autonomy.	Marxists and Traditionalists.	Frustration with corruption of democratic institutions.	Produced disillusionment with liberal democratic models.
	Commercial interests.	To create a private sector of Secondary and Higher Education.	Radicals and Liberals.	Successful expansion of private education as commercial activity.	Undercut public educational system.

The Castro Revolution (1959-?)	Castro, Communist Party, State organizations, Mass organizations.	Value change --the creation of the new Socialist Person. Structural change -- comprehensive, universal, applied. Pedagogic change -- Education now viewed as Social, not Private Capital. Combination of study and productive labor. Link education with international class struggle.	Abroad, Cuban exiles in the U.S. In Cuba, mostly passive resistance from religious groups, anti-communists, and pro-democracy elements.	Value change -- creation of new man problematic. Structural change -- reforms accomplished. Reorientation of education to production and technical functions. Pedagogical change -- Many third world students educated and indoctrinated. Cuba far surpasses U.S. Alliance for Progress goals for educational reform in Latin America.	Value shift -- Cuba realizes Marti's political/ educational goals. Structural shift -- Educational theory and practice transformed at all levels, with heavy dependence on Eastern European models and technical inputs. Shift in higher education from a liberal humanist pedagogy to a commanded pedagogy.
"Post-Castro Period"	Military (?) Professional Elites (?) Reformist Students (?)	Economic Realism, ie, increased efficiency and productivity. Human rights. Re-emergence of a private educational sector.	Marxist ideologues. Privileged Bureaucrats. Beneficiaries of Marxist redistribution.	Increased participation of major interest groups. Education becomes less ideological and commanded.	Reintegration of Cuba into Western Hemispheric context. Cuba rejoins OAS educational organizations.

American reform efforts. Because this critical historical perspective represents a conflictual world-view of reform efforts, the relationships of political, economic, and educational systems as they impact on each other will be instrumental in gaining a representation of the Cuban case. In previous publications, revolutionary educational systems have been defined as those in which there is a clear and systematic use of educational policy in leading cultural and social reconstruction (Paulston, 1972). Although the term "educational reform" is used here for consistency with terminology in the encyclopedia, we prefer the more value-neutral term "educational change," that is, a term free from the Victorian notion of privileged or foundational knowledge in theory, and the linked idea of progress that infuses both the structural-functionalist and the Marxist literature on reform theory and practice (Paulston, 1993).

This study examines reform from the inside out by describing reform advocates and their opponents within chronological periods, and then by representing characteristics of immediate and long-range change associated with educational reforms/changes at each particular time period. The data procedures used include secondary analysis of current and archival literature, especially interviews of participants in past reform with first-hand knowledge of reform practices and outcomes.

THE SPANISH COLONIAL PERIOD, 1842–1898

Front-line efforts to achieve educational reform in Cuba have historically been in the minds and hands of university students. While Cuban students did not gain recognition as an organized group until after 1920, the early beginnings of their influence date back to the Spanish colonial period. At that time, the hierarchical educational structure closely tracked Cuba's plantation society dominated by Hispanic social elites and Hispanic culture. In the newly independent Latin American republics, ideas about instruction of citizenship concepts, state responsibilities for public instruction, and the need for education of a utilitarian nature found a lively public debate. In colonial Cuba, the Catholic Church provided classical education of the elite, while the vast majority of Cuban children went unschooled. For over 300 years Spanish colonialists had presented themselves to the New World as ambitious visitors seeking to extract wealth and return home. Accordingly, the colonial period saw few, if any, reform efforts from the top-down.

Rather, Spanish rulers and the Catholic Church designed and implemented limited educational programs to meet their own ends. The affluent sent their children abroad or to private schools, while the small middle sectors supported a few public schools with religious affiliation at the local level. The masses of rural poor remained untouched by education.

In Spain's defense, plans for educational development existed (Epstein, 1987:6). But without elite support, implementation faltered. In 1842 a law established municipal funding of public instruction, and a revision of this law in 1880 provided for free instruction of primary children whose parents could not afford tuition. The law required that children between the ages of six and nine attend school, and that the granting of teaching appointments be based on competitive exams (Report of the Civil Department, 1899:843–845). Yet the Hispanic class hierarchy changed little by extending the promise of free education to young children, and only rarely did students use education to rise above their socioeconomic class. Emphasis on moral and religious teachings rather than subjects appropriate for economic advancement also served to reproduce hierarchical and semifeudal relations. A few separate schools for black children were established, but attendance was not required and was infrequent. Separation of the sexes was maintained in all but the most impoverished rural schools. Under Catholic Church control, Cuba developed something of a dual educational system. Church-supported facilities had better physical plants and better trained teachers, which served to further distinguish between the religious, private system and the legally enabled but largely unfunded public system.

The aspirations of the poor could not be realized within this Spanish educational system, and it fell far short of stated outcomes. In spite of the structure it established in terms of written laws, the funding of two separate systems served to maintain the historic alignment of church and state that gave religious sanction to the hierarchical order of the elite ruling class (Epstein, 1987:7). Thus, the social and economic conditions of colonialism precluded significant educational reform. For many more years than the rest of its Latin American counterparts, Cuba followed this educational pattern under the domination of the mother country. Nonetheless, the imbalance in this system of the rich few controlling the poor masses eventually set the stage for revolution against the Crown.

Within this context, university students under José Martí looked not only to Cuba's liberation from Spain, but perhaps more intensely also to liberation from the legacy of Hispanic culture and its strict adherence to social class hierarchy. Martí's vision for an independent homeland called for private landownership by the masses, a reduced economic dependency on sugar, a political structure that would foster law and order instead of individual social advancement, and an educational emphasis on practical, utilitarian instruction instead of classical studies.

Following the execution of eight university students and the imprisonment of thirty-four others as punishment for revolutionary action against Spanish colonial rule, Martí led other students in the forefront of the independence movement (Pera, 1900:39–44). Martí's greatest fear in the struggle for national independence was United States military intervention. Unhappily, this fear was realized. Following decades of struggle for independence from the mother country, the reins of domination passed from the hands of one outside power to another.

Over the succeeding five decades, Cuba's retarded development as a semi-independent nation and the struggle for liberation and for educational reform continued.

U.S. OCCUPATION, 1889–1902, 1906–1909, AND ECONOMIC DOMINATION, 1909–1933

The years immediately following the Spanish-American War saw American military occupation and, under the direction of General Leonard Wood, the energetic construction of roads, sewers, and schools. Wood viewed education as the main tool in his plan to cleanse not only the island of Spanish influence, but also the bodies and minds of the Cubans (Epstein, 1987:2). Decades of war had devastated Cuba and taken an enormous toll in lives and property. Hugh Thomas estimated that over one-tenth of the population had perished and that one-third of the island's farms and plantations lay in ruin (Thomas, 1971:423–424). Only about one-half of the schools open before the war were still open in 1889, and most of these lacked supplies, texts, and desks. Sixty percent of the total population and 77 percent of the rural population were illiterate at this time (Perez, 1945:308–311). Against this backdrop, American reconstruction produced dramatic structural changes.

With an American public school model from the state of Ohio, school administrators and teachers were trained in both Cuba and the United States. American reformers introduced an American curriculum and American texts. Enrollments soon quintupled. By February 1902, 40 percent of the school-age population was enrolled in school, an increase of 24 percent over 1899, and the rate of attendance reached a high of 76 percent (Trelles, 1923:36). The urban/rural educational gap narrowed, and the educational system became accessible to the black population. While private and religious schools continued, they played a diminished role during the U.S. occupation (Epstein, 1987:10). In addition, the American school reform efforts shared a good deal of Martí's educational reform vision. They attempted to inculcate utilitarian skills rather than memorization and drill. They separated church teachings and authority from the new public education, and they attempted to enforce attendance laws. Teacher education programs flourished, and access to free public education was extended to all socioeconomic sectors. Why, then, did the U.S. reforms largely end with the departure of U.S. troops?

The U.S. system, which had proven workable in Ohio, for example, stressed local control. It developed slowly in incremental steps under the direction of a literate population. It could not be easily and quickly transplanted to a largely illiterate plantation society without any experience in self-government. Additional insight is provided by José Martínez Díaz, a schoolteacher under the American occupation, who thought the human element was much of a problem as the structural. Martínez reported that, although many teachers from the colonial period renounced their Spanish citizenship, they remained in the newly Americanized classrooms, still implementing their previous training in hierarchical patterns of authority rather than the American methodology and democratic models. These teachers had been attracted by the high salaries paid by the Americans (80 percent higher than their North American counterparts) (Hanna, 1901:57), but they were not attracted by the new methodology.

Another severe problem was the prevailing tendency of local boards to look more to personal conditions for employment than to professional qualifications, thus fostering a system of nepotism and bribery. By giving the local school boards this responsibility, which had worked well in Ohio, the Americans had assumed that Cuban officials would act competently and democratically. Quick and effective educational success in Cuba was as much a part of Wood's vision and reform as a fast and decisive war against Spain had been a part of Martí's vision. Both dreams went unrealized.

Whereas the Spanish planned a system of schooling that was never delivered, the American resources secured Wood's reforms, at least in terms of initial enrollments and buildings. His efforts to increase literacy, which were largely successful in the first two decades of the twentieth century, sought to create a democratic foundation, but they lacked an underlying national support structure in which literacy might be made functional with increased political and economic participation. By midcentury the literacy rate had slipped from that of previous decades (International Bank for Reconstruction and Development, 1951:406). Indeed, American resources had enabled the construction of schools and the training of teachers, and significantly increased enrollments. But the superficial understanding of Cuban society by U.S. reformers resulted in a treatment of symptoms throughout the occupation at the expense of getting to the causes of abuses that had not been effectively addressed. The War of Independence rid Cuba of domination by Spain, but it resulted in the attempted imposition of a pragmatic, foreign North American cultural system, rather than Martí's idea of individual empowerment of the Cuban people through education.

While U.S. reformers for the most part ignored university education, enrollments increased during the occupation, and tuition fees decreased (Suchlicki, 1969:18). In spite of some growth in budget and faculty, the university failed to address educational tasks essential for the nation. Law and medicine, the most popular professions, continued to serve as important stepping stones for political prominence and social status. University students blamed the problem of educational inequalities, along with most other Cuban problems, on the United States.

Julio Antonio Mella, an articulate critic of U.S. imperialism, organized the First Congress of Cuban Students in 1923 to form a university that would be more cognizant of the needs of Cuba and less allied with the privileged of society. In his attempt to combine university reform and class struggle, Mella allied with several communist groups and later with the Communist International. He became a leading opponent of President-elect Gerardo Machado, who was seen as a U.S. puppet and a continuation of earlier American intervention. Confrontational activities led to Mella's expulsion from the university and to his temporary incarceration by Machado's police. A nineteen-day hunger strike roused public support for his release. After a break with the communists and his expulsion from the Mexican Communist party where he had learned revolutionary tactics, Mella died under "mysterious" circumstances. Some blamed his death on Machado, others on the Communist International. In any case, Mella's assassination in 1929 provided the students with a martyr to use in agitation against the hated Machado and his American business supporters. With the dictator's unopposed reelection, demonstrations, student beatings, deaths, and urban violence increased over the next several years, and Machado closed the university from

1930 to 1933. The educational dissatisfaction did not remain dormant, however, and students continued to agitate for democratic reform. They fought to terminate the humiliating Platt Amendment, which permitted direct U.S. intervention in Cuban affairs, and to achieve land reform and the eventual nationalization of the sugar and mining industries, the largely U.S.-owned commercial interests.

QUASI-REPUBLICAN PERIOD, 1933–1959

Franklin Roosevelt's Good Neighbor Policy for the first time enabled the Cubans to experience some sense of independent action. Although U.S. troops had long departed the island, the continual threat of the Platt Amendment provided for their reintroduction whenever the U.S. government deemed it necessary. Although the Cubans had begun political representation based on a modified American model, they lacked political structures and the experience necessary to put a democratic process into operation. In this demoralized period of Cuban history those in government, in education, and in society as a whole used the system to serve self-interest. The two political powers of this time, the dictators Machado and Juan Batista, both ruled with U.S. government and commercial support. Not surprisingly, most Cubans saw them as tyrants, as detestable U.S. puppets.

University student reform leaders of the 1930s saw themselves as advocates of Martí's nationalist vision in spite of their inability to attend classes. September 1933 marked a turning point in their unequal struggle, with the army's entry as an organized force into politics under Batista's leadership. Students and military, two armed groups accustomed to violence, united to rule Cuba (Suchlicki, 1969:35). The Roosevelt administration refused to recognize their five-man government, and in a meeting with Batista and the army, Dr. Ramon Grau San Martín was appointed provisional president with student support but with no political experience for the job. By January 1934 Batista overthrew Grau. This overthrow dealt a severe blow to student dreams of reform, and many left Cuba. Some turned to fascism, and others entered the elitist professional system that they had once been determined to change.

The largely neglected rural population continued to be bypassed in educational efforts, and the gap between modern urban Cuba and backward rural Cuba grew steadily. Corruption in education spread throughout the system. The minister of education under President Grau San Martín (1944–48) became one of Cuba's richest men at the expense of the education budget (Mesa-Lago, 1971:382). Cuban teachers held life tenure whether or not they taught, and appointments sold for large sums. The patronage system resulted in the hiring of many unqualified teachers, who sometimes sold their positions to others and left their teaching post or even the country itself while still collecting a salary. World Bank reports criticized "specialists" who had little knowledge in their professed specialties, and the organization stressed that unless Cuba greatly improved the education system, there was little reason to be optimistic about social or economic development (World Bank 1958 Report from Mesa-Lago, 1970:384). Professor Pablo Lavin pointed to the growing divorce between education and the social and economic needs of his country (Lavin, 1947:232–331). Society's failure to absorb university graduates in a practical way led to a generation of unemployed with little hope of ever applying their newly acquired knowledge. Unemployment provided long periods of time for dissatisfaction to grow and for revolutionary plans to take shape.

In the 1950s the number of primary-aged children enrolled in school was only 6 percent higher than it had been fifty years earlier, and Cuba's total enrollment was well under the 64 percent average for the remainder of Latin America (Unesco, 1962:146). During this same period, Cuban university enrollment ranked among the top three in Latin American universities. This disparity reflected the continuation of an elite system which in the middle of the twentieth century was as much a part of the Cuban educational scene as it had been when José Martí and his fellow students cried out against the class-oriented colonial system. American practices had reshaped and renamed the educational system, but the Spanish tradition of elitism continued to thrive.

REVOLUTIONARY REFORM, 1959–PRESENT

Cuba had arrived at self-government a century later than its Latin American sisters, and that arrival occurred with a great deal of pent-up resentment against U.S. military, commercial, and educational influence. The sweeping educational changes that followed the 1959 Cuban revolution altered structures and ideology in order to facilitate a move from a distorted capitalist economy to a centrally planned socialist state. Education would play a central role in creating a changed value system and a "New Socialist Person." It was Castro's belief that education was the country's most important task after having made the revolution, for it would create the ideological framework for the new generation. This, too, set Cuba apart from other Latin American regimes that viewed education more as a means of individual mobility and social control. Where other regimes saw education as private capital to be used for personal and family advancement, revolutionary education in Cuba had become social capital to enable individuals to do what the revolution required.

The educational reform best representing this new reform rationale can be seen in the Campaign Against Illiteracy. Fidel Castro developed the pedagogy of this program during his months in the mountains of the Sierra Maesra in the summer of 1957. Despite General Wood's historic efforts to expand enrollment in primary schools via a series of legal enactments establishing free and compulsory education, rural Cuba in 1960 had a population of largely illiterate adults. Now Castro's revolution sought to bring rural workers literacy and a deeper understanding of national problems, a new conception of citizenship, and a new willingness to work and be examples to their children in order to transform the old society. After a census was taken to identify all illiterates, secondary school students, mainly from middle-class families, responded to Castro's challenge to create an exciting literacy adventure. These urban youth formed the corps of the first "army of education." When their training program at the once-elegant Varadero Beach resort ended, 105,700 young people had been trained and indoctrinated. Following seven days of intensive instruction in the use of Venceremos and Alfabeticemos, Castro sent his young army away from their parents with his moving Mothers' Day Speech of 1961.

Castro's emphasis on youth was more than a response to personnel shortages. Youth, he claimed, were uncorrupted and pure enough to be formed into true communists. And they were at precisely the developmental stage of their lives when searching for a sense of self allowed their physical energies and their searching minds to respond to an action-oriented ideology. Castro knew that success did not depend on literal truth but instead on motivating power under prevailing conditions. He also knew well that many of the families of the youth he needed for his initial literacy campaign were planning to leave Cuba for the United States. His Mothers' Day appeal to Cuban youth sought to enlist their energies in doing great deeds for Cuba and the revolution. His intent was to do far more than raise the consciousness of these young men and women; rather, his aim was to give them new families, new responsibilities, and a new societal ego. And he succeeded.

Jonathan Kozol's comprehensive and vivid account of the literacy campaign describes how most of the new literacy "teachers," themselves barely past childhood and from bourgeois backgrounds, had never lived without electricity or running water. Away from home for the first time, they found themselves sleeping in a hammock or on a dirt floor, eating an entire meal with a spoon, and washing in the river. Living conditions in the countryside were usually primitive and unsanitary. Daily farm work prior to evening literacy instruction exhausted most.

Few of these youth were socialists or Marxists. They had merely responded to a challenge of revolutionary nationalism. Kozol points out that, although the university student leaders were already committed to the socialist ideal, at this early period it had not been thrust on the public mind. To miss this point is to miss the long-term consequences of Castro's influence. It was *not* socialist conviction that prompted thousands of adolescents to spend nearly six months of their lives sleeping little more than six hours a day. Rather, it was the result (Kozol, 1978:7). The literacy struggle marked the first time in Cuban history that women had equal roles with men in bringing about social change.

After the primary schools closed for the summer, many thousands of teachers also joined the campaign. Some served as brigade leaders, and others as overseers of the literacy work in factories and municipal areas. With the minister of education, Armando Hart, in Eastern Europe during the spring training thrust, Castro took direct control of the 1961 literacy army. By fall, the bureaucratic apparatus had become totally operational, and in order to continue the initial "thrust," Castro ordered schools to participate in a mandatory September to January 1962 additional literacy campaign period. This meant that most Cuban schools remained closed for the fall session, the period totaling eight months including the summer break. During this time Conrado Benitez brigades were established in order to occupy the time of the children whose parents were being schooled. Youngsters planted flowers, learned national songs, and visited museums and factories. Canceling three months of academic instruction for pupils was not considered too great a sacrifice in the final push of the literacy campaign, and in December mass graduations took place nationwide.

The system did not work perfectly. Some illiterates had been overlooked in the census, some teachers occasionally failed to show up for evening classes, and pupils were often unwilling or too tired to learn at the end of a day's work. Critics pointed out that, with only first grade levels in reading and writing, new literates had skills much too low to be of use at work or home and that such marginal skills would be lost without follow-up work. Nonetheless, the literacy reform was an important first step in the unfolding of educational revolutionary reforms yet to come. Nothing of this magnitude had ever been attempted in Cuba before. Theodore McDonald sees the Cuban literacy campaign of 1961 as one of the truly great achievements of humankind, because, unlike many Third World literacy campaigns which received mixed evaluations, this one actually worked (McDonald, 1985:54). The campaign also demonstrated the feasibility of mass mobilization, and it affected the new belief system in several important ways. Cubans came to see that the literacy organization had grown from revolutionary activity rather than bureaucratic organization. The effort demonstrated to the population that reform programs were not necessarily limited by resources. It taught the nation that development projects needed to be political projects. And the campaign mixed urban resources with revolutionary values and converted them into virtues and heroic experiences (Fagen, 1969:55–63).

Literacy followups in revolutionary instruction took the form of weekly neighborhood meetings or seminars in which governmental programs were explained and the manual of the rebel army was studied. To meet the demand for instructors who could stay at least one lesson ahead of their students, the Committees for Defense of the Revolution (CDR) recognized for leadership any committee member who showed some talent or motivation for such work (Fagen, 1969:42).

Schools of Revolutionary Instruction—Escuela Instruccion Revolucionaria (EIR)—on the other hand, operated mainly in secret from 1960 to 1967 and one had to be chosen or appointed to attend them. The Cuban revolution of 1959 was identifiably the turning point in educational change in Cuba. The expansion that followed took place in stages, closely paralleling the economic policy of that time. Following the initial literacy thrust and until 1964, basic education in the rural primary school was emphasized during the failed attempt to industrialize under the Soviet model. Now the government viewed the schools as the change agent. New ideology effectively could be channeled through an educational framework. In 1964 the "schools to the countryside" movement sought to increase agricultural production and to inculcate socialist values. Martin Carnoy describes how for forty-five days of summer vacation students and teachers worked side by side at the difficult task of harvesting sugar cane as part of the new curriculum. The disillusionment that accompanied the failure to meet the sugar quotas, in 1969–1970, raised the likely possibility that trained managers and technicians would contribute far more to the economy than the students ever could. Although the use of student labor to increase quotas did not have its expected impact, the underlying concept involved, combining manual labor and mental work, continues to be an integral part of Cuban educational policy.

During 1965, the EIR moved into technological reform in education in the service of agricultural development. The importance of technology presented itself as more pragmatic than "winning the consciousness." Richard Fagen has looked at educational reform in a political context and notes that one of the least talked about but perhaps most important characteristics of the Schools of Revolutionary Instruction was the low educational level of their students. Only one in five had as much as a sixth grade education. Teaching technology to such students was extremely difficult, if not impossible, because the Soviet materials that were used were designed for far more sophisticated audiences. One reason for this problem was the Castro selection policy which consciously favored those of lower social and consequently lower educational origin (Fagen, 1969:131). Group commitment and solidarity, it seems, may have been purchased at the expense of problem solving.

This turn from an agricultural to an industrial base marked Cuban educational change throughout the 1970s. The decade saw a decided movement toward academic excellence and competition in an effort to raise educational standards (Carnoy, 1981:7). Nonetheless, these vocational schools did require students to be involved in work programs twenty hours a week, as did the schools in the countryside.

Higher education has remained a monopoly of the state. All policy is centrally developed, implemented, and evaluated within a Marxist-Leninist "scientific" world-view. The rationale for higher education is to provide a communist education, where study, work, sports, and military training combine to serve state interests (Paulston, 1989:1).

The university of the postrevolutionary period saw seven universities become three, faculty tenure end, and the number of professors increase fourfold. Most importantly, the revolutionary university sought to prepare students for meeting personnel needs in industrial engineering and agricultural sciences, whereas the prerevolutionary university had prepared students for professional careers. This new vocational and applied emphasis at the university level sought to integrate science and technology in national development. Carnoy notes that since 1975 the university has increasingly emphasized economic needs. In spite of Cuba's small size lending itself well to central planning, Castro has always been plagued with the problems of bureaucratic inefficiency. Moreover, attempts to educate planners and managers are producing a new elite in the old Hispanic tradition.

Although their salary is not more than double that of the average worker, they have numerous privileges, such as access to a car or an apartment, that the average Cuban does not have.

The gains Castro produced in the Cuban educational system are undeniable. Six years before the revolutionary takeover, he stated that an integral part of the creation of a new society would be the government's reform of education, and he made good on his promise. In the decade after 1959, the number of primary and secondary public schools doubled, and the accessibility of education for rural children improved greatly for the first time in Cuba's history. The matriculation rates of students increased twofold at the primary level and threefold in secondary schools. In addition, special provisions for preschool education and special education for the handicapped, along with school health services, evidenced significant gains (Paulston, in Mesa-Lago, 1971:386).

What factors limited this monumental reform? Programs that expanded at rapid rates resulted in shortages of teachers. The departure of thousands of teachers after the revolution intensified the problem. The use of untrained volunteer teachers, as well as teachers who had been pushed through training programs at rapid rates, undermined quality. A textbook shortage following the Bay of Pigs invasion reached critical proportions by 1966–1967, and technical training activities were severely hampered by lack of access to U.S. book suppliers. By 1969 the Cuban Book Institute declared that the contents of books could not be regarded as private property, and proceeded to print cheap editions of copyrighted titles, producing about 1.5 million copies of works by leading authors from around the world, without payment of royalties (McDonald, 1985:129). Later, Eastern European textbooks became widely available for scientific and technological studies.

In an evaluation of Cuban revolutionary education, Manuel Pastor finds that the cultural inequalities of gender and race have been addressed, while class inequalities are never discussed. Cuba has experienced what Eastern Europe and the Soviet Union had already recognized—that the development of high-level scientists and technicians creates a new privileged elite (Pastor, 1983:9–11).

In Geneva in 1977, Paulo Freire said that those who would study educational reform in Cuba, the re-creation of a people, would have to approach the subject with open eyes and unfrightened minds (Kozol, 1978:preface). He analyzed the educational change as one in which the Cuban people finally took history into their own hands and discovered that in making their history, they could also remake themselves.

In contrast, Eusebio Mujal-Leon likens Cuba to the Soviet Union in the 1920s, China in the 1950s, and Vietnam in the 1960s, with their myths about popular power and the creation of the "new" man (Mujal-Leon, 1988:46). Mujal-Leon claims that Castro's major goal since taking power in 1959 has not been educational reform, but the projection of himself and Cuba intertwined into the international spotlight. This view sees Castro as using the educational system as a tool, as an instrument of change in the creation of a new social order.

In her evaluation of the Cuban revolution at thirty, George Geyer concluded that Castro had become the epitome of a traditional Spanish *caudillo*. He only needed a modern philosophy to keep him in power, and communism, not fascism, provided the perfect ideology. The ideology was totalitarian and anti-American, and he had to be anti-American to be a world leader. Thus, Castro created power out of powerlessness, but more for himself than for his people. He has never hesitated to kill or exile his critics. He rid himself of those in a social class capable of questioning him—over 10 percent of all Cubans have abandoned Castro's utopia, and his interest in ideology has been a technique of personal power acquisition, not educational reform (Cuban American National Foundation, 1989a:41).

Jaime Suchlicki, an authority on Cuban university reform, claims that the ultimate educational goal of creating the New Socialist Person has not been realized, that the new university population is not interested in failed rhetoric. Castro's Rectification of Errors Campaign is seen as reminiscent of China's Cultural Revolution. Castro quickly stepped back onto center stage after a temporary venture into an experimental period of *perestroika*. "Fidel Castro is less concerned about whether the Cubans eat better and more concerned about his position in history and his position in the world" (Suchlicki, CANF *Conference Proceedings*, 1989:5). According to Suchlicki, he does not model educational reforms to the Third World; rather, he models violence as the way to power, bullets instead of the ballot box, and never mentions the educational road to the new order he advocated previous to 1959. Irving Horowitz views the great loss in this revolutionary period of educational reform as the loss of vivacity in private life (Horowitz, in CANF *Conference Proceedings*, 1989:17). He notes that Castro, like Lenin before him, predicted that communism would spread like wildfire, and this has not been the case. The consensus of the summer 1989 conference sponsored by the Cuban American Foundation was that Castro is now an anachronism and does not fit into the current era. Even the Soviet press affirms this view (Cuban American National Foundation, 1989b:36).

How then is one to assess Castro's revolution? A betrayal of the Cuban people, say the exiles. But friend and foe alike recognize he has created one of the most radical educational change movements in history. Castro's iconoclastic perspective inspired his belief in the perfectibility of human nature, with the reconstruction of society along socialist lines (Fagen, 1969:1). Historically, those who have dominated Hispanic culture have been able to hold up a gilded image of the future to give spiritual quality to the workaday world. The difficulty in changing the inertia of their cultural system has been the hardest lesson for Cubans to learn. It is not in the Hispanic tradition to favor hands dirtied by physical labor. Peasant families are still reluctant to send their children to new schools. High absenteeism and low productivity continue to characterize the Cuban workforce.

While the Cubans have undeniably enriched the tradition of revolutionary educational change, there is little reason to believe that future movements will be triggered by or modeled after the Cuban experience. Reform movements in Latin America have traditionally been blocked by the privileged elites, and they are not willing to facilitate a resource distribution, as in Cuba, in favor of the deprived and impoverished majority. While revolutionary Cubans successfully exploited cold war opportunities to realize Martí's frustrated goals for Cuban independence and educational reform, future developments will more likely see Cuba's reintegration into a Latin America racked by post–cold war debt and growing inequality. The challenge for Cuban educators will soon be to adapt and protect past reform gains, as Cubans struggle to adjust to harsh new economic realities and more pluralistic politics.

REFERENCES

Aigüesvives, Eduardo. 1989, January 30. "University Reform in Cordova and Cuba." *Gramma Weekly Review* 2.

Caberra, Olga, and Carmen Almodobar. 1975. *Las Luchas Estudiantiles Universitarias*. Habana: Editorial de Ciencias Sociales, pp. 22–30.

Carnoy, Martin. 1981. "Educational Reform and Economic Development in Cuba: Recent Developments." Paper presented at the annual meeting of the American Research Association, Los Angeles.

Castro, Fidel. 1982. *Speeches and Interviews from Castro's Tour of Chile*. New York: Pathfinder Press.

Cuba, Ministerio de Education. 1972. "A Decade of Adult Education in Cuba." Paper presented to the Third World Conference on Adult Education. Tokyo, Japan.

Cuban American National Foundation. 1989a. "Aftermath of the Purge." *Cuban Update*. Washington, D.C., (CANF).

———. 1989b. "The Cuban Revolution at Thirty." *Conference Proceedings*. Washington, D.C., (CANF).

Epstein, Erwin. 1987. "The Peril of Paternalism." *American Journal of Education* 96(1): 1–23.

Fagen, Richard. 1969. *The Transformation of Political Culture in Cuba*. Stanford, Calif.: Stanford University Press.

Figueroa, Max. 1974. "The Basic Secondary School in the Country: An Educational Innovation in Cuba." A Paper prepared for the International Bureau of Education. Paris: Unesco Press.

Geyer, Georgie. In CANF Conference Proceedings, 1989. *The Cuban Revolution at Thirty*. Washington, D.C.

Gramma Weekly Review. 1989, November 5. "Fidel at Ceremony Marking 30th Anniversary of Camilo Cienfuego's Death." Havana.

Groth, Alexander J. 1987. "Third World Marxism-Leninism: The Case of Education." *Comparative Education* 23:329–344.

Hanna, Matthew. 1901. "Report of the Commissioner of Public Schools." *Records of the Military Government of Cuba*. National Archives file n.LDC (LR)57.

Horowitz, Irving. In CANF Conference Proceedings, 1989. *The Cuban Revolution at Thirty*. Washington, D.C.

Howes, R. W. 1982. "Publishing and Libraries in Cuba." *International Library Review* 14: 317–334.

Kozol, Jonathan. 1978. *Children of the Revolution: A Yankee Teacher in the Cuban Schools*. New York: Delacorte Press.

Lafitade, Juan M. 1983. *Brigada Universitaria Jose A. Echeverría y Bon 154*. Havana: Editora Politica, pp. 33–35.

Lavin, Pablo. 1947. "El estado cubano y sus problemas educacionales." *Universidad de la Habana* 24:323–331.

Leiner, Marvin. 1973. *Major Developments in Cuban Education*. Andover, Mass.: Warner Modular Publications.

Lent, John A. 1984. "Journalism Training in Cuba Emphasizes Politics and Ideology." *Journalism Educator* (Autumn):12–15.

McCall, Cecelia. 1987, January. "Women and Literacy: The Cuban Experience." *Journal of Reading* 87:318–324.

McDonald, Theodore. 1985. *Making a New People: Education in Revolutionary Cuba*. Vancouver: New Star Books.

Marinello, Juan. 1960. *Revolución y Universidad*. Habana: Gobierno provincial revolucionario de la Habana, p. 65.

Martuza, Victor. 1986. "Evaluation of Reading Achievement in Cuban Schools: A Comparative Perspective." *Journal of Reading* 30(4):318–324.

Mesa-Lago, Carmelo, ed. 1971. *Revolutionary Change in Cuba*. Pittsburgh: University of Pittsburgh Press.

————, and Jorge Pérez-López, response to Brundenius, Claes, and Andrew Zimbalist. 1985. "The Endless Cuban Economy Saga: A Terminal Rebuttal/Cuban Growth: A Final Word. *Comparative Economic Studies* 27:67–84.

Ministerio de Educación. 1981. "Cuba, Organización de la Educación." Paper presented to the Conferencia Internacional de Educación. Habana, Cuba.

Mujal-León, Eusebio. 1988. *The Cuban University Under the Revolution*. Cuban American National Foundation.

New York Times. 1989, December 11. "The Fossil Marxist." p. 24.

————. 1990, January 18. "Cuba Loses Allure for Nicaraguans." p. 1.

Pastor, Manuel. 1983. "Cuba." *Integrated Education* 39(3):12–15.

Paulston, Rolland G. 1972. "Cultural Revitalization and Educational Change in Cuba." *Comparative Education Review* 16(2):475–485.

————. 1976. "Preconditions for System-Wide Educational Reform: Learning from the Cuban Experience." Paper presented at the Conference on the Future of U.S.–Cuba Relations. University of Kentucky.

————. 1980. "Impacto de la Reforma Educativa en Cuba." *Latin American Reprint Series*. Center for International Studies, University of Pittsburgh Press.

————. 1989. *Higher Education and the State in Revolutionary Cuba*. Pittsburgh: University of Pittsburgh.

————. 1993. "Ways of Seeing Latin American Educational Change: A Phenomenological Perspective." *Latin American Research Review*.

Pera, Enrique Varona. 1900. *Las reformas en la enseñanza superior*. Habana: El Figaro.

Pérez, Emma. 1945. *Historia de la pedagogía en Cuba: Desde los orígenes hasta la guerra de independencia*. Habana: Cultural S.A.

Report of the Board Appointed by General Orders, no. 2, Headquarters, Department of Santiago de Cuba, Civil Department. 1899, January 4. Washington, D.C.: U.S. Government Printing Office, pp. 843–853.

Suchlicki, Jaime. 1969. *University Students and Revolution in Cuba, 1920–1968.* Coral Gables, Fla.: University of Miami Press.

———. In CANF Conference Proceedings, 1989. *The Cuban Revolution at Thirty.* Washington, D.C.

Thomas, Hugh. 1971. *Cuba: The Pursuit of Freedom.* New York: Harper and Row.

Trelles, Carlos M. 1923. "La Instrucción primaria de Cuba comparada con la de algunos páises de America, Asia, Africa y Oceanía." *Cuba Contemporánea* 26:36–37.

Unesco. 1962. "Report on Cuba." Paris: Unesco Press.

Urivazo, Renaldo. 1982. "Introducing Students to Mass Media: Radio Victoria de Giron." *Prospects* 12(3): 387–394.

Wald, Karen. 1978. *Children of Che.* Palo Alto, Calif.: Ramparts Press.

Zimbalist, Andrew. 1988. "Cuba's External Economy: Reflections on Export Dependence, Soviet Aid, and Foreign Debt." *Comparative Economic Studies* 30:21–46.

9

ARAB REPUBLIC OF EGYPT

Samir A. Jarrar and Byron G. Massialas

The Arab Republic of Egypt possesses the longest recorded history of any modern nation, dating back to approximately 3200 B.C. In its long history, Egypt experienced periods of strength and expansion when it dominated neighboring lands and periods of weakness when it fell under the control of foreign powers. Greeks, Romans, Persians, Arabs, Ottomans, French, and British forces controlled different parts of Egypt over the centuries.

Education in Egypt dates back to the early days of settlement in the Nile Valley and the unification of Upper and Lower Egypt in 3110 B.C. At the time education was confined to the religious hierarchy and a few of the fortunate elites. It was not until the middle of the seventh century A.D., the Islamic era, that education was introduced to the populace in a formal manner. The Kuttab or Quranic schools and the Madrassa became the neighborhood educational institutions.

The basic learning skills and religious studies dominated the Kuttab curriculum, whereas the Madrassa catered to adults and graduates of the Kuttab. With time, the Madrassa became a higher education institution and a specialization center. These institutions laid the foundations for establishing one of the first, continuously operated universities in the world at Al-Azhar Mosque in Cairo in the tenth century (Massialas and Jarrar, 1983: 352–353).

Traditional education emphasizing religious studies and the basic skills formed the basis of the educational system in Egypt until the first half of the nineteenth century. It was provided at minimal cost through mosque-affiliated centers and philanthropy with little, if any, public funds. Mohammad Ali (1805–1849), the founder of a dynasty that ruled Egypt until the "free officers" revolution of 1952, established a public and secular educational system in the country. This system, motivated by Mohammad Ali's need for a modern army, was parallel to the traditional religious-based system. The system was run by the Department of War and started with institutions of higher education; it then added lower level institutions to meet the need to graduate army officers and bureaucrats to run a war machine. This system was elitist and was based on the needs of the ruler rather than those of the people. Mohammad Ali encouraged the sending of students abroad to pursue higher education.

Efforts to modernize and improve the educational system were led by members of the cultural and scientific missions upon their return. Kuttabs and schools were founded in remote areas of the country under the auspices of the Department of Education. A girl's school and a teacher training institute were established. By 1887 there were 270 primary schools and 200 European missionary and private schools, besides hundreds of Kuttabs (Massialas and Jarrar, 1983: 353).

The first real educational reform took place in Egypt in 1868 when the Shura Council (the Senate) introduced a new law promulgating that

Admission to primary school should be made available to all citizens without discrimination.

The Department of Education was responsible for supervising all existing schools.

The department should organize the establishment of new schools in the provinces, districts, and villages.

This law was instigated by Ali Mobarak, the secretary of education, who believed in the democratization of the educational system and considered education to be a right for all classes of the population. He also propagated the proper training of teachers and laid the foundation for one of the first primary teacher training institutes in the area, Dar-El-Aloum, founded in 1882 (Sorour, 1989: 41).

These reforms were short-lived, for Egypt was colonized by Britain in 1882. According to Lord Cromer's report of 1889, the new regime opposed national public education, imposed foreign curricula and language, and restricted attendance in public schools to a few, satisfying only the needs of the bureaucracy for clerks and employees. Thus, a dual educational system was established in Egypt—(1) a traditional scheme represented by Kuttabs and some primary schools that were once again run and financed by the private and religious sectors, and (2) a public school system.

The traditional scheme enrolled most of the students and did not allow graduates to pursue any other kind of education. The public system under British control comprised elementary schools that were attended mainly by foreigners and few Egyptians. Graduates of these elementary schools were allowed to continue their education in secondary schools, and thus they could join institutions of higher education upon graduation. Conditions did not change much during the British hegemony that lasted until 1922.

Attempts to reform education during the British era were unsuccessful. However, nationals were able to establish the "People's University" in 1908 under private auspices.

Educational reform took a positive turn in 1923 when Egypt adopted its first Constitution. Article 19 promulgated free and compulsory education for all Egyptians, male and female, in public schools, starting at the age of seven for a five-year cycle. A series of laws and decrees followed that set the tone of reform until the revolution of 1952. The reforms that took place prior to 1952 included democratization of education, with free and compulsory education, encouraging female education and improving teacher training.

A series of decrees in 1944, 1950, and 1951 promulgated free elementary education, followed by free secondary education. Compulsory education was extended to cover the six to twelve age group. Law No. 143 of 1951 unified the different types of schools that existed at the time into one type of elementary school catering to all students (Sorour, 1989: 42). This step aimed at institutionalizing equality of educational opportunity for all Egyptians.

The other areas in which reforms were introduced prior to the 1952 revolution were teacher training and vocational education. Teacher training institutes were established in rural areas. However, more attention was paid to vocational education. Law No. 142 of 1951 divided secondary education into an academic and a technical track, formalizing the two tracks.

Egypt has tried to attain total compulsory education for many years. The first attempt was a law in 1925 that planned to achieve universal enrollment in fifteen years. Lack of funds, among other factors, played a major role in derailing these plans. The pressures of World War II did not help either. Many types of schools were experimented with during this period in order to reach different strata of society that were not reached by the system. As a result, Egypt witnessed the establishment of primary rural schools and primary experimental schools. The rural schools sought to prepare its students for life and were conceived of as terminal. On the other hand, experimental schools were geared toward allowing their graduates to continue their education into higher levels. The search for the proper system continued during the 1940s without ever reaching universal compulsory education as originally planned. All changes and reforms that were introduced stressed mainly expansion, with little attempt made to modify the quality or philosophy of the system.

The 1952 revolution brought about a new philosophy and approach to education. The revolutionary regime preached uniformity, equity, equal opportunity, and access for all at all levels of education. Different types of schools, remnants of earlier years, were replaced by one-track public elementary schools. In 1956 the first Constitution issued after the revolution promulgated the following:

- Education is free within the limits of the law and public decency (Article 48).

- Education is a right to all Egyptians, guaranteed by the state which will gradually establish all types of schools and educational institutions (Article 50).

• Education is free and compulsory at the elementary cycle in all public schools (Article 51).

The new Constitution of 1971 reiterated that "education is a right guaranteed by the government. It is compulsory at the elementary level. The government is to extend it to other cycles" (Article 18). Article 19 of the new Constitution stated that "Religious education is a basic course in the general curricula." The prominence given to religious education by the Constitution reveals the interplay between the religious and the secular forces in the community (Kandil, 1989: 25).

Through the 1980 amendment to the Constitution, the government guaranteed equality of educational opportunity to all Egyptians and stipulated education to be free at all cycles. Eradication of illiteracy was considered a national requirement, and the population was supposed to be mobilized to participate in literacy courses (Article 21).

As revealed in the different ministerial declarations and policy papers, the Egyptian government is trying to address the needs of the people by proclaiming free and compulsory education and equality of educational opportunity. These declarations also affirm the government's educational vision which gives attention to expanding compulsory education and relating education to development and productivity. All these declarations concentrated on presenting general aims and goals without any comprehensive strategy or clear objectives for the educational system. This pattern, that is, goals but no commensurate means of implementation, dominated educational policy through the 1950s.

Planning and the linkage between education and development started in the 1960s with the declaration of the first five-year plan for education in Egypt (1960–1965). The first five-year plan called for absorbing all children of school age in schools aiming at universal attendance at elementary schools by 1970. The second five-year plan (1965–1970) was directed at controlling dropouts and increasing the efficacy of the system.

The 1967 Arab-Israeli War disrupted the plan and led to a major reevaluation of the system. As a result, a series of "declarations" were issued in March 1968 and the 1974 "document." The declarations stated that a modern state should be based on science and technology. Therefore, a number of specialized councils were to be started, aiming at improving the quality of the different subsystems of the government including the educational system. It was not until the early 1970s, however, that real action was taken. First, as we saw earlier, the Constitution was revised, and then a new paper was issued in October 1974. This paper stated the need for a new strategy, one based on a total restructuring of the concepts and systems of the educational and cultural milieu. The October declaration mentioned that "education is not only a number of static courses that students should comprehend. Education is directly linked to society and its needs. Therefore the educational system has to respond to these needs and react to them." It was the first time that an official statement addressed the rigidity of the educational system calling for its flexibility and for closer ties between education and the workplace. The declaration addressed the information explosion, witnessed worldwide, and the need to keep up with the expansion of knowledge and the advancement of science and technology. It also called for life-long education to keep up with developments and for the need for coordination between the different educational and research institutions (Kandil, 1989: 27).

An analysis of the official educational pronouncements in Egypt reveals that, up to the 1960s, the policy concentrated on establishing a wider educational base by trying to achieve equity, reaching the different strata of the society. The goals and aims of the educational system were general and unfocused. Quantity was the undeclared aim, and little attention was given to quality. After the June 1967 war, the quality of the educational systems became the focus of reform. Education was to become relevant, and this goal could be achieved only by training a skilled labor force that could meet the challenges of development and match the higher productivity requirements.

BASIC AND SECONDARY EDUCATION

The most significant attempt at educational reform in Egypt in the past quarter century has been the one that relates to the introduction of basic education in the late 1970s. Basic education is a program of studies, grades 1 through 9 (now through 8), which seeks to modernize the curriculum and the methods for delivering it in the classroom. Under Law 139 of 1981, the aims of basic education were formulated emphasizing the following:

- "Religious and national education, as well as the teaching of good manners and sports."
- "The relation between education and productive work."
- The establishment of a closer link between students and the environment through the diversification of practical and vocational programs "in accordance with the circumstances of the local environment and demands of its development."
- "Achieving integration between the theoretical and applied aspects of the syllabi, study plans and curricula."
- "Linking education with the lives of the rising generation and the realities of the environments they live in so that the relation between learning in theory and the applied aspects is highlighted provided the environment and socioeconomic activities therein are among the major sources of knowledge, research and activity related to the various areas of study" (quoted by Massialas and Jarrar, 1988: 359).

Obviously, the aims of education, as stated above, represent a new philosophy of education for Egypt. Have these aims been accomplished? First, one of the prerequisites in implementing basic education was the universalization of education for the school levels under consideration. Most recent data on enrollments for primary education (grades 1 through 5) indicate that by 1966, 91 percent of school-age children, six to eleven years old, would be enrolled in primary schools. This would constitute a 10 percent increase from enrollment at this level recorded in 1986 (Reform of Educational System of Egypt, 1990, p. 5). Commensurate growth in enrollment has been recorded in the preparatory school level as well (grades 6–8).

Religious and national education offerings in the curriculum have remained intact in the new program. There were curriculum changes, however, which relate to the aim of establishing a "closer link between students and the environment." In this regard, the new curriculum introduced "general knowledge and environmental activities." This subject is taught three periods per week in grades 1 and 2 and six periods per week in grades 3 and 4. Presumably, the subject incorporates material that was previously taught under the label of "science and hygiene"; the requirement of two hours per week of "fine arts" has also been dropped. Given the lack of assessment data, it is virtually impossible to determine whether or not the aims of the reform-minded educators as represented in Public Law 139/81 have been or are likely to be achieved. Of course, the success of a curriculum reform depends to a large measure on the ability of teachers to apply the new concepts and methods. In this respect, provision has been made to train and retrain teachers who were responsible for delivering the new program. According to published reports (ARE, 1989: 71), 42,305 teachers of basic education in the primary school level were enrolled for training during the 1987–1988 academic year. These teachers were trained in 113 centers, which were connected with ten university schools of education. Teachers who successfully completed the program of studies in basic education earned a certificate in education, a certificate that had equivalency with a bachelor's degree awarded by an accredited university. In addition to the teachers above, it is reported that in-service teacher training programs have trained nearly 26,000 educational leaders in the components of the new curriculum. Of these leaders, 50 were master trainers, 500 senior supervisors, and 25,000 junior supervisors, headmasters, and teachers.

Along with teacher training, the authorities, assisted by funds and technical know-how from international donors, established as part of the Ministry of Education, a Curriculum Development Center to implement the aims of basic education. The center undertook to develop the plan for the new curriculum, prepare manuals for selected teachers in experimental schools to field test the new materials, and develop prototype materials in each subject taught in school to form the basis for new textbooks and instructional aids. Plans for educational evaluation and for construction of new school buildings were also developed and partially implemented as part of the overall effort to spearhead a coordinated reform act. To this end, the Educational Planning Division at the Ministry of Education was strengthened, and new studies and services were initiated.

At this juncture, it appears that the government is genuinely interested in school reform. The educational reform plan appears to attend to some of the critical issues facing educational development in Egypt—obsolete curricula and instructional methods, unqualified teachers, and lack of resources such as school buildings and equipment. The curriculum issue has been a critical one. Traditionally, humanistic subjects such as language and religion dominated the school curriculum. Under the revised first level of the basic education curriculum (see ARE, 1989: 31), the humanistic focus continues. In grades 1 and 2, for example, religious education constitutes three periods per week; Arabic language is offered for ten periods. If one were to add art education (two periods) and music (one period), then humanistic education would constitute about 59 percent of the total curriculum (sixteen periods out of a grand total of twenty-seven). Changing science to "environmental activities," is an innovation, but will this change substantially affect the manner in which Egyptian children learn to think scientifically? Will the so-called new curriculum be able to help children bridge the gap between theory and practice, something that is pivotal in the basic education plan?

Teaching methodology has also traditionally caused problems. Students were taught to memorize and recite ideas handed out by the teacher, either in lectures or through assignments in the textbook. Studies of the Egyptian classroom at all levels reveal, with monotonous regularity, that the dominant instructional methodology is teacher "talk and chalk." Students rarely, if ever, are given the opportunity to raise questions or discuss issues. This type of instruction is, as per Sharabi (*Neopatriarchy*, Oxford, 1988) monologic and discourages students from developing problem-solving skills and abilities. Given this school environment, it is not unreasonable to expect that students, partly as a result of the traditional teacher approach to learning and instruction, will be limited in their ability to make effective decisions as adults. Although the basic education reform plan calls for a more open classroom climate where students are given the opportunity to engage in dialogue, rather than always passively listening to teacher monologue, most of the in-service education instruction for teachers observed by the authors was monologic. In other words, teacher education provided through in-service programs for teachers for a degree, or for upgrading, still use the lecture as a means of conveying the tenets of school reform. The new or upgraded teachers, modeling their university and teacher institute instructors, inescapably use lecturing as the primary mode of approaching their students in the classroom. Accordingly, it is very unlikely that the proposed reform will affect student learning in the years to come. Unless teachers are continuously exposed to other teachers who employ problem-solving and inquiry methods in their instruction on a daily basis, they will not be able to introduce the new materials that the Curriculum Development Center is producing.

The quality of instruction in the classroom is low because existing school facilities are inadequate for housing the dramatically expanding student population, for example, from 6,002,850 students in general primary in 1985–1986 to 6,631,265 in 1987–1988, an increase of 9 percent. It was estimated that for 1991–1992 there were 169,631 classes for use by students, but given the enrollments, a minimum of 207,234 was needed (Sorour, 1989: 141). As a result of this overcrowding, schools have been forced to hold two or even three shifts per day. This, in turn, has necessitated shorter instructional periods and an overall reduction in the number of instructional subjects offered. Thus, the quality of instruction has been inescapably affected. Current efforts are directed toward (1) reducing class size to less than forty students per class and (2) abolishing the shifts. To accomplish the first objective, 37,605 new classes would be needed by 1991–1992; to accomplish the second objective, 38,725 new classes would be needed, for a total of 76,330 classes in the primary grades. Given other pressing needs in the system, it is unlikely that school construction will keep pace with the need as documented in the five-year plan. Even if more classrooms were to be added, there would still be a school maintenance problem. It has been observed, for example, that newly constructed schools deteriorate shortly after they are built (about two years). Without any substantial maintenance after the first two-year period, they become almost uninhabitable. The reformers are now trying to introduce the position of school "janitor" to take care of things. Whether this would resolve the maintenance problems remains to be seen.

The educational system in Egypt is undergoing a new and comprehensive reform that was initiated during a new five-year plan (1987–1988/1991–1992). After a series of high-level consultations, conferences, and external technical assistance, the ministry launched a new strategy and a new set of policy guidelines. The proposed long-term goals of the proposed reform include the development of the Egyptian character and the achievement of comprehensive development via the integration of education with the cultural, social, economic, and political systems. To achieve these goals, the proposed strategy aims at linking education with the human resource requirements of the economy in order to construct a more productive society that is based on a generation that better understands and interacts with science and technology (Sorour, 1989: 120–135).

Four major groups of objectives have been developed to meet the long-term goals. These include increasing access to achieve universal primary education, improving the quality of education, and increasing the relevance of curricula, improving the efficiency of the system resources, and mobilizing additional resources.

A torrent of new laws, decrees, and regulations were promulgated in order to affect all levels of the system. Law No. 233/1988 amended Basic Education Act 139/1981. It stipulated that the pre-university cycle would consist of eight years for compulsory basic education (instead of nine). Basic education was divided into two cycles: a primary cycle consisting of five years and a preparatory cycle of three years. The secondary cycle for both the general education and the technical education would consist of three years. The advanced technical education and teacher training institutes would comprise five years each (Article 4). The new law also stipulated that promotion from one cycle to the other should be regulated through an examination at the governorate level. A certificate of completion of the primary cycle allows the graduate to attend the general basic preparatory cycle or a technical cycle (Article 18). The first two years of the secondary cycle would be similar for all students. The third year of this cycle would consist of different specialties of which the student would choose one. The different choices would be regulated by the minister of education after coordinating with the Supreme Council for Universities (Article 26). At the end of the secondary cycle, students would sit for the General Secondary School Certificate exam. They would be allowed to take the exam up to three times. To qualify for taking the exam the third time, a student would have to pay an examination fee of 100 Egyptian pounds (Article 29) (Ezzat, 1990: 77–82). This law became effective in the 1988–1989 academic year. The new reform builds on and refocuses the Basic Education Act of 1981 which combined academic and productive work, linking education with the needs of the community. The original basic education cycle of nine years failed to implement curricula reforms, because the participants did not understand the objectives, the teachers and administrators were insufficiently trained, and the curricula were prepared and introduced in a hurried manner.

Other laws and regulations dealt with increasing the school year to thirty-eight weeks instead of the present thirty-two weeks; abolishing the multiple shifts in school buildings; and increasing the number of contact hours in the school day. The school year at the secondary level was reorganized on a two-semester basis (in 1989), each consisting of seventeen weeks, with two-week midyear vacation (the second half of January). The two-semester system was extended in 1990 to apply to the preparatory cycle of basic education.

Along with these administrative changes, a set of other directives were issued to improve the quality of the system by establishing a National Testing Center. The center was charged with developing standardized tests for the General Secondary Certificate Exam that measures students' achievement, knowledge, and ability to comprehend ideas and be creative. Sample question guides were to be prepared and distributed to students and teachers. Computer education would be introduced on an experimental basis in some secondary schools. New regulations would allow secondary school students to join technical tracks in their third year.

It is too early to assess the results of these reforms. The important thing to mention here, however, is the comprehensiveness of the approach that was taken after involving a wide range of educators, administrators, and community figures. The steps taken to improve the quality of the system within an integrated strategy targeted several subsystems, which include access to schooling, diversification in the educational ladder, especially at the secondary level, improving teacher education and training, improving the management and administration of the system (an effort to be accomplished by accelerating decentralization), reforming the curricula, and responding to human power needs of development.

To introduce the reforms stipulated in the new strategy, the ministry embarked on an ambitious five-year plan that includes forty-two projects dealing with basic, general, and technical secondary, nonformal, and higher education. These projects deal with student school admission and evaluation, teacher training, physical facilities, curriculum and materials development, administration and management, including information systems and finance (MOE, 1990: 2).

New centers, units, programs, and councils were established to implement the suggested reforms. Centers were developed after studying the needs, identifying capable Egyptian educators, and establishing proper channels and linkages between the ministry, institutions of higher education, teacher training institutes, and research centers. As a result, the National Center for Educational Research and Development (NCERD) was established in 1987. The center includes an Educational Planning Unit, a Physical Planning Unit, a Curriculum and Materials Development Center, and a Policy Analysis and Research Unit. Bilateral aid was utilized in securing technical assistance for the NCERD staff. A Higher Council for Examinations and Educational Evaluation was created to change and improve the procedures for student evaluation. The center is in the process of establishing a bank of test items that are linked to the curriculum objectives under adoption. It will also prepare items for examining students in grades 2–8 for promotion purposes, after abolishing the automatic promotion procedure. New requirements for teacher certification have been established. Primary school teachers are to be trained for four years after matriculating from secondary schools. Programs have been started in colleges of education to meet the new requests.

At the secondary level, students study a common core for the first two years. In the third year they can choose among several streams offered, for example, humanities, sciences, math, or technical streams. Comprehensive secondary schools have been established on an experimental basis. Their focus is on combining academic and practical skills. Preprofessional secondary schools offering courses in education for students interested in pursuing teaching careers have been established. Gifted students who complete the Preparatory Certificate Examination can join some of the newly established experimental schools for the gifted.

Changes that were introduced at the secondary level are too early to evaluate. The one striking feature, however, is the number of new reforms and the short period within which they were introduced. Although most of these reforms have been long overdue, the ambitious schedule adopted to introduce them may be counterproductive. Many programs had to be introduced without sufficient training of key personnel. The system was originally underfinanced and overburdened. Unless new resources are made available and proper development, testing, and training take place, the newly adopted strategy may not succeed in achieving all its goals and objectives.

While there are plans to affect long-term reform, status reports reveal that the current school situation leaves much to be desired. The most recent survey (*Abstract: Basic Education II; USAID Project in Egypt*, 1990: 2) concludes with the following statements:

At present, curriculum content is not well integrated so that different subjects do not relate well to one another within grades; nor is the content within each subject sequenced effectively from one grade to the next. In addition, it is not relevant to the needs of Egyptian society. Textbooks and educational aids are severely lacking and of poor quality. Pedagogy relies almost entirely on uncreative, cumbersome and poorly sequenced books. Teacher guides are nearly nonexistent. Teacher training, curriculum content and student testing are inappropriately linked, thus, contributing to poor achievement rates, repetition and drop out and thus to a costly and inefficient educational system.

TERTIARY EDUCATION

The establishment of the Alexandria library in the third century B.C. marks the beginning of advanced studies and research in Egypt. This tradition was formalized with the establishment of the Al-Azhar University, in the tenth century A.D. The government did not formalize the institutionalization of higher education until the early nineteenth century, when Mohammad Ali established a military academy and a school of engineering in 1816.

By 1835 the War Department was administering a number of institutions of higher education that included Qasr-al-Aini Medical School, schools of agriculture, administration, accounting, pharmacy, veterinary medicine, languages, industrial arts, and an institute of music. Most of these schools followed the French model and curriculum. Instructors were mainly foreigners until Egyptians who studied abroad were recruited. By 1880 a teacher training institute was established (Jarrar, 1991: 1000). The first secular university was founded in Cairo in 1908 by private initiative. The National University was supposed to enhance the knowledge base and character of the Egyptian youth, rather than to train them to become bureaucrats and officers. The government tried to integrate the different institutions of higher education as early as 1917. An agreement was finally reached with the National University, and in 1925 Fuad the 1st University was established (later known as Cairo University). The new institution had four colleges: humanities, sciences, medicine, and law. Later, a college of agriculture, a commerce institute, and a veterinary institute became colleges at Cairo University. By 1942 another university was established in Alexandria (Jarrar, 1991: 1001). By 1950 Ain Shams University was established in Cairo. The need to regulate higher education in the country led to the development of the Higher Council for Universities in 1951 and the Ministry of Higher Education, ten years later.

Promoting social mobility through education was a major aim of the postrevolutionary regime. This led to the establishment of branch colleges in some of the major cities. By the mid–1970s new universities were established in Tanta, al Mansoura, Zagazig, Helwan, Menia, and Menofia. By 1990 there were twelve public universities and one semiprivate, the American University in Cairo. These universities incorporated colleges and institutes of higher education that were operating in the region. At present the thirteen universities have twenty-one affiliated branches and include 280 colleges enrolling over 800,000 students, of which around 88 percent are in undergraduate programs. One-third of the enrollees are female, with a high concentration in certain colleges such as education, liberal arts, and mass communication where they exceed male enrollees (Jarrar, 1991: 1003–1006).

Technical education at the tertiary level was expanded after the 1952 revolution. With the establishment of the Ministry of Higher Education (MOHE) in 1961, special attention was given to technical education. As a result, major curricular reforms were introduced in 1962. By 1970 a new law was promulgated to increase the number and improve the quality of technical institutes. In the early 1980s the government decided to increase admissions to technical institutes to meet the new developmental challenges and to relieve some of the pressures on university admissions. By 1990 more than half the graduates from secondary schools entering tertiary education enrolled in technical institutes. There are around fifty-five two-year technical institutes offering diplomas in a wide range of programs spanning from electronics, social services, laboratory specialists, and mechanics to secretarial services. In addition, over forty colleges offer four- or five-year specialized programs leading to baccalaureate degrees. Twenty-four of these prepare specialized teachers in early childhood, home economics, music, and arts education. These colleges cover all the governorates of Egypt. Others offer degrees in social work, agricultural extension, technology, cooperation, and administrative sciences. Some of these institutions are private, whereas others are established for a certain period of time to meet shortages in certain skill areas (Jarrar, 1991: 1000–1001).

Tertiary education is publicly financed and highly centralized. The minister of higher education (who currently serves as the minister of education as well) is aided by an undersecretary of higher education and an undersecretary for technical education. Two Supreme Councils, one for universities (SCU, established in 1950) and a Supreme Council of Institutes (SCI, established in 1988), share the responsibilities with MOHE in providing policy guidelines and coordination among universities and institutes. In addition, they approve new colleges, universities, and institutes, set admission standards, develop local linkages with industry and commerce as well as international linkages and graduates studying abroad. There are sector committees covering major disciplines and professional fields as well as committees for the evaluation of academic work.

As we saw earlier, the Egyptian Constitution guarantees the independence of higher education, institutes, and centers of research. Article 18, 1971, provides that these institutions serve the community and help increase its productivity.

It is noteworthy to mention that independence of tertiary education is no more than autonomy in the management of academic offerings, since financing is publicly controlled. Presidents and vice-presidents of universities are appointed by presidential decree upon their nomination by the minister. The Supreme Council of Universities shares the powers of the minister of higher education since the Higher Education Law (No. 49, 1972) stipulates that SCU sets policies and monitors their execution. Given these practices, one wonders how free and independent the Egyptian tertiary institutions are.

The official discourse, represented in ministerial platforms and official pronouncements as well, through political parties and union proclamations, has been calling for the reform of tertiary education. These pronouncements include calling for full independence, making sure that no new institutions are established until the existing ones are provided with all the resources required to achieve their goals and improve their quality. Other issues facing tertiary education include monitoring admission and changing current practices that depend on the grades attained by students in the General Secondary Certificate Examination, without any attention to students' capabilities, career interests, or skills. The need to reform student unions by laws and the establishment of private and open universities are among the debated issues.

Tertiary education in Egypt passed through three phases. The first phase was dominated by religious education. Al-Azhar institutions represented the best in Islamic education, its graduates serving as theologians, judges, teachers, scholars, and arabists. They were spread all over the Muslim world. The reform of this system in the early 1960s led to the addition of nonreligious colleges like medicine, agriculture, and education. Currently, Al-Azhar University enrolls over 115,000 students in eight disciplines.

The second phase was the military phase, in which higher education was geared to serve the military institution. Colleges were established to graduate officers and bureaucrats, starting in the early nineteenth century. This system was elitist, and admissions were limited.

The third phase may be called the social or popular one. Commencing after the 1952 revolution, higher education was opened to the masses as a means of social mobility. Admission was free and open to all who passed the General Secondary Certificate Exam (GSCE). Enrollment in colleges and universities was based on GSCE scores. Students with high scores were admitted to more prestigious colleges and universities without regard to their abilities, skills, or career orientation or preferences. Few colleges had other requests for admission. As a result, the system rewarded rote memorization, measured in endurance tests based on essay examinations. Score reliability and the test-predictive validity are questionable at best. Very few if any studies exist to determine the correlation between the GSCE scores and the students' performance in colleges.

The proliferation of higher education in the 1970s continued unchecked to the mid–1980s, when measures were introduced to check the rapid expansion and the general decline in quality. The Ministry of Higher Education introduced a series of measures aimed at reforming the system. These included controlling admissions and linking them to development needs; improving the quality of programs to enhance development and productivity by reforming the testing and evaluation system; improving efficiency by promoting more responsible fiscal management, along with introducing measures to effect some cost recovery (MOE, 1990: 23).

As a result of these measures, MOHE established a Center for Higher Education Research (CHER). The center was charged with providing information, analyses, and recommendations in support of policy development; conducting research studies of major issues and needs in higher education; identifying and supporting achievement of major cost-effective innovations in higher education; and assisting MOHE with implementing pertinent improvements.

A National Center for the Development of Testing and Evaluation was established in 1990. Although the center was established under the jurisdiction of the Ministry of Education, it has major impact on tertiary education. It was charged with developing policy and criteria for all public examinations; reforming the testing and evaluation system, especially the secondary school learning examination; collaborating with the NCERD to effect curricular reforms; developing in-service training programs in evaluation and measurement for teachers; and improving the criteria for selecting students to be admitted to universities (Ezzat, 1990: 151–152). The center is in the process of developing a new strategy and a standardized examination that would test knowledge, as well as higher level skills like reasoning and creativity, and would serve as an entrance exam to universities.

Although most reforms in tertiary education have not yet been fully implemented, limiting admissions to universities led to sharp increases in admissions to technical institutes. This may in turn result in more problems in the near future unless a full revision of the curricula and methodology occurs, as well as preparing better instructors and providing sufficient resources for improving the laboratories, workshops, and libraries. Since the question of employability of these graduates, because of their limited skills, has always been a problem, employers should be more involved in decision making at all levels and in providing practical training and on-the-job training. The involvement of employers will help achieve one of the major goals of higher education reform, namely, increasing the productivity and skill levels of graduates.

MOHE is currently experimenting with the concept of a correspondence or open university. It has allowed certain departments and facilities in existing universities to engage in distant learning. This approach may backfire since it may draw upon already overburdened resources. Faculty members who have active associations should be more fully utilized in reaching some of these policy decisions so that they can be more effective in the implementation phase of all intended reform measures.

THE LITERACY CAMPAIGN

As reported in figures released by the United Nations, in 1986 there were 15,298,800 illiterates in Egypt or 55 percent of the total adult population. Of these illiterates, 42.4 percent were male and 68.2 percent female (Massialas–Jarrar, 1991: 61). Apparently, little progress has been made in a decade, for in 1976 the estimated illiteracy rate among adults was 56 percent (Massialas-Jarrar,

1983: 272). The main reasons for this relatively high rate are (1) the problem of student dropouts and (2) the system's inability to enroll all children in school as per the compulsory education laws (Sorour, 1989: 154). Actually, the campaign to eradicate illiteracy only began in 1971.

Although the problem of illiteracy was national in scope, a multitude of agencies tried to resolve it without proper coordination among them. As a result of the authorities' realization that individual agency-sponsored programs could not attend to the problem, an educational reform plan was instituted in 1990 aiming at a coordinated national literacy campaign. Building on the existing organizational arrangements, the reform plan sought to focus on clearly defined targets of people needing training and then concentrate on the delivery of this training through various programs. Beginning in 1987, the Higher Council for Adult Education and Elimination of Illiteracy assumed the leadership in organizing these programs.

The first task in resolving the problem was to ensure that there was a sufficient number of teachers who could deliver effective literacy instruction. In this regard, postsecondary school graduates were enlisted to provide literacy instruction as part of their year-long public service requirement. In addition, educated young men serving their military duty were asked to serve as part-time literacy instructors to attend to the special needs of each governorate in which they were stationed. Incentives such as financial gains, as well as a reduction of time they had to serve in the military, were applied to this group of instructional personnel. Teachers in the formal school sector with special skill in literacy instruction were enticed to participate in the national literacy campaign, especially in training other potential instructors.

Four target groups of illiterates or semi-illiterates based on age were identified: (1) boys who are between ages of twelve and fifteen and who are not of age to be gainfully employed; (2) boys and girls who went through school but because of the existing automatic promotion practice and the low quality of instruction were never properly educated, thus becoming illiterate or semiliterate; (3) young men approaching conscription age (sixteen to twenty-one years of age) with no education whatsoever; and (4) illiterate laborers through the age of forty-five, employed in either the public or private sector. Housewives of similar ages were included in this category (Sorour, 1989: 159–161).

The illiterate females, much more numerous than their male counterparts, were to be given special incentives so that they would enroll in the appropriate programs. For example, certain vocational skills were offered to them along with literacy training. Those who excelled and successfully completed the program received a sewing machine or a similar prize for their accomplishment. A system of periodic exams was put in place to monitor the outcomes of the program and to ensure that graduates did not relapse into their former state.

The illiterate males, especially those of working age, fell into two categories: the jobless and the employed. The first group may receive literacy training along with vocational training in adult education classes in all governorates sponsored by the Ministry of Education. In collaboration with Unesco, a multipurpose adult education center was created in 1987 to address the needs of this particular group of illiterate adults. As far as the "employed" category of persons is concerned, regular literacy training is expected from the employing establishments, in both the public and private sectors. These programs are monitored by the Ministry of Education. The armed forces also have a number of literacy programs for those who are on active duty. As a rule, the curriculum providing literacy skills to adults is based on skills normally learned in the fourth grade of the primary school. Special textbooks have been developed for use with these students. Upon successful completion of the program, students are given a certificate of literacy. Most programs are of nine-month duration and are housed in public primary schools, with the instructors drawn from the cadre of existing teachers, at an additional remuneration. The ministries of Interior, Agriculture, and Housing conduct their own literacy programs as well. The Ministry of Information provides instruction through radio and television; the Ministry of the Interior provides similar training to members of the police forces and to prisoners.

To ensure progress in combating illiteracy, the government has currently undertaken the following: (1) in order to prevent students from dropping out of school, vocational programs are being put in place so that students who are not academically inclined are enticed to stay in school; (2) automatic promotion in the primary grades has been eliminated, thus making it difficult for students to continue without exhibiting some mastery of basic skills; (3) parent councils have been formed to increase parental involvement in the education of their offspring: (4) the content of the vocational training program in school seems to relate to the peculiarities of local work conditions and focuses on local work activities, work tools, and work ethics; literacy skills—reading, writing, and numeracy—are integrated into the entire school program; and (5) new teaching methods are being introduced which allow wide student participation in discussion and in learning how to learn—away from rote memorization.

The sector assessment concerned with the reform of the educational system in Egypt (MOE, 1990: 21–22) confirmed the perennial problems in the campaign for literacy and pointed to additional means for the successful program implementation. For example, a powerful means is the expanded use of media in literacy training, including what is known as distance education methods such as use of the radio in teaching basic concepts to the populace. The sector assessment also stresses the need to monitor progress in this area and, as a result, redesign campaign elements that have not been very successful.

The task to reduce the illiteracy rate in Egypt, as elsewhere in the world, is a most difficult one. Presently, the authorities realize that unless a concentrated and well-coordinated campaign is put in place, there will be very little chance to eradicate illiteracy in the near future. While the government marshals some financial assistance to the campaign (see Sorour, 1989: 164–165), there is still a lack of substantial resources to make the program viable. Given the present-day tight budget in all areas of education, it is unlikely that additional money will be earmarked for literacy training per se, thus forcing the ongoing program to be only moderately effective.

SUMMARY AND CONCLUSION

The Egyptian education system is deeply rooted in tradition and ritual but is struggling to catch up with development. The system is suffering from a state of "congestion and stagnation" that limits its delivery capabilities and makes it less responsive to development needs and requirements. This is due to a number of factors, including a rapid increase in population coupled with an increase in social demand for education, resulting in an "expensive and expansive" system. The limited resources available, coupled with statutory requirements of free education, makes the system incapable of expanding quantitatively and maintaining qualitative improvement, which leads to stagnation. Since there is a heavy influx of students at the base of the system, congestion problems are rampant (Abdel-Mawgood, 1989: 1–3).

The education system is fraught with marginal private funding. Parents spend a substantial amount of funds on private tutoring at all levels. If a way can be found to channel some of these funds (estimated at 600 million pounds) to the system, many problems will be alleviated.

The system is plagued with obsolete administrative and management procedures. Centralization is still a fact in spite of attempts at decentralization. The system is based on seniority rather than merit. Duplication of effort is common, and communication between and among the different levels, sectors, and departments is weak. As a result, schools normally get little information about the decision process, which makes implementation lag.

Studying the reform attempts for the last four decades, one is struck by the similarities and persistence of problems, for example, teacher shortages and lack of training, the development of curricula, the lack of physical facilities and instructional materials, academic versus technical education, the need to improve technical education, dropouts and repetition (educational wastage), universalization of basic education, illiteracy, the mismatch between skills acquired and skills required in the job market.

The government of Egypt has undertaken a major effort to reform the educational system in the last few years. However, the persistence of the same problems suggests either faulty policies or lack of resources, or both. A more realistic approach that involves all players in the process of education may be needed. Specifically, to survive as an educational reform basic education needs (1) a cadre of practitioners thoroughly trained in the principles and procedures of the reform plan to demonstrate to others how the innovation works when put in place; (2) a continuous in-service training program for teachers by instructors who are completely familiar with the philosophy and application procedures of the program (not proceeding as in the past on the principle of business as usual, generating memory-type learning; and (3) a set of new textbooks and materials which are provided on the basis of psychological and substantive principles in line with the new philosophy of education.

The illiteracy problem persists. The effort to centralize the decision-making power and to make one agency responsible for overseeing action-type programs (the Higher Council for Adult Education and Elimination of Illiteracy) was certainly a step in the right direction. Nevertheless, as in the case of the implementation of basic education and higher education reform, plans designed in Cairo often do not reach the countryside and the target groups these plans are designed for. International donor agencies provide financial and technical assistance to the Egyptian government. The record suggests, however, that once the support is removed and the agency withdraws, arrangements revert to their previous state. What is needed is to provide for a cadre of professionals (an "elite corps") who are personally rewarded and are committed to carrying out the purposes of the reform. To be successful a reform needs to have a skilled and dedicated group that would sustain the momentum and ensure its proper implementation.

As we enter a new era, the Egyptian leadership realizes that reform is needed and is possible. With foresight, persistence, and cooperation with knowledgeable professionals in the field, the reform movement can succeed. Is there a will to proceed?

REFERENCES

Abdel-Mawgood, M. E. 1989. "Policy Options for Achieving Educational Equity in Egypt." Paper presented at Policy Options for Educational Reform Conference, Cairo.

Arab Republic of Egypt (ARE). 1988–1989. "Development of Education in the Arab Republic of Egypt." National Center for Educational Research, Cairo.

Bashshur, Munir. 1988. "Takafu al Furas al talimiah Filbilad al-Arabaia" [Equality in educational opportunity in the Arab world]. In "Altoufula al-Arabia waadalaht al-Tarbaieya Al-ghaebah" [Arab childhood and the absent educational equality], ed. M. J. Rhida. Kuwait Society for the Advancement of Arab Children, Fifth Annual Yearbook (Arabic).

Educational Planning Unit, Ministry of Education, Government of Egypt. 1990. "Reform of the Educational System of Egypt. Sector Assessment" (mimeograph).

El-Shikhaby, Aly. 1984. "Equality of Educational Opportunity, the Contradiction Between Idea and the Reality in Egyptian Society." Ain Shams University, paper presented at the Democracy and Education Conference in Egypt.

Ezzat, Mohammad Said. 1990. "Hawla Tatweer Al-Taleem Fi Misr." About the Development of Education in Egypt, a series of articles, Ministry of Education, Educational Development Series, Vol. 2.

Jarrar, Samir A. 1991. "Egypt." In "International Higher Education, An Encyclopedia," ed. Philip G. Altbac. New York and London: Garland Publishing, pp. 999–1014.

Kandil, Amani. 1989. "Siasat al-taleem Fi Wadi El Neel wasomal wa Djibouti." [Educational policies in the Nile Valley, Somalia and Djibouti], Arab Thought Forum, Amman, Jordan (Arabic).

Mahmoud, H. B., Shehab, M. M., Haikal, M. S., and Ghanew, A. 1990. "Majalat al-taleem Liljamie'h Fi Misr" [Spheres of education for all in Egypt]. National Unesco Unit, Cairo (Arabic).

Massialas, Byron G., and Samir A. Jarrar. 1983. *Education in the Arab World.* New York: Praeger.

———. 1988. "Egypt." In *World Education Encyclopedia*, ed. G. T. Kurian. Vol. 1. New York: Facts on File Publications, pp. 352–372.

———. 1991. *Arab Education in Transition: A Source Book.* New York and London: Garland Publishing.

Ministry of Education (MOE). 1979. "Working Paper for Developing Innovating Education in Egypt." Cairo (Mimeograph, Arabic).

———. 1990. Reform of Educational System of Egypt: A Sector Assessment (Executive Summary). Educational Planning Unit (Mimeograph).

Sara, Nather. 1990. "Al Tarbiah-al-Arabia, Minthou 1950, Injaratiha, Mashkalateha, Tahaditehe" [Arab education since 1950, its achievements, problems and challenges] Arab Thought Forum, Amman.

Sharabi, Hishan. 1988. *Neopatriarchy: A Theory of Distorted Change in Arab Society.* New York: Oxford University Press.

Soliman, S. G. 1989, January. "Planning Educational Reform in Egypt: Some Proposals for Workability." Paper presented at the Policy Options for Educational Reform held at the National Center Educational Research and Development, Ministry of Education, Cairo. (Mimeograph).

Sorour, A. F. 1987. *Strategy for Developing Education in Egypt.* Cairo (Arabic).

———. 1989. *Educational Development in Egypt: Its Policy, Strategy and Implementation Plan.* Cairo (Arabic).

10

FRANCE

George A. Male

The basic characteristics of education in France have persisted for so long as to become stereotypes, and much of the effort to reform education focuses on these basic characteristics which, not surprisingly, are resistant to change.

French education can be described as:

1. *Public.* Only 15 percent of the enrollment is in private schools.

2. *Centralized.* The power of the national government is legendary.

3. *Dualistic.* Traditionally, there have been two public school systems, one for the ordinary people and one for the elite. Starting as early as World War I, the reformers sought to end this dual system with only partial success. Beginning in the 1960s, an all-out effort began to establish comprehensive lower secondary schools where everyone would be brought together under the same roof. Reforms of the 1970s, 1980s, and 1990s have sought to make this comprehensive system work.

4. *Hierarchical.* Some types of schools and teachers are given high status, while others find themselves in a more lowly position, as do the students enrolled in the lesser institutions. The low status of vocational education is a case in point and is especially worrisome to education policymakers interested in strengthening the link between education and the economy.

5. *Class ridden.* The socioeconomic status of one's parents has a great deal to do with whether one ends up in high-status schools. This conflicts with repeated reform efforts to make educational opportunity more widespread and to "democratize" education.

6. *Excessively verbal.* Verbal skill in framing ideas has, according to the critics, become an end in itself, at times almost a matter of aesthetics. As one study of French education put it: "Among the notable features . . . which attracted

the attention of educational reformers in France was the emphasis on verbal and theoretical analysis, by itself considered a virtue, but not when combined with under-attention to application of ideas'' (Male, 1963: 3).

7. *Overly intellectual.* Developing an intellectual stratum is frequently the starting point in describing the goals of French education. Until recently, few students were judged capable of becoming intellectuals. Indeed, at various points along the way students were encouraged to drop out or to settle for a lesser type of education, such as vocational education. There is also some criticism of how "intellectual" is defined. Some of the reformers would lessen the stress on mathematics and other theoretical kinds of analysis and would instead give greater attention to the application of ideas in various fields of knowledge.

8. *Exam ridden.* A ruthless and efficient sorting out of students by the use of exams is a tradition with a long history in France. The stereotype of this includes the concept of letting only a small percentage pass the entrance exams to the more prestigious educational institutions.

9. *Meritocratic.* French parents and teachers alike believe that the educational system, especially because of the emphasis on examinations, provides an opportunity for those with high academic ("intellectual") ability. Attempts to "democratize" the system by increasing the percentage passing the exams are often resisted. "They [French parents] want educational achievement to be a mark of distinction, thus, the fewer people attaining it, the more rewarding it is" (Carduner, 1987: 90).

10. *Competitive.* Emphasis on exams, meritocracy, sorting and selecting, status, and so on produces an atmosphere of fierce competition. Various reform efforts to lessen the competition have been met with resistance.

Another stereotype about education in France has to do with the failure of education reform plans ever to amount to much. There has been no lack of reform proposals; in fact, almost every head (minister) of the national government's Ministry of Education seems to come up with a new reform plan, which usually has his name attached. When combined with frequent changes of ministers of national education, the result is much discussion of reform proposals and plans; implementation is another matter.

In some cases a particular reform seems to be underway, but closer scrutiny reveals that it consists mainly of names being changed. (The first few years of secondary education with great fanfare become the "first cycle.") The basic characteristics, and flaws, of French education continue with relatively few real changes.

To be fair, other countries, including the United States, find it difficult to carry out reform plans. Hans Weiler has also noted this fact, but he takes French educators and government officials to task for three decades (1960s, 1970s, and 1980s) of reform plans but little significant change (Weiler, 1988: 251). Others have noted that the reform talk goes all the way back to World War I (Male, 1963: 23–24).

Weiler argues that in recent decades education reform in France has been a weapon used for symbolic purposes—to get support, or "legitimacy" for the government in power, but reform, he asserts, was never as serious a goal as it was made out to be (Weiler, 1988: 251–265). France, he argues, was under pressure in the 1970s and 1980s to show evidence that it was modernizing and keeping up with other countries. Thus, education reform proposals are strategies or weapons for politicians, even if the reforms do not materialize.

Weiler also suggests that the great inertia in France's education system holds back reform; related to this lack of energy is the tendency of vested interest groups, including the teachers' unions, to resist change.

Looking at the 1980s, Weiler asserts that the proposed reforms got sidetracked by a revival of the church–state–education conflict as the socialist government of President François Mitterrand proposed a very controversial reform in 1984. The reform would have either revised arrangements so that private Catholic schools would have lost their large grants of public tax money or would have had to submit to such close government inspection and regulations as to make them into quasi-public schools. The opposition of private school supporters was fierce, and the national government dropped the matter (Glenn, 1989: 31–35).

After the failure of 1984, the socialist government turned very conservative in its education policies and spent its time trying to demonstrate that public schools were better than private schools in terms of scores on examinations and the like. The term in vogue was "quality of instruction." Not surprisingly, educational reforms stressing equality of opportunity had a more difficult time in France in the 1980s (Weiler, 1988: 265).

Much of the effort to extend educational opportunity over the last thirty years has centered on secondary education. Until the 1960s France had a system of separating out a small percentage of an age group at age eleven and admitting them to a prestigious secondary school (*lycée*) which was the route to higher education. Most of the rest of the age group remained in an elementary school until they reached the age of fourteen when they dropped out of school (Neave, 1985: 13). Less than 20 percent of an age group entered the *lycée*, and less than 10 percent of an age group finished the *lycée* and were thus eligible to enter higher education (Male, 1963: 76).

The reforms instituted since 1963 have been designed to bring all secondary school youth together under the same roof for the first four years of lower secondary education. At the same time, the reform has tried to reduce the separation ("tracking") of vocational-type students from academic-type students "often in the face of ferocious resistance of teachers" (Neave, 1985: 14).

Those who finish lower secondary education and decide to continue their education are sent either into the academic branch of the upper secondary school or the vocational branch. An attempt to raise the status of the vocational branch involved adding the prestigious word *lycée* to the name of the vocational schools. The academic branch of the upper secondary schools ends with a rigorous ex- amination, the *baccalauréate* exam, which traditionally only slightly more than half of those still in school passed. Passing of the *baccalauréate* exam gives the individual the right to enter a university. Many of the reforms which never got beyond the proposal stage have involved attempts to lessen the ruthless sorting and eliminating of people which the *bac* (short for *baccalauréate* exam) represents.

Other attempts to lesson the sorting and grouping of students have focused on the lower secondary school, or what American educators would call grades 6 through 9. The "Haby Reform" of 1977, for example, called for the gradual abolition of grouping by ability and proposed a common curriculum for the first two years of the lower secondary school (Halls, 1987: 50).

The 1982 LeGrand Report on the eleven to sixteen age group called for (1) team teaching, (2) more initiative and responsibility to be assumed by students, and (3) changes in the curriculum to give greater weight to the technological and the aesthetic. There was some opposition to the LeGrand Report by teachers who saw their workload increased by such innovations as team teaching and the fact that the national government proposed to increase the workload for teachers to twenty-two hours per week. The national government later dropped the idea of a twenty-two-hour work week, and the minister of national education ended up asking the teachers of France to voluntarily implement the LeGrand Report (Halls, 1987: 57). The voluntary approach was unusual for France where the central government customarily orders changes to be made.

The Prost Report of 1987 investigated the upper secondary school (*lycée*). The commission found that there were too few guidance counselors; that the school day and school week were too long but the school year too short (177 days); that linkages between subjects (fields of knowledge) were inadequate; and that students did too much cramming for exams and achieved too little assimilation (retention) of knowledge (Halls, 1987: 61).

The complaint about cramming and memorizing for the *bac* exam was an old story as indicated by similar criticisms twenty-five years earlier.

For at least a month before the *baccalauréate* examinations, students and parents can think of little else, and teachers complain that the latter part of the school year is completely disorganized and sacrificed to feverish preparation for the examinations. . . . Much of the criticism centers on the excessive strain placed on the students and on the substitution of "examination passing" for the legitimate goals of learning (Male, 1963: 106).

Defenders of cramming (*bachotage*) and memorization spoke up in 1961, asking for a delay in impending reform suggestions which included one from a 1955 national commission that the *baccalauréate* exam be abolished. Defenders of the exam argued:

Reviewing has its merits: it not only consolidates learning, it also makes comparisons possible and reveals the interest of a question. Such strengthening of knowledge should always be encouraged. Any future reform of the *baccalauréate* should be concerned less with reducing bachotage [cramming] than with proposing more concise programs of study and making sure that the subjects are better learned (*l'Education Nationale*, 1961: 11).

Reform has occurred in the *bac* exam in that a large number of alternative programs of study have been created in place of the previous system where one either took the exam in mathematics or philosophy and literature or science. In the 1980s there were eight options under the general education category, sixteen options under the fairly new *baccalauréate* in technology, and since 1987 a new vocational *baccalauréate* with fourteen options. So the four options in 1950 had grown to thirty-eight near the end of the 1980s (Eckstein and Noah, 1989: 314). A hierarchy of prestige and status has emerged, as one would expect in France, "with the mathematical options at the head and the vocational options forming the tail" (Eckstein and Noah, 1989: 314).

The offering of more options has increased the percentage of an age group passing the *baccalauréate* exam. In 1953 it was 6 percent of the eligible age group (eighteen or nineteen year olds), and in 1983 it was 27 percent (Halls, 1987: 59). The national government has announced that its goal is to get 80 percent of an age group to get a secondary school diploma (*baccalauréate*) by the end of the 1990s.

In 1988 40 percent of the age group attempted the *bac* exam, and 28 percent passed. Some of the critics claim that standards for the *bac* exam are being lowered, but the Ministry of National Education claims that is not so. The ministry does admit that an increasing number of students are spending a fourth year in the upper secondary school (*lycée*) rather than the usual three years in order to better prepare for the *bac* exam (*Times Educational Supplement*, October 27, 1989: 13).

The reform of the *bac* exam was partly a response to pressures to provide more opportunities for more young people to enter higher education and partly an attempt to meet the demand for studies with more relevance (Eckstein and Noah, 1989: 314). Relevance meant different things to different people, but national government planners and policymakers saw technical and vocational studies as relevant to the issue of improving France's economy.

As more students stay on in the upper secondary school, problems of over-crowded schools and classrooms have surfaced. In 1990 the national government was less interested in reforming secondary education than in trying to raise additional money to meet salary raises demanded by teachers and to hire thousands of additional teachers needed to fill the classrooms.

The expansion of secondary education has inevitably led to a larger percentage of an age group entering higher education. Whereas in 1955 only 5 percent of the eligible age group entered university in France, by the late 1980s the figure was over 20 percent.

There was also a movement to democratize higher education in terms of reaching the children of small farmers and factory workers. This movement began after World War II and moved ahead very slowly. It was reported in 1962 that "the son of a doctor or lawyer . . . has a 200 times greater chance of entering higher education than the son of a laborer" (*Education in France*, 1962: 28). Twenty years later (1981) it was claimed that senior executives' sons had seventeen time more likelihood of entering higher education than sons of blue-collar workers (*Times Education Supplement*, September 4, 1981: 11). Martin McLean, writing in 1985, reported no significant change in the social class composition of the student body in higher education in France (McLean, 1985: 93).

Aside from reforms related to democratization, significant reform efforts have been made in higher education in the last three decades, particularly those designed to establish closer links between higher education and the economy. The university institutes of technology established in 1966 were forerunners of abortive efforts in the 1980s to give an applied or vocational emphasis to most courses in the universities. Guy Neave has characterized this as the "vocationalization" of higher education and asserts that it was not too successful (Neave, 1985: 27–28).

Neave also notes that reforms did not touch the elite part of higher education, namely, the *grandes écoles*; these are small, specialized institutions offering what Americans would call undergraduate education to a very select group of students (about 10 percent of the total higher education enrollment) who spend a year or two in preparatory classes cramming themselves with information to pass the difficult entrance exams. Neave attributes the failure of reforms to touch the *grandes écoles* to the fact that many high-ranking policymakers in the national government are proud alumni of these *grandes écoles* (Neave, 1985: 11). Neave claims that "without exception, both in secondary education and higher education reform applied [only] to nonelite institutions" and the *grandes écoles* "were not touched by the reforms" (Neave, 1985: 11).

McLean suggests that the existence of the *grandes écoles* may have made it easier for reforms in the other parts of higher education since the intellectuals, who often were educated at the *grandes écoles*, see the rest of higher education as being for lesser people and, therefore, of less concern to them (McLean, 1985: 91). The opposition of intellectuals has killed or slowed down many education reforms in France in the past.

Neave claims that the prestige of the *grandes écoles* probably increased in the 1980s, in part because the systematic rejection of a large percentage of applicants, seemingly well endowed intellectually, gives the *grandes écoles* a special mystique. In addition, says Neave, there is widespread belief that the training offered by the *grandes écoles* meshes well with the demands of high-level technology and with the bureaucratic and administrative skills needed by the centralized and bureaucratic national government.

In a curious way, says Neave, the French have retained their traditional emphasis on elitism, selectivity, and high intellectual quality by retaining the *grandes écoles*, untouched by reform, while meeting demands for mass higher education by encouraging the universities to expand and to offer new programs (Neave, 1985: 11).

The rising enrollments in French universities in the last five years (1986–1990) have reached a crisis stage with regard to inadequate library facilities, badly overcrowded classrooms, and shortage of qualified instructors. One is reminded of a similar situation in 1968 which helped produce the student protest movement that almost toppled the French government (Male, 1970: 349–358).

In 1986 the national government responded to the overcrowded universities with a reform proposal that would have allowed the universities, and the departments within the universities, more autonomy in rejecting applicants in place of the traditional system of accepting all applicants with a secondary school diploma (*baccalauréate*). The proposal generated strong student protest and political opposition, and the national government dropped its efforts to get the needed legislation through the French Assembly (Eckstein and Noah, 1989: 309).

The minister of higher education reported two years later (1988) that French universities were worse than any in Europe (*Times Educational Supplement*, January 1, 1988: 9). In 1989 the president of the largest university in Paris (Paris I) said that he had 10,000 more students than his institution could handle, while the teaching staff was the same size as it had been ten years earlier. Other universities reported similar problems (*Times Educational Supplement*, December 1, 1989: 16). In January 1990 the minister of national education announced plans to build five new universities and to increase the budget for existing universities by 12 percent.

The national government has a five-year plan to double the existing library facilities and build other facilities to accommodate an expected increase of 300,000 students over the first half of the 1990s (*Times Educational Supplement*, June 15, 1990: A21). The increased government efforts coincide with considerable talk about possible student unrest (*Times Educational Supplement*, January 19, 1990: 14).

Student unrest in 1990 was partly a result of a failure to improve the defective atmosphere surrounding teaching and learning in the universities, which was an important factor in the 1968 protest and remained a problem twenty-two years later. The problem was described in 1970 as follows:

More important than lack of physical facilities is the defect in spirit and atmosphere of French universities. The stereotype of French university teaching . . . includes rigidity, dull lectures, copies of lectures circulated and memorized for examinations, professors pouring out a stream of knowledge and not appearing to care whether it was understood or not . . . and generally poor contacts between professors and students (Male, 1970: 351).

Recently, some of the French universities have formed committees to try to improve the atmosphere. In 1989 the university at Orsay instituted a reform that reportedly "was entirely centered on student-teacher relations. It aimed at abolishing the traditional image of the distant professor who cares nothing about his students" (*Times Educational Supplement*, September 8, 1989: 21).

Partly because of the defective atmosphere and partly because of the ruthless exams given at the end of the first year of university study there is a massive dropping out, with 40 percent or more of the first-year students leaving. At the end of the 1980s the national government announced plans to establish the first two years of university study as a kind of junior college American style, with emphasis in the first year on getting the students "oriented." At the end of the second year a diploma will be issued, and many presumably will not go on for the regular undergraduate degree (*licence*). The junior colleges, or "university colleges" as they are called, will be part of the university but will have administrative and teaching autonomy.

Autonomy for universities is part of a larger reform effort to decentralize education. Traditionally, the Ministry of National Education at all levels of education has defined courses to be taken, length of study, hours per year, and so on. The result of such actions, says Neave, is that "they have the not inconsiderable drawback of making reform extremely difficult since, if reforms are to have any standing at all, they have to be introduced at a system level rather than at the individual establishment" (Neave, 1985: 19).

Starting in the 1970s, various attempts have been made to give some control over courses, examinations, and so on to local governments so that they could to some extent reflect local or regional needs. The Prost Report of 1983 on the secondary school (*lycée*) recommended that at least one-third of the curriculum should not be specified by the national government but rather should be decided at the local level to reflect local interests (Halls, 1987: 61). Even more surprising are efforts beginning in the second half of the 1980s to give some autonomy and decision making to individual schools. For example, some schools have been authorized to vary the timetable of courses to fit the needs of local industries (Halls, 1987: 66).

Unlike reforms in the United States in the late 1980s, there is little expectation that educational reform in France will be initiated by teachers as decentralization proceeds. As McLean put it, "There is little incentive for teachers . . . to initiate curriculum reforms" (McLean, 1985: 89).

Part of the teachers' resistance to reforms has to do with the fact that different kinds of teachers get different amounts of respect and power and organize themselves into different unions.

The vertical organization of the teaching profession [in France] discourages school-based internal reforms. Different grades of teachers in second-level education are divided against each other and are represented by different teacher unions. Furthermore, there are few senior teachers who are encouraged and rewarded for taking responsibility for internal school management and leadership (McLean, 1985: 89).

Decentralization has also been slowed down by the fact that often it only means that local areas are being asked to assume new financial burdens as the national government tries to balance its budget. Thus, under decentralization, starting in 1988 local governments were ordered to provide computers for schools rather than relying on the national government. Similarly, the local regions of France were asked to pay for the building and maintenance of secondary schools (*lycées*). At the higher education level, the building of several new universities in the 1990s will depend partly on funds supplied by regional governments, which in return will have some say about the programs to be offered and the exact location of the new universities. Consulting the local governments in this way is seen as a significant break from the traditionally centralized decision making (*Times Educational Supplement*, June 15, 1990: A21).

Another significant change is that in some parts of France parents are being allowed to choose among three or four nearby schools. The Ministry of National Education publicly asserts that it is not worried that this could lead to certain schools emerging as the preferred institutions. A spokesman for the national government said, ''The elite schools are already there despite catchment boundaries. We are only authorizing what already exists'' (*Times Educational Supplement*, January 1, 1988: 9).

In fact, as the study by Didier Maupas in 1984 reported, middle-class parents had found ways to ignore school attendance zones and get their child into a school with a good reputation (Maupas, 1984: 19, as cited in Glenn, 1989: 36).

Interest in choice of school may continue to grow in France as it has in the United States, although in the case of France it is not a matter being pushed by the political party in power. Decentralization in general does have official approval, but it is likely to move slowly in the 1990s for a variety of reasons including (1) the opposition of some of the teachers unions, which see it as a threat to their existing arrangements with the national government, (2) the lack of a tradition of parent or citizen involvement in educational policymaking; as Wanner put it: ''In a land where the central Ministry of National Education has exercised control over every aspect of education for more than a century citizens do not have the tradition of involvement in the schools that they do in certain other countries'' (Wanner, 1988: 423); and (3) the power of the bureaucrats in the national government and their skill in retaining control; as Burton Clark noted: ''In the most highly bureaucratized state among the Western democracies, power remains with, and keeps rebounding back to, the central bureaucratic elite. . . . The French institutions of centralization have much stability and endurance'' (Clark, 1983: 199).

The slowness to decentralize is also a result of almost two centuries of national government control of education. In addition, some educators see a positive side to strong national government control to insure uniformity of standards and to minimize regional inequality of educational opportunity. McLean, for example, sees France as more successful than some other countries in approaching the goal of equal provision of educational opportunity.

Similarly, the education system [of France] has been relatively successful in accommodating the ideal of equality of opportunity. Central allocation of resources has reduced the geographic inequalities found in some other education systems [Kentucky, Texas, New Jersey, etc. in the United States in 1990]. Central direction of reform has meant that the structure of second-level education [secondary education] has become more egalitarian in a fairly short space of time (McLean, 1985; 94).

In the name of uniformity, the minister of national education in 1989 ordered all public primary schools to test children at age eight and eleven. The elementary schools in France (called primary schools) have received less attention from reformers, but some problems surfaced near the end of the 1980s. The new testing procedures are designed to find out whether children are being prepared for secondary schools in such basics as reading. Reportedly, two out of three children could not read at the needed level as they enter the secondary schools (*Times Educational Supplement*, March 2, 1990: 18). The head of the Ministry of National Education said that he also hoped to cut down on the tendency of teachers to make large numbers of children repeat a grade in the primary school. As part of the same reform effort, the national government authorized public primary schools to end the tradition of closing for half of Wednesday so that those children who wished could attend catechism classes offered by the Catholic Church. Catholic bishops have announced their opposition to the change and want the national government to order the public schools to reserve one-half of Wednesday for religious education (*Times Educational Supplement*, March 2, 1990: 18).

The Catholic bishops are even more concerned about their private Catholic schools, which after a century or more of conflict with the national government are funded almost completely by public tax money. The funding breakthrough came in the 1950s with the passage of two important laws (Fowler, 1987: 356).

According to Richard Teese, the effect of massive national government tax aid on the Catholic schools has been a raising of the level of teacher qualifications, a general alignment of the Catholic secondary school curriculum with that of the public schools, and a growing secularization of Catholic schools (Teese, 1986: 251). With the growing secularization of the Catholic school curriculum and a dramatic increase in lay teachers, a new problem has emerged, says Teese, of trying to retain a distinctive identity. Teese also notes a curious development over the last thirty years whereby a centralized bureaucracy has developed to take charge of what previously was a loose assortment of Catholic schools, each more or less on its own (Teese, 1986: 251).

More recently, teachers in Catholic schools have formed unions and have pressured for tenure-like protection as in public schools. Teese claims that the Catholic hierarchy has been successful in diverting these Catholic teachers unions from pay demands by getting them to focus on the defense of the right of Catholic schools to receive public tax money (Teese, 1986: 254).

Public school teachers in the late 1980s were not reluctant to demand higher pay and to resort to strikes and threats of strikes. In 1988 one of the secondary school teachers unions, Syndicat National des Enseignements du Second Degré, called a strike, and threats of strikes were made by one of the primary school teachers unions, Syndicat National des Instituteurs. Over the last two years (1988–1990) the Ministry of National Education has tried to placate the teachers by offers of pay raises, including bonuses for spending more time with individual students to counsel them. At the same time the Ministry of National Education has laid aside a proposed reform that would have pressured teachers into a new style of teaching which would focus on the needs of the students rather than on an accumulation of knowledge (*Times Educational Supplement*, December 29, 1989: 8).

One could have predicted trouble for any reform calling for a change in teaching methods. As William Halls put it, "The conservatism of French teachers as regards methods is notorious" (Halls, 1987: 54). The teaching methods in the academic branch of the secondary school has been described as follows: "In France the teacher in the academic secondary school sees his task as that of developing the intellect of the few who get into these schools. Prompted both by the government circulars and by tradition he encourages the students to memorize large portions of assigned materials" (Male, 1963: 111).

Those who fail to memorize enough material have traditionally been held back and made to repeat the year. In 1990 the national government took away the right of secondary school teachers to hold back a student. Henceforth teachers can only "suggest" that students be held back, but the head administrator of the school will decide. Reportedly, the teachers unions have grudgingly accepted this reform (*Times Educational Supplement*, April 27, 1990: A16).

The national government has also taken steps to change the teaching in elementary schools by abolishing the old teacher training schools (*écoles normales*), which as late as the 1960s took students at age fifteen, finished their secondary schooling, and added on a year or two of postsecondary teacher training. In 1990 the national government ordered all twenty-six educational regions (*académies*) in France to establish institutes where prospective teachers would get the equivalent of a university degree along with teacher training. The hope is that by the end of 1991 every region of France will have one of these institutes (*Institutes d'Universitaires de Formation des Maitres*).

The teaching in vocational schools has also come under attack, as has the general effectiveness of vocational training. This presents a problem for planners in the national government who see a link between vocational education and improving France's economy. Halls has raised doubts as to whether efforts to improve vocational education will succeed. He speaks of "the lingering disdain still felt for technical and vocational courses, as courses for the second-rate" (Halls, 1987: 67).

Inspectors from the national government in 1989 reported that morale was low in the vocational schools "partly because the vast majority of pupils never wanted to go there in the first place" (*Times Educational Supplement*, May 19, 1989: A17). The provision of secondary school diplomas (*baccalauréate*) in the 1980s for certain vocational and technical programs has helped, but many students leave vocational programs without adequate job preparation. Part of the problem relates back to the highly centralized French system which makes it difficult to respond to local industry needs.

In 1984 the Bloch Commission was appointed to seek ways of bringing "closer collaboration between education and business/industry." The commission included employers, school administrators, and representatives of trade unions. The commission's 1985 report (*Mission Education—Entreprise: Rapport et Recommandations*) set out procedures for involving business and labor leaders in educational policymaking. As Eckstein and Noah put it, "An important outcome of the Bloch Commission's work has been the legitimation of participation by associations of employers and organized labor in the policy and practice of general 'education and vocational training" (Eckstein and Noah, 1987: 25). Eckstein and Noah see this new development as a significant deviation from the tradition of centralized control.

Instead of detailed direction from the center, the central authorities and the national organizations have chosen recently to promulgate general frameworks of law and encouragement, leaving the regional and local organizations to determine the extent and the form of their activities in detail. As a consequence, there are substantial differences in employers' involvement to be observed, both among the various geographic regions of France and from one economic sector to another (Eckstein and Noah, 1987: 28).

Another area that has recently received belated attention is the existence of a sizable amount of illiteracy in a country that prides itself on fostering intellectualism. Even though there is an obvious connection between large numbers of illiterates and the economy, France did very little about the problem until the 1980s. "France, like a number of other industrialized countries, has been extremely slow to recognize that it may have a large number of adult illiterates in its own population" (Limage, 1986: 62).

The first official recognition of the problem came in 1981 with the publication of a report (the Oheix Report) on poverty which called for an adult literacy campaign. In 1984 a report from a commission set up to study illiteracy called for the establishment of a permanent agency to deal with illiteracy. Limage argues that the minister of national education seemed reluctant to become involved in the illiteracy problem (Limage, 1986: 62). He is not optimistic that France will move forward to eradicate illiteracy because its attention is elsewhere.

Also given retrenchment in educational spending, the recent [1984] capitulation by the government to conservative forces seeking to maintain the autonomy of the private, primarily religious, schools subsidized completely by the nation [public tax money]; and the recent "Back to Basics" discourse of the present minister of education, it appears unlikely that France will undertake a major effort to eradicate illiteracy (Limage, 1986: 66).

In 1989 the minister of national education did promise to seek to reduce illiteracy (*Times Educational Supplement*, January 6, 1989: 14).

Another problem that had received little attention is the education of minorities. Reform proposals rarely acknowledge any problem, although the growing number of Muslim immigrants from North Africa has created housing and other kinds of problems.

The number of Muslims living in France has been estimated at 4.5 million, or about 8 percent of the population. In the last three years (1988–1990) a number of school incidents have received public attention. In several cities (Paris, Marseille, Montpelier, Avignon, Lille), Muslim girls were ordered to stop wearing headscarfs (*hijabs*), which are part of their observance of their religious faith. When Muslim girls refused to stop wearing the scarves, they were threatened with expulsion from school.

At first the minister of national education took the rather mild step of suggesting that more religious toleration was needed. In 1989, when the issue became inflamed by a political group on the far right (the National Front) that advocates a policy of sending immigrants back to their home countries in order to keep French culture pure, the Council of State of the national government intervened. The Council issued an order that said schools could forbid Muslim girls from wearing the scarves, but the school would have to secure permission from the Council of State. Teachers were forbidden to wear such religious symbols under threat of dismissal (*Times Educational Supplement*, December 8, 1989: 14).

In 1990 the prime minister of France announced a program to combat racism in France after the appearance of a report from the National Advisory Committee on Human Rights. The report claimed that "anti-North African racism is spreading everywhere like an oil slick" (*Times Educational Supplement*, April 6, 1990: 14).

The Ministry of National Education has been accused of doing nothing to solve the problem over the last five years (1986–1990); its response is that teachers have already been instructed to promote citizenship education (*Times Educational Supplement*, April 6, 1990: 14).

As France enters the last decade of the twentieth century, it faces a number of educational problems. Among the easier problems will be the matter of raising the needed money to hire many more teachers to handle growing enrollments. The harder problems lying ahead include trying to change some of the basic characteristics, such as ruthless elimination of students by exams and the heavy emphasis on accumulating knowledge to pass the tests.

The basic characteristics of French education listed at the beginning of this chapter remain intact, although each has been modified somewhat by various reform efforts. In the immediate future, French education will continue to change, but slowly. Most resistant to change is the French outlook, which pervades French education. This will change most slowly of all since it pervades other aspects of French life and is basic to the culture.

REFERENCES

Carduner, Jean. 1987. "The Making of French Citizens: Conflicts Between Fading Traditions and Emerging Values." *In the Nation's Image: Civic Education in Japan, the Soviet Union, the United States, France, and Britain*, ed. Edgar Gumbert.

Atlanta: Center for Cross-cultural Education, Georgia State University, pp. 87–103.

Clark, Burton. 1983. *The Higher Education System: Academic Organization in Cross-National Perspective*. Los Angeles: University of California Press.

Coombs, Fred. 1978, October. "The Politics of Educational Change in France." *Comparative Education Review* 22: 480–503.

Eckstein, Max and Harold Noah. 1987. *International Study of Business/Industry Involvement with Education*. New York: Teachers College, Columbia University, Institute of Philosophy and Politics of Education, Occasional Paper No. 4.

———. 1989, August. "Forms and Functions of Secondary-School Leaving Examinations." *Comparative Education Review* 33: 295–316.

Education in France. 1982, May. No. 18: 28–30.

l'Education Nationale, 1961, September 22. P. 11.

Fowler, Frances C. 1987, January. "The French Experience with Public Aid to Private Schools." *Phi Delta Kappan* 69: 356–359.

Glenn, Charles L. 1989. *Choice of Schools in Six Nations*. Washington, D.C.: U.S. Department of Education ("France," pp. 9–43).

Halls, William D. 1987. "The French Secondary School Today." In *Changing Patterns of Secondary Education: An International Perspective*, ed. Robert F. Lawson. Calgary, Canada: University of Calgary Press, pp. 47–71.

Limage, Leslie J. 1986, February. "Adult Literacy Policy in Industrialized Countries." *Comparative Education Review* 30: 50–72.

Male, George A. 1963. *Education in France*. Washington, D.C.: U.S. Office of Education.

———. 1970. "Student Protest in France." In *Conflict and Change On the Campus*, ed. William Brickman and Stanley Lehrer. New York: School and Society Books, pp. 349–358.

Maupas, Didier, 1984. *L'école en accusation*. Paris: Albin Michel.

McLean, Martin. 1985. "Education in France: Traditions of Liberty in a Centralized System." *Equality and Freedom in Education: A Comparative Study*, ed. Brian Holmes. Boston: George Allen and Unwin, pp. 63–104.

Neave, Guy. 1985. "France." In *The School and the University: An International Perspective*, ed. Burton Clark. Los Angeles: University of California Press, pp. 10–44.

Teese, Richard. 1986, May. "Private Schools in France." *Comparative Education Review* 30: 247–259.

Times Education Supplement (London).

Wanner, Ray. 1978. "The Case of France." *Western European Education* 10(Spring): 33–39.

———. 1988. "France." In *World Education Encyclopedia*. Vol. 1. New York: Facts on File Publications, pp. 422–423.

Weiler, Hans N. 1988, August. "The Politics of Reform and Nonreform in French Education." *Comparative Education Review*, Vol. 32, no. 3, pp. 251–265.

11

GERMANY

Wolfgang Mitter

THE HISTORICAL CONTEXT

Educational reform in Germany has always been closely linked with the general development of its school system. The system can be traced back to the Middle Ages and the period of humanism; its modern history, however, comprises only the past four centuries. It began with the school statutes of the seventeenth and eighteenth centuries which bear witness, on the one hand, to the far-sightedness of German princes whose policies were aimed at the struggle against illiteracy and the introduction of compulsory education at the elementary level. On the other hand, they reflect the contribution, if not even the authorship, of prominent pedagogic reformers to the progress of schools. The alliance of reform policy, prospective theory, and innovative experiment is also characteristic of the "classical" educational reforms of the nineteenth century which, taken as a whole, were based on an idealistic concept of personality development. Of particular note are Wilhelm von Humboldt who influenced the Prussian and German universities and grammar schools (*Gymnasien*), and Heinrich Pesklozzi and Johann Friedrich Herbart whose pedagogic theories and methodic guidelines for action influenced the elementary school and the training of elementary school teachers (Blankertz, 1982).

After World War I, the whole of Germany was affected by a strong innovative wave. It was part of the worldwide movement for educational reform (*Reformpädagogik*). Among German protagonists, especially the outstanding educationists, were Eduard Spranger, Paul Oestreich, and Georg Kerschensteiner. The last named gained special importance in preparing the way for modern vocational education. This reform wave concentrated on an assault on traditional schooling which, in general terms, was marked by rote learning and the assimilation of encyclopedic facts. At the same time it mirrored, to a considerable extent, the stagnation of the aforementioned approaches or even their perversion into opposite purposes.

During this first reform period of the twentieth century, open methods of teaching and learning, such as group instruction, which aimed to arouse children's desire to know and their imaginative powers, found their way into the elementary schools. Even grammar schools were affected by the movements to reform education. At this level such innovative approaches could be seen particularly in the preference for interpreting individual works of literature and historical events as opposed to the traditional transmission of encyclopedic knowledge.

The partition of Germany in 1945 entailed the emergence of two separate education systems that sharply diverged with the establishment of two republics, the Federal Republic of Germany (PRG) and the German Democratic Republic (GDR) in 1949. Yet, the period between 1945 and 1949 requires special attention, for efforts were then aimed at rebuilding education from the chaos that the collapse of National Socialism had left behind. A common core could be made out in all four occupation zones. It consisted of the elimination of the National Socialist ideology, which had been focused on racism, nationalism, anti-Semitism, and militarism, and had particularly dominated the syllabi of history, German literature, biology, and physical education. The divergent tendencies, on the other hand, were caused by the military governments and their German counterparts in West and East. Soon it became evident that these strategies were the outcome of divergent philosophical concepts of people and education.

In the Western part of Germany, particularly in the American and British occupation zones, education officers in the military governments of the reestablished states (Länder), as well as German educationalists and politicians, used their joint powers and energies. In spite of the manifold differences of opinion between both counterparts on the one hand and among the political parties on the other, there was a widespread consensus with regard to the basic aims of the new policy for education: the resuscitation of respect for the dignity of people and the promotion of equity of opportunity and fairness in education. As regards the structure of the education system, the German educationists and politicians shared the idea of reestablishing the system as it had existed in the Weimar Republic, namely, focused on four-year primary schools and a secondary level organized according to the vertical principle with grammar schools (*Gymnasien*), intermediate schools (*Realschulen*) and the upper stage of elementary schools (*Volksschulen*). At length, they asserted themselves against the preference for comprehensive schools which had been favored by the American and British military governments (von Friedeburg, 1989).

Education in the Soviet occupation zone pointed to an opposite direction from the beginning (Anweiler, 1990). The Soviet military government set up a central education administration. Its early policy culminated in the Education Act of May 1946 which was adopted by the parliaments of the—at the time still existing—East German Länder. This act focused on introducing an eight-year uniform school built on unified syllabi for all children (grades 1 to 8) and the entire secularization of the school system which, in German historical terms, included the closing down of denominational schools as well as the abolition of religious instruction in all state schools. While this bill still reflected some impacts of the aforementioned Weimar inheritance, the rapidly increasing dominance of the Socialist Unity party (SED) led to the infiltration of the Marxist-Leninist ideology throughout the education system at the end of the 1940s, that is, even before the installation of the German Democratic Republic.

The collapse of the socialist regime in the Eastern part of Germany in 1989 has consequently vindicated those who maintained that socialist education in the German Democratic Republic had been a failure from its start. This opinion is rooted in solid ground, insofar as governance, syllabi, and pedagogy were strictly subjected to the Marxist-Leninist ideology and the totalitarian policy of the Socialist Unity party. Moreover, the establishment of the socialist regime was followed by the consistent adjustment of the education system to the uniform political and ideological power structure and was manifested by an articulate and gradually achieved retreat from what was called the bourgeois past. The "change" (*Wende*) of 1989 and 1990 has brought to light how little impact the "command education" (*Kommandopädagogik*) has had on most youth as regards their political and ideological commitment.

Yet, certain "innovative" components of school development in the past forty years can be identified, especially vocational education, and polytechnic education and training as a school subject and a cross-disciplinary learning area. The development of vocational education was widely similar to that in West Germany, going back to the common base promoted by Georg Kerschensteiner. (It will be dealt with in detail later in this chapter.) Polytechnic education, however, turned out to be a "specific" curricular field of socialist education. Its implementation in the Ten-General Polytechnic Secondary School (*Allgemeinbildende Polytechnische Oberschule*) and its continuation in the two-year Extended Secondary School (*Erweiterte Oberschule*) put the East German education system in a special position even among the other socialist countries including the Soviet Union (Mitter, 1990). After the end of the 1960s, however, the development was marked by increasing curricular stagnation and ideological torpidity.

The development of education in the Federal Republic of Germany was at first characterized by widespread consolidation of the preceding "second innovative wave," as related to the twentieth century as a whole. On the one hand, this led to the stabilization of the existing system. On the other hand, more and more people felt that progress in achieving equity of opportunity was inadequate. Hence came the criticisms that laid the basis for the large-scale reforms characterizing educational development in the late 1960s and early 1970s.

Since this "third wave" continues into the present era, we will confine ourselves to a few comments to describe its most important indications. First, the student movement must be mentioned. Its spectacular expressions, though short-lived, had far-reaching effects because they marked the start of changes in social and political development and in matters hitherto taken for granted in the universities. Second, reference must be made to the extensive work of the German Council for Education (*Deutscher Bildungsrat*), an advisory body which during its existence (1965–1975) published a large number of remarkable reports and recommendations. Finally, the change in the federal government in 1969, which led the social-liberal coalition to power (1969–1982), brought to maturity the first visible result of an educational policy at the federal level that was clearly expressed in the publication of the Education Report, 1970. In addition to equity of educational opportunity, the following aims were listed in the program of educational reform (Führ, 1989, von Friedeburg, 1989):

- Modernization of the education system with reference to planning, school building, and organization.

- Democratization of education in which the German interpretation involves not merely the opening of school and society to strata of population hitherto underprivileged, but also cooperation and joint decisions by teachers, parents, members of the community, and finally even students in the way schools are set up and organized.

- Introduction of curricula aimed at replacing or, at any rate, restricting the function of traditional syllabi by subsuming aims and objectives, contents, methods, and evaluative guidelines in a superordinate concept of schooling (Robinson, 1975).

- Structural reforms concerning lower and upper secondary education as well as the preschool level (to be analyzed in detail later).

- Reforms in higher education with special regard to planning, organization and governance.

The third innovative wave was embodied in what has been called the period of large-scale reforms. It became separated from the turning point of the spirit of the age as soon as the conservative politicians and intellectuals designated (and welcomed) the subsequent period as one of consolidation again. This last distinct change in the education system made itself known as early as the mid–1970s—long before the change of government in October 1982 which brought the Christian-liberal coalition to power. It has been confirmed by the (West German) elections in 1987 and the (first all-German) elections on December 2, 1990.

In summary, all innovative waves of the twentieth century resulted variously in consolidation, stagnation, or even destruction. Acceptance of such an appraisal depends not only on what in fact has happened, but also on the individual critic's point of view. The Weimar Republic's reforms were given up or perverted into purposes that the National Socialist officials declared to be "true" German education. The radical initiatives of the postwar period after 1945 were slowed down in the early 1950s by an educational policy that critics have called "restoration." Indeed, this may be the characteristic of the whole period from the end of the 1940s to the mid–1960s. Although such a harsh criticism should be seen as biased and even exaggerated, it does show that the education system in

West Germany (up to 1989) has been linked directly to that of the Weimar Republic in both their reformative and their conservative components.

The "consolidating" forces scaled down or even suppressed the reformative achievements of the previous innovative waves. In general, however, it can be stated that in given circumstances these achievements had been absorbed into the forty years' history of formal and nonformal education in the (Western Länder of the) Federal Republic of Germany.

ECONOMIC DEVELOPMENT AND EDUCATIONAL REFORM

The three waves of educational reform in the twentieth century have been caused by political changes and philosophical concepts. Yet, they also demonstrate immediate reactions to radical economic challenges. In the first two waves these were the inevitable corollaries of postwar crises following lost wars. It seems that the economic impulses of the third wave in the Federal Republic were deeper, insofar as they mirrored the invasion of the new technologies into the economy and the demand for people with advanced qualifications. "To increase the number of secondary school-leavers" turned out to be a widespread slogan at the end of the 1960s. From today's viewpoint it has proved to be legitimate in spite of its one-sidedness twenty years ago, when Georg Picht (1964), one of its most prominent proponents, overemphasized the need for academic versus vocational education.

Generally, educational reform in the Federal Republic has coped with the demands posed by the country's continuously high industrialized production and rapid growth of the service sector. Of course, educational innovations have not overcome the disparities between economic and educational progress. In particular, deficits in the output of skilled workers for the "middle range" of the employment ladder have continually caused labor shortages. Yet, these shortages could, in general, be ended mainly by Gymnasium leavers taking vocational training courses. The recruitment of unskilled workers has remained on the agenda over the past twenty years. This gap has been widely filled by migrant workers; the undesirable sociopolitical side-effects of the arrival of the "new minorities" must not be overlooked, however. The history of education in the GDR, compared to that of the Federal Republic, demonstrates a higher degree of "compatibility" with the labor market, insofar as recruitment and output were derived from the rigidly fixed quota that was part of the GDR's five-year plans. Therefore, the official statistics were used to reveal permanent efforts to eliminate or, at least, to minimize disparities between economic and educational progress.

Summing up, Germany's education system (until 1989) developed according to the needs of highly industrialized economies. It seems that the 'liberal" variation in the Federal Republic, rooted in the close interaction between a market-oriented economy and a school system predominantly financed and governed by the state, met the challenges of modern economic progress and change more efficiently than did the "totalitarian" variation in the German Democratic Republic.

THE ROLE OF THE STATE

In Germany the state plays the leading role in the organization, administration, and control of schools and other educational institutions. This feature can be traced back directly to the period of early absolutism. The "state," as the Germans understand the term, signifies the centralized structure for legislation in government which can make use of a hierarchically constructed administration headed by the minister of education and culture (*Kulturminister*). The general nature of this fundamental stipulation was laid down in Article 144 of the 1919 Constitution (the Weimar Constitution).

In the Federal Republic of Germany this stipulation was confirmed by Article 7 of the Basic Law (*Grundgesetz*) of 1949: "The entire school system is subject to the supervision of the state." As for the interpretation of this article, in particular the notion of "supervision," however, controversial debates have been going on for the past four decades. The Supreme Court's decisions and the jurisprudential literature have been dominated by the traditional version which states that "supervision" means all-embracing state control through decision-making administrative authorities according to the valid laws, decrees, and orders. This interpretation has been continually criticized long since (cf. Becker, 1968); the outcome of this criticism is discussed later in this chapter.

State responsibility applies to all types of primary and lower secondary education, as well as to the school sector of upper secondary education, including, besides the academic institutions (*Gymnasien*), both full-time and part-time vocational schools. But at the university level the state's influence is restricted to supervision in the real sense of the word, for, within this framework, the universities are allowed considerable autonomy.

In principle, the state monopoly is limited to preschool education. Thus, it is in favor of the local authority units and the churches, as well as of private individuals and institutions. Another limitation occurs in the field of apprenticeship training at the workplace as part of the dual system of vocational education. Here the state is content with outline legislation and allows the nonstate chambers of trade, commerce, and agriculture extensive rights to regulate their forms of training.

State monopoly in the education system and political and administrative federalism do not present a paradox because each state (Länder) of the Federal Republic possesses a centralized administrative structure. Until 1989 the school system was de facto an agglomeration of eleven systems; the reunification has entailed a change only insofar as five additional Länder have been (re-)installed in the former German Democratic Republic. Certainly, the history of German education bears witness to remarkable efforts to achieve a national education.

These efforts found expression with varying degrees of intensity from the beginning of the nineteenth century and have three roots: the spiritual impetus given to educational theory in Germany in the nineteenth and twentieth centuries; the political movement at the beginning of the twentieth century which produced converging tendencies that were revived after 1945 and continue even today; and the economic expansion and its impact on people's mobility which, in turn, has been enormously reinforced by millions of refugees from Eastern Europe and (up to 1989) Eastern Germany accelerating the emergence of a "mixed" population in regard to its members' regional descent.

Not surprisingly, there is an educational public that disregards Länder boundaries and ensures that, even allowing for their important status in matters of education, a core of common concerns continues to be effective. While this core encompassing structures, syllabi, certifications, as well as the qualifications and remunerations of teachers, is acknowledged by all Länder authorities, there are wide-ranging differences concerning the transfer of these features to laws, decrees, and statutes and to their implementation in everyday practice (Frey, 1976).

The education system of the German Democratic Republic, after a short transitional period, was entirely centralized. According to Article 71(1) of the education Act of 1965, "the Ministry of Education is responsible for the uniform planning and steering of socialist education in its subordinate institutions, and it ensures the uniform school policy." This authorization included not only primary and secondary schools, but also preschool education, the whole area of vocational education, and higher education. Consequently, the universities were deprived of any autonomy. With the German reunification the Basic Law of the Federal Republic has been extended to the former GDR, and the (re-)constituted Länder are likely to orient their legal foundations to those of their Western counterparts. Therefore, the following considerations will be confined to the Western part of Germany.

The supervision of the state as a principle laid down in the Basic Law as well as in the constitutions of all the Länder, can be considered the most substantial feature of the core of common concerns. Its importance is underlined by the fact that the private school sector has always been very limited and subject to the principle of equivalence to the state sector, including certifications of students and teachers (Behr, 1988). Its recent increase does alter this statement. In all Länder the supervision of the state is exercised by the ministers of education and culture who are members of their respective state (Land) government (and, in this capacity, responsible to their Landtag) and the heads of a hierarchically structured bureaucracy, with the headteachers of the individual schools at the bottom of the ladder. The functioning of the supervision is formally guaranteed by the teachers' status as civil servants with special rights and duties. In some Länder the recent trend has been to appoint teachers with the status of employees. This, however, has affected only a small number so far, and therefore, its effect cannot yet be evaluated. The headteachers' role is also ambivalent because they must reconcile their position as the "lowest bureaucrats" with their "pedagogic ethos" which includes protecting and promoting their "pedagogic freedom" which is of greatest relevance to the initiation and realization of reforms.

According to Article 7 of the Basic Law, "a total autonomy of the individual educational institutions is excluded by constitutional law" (Horn, 1976: 43). Nevertheless, there is a growing opinion that a limited autonomy remains possible. Consequently, the Länder have passed laws and issued decrees and directives setting the framework for "autonomous" spaces. This process as a whole has been closely connected with efforts to define and describe participation at the levels of the individual schools as well as of the municipalities, districts (*Kreise*) and the Land as the holder of cultural sovereignty (*Kulturhoheit*). In this context, the recent decentralization of school administration in favor of district and municipal authorities must be mentioned. Yet, delegation of responsibilities includes mainly the "material sector": to build and maintain schools, to care about equipment (laboratories, learning aids etc.), and to appoint (and fire) nonteaching personnel (secretaries, technical workers, housekeepers, etc.). This form of regional autonomy includes responsibility for financing this sector, whereby the Land provides subsidies in cases of emergency and, above all, of exceptional expenditure.

Admittedly, a change in the Basic Law in 1969 gave the federal authority legislative powers for initial development of the university system and for collaboration in educational planning. Even in these fields the Länder remain responsible for legislation affecting any changes in normal standards and practices. Accordingly, the state-supervised nature of the education system is, in essence, to be seen in the jurisdiction of the Länder, which collaborate in various specialized bodies. With regard to educational reform, two bodies are of particular importance. One is the Standing Conference of Ministers of Education and Culture which has existed since 1948 (i.e., it was established before the foundation of the Federal Republic of Germany). Through this body the Länder governments coordinate their educational policies on the basis of their cultural sovereignty. The second body is the Federal-Länder Commission for Educational Planning and Promotion of Research which was formed in 1970 in conjunction between the Länder and federal governments. This body has gained particular importance because of its contribution to supervising educational pilot projects and to financing educational research. It has worked closely with the representatives of schools, regional administrations,and research institutions (Führ, 1989). However, even within this new framework the Länder remain formally autonomous in the initiation and development of innovations, as they do in general in regard to their competency for introducing, revising, and withdrawing syllabi and for qualifying teachers.

EDUCATIONAL EXPANSION AND STRUCTURAL REFORMS

Like other European countries, Germany has a centuries-old history of education, and the dominant principle in the organization of education was a vertical one. This organization was determined by the parallelism between the grammar schools (*Gymnasien*)—with, in Prussia, their preparatory establishments—and the elementary schools (*Volksschulen*). A boy's schooling was usually predetermined from his sixth year onward: either from a preparatory school to the grammar school, and thence to the university or, alternatively, from the elementary school to vocational training at a trade and later in industry. (Education for girls was not systematically developed until the end of the nineteenth century.) The vertical principle was clearly affected by the existence of a manifold intermediate area which, since the 1920s, has coalesced into the intermediate schools (*Realschulen*) of today. The cultural difference between town and country schools was also opposed to the vertical principle without, in fact, calling its existence into question.

The vertical principle was broken by two educational reforms, both of which were far-reaching and were joined in a historical compromise between ideal conceptions and political reality.

1. The demarcation of *Gymnasium* and university, the dividing point being the school-leaving examination qualifying for university entrance (*Abitur*).

2. The Elementary School Act of 1920, as a result of which the compulsory four-year primary school (*Grundschule*) was created as part of the remaining eight-year *Volksschule*. The abolition of the preparatory school devised (in Prussia) to secure entry into the *Gymnasium* was confirmed in 1949 by the Basic Law of the Federal Republic of Germany.

In contrast to this primary school reform, the organization of the compulsory full-time lower secondary stage, with the *Gymnasium* at one extreme and the upper stage of the *Volksschule* (classes for age groups eleven to fourteen) at the other, with the intermediate sector in the middle, remained unchanged until 1945. The way from the upper stage of the *Volksschule* led to practical vocational training (mainly in the dual system to be described later); from the intermediate sector the way led to the extended and specialist full-time vocational (technical) school sector; and from the sixth grade of the *Gymnasium* the way led to its three-year upper stage and from there to the university.

Both the ''second innovative wave'' of educational reform and the subsequent 1950s and early 1960s passed without any relevant changes. But the developments described next have affected the primary and secondary levels of the education system, mainly as a result of the third wave of the late 1960s and early 1970s.

General Education

Whereas primary education (except for the six-year course in West Berlin) has remained fixed at four years, there has been a remarkable expansion of preschool education. During the 1960s animated public debate about preschool education accelerated the construction of kindergartens and renewed people's awareness of their significance. In 1960 only around 817,000 kindergarten places were available. The number had reached 1,392,000 by 1980, and 1,440,000 by 1989 (Basic and Structural Data, 1990–1991). At the start there were places for only a third of all three to six year olds, but in 1986 the figure rose to over 80 percent of all three to six year olds—with a decline in birthrate playing a part in this development. Preschooling attracted growing public attention in the 1960s and 1970s, but interest has dwindled in recent years. Nonetheless, that does not affect the high status which kindergartens continue to enjoy.

The classes for eleven- and twelve-year-old students act as an orientation level (*Orientierungsstufe*) for all students, easing their transition into the secondary stage. Its most important function is to postpone the decision about what the student wants to do (and should do) at the age of ten plus, and thus ensures a more reliable decision. To this end, various models of external and internal differentiation have been developed, especially in mathematics and foreign languages (mainly English). According to these models, students are allocated to special achievement groups (usually three in each grade, with the possibility of transfer between them). Since its introduction at the end of the 1960s the *Orientierungsstufe* has been a controversial aspect of school policy. In the Länder governed by the Social Democrats, it has been established as an "independent" stage for all students of the respective two age groups. In contrast, the Länder governed by the Christian Democrats have tended to establish separate orientation classes with traditional secondary school types. This tendency has, of course, relativized the original concept of postponing the decision for the students' subsequent school careers. Accordingly, the proposals that allowed teachers to direct their students to the different forms of the tripartite system of secondary education came to grief. The choice of secondary school courses for the children continues to be the parents' responsibility.

The lower stage of the secondary level continues to be dominated by the tripartite system. Compared with the vast majority of education systems in Western Europe, Germany, as a whole, was in the last rank in the program to achieve comprehensiveness in the 1960s and early 1970s. Even the Länder, which were governed by Social Democrat-Liberal coalitions at that period, were not eager to push the "comprehensivising" reform along and refrained from making lower secondary education in toto comprehensive. Therefore it should not be astonishing to state that in the traditionally conservative Länder of Southern Germany, namely Bavaria, Baden-Wuerttemberg and Rhineland-Palatinate, the few comprehensive schools (*Gesamtschulen*) that were established never lost their status as experimental schools. On the other hand, the belief in the irreversible nature of the traditional tripartite system (with selective *Gymnasien* and *Realschulen*, and nonselective secondary modern schools/*Hauptschulen*) somehow lost ground in that period. This explains why even conservative politicians, as well as tradition-oriented educationists, had difficulty formulating appropriate arguments against the need for structural reforms in favor of comprehensivization in lower secondary education.

In the 1980s, the pendulum swung back toward consolidation or even restoration of the tripartite system. In Southern Germany most of the few comprehensive schools were dissolved. In the rest of West Germany, the general development has been rather wavelike, caused in particular by several changes of party majorities and, consequently, governments. Compared to the early 1970s, even in the Länder ruled by Social Democrats, we cannot speak of clear strategies—the more so as the majority of the population (in all Länder) seems to continue favoring the tripartite system, although the arguments are differently oriented and need to be explained by the following considerations.

The secondary modern school (*Hauptschule*), as an independent type, emerged from the upper stage of the former *Volksschule* in the 1950s. Its official function is to prepare its students for vocational training in the dual system: for work in the lower or intermediate range of public service (combined with training which includes attendance at a part-time vocational school; or for attendance at a full-time vocational (technical) school. In spite of the Länder authorities' attempts, the *Hauptschule* has reached a critical point as far as its achievement levels and socials status are concerned. Its official function can be fulfilled, more or less, only in rural areas. In towns it finds it increasingly difficult to compete with the expanding *Realschulen* and *Gymnasien*. The *Hauptschule* is in constant danger of declining into a school for "leftovers," that is, one that is intended for boys and girls of low achievement and also for the majority of children of migrant workers.

Between the selective *Gymnasium* and the nonselective *Hauptschule*, the *Realschule* has not only established itself but also, during the last thirty years, has expanded as an alternative selective institution. It is different from the traditional *Hauptschule* in offering an additional year (age fifteen–sixteen) and a wider range of subjects (e.g., English as a compulsory and French as an optional foreign language). Therefore, at the end of its course the way is open to full-time vocational training (in advanced technical schools) and also to the dual system as well as to the upper stage of the *Gymnasium*. For the latter purpose, special classes have been organized in many *Gymnasien*.

The *Gymnasium* has probably undergone the greatest changes during recent decades. From a basically elitist school with relatively strict selectivity, it has become a school for students of all strata of the population. These students are young people who are planning to go to university or, at least, to complete the medium stage (to age sixteen plus). In earlier times the *Gymnasium* was criticized for its selectivity, which was geared to social factors. This is not the case today, or, at least, not to the same extent. What continues to be a matter of dispute is the gearing of all school work and subjects to university entrance. In the late 1960s and 1970s, that is, at the crest of the third wave the *Gymnasium* was often regarded as out of date, and its position in the field of secondary education was attacked, particularly in connection with efforts to introduce comprehensive schools (as the monopolizing type of compulsory secondary schools). By contrast, in recent years, the reputation of the *Gymnasium* has again risen among many of the population—admittedly nowadays as an institution through which many rise, and not, as in earlier days, through which only a few could do so. The *Gymnasium*'s changed position can also be seen in the increasing number of students who leave at sixteen plus to begin vocational training in the dual system, or what is more frequently the case, to begin a full-time course of technical training. For such students the *Gymnasium* fulfills the same educational function as the *Realschule*.

The three-year upper stage of the *Gymnasium* covers the age groups seventeen to nineteen. In 1976 this course was reorganized to become the so-called Reformer Upper Stage Course, in accordance with the decision of the Standing Conference of Ministers of Education and Culture of 1972. Instead of the traditional system of teaching, in which the subjects were taught in self-contained class groups (as continues to happen in all types of lower secondary education including the lower and medium stages of the *Gymnasium*), a course system was established. Like the *Gymnasium* as a whole, the Reformed Upper Stage Course reflects a basic dissension insofar as it has not expressly adjusted to its changed function in respect to the requirements of the employment system. In this connection we may state that, in addition to its traditional function of preparing its students for the university, for an increasing number of students the *Gymnasium* has become a course that leads to vocational training (of the intermediate level) or even directly to a job in the employment system. In spite of these far-reaching internal changes the Reformed Upper Stage Course has also retained the traditional concept of the *Gymnasium*, according to which its function is defined solely as being preparatory to the university.

In summary, the general education sector, from the preschool to the upper secondary level, obtained its overall shape during the 1970s, whereby the above-mentioned steps toward consolidation covering the events of the late 1970s and 1980s must also be taken into account. In the German Democratic Republic, on the other hand, the period of its large-scale reforms, which aimed at establishing a socialist education system, culminated in the Education Act of 1965. The act focused on stabilizing the compulsory Ten-Year General Polytechnic Secondary School (*Zehnklassige Allgemeinbildende Polytechnische Oberschule*) as the center of an integrated education system beginning at the preschool stage (with crèche and kindergarten) and ending at the higher and adult education level. Special mention has to be made of the Extended Secondary School (*Erweiterte Oberschule*), that is, the two-year type of upper secondary education that was built on a highly selective admission procedure and established as a school with the distinct function of preparing youngsters for studies at universities and other higher education institutions.

Vocational Education

In contrast to the general education sector which differed markedly in the two former German education systems, the differences in the vocational educational sector have been less pronounced. This phenomenon can be attributed to the historical fact that both West and East Germany accepted and developed the former German vocational education system which it had adopted at the beginning of this century. This observation is true both of the compact sector in full-time technical schools and of the dual system. This sector of vocational education has recently attracted great attention in many countries of the world. It is based on the principle that until the age of eighteen all boys and girls not in full-time attendance at the upper stage of secondary school (whether for general or vocational education) are obliged to attend part-time vocational schools for the purpose of enriching their apprenticeship training in the workplace.

Below the common acceptance of the German "inheritance," both Germanies developed their own particularities with regard to legal and administrative allocations. While the dual system in the GDR had been the full responsibility of the centralized state authorities, the regulations in the West German Länder are highly complicated owing to the division of competences between federal and Länder authorities on the one hand and between state and employment agencies on the other.

Germany's vocational education presents a highly differentiated system that consists of technical schools of various types and a multiplicity of specialist courses. Attendance at an advanced technical school can also lead to a general secondary school-leaving certificate (*Abitur*) or a specialist one, or to the right of admission to a technical university. In West Germany in the early 1970s, some reformers, seeking to merge general and vocational education, demanded that integrated forms be developed. Their aim was to achieve cooperation between, or even amalgamation of the top grades of, *Gymnasium* and full-time vocational education. Such moves have still not gotten beyond the experimental stage. In the German Democratic Republic, however, comparable efforts led to the establishment of a sector called vocational education with Abitur (*Berufsausbildung mit Abitur*) as a special type existing alongside the *Erweiterte Oberschule*.

In Germany the dual system, like full-time vocational education, can be considered part of the upper secondary level. In the same way it presents a highly differentiated system. Efforts to modernize it as a whole have in recent years included (1) a training organized in stages starting with a first year of apprenticeship as a period of basic training when fundamental knowledge and skills over a wide range are given; and (2) significant reductions of the specializations of training which have responded to the increasingly important principles of mobility and adaptation to changing work conditions.

In both German systems in the area of full-time schooling and, in particular, in the dual system, innovative approaches had to cope with the rapidly changing circumstances of the employment market and the need to find an equilibrium between short-term expectations and middle-term (or long-term) predictions. The West German variation was more successful, because the bureaucratized rigidity of economic planification in the German Democratic Republic proved obstructive to the adjustment requirements of the labor market. In West Germany the big firms developed well-functioning vocational training schemes, whereas small firms and particularly crafts find it more difficult to keep pace with modernization needs. An innovative approach can be observed in the establishment of joint workshops organized by several firms (Mitter, 1987).

CURRICULAR REFORMS

Our comments here are restricted to the curricular issues relating to the lower and secondary general education level. Curricular concepts and programs in Germany have always emphasized the idea reflecting the philosophy of general education, traced back to Wilhelm von Humboldt. Here, too, let us first look for a brief measure of agreement with the past. In all schools that offer a general education, certain specific practices existed. The standards of higher scientific education in the *Gymnasium* or popular education in the elementary school were indeed strictly distinct from each other in the vertical system. The claim that the system transmitted to the students a core of curricular content which society and state regarded as compulsory, nevertheless applied to all children and young persons. Moreover, this philosophy was supported by the assumption that acquiring the core curriculum was essential to the students' personality development, because it strengthened both the cognitive and emotional aspects of human personality.

Identifying the content of the core curriculum in detail has always been controversial. Apart from the fundamental difference between higher scientific education and popular education, one has to take into primary account the replacement of von Humboldt's focus on the students' acquisition of the genuine "core" (namely Greek and Latin language and literature linked with history and mathematics) by a growing tendency toward encyclopedism (McLean, 1990). Once this change had taken place, a good deal of arbitrariness made itself felt in determining the components of the curriculum in practical terms. This is common knowledge to theoreticians and historians of education. They encounter this set of problems particularly when they see obsolete syllabus content in school subjects persisting on the one hand, and the struggle to put into practice new and legitimate claims on the other. An example of the complexity of this problem is the present-day discussion of the value of teaching Latin in the *Gymnasien*.

The general education core of subjects always included German, arithmetic or mathematics, natural and social sciences in *Gymnasien* (or natural study and local history and geography in intermediate and elementary schools), as well as religious knowledge (as related to the doctrines represented by the Christian denominations). Any forms of specialization were placed in a lower category, being regarded as essentially a matter for vocational education. In secondary education, at least one foreign language was part of the core curriculum. As a rule, there were two, possibly even three and, indeed, classical and modern languages in various combinations, the major position moving from Latin to English by the beginning of the twentieth century.

This fundamental situation has remained unchanged to this day, insofar as the primary school and the lower stage of the secondary school are concerned. The education system of the former GDR, emphasizing its appreciation of socialist general education and allocating more than 90 percent of the timetables to mandatory subject matter, can be placed nearer the traditional German philosophy than the West German variant which came out of the reforms of the late 1960s and early 1970s. West German curricula are the responsibility of the Länder authorities which have issued syllabi with the tendency to reduce "frame guidelines" (*Rahmenrichtlinien*) with even more choice for the individual schools and teachers. In contrast, the Curriculum Network (*Lehrplanwerk*) of the GDR was clearly characterized by an arrangement of close mandatory prescriptions. In this connection one is reminded of the different ranges concerning the power and competency of the school inspectorates. Their supervisory competitions were wide ranging in the GDR compared to the current West German trend toward strengthening their advisory tasks.

On the whole in both German systems, the core curricula were extended during the past four decades. First, this is true of the field of social and political education where, of course, the divergences are sharpest. Whereas the West German variant has been based on democratic principles comparable to the social studies concept in the United States, "civics" (*Staatsbürgerkunde*) in the GDR was rigidly subjected to the Marxist-Leninist ideology.

Second, in the educational field covering the working world, the introduction of polytechnic education and training as a school subject and as a cross-disciplinary learning area was one of the GDR's most significant educational innovations after 1960. As already mentioned, this curricular field focused on the four upper grades of the Ten-Year General Education Polytechnic Secondary School and continued in the Extended Secondary School under the category scientific-practical work. Polytechnic education and training was a curricular field that was mandatory for the uniform school system as a whole. On the other hand, the subject *Arbeitslehre* (teaching about work) which is taught in the Western Länder has been, in principle, constricted to the nonselective *Hauptschule*.

Third, until now the diversified development for foreign language teaching has mirrored the supra- and international ties of the two Germanies. In particular, this is true of the first foreign language which appears in the syllabi mainly from the fifth grade upward. While in the GDR Russian was mandatory in all schools, in the Western Länder, as a rule, English was the first foreign language, with a minor group of schools offering Latin or French as alternatives.

All curricular reforms that have taken place in Germany over the last forty years have focused on the traditional German philosophy of the broad core curriculum. Within this framework, efforts were made in both Eastern and Western systems to build bridges between the hitherto strictly segmented syllabi whose subjects were derived from the academic disciplines of the universities. In several West German Länder, steps aimed at such a linkage pertained to the area of social studies composed of history, geography, and sociology. Moreover, pilot projects were launched in the natural sciences to promote interdisciplinary liaisons among physics, chemistry, and biology. These attempts have more or less stagnated in the recent period of consolidation.

In the GDR students in the extended secondary school had to take ten mandatory subjects throughout the two-year course up to the final *Abitur* examination (Baske, 1990). Contrary to this policy, the West German *Gymnasien* were strongly affected by the introduction of the Reformed Upper Stage during the 1970s. Departing from the traditional system of instruction whereby subjects were taught in self-contained classes according to the age-group criterion, it substituted a system of course instruction. Requirements for individual subjects or groups of subjects remained, but students were given ample opportunities to choose the subjects they wanted and to specialize within an extended range of available subjects (Mitter, 1987).

With regard to the traditional *Gymnasium*, the reform of 1977 has been of great significance in two respects:

1. Compared with the compactness of the traditional syllabi which the students were required to take, though in three different combinations, four major and eleven minor subjects up to the *Abitur*, the "reformed" syllabi were characterized by a significant reduction to two major and approximately six minor subjects. American observers will certainly notice that the core curriculum has been maintained rather widely. Nonetheless, the reform of the upper stage has been regarded as a break in the history of the *Gymnasium*.

2. The second component of the reform has proven to be even more revolutionary. While in the previous system there had been a consensus that in each combination the group of major subjects had to consist of German, mathematics, and one foreign language, the reform opened the door to the formal equality of all subjects.

From its beginning, however, the Reformed Gymnasium Upper Stage was faced with criticism from various sides. During the 1980s, the debate widened into fundamental controversies about the extent of the mandatory core curriculum and the range of the options to be given the students. Beyond the issue of defining the concept of general education, the requirements in single subjects were debated. For example, in German-language studies, the question was raised whether, or to what extent, traditional literature studies should be replaced by analyses of actual texts written in everyday style, such as newspapers or magazines. As regards literature studies as such, conflicts arose with regard to the proportion between mandatory and optional subject matter. Here the freedom of choice (by the individual teacher, the whole team of subject specialists or, in participatory pilot projects, also the students) created an additional item in the debate.

The division of the German literature curriculum into mandatory and optional units has existed for decades, being traceable to the first innovative wave. Nevertheless, until the reforms of the late 1960s and early 1970s, the universal consensus was that certain works of the German classics, in particular Goethe's *Faust*, were a mandatory component of the German literature curriculum. Precisely the abandonment of this consensus captured the attention of policymakers and public alike. Their respective conflicts crystallized into the controversial appraisal of the school's duty to impart the classics. Opponents of the conventional view argued that the choice of texts and works must not be slanted toward traditional concepts, but rather should be derived from issues and problems now affecting students' minds and perspectives.

In the late 1980s controversies increasingly affected the educational policies of the big political parties and, consequently, their representatives in the Länder governments, above all the ministers of education and culture. Whereas the governments formed by the Social Democrats advocated the state of affairs that had been achieved in the 1970s, their Christian Democrat counterparts stood for its modification. After several meetings, the Standing Conference of Ministers of Education and Culture came to an agreement in 1987 which, in principle, confirmed the essentials of the Reformed Gymnasium Upper Stage but reintroduced the central position of German, foreign languages, and mathematics as the major subjects to be taught and certified (Führ, 1989).

THE STATUS AND FUNCTIONS OF UNIVERSITIES

In both Germanies the universities underwent considerable changes during the past four decades. While these changes began in the GDR as early as the 1950s, the reforms in West Germany were one of the indirect outcomes of the student movement of the late 1960s and the third wave in general. The changes concerned particularly the right to attend university and their internal organization (participation in certain decision-making processes by assistants, students, and members of the nonacademic personnel; closing down traditional faculties in favor of departmental structures; introducing the presidential system instead of the traditional rectorial one, etc.). The 1980s achieved a degree of stabilization at this level too. On the other hand, the West German universities have inherited and continued the traditional confrontation between their profession-oriented and personality-developing functions. Harmonizing these two functions has created many problems for research and teaching in the past two decades, caused by the rapid expansion from the former elite to today's mass universities and polytechnics (*Fachhochschulen*).

Finally, the universities continue to be burdened with an ever-growing number of students which long ago passed the 1 million mark (Basic and Structural Data 1990–1991). It seems unlikely that the crisis which this has caused will diminish during the last decade of the twentieth century. This crucial issue must be particularly related to the legal position according to which, in the "old" Federal Republic of Germany as well as now also in the newly established Länder in East Germany, admission to university education is regarded as a fundamental right. In a number of disciplines, such as medicine, restrictions on admissions have been introduced (in the shape of regulations imposing fixed numbers). Quite apart from the fact that, in the disciplines concerned, conditions of study are not even improved by these regulations, these fixed numbers merely force the students to apply for admission to other fields of study, which thereby become overcrowded too. Among the fields of study that in recent years have attracted financial grants and the establishment of chairs are communication and information studies in particular. This reorientation has occurred in many countries at the expense of the humanities and the social sciences.

The universities in the GDR had not been affected by any expansion, because the admission quota had always been retained, that is, at 10 percent of the age group against 25 percent in West Germany at the end of the 1980s (Köhler and Schreier, 1990). Yet, as regards its total societal function, the whole area of higher education had undergone radical internal changes toward professionalization. This resulted in the predominance of industry-oriented research and the transformation of most of the fundamental research to extra-university tradition which has continued to exist in the universities of West Germany, namely, built on the linkage of teaching and research.

PEDAGOGIC REFORMS

Pedagogic reforms in both Germanies were significantly influenced by the sociopolitical framework of the education systems. Above all, we must consider the ties of the curricula to the overarching philosophical and political norms in both Germanies, which mirror basic ideas about the education and socialization of youth and, beyond that, about the relation between individual and society. Comparative indicators are offered by the extent to which the teacher is conceded the choice of methods (linked with the range of freedom in curricular decision making, e.g., in the field of literature), as well as by the methodic approaches as such. Here the contrasting positions are represented by receptive learning and authoritarian teaching and by communicative teaching and learning which can be traced back to the big reform movement of the 1920s (*Reformpädagogik*). Generally, the education systems of the two Germanies embodied the contrast between these two fundamental methodic models.

In-depth comparison leads to more complex insights. First, as in other countries, the everyday teaching and learning practice has never entirely abandoned the traditional schooling outlined earlier in this chapter. Second, the *Reformpädagogik* gave the initial impulse for all the pedagogic reforms of the twentieth century. Therefore, the contrasting position of the two German education systems can be best investigated by asking whether and how the heritage of the *Reform-pädagogik* was accepted and pursued after its suppression during the Nazi period.

In West Germany this heritage has never been excluded from either experimental or everyday practice. It is precisely the *Reformpädagogik*'s emphasis on pedagogy at the micro-level of the classroom against the somewhat illusive confidence in the short-term effects of large-scale reforms dominating the third innovative wave that has stimulated the recent "rediscovery" of this heritage. While the macro-level of structures and curricula has been characterized by the aforementioned consolidation, the call for quality in the classroom, school ethos, and, in general, for more pedagogy has awakened widespread response in the form of pilot projects and other innovative activities.

This movement has been supported by the delegation of pedagogic freedom to individual schools and, in particular, to individual teachers and teaching teams. In several Länder this policy has been enacted by special decrees reducing the range of the mandatory syllabi in favor of optional choice. In this connection we should consider that in Germany this kind of pedagogic freedom focused on the arrangement of experimental lessons in the sciences, the interpretation of literary works and historical events, the organization of extramural activities, and, finally, the choice of instruction methods in general. Pedagogic freedom has a long history, though it was mainly reserved for the *Gymnasium* teacher before the first innovative wave. Of course, it has always prospered under the favorable conditions of an open school climate and liberal school inspectorates. Furthermore, in the Länder North to the Main, the teacher's pedagogic freedom at the stage of upper secondary education has been supported by his or her traditional function as an examiner in the *Abitur*. The individual teacher examines his or her students in the oral part of this important examination and in the submission of three topics to be chosen by the minister for the examination papers. The assessment of the examination papers is again the responsibility of the individual students' subject teacher. In Southern Germany (Bavaria, Baden-Wuerttemberg, Rhineland-Palatinate), this competency has been constricted by the fact that, according to the Napoleonic tradition, the minister prescribes the topics of the examination papers. However, in these Länder the oral examinations are also the individual teachers' responsibility.

In the post–World War II period the *Reformpädagogik* exerted some influence in the Soviet zone too, because a few of its proponents were given the opportunity to reactivate their experiences from the Weimar period in order to reconstruct the education system. This period of relative liberalism came to a definitive end with the foundation of the GDR and the total subjection of education (with its theoretical and practical components) to the Soviet model, and that just at the climax of its Stalinist variation. The radicality of this pervasion determined pedagogy in the GDR throughout the four decades of its existence. Yet, during the 1980s one could observe some tentative steps toward more individualization and flexibility and even toward communicative teaching and learning (Anweiler, 1988; Neuner,

1989). Whether these modest steps might have led to genuine pedagogic reforms remains a question that recent historical events have forever muted.

MINORITY GROUPS AND WOMEN

This chapter deals with educational reform as it affects the great majority of youth in Germany. The special concerns of the particularly advantaged or disadvantaged have not been taken into special consideration. This does not mean that the problems concerning mass education do not affect the peculiar provisions for minorities to a certain extent. Nevertheless, for the sake of completeness, some remarks should be devoted to these "outsiders" of the system.

As regards particularly advantaged students, we have to think, above all, about highly talented youngsters. The special issues concerning their education and training have been neglected during the past decades. The reason why is to be seen in the prevailing trend toward achieving equity of opportunity and providing educational facilities for disadvantaged groups. During recent years, however, the question of how to provide special opportunities for highly talented youngsters has come up and has been addressed in publications, conferences, and pilot projects in schools. In West Germany educationists as well as the majority of politicians hold that such provisions should be part of the tasks of the ordinary schools and should not be sought in separate institutions. In contrast, the GDR established so-called specialized schools for highly talented youngsters in the fields of mathematics, sciences, and foreign languages as well as in music and physical education.

Among disadvantaged youngsters we must distinguish between the physically and mentally handicapped, and the migrants' children. The care of handicapped youngsters in special institutions throughout Germany has reached a fairly high standard, including vocational education. The training and schooling efforts are compensated by legal measures that encouraged firms, or even legally obliged them, to reserve a certain number of jobs for handicapped people. This specific problem has in no way been satisfactorily solved, and improvements in the education system are still needed, whereby current projects in West German schools dealing with the "integration" of handicapped youngsters into ordinary classes attract particular attention. The GDR had no such projects at all. Yet, compared to efforts in other countries, such as Sweden, Italy and the United States, West Germany has not proved to be stimulating in this field either, which continues to be dominated by those who advocate separate institutionalization.

Special provisions are also required for the migrants' children in Germany. The GDR did not have to cope with this problem, since its migrants (mainly from Vietnam) were not given the chance to bring their families. Although the shortcomings are still enormous, efforts are being made to help and encourage these students, for instance, by offering in-service training activities to operating teachers, and to develop teaching in the relevant native language as well as in

German. In addition, agreements by treaty have been made with some countries (e.g., Italy and Greece) to send appropriate native teachers to Germany for a specified period. For upper secondary education in particular, one has to take into account the special provision in the dual system regarding language teaching and remedial care for youngsters who have not reached formal certification during compulsory education because they arrived in Germany after the age of six. Furthermore, measures aimed at encouraging youngsters to continue their education at the *Realschule* or *Gymnasium* have led to promising results. This encouragement has been, among other efforts, realized by giving students the opportunity to choose their mother tongue as one of the required "foreign" languages. As a corollary of decreasing enrollments, some *Gymnasien*, especially in urban areas, have organized specific courses for migrants' children, thus attracting this group as a whole. In principle, however, all these efforts are complicated by the political and legal framework according to which non-German children (and their parents) do not have German citizenship. Consequently, tension persists between the demands for integration and reintegration (i.e., return to the countries of origin).

As regards the education of women and girls, analysis of enrollment ratios indicates increasing numbers throughout Germany, particularly at secondary education levels (Köhler and Schreier, 1990). In this respect we may speak of continuous progress. However, here too the situation is still unsatisfactory. Special educational effort is required to overcome the underrepresentation of women in a great number of vocational training tracks, particularly in technology and engineering. This equity continues into employment, where the traditional attitudes of employers to females and of females about themselves reinforce each other. Moreover, the quantitative enrollment and success of girls in secondary and in higher education as well do not mean that they receive the instruction and care they especially need. Inquiries have shown that in instruction patterns coeducational schools often follow traditional styles that have been developed solely according to male needs and desires. Educationists have reacted by advocating the partial segregation of boys and girls with regard to the instruction of certain subjects, above all mathematics and social sciences, especially for the age groups thirteen to seventeen. The outcomes of respective pilot projects are not yet available, but evidently they are not aimed at a return to traditional segregation. Their advocates represent a rather wide spectrum of opinions and approaches, ranging from conservative to feminist.

This reference to the recent "revision" of unlimited "coeducationalism" was confined to West Germany. The GDR had made considerable progress with regard to increasing the proportions of women in technical occupations. Despite all these efforts, taken as a whole, women in the GDR did not have any significant advantage over women in the Western Länder. A fundamental reason is to be found in the persisting religious and ideological attitudes rooted in society. Reforms in this area demand permanent efforts, although the progress reached in the whole of Germany should not be underestimated.

PROSPECTS AFTER GERMAN REUNIFICATION

German reunification took place on October 3, 1990, and was formally based on the "accession" of the German Democratic Republic to the Federal Republic of Germany, according to Article 23 of its Basic Law. Consequently, responsibility for the education system has become the prerogative of the (reconstituted) five Länder and the reunified Land Berlin. As of February 1991, no legal provisions concerning educational structures have been made. However, radical changes have been initiated in the curricular area, particularly the humanities and social sciences, which have been, more or less, adapted to West German "examples." The near future is likely to be characterized by the inclusion of the East German Länder into the controversial deliberations regarding "comprehensive schools versus tripartite system."

Beyond the structural and curricular areas, schools in East Germany are today facing numerous pedagogical challenges. Above all, they must cope with the attitudes that have survived the collapse of the Marxist-Leninist ideology. In particular, students must learn how to overcome their internalized shyness of making choices and decisions. These challenges are exacerbated by the fact that the problems must be solved with thousands of teachers who had been loyal executors of the hitherto official doctrines. Of course, teacher education is highly involved in the reeducation process. At the end of 1990 all the departments and faculties of education at the East German universities were dissolved and replaced by newly organized units in the course of 1991, and the former professors and lecturers were given the chance to apply for reappointment. In short, East Germany is presenting itself as a huge laboratory for educational reform. It seems that the overall trend toward adjustment to the West German counterpart will dominate the near future. Whether the assets of the former GDR system will be thoroughly evaluated, as would be beneficial for the whole of Germany, remains open. In particular, they refer to the experiences the GDR has gained in the field of polytechnic education, although the theoretical concept, as well as its implementation, needs to be reconsidered. The teaching of Russian must also be taken into special account in view of the increasing need of the areas of economy, science, and culture for people with competence in Russian.

Since the current debate and policy in Eastern Germany mirrors issues of an all-European and even global range, education in West Germany will hardly be left unaffected. Although structural and curricular issues were handled quite smoothly in the late 1970s and 1980s, some symptoms signalling the abandonment of this "stability" were apparent. Here the all-German situation may operate as a stimulating and reinforcing incentive. In this connection, the following considerations can serve as examples (cf. Mitter, 1990).

First, the "revision" of the large-scale reforms that were initiated and implemented by the third innovative wave must not be simplistically labeled political "conservatism." The search for an explanation must be more open and multi-faceted. The observer should take into special account that conservatives, but also liberals and even Social Democrats, prefer to maintain or reestablish separate (parallel) schools past the lower secondary level. The renaissance of the *Gymnasium* as a concomitant of the recent trend toward decomprehensivizing secondary education by (re)stabilizing the traditional tripartite system has been affected by the growing awareness of the importance of new technologies for content, method, process, and achievement in learning. Consequently, an increasing appreciation of excellence and selection has emerged instead of equity and support (which reaches its top in the promotion of highly gifted youngsters). Yet, the widespread acceptance of the link between excellence and aversion against separate schools for highly talented students prevents the pendulum from swinging too far toward disregarding equity.

Second, Germany is characterized by a de facto revival of the *Gymnasium* and, consequently, by a declining interest in the "comprehensive" concept, let alone its implementation. Nonetheless, we should not ignore the remarkable number of multifarious pilot projects and innovative activities within the traditional school type. We can even point out that the principals and teaching staffs of *Gymnasien* have fewer scruples in such engagements, because the existence of their schools as such, contrary to that of comprehensive schools (*Gesamtschulen*), is not endangered or contested. These pilot projects help strengthen the move toward internal school reforms at all levels of the education system. Their goals are defined mainly as quality in education and school ethos (climate, chemistry).

Third, a manifest drive among parents and the public in general has crystallized into changing conceptions of schools from governmental institutions to service agencies. For the time being, public expectations indicate a significant preference for the tripartite system. In a growing number of places, however, principals and teachers of comprehensive schools have succeeded in making their social reputation and in consolidating their positions in and beyond their communities. This trend, taken as a whole, signals changes in public attitudes, tending to more flexibility on the one hand and to more democratization on the other. Among the social groups that made known their expectations and demands, we must not forget the youngsters themselves who, compared to their "ancestors," seem to have learned much more how to express their attitudes and aspirations, including critical judgments and utterances. In this respect, students attending *Gymnasien* today have little in common with those of previous generations.

The apparent consolidation that has resulted from the "revision of the reform" in the Western Länder of the Federal Republic of Germany is far from attaining that kind of "stabilization" that some people and, particularly, politicians may have dreamed of in the early and middle 1980s. This observation justifies the overall prediction that hopes for a fourth innovative wave may not end in an academic debate, but may be translated into political and pedagogic action. The reunification of Germany, the need to integrate the "new minorities," and the march toward the single market and toward a "wider Europe" are likely to reinforce this challenge.

REFERENCES

Anweiler, Oskar. 1988. *Schulpolitik and Schulsystem in der DDR*. Opladen: Leske and Budrich.

————. 1990. "Grundzüge der Bildungspolitik und der Entwicklung des Bildungswesens seit 1945." In *Vergleich von Bildung und Erziehung in der Bundesrepublik Deutschland und der Deutschen Demokratischen Republik*, ed. O. Anweiler et al. Cologne: Verlag Wissenschaft und Politik, Chap. II.1.

————, and Arthur Hearnden, ed. 1983. *From Secondary to Higher Education*. Cologne, Wien: Böhlau.

Basic and Structural Data. 1990–1991. *Education Statistics for the Federal Republic of Germany*. Bonn: Federal Ministry of Education and Science.

Baske, Siegfried. 1990. "Die Erweiterte Oberschule in der DDR." In *Vergleich von Bildung und Erziehung in der Bundesrepublik Deutschland und der Deutschen Demokratischen Republik*, ed. O. Anweiler et al. Cologne: Verlag Wissenschaft und Politik, Chap. III.2.2.2.

Becker, Hellmut. 1968. *Quantität und Qualität. Grundfragen der Bildungspolitik*. 2nd ed. Freiburg i.Br.: Rombach.

Behr, Michael. 1988. *Freie Schulen und Internate. Pädagogische Programme und rechtliche Stellung*. Dusseldorf: Econ.

Blankertz, Herwig. 1982. *Die Geschichte der Pädagogik von der Aufklärung bis zur Gegenwart*. Wetzlar: Büchse der Pandora.

Frey, Kurt. 1976. *Konstruktiver Förderalismus. Gesammelte kulturpolitsche Beiträge 1948–1975*. Weinheim, Basel: Beltz.

Friedeburg, Ludwig von. 1989. *Bildungsreform in Deutschland. Geschichte und gesellschaftlicher Widerspruch*. Frankfurt am Main: Suhrkamp.

Führ, Christoph. 1989. *Schools and Institutions of Higher Education in the Federal Republic of Germany*. Bonn: Inter Nationes.

Hearnden, Arthur. 1974. *Education in the Two Germanies*. Oxford: Blackwell.

Horn, Peter. 1976. *Partizipation und Schulverwaltungsstruktur*. Cologne, Berlin, Bonn, Munich: Carl Heymann.

Köhler, Helmut, and Gerhard Schreier. 1990. "Statistische Daten zum Bildungswesen." In *Vergleich von Bildung und Erziehung in der Bundesrepublik Deutschland und der Demokratischen Republik*, ed. O. Anweiler et al. Cologne: Verlag Wissenschaft und Politik, Chap. II.5.

Leschinsky, Achim, and Karl-Ulrich Mayer, ed., 1990. *The Comprehensive School Experiment Revisited: Evidence from Western Europe*. Frankfurt am Main, Bern, New York, Paris: Peter Lang.

McLean, Martin. 1990. *Britain and a Single Market Europe. Prospects for a Common School Curriculum*. London: Kogan Page.

Max Planck Institute for Human Development and Education. 1983. *Between Elite and Mass Education. Education in the Federal Republic of Germany*. Albany: State University of New York Press.

Mitter, Wolfgang. 1986. "Continuity and Change—A Basic Question for German Education." *Education* 33:7–23.

————. 1987. *The Organisation and Content of Studies at the Post-secondary Level. Country study: Germany*. Paris: OECD (OECD Educational Monographs 7569).

————. 1989. "Recent Trends in Educational Policies in the Federal Republic of Germany." In *Teachers' Expectations and Teaching Reality*, ed. W. Tulasiewicz and A. Adams. London, New York: Routledge.

———. 1990. "Educational Reform in West and and East Germany in European Perspective." *Oxford Review of Education* 16:333–341.

Neuner, G. 1989. *Allgemeinbildung. Konzeption–Inhalt–Prozeβ*. Berlin: Volk und Wissen.

Oehler, Ch. 1989. *Geschichte des Hochschulwesens in der Bundesrepublik Deutschland*. Frankfurt, New York: Campus.

Picht, Georg. 1964. *Die deutsche Bildungskatastrophe. Analyse und Dokumentation*. Freiburg: Walter.

Robinsohn, Saul. 1975. *Bildungsreform als Revision des Curriculum*. 5th ed. Neuwied: Luchterhand.

Waterkamp, Dietmer. 1987. *Handbuch zum Bildungswesen der DDR*. Berlin: Verlag Arno Spitz.

Weishaupt, Horst, et al. 1988. *Perspektiven des Bildungswesens in der Bundesrepublik Deutschland. Rahmenbedingungen, Problemlagen, Lösungsstrategien*. Baden-Baden: Nomos.

12

GREAT BRITAIN

Geoffrey Walford

In Great Britain, the 1980s will be remembered as a decade of major changes within education. The decade saw a series of reforming education acts that culminated in the Education Reform Act of 1988. This act fundamentally restructured the organization and content of education in schools, colleges, and universities and will come to be seen as a milestone in the history of British education. This chapter describes and examines the nature of the changes made to schools and schooling during the 1980s, and begins to assess their equity effects in terms of social class, gender and ethnic group differences. The first step toward such a discussion, however, must be to set these reforms in their political, social, and historic context.

THE DEVELOPMENT OF SCHOOLING IN GREAT BRITAIN

Throughout much of its development, British education has reflected and perpetuated inequalities of gender, class, and ethnic group. Before the nineteenth century, the education of children was considered to be the private affair of parents. All schools were private schools, with differential provision according to social class and gender—private tutors or grammar schools for those with sufficient means, and dame schools, charity schools, or nothing at all for the poor. As urbanization and industrialization progressed, the sometimes contradictory drives of philanthropy, religious conviction, and the practical need for a better educated and disciplined workforce led to the gradual expansion of a network of charity schools for the poor. Schooling for the bulk of the population developed gradually and unevenly, and was largely under the control of a diversity of religiously based organizations (Walford, 1990a).

Even at this early stage of development, there were differences between England and Wales and Scotland, and this remains true today. Government changes to education in Scotland require separate legislation and, as the political complexities of Scotland differ markedly from those of England and Wales, the parallel legislation is often far from identical (Anderson, 1983; Scotland, 1969; Walford, 1989). Unfortunately, lack of space in this chapter necessitates that we limit most of the discussion to England and Wales.

Early attempts during the nineteenth century to establish a national education system for all children in England and Wales met with opposition from the churches—the Church of England wanted overall control of any new system, while, not surprisingly, the Roman Catholic and other Protestant churches objected. Instead, in 1833, when the government of the day made the first of many annual grants to schools, it was paid to the two main religious providers of schooling at the time—the National Society for Promoting the Education of the Poor and the British Foreign School Society. Grants to these charity schools grew rapidly so that by 1858 government established an Education Department to control this funding. This was followed by a series of three commissions into educational provision, each commission—Clarendon, Taunton, and Newcastle—largely concentrating on arrangements for a particular social class. The 1870 Education Act which followed led to the beginnings of a national system, with the government establishing its own elementary schools to fill the gaps in church and charity provision. The problem of Church of England control was avoided by providing for the continued existence of voluntary church schools alongside the state—maintained schools. This compromise is at the heart of the dual system that still exists today, whereby what are now called county schools are under the control of Local Education Authorities (LEAs), while the church voluntary-aided schools remain in ownership of the church denominations but are heavily funded by the state through the LEAs.

Although there were several intervening education acts, the 1944 Education Act led to the next significant restructuring of the developing system. Essentially, it established a national education system for England and Wales which was locally administered and which was part of an integrated public service welfare state (Finch, 1984; Shipman, 1984). It provided for free education for all children and made secondary education a distinct stage for all children. Most of the remaining church schools were further integrated into the state-maintained system through a system of voluntary-aided or voluntary-controlled schools leaving, by 1951, only some 9.2 percent of the school-age population in private schools (Halsey, Heath, and Ridge, 1984). The 1944 act stated that provision for older children was to be made according to "age, ability, and aptitude," but did not stipulate whether this was to be in comprehensive schools or in separate schools that selected according to ability and achievement. In practice, different LEAs chose their own scheme, but most initially followed the ideas of the earlier Norwood and Spens reports which argued for separate provision for three types of pupil in grammar, technical, and secondary modern schools.

The only element of the curriculum to be made compulsory in all state-maintained schools was that of religious education which was explicitly included in the 1944 act as part of the compromise with the churches. The three different types of school that made up the tripartite system did, however, develop their own curricular emphases, with greater "practical" teaching in the secondary modern and technical schools, while the grammar schools retained their academic curriculum designed for university entry. There were also major differences between the curriculum for boys and girls. Girls in secondary modern schools, for example, were prepared for their role as wives and mothers, while girls in grammar schools had little comparable instruction.

The tripartite system did not last long. In most areas there were never more than a few technical schools, so selection at ten became a contest where those who "passed" went to grammar schools, while those who "failed" ended up in the secondary moderns. However, as the 1950s and 1960s progressed, evidence was gradually gained showing that there was considerable class bias in the way in which children were selected (Floud, Halsey, and Martin, 1956). The tests themselves came under severe criticism (Ford, 1969), and there was growing concern about the social effects of selection and differentiation at an early age (Hargreaves, 1967; Lacey, 1970). The postwar "baby boom" and rising expectations on the part of parents brought an increasing demand for a grammar-school-type education at a time when there had been little increase in the number of grammar school places. In 1955 the Labour party became firmly committed to the abolition of selection and the introduction of comprehensive schools. It strongly encouraged LEAs to change to comprehensive schools during its term of government from 1964 to 1970—a period that coincided with a widely held public desire for greater equality of educational provision. In 1960 the majority of LEAs had a selective system of schools, but by 1979 practically all LEAs had changed to comprehensive schools. Strangely enough, these changes continued unabated throughout the Conservatives' short period of government from 1970 to 1974 when, ironically, Margaret Thatcher was secretary of state for education.

THE BEGINNINGS OF REFORM

The optimism and vitality that characterized the 1960s were rudely disturbed by the oil and inflation crises of the early 1970s. The extended economic recession of the 1970s and 1980s, and the accompanying high levels of unemployment, brought growing disenchantment with education and led to renewed attempts by pressure groups and policymakers to strengthen the links between education and the economy. Such attempts to link the education system more closely to the perceived needs of industry for a well-skilled, motivated, and disciplined workforce are far from new (Davies, 1986). Although the argument has ebbed and flowed over time, Reeder (1979) has shown that criticisms from industrialists about schooling have intensified at times of economic underperformance and decline, as industry searches for a scapegoat for its failures. Thus, it was to be expected that such arguments would gain increased prominence as the economy began to slow in the 1970s.

Concern about the relationship between education and industry was projected into the public arena by James Callaghan (then Labour prime minister) in his speech in 1976 which launched what he called the "Great Debate" on education. He cast doubts on the benefits of progressive education and suggested that schools had perhaps overemphasized their social role and underplayed their duty to prepare children for the world of work. The Great Debate that followed the speech occurred too near the next general election for much to change as a result, but the incoming Conservative government of 1979 clearly had the political will to bring about radical change.

The newly elected Conservative government quickly overturned Labour's 1976 Education Act which had made moves toward comprehensive education obligatory for all LEAs, and encouraged those few LEAs which still had grammar schools to retain them. It perceived that greater harmony between industry and education was likely to be brought about through greater differentiation between schools and the reintroduction of selection, so that children could be taught the skills and knowledge appropriate to their probable future position in society.

The government further signalled its desire for greater differentiation through the introduction of the Assisted Places Scheme (APS) in the 1980 Education Act. This scheme supported the private sector of schooling, and encouraged the idea that maintained schools were not able to provide adequately for all children, by giving means-tested assistance with fees to selected children who wished to attend named private schools. The major evaluation of the APS (Edwards, Fitz, and Whitty, 1989) has shown that the scheme has been a major financial and ideological support for private schools, that there is bias in the number of places in favor of boys, and that far from all the parents receiving help with their fees could be considered to have genuine financial need. In Scotland, where the idea of egalitarianism was strong and deep, there would have been little support for a scheme based on academic selection. In consequence, the APS in Scotland was presented in terms of increased parental choice (Walford, 1988).

This theme of greater parental choice was also central to the second main part of the 1980 Education Act for England and Wales, which gave parents a right to express a preference between maintained schools for their children rather than being automatically allocated a neighborhood school, or a church school if applicable (Walford, 1990b). The act required schools to publish information on examination performance, facilities, philosophy, curriculum, and so on, so that parents could have more information on which to base their preference. In turn, the LEAs were obliged to take this preference into account in allocating children to schools, but the act also allowed the LEAs to retain powers to manage falling school rolls and to plan the overall provision in their areas in an efficient and effective way. This was a particularly important provision given that the number of secondary school children was set to fall by about a third in the years from 1978 to 1990. Stillman and Maychell (1986) have shown that the effect of this legislation was extremely variable, as some LEAs tried to encourage parental choice, while others endeavored to restrict it. Those offering minimal choice justified their behavior mainly in terms of catchment area schools fostering better links with the local community, and observed that this ensured that the LEA could engage in long-term planning.

The high degree of autonomy that LEAs had in the early 1980s made the implementation of central government's educational policies extremely difficult. Not only could individual LEAs go their own way, but it was also widely believed by government that Department of Education and Science (DES) officials were likely to obstruct major changes (Cox and Marks, 1988). In November 1982 the central government announced an alternative strategy for educational change which simply bypassed the DES altogether and provided money for educational innovation through the Manpower Services Commission (MSC). The MSC was a government agency that was started from some sections of the Department of Employment in 1974. At first, it simply provided work and work experience for the unemployed, but it gradually developed major vocationally oriented training programs for young people and others out of work. By 1981 the government had launched the one-year Youth Training Scheme for unemployed sixteen-year-old school-leavers, but the announcement of the Technical and Vocational Education Initiative (TVEI) brought the MSC into school-age provision. TVEI was established without any consultation with LEAs and was administered by the MSC rather than the DES to ensure that it was quickly put into effect. A small number of pilot schemes for technical and vocational education for fourteen to eighteen year olds were to be generously funded for September 1983, and LEAs were invited to bid to take part in the program. At a time when resources were scarce, the opportunity to purchase new scientific and technological equipment and employ more teachers at no cost to the LEA led many to apply. The popularity of the scheme led to its rapid expansion such that all LEAs now take part, but on far less generous funding. TVEI has been widely criticized (for example, Holt, 1987; Holt and Reid, 1988), and its achievements have been variable, but there is little doubt that it has brought about a major reorientation of secondary education (Dale et al., 1990; Gleeson, 1987). Its influence has extended far beyond its original brief and includes staffing, resources, teaching relations, evaluation, appraisal, and curriculum development, in addition to the far closer links between schools and industry.

The next major legislative change came with the 1986 Education Act which greatly increased the powers of school-governing bodies (Deem, 1990). The governing bodies established in the 1944 Education Act had previously played a trivial role in the everyday management of schools. Many schools shared their governing body with other nearby schools, and in a few LEAs all schools were served by a single committee. The 1986 Education Act revitalized governing bodies by ensuring that each school had its own committee and by giving it real powers and responsibilities over appointments, the curriculum, and the management of the school. The act also reconstituted the membership of governing bodies such that local politicians and their nominees were no longer in the majority. The aim was that they were to be largely replaced by members of the local community (in particular, people in business and commerce), and parents of children in the school. The changes were justified in terms of increasing local accountability and fostering stronger links between schools and the world of work, but they can also be seen as encouraging differentiation and generating competition between schools. Reorganization and strengthening of the powers of governing bodies were also necessary prerequisites for the greater role they were later asked to play in the local management of schools, where they have come to control the overall budget of their school.

THE 1988 EDUCATION REFORM ACT

The Conservative party's 1987 general election manifesto put forward radical proposals for change within education. First, a national curriculum was to be established, with attainment targets and associated testing of performance at around age seven, eleven, fourteen, and sixteen years. Second, the governing bodies of all secondary schools and many primary schools were to be given control over their own budgets and were to become the unpaid managers of enterprises often with an annual turnover of over a million pounds. Third, parental choice was to be strengthened by ensuring that pupil numbers in state-maintained schools could not be artificially restricted by LEAs to help in their overall planning. Fourth, a pilot network of City Technology Colleges (CTCs) was to be established. Fifth, state schools were to be given the right to opt out of local education authority control and become directly funded by the Department of Education and Science instead.

Any of these five changes would have presented a major challenge to the nature and administrative structure of the existing system of the state-maintained schools. All five together were designed to bring about a revolution, and this is indeed what is in the process of occurring as a result of the 1988 Education Reform Act. The main thrust of this complex act is best seen as part of a process of privatization, differentiation, and extension of the market principle to schools (Walford, 1990a). Schools are to compete with each other for pupils and teachers and to be run as separate nonprofit organizations rather than being part of a wider educational and social service to the whole community. Schools were to have closer links with local industry and commerce.

Not all the changes in the act are the direct result of an ideological commitment to privatization, open competition, and vocationalism. Conservative policy toward education is more contradictory than this and has developed unevenly. The act has received much critical comment, with various authors emphasizing different ideological thrusts (see, for example, Bash and Coulby, 1989; Flude and Hammer, 1990; Lawton, 1989; Maclure, 1988; Morrell, 1989; Simon, 1988). There are also inconsistencies between various government policies as they have developed over the decade. Perhaps the most stark illogicality is that the powers that governing bodies were given over control of the curriculum in the 1986 act were taken away again by the 1988 act through the imposition of a national curriculum! The strong attack on LEAs in the 1988 act is also a prominent feature and can be seen as the reaction to firm egalitarian stands taken by some Labour-controlled councils, particularly in the implementation of antiracist and antisexist policies. Some LEAs also attempted to implement anti-heterosexist initiatives which, in the moral panic surrounding AIDS, provoked some extreme reactions. Labour LEAs, taking all these issues seriously were frequently labeled the ''looney left'' by popular newspapers and by various Conservative Members of Parliament, and regarded profligate. In particular, it galled many Conservative Members of Parliament that the Inner London Education Authority (ILEA) was controlled by Labour and invested heavily in equal opportunities policies. To solve this perceived problem, the act simply abolished the ILEA and devolved the responsibility for education down to the constituent local councils within the inner London area (Blackstone, 1989).

Some commentators on the 1988 act have highlighted the strong tendency toward greater central control of education (for example, Bash and Coulby, 1989; Lawton, 1989), for many new powers have been given to the secretary of state for education and science. However, much of this greater central government power can be seen as an accompaniment to the privatization process. Parents are to be seen as customers of individual schools, but the government wishes to ensure that minimum standards and the needs of the country as a whole are met. Requiring the national curriculum and associated testing of pupils, in particular, can be seen as the government acting to ensure that all schools that they are funding in the free market meet minimum standards.

THE NATIONAL CURRICULUM

The 1944 Education Act was unconcerned with the content of education and ceded power over the curriculum to teachers, who were constrained only by the demands of a range of external academic examinations at postcompulsory school age. Technically, only religious education was compulsory, and that was the very subject that was often omitted in many schools. With a population that was increasingly mobile geographically, the need for greater similarity in what was taught in various schools was evident, and there was little direct controversy about the principle of a national curriculum. Nevertheless, considerable debate arose over exactly what the national curriculum should entail and even more over the nature of the associated testing of attainment.

In outline, the idea is simple. After a phasing-in period, all maintained schools will follow a ''broad and balanced curriculum'' that consists of the core subjects of mathematics, English, and science, and the foundation subjects of history, geography, technology, music, art, physical science, and a modern language at secondary school. Religious education is also a compulsory part in the curriculum, and Welsh is ''core'' in Welsh-speaking Wales and ''foundation'' elsewhere in Wales. Three new councils, each with a myriad of subcommittees, have been established to develop the detailed programs of study, to specify up to ten attainment targets, and to develop examinations and assessments for all subjects, covering the whole age range from five to eighteen. All children are to be tested at around ages seven, eleven, fourteen, and and sixteen, as well as having regular assessments of their levels of attainment. Teachers and schools will still be able to choose whatever textbooks they wish, but they must show that the attainment targets are covered.

In practice, schools have been inundated with booklets, leaflets, circulars, and ring binders, and teachers have found their workloads escalating. Assessment trials in primary schools during early 1990 showed that the burden of extra work required to give standardized tests to all children would severely prejudice good teaching. The tasks were time consuming, unwieldy, and largely confirmed what teachers already knew about pupils' abilities. Teachers were overwhelmed by the task, and children were put under undue stress. Teachers, headteachers, and unions protested strongly, and, to some surprise, the government announced that testing at seven and eleven would be conducted only for the three core subjects—mathematics, English, and science—rather than for all subjects. It was further announced that the curriculum and assessments for the foundation subjects were to be more flexible and would allow greater scope for choice by teachers and pupils.

Meanwhile, secondary teachers were facing a "quart into a pint pot" problem with their part of the national curriculum. As they began to prepare for the new system, it gradually became evident that there was simply not enough time to cover all they were expected to do. The first break from the original plan came in science, when it was announced that not all students would have to follow the same program of study, but could choose to follow a more restricted program if they wished. By July 1990 it had been announced that students would be able to drop some whole subject areas and that history, geography, music, art, and physical education were effectively being made more optional after age fourteen. The concluding section of this chapter shows that these decisions, and many others that have been taken on the nature and content of the national curriculum, have severe equity implications, in particular for women and ethnic groups.

TWO NEW TYPES OF SCHOOL

Two completely new types of school have been introduced since 1988—the City Technology College (CTC) and the Grant-Maintained School (GMS). The City Technology Colleges represent the most obvious moves to diversify the range of schools available and to support and extend the private sector of education and the gradual privatization of the maintained sector. The idea presented in October 1986 by Kenneth Baker, then secretary of state for education and science, was that he would be creating a network of twenty CTCs jointly funded by government and industry. These schools were to be established outside the

LEA system and would cater for eleven to eighteen year olds. They would be private schools, run by educational trusts closely linked to industry but directly government-funded in line with per capita expenditure for schools in similar areas. The colleges would charge no fees, but sponsors would be expected to cover the extra costs involved in providing a highly technological curriculum and would make substantial contributions to both capital and current expenditure. But, as is explained more fully elsewhere (Walford, 1990c), while the desire to increase technological education was a major feature of the plan, the CTCs were also about reintroducing selection, destroying the comprehensive system, and reducing the powers of the LEAs.

It was intended that the colleges would be established in urban areas, especially the "disadvantaged" inner cities, and that the first CTCs would come into operation in 1988. They were to serve substantial catchment areas, which would be defined in such a way that places would be offered only to about one in five or six children from within the areas. In order to dampen criticism that the colleges were equivalent to reintroducing grammar schools, they were to admit pupils spanning the full range of ability. Nevertheless, selection was a major feature of the plan, not according to ability alone, but based on general aptitude, readiness to take advantage of the type of education offered, and on the parents' commitment to the college and to full-time education or training up to age eighteen. Selection was thus to be based on the motivation not only of the child but also that of its parents.

The reality of the CTCs has thus far not matched the rhetoric. The government has found it difficult to find industrial and commercial sponsors prepared to donate funding on the scale anticipated, the cost of establishing the colleges has been far greater than expected, and the aim to locate the colleges in inner city areas has brought the scheme in direct conflict with Labour-controlled local councils who fiercely oppose it. The first CTC at Solihull in the West Midlands has been investigated in depth (Walford, 1991; Walford and Miller, 1991), and it has been shown that, while the college is giving advantage to the children it accepts, it is not acting as a catalyst for raising the quality of education in the schools in the nearby area. In fact, it is doing the reverse, and taking from those schools the very children and parents who might otherwise have fought for those schools and encouraged teachers and other pupils.

When the CTC idea was launched, the intent was to have all twenty colleges in operation by 1990. In practice, the College at Solihull which opened in 1988 was followed by two more in 1989, and just four more in 1990. Nine more were due to open in September 1991, but there is now little expectation that the target of twenty will ever be reached. The whole scheme has been engulfed in controversy and difficulty through lack of sponsors, rising costs, and opposition from LEAs and parents. While the government expected industry and commerce to quickly volunteer to support the new concept, the reality has been that few have seen it as a worthwhile investment. Ironically, the main reason for this reluctance stems from the very success of an earlier government policy that aimed to link schools and industry—the Technical and Vocational Education Initiative (TVEI). This scheme, which was discussed earlier, led to great involvement of industry in schooling for the fourteen to eighteen age group. Teacher secondments, pupil industrial visits, work experience placements, and direct involvement of industrialists in the classroom and the curriculum have all flourished, and there has been a major reorientation of education and training toward the new vocationalism. Since this has occurred in the vast majority of secondary schools and there are parallel changes in many primary schools, there is little reason why companies should wish to concentrate their efforts on CTCs rather than spread their interest far wider into many maintained schools. Indeed, there is every good reason to continue to influence the bulk of mainstream schooling, where the financial and other investment is smaller and the effect proportionally greater.

Industry's reluctance to fully support the CTC concept forced the government into a difficult position. It had no wish to make massive expenditure on a few schools, but it was forced to do so to save the scheme from becoming an embarrassing disaster. The vast majority of funding for the new colleges has actually come from the government, but the level of government support has become less and less generous since 1988, giving the colleges the task of being highly technological without providing sufficient technological equipment. Moreover, with time, the original idea of establishing completely new colleges has been gradually modified, and the range of supporters has diverged from the initial intention. The CTC at Gateshead, for example, has found its major supporter in a second-hand car dealer with fundamentalist Christian beliefs. This CTC is open to children of all faiths, but has a firm Christian emphasis to its teaching and moral standards are expected. In Croydon and Kent, two of the CTCs that opened in 1990 are actually conversions of existing LEA schools that had been sold to new trusts, against the wishes of many parents. The existing pupils were transferred with the sale. At Lewisham, two former voluntary-aided schools owned by the Haberdashers' Aske's Charitable Trust have been converted into CTCs after a long legal battle. The parents of the girls' school voted against the change but were overruled by the numbers in favor from the boys' school.

The present reality for the CTCs is, therefore, far from the optimistic future presented in 1986. Nevertheless, the significance of the CTCs is far greater than the number of pupils involved would signify. Fundamentally, the CTC idea made it clear that the government wished to develop an educational system based on inequality of provision and on selection of children for specific schools with better facilities, funding, and support than are available for the majority. Furthermore, the CTCs made it clear that new types of school were possible and that the government wished to see a greater diversity of schools and a decline in LEA power. The solution proposed by the Hillgate Group (1986) was that all schools should be owned by individual trusts and released from the control of LEAs. Stuart Sexton (1987), a one-time adviser to various secretaries of state for education, argued that schools should be able to opt out and become a new form of private school directly funded by government. His wish was granted in the 1988 Education Reform Act in the form of Grant-Maintained Schools.

The basic idea behind Grant-Maintained Schools (GMS) is that the parents and governing body should be allowed to choose whether they wish to take over the entire running of the school or remain within overall LEA control. If the parents vote in favor, the secretary of state for education examines the case and, if it is thought to be viable, authorizes the change of status. Funding from central government is on a per capita basis at exactly the same level as the relevant LEA (from which the DES claims back its costs), but the advantage is that a GMS also receives its share of the LEA administration, facilities, and service costs, which it can then use as it wishes. As with CTCs, the initial reaction to the proposal was highly negative from practically all groups involved with education (Haviland, 1988). Many LEAs were concerned that it would lead to inefficiency and a planning nightmare at a time of falling school rolls, and would lead to a network of schools that did not best serve the needs of the community. Even the government's Audit Commission pointed to the possibility of perpetuating a wasteful distribution of resources through the opting-out process. Those on the political left were also aware of the inequality between schools that such a move would engender. Schools in affluent neighborhoods would be well supported by parents and would be able to attract additional sponsorship from local industry and commerce, while those in poorer districts were likely to become ''sink'' schools for those children not accepted elsewhere.

In practice, the GMS option was initially not as popular as had been expected, and a high proportion of the early applications to opt out were a last resort for a school faced with closure or reorganization by its LEA. The fact that the school was due to be closed has not stopped the secretary of state from granting GMS status, and there are several cases in which a LEA's plans for reorganization have been interrupted by such a move. Lawyers have done well in the several legal fights between LEAs and central government. The initially slow flow of applications was increased by the government making available considerable amounts of money to new GM schools for capital expenditure, and by allowing primary schools as well as secondary schools to opt out. Government policy is now that it would like to see the majority of schools become grant maintained. By April 1991 a total of sixty-six grant-maintained schools were established, and a further one hundred were under discussion. The government's initial expectation that the majority of schools wishing to opt out would be popular schools within Labour-controlled LEAs has not been fulfilled. In practice, many GM schools have been from Conservative areas and have been in weak positions when applying. The policy has also been used against the government's general intentions by two well-known progressive comprehensives in Milton Keynes (both part of Stantonbury Campus) which have opted out of the control of Conservative Buckinghamshire County Council to counter the council's continued threats to make the schools academically selective, and to reduce their well-established community role.

Overall, however, both new types of school that have been introduced have been less important to the educational restructuring process than had been expected. In practice, the changes in open enrollment and local financial management of schools have together wrought greater changes throughout the maintained sector.

LOCAL MANAGEMENT OF SCHOOLS AND OPEN ENROLLMENT

The increased power given to school governing bodies was a precursor to delegating greater financial decision making to individual schools. For many years heads have been given the freedom to spend a small proportion of the budget as they feel best suits their school, but the 1988 Education Reform Act gave schools autonomy over practically all their spending, including, most importantly, staff salaries. After a planning stage, all schools will have delegated budgets, and governing bodies will be responsible for expenditure on all manual, technical, secretarial and teaching staff, books and equipment, heat and light, and cleaning and rates (local property taxes). The school's share of LEA funding is calculated on a formula basis, which depends mainly on the number and age of pupils in the school, but also includes allowances for some special circumstances of the school.

Some LEAs, such as Solihull and Cambridgeshire, had experimented with the delegation of part of the budget during the early and mid–1980s (Downes, 1988; Humphrey, 1988), but these experiments had excluded staff salaries. Although they experienced teething problems and heads were left with a higher workload, delegated budgets had generally been popular with heads and teachers, and this part of the Education Reform Act at first caused little comment. Gradually, however, it began to be recognized that when this measure was coupled with the open enrollment legislation that obliged schools to take all applicants up to the maximum the buildings could hold, there was very little difference between maintained schools under the new regulations and Grant-Maintained Schools. All schools are now under the management of a powerful governing body, and the pupil-number-based formula funding ensures that they compete with each other in the market for pupils. Popular schools take in more pupils than the less popular ones, with the result that these schools either compete further for pupils or enter a downward spiral of decay, with fewer pupils leading to fewer teachers and eventual closure. Yet not all children will be able to attend the popular schools, for they will eventually become unable to accommodate all who apply. Selections will thus become a necessity whether or not the schools are nominally comprehensive.

Philippa Cordingley and Peter Wilby (1987), writing before the act became law, point out that taken together the various changes amount to the introduction of a voucher system.

The differences between what the government proposes and how a voucher system would operate are trivial. Under the latter, parents would receive a voucher, equivalent to the average cost of educating a child, which they could present to the school of their choice. The school would then redeem the voucher for cash from the government or local authority. The government's scheme works on exactly the same principle, except that there is no voucher. Instead parents simply present their child. Of course, there are limitations, but so would there be with any voucher system. For example, parents will not get places if a school is full. Holding a voucher would make no difference any more than cash in the pocket will get you on to a bus or into a theatre that is full.

This is an interesting analysis and one that highlights the full extent of the privatization process that has occurred as a result of the Education Reform Act. The idea of the educational voucher has been a central one for the radical right for many years, but those involved in education have attacked vouchers too frequently for the government to risk openly introducing them (Seldon, 1986). Instead, it has followed the program outlined by Sexton (1987) and "privatized by stealth." What at present is a direct grant could be renamed an educational credit or an educational voucher, for parents are in the position of consumers picking and choosing in the marketplace.

The difficultly with Cordingley and Wilby's analogy is that we all know that money in the pocket *can* get us into a full theater if we are prepared to supplement the ticket price, or it can allow us to travel by taxi when the bus is full. Once popular schools are allowed to select children, there will be no orderly line to get on to the bus; instead, affluent parents will ensure that their children force their way forward and are able to gain access. Initially, they may simply have to show that they are prepared to give their children an abundance of support (as with selection for CTCs). However, Sexton's (1987) plan envisages that many parents will wish to "top up" the value of their educational credit, and it will be hard for schools to resist selecting those parents who are most likely to do so. The result will be the gradual privatization of the entire system and the development of a hierarchy of schools with differential facilities and opportunities for personal fulfillment, development, and progress. Selection for specific schools is likely gradually to become more and more dependent on parental attitudes, wealth, and income.

THE OBJECTIVES AND CONSEQUENCES OF EDUCATIONAL REFORM

The organization and content of schooling are continually changing, but the concept of "reform" signifies a belief that there was previously something fundamentally wrong. The 1988 Education Reform Act was justified on the basis that it would raise educational standards and give greater choice to parents, but there was actually little evidence that educational standards were a problem. On the contrary, the 1970s and 1980s had seen substantial rises in the number of children staying on at school beyond compulsory school-leaving age, and in the number taking and gaining success in external examinations. While those on the political right claimed to have evidence that children in comprehensive schools did less well than those in a selective system (Marks, Cox, and Pomian-Szrednicki, 1983), there was no systematic evidence to back this assertion, and the claim was strongly challenged by most academics (see Steedman, 1987). In addition, by 1988 there were more people studying and gaining degrees in higher education than ever before, with no evidence of any decline in standards.

One major problem was certainly that teacher morale was low by 1988. Throughout the 1980s they had been the recipients of abuse from various government ministers as the blame for poor economic performance was heaped onto schooling. Both pay and status had declined, there were serious shortages of teachers in key subject areas, and a succession of Her Majesty's Inspectorate Reports catalogued poorly decorated and maintained school buildings with inadequate resources. After a long and bitter period of teacher industrial action from 1984 to 1987, teachers' negotiating rights were withdrawn by an Act of Parliament and new pay and working conditions were imposed. There was nothing in the 1988 Education Reform Act which was aimed at raising teachers' pay or morale. Instead, it offered a heavier workload and greater responsibility with no increased rewards.

In practice, the perceived need for educational reform stems from its very success rather than its failure. Educational success raises expectations which society may not be able to fulfill, so that unskilled jobs remain unfilled while well-qualified young people are unemployed. As the number of young people declines owing to demographic factors, employers of manual and low-skilled workers are finding it increasingly difficult to find recruits. In response, the DES and other educational officials interviewed by Stewart Ranson (1984:241) argue that "We need to select: to ration the educational opportunities to meet the job opportunities so that society can cope with the output of education," or, more bluntly, "People must be educated once more to know their place."

Fundamentally, the 1988 Education Reform Act is concerned with increasing inequalities rather than reducing them. It is designed to bring into existence a continuum of different types of school with unequal provision, into which various children will be fitted through a process of mutual selection closely linked to social class, gender, and ethnic group. There will be a shift toward greater inegalitarianism within a more self-consciously stratified society. There will be increased vocationalism, with schools having links with particular types of industrial or commercial organization. This will lead to growing differentiation between groups, as children are more clearly channeled into "appropriate" occupational positions. At the top of the continuum will be the fee-paying private schools, some of which will be overflowing with expensive teaching and leisure facilities and may become places where real privilege can be bought (Walford, 1986, 1990). About 7 percent of pupils now attend private schools, with fewer girls than boys and a disproportionately low number of Afro-Caribbean children. These schools are not forced to adhere to the national curriculum and its associated testing, and are thus freer to encourage critical thought in their pupils and develop a curriculum appropriate to the needs of these potential leaders of tomorrow. The majority of places at these schools are still available only to children of those parents with sufficient means to pay the fees, but a substantial minority of children from less wealthy (but still predominantly middle-class) backgrounds are selected for this type of schooling and are financed through the Assisted Places Scheme. It is unlikely that there will be any change in the disproportionately small number of girls and Afro-Caribbean children so far accepted on the scheme (Edwards, Fitz, and Whitty, 1989).

Exactly how individual schools and types of school will fit into this new hierarchy is yet to be seen, but the next rank of school will surely include CTCs and GMSs. Both are new forms of non-fee-paying private schools, controlled by independent governing bodies and at least partly funded by the state. As time passes, the degree to which individual schools draw income from other sources will differ. Some will be able to attract income and support from industry and commerce in their attempts to attract future employees, but other schools will have to rely more on voluntary donations from parents. And it is clear that such supplementary income will be necessary if these schools wish to enhance their teaching and facilities beyond the level available in LEA schools. As these schools become more popular, they will be forced to become selective, and it is likely that such selection will be related to pupil and parent motivation and enthusiasm, as it is currently for CTCs. Quite explicitly, those children from disadvantaged homes, who may receive inadequate encouragement, may be excluded regardless of their ability.

Finally, at the bottom of this new continuum of schools will be a mixture of those state-maintained schools that are still under the control of the LEAs and those church voluntary schools that have not become grant maintained, but each school now with individual budgets and competing in the market for pupils. Eventually, greater differences between these schools will develop, and some schools will become more popular than others. This popularity will lead to greater total income for the school, and a downward spiral for the competitors, leading to closure. However, once schools have closed, parental choice will be restricted to just the now overcrowded popular schools. The Education Reform Act contains no measures to encourage the opening of new schools, but simply provides a method whereby expenditure can be saved by closing them.

The divisions between types of school are unlikely to be clear cut. For example, some LEA schools will undoubtedly offer a better educational and social experience than some GMSs or private schools. Some church voluntary-aided schools will probably be more popular than some of the Grant-Maintained Schools. The details are unclear, but what will develop is a continuum of differentiated schools that are likely to attract and select children according to inegalitarian criteria. In theory, all these schools will be open to any child who applies and is accepted. In practice, such a mutual choice process cannot fail to be discriminatory, for it is the parents who must apply to CTCs, GMSs, and for

Assisted Places on behalf of their children, and who must be prepared to be interviewed and supportive of the education provided. Obviously, some working-class and ethnic minority parents will seize the chance to take advantage of the better facilities, staff, and teaching that will probably be available in the schools at the top of the hierarchy, but the fact has to be faced that working-class and ethnic minority parents are likely to have had a poorer education and be less knowledgeable about education than their white middle-class competitors. Even if they apply on behalf of their children, they are less likely to be able to negotiate educational bureaucracies or to present themselves as "supportive" parents in interview with headteachers or other selectors, who are themselves mostly white and middle-class.

The nature of the national curriculum will also act against ethnic minority pupils, for it is fundamentally based on an ideology of assimilationism, and takes no account of cultural differences. Whitty and Menter (1989:53) indicate some examples:

... the very emphasis on "national" in the proposed national curriculum, the centrality of a notion of national testing with all the cultural and linguistic bias which that implies, the failure to recognise languages other than Welsh and English as pupils' first language, and the omission ... of any reference to the 1985 report of Lord Swann's Committee of Inquiry into the Education of Children from Ethnic Minority Groups, entitled "Education for All."

Since that article was written, intense pressure on the government has brought some positive changes. It was originally intended that only European Community working languages would be included as options within the modern foreign languages part of the national curriculum, but this has been replaced by a two-tiered system whereby ethnic minority languages such as Urdu, Punjabi, and Gujerati can be included as long as the school also offers at least one of the European Community languages. This compromise still retains implications of "second-class" languages, but does actually enhance the status of the ethnic minority languages compared with their previous position. Young pupils will now also be able to be assessed in the language of their home for their math and science tests of attainment. However, major inequalities remain in the form of collective worship and religious education introduced by the act. Ethnic minority religious values have been devalued by amendments to the act which ensured a place for religious education in the basic curriculum, and reaffirmed the need for a compulsory act of school worship each day. Moreover, for the first time the legislation states that (with a few exceptions) both of these must be wholly or mainly of a broadly Christian character. In addition, battles have been fought about the content of geography and history, but both now center on Britain and Europe rather than on promoting a world-view. Multicultural and antiracist education are clearly under attack (Ball and Troyna, 1989; Troyna, 1990).

The move toward individually competitive schools is also unlikely to favor ethnic minority pupils, or wider social aims for interethnic understanding. Many LEAs targeted equal opportunities and antiracism as areas where additional support and training were given, but schools controlling their own budgets may well place these vital issues low on their list of priorities. Indeed, this is the government's expectation, as the attack on LEAs was often explicitly in terms of their "profligacy" in funding antiracist, antisexist, and antiheterosexist programs. What school is going to "waste" money on multicultural or antiracist education when it has few black or Asian pupils?

In a similar way, local management of schools will likely lead to less emphasis on gender equality and antisexism. Formal policies will undoubtedly remain, but monitoring and implementing a program of antisexism may well cost more than the school is prepared to spend. Moreover, the hope that greater equality between the sexes might be encouraged through the national curriculum has turned out to be false. Since 1976 all curriculum subjects on offer at a school have had to be open to both boys and girls, but there were still gender biases in the subjects chosen for options at age thirteen or fourteen. The national curriculum as originally proposed would have ensured that all pupils take all subjects up to sixteen, which might have encouraged, for example, more girls to enter scientific and technological jobs. The revisions allowing pupils to drop certain subjects and to choose a restricted science program mean that this possibility has been lost.

Greater parental choice often may not act in the best interests of all children or the wider society. There have already been several cases of parents choosing to move their children from a school on the basis of its ethnic mix, and the government has admitted that parental choice could lead to some schools becoming all black, but that this was the "price that had to be paid" for greater choice.

In summary, the educational reforms of the last decade have been designed to widen differences between the educational experiences of various children, and to link them more closely to their most probable occupational destinations. The result is that schooling is likely to become more closely linked to social class, gender, ethnic group, and geographical regional differences. Rather than aiming to increase equity, these reforms are likely to confirm and reinforce the preexisting social order of wealth and privilege.

REFERENCES

Anderson, R. D. 1983. *Education and Opportunity in Victorian Scotland.* Oxford: Clarendon Press.

Ball, Wendy, and Barry Troyna. 1989. "The Dawn of a New ERA? The Education Reform Act, 'Race' and the LEAs." *Educational Management and Administration,* 17:23–31.

Bash, Leslie, and David Coulby, eds. 1989. *The Education Reform Act, Competition and Control.* London: Cassell.

Blackstone, Tessa. 1989. "The Abolition of the ILEA." In *The Education Reform Act: Choice and Control*, ed. Denis Lawton. London: Hodder and Stoughton.

Cordingley, Philippa and Peter Wilby. 1987. *Opting Out of Mr. Baker's Proposals*. Ginger Paper 1. London: Education Reform Group.

Cox, Caroline, and John Marks. 1988. *The Insolence of Office*. London: Claridge Press.

Dale, Roger, Richard Bowe, David Harris, Mark Loveys, Rob Moore, Chris Shilling, Pat Sikes, John Trevitt, and Vicki Valsecchi. 1990. *The TVEI Story, Policy, Practice and Preparation for the Workforce*. Milton Keynes: Open University Press.

Davies, Bernard. 1986. *Threatening Youth, Towards a National Youth Policy*. Milton Keynes: Open University Press.

Deem, Rosemary. 1990. "The Reform of School-Governing Bodies: The Power of the Consumer over the Producer?" In *The Education Reform Act 1988*, ed. Michael Flude and Merril Hammer. Lewes: Falmer.

Downes, Peter. 1988. *Local Financial Management of Schools*. Oxford: Blackwell.

Edwards, Tony, John Fitz, and Geoff Whitty. 1989. *The State and Private Education: An Evaluation of the Assisted Places Scheme*. Lewes: Falmer.

Finch, Janet. 1984. *Education as Social Policy*. London: Longman.

Floud, J., A. H. Halsey, and F. M. Martin. 1956. *Social Class and Educational Opportunity*. London: Heinemann.

Flude, Michael, and Merril Hammer, eds. 1990. *The Education Reform Act, 1988. Its Origins and Implications*. Lewes: Falmer.

Ford, Julienne. 1969. *Social Class and the Comprehensive School*. London: Routledge and Kegan Paul.

Gleeson, Denis, ed. 1987. *TVEI and Secondary Education: A Critical Appraisal*. Milton Keynes: Open University Press.

Halsey, A. H., A. F. Heath, and J. M. Ridge. 1984. "The Political Arithemetic of Public Schools." In *British Public Schools: Policy and Practice*, ed. Geoffrey Walford. Lewes: Falmer.

Hargreaves, David. 1967. *Social Relations in the Secondary School*. London: Routledge and Kegan Paul.

Haviland, Julian, ed. 1988. *Take Care Mr. Baker!* London: Fourth Estate.

Hillgate Group. 1986. *Whose Schools? A Radical Manifesto*. London: Hillgate Group.

Holt, Maurice. 1987. "Vocationalism on the Hoof: Observations on the TVEI." In *Skills and Vocationalism*, ed. Maurice Holt. Milton Keynes: Open University Press.

———, and William A. Reid. 1988. "Instrumentalism and Education: 14–18 Rhetoric and the 11–16 Curriculum." In *Education, Training and the New Vocationalism*, ed. Andrew Pollard, June Purvis, and Geoffrey Walford. Milton Keynes: Open University Press.

Humphrey, Colin. 1988. *Financial Autonomy in Solihull*. London: Institute of Economic Affairs.

Lacey, Colin. 1970. *Hightown Grammar*. Manchester: Manchester University Press.

Lawton, Denis, ed. 1989. *The Education Reform Act: Choice and Control*. London: Hodder and Stoughton.

Maclure, Stuart. 1988. *Education Re-formed*. London: Hodder and Stoughton.

Marks, John, Caroline Cox, and M. Pomian-Srzednicki. 1983. *Standards in English Schools*. London: National Council for Educational Standards.

Morrell, Frances. 1989. *Children of the Future*. London: Hogarth Press.

Ranson, Stewart. 1984. "Towards a Tertiary Tripartism: New Codes of Social Control and the 17 + ." In *Selection, Certification and Control*. ed. Patricia Broadfoot. Lewes: Falmer.

Reeder, David. 1979. "A Recurring Debate: Education and Industry." In *Schooling in Decline*, ed. Gerald Bernbaum. London: Macmillan.

Scotland, James. 1969. *The History of Scottish Education. Vols. 1 and 2*. London: University of London Press.

Seldon, Arthur. 1986. *The Riddle of the Voucher*. Hobart Paperback 21. London: Institute of Economic Affairs.

Sexton, Stuart. 1987. *Our Schools—A Radical Policy*. London: Institute of Economic Affairs.

Shipman, Marten. 1984. *Education as a Public Service*. London: Harper and Row.

Simon, Brian. 1988. *Bending the Rules. The Baker "Reform" of Education*. London: Lawrence and Wishart.

Steedman, Jane. 1987. "Longitudinal Survey Research into Progress in Secondary Schools, Based on the National Child Development Study." In *Doing Sociology of Education*, ed. Geoffrey Walford. Lewes: Falmer.

Stillman, Andy, and Karen Maychell. 1986. *Choosing Schools. Parents, LEAs and the 1980 Education Act*. Windsor: NFER–Nelson.

Troyna, Barry. 1990, April. "Reform or Deform? The 1988 Education Reform Act and Racial Equality in Britain." *New Community*.

Walford, Geoffrey. 1986. *Life in Public Schools*. London: Methuen.

———. 1988. "The Scottish Assisted Places Scheme: A Comparative Study of the Origins, Nature and Practice of the APS in Scotland, England and Wales." *Journal of Education Policy* 3 (2):137–153.

———. 1989. "Scotland: Changes in Government Policy Towards Private Schools." In *Private Schools in Ten Countries: Policy and Practice*, ed. Geoffrey Walford. London: Routledge.

———. 1990a. *Privatization and Privilege in Education*. London: Routledge.

———. 1990b. "Developing Choice in British Education." *Compare* 20 (1):67–81.

———. 1990c. "The Education Reform Act for England and Wales: Paths to Privatization." *Educational Policy* 4 (2):127–144.

———. 1991. "City Technology Colleges: A Private Magnetism?" In *Private Schooling: Tradition, Change and Diversity*, ed. Geoffrey Walford. London: John Chapman.

———, and Henry Miller. 1991. *City Technology College*. Milton Keynes: Open University Press.

Whitty, Geoff, and Ian Menter. 1989. "Lessons of Thatcherism: Education Policy in England and Wales 1979–88." *Journal of Law and Society* 16(1):42–64.

13

HONG KONG

Gerard A. Postiglione

The greatest challenge facing Hong Kong society concerns its reunification with China (Burns and Scott, 1988; Buruma, 1990; Clark and Chan, 1991; Emmons, 1988; Mushkat and Cheek-Milby, 1989; Zeng, 1989). Education is expected to play a major role in the transitional period. Therefore, educational reforms are viewed with increasing importance (Postiglione, 1991). Educational reform in Hong Kong hinges on a number of sociohistorical processes, most notably decolonization, localization, and democratization (Sweeting, 1991). Other relevant factors include Hong Kong's Chinese heritage, its position in the world economy, and problems associated with the large-scale emigration of those with high levels of education (Kwong, 1991; Peebles, 1988; Shive, 1991; Wong, 1986). Many of Hong Kong's educational reforms occurred before the question of reunification with China was settled in 1985. Nevertheless, the major problem involving educational reform in Hong Kong has become increasingly concerned with reconciling the contradictions between capitalism, socialism, and patriotism during the transition to 1997 and beyond (Postiglione, 1991b). This chapter deals with the subject in several parts. First, a brief outline of the system of education in Hong Kong is given, along with background information regarding the growth of the system and its relationship to the developing economy. Second, educational reform is discussed as it relates to the policy process. Third, the major reform orientations of Hong Kong's transitional period are identified. Finally, selected educational reforms are reviewed as they relate to the macroscopic social transformations.

EDUCATION AND THE HONG KONG CONTEXT

In 1997 Hong Kong will become a Special Administrative Region of the People's Republic of China under a "one country, two system" arrangement by which it can maintain its capitalist system for another fifty years and enjoy a high degree of self-government with "Hong Kong people ruling Hong Kong." Confidence in this agreement on the part of the people of Hong Kong has fluctuated, however. The underlying rationale is that China, which gains one-third of its foreign currency from Hong Kong and much more, will want to preserve the Hong Kong system, even allowing it a great degree of autonomy, if necessary (Lau, 1988; Youngson, 1983). While Hong Kong and China have already achieved successful economic integration and mutually beneficial economic cooperation, other institutions including education have yet to show how well they can weather the transitional period (Leung, 1991). The political system will be transformed according to the new Basic Law, Hong Kong's post–1997 mini-Constitution, which has been promulgated by the Chinese government. Yet, controversies remain with regard to the pace of representative government and a bill of rights (Tsim, 1991).

According to the Sino-British agreement restoring Chinese sovereignty over Hong Kong, and the Basic Law of the Hong Kong Special Administrative Region, education will maintain a great degree of autonomy.

The Hong Kong Special Administrative Region Government shall on its own decide policies in the field of culture, education, science, and technology, including policies regarding the education system and its administration, the language of instruction, the allocation of funds, the examination system, the system of academic rewards and the recognition of educational and technological qualifications (Sino-British Joint Declaration, 1984:17).

Community organizations and individuals may, in accordance with law, run educational undertakings of various kinds in the Hong Kong Special Administrative Region. Educational institutions of all kinds may retain their autonomy and enjoy academic freedom. They may continue to recruit staff and use teaching materials from outside the Hong Kong Special Administrative Region. Schools run by religious organizations may continue to provide religious education, including courses on religion. Students shall enjoy freedom to choose between educational institutions and pursue their education outside the Hong Kong Special Administrative Region (Draft Basic Law, 1988: 67–68).

For most of Hong Kong's history, educational developments occurred within a colonial society built on an entrepot trade economy (Sweeting, 1990). Beginning after 1949, skills and technology transferred from Shanghai, a steady immigration from the adjoining region of Guangdong, and increasing amounts of local investment combined with a laissez-faire economy and a British-style colonial government to promote Hong Kong's industrial foundation (Wong, 1986). Successful textile manufacturing followed by new international investments in other infant industries, including electronics, through the 1960s and 1970s contributed to the socialization of the workforce (Chen, 1983). Government land sales, efficient infrastructural planning, and a growth rate averaging 10 percent per year further improved the investment climate even as the British government entered into negotiations with the People's Republic of China on the question of sovereignty over Hong Kong. By 1990 Hong Kong had become a major international financial center with the second highest living standard in Asia, a key regional center for semiconductor manufacturing, and an important point for technology transfer to China (Henderson, 1987).

Hong Kong's burgeoning position as a textile trader within the European Community in the 1970s led to pressure on the governor to insure that child labor was not a factor in Hong Kong's economic success. The implementation of free and compulsory schooling was used to indicate compliance. The rapidly expanding educational system, funded through both public and private efforts and managed through a combination of voluntary, government, and semigovernment arrangements, was brought under the Education Department's inspection system. The British tradition of elite education combined well with the Chinese tradition of examination-oriented selection for positions in government. By the early 1980s Hong Kong had a highly bureaucratized, well-monitored, and tightly structured system of schools.

Throughout a 140-year history, the sociopolitical system remained virtually unchanged (Miners, 1986). An atomistic Chinese society remained insulated from a secluded bureaucratic polity (Lau, 1982). The government was not directly elected and less representative of the general population than it would come to be as the date for the recovery of sovereignty by China approached. Until the late 1980s, schools did little to promote democracy but instead reflected the seemingly apolitical nature of the society. Classroom and school social interaction was highly regulated and ritualized, and student participation in school politics was virtually nonexistent, owing in part to a government ban on any semblance of political activity in schools. The 1989 military crackdown on the democracy movement in China slightly altered the situation by temporarily removing the ban on politics in schools. During this period hundreds of thousands of students joined street demonstrations, and political activities inside many schools, including speeches, rallies, poster displays, and letter writing, increased. The regulation regarding political activity in schools was later revised and reinstituted to allow teachers more flexibility when teaching topics of a political nature.

THE STRUCTURE OF THE HONG KONG EDUCATIONAL SYSTEM

Throughout Hong Kong's history, a combination of government, government-subsidized, and private forms of education flourished (Sweeting, 1990). For most of its history, education in Hong Kong generally followed colonial lines, although Chinese education was always an accepted part of the system (Ng, 1984). However, after World War II, a gradual move away from traditional colonialism took place as educational influence shifted away from much of its lock-step dependence on developments in the United Kingdom. Hong Kong has a 98 percent Chinese population, and, aside from the few schools established specifically for

Table 13.1
Enrollment in Day Schools by Level and Sector, 1981–1990

Level	Sector	1981	1982	1983	1984	1985	1986	1987	1988	1989	1990
Kinder-garten	Private	200426	205200	209869	226450	229089	231610	225108	214703	201750	196466
Primary	Government	32055	33961	35538	36302	37028	36380	35696	34906	34112	33146
	Aided	439572	442423	445140	443772	443240	443255	446557	448326	449079	441908
	Private	65496	62074	59178	56146	54635	52358	52056	51805	51259	49865
	All Sectors	537123	538458	539856	536220	534903	531993	534309	535037	534450	524919
Secondary	Government	29684	31833	33145	34616	35437	36279	36064	36331	36654	37625
	Aided	182807	261587	269042	276761	283528	294351	302574	311086	318695	325604
	Private	252432	166191	151182	136436	125556	117128	109391	96484	82946	69979
	All Sectors	464923	459611	453369	447813	444521	447758	448029	443901	438295	433208

Special Education+	Government	176	208	230	280	369	522	709	907	1111	1298
	Aided	7823	7976	7741	7719	7740	8103	8766	9715	10555	10819
	All Sectors	7999	8184	7971	7999	8109	8655	9475	10622	11666	12117
College of Education @	Government	2663	2351	2355	2435	2573	2614	2774	2519	2196	1732
Approved @ Post-secondary	Private	4730	5049	5230	5426	5253	4789	4634	7084	7377	7543
Adult Education @ & Others	Private	22993	28074	2717	28154	21854	24925	21849	19636	18219	18065
All levels	Government	73610	73325	73822	74475	75601	75631	74401	72109	69101	64769
	Aided	775335	775750	767153	756850	745346	734871	729299	723897	714565	633198
	Private	344033	369078	395396	420135	428203	438994	445515	446949	459061	543962
	All Sectors	1192978	1218153	1236371	1251460	1249150	1249496	1249215	1242955	1242727	1241929

+ Including Special Schools and Special Classes in Ordinary Schools.
@ as at October of the Year.

the children of expatriates, the school system is designed to serve the needs of the local populace.

In 1978 Hong Kong achieved a nine-year universal, free, and compulsory education system (Table 13.1). By 1980 most (87 percent) of the student population chose to continue beyond the nine years, with 40 percent studying in government or government-aided schools and the rest in self-financing private schools. The number of private schools continually declined until 1988 when a Direct Subsidy Scheme (discussed later in this chapter) was proposed as a measure by which more private schools could survive.

The government allocates students according to a Primary One Admission Scheme after kindergarten, a Secondary School Allocation Scheme after primary school, and a Junior Secondary Education Assessment (JSEA) after junior secondary school. The JSEA, which will be gradually phased out as the number of subsidized places in senior secondary schools increases, is aimed at insuring fairness and equal opportunity. Yet, while its standardized testing insures a more objective means of allocation, social class and gender-related factors have already worked themselves into the system in a systematic way by the time the JSEA is administered.

Students who remain in secondary school until form five will sit for a public Certificate of Education Examination. About a third of these students go on to the two-year sixth form education. They may sit for the Higher Level examinations after the first year to gain entrance to the four-year program of the Chinese University of Hong Kong, or the Advanced Level examinations after the second year to gain entrance to the University of Hong Kong. Reforms in 1988 called for a change leading to a unified admission system for a standard three-year university education.

The vocational-technical sector of the school system has grown since 1981 when only 3 percent of the form three leavers continued their studies in technical institutes. By the end of the 1980s this figure more than doubled as the number of these institutes grew to eight. Aside from offering post-form three craft courses lasting two years, the technical institutes also offer post-form five technical courses that have taken in an increasingly larger segment of the population as opportunities to enter universities expanded less rapidly than the levels below it (Figure 13.1).

University entrance increased from 2 percent of the relevant age group in 1980 to 8 percent in 1990. Other postsecondary institutions including the two polytechnics, teacher and nurse training institutes, and the other colleges, including the Hong Kong Baptist College and Lingnan College, have provided places for about another 8 percent of the age group. Many of these institutions are upgrading their diploma and certificate courses to degree-level offerings.

EDUCATIONAL POLICY AND REFORM

Under the Educational Ordinance, the director of education controls all government schools, and supervises all other kindergarten and primary and secondary

Figure 13.1
Departments Within the Hong Kong Educational System

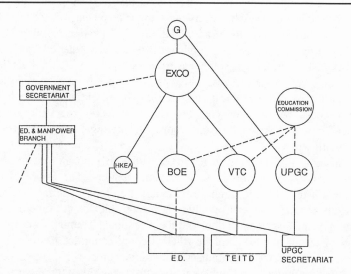

G: Governor; **EXCO:** Executive Council; **HKEA:** Hong Kong Examinations Authority;
BOE: Board of Education; **VTC:** Vocational Training Council; **UPGC:** Universities and
Polytechnics Grants Committee; **ED:** Education Department; **TEITD:** Technical Education
Industrial Training Department.

Source: Developed by Leung Kam Fong.

schools in the territory (Luk, 1989). He also supervises postsecondary institutions
with the exception of the universities and polytechnics. The ordinance provides
the director with broad-ranging powers over the life and practice of schooling,
its staff and pupils, and particularly anything that seems like politics in schools.
Most of the schools in the territory are publicly funded but privately operated.
Each school has an unpaid management committee and supervisor appointed by
the sponsoring body. In most cases, members of the committee are laypersons
who are not involved with policymaking or the day-to-day affairs of the school.
The supervisor has considerable legal responsibility and usually works closely
with the school head in policy and personnel decisions. The school principal has
absolute power over the staff and pupils. Heads of the government schools are
appointed by the Education Department and those of other schools by the sponsoring agencies. According to the government's Code of Aid, all aided schools
are funded according to the same formula, regardless of location, sponsorship,
or prestige. Schools in the small private sector are financed mainly by fees paid
by the students' parents, but the government purchases places in these schools
when the government and government-aided schools cannot accommodate all
their form one to three students.

Educational policy in Hong Kong has been characterized as somewhere between a centralized and a decentralized system. It would be more accurate to say that decision making and policy are part of the centralized system, yet a broad and complex consultative process has evolved since the late 1970s. Although the education system is very much modeled on that of the United Kingdom in its structure, organization, admission and examination regulations, and curriculum, it is far from being a duplicate of that or any other educational system. Traditionally, educational policy has been the province of an influential elite of the colony who are not representative of the people as much as reflective of the powers that be. As the education system expanded in the 1960s and 1970s, the policy process became more complex with the flowering of a variety of education associations, unions, and pressure groups, all entering into the educational policy consultative process.

In general, the highest decision maker is the governor in Council. Four committees advise the governor on educational matters. The Board of Education concerns itself with education from kindergarten to sixth form, the Universities and Polytechnics Grants Committee is responsible for the funding and development of university education, and the Vocational Training Council is responsible for technical education. Insufficient coordination led to the founding of a fourth committee, the Educational Commission, composed of appointed members from the community and representatives from the other three committees and the Education Department. It provides consolidated advice to the governor on the overall development of the education system (Cheng, 1991) (Figure 13.2).

The legitimacy of the educational policy process has come to be increasingly tied to the membership of such committees. The most controversial issue on membership concerned Mr. Szeto Wah, president of the Hong Kong Professional Teachers Union and one of the few elected (rather than appointed) members of the Hong Kong Legislative Council. As a long-time critic of the Government Education Department and a liberal member of the Legislative Council who opposes many of the policies of the Beijing government toward Hong Kong, Szeto was not appointed to the Education Commission until 1990, even though he enjoyed broad support among the rank and file of the teaching profession and large sectors of the community. Until his appointment, this became a challenge to the government's legitimacy in matters of educational policy.

EDUCATIONAL REFORM ORIENTATIONS

Educational reform policy has its intervention points in Hong Kong's transitional period. It has a shaping influence on the thinking of the generation that will lead Hong Kong after 1997; it influences the selection criteria for recruitment into important positions within the transitional government civil service; it works to maintain a highly skilled labor force in the face of the large-scale emigration of talented people from the territory; it determines to some extent the degree of interaction between the educational systems of Hong Kong and other parts of China; it influences school socialization processes that build a cultural identity

Figure 13.2
Education System of Hong Kong

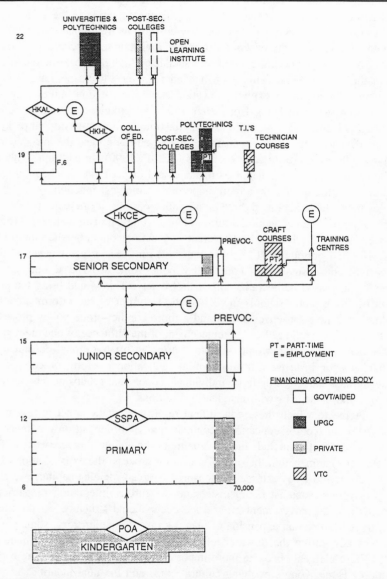

GOVT/AIDED: Government and Government-Aided Sector; **UPGC:** Universities and Polytechnics Grants Committee; **PRIVATE:** Private School Sector; **VTC:** Vocational Training Council; **PT:** Part-time; **E:** Employment; **POA:** Primary One Allocation Scheme; **SSPA:** Secondary School Placement Allocation Scheme; **PREVOC:** Prevocational Schools; **E:** End (Terminal); **TI:** Technical Institute; **HKCE:** Hong Kong Certification Examination; **HKHL:** Hong Kong High-Level Examination; **HKAL:** Hong Kong Advanced-Level Examination.

Source: Developed by Cheng Kai Ming.

essential for reuniting people in Hong Kong with the rest of China; and, finally, it bolsters or restrains the general process of democratization in the society.

Education in Hong Kong has not yet veered from its traditional role within a colonial setting. With the exception of minor revisions to the content of some school textbooks, schooling continues to socialize children into a sociopolitical system that has remained almost unchanged for over 140 years (Lau, 1982). Moreover, China has no explicit education strategy of nation building that it plans to implement in Hong Kong after 1997. Nevertheless, as noted above, education is increasingly regarded as a key institution in the transitional period. Specific decisions about the expansion of higher education and the introduction of civics education are just two examples (SCMP, 1990). In addition, without a military acting to strengthen a particular brand of patriotic socialization, education can come to take on a more important ideological function.

Elsewhere I have identified three broad policy options or orientations relating to school politics and education reform in Hong Kong's transitional period (Postiglione, 1991a). Each deals in a different way with reconciling emerging problems. The first option, most likely in the short run, sees a maintenance of the status quo, consensus-bound, consultative policy process. The second option hinges on increased democratization of the society. This would bring the pluralism of Hong Kong schools more into the forefront of the reform process, resulting in a less consensus-bound and a more conflict-prone policy process. The third option would reflect the replacement of the influence of one metropole by another. This option would see the shoring up of traditional consultative mechanisms for insuring legitimacy of the educational reform process, with greater influence exerted by those individual schools and groups of schools that have or build closer ties with mainland institutions.

The degree to which these educational reform orientations act to lessen or intensify Hong Kong's educational contradictions will depend on a number of factors. These factors include the positioning of the unique characteristics of the educational system within the overall transition process, the expansion of what might be referred to as externally sponsored national socialist capital, namely, the growth of a socialist bourgeoisie, and the further integration of patriotic elements into the government organs and occupational structure. At the same time, there has been an expansion of liberal groups in the territory, some going as far as advocating the downfall of the Beijing government or communism itself. These elements become more important when viewed against the background of Hong Kong's evolving cultural ethos and the dual identities it represents, that of Chineseness and Hong Kongeseness (Lau and Kuan, 1988). As a Chinese society under a long history of colonial rule, Hong Kong possesses structural elements distinguishable from those of both traditional and modern China. This has fostered an ethos that represents "at once a departure from dominant Chinese values and a continuation of Chinese heritage." The dual nature of the ethos is visibly a postwar phenomenon and has been particularly salient with the advent of the 1997 issue and the rise to prominence of the younger generation. Furthermore, the sharp value differences that are reflected in these two identities become more distinct as they are situated within selected types of schools. These types differ on such important cultural, social, and political features as the medium of instruction (English or Chinese), the political leaning of the school (in support of Beijing or Taipei), the connection of the school with various clansmen and provincial associations in China, and the social class composition of the schools (Huo, 1988).

EDUCATION REFORMS AS REACTIONS TO THE TRANSITION

Since the agreement between China and Britain over Hong Kong's future, several educational reforms have been instituted that have direct implications for the transition. These reforms have been related to the structure of sixth form education, language medium of instruction, school curriculum, and private schools. While some might argue that many of the educational reforms were fashioned without special consideration being given to the 1997 issue, however, the sovereignty issue certainly had an indirect influence on the formulation of all the reforms.

Reforming the Transition from Secondary School to the University

By far the most controversial reform to date was initiated by the Education Commission in its third report of June 1988. This reform was directed at sixth form education but had major implications for Hong Kong's two universities. The reform was designed to standardize sixth form education, reduce examination pressure, and unify the admission scheme to universities. In effect, it brought the issue of length of university education to the forefront.

Prior to the Education Commission's recommendations, the University of Hong Kong had recognized the problem of sixth form education as it affected the quality of the pool of candidates from which it drew its students. The university decided to launch into the development of a foundation year that would be attached to the beginning of the already existing three-year program. This foundation year was designed to provide a broad curriculum and language improvement opportunities for new students. This change would bring the University of Hong Kong into line with Hong Kong's other university, thus eliminating the need for sixth form students to surmount the dreaded advanced-level examinations before entering university.

The Education Commission's third report cited the narrowness of sixth form education and how it fostered students "who lack maturity, initiative, and innovation" (Education Commission, 1988). However, the commission favored broadening the upper sixth form rather than making modifications at the university level. A major reason cited was the high financial cost of extending university education and the concern with finding lecturers to staff it.

This reform was unique in the sense that it broke the past pattern of consensus-bound educational reform and delivered the policymaking process into the conflict-prone mode of educational reformation. Before the date arrived to debate the implementation of the reform in the Legislative Council, as many as 4,000 students marched to the government house to protest the reform. Many educational groups in Hong Kong entered the fray, revealing a deep split in preference for and against the reform. Although the heads of the major postsecondary institutions were opposed to the reform, the Legislative Council voted, by a narrow margin, in favor of the reform.

The government's strong ties to British higher education were enough to deaden any movement toward a four-year university system. With encouragement from the government, the influential subsidized secondary schools council came out in favor of the proposal and tipped the balance in favor of maintaining upper sixth form schooling. The proposal had important resource implications, thus acting to unite secondary school principals who received government subsidies for the upper year of their secondary schools. This upper year stood to be eliminated if a four-year university structure came to prevail.

Although not part of any colonial conspiracy, the Hong Kong Education Commission appeared to be working toward insuring a continuation of the three-year British system of higher education while under great pressure by many sectors of the education community to bring the University of Hong Kong into line with universities in China, the United States, and elsewhere. The result of this proposal was to pressure the Chinese University of Hong Kong to cut its academic program from four to three years. At one time, opposition groups even appealed, though unsuccessfully, to China's quasi-ambassador in Hong Kong, asking him to intervene and support the four-year structure of higher education since it coincided with that in the rest of China. The result of this case can be viewed not so much as signifying an abandonment of the Chinese character of the Chinese University of Hong Kong, or the embracing of colonial values, but rather as an acknowledgment that groups in Hong Kong are prepared to exercise their right, as spelled out in the Joint Declaration, to resist following the model of education in China. Moreover, since that time, the government has appeared less willing to activate the elaborate consultation process it had knit over so many years, and thus less concerned about its legitimacy in educational matters. This was most evident a year later, when following the June 4 incident in Beijing, the government acted without consultation and proposed to double the number of places in tertiary education by 1996. In contrast to the reform of a year or so earlier, the government was no longer as concerned with the financial cost of expanding university education or the difficulty in finding competent lecturers. While some have seen this as a way of rewarding tertiary institutions for their compliance with the earlier reforms, others saw it as a genuine effort to develop human resources lost due to the exodus of talented people following the crackdown on the democracy movement in China.

Language Reforms

Of all the educational reforms, those dealing with language have received the most attention by the Education Commission. In fact, the issue has found its way into almost every major report on education since the founding of the colony. This should hardly be surprising since language lies at the heart of culture; it binds society, acts as a mark of identity, and in the case of Hong Kong it is taken especially seriously by a people who have been united by the same common written language for thousands of years. Moreover, the issue gains added complexity in Hong Kong where most people do not use the standard dialect known as Putonghua (Mandarin), but rather the regional dialect Guangdonghua (Cantonese) in their daily lives.

Although Hong Kong's return to China increases the status value of the Chinese language, especially Putonghua, the reality is that fluency in English still promises more opportunities in the society. Moreover, English proficiency in learning the secondary school curriculum can make university admission and overseas employment more attainable. Unlike many British colonies in the past where English acted as a bridge between peoples of different languages and dialects, the English language did not serve to improve communications between indigenous peoples. Most people communicate in Cantonese and read a Chinese script almost identical to that in other parts of China. When Cantonese speakers interact with Chinese speakers from other dialect regions, they prefer to find a way to communicate across their often mutually unintelligible Chinese dialects rather than resorting to the use of English. The reasons for this have much to do with culture and identity.

Language policy in education has been increasingly fashioned so as to dovetail with the recruitment of native Hong Kongese to the civil service by establishing the mechanism to develop an explicit English-language facility necessary for succeeding on linguistically based civil service examinations. This has been accomplished through a policy process reflecting the colonial support of elite schools and the preservation of the University of Hong Kong as a wholly English-medium institution. English-language facility and cultural consonance are essential to the recruitment and promotion of graduates from the University of Hong Kong in the civil service.

This emphasis also led to a large Anglo-Chinese system of secondary schools. By the early 1980s this sector of the educational system peaked, thus surpassing the number of Chinese-medium schools by a proportion of 9 to 1. However, although the official medium of instruction in the Anglo-Chinese schools was English, a different reality prevailed in most schools. The limited number of competent English-speaking teachers led to many variations in the quality of language instruction. Even when competent English-speaking teachers were available, it was evident that a great many students were not able to learn through this medium. Parents resisted pleas by educationalists to reconsider choosing Anglo-Chinese schools instead of Chinese-medium schools for their children. The Education Department eventually took steps to increase the number of schools in the Chinese sector by providing incentives to those questionable Anglo-Chinese Schools to convert to Chinese-medium instruction. This resulted in an increase in the number of Chinese-medium secondary schools and a corresponding influence on the ethos of many Hong Kong secondary schools.

The medium of instruction in most secondary schools in Hong Kong is still officially English, a fact of educational life that places a tremendous burden on students, especially since most have little contact with native English speakers. The effects of this practice on culture and identity are of more interest to researchers than to parents, most of whom continue to opt for as much English-medium education for their children as possible (Gibbons, 1982). This places children attending elite English-medium schools at an advantage in terms of being recruited to government civil service posts. Public policies do not seek to redress this, as noted again by a visiting panel.

There also seems to be an element of safeguarding privilege by an elite whose children are more or less bilingual. Everyone should try by the best legitimate means to secure the best start for his own child, but we feel the public policies should look particularly to the needs of those whose starting positions are not so favorable (Visiting Panel, 1982).

This pattern may be further reinforced by a new set of language policy proposals that the government is considering. These would make entrance into English-language secondary education dependent on an examination administered after primary six (Working Group, 1989). The stated aims of the proposal are to improve competency in at least one language and to eliminate the use of "chinglish," a mixture of English and Chinese words in the teaching-learning process. The reality of this proposal, as explained elsewhere, is that it will further extend elitist elements in the educational system and further restrict access to the University of Hong Kong and to government civil service positions to those in the English streams (Postiglione, 1989).

All past government-initiated language proposals have fallen short of implementation, however. The medium of instruction controversy dates back to the end of World War II, the government forever being in the bind of eliminating either parental choice in medium of instruction on the one hand, or good sound educational practice on the other. Some accuse the government of being half-hearted, as has been the case with Putonghua (Mandarin) teaching. In this respect it never went beyond recommending Putonghua teaching as an option of the curriculum, failing to make it a requirement. The Education Commission recommended that the schools be encouraged to teach Putonghua either before or after hours or as an extra-curricular activity. However, only two schools use it as a medium of instruction (Kwo, 1991). Some researchers like Pierson are confident that Putonghua will replace English and Cantonese to become the language of power and the official language of government, and that everyone will be required to learn it (Pierson, 1991).

Growing business opportunities in the China trade and investment area, along with the expanding interactions between China and Hong Kong, have added to a new groundswell favoring Chinese mother-tongue schooling over English-medium schooling. In fact, the battle to preserve Hong Kong's status as an English-speaking territory is far from being won. At the same time, many educationists in China have criticized Hong Kong's return to Chinese mother-tongue education. This is because Hong Kong Chinese consider Cantonese rather than Putonghua, the official language of China, as their mother tongue (Wai, 1986). The majority of Hong Kong educators strongly resist the use of Mandarin as a learning medium in their schools. This represents yet another example of how the dual identity of Hong Kong's cultural ethos manifests itself within educational issues even as they impinge on localization and recruitment into the government civil service. Thus, school language policy, and the extent to which individuals can function competently in Putonghua, Cantonese, and English, can easily come to influence the legitimacy of emerging political leaders and the type of orientation that educational policy will take.

Curriculum Reforms

The only area of educational reform that has been explicitly tied to the transfer of sovereignty has been the reform of the school curriculum. The first example occurred soon after the Sino-British agreement was formalized. At that time, the Education Department issued a set of guidelines for civics education. Until the late 1980s, the school curriculum virtually ignored raising political consciousness. The planned return of sovereignty changed that to some degree by leading to minor modifications of the school curriculum. However, political democracy, as noted by Paul Morris (1988), remained an avoided topic. "The decision to return the sovereignty of Hong Kong to the PRC has created pressure to prepare pupils for their future as citizens of the PRC. This influence has come primarily from the government, whose primary goals are to ensure minimal disruption prior to 1997 and a trouble free handover in 1997" (1988:514).

Such curriculum changes also provided much needed legitimacy to a colonial government often accused of dragging its feet for many years before introducing opportunities for representative government. In this sense, the curriculum appears to the populace as an instrument used to bolster attempts at expanded representative government.

After 1985, the year of the signing of the Joint Declaration, the number and range of school curriculum topics dealing with political awareness increased. Although this may be associated in any society with a general trend toward more affluence and a growing middle class, it derived at least equally from the expected return of sovereignty in 1997. For example, civics education made its appearance during this time. Its implementation was difficult owing to the general political apathy of the populace spawned over many decades. Yet it constituted the most direct attempt to influence the curriculum with regard to Hong Kong's future. However, the greatest stress is placed on the responsibilities of good citizenship. Activities that encourage political involvement are minimized. Several quotations from the Government Guidelines on Civic Education (1985) reflect this emphasis: "in light of Hong Kong's recent political development, evolution should be the watch-word and the emphasis in this guide will be on civic education as a politically socializing force for promoting stability and responsibility." And, "Democracy means different things to different people. . . . So education for democracy per se would be difficult to interpret."

Moreover, education officials have lifted the taboo on teaching about post–1949 China. However, many school principals want to teach children about modern China but are encountering difficulties. In particular, it is difficult to get teachers to analyze the present regime. Most teachers are reluctant to discuss Beijing's generally feared and despised regime, with the result that Hong Kong is fostering a generation of young people who have only the slightest under-standing of their future as Chinese citizens. Although some academics support the new courses, others criticize them as reflecting a new defensiveness in the Education Department to appease Beijing (Glain, 1990).

The most recent curriculum reforms concern the introduction of a liberal studies component to the sixth form curriculum. In its second report, the Education Commission suggested the abolition of higher-level examinations, taken at the end of the first year of the sixth form to gain admission to the Chinese University of Hong Kong, and the introduction of a new curriculum termed intermediate levels (I-level). This I-level examination would be developed from, and as part of, the advanced-level (A-level) curriculum. These would be half subjects in that they would represent half the teaching syllabus of and half the teaching time required for the comparable A level. All sixth form courses would last two years and should lead to the existing A-level examination, but students could take the I-level examinations after one year of their studies in the sixth form. The Education Commission also recommended that more subjects of a less academic nature be introduced at A level and I level. It was believed that the introduction of I-level subjects would broaden the course of study undertaken by sixth form students. The commission contended that the I levels would be a way of establishing a certificated area of study for those who leave the sixth form after one year. In 1988 the government modified the proposal, saying that the sixth form curriculum should be broadened by offering new subjects of a technical and practical nature at A and I levels. In 1989 the I-level examination was renamed the Advanced Supplementary Examination (AS level).

Following the recommendation of the Education Commission Report Number Three, a working group named Working Group on Sixth Form Education was set up in June 1988 to consider the reform of the sixth form curriculum. In July

1989 the working group submitted its report to the secretary for education and manpower who endorsed the recommendations. One recommendation was the introduction of a new course entitled "Liberal Studies," which along with the "Use of English and Chinese Language and Culture" would be AS-level core subjects beginning in September 1992. Several modules were proposed, with students being required to take two, one at least to contrast with their main course of study. The modules eventually named were: Hong Kong Studies, Environmental Studies, The Modern World, Science Technology and Society, China Today, and Human Relationships. Despite the benefits of such a long overdue reform, the fact that the curriculum will be limited to the sixth form and that it may remain an optional course acts to relegate this reform to the backwaters. Its successful implementation, therefore, has much to do with how the universities choose to act regarding whether or not to make it an admissions requirement.

These curriculum changes are occurring with a backdrop of important changes in the political culture of Hong Kong during the late 1980s. The sociopolitical landscape has gradually been transformed away from its traditionally apolitical orientation. Rapid economic growth, expanded educational opportunity, and a younger population have led to a decline of traditional institutions and social customs. Social and economic issues have been pushed into the political arena, and this has led to demands for more government action. After a long period in which a secluded bureaucracy existed apart from the Chinese society, new efforts have been made to formalize government–people relationships. An increasing number of people hold that the government is responsible for solving their personal and family problems. The people of Hong Kong are rapidly adapting an active, and even interventionist, conception of government, and they would also like to see the government measure up to their expectations. Moreover, it is apparent that the people of Hong Kong are becoming more favorably disposed toward political activism of many kinds as the growth of political pressure groups continues. A prominent Hong Kong political scientist notes that "tactics which involve a quantum of confrontation or violence are increasingly rated as effective means to compel the government to give in" (Cheng, 1986:37–38). This is no small change. However, there is still a lack of adequate local structures for social and political participation, including areas of education decision making.

Privatization and Educational Reform

When a large-scale international move toward privatization of education occurred in the 1980s, Hong Kong was driving in the opposite direction. Private schools flourished in Hong Kong during the 1950s and 1960s when the school system was experiencing its initial expansion. Private primary schools virtually disappeared as the government's inspection standards under its Code of Aid became the measure of the viability of keeping a school open. By the 1980s the Code of Aid was used to bring all primary and most secondary schools under the umbrella of the Education Department. When three years of junior secondary education became universal, free, and compulsory, there were not enough places for students in the government or government-subsidized schools. Therefore, the government began to buy places from the private schools. Private school places were generally inferior to those in the government sector. The government increased the number of schools under its control, and at the same time the number of private schools declined. However, beginning in the late 1980s, a number of factors including organized opposition by the private schools led to a new reform proposal that would lend salvation to private schools. The major change came in 1988 with a new proposal by the Hong Kong Education Commission.

The Education Commission recommended that the Bought Places Scheme be phased out. This scheme permitted the buying of places from private secondary schools as a way of supplementing the supply of free secondary school places. While one of the major selling points of this proposal is that it throws a lifeline to the private schools by allowing them to apply for government subsidies, there are other implications as well. The secondary schools of a high standard will likely opt to come under this Direct Subsidy Scheme (DSS) rather than the existing Code of Aid. Under the DSS scheme, schools that receive financial subsidy from the government could charge school fees. Moreover, they would not have to accept students through the government's centralized scheme. The other selling point of this scheme is that it expands parental choice. Parents could send their children to DSS schools by applying directly to them.

Critics of the scheme note that the new system would allow parents who are willing to pay a weighty school fee to send their children to the exclusive secondary schools which would still be supported by public funds. For the first time, these publicly subsidized schools could have the power to accept or refuse students as they saw fit. Thus, the financial scheme evolved over several decades to insure more equality of educational opportunity would be severely compromised. Social distinctions would become further institutionalized.

Research on family background in Hong Kong has consistently confirmed what has been all too evident in the Western developed nations—that family background, however measured, is the best predictor of school achievement (Brimer and Griffin, 1985; Mitchell, 1972; Ng, 1985; Post and Pong, 1989). School factors also play a large role. In this regard, there is great disparity among schools, as confirmed in a recent report by a visiting panel:

There are striking variations indeed. Hong Kong has some of the best schools in the world in terms of student attainment . . . most of the schools, however, leave something to be desired. Facilities, teacher qualifications, examination results and other indicators of quality rank low. Students are allocated to these schools for various reasons, including their test performance and lack of opportunity owing to the educational and economic status of their parents (Visiting Panel, 1982).

Little has been done to relieve this problem, and if, as expected in the early 1990s, the economy goes through a period of crisis, this could highlight the gap between the social classes. It is more likely than that the schools will become an arena of social class conflict. It remains an important question as to whether or not social class conflict can work itself into the cultural fabric of Chinese society in Hong Kong in such a way as to avoid becoming dangerously divisive. If it cannot, then it poses perhaps the greatest threat to realization of an extended democratic educational policy process.

Nevertheless, the DSS proposal has been welcomed by a number of educators who point to international trends and who contend that the system would more closely match Hong Kong's free market ideology. Naturally, the heads of the most prestigious schools welcomed the proposal. The proposal also received support from the pro-Beijing or patriotic schools which have long been excluded from financing through the Code of Aid.

THE FUTURE OF EDUCATIONAL REFORM IN HONG KONG

Aside from reconciling or heightening the contradictions between capitalism, socialism, and pariotism, Hong Kong's educational reforms have a second major challenge to confront during its transitional period. A central question facing Hong Kong concerns the role of the education system in producing the kind of popular political leaders that will bolster confidence of the local population enough to take Hong Kong through the transitional period. When colonial rule ended in former British colonies, it led to a form of independence either through peaceful or violent means. In the case of Hong Kong, the end of the colonial period leads directly to a restoration of sovereignty by China in 1997. The agreement between Britain and China promises that the post–1997 period will include a preservation of the capitalist system, a high degree of self-government, and "Hong Kong people ruling Hong Kong." Lau Siu-kai points out that "with only seven years remaining before 1997, Hong Kong is still in search of an organized group of political leaders who can be trusted by the people of Hong Kong and the two governments to make the arrangements stipulated in the Sino-British agreement and the Basic Law work" (1988:1). The formula of "Hong Kong people running Hong Kong" cannot be successfully implemented without indigenous popular political leaders.

As 1997 approaches and Hong Kong becomes more and more a part of China, the decolonization process and the accompanying social transformation are gradually unfolding. Education's transformation potential is closely tied to its ability to produce political leaders. This will require a fundamental change in the manner of political socialization in secondary schools and tertiary institutions. The government's guidelines on civics education, the modification of the ban on political activity in schools, and the liberal studies curriculum go part of the way to this end. Moreover, an increasing number of teachers and school principals are becoming active in local elections aimed at insuring more representative government. However, much more will have to be done to have any effect on the impediments that have mitigated against the formation of such leadership, including the nature of colonial governance; the character of the Chinese community; the institutional features of the local sociopolitical system; the constraint of time; the inconsistent and incoherent leadership policy of the British and Chinese governments; and the elusive and erratic mass support for leaders. Although the reforms discussed above have only begun to approach this important challenge, future educational reforms can be expected to give increasing consideration to this important issue.

REFERENCES

Brimer, A., and P. Griffin, 1985. *A Study of Mathematics Achievement in Hong Kong*. Hong Kong: Centre of Asian Studies Monograph.

Burns, John, and Ian Scott. 1988. *The Hong Kong Civil Service and the Future*. Hong Kong: Oxford University Press.

Buruma, Ian, 1990, April 12. "The Last Days of Hong Kong." *The New York Review*, pp. 41–46.

Census and Statistics Department. 1986. *Hong Kong Annual Digest of Statistics*. Hong Kong: Government Printer.

———. 1989. *Hong Kong Annual Digest of Statistics*. Hong Kong: Government Printer.

Chan, M. K., and David Clarke. 1991. *The Hong Kong Basic Law: Blueprint for "Stability and Prosperity" Under Chinese Sovereignty*? Armonk, N.Y.: M. E. Sharpe.

Chen, Edward K. Y. 1983. *Multinational Corporations, Technology & Employment*. New York: Macmillan Press.

Cheng, Joseph Y. S., ed. 1986. *Hong Kong in Transition*. Hong Kong: Oxford University Press.

Cheng Kai Ming. 1991. "Education Policy Making in Hong Kong: The Search for Legitimacy." In *Education and Society in Hong Kong*, ed. G. Postiglione. Armonk, N.Y.: M. E. Sharpe.

Clark, David, and M. K. Chan. 1991. *Hong Kong's Transition and the Basic Law*. Armonk, N.Y.: M. E. Sharpe.

Draft Basic Law. 1988. The Secretariat of the Consultative Committee for the Basic Law. *The Draft Basic Law of the Hong Kong Special Administrative Region of the People's Republic of China*.

Education Commission. 1984. *Report Number 1*. Hong Kong: Government Printer.

———. 1986. *Report Number 2*. Hong Kong: Government Printer.

———. 1988. *Report Number 3*. Hong Kong: Government Printer.

———. 1990. *Report Number 4*. Hong Kong: Government Printer.

Emmons, Charles. 1988. *Hong Kong Prepares for 1997: Politics and Emigration in 1997*. Hong Kong: Centre of Asian Studies.

Gibbons, John. 1982. "The Issue of the Language of Instruction in the Lower Forms of Hong Kong Secondary Schools." *Journal of Multilingual and Multicultural Development*, no. 3: 117–128.

Glain, Steve. 1990. June 18. "The China Story, All of It: Hong Kong Schools End Taboo on Communism." *International Herald Tribune*, p. 5.

Guidelines on Civics Education. 1985. Hong Kong: Education Department.

Henderson, J. 1987. "Hong Kong: High Technology Production and the Makings of a Regional Core." In *Global Option: Society, Space, and the Internationalization of High Technology Production*, ed. J. Henderson. London: Croom Helm.

Hong Kong Government. 1981. *Overall Review of the Hong Kong Education System*. Hong Kong: Government Printer.

Huo Guoqiang. 1988. *Xianggong zhongxue gailan*. (Xianggong: Xianggong zhonghua jidujiao qingnianhui).

Kwo, Ora. 1991. "The Political and Social Context of Putonghua Teaching." In *Education and Society in Hong Kong*, ed. G. Postiglione. Armonk, N.Y.: M. E. Sharpe.

Kwong, Paul C. K. 1991. "Education and Manpower." In *The Other Hong Kong Report 1990*, ed. Richard Y. C. Wong and Joseph Y. S. Cheng. Hong Kong: Chinese University of Hong Kong Press.

Lau Siu-kai. 1982. *Society and Politics in Hong Kong*. Hong Kong: Chinese University of Hong Kong Press.

———. 1988. "Basic Law and the New Political Order of Hong Kong." Hong Kong: Center for Hong Kong Studies.

———. and Kuan Hsin-chi. 1988. *The Ethos of the Hong Kong Chinese*. Hong Kong: Chinese University Press.

Leung Yat-ming. 1991. "Education in Hong Kong and China: Toward Convergence." In *Education and Society in Hong Kong*, ed. G. Postiglione. Armonk, N.Y.: M. E. Sharpe.

Luk Hung-kei. 1989. "Education." In *The Other Hong Kong Report*, ed. T. L. Tsim and H. K. Luk. Hong Kong: Chinese University of Hong Kong Press.

Miners, Norman. 1986. *The Government and Politics of Hong Kong*. 4th ed. Hong Kong: Oxford University Press.

Mitchell, Robert E. 1972. *Pupil, Parent and School*. Hong Kong–Taipei: Orient Culture Service.

Morris, Paul. 1988. "The Effects on School Curriculum of Hong Kong's Return to Chinese Sovereignty in 1997." *Journal of Curriculum Studies* 20 (6):509–520.

Mushkat, Miron. 1990. *The Economic Future of Hong Kong*. Hong Kong: Hong Kong University Press.

———. and Kathleen Cheek-Milby. 1989. *Hong Kong: The Challenge of Transformation*. Hong Kong: Center of Asian Studies.

Ng Lun Ngai-ha. 1984. *Interactions of East and West*. Hong Kong: Chinese University Press.

Ng, Pedro. 1975. "Access to Educational Opportunity: The Case of Kwun Tong." Social Research Center, Chinese University of Hong Kong.

Peebles, Gavin. 1988. *Hong Kong's Economy*. Hong Kong: Oxford University Press.

Pierson, Herbert. 1991. "Cantonese, English, or Putonghua—Unresolved Communicative Issues in Hong Kong's Future." in *Education and Society in Hong Kong*. ed. G. Postiglione. Armonk, N.Y.: M. E. Sharpe.

Post, David, and Suet Ling Pong. 1989. "Trends in Gender and Family Effects on School Attainment: The Case of Hong Kong." The Comparative and International Education Society Annual Meeting, Harvard University, April 3–4.

Postiglione, Gerard. 1989. See Hong Kong Chinese Newspapers (1) *Jingji Ribao*, November 24, and (2) *Xinbao*, November 27.

————, ed. 1991a. *Education and Society in Hong Kong*. Armonk, N.Y.: M. E. Sharpe.

————. 1991b. "Hong Kong Education Within a Transition Society." *Comparative Education Review*, 35(4):627–649.

————. 1991c. *Education and Society in Hong Kong*. Armonk, N.Y.: M. E. Sharpe.

SCMP. 1990. "Tertiary Doors Will Open to More Students." *South China Morning Post: Year in Review*, January 14, and *South China Morning Post*, "Academic Hits Out at Crisis Intervention," November 5, 1989.

Shive, Glen, 1991. "The Expansion of Higher Education and the Work Force." In *Education and Society in Hong Kong*, ed. G. Postiglione. Armonk, N.Y.: M. E. Sharpe.

Sino-British Joint Declaration. 1984. Xinhua News Agency (Hong Kong Branch). *Sino-British Joint Declaration on the Question of Hong Kong*.

Sweeting, Anthony. 1990. *Education in Hong Kong Pre–1841 to 1941*. Hong Kong: Hong Kong University Press.

————. 1991. "Hong Kong Education and Historical Processes. In *Education and Society in Hong Kong*, ed. G. Postiglione. Armonk, N.Y.: M. E. Sharpe.

Tsim Tak-lung. 1991. "The Implementation of the Sino-British Declaration." *The Other Hong Kong Report*. Hong Kong: Chinese University of Hong Kong Press.

Visiting Panel. 1982. *A Perspective on Education in Hong Kong*. Hong Kong: Government Printer.

Wacks, Raymond, ed. 1990. *Hong Kong's Bill of Rights: Problems and Prospects*. Hong Kong: Faculty of Law, University of Hong Kong.

Wai, S. W. 1986, November 12. "Secondary Schools Favor Teaching Through Chinese." *South China Morning Post*, p. 3.

Wang, Qile. 1982. *Xianggong zhongwen jiaoyu fazhowshi*. Xianggong: Po Wen Shuju.

Wong, S. L. 1986. "Modernization and Chinese Culture in Hong Kong." *The China Quarterly* 106: 306–325.

Working Group. 1989a. *Report of the Working Group Set Up to Review Language Improvement Measures*. Hong Kong: Education Department.

————. 1989b *Report of the Working Group on Sixth Form Education*. Hong Kong: Education Department.

Xinhua News Agency (Hong Kong Branch). 1984. *Sino-British Joint Declaration on the Question of Hong Kong*.

Youngson, A. J., ed. 1983. *China and Hong Kong: The Economic Nexus*. Hong Kong: Oxford University Press.

Zeng, Yu Shuo. 1989. *Guodugide xianggong*. Hong Kong: Joint Publishing.

14

HUNGARY

Cathy C. Kaufman

This chapter examines educational reform in Hungary as part of a larger social transition in that country. French sociologist Alain Touraine argues that interacting social elements are of special significance at the beginning of new historical periods when fundamental questions about a changing society and its educational system are defined and established (Touraine, 1989:70).

A pattern of reform prompted by crisis and instituted through adaptation marks Hungary's response to external forces that have changed geographic borders, the political and economic system, and the educational structure as well. During the current transition period, as Hungary shifts from an imposed value system to a plurality of values, the society and the educational system are seeking to define reforms that will facilitate this transition.

This chapter combines a secondary analysis of archival and current literature with recent qualitative research conducted by the author's examination of Hungarian educators' perspectives on reform during the 1989–1991 time period. An historic perspective will allow the reader to evaluate current reform efforts in relation to past patterns of change. The important relationships of the economic, political, cultural, and educational systems in Hungary are examined within seven time frames: the Turkish period, the feudal period under the Hapsburg influence, the Enlightenment, liberalism, nationalism, the imposed Soviet model, and the current transition period. Dennis Rondinelli argues that reforms fail primarily because of social conflict and resistance rather than because of flawed intent (Rondinelli, Nellis, and Cheema, 1983). Both educational policies and acceptance and resistance to the reforms, therefore, are examined within each time period. Education historically has transmitted the political aims of the dominant power. Occasionally, the purpose of reform was established as the propagation of culture, but reforms were most purposefully motivated by faltering economies. From the past to the present, educational reforms in Hungary have traditionally grown from economic crisis. In 1846 Jozset Etos, minister of education, wrote, "The major and surest method of promoting our material interest is public education" (Carron and Chau, 1980:4). A. Horvath, in a recent report to Unesco, argues that Hungarians must "tie ourselves to the rest of the world with all the strings possible" (Horvath, 1990:214).

THE TURKISH PERIOD

During the 360 years between 1339 and 1699, the Ottoman Empire exercised control over areas in the Balkans, but it only occupied Hungarian territory for the 175 years between 1526 and 1699. Until their defeat at the hands of the Turks, the Hungarians, or Magyars, had been the dominant nationality in the area for 500 years. The Ottomans imposed political and economic reform, but they rarely destroyed the religious and ethnic elements of Hungarian society on which the responsibility of education and cultural transmission rested. In spite of Hungarian resentment of their subjugation, the flourishing economy during this period brought a measure of prosperity to the native population (Walters, 1988:26). The major point of educational contention during the period was that the children of Christian families under a child levy act could be taken from their parents and educated as professional soldiers for the sultan's army (Walters, 1988:27). Hungarian attempts at resistance focused on turning to neighboring nobility to rescue their lands. They were failed first by Frederick I of Hapsburg, and later by Zapolya of Transylvania, who was coopted by the Turks in return for peace in his region. In 1657, when the Turks were preoccupied during the Swedish invasion of Poland, Leopold I, the Hapsburg emperor, took the initiative against the Turks, and the immediate future of Hungary rested and remained in the hands of the Hapsburgs (Radkai, 1989:43–45).

THE FEUDAL PERIOD UNDER HAPSBURG DOMINATION

The basis for a formal Hungarian educational system emerged from the absolutism of the Hapsburgs. The intent of the 1777 decree Ratio Educationis to eliminate illiteracy is recognized as an important factor in accounting for the current high national literacy rate (Okey, 1982:24). The foremost structural reform was a decisive break between Roman Catholic and Orthodox tradition and established a Western rather than an Eastern focus for Hungarian education, with a formal linking to Rome rather than to Constantinople. Content reforms involved an alphabetic choice of Latin over Cyrillic, and the instructional language choice of Latin over Greek.

A second reform goal was to eliminate Protestantism from Hungary. The continued exposure of upper class children who were educated in Geneva to Calvinism, however, negated this attempted reform. Another short-term reform project was directed at a minority of Hungarian Gypsies. Maria Theresa sought to make "New Hungarians" of this segment of the population. She forced all Gypsies to sell their horses and coerced landowners into giving land and building materials to construct permanent housing for the group. She forbade the Gypsies to leave their villages without written authorization, to speak their own language, or to wear other than the locally determined clothing. In addition, at age four Gypsy children were handed over to local non-Gypsy families, and the village priest was responsible for their education (Liegois, 1987:99, 100). Nevertheless, the Gypsies' active resistance caused the failure and ultimate abandonment of this reform effort.

Hungary was considered the peasant sector of the Hapsburg Empire, but those who were able to gain access to the elitist educational system received a classical training equal to any in Europe. Hungarian educational excellence, however, was grounded in principles of social, religious, and gender inequality. Education in this feudal state was delegated to the guilds and to the churches, and educational training depended totally on one's social rank, religious affiliation, and gender. The masses of Hungarian peasants were still untouched by formal education (Okey, 1982:20).

THE ENLIGHTENMENT PERIOD

The second half of the eighteenth century, the Hungarian Enlightenment, was a major turning point in the educational reform of attitudes, but not of content or structure. Historian Robin Okey's assessment of enlightened despotism in Eastern Europe suggests that reform was more despotic than enlightened, and that educational change resulted from the political ambition of a few rather than from a philosophical enthusiasm that more typified Western Europe. Reform in education was not a central societal ideal. Rather, reform ideas were presented by the peripheral fringe groups of Hungarian society, such as the Hungarian Protestants, who had been exposed to alternative ideas from an education abroad (Okey, 1982:38).

Okey argues that, in spite of Marxist attempts to historically root the Hungarian Enlightenment in the context of socioeconomic change from the few to the masses, the peasants of the period were more interested in personal welfare than in social and educational emancipation reforms. Enlightenment reforms established an important "mood" more than it changed the educational framework, with the most influential reform component being the legacy of an intellectual and liberated spirit that historically differentiated East European education from its Soviet counterpart (Okey, 1982:46 and 58).

LIBERALISM

Until this time, the Austrian Catholic Church dictated educational direction. Following the Crimean War (1853–1856), however, Franz Joseph had to accept the capitalists' request for a constitutional government in return for the funding necessary for his country's economic recovery. The Hungarian terms of this agreement demanded two equal states, Austria and Hungary. At this juncture, the church lost its essential control over education. The major educational reform growing from this period was the replacement of the imperial and church language of Latin by German.

Hungary has historically placed its own interpretation on transplanted concepts and ideals. Janos Kadar's reinterpretation of Stalin's statement, "He who is not with us is against us," to "He who is not against us is with us," is perhaps the best known of the twentieth century. During the nineteenth century, too, Hungary's interpretation of liberalism differed markedly from that of the rest of Europe, where liberalism was the creed of the middle classes, signalling the reorganization of society according to the individual rather than the more traditional concept of inheritance. In Hungary, the period of liberalism, by contrast, was dominated by the noble class. The nobility of the old Austro-Hungarian Empire occupied the middle ground between the masses and the new governing elite, similar to a West European middle class. There were extremely large numbers of nobles in Hungary, compared to the diminishing numbers of elites in England and France. This intelligentsia, built up largely from impoverished but well-educated nobles, some 544,000 strong, was almost as large as the urban population itself in 1840 (Okey, 1982:70). Only these nobles had political rights, and educational decisions were in their hands.

The nobility set forth various aims to educate the entire population, but educational access remained restricted. Social sorting affected not only peasants, but the working class as well. While nearly all bourgeois children went to secondary school, less than 2 percent of the agricultural population gained entry to the educational system (Carron and Chau, 1980).

Educational reforms during the period were legally enabled but were seldom actualized. Visions and rhetoric were present, but action and change were absent.

NATIONALISM

The years between 1918 and 1939 are unique in East European education because for the first time since the Middle Ages, democratic nation-states replaced semi-aristocratic authority in establishing policy. These states were not independent economic units in their own right. Rather, they exchanged tutelage of the Austro-German capital for that of Western Europe and America. The collapse of the old empires merely transposed the problems to another sphere of influence. Nation-states were not nearly as nationalistic as the terminology implied (Okey, 1982:180).

Socially and educationally, the interwar period is nationalistically portrayed as one of great progress. Simple entrepreneurial enterprises of the nineteenth century were replaced by more complex managerial enterprises led by professionals. At a time when a basic education was no longer considered sufficient, elite preparation for university resulted in an extension of mass education and a broader basis for the extension of higher education. Ivan Berend argues that resulting reforms consisted mainly of an extension of the structural framework rather than improvement of educational content. Hungarian educational facilities and enrollments evidenced improvement, but the character of education remained unchanged. It remained high quality and was almost solely limited to the elite process (Berend, 1980:169, 170).

Structural reforms of the period resulted in the establishment of teacher training schools and technical secondary institutes. Reforms in the content of education allowed for a literary language based on living Slovak dialects.

Okey takes a cynical look at nationalism, arguing that it was not an altruistic devotion to national destiny but middle-class competition for clerical jobs. He views the educational system as a functional matter of group dynamics rather than ideological progressiveness in reforming society, and he cites a Rumanian critic who pointed out, "Hungarians say they want democracy but what they really want is a thousand year old Hungarian state" (Okey, 1982:96). It should be noted that Germans and Magyars in Hungary have historically refused to others the national rights they demanded and claimed for themselves. Nationalism promised educational reform, but in actuality schools were used as assimilation agencies of Magyarization.

Garrison Walters defines reforms in the nationalism period in terms of attention to linguistic groups. He argues that this language base has been the root of national minority group dissatisfaction and notes that the concept of fusions of nationality and state in a nation-state is a problem not only of complexity but also of conflict in Eastern Europe (Walters, 1988:32, 33). Ethnicity and diversity serve as additional organizing elements in examining Hungarian education because Hungary essentially has three major minority classifications. The first, ethnic minorities, are those populations who have immigrated to Hungary, usually for economic reasons, and have assimilated into the host societies. The second, national minorities, have not moved anywhere but have been created by peace treaties that have changed official boundaries (Kozma, 1990:10, 11). The third group is the population of Gypsies or Travelers, who in Hungary have generally been absent from consideration in most educational policy documents. The modernization attempted during this period of nationalism only served to amplify existing ethnic grievances.

Hans-Georg Heinrich, too, is critical of educational equity during this time, arguing that nationalism was an ideological vehicle by which Hungarian aristocratic-bourgeois elites could embark on modernization while remaining free of former Austrian interference. To defuse minority issues, one nationalistic thrust was to encourage national minorities to have their own associations, press, and broadcasting, and to establish their own minority areas of educational focus. Any form of identity was critical to Hungarians at this time. They had lost 75 percent of their physical territory following World War I, a loss that ultimately accounted for their siding with the Axis powers in World War II. Hitler had promised to regain the lost Hungarian territories. Instead, Hungary lost over half its male population during World War II.

THE SOVIET MODEL

Following a brief period of national rule between 1946 and 1948 and the concomitant European-oriented school curriculum, the Soviet model was externally and forcibly imposed when Stalin reneged on his postwar agreement. Every teacher in every school taught children the same content from the same textbooks during this period of reeducation. The political content of communist education was clearly expressed in the reformed curricular content, including the mandatory study of the Russian language and Marxist ideology (Horvath, 1990:209).

Soviet education reflected the dual reform goals of providing enough workers to meet industrial goals (manpower planning) and of abolishing the historic elitist educational privileges in Hungarian education (Volgyes, 1982:152). These two concerns of the Soviet model resulted in structural reforms that attempted to provide industrial matches and in curricular content changes that mandated teaching of the Russian language and Marxist political ideology. Ironically, the theoretical structure of the new education did not differ greatly from that of earlier Catholic domination. The foundations for both were authoritative and absolute, administered in the earlier instance by the church and in the latter by the state (Horvath, 1990:209, 210).

Hungary, like other East European socialist countries, entered a phase of intensive growth after 1950 that reflected a belief in limitless expansion. This belief was linked to reforming the structure of education in order to produce the needed personnel for the task. In 1958 long-range planning of the national economy started in Hungary, as did the personnel planning of education for the needed labor force. Reforms during this period were marked by redefinition of the educational framework and by the educational content itself. The four- to six-grade elementary schools were abolished, and a unified system of eight-grade primary schools was created. In the 1950s the spreading of secondary education was based primarily on the traditional *gymnasium*, and the rapid growth of secondary education put an end to its earlier elite character. The school reform of 1961 was aimed not only at making the secondary education of the 1950s compulsory, but also at mandating the changing of its structure and content in order to link education with vocational training (Berend, 1980:171).

Hungary presents a situation in educational reform that is not found elsewhere in the rest of the Eastern Europe. Hungary's dual economic system (NEM), a socialist planned economy side by side with a market economy, began in the 1960s and set the stage for a different agenda in central planning for education. During the past twenty years, Hungary has also allowed the emergence of conflicting interest groups in educational policy formation, in conjunction with the overall context of changing economic emphasis. During the 1960s, 1970s, and 1980s, Hungarians experimented with and revised the processes of economic and educational reforms that are now just beginning to emerge in neighboring former Eastern bloc nations. Nonetheless, educational decision making was determined and did not seek public input.

Gabor Halasz's work established a framework that identified the shapers of educational policy over a twenty-five year period prior to the 1985 decentralization reforms. Conflicts regarding the economic versus the ideological aspects of reform eventually fractured party unity. According to Halasz, conflict resulted from attempting to realize the egalitarian ideology of the Soviet model within a context marked by economic backwardness. The most important reform to those with an economic orientation was equated with early manpower approaches. The role of education was to rapidly provide the labor force for a backward economy. In the early 1960s this economic focal point of reform was paramount in the formation of educational policy. It enabled schools to put out masses of young people just at working age and able to cope with simple, physical labor tasks (Halasz, 1986:126).

In the late 1960s, however, reform shifted to the emphasis of ideology and defining schools as melding institutions for the teaching of the practical tasks of Marxist political ideology. This reform reflected the polytechnical concerns of the Soviet model and was equated with later polytechnical, vocational approaches. Those holding this strong vocational commitment for secondary students placed the concept of upbringing before instruction at the primary level. They favored nonacademic, nonformal, collective group activities in and out of school. Later reforms were influenced once again by an economic need, but they favored a subject-oriented curriculum, measured performance, individual differentiation, and special provisions for students whose performance was outstanding.

By the 1970s over half the pupils in Hungary along with students in other Comecon countries were receiving a secondary education where vocational elements dominated. The 5 + 1 system (five days of general education and one day of vocational training), however, failed for lack of funds. Berend notes the absence of school workshops and qualified teachers of the various professions, the shortage of equipment, and the oversupply of pupils per teacher (Berend, 1980:172). Horvath argues that the fundamental reforms of the 1970s were launched because Hungarian education was forced to confront the reality that the ideological content of education contradicted economic reality (Horvath, 1990:210).

Educational policies based on the common belief that vocational education was the cheapest way to match educational preparation with economic need were incorrect. Vocational education was very expensive, and the physical work necessary in the future economy was not the type of work students of traditional vocational education had trained for (Horvath, 1990:129). Clinging to the traditionally established educational approaches, in spite of a reforming economy, in large measure accounts for the economic crisis of the 1980s and mandatory lower grade jobs for the now more highly qualified generation. The result is that today's workers must either take jobs below their competencies or become long-distance commuters. Youth are guaranteed a job but not a career. This is what Julia Szalai refers to as hidden unemployment (Szalai, 1984:270). As another result of Soviet educational approaches, age, not education, became the significant factor in the 1980s in determining a Hungarian's place in the social hierarchy. Szalai's research identifies a critical mid-age group threatened by the current phenomenon of job displacement. Those in the 35 to 40-year-old bracket entered the labor market when the population was already enjoying full employment. Since then, new entrants have demonstrated increasingly higher qualifications. Although hardly any change was made to the structure itself since the hiring of the thirty-five- to forty-year-old group, significant changes were made in the training of the entrants. With their higher qualifications, they were in a position to advance more rapidly than older employees with less education but with more years of experience.

THE CURRENT TRANSITION PERIOD

Tamas Kozma of the Hungarian Institute for Educational Research argues, "What [goes] on in the classroom influences the political future of Eastern Europe much deeper than what [happens] in the public arena" (Kozma, 1990:12). How will the changing Hungarian educational system evidence reform of the former Soviet model?

Eighteen Hungarian educators, representing instructors at the university, secondary (gymnasium), and elementary (primary) levels of the Hungarian educational system, described to the author current reform in relation to visible change, economic and political factors, comparisons to other Eastern European nations, opposition factors, and equity. Five questions framed their responses.

1. What were the most significant changes that occurred in education in the past year?
2. How are economic and political factors in Hungary influencing educational policy?
3. How do teachers compare educational changes in Hungary to changes in other East European nations?
4. What opposition to change exists?
5. Is any minority group large enough to have a voice in educational change?

Within the theme of change, these educators identified three distinct domains: the curricular change dropping mandated Russian-language instruction, redefinition of the meaning of "school," and restructuring of the educational system most directly impacted by a legally enabled, though minimally actualized decentralized educational plan.

Educators indicated that the single most dramatic change following the 1989 political changes was the removal of the Russian language from a place of curricular prominence. For forty years competency in Russian was an undisputed educational requirement. Consultants described this as an "overnight difference" that resulted in an immediate decrease in enrollment in Russian-language classes.

Second, Hungarians are redefining the socialist meaning of schooling. Formerly, schooling was a state concern. Present transitions represent the dimensions of private language schools and church-affiliated schools. Hungary is witnessing a rapid growth of private schools that are sponsored by religious groups or private organizations. The growth of such schools produces both positive and negative educational changes. Parents who can afford it now have greater latitude in the education they choose for their children. Many language classes have been added as an after-hours opportunity, but students who cannot afford the tuition or a way home cannot participate. Churches are reclaiming the physical plants (cathedrals, convents, and monasteries) taken from them under Soviet rule, resulting in displacement of state-operated programs, such as art institutes, which formerly occupied these sites. Students now remain "stranded" midway through disbanded programs.

Third, decentralization of the economy in 1977 established a need for a decentralized educational system. Educational decentralization was legally enacted in 1985, and the "free" elections of 1987 gave added credence to the idea of public input. Political restructuring in 1989 lent attention to decision making at the local level, but currently it appears that what was legally enabled has not been largely actualized. As part of a structural change, local municipalities are entitled to elect their own local boards and hire their own supervisors and principals. In terms of changed content, educators can add previously prohibited courses to the curriculum and access textbooks from inside or outside the country. Changed courses include religious instruction if there is local demand, additional languages, and literature of the instructor's choice.

Local citizens have no prior experience in setting up or conducting such elections for local governance boards. As a result, 92 percent of the authorities in local governing positions in the schools prior to 1985 were still in those positions in 1990. Passivity and nonaction constitute a safe stance in light of the past. Whenever Hungarians have attempted to rectify social injustice in the past, they have paid dearly for it. In 1919, for example, protestors and innocent bystanders alike were slaughtered by communists and rightists. And in 1956, thousands lost their lives in the quashed rebellion against Soviet occupation. Martha Lampland contends that the real reluctance to embrace radical change rests on pragmatic experience (Lampland, 1989:15). Timothy Ash claims that recent social change has revealed just how important the "residual veil" of Marxist ideology currently is as it performs a blocking function to reform (Ash, 1990:6).

Moreover there is no provision for the national exams to be changed. Therefore, teachers say that deviating from what is currently taught, and choosing other materials and subject areas within the curriculum, will cause their students to fail the tests. As a result, local parents, teachers, and students alike resist curriculum change.

With regard to the second question, the economic and political influences, educators refer to the past system as socialism, totalitarianism, state capitalism, dictatorship, or the Soviet system. All, however, identify economic change as the catalyst to the current social and educational change, and all agree that the current emphasis on learning English and German reflects the concern over establishing international business ties.

On the eve of the French Revolution Mirabeau said that, "The nation's deficit is the nation's treasure." Timothy Ash claims that if we substitute "hard currency debt" for "deficit" we have the main reason why Hungary led in the reform movements of the 1960s and 1970s, in the free elections of 1987, and in the 1989 break with socialism (Ash, 1990:3). Everyone today has some stake in the faltering economic system, and however small that stake—an apartment, a car, a German stereo set—it is more than owners care to lose (Volgyes, 1982:57). It is, therefore, a common practice for Hungarians to hold three or four jobs. Occupational status and job affiliation are dependent not as much on the choices of occupation as on the numbers of occupational opportunities.

Educators today say that they now realize that what came about politically in 1987 could have happened in the late 1970s if the people in general had known how fractured the party was during that period. Educators, who see themselves as change agents, criticize a lack of commitment on the part of local parents to help change schools (Kaufman and Paulston, 1991:8,10). They also note the parental fear that if they vote against the current director they or their children as students will be "hurt."

Only 24 percent of Hungarians surveyed by the press, *Magyar-Nemzet*, in 1989, considered themselves active participants in political life (*Magyar-Nemzet*, 1989, 5). Many believe that the plans put forth by educators, whom they view as the current elite intellectuals, will leave them as much in the cold as the old socialist practices did. There is a lack of belief that the new system will work any better than the old.

An area strongly tied to possible curricular content reform within schools, but motivated by political bias, is the key issue of nationalism. Hungarians differ regarding the emphasis which new social science programs should place on "What it means to be Hungarian." A minority of educators feel that Hungarians should look inward, build national pride, and concentrate on national uniqueness. The majority currently favor a Western focus. They express concern that the European Community views Hungarian culture as "not as accepted as are the German, French, or British cultures." Although teachers themselves are proud to be Hungarians, they contend that a national educational movement would isolate them at precisely the time when international financial agreements are integral to the success of the national economy.

Concerning the third question, the comparison of Hungary to other nations in Eastern Europe, Hungarians see their nation as a leader in change for the former Eastern bloc. Interviewed educators see themselves in a position to establish the direction of reform. They emphasize the importance of decision making at the major universities in spite of the fact that the educated intelligentsia is a small minority of the general population and that there are only four universities in the entire country.

Hungarians point out that they have been Eastern bloc leaders since the Hungarian revolution of 1956. They claim that the revolution brought the concept of political enlightenment to Eastern Europe in spite of the disastrous immediate results. In addition, they cite the dual economic system, operating for the past thirty years, in conjunction with central planning as evidence of the unique effectiveness of Hungarian reform.

Opposition to change, the fourth question, exists in the form of resistance to a knowledge hierarchy in education that is currently emerging, where certain teachers are more highly valued for their subject knowledge than others and are paid accordingly. This creates dissension within the profession. For example, teachers of German and English have greater earning power than teachers of the natural and the social sciences. In addition, conflict exists within the ranks of the language teachers themselves. Although a ten-year period has been established to get the new curriculum in place, former Russian-language teachers are being given only two years by the government to update their skills. They have been given time off and paid an expense budget to obtain twelve hours per week of English or German instruction. Those who are financially able or who can make exchange arrangements with colleges in Europe or America are perfecting their English while teaching Russian to local college students. Teachers within Hungary repeatedly use the term "disillusionment" when describing their contrasting situation. They claim that, although they have been trained as linguists, they "cannot cope" with the pressure of learning all the subtleties of a new language in two years, with only twelve instructional hours per week and limited opportunity for oral practice.

Interviewees acknowledge that reform is now occurring through trial and error. Most of the old established lesson formats are still in use because of the national exams, which have not been altered, and because they "need something to go by." Teachers who are innovating new class ideas complain that the sharing of successful teaching ideas is difficult in the absence of a network of colleagues. Teachers classify themselves into two basic groups: the few, who embrace the idea of making curriculum and instructional determinations, and the majority, who wish to be guided in the instructional process. Hungarians conditioned to take orders resist taking control and making decisions. They see their choices as resting on the advisement and decisions of others.

Lastly, although no minority group exerts "influence" in decision making, there is a minority large enough to "require the immediate attention" of educational policy planners. This group is a Gypsy population of 500,000 Hungarians. Government policies are currently designed to improve the health, employment situation, and education of Gypsies. There is now, for the first time in the curricular content reform, the plan to instruct children in their own language. Previous access to state education by Gypsies was not sought either from within or without in either the educational community or the Gypsy community itself. Under the former Soviet system, parents frequently kidnapped their children from schools and represented the most overt social resistance to Marxist policies. Hungarian Gypsies define themselves as Gypsies who are Hungarian, not as Hungarian Gypsies. Because they represent a large segment of the population, they have been the focus of current policy changes. They themselves have not initiated such educational changes, and in areas where change has been implemented, resistance is more common than acceptance. There exists an attitude ranging from extreme negativity to great skepticism on this subject with the educators themselves. Teachers express lack of preparation for the task. Wolfgang Mitter argues that teachers trained in a socialist environment currently do not have the skills to implement innovative change (Mitter, 1987:55).

CONCLUSION

Reform strategies in Hungary grew from desperation rather than design, resulting in the achievement of temporary periods of social stability. They were seldom linked with progressive educational change. The predominant historical characteristic from the Ottoman Empire, through the long Hapsburg reign, to Soviet domination was control. Hungary has evidenced an elitist, class-oriented structuring of education, a structure that forty-five years of Soviet domination failed to eradicate. From a population used to a central government dealing with problems while the people wait, there is today a great resistance to change. Hungarians have no behavioral history of effecting change, only a history of waiting for decisions to be made elsewhere. Learning to survive has meant learning to deal with the system. To Hungarians, a large part of such "dealing" means basing their transactions in life on each other, in one-to-one relationships with acquaintances. Reform is further impeded by this factor similar to the Soviet concept of *blat*, since people trust only those who have proven themselves on the basis of personal favors. Change and action in Hungarian daily life take place through personal relationships; there is a lack of identity with change through impersonal election.

Social and educational reforms in Hungary have been slow, incremental changes over the past thirty years. The dramatic events of the fall of 1989 were not an impetus for Hungarian reform, but rather the confirmation of past economic and educational change efforts. Accelerated political change since the free elections of 1987 and the break with Moscow in 1989 give added credibility to such educational reform efforts as decentralization, which if successfully enacted will enable Hungary to serve as a reform model for social and educational de-Sovietization.

REFERENCES

Antweiler, O. 1975. "Towards a Comparative Study of the Educational Systems in the Socialist Countries of Europe." *Comparative Education* 11(1):3–11.

Ash, T. G. 1990, January 18. "Eastern Europe: The Year of Truth." *The New York Review*, 1–8.

Berend, I. 1980. "Educational Reforms in East-Central Europe: The Hungarian Example." *Prospects Quarterly Review of Education* 10(2):169–173.

Carron, G., and Ta Ngoc Chau. 1980. *Regional Disparities in Educational Development*. Paris: Unesco Press.

Halasz, G. 1986. "The Structure of Educational Policy Making in Hungary in the 1960s and 1970s." *Comparative Education* 22(2):123–132.

Heinrich, H. 1986. *Hungary: Politics, Economics, and Society*. London: Pinter.

Horvath, A. 1990. "Tradition and Modernization: Educational Consequences of Changes in Hungarian Society." *International Review of Education*, Unesco Institute for Academic Publishers, Netherlands 36(2):207–217.

Kaufman, C., and R. Paulston. 1991. "Hungarian Education in Transition." Paper presented to the American Educational Research Association.

Kozma, T. 1984. "Teacher Education in Hungary: System, Process, Perspectives." *European Journal of Teacher Education* 7(3):255–265.

———. 1985. "Conflict of Interests in Educational Planning." *Prospects Quarterly Review of Education* 15(3):347–360.

———. 1989. "Education in Eastern Europe: Recent Changes, Future Prospects." *Homework, a Newsletter of the School of Education, Syracuse University* 1(5):1, 7.

———. 1990. "Education in Eastern Europe: The New Conservative Wave." Fulbright Lecture to the Department of Cultural Foundations, Syracuse University.

Lampland, M. 1989, April 14. "Hungary and Transistion Opportunities and Challenges." Paper presented to Congressional Seminar, University of California at San Diego, pp. 3–16.

Liegois, J. 1987. *Gypsies and Travelers. Social-Cultural Data, Social-Political Data*. Strasbourg.

Magyar-Nemzet. 1989. "Editorial Commentary: Equity Issues." Vol. 1, No. 6, p. 5.

Mitter, W., ed. 1983. Multi-culturalism. T. Kozma (presenter.) "Multiculturalism and Educational Developments in Hungary: A Multicultural Approach to Policy Alternatives." [Conference Proceedings/Wurtzburg]:366–378.

———. 1987. "The Teacher and the Bureaucracy: Some Consideration from a Soviet Case." *Compare*, Vol. 17, No. 1, pp. 47–60.

Okey, R. 1982. *Eastern Europe 1740–1985*. Minneapolis: University of Minnesota Press.

Radkai, M. 1989. *Hungary*. Singapore: Hoefer Press.

Rondinelli, D., J. Nellis, and G. Cheema. 1983. *Decentralization in Developing Countries: A Review of Recent Experiences*. Washington, D.C.: World Bank.

Szalai, J. 1984. "Youth and Unemployment: The Case of Hungary." *Prospects Quarterly Review of Education*: 270–276.

Touraine, A. 1989. *Return of the Actor: Social Theory*. Minneapolis: University of Minnesota Press.

Volgyes, I. 1982. *Hungary. A Nation of Contradictions*. Boulder, Colo.: Westview Press.

Walters, G. 1988. *The Other Europe*. Syracuse, N.Y.: Syracuse University Press.

15

INDIA

Ila Patel

Recent educational reforms in developing countries are set in the context of world economic crisis. Worldwide educational planners face economic constraints to finance the existing system of education and expand it further to meet the growing social demand for more and better schooling (Carnoy, 1986). However, educational decisions about whether to expand or improve the existing education system, and how to reform education, are part of a wider economic and political-ideological conflict over the educational system and resources in a given society. What kind of educational reforms are proposed in the context of the present "crisis" of education? To understand the economic and political dynamics that condition recent educational reforms in developing countries, this chapter presents the case study of India's new educational reform in the 1980s.

Since independence, the Indian government has routinely reviewed the country's educational system. There is no dearth of reports by various committees, commissions, and experts on ways of reforming the existing system. However, only twice during the postindependent period has a national policy on education been formulated by the government to reform the entire system of education. First, a National Policy on Education (1968), based on recommendations of the Education Commission (1964–1966), was put forth to restructure the existing educational system in order to create a skilled labor force and a "modern" citizenry for the gradually modernizing economy and nation building.[1] Second, the National Policy on Education (1986) proposed a major educational reform to gear the existing educational system toward new development priorities (Ministry of Human Resource Development 1986a). This second reform is a landmark in the history of Indian educational planning. It marked the beginning of the new direction of educational development in India, a shift toward greater efficiency in the educational system for the privileged sections of society rather than toward educational equity, equality, and access for marginal groups.

There is no dearth of descriptive studies on educational reforms in India. But even the most recent and voluminous work on Indian educational reforms (Panchamukhi 1989a, 1989b and 1989c) does not pay adequate attention to the study of educational reforms in the broader social, political, and economic context of Indian society. The new educational reform proposed by the National Policy on Education (1986) was widely discussed and debated by the government.[2] Although it was debated among academicians,[3] no serious attempt has yet been made to critically examine it from the perspective of political economy.

Unlike the traditional human capital theory of education, which emphasizes the role education plays in economic growth, the political economy theory of education treats education as part and parcel of power relations among different groups in society.[4] The political economy perspective does not examine an educational system as an independent force in changing social/economic inequality or in altering individual characteristics. Rather, it argues that the way different levels of the educational system expand, who goes to what level, what kind of education is obtained, and the value attached to different levels of schooling in the labor market are conditioned by the class structure of society and continuous power struggle in society for control over resources and the state. Because of the relative weakness of the local bourgeoisie in developing productive forces and in establishing its dominance over the state and society, the state in the Third World plays a direct and active role not only in the economy but also in establishing its hegemony in society.

Within this perspective, a study of educational reform cannot be separated from implicit or explicit analysis of the state, understanding broadly the government. The state plays a central role in maintaining or restructuring the existing system of education in a given society. Hence, a study of state intervention in education is necessary in the political economy theory of education and social change. In the context of Third World capitalism, education serves an important function in the reproduction of relations of production and the political legitimation of the state.

Formal education partakes in the reproduction of the social division of labor by supplying skills for production and allocating the skilled labor to hierarchical workplaces. It promotes the process of capital accumulation by providing the skilled labor in abundant quality, the "reserved army" of the educated population, to the private and public sectors. The political-ideological role of education is equally important. Education contributes to the creation of a dominant set of beliefs and values which promotes existing social and economic inequalities as just and rational. At the same time, in the situation of high symbolic value of formal education as a vehicle to achieve social mobility and to gain political power, education also serves an important role of political legitimation of the capitalist state.

The kind of knowledge imparted through the educational system and struggle in educational institutions can contribute to the process of change and can adversely influence the processes of capital accumulation and of political legitimation. The existing educational system has the potential to transmit progressive knowledge that can enable workers and citizens to demystify the state and wage a struggle against an unequal social order. With a low level of economic development, neither the state nor the private sector can provide employment opportunities to the entire educated population. The rising frustrations of the educated unemployed or underemployed and the inability of the state to expand education exponentially can also delegitimize it as a welfare state and lead to a politically unstable situation.

Why does the state propose an educational reform at a particular historical juncture? What kind of educational reform is undertaken? Who are the actual beneficiaries of the reform? These are some of the key questions that we will examine in this chapter.

EDUCATIONAL EXPANSION AND ECONOMIC CRISIS

Indian's educational reform in the 1980s was set in the context of economic crisis and the growing social demand for further expansion of education. After independence, the Indian state undertook the task of educational reconstruction against the legacy of a hierarchical system of colonial education through a powerful apparatus of planning. Educational expansion during 1951–1981 took place in the context of a low level of economic development and a high social demand for formal education as an avenue to social mobility. For the Indian state, formal education has remained an important sector in development plans to facilitate the process of capital accumulation and political legitimation. However, with sluggish economic growth since the 1970s, the state is constrained to pursue rapid expansion of the educational system. This section highlights the salient aspects of the educational expansion in India before the 1980s.

Educational statistics reveal the story of an unprecedented expansion of the formal educational system in the history of Indian education during the first three decades after independence. Educational institutions and enrollment increased at each level of schooling (see Table 15.1). Expansion of the educational system has taken place with large investment in education by the government. Since 1950–1951, government expenditure on education (both plan and nonplan)[5] steadily increased from Rs. 1,140 million in 1950–1951 to Rs. 37,460 million in 1980–1981.

The expansion of the lower levels of education (primary and middle) also helped democratize the existing system of formal education for socioeconomically disadvantaged groups, such as scheduled castes, scheduled tribes, and girls.[6] Considerable progress has been made in terms of their participation in education, which is reflected in a rise in the literacy rates (Table 15.2) and the enrollment ratio in elementary education. The participation of the scheduled castes and tribes in elementary education has also improved over time—from 5.1 million in 1951

Table 15.1
Educational Development in India, 1951–1981

	1951	1961	1971	1981
Educational Institutions				
Primary	209,671	330,399	408,378	485,538
Secondary	13,596	49,663	90,621	116,447
High/Higher Secondary	7,288	17,257	36,738	51,594
Higher Education				
Arts, Science and Commerce Colleges	548	1,161	2,587	3,393
Professional Institutions	147	381	1,017	1,382
Universities and Deemed Universities	28	44	93	123
Enrollment by Level of Education (in millions)				
Primary (Grades I–V)	19.16 (42.6)	34.99 (62.4)	57.04 (76.4)	72.68 (83.1)
Middle (Grades VI–VIII)	3.12 (12.7)	6.70 (22.5)	13.32 (34.2)	19.84 (40.0)
High/Higher Secondary/ Intermediate	1.48	3.48	7.17	11.28
University and Above (first degree)	.17	.56	1.96	2.75
Expenditure (Rupees in Millions)				
Total	1,140	3,440	11,180	37,460
Plan	200	900	1,150	5,200
Non-Plan	940	2,540	10,030	32,260

Figures in parentheses indicate gross enrollment ratio as percentage of the total population in that age group.

Source: Planning Commission (1985b:265)

Table 15.2
Progress of Literacy Among Socioeconomically Disadvantaged Groups, 1961–1981

	Scheduled Castes	Scheduled Tribes	Rest of the Population	
			Total	Female
1961	10.27	8.53	27.86	16.59
1971	14.67	11.30	33.80	17.11
1981	21.38	16.35	41.22	29.51

Figures indicate percentage of the literate population in the corresponding population

Source:Planning Commission (1985b:330)

to 18.6 million in 1981 (Ministry of Education and Culture, 1984: 2; National Institute of Educational Planning and Administration, 1990: 14). The proportion of girls to total enrollment in elementary education increased from 26.5 percent (22.3 million) in 1951 to 37.5 percent (92.6 million) in 1980–1981 (ibid.: 11).

The situation has been far from satisfactory, however. The lopsided development of the formal educational system is evident in terms of the uneven growth rate of different levels of education. Higher education has expanded at a faster rate than elementary education. In higher education the enrollment has increased at the annual rate of 9.7 percent per year, while it was never more than 6.2 percent in elementary education (Ministry of Education and Culture, 1985). High primary school enrollment percentages also disguise the low percentage of children who finish primary school. The magnitude of the problem is evident from cohort analysis. Although the retention rate in primary education (grades 1–4) improved from 33 percent in 1951 to 52 percent in 1981, a vast majority of children (six to eleven years) drop out (National Institute of Educational Planning and Administration, 1990: 15–16). In the absence of a radical restructuring of a class-based division of labor and knowledge, equality of opportunity to the disadvantaged groups, the expansion of the subsidized system of formal education has not succeeded in drastically improving their educational situation. The level of literacy among scheduled castes, scheduled tribes, and the female population continues to be very low, and dropout rates in elementary education have also remained higher among these groups compared to the general population (ibid.: 31–37).

The fact that development of the formal educational system has been impressive does not mean that the large majority of the Indian population has received even a minimal education. The literacy rate increased from 16.7 percent in 1951 to 36.2 percent in 1981. However, the absolute number of illiterates has increased over time. Table 15.3 shows the magnitude of illiteracy in India and urban-rural and gender disparities in literacy.

Table 15.3
The Magnitude of Illiteracy in India, 1961–1981

Year	Area	Number of Illiterates+ (in millions)		
		Male	Female	Total
1961	Total	148.4 (65.5)	185.4 (87.5)	333.8 (76.0)
	Rural	130.2 (70.9)	161.7 (91.5)	291.9 (81.1)
	Urban	18.2 (42.5)	23.7 (65.5)	41.9 (53.0)
1971	Total	172.0 (60.5)	214.7 (81.3)	386.7 (70.5)
	Rural	149.3 (66.2)	185.5 (86.8)	334.8 (76.3)
	Urban	22.7 (38.7)	29.2 (57.9)	51.9 (47.6)
1981*	Total	182.6 (53.1)	241.7 (75.2)	424.3 (63.8)
	Rural	153.9 (59.2)	203.2 (82.1)	357.1 (70.4)
	Urban	28.7 (34.2)	38.5 (52.2)	67.2 (42.6)

+ Number of illiterates in all ages exclusive of 0-4 years of age. Figures in parentheses indicate percentage of the corresponding population.

* Excludes the state of Assam where the Census of 1981 was not held.

Source: Directorate of Adult Education (1988:7)

A major constraint to continue further educational expansion is the inadequacy of financial resources owing to sluggish economic growth. The overall growth rate of the Indian economy as a whole between 1950 and 1980 is approximately 3.5 percent per year. However, the increase in population growth absorbs gains in terms of per capita income. India's rate of economic growth goes down to a

Table 15.4
Plan Allocations on Education, 1951–1985 (figures in millions)

Plan	Outlays for Education to the Total Plan	Elementary Education	Higher Education
First Plan (1951–1956)	153 (7.2)	93 (55)	15 (9)
Second Plan (1956–1961)	277 (6.2)	93 (34)	47 (17)
Third Plan (1961–1966)	560 (7.5)	209 (37)	82 (15)
Fourth Plan (1969–1974)	822 (5.2)	256 (31)	183 (22)
Fifth Plan (1974–1979)	1,726 (3.3)	410 (32)	292 (23)
Sixth Plan (1980–1985)	2,524 (2.6)	905 (36)	486 (19)

Figures in parentheses indicate percentages of the total.

Source: Ministry of Education and Culture (1983: 241–43 and 246–47).

very modest 1.3 percent per year after deducting the 2.2 percent annual rate of population increase (Balasubramanyam, 1984: 30–31).

A cursory look at the trends in public expenditure on education shows that, over the years, it increased as a proportion of gross national product (GNP) from 1.2 percent in 1950–1951 to 3.1 in 1980–1981 (National Institute of Educational Planning and Administration, 1990: 107). However, in the 1980s, the percentage of GNP going to education increased at a slower rate.

Plan allocations to the education sector do not represent the total public outlays on education. However, the figures in Table 15.4 suggest the declining share of education in the development plans. Except for the Third Plan, the share of education in the total plan allocations declined from 7.2 percent in the First Plan to a mere 2.6 percent in the Sixth Plan. The share of elementary education in the plan allocations to education has also decreased from 55 percent to 36 percent between these plans.

Much of the growth in expenditure on education has been offset by an increase in prices and a rapid increase in the student population. In terms of expenditure per student, the educational system is managing with more or less the same amount of money in real terms.

Thus, the economic reality of unprecedented educational expansion in India since the 1980s is pessimistic. However, decisions about which level of education to expand and for whom during the period of austerity are not economic or technical, but political decisions. Before examining the nature of the proposed educational reform, we will turn to the circumstances that led to the introduction of a new educational reform in the mid–1980s.

CHANGES IN INDIA'S DEVELOPMENT STRATEGY

Political transition to a technocratic regime under the leadership of Rajiv Gandhi in 1984 marked a significant change in India's development approach. The new educational reform, proposed by the new regime, was conditioned not only by the fiscal crisis of the Indian state, but also by the changed political and economic context of Indian society.

The parliamentary elections in 1984 introduced a new generation of rulers from the urban middle class who were attuned to the metropolitan culture and economic outlook (Gould, 1986: 645–648). The bifurcation of the state and national political systems also became apparent in the mid–1980s elections. The new regime undertook the task of political and economic transformation against the background of a nation torn by divisive and communal forces, and a sluggish economic growth. It assigned priorities to unity and integrity of the nation, rapid modernization of the industrial sector, and efficient administration.

Modernization of the economy has been a pervasive goal of the Indian state since independence. However, with the advent of a new regime, it acquired new meaning. External pressures to change the domestic industrial policy, domestic pressures from the Indian bourgeoisie for liberal economic policies toward the private sector and foreign investment, and contradictions developed during earlier regimes paved the way to an export-oriented development strategy for rapid modernization of the economy (Patnaik, 1986; Sathyamurthy, 1985). The new development strategy represented a marked shift in the Indian economic policy away from a left-of-center, socialist, and regulatory orientation toward a more centralist, private sector, and market-oriented approach. The accent of new development strategy was on accelerating economic growth through liberalization of one of the most controlled and regulated economies in the nonsocialist world. The regime introduced a series of far-reaching changes in earlier economic policies in the areas of taxation, industrial licensing, control of monopoly and foreign capital, import/export rules, and industrial planning (Kochanek, 1986). It proposed modernization for export-oriented growth. It was assumed that the new economic policies would improve the performance of the Indian economy and would help alleviate the problems of rural poverty and unemployment.

Politically, the new development approach was geared toward the top 10 percent of the population, represented by India's new urban-based, middle class. The new development approach was based on the assumption that India's new middle class of 100 million would provide the domestic market for an accelerated and sustained economic growth and that improved economic growth would alleviate rural poverty and unemployment.

To improve the efficiency of administration in the implementation of new development policies, the regime proposed several administrative measures (Rudolph and Hoeber, 1987: 82–83). It also reorganized the ruling party (Congress I) to prevent further deinstitutionalization, to bring the party organization under the managerial and professional style of new leadership, and to prepare the new cadres of party leadership at all levels (ibid.: 148–158).

The new development approach was translated into concrete policies in the Seventh Plan (1985–1990).[7] The plan envisioned the emergence of India as a modern industrial society guided by a welfare state in which poverty, illiteracy, and unemployment would be eliminated and basic social services would be made available to all. Given the resource constraints on the domestic economic policy, the plan adopted the policy of deficit financing and external financing (foreign aid). To attain the higher growth rate for the industrial sector, the private sector was assigned a very prominent role for the first time in decades. Private sector investment increased to 52 percent of the plan outlays. Furthermore the plan emphasized the consolidation rather than expansion of the public sector and improvement in management and efficiency of existing units.

On the other hand, to show the regime's commitment to the rural poor, a populist package of development programs of the earlier regime (the twenty-point program) was continued and several antipoverty programs were introduced.[8] The Seventh Plan continued the employment-oriented programs of the earlier regime for the rural population and assumed that the expansion of the private industrial sector would generate employment in urban areas. Given the major thrust of the plan on rapid modernization of industrial sector, the agricultural sector was not emphasized in the Seventh Plan. However, earlier modernization policies for agriculture that favored rich peasants continued.

Against this background of the new development approach of the technocratic political regime, we will examine the educational reform proposed to meet changing requirements in skills and values for new development priorities.

DIRECTION OF THE EDUCATIONAL REFORM

The new regime proposed the educational reform in response to changed development priorities.[9] The proposed reform focused on slowing down educational expansion while improving the efficiency of the existing system and quality of education for a few. It also concentrated on preparing a skilled labor force with appropriate ideological orientation for the modernizing economy with high technologies and foreign investment. On the other hand, the concerns for equality and the democratic goals of education, which were emphasized by the earlier educational reform, were diluted and neglected in the educational reform in the 1980s.

The Ideology of Efficiency

With changes in development priorities, a marked shift occurred in the conceptual framework of the educational reform. The reform in the 1980s viewed education as an important input for economic growth instead of a source of participation and social mobility for all sections of society. It placed emphasis on improving the existing educational system by relating it more closely to the changes in the production system. The assumption underlying such a view of education is that the relationship between education and the workplace is an efficiency problem that can be solved through better management of resources and better integration of students into the work system. By ''efficient'' investment in education and management of educational resources, eventually everybody (schooled and unschooled population) will benefit.

Within this perspective, the major achievements of the Indian educational system were viewed in terms of the quantitative expansion of each level of the educational system since independence. Although the reformers acknowledged the unequal expansion of different levels of education, no attempt was made to explore the possible role of education in maintaining the inequality. Instead, the educational problems of access, quantity, quality, and utilization of financial resources were attributed to ''inefficient'' implementation of educational strategy and management of resources. Implicit in this view was an optimism that educational problems could be solved by efficient management of the educational system through expertise and improved use of capital.

With the shift toward the technocratic view of education, the new educational reform stressed the reproductive role of education in preparing and training skilled human resources for ''self-reliant'' economic development and in inculcating a scientific temper, modern attitudes, and values to support production activities. Since the major concern of the reform was to restructure the educational system to prepare the workforce for the economy, it selectively omitted the democratic and egalitarian role of education in society. However, in the context of growing religious revivalism among Sikhs, Hindus, and Muslims and related political movements and violence in the 1980s, which posed a serious threat to the unification of the Indian nation and the system of Indian federalism, the role of education in homogenizing divergent sections of Indian society and creating national identity was also emphasized.

Major Areas of Educational Reform

Despite lip-service to the slogan ''Education for All,'' the new educational reform favors consolidating the formal educational system and restricting its access to a few. The educational strategy of the reform centered on promoting nonformal education to diversify social demand for formal education, while advocating a different quality of education with differing prices. The elitist nature of the reform is visible in the following main proposals.

Universalization of Elementary Education through the Channel of Nonformal Education. In the area of elementary education, the educational reform made the most glaring departure in the general direction of the earlier educational strategy followed since independence. In the period of austerity, the new reform proposed neither expansion of elementary education nor radical improvement in the quality of primary schooling for the poor and marginal groups. Instead, nonformal education was perceived as a panacea to fulfill the constitutional promise of universalization of elementary education for children up to the age of fourteen years. Nonformal education was proposed specifically for dropouts and for those children who have remained on the fringe of the formal educational system.

Without radically improving the quantity or quality of primary schooling in rural areas, advocacy for nonformal education at the elementary stage can be seen as a promotion of low-cost strategy to extend a compensatory type of elementary education for solving the problem of universal enrollment and universal retention in primary schools. Instead of making good quality elementary education widely accessible to the marginal groups, the reform restricted their access to the lowest level of formal education by slowing down its expansion, and channeling them to a compensatory type of elementary education through nonformal education programs. In practice, nonformal is not interchangeable with primary schooling. In the context of credential-oriented formal education and competitive job markets, nonformal education offers very limited access to higher levels of formal education and to jobs. In fact, nonformal education at the elementary stage adds one more layer of educational inequality to the existing system of formal education.

Navodaya Vidyalaya for Quality Improvement. Instead of improving conditions of mass primary schooling in rural areas, the new educational reform proposed government-sponsored, meritocratic residential schools known as *Navodaya Vidyalayas*, or model schools, starting from Grade 6 at the district level. These pace-setting schools in the countryside were justified on the ground that the brightest children from rural areas must receive good quality education at state expense. Navodaya Vidyalayas were also advocated as a step toward equal educational opportunity by making provision of quality education for meritorious children from socioeconomically disadvantaged families. English was suggested as a medium of instruction in these schools, so that their graduates could gain access to prestigious institutions of higher education and compete for lucrative positions in the "modern" sector.

The assumption underlying such schools in the countryside was that the meritocratic selection of students would be "objective" and would not legitimize the interests of the privileged sections of agrarian society. In fact, class bias is inherent in the differentiation of students on the basis of merit. In the first place, children from poor and marginal groups can get access to these schools only if they survive in schools up to Grade 5 and do well in academic work to pursue further education. In the context of the low participation of children from the families of rural poor in the existing educational system, and the low-quality education they receive in rural schools, it is not clear how they will get access to merit-based and competitive model schools.

In practice, Navodaya Vidyalayas are for the children of the rising class of rich peasants in the name of the poor. Rich peasants have become an important economic and political force in the Indian polity since early 1970s. They have money but not the facilities for good quality education in rural areas. Navodaya Vidyalayas will enable their children to receive quality education at state expense and compete with their urban counterparts for access to lucrative professions. Such schools can also be seen as an attempt to prepare a skilled labor force in rural areas with "modern" values, outlook, and cultural orientation for the economy modernizing with the support of transnational capital.

Vocationalization. The new educational reform in secondary education focused on vocationalization. Vocational education was proposed as a distinct stream to prepare students for selected occupations. It was advocated to meet three objectives: "to enhance individual employability, to reduce the mismatch between the demand and supply of skilled manpower, and to provide an alternative for those pursuing higher education without particular interest or purpose." (Ministry of Human Resource Development, 1986a: 13). The proponents of vocationalization perceived it both as a solution of the unemployment problem among educated youth and as a strategy for cooling down the high social demand for higher education.

The reform's technocratic perspective on the relationship between education and work is perhaps most visible in its proposal for vocationalization at the secondary stage. The unemployment problem in this perspective is seen as much more related to education itself (what is taught in the schools and how students are prepared for work) than the structure of the labor market. The "mismatch" between jobs and schooling is viewed as an efficiency problem to be solved by better integration of students into the type of work available through appropriate vocational training. It is assumed that vocational education will enable students either to find suitable employment or to promote self-employment.

In the context of changes in industrial and trade policies for export-oriented economic growth, the proposal for vocationalization can be seen as an attempt to prepare skilled technicians for the new "screw-driver" technology. In the short run vocational education may increase the employability of labor in the technologically advanced sectors of the economy. However, vocational training per se does not reduce unemployment. Overall employment or unemployment is not so much a function of the kind of education the labor force receives as of the way economy is organized. In other words, unemployment among the educated population is not an educational problem but a structural problem of an underdeveloped economy, which is unable to absorb its labor force.

Furthermore, the proponents of vocational education assume that secondary school graduates with vocational training will be treated equally in the labor market. However, labor markets in highly stratified Indian society are segmented.

People in the different segments of the markets with the different or same level of schooling are treated differently. In the class-based educational system, vocationalization will further accentuate inequalities by channeling students from rural or lower class urban backgrounds, who are not oriented to "academic" work, into low-paid occupations in the secondary labor markets. Finally, the introduction of vocational education may not serve to diversify social demand for higher education. Unlike higher education, vocational training lacks the social power to bestow its clientele with a legitimate claim for lucrative jobs in the primary sector of the labor market.

Restructuring Higher and Technical Education. Reorganizing the system of higher education was necessary in the light of diversifying growing social demand for higher education and changes taking place in the economy with the new technology. Hence, higher education and technical education received maximum attention in the new educational reform.

The reform in higher education was not primarily concerned with the further expansion of higher education. The educational strategy centered on consolidating the existing institutions, while improving the quality of higher education and restructuring the existing administrative structure of the higher educational system to facilitate the linkage between higher education and employment. The reforms proposed three main areas of change: autonomous colleges, the open university, and delinking degrees from jobs to restructure higher education.

A thrust toward privatization in higher education was visible in the proposal of granting autonomy to private colleges. Autonomous colleges were proposed in the name of better quality education. However, with the "autonomy" of higher education institutions, a whole range of qualities in higher education with different prices will emerge. Such a strategy will further widen the educational disparities between different social classes.

The second important proposal in higher education was the introduction of the open university and distance learning. The open university system was envisaged to democratize education by expanding opportunities for higher education. In reality, it can be seen as an attempt to diversify the social demand for higher education by adding one more layer to the hierarchical system of higher education. Far from equalizing educational opportunities, the open university system can further accentuate educational inequalities.

Finally, to tackle the problem of unemployment among the educated population, the reform proposed delinking jobs with degrees in the selected fields in which a university degree was not a necessary qualification. The assumption underlying this view was that the strategy of delinking degrees from jobs would cool down the social demand for higher education and, consequently, would reduce excessive pressures on the government for the expansion of higher education. It was assumed that the labor markets can absorb the graduates without university degrees. However, in the situation of high popular demand for higher education as a route to social mobility, such a proposal will probably not be effective in cooling down the educational aspirations and demands of the people.

With rapid modernization of the economy through high technology, the reform assigned considerable importance to technical and management education. The focus in technical education, however, was not on consolidation, but on the expansion and creation of an infrastructure in new areas of emerging technology vital for the economy and the provision of necessary facilities for education, training, and research in those fields. For new technological development, effective management education was also emphasized. A drive for high-level skills in a period of "austerity" further suggests the promotion of high-quality schooling for the few, particularly the students from the middle-class and affluent sections of society who have access to exclusive educational institutions.

Neglect of the education of the educationally disadvantaged sections of society (women, the scheduled castes and tribes, and adult illiterates) further reveals the inegalitarian nature of the reform. The reformers recognized disparities in education at each level of education. However, the reform did not propose to solve them through expansion of the good quality of primary and secondary education for the majority of the Indian population, but through special measures. Advocacy for a meritocratic educational system in secondary education through Navodaya Vidyalaya also indicates a redefinition of the concept of equality of opportunity in favor of the privileged sections of society.

In summary, the new educational reform favored consolidation of the formal educational system in the period of austerity while restricting its access to a few and improving educational quality for those who already do well in schools. Democratic concerns for equality in education and education for all were relegated to benign neglect.

Limits of the Educational Reform

Implementation of the new educational reform was conditioned by the economic and political constraints of the technocratic regime. In general, the regime was unable to translate fully its new development approach into practice.

First, the new regime faced substantial difficulty in translating its goals and objectives into effective policy and meeting rising popular expectations. Given the domestic and international financial and trade constraints, the regime had limited resources to implement its policies. Second, it was constrained by the existing bureaucratic structure to facilitate speedy implementation of new policies.

Second, the regime was situated in the less favorable political context characterized by growing unrest and an upsurge of divisive forces in almost every part of the country, the rise of Hindu revivalism and Muslim fundamentalism, and the problem of accommodating regional aspirations and identities in the existing structure of Indian federalism. The parliamentary victories strengthened the ruling party's political position to establish its hegemony over the state and to institute its development strategy. However, bifurcation of state and national political systems in the mid–1980s weakened the federal government's ability to implement its policies at the state level.

With these constraints on general implementation of the new development strategy, the new educational reform was not fully translated into practice in the Seventh Plan (Planning Commission 1985b: 252–269). For the ambitious educational reform, the plan allocated 3.6 percent of the total plan outlays. Given the limited financial resources to implement the new educational plan, the ambitious educational reform of the technocratic policy planners did not fully materialize. Nonetheless, the new education policy laid down the parameters of the future direction of educational development in India.

CONCLUSION

In the context of deepening world economic crisis, educational planners in developing countries face economic constraints to expansion of the existing educational system to meet the undiminished demand for more and better schooling. However, solutions to the present crisis of education may be found in the historical context of a given society. India's educational reform in the 1980s shows the momentum to slowing down educational expansion while restricting its access to a few. However, the implementation of the reform is constrained by the economic and political climate in which the reform is framed.

NOTES

1. See the report of the Education Commission (1964–1966), popularly known as the Kothari Commission, for details on the proposed reform (Ministry of Education and Youth Services, 1971), and Naik (1980) for analyses of the reform from a liberal perspective. For the policy statement on the National Policy on Education (1968), refer to the Ministry of Education and Youth Services (1968).

2. The new educational reform was primarily the work of the national bureaucracy. However, to create a consensus around its policy and to win the political support of wider sections of society, the central government widely circulated the policy perspective of the reform, "Challenge to Education: A Policy Perspective" (Ministry of Education and Culture, 1985), among different government and semigovernment agencies and the educated sections of society.

3. For example, refer to special issues on the National Policy on Education (1986) in *Indian Journal of Public Administration* 32:3 (July–September 1986); *New Frontiers in Education* 16:2 and 3 (1986); *Social Scientist* 14:2–3 (February–March 1986); and *University News* 25:50 (December 1986) for details on the academic debate.

4. See Carnoy (1985) for a brief analysis of the political economy approaches to education.

5. Plan expenditure refers to expenditure incurred in development plans for further development of education. Nonplan expenditure includes expenditure for the general operation and maintenance of the educational system.

6. Besides expansion of educational infrastructure, the introduction of several special measures, such as the provision of financial incentives, construction of hostel facilities,

reservation of seats in educational institutions, and relaxation in admission criteria have helped improve the general educational situation of scheduled castes and tribes. The government has also taken some measures to improve the conditions of girls' education.

7. Refer to the Seventh Five-Year Plan for a detailed discussion on the new development strategy and the underlying perspective (Planning Commission, 1985a).

8. See Bagchee (1987) for a review of how the Seventh Plan proposed to tackle the problem of poverty.

9. This discussion of the educational reform is based on three government documents circulated by the new regime: (1) *Challenge of Education: A Policy Perspective* (Ministry of Education and Culture, 1985), (2) *National Policy on Education—1986* (Ministry of Human Resource Development, 1986a), and (3) *National Policy on Education—1986; Programme of Action* (Ministry of Human Resource Development, 1986b).

REFERENCES

Bagchee, Sandeep. 1987, January 24. "Poverty Alleviation Programmes in Seventh Plan: An Appraisal." *Economic and Political Weekly* 33: 139–148.

Balasubramanyam, V. N. 1984. *The Economy of India*. London: Weidenfeld and Nicolson.

Carnoy, Martin. 1985. "Political Economy of Education." In *The International Encyclopedia of Education*, ed. Husen Torsten and T. Neville Postlethwaite. Oxford: Pergamon Press, pp. 3964–3974.

———. 1986. "Educational Reform and Planning in the Current Economic Crisis." *Prospects* 26:205–13.

Gould, Harold A. 1986, June. "A Sociological Perspective on the Eighth General Election in India." *Asian Survey* 26: 630–652.

Kochanek, Stanley A. 1986, December. "Regulation and Liberalization Theology in India. *Asian Survey* 26: 1284–1308.

Ministry of Education and Culture. 1983. *A Handbook of Educational and Allied Statistics*. New Delhi.

———. 1984. *Selected Statistical Information on Education*. New Delhi.

———. 1985. *Challenge of Education: A Policy Perspective*. New Delhi.

Ministry of Education and Youth Services. 1968. *National Policy on Education, 1968* New Delhi.

———. 1971. *Education and National Development: Report on the Education Commission 1964–66*. 2nd ed. New Delhi.

Ministry of Human Resource Development, 1986a. *National Policy on Education—1986*. New Delhi.

———. 1986b. *National Policy on Education—1986: Programme of Action*. New Delhi.

Naik, J. P. 1980. *The Education Commission and After*. New Delhi: Allied Publishers.

National Institute of Educational Planning and Administration. 1990. *Education for All by 2000: Indian Perspective*. New Delhi.

Panchamukhi, P. R., ed. 1989a. *Studies in Educational Reform in India, Volume 2: Educational Reform at Different Levels*. Bombay: Himalayan Publishing House.

———. 1989b. *Studies in Educational Reform in India, Volume 3: Reform Toward Quality and Relevance*. Bombay: Himalayan Publishing House.

———. 1989c. *Studies in Educational Reform in India, Volume 4: Medium of Instruction and Examination Reform at Different Levels.* Bombay: Himalayan Publishing House.

Patnaik, Prabhat. 1986, June 7. "New Turn in Economic Policy: Context and Prospects." *Economic and Political Weekly* 21: 1014–1019.

Planning Commission. 1985a. *The Seventh Five Year Plan: 1985–90, Volume I, Perspective, Objectives, Strategy, Macro-dimensions and Resources.* New Delhi.

———. 1985b. *The Seventh Five Year Plan: 1985–90, Volume II, Sectoral Programmes of Development.* New Delhi.

Rudolph, Lloyd I., and Susanne Hoeber. 1987. *In Pursuit of Lakshmi: The Political Economy of the Indian State.* Chicago: University of Chicago Press.

Sathyamurthy, T. V. 1985, July 20. "Piloting a Nation into the Twenty-First Century: Changing Political Context of State Power and Class Contradictions in India." *Economic and Political Weekly* 20:1218–1222.

16

IRAN

Golnar Mehran

Education in Iran has historically been used to serve the purposes of three main political actors within Iranian society: the ruling power, the reformists, and the revolutionaries. Each has utilized the system of education to further its cause and advocate its message. The ruling power has aimed at ensuring a close relationship between education and the prevailing social, political, economic, and cultural system so that it would reflect the dominant ideology of the authorities. The reformists of the nineteenth and early twentieth centuries regarded education as the panacea for the problems faced by a society experiencing domestic despotism and foreign domination. The revolutionaries have also viewed education as an instrument of change to be used in transforming the Iranian society. Educational reform in Iran, therefore, has served to maintain the status quo; to introduce gradual change through reform; and to contribute to fundamental transformation in the values and ideology of a nation.

THE HISTORICAL CONTEXT OF EDUCATIONAL TRANSFORMATION

The educational system of any nation reflects its social, political, cultural, and economic system. Thus, the study of educational reform efforts in Iran will provide the reader with a clear picture of the sociopolitical changes occurring in the nonstatic Iranian society.

A historical study of educational transformation in Iran points to four major types of schooling, reflecting the religious or secular nature of the state at different times: Zoroastrian education (550 B.C.–A.D. 642); Islamic education (A.D. 642–present day); modern, secular education (1851–1979); and education in the Islamic Republic (1979–present day).

Zoroastrian Education

The state religion of the Persian Empire, founded by Cyrus in 550 B.C., was Zoroastrianism, and the religion and teachings of Zoroaster formed the basis of schooling at the time. Zoroastrian education was geared toward preparing religious leaders and educating the sons of the nobility, thus enforcing the rigid stratification of the caste-like society and maintaining the dominant role of the priesthood and aristocracy. Zoroastrian education placed heavy emphasis on moral and religious training and character building, as well as physical education and military training, and included some reading, writing, and arithmetic taught by Zoroastrian priests (Arasteh, 1962). An important achievement of pre-Islamic education in Iran was the establishment of an institute of higher learning known as Jundishapur. Founded in A.D. 260, Jundishapur was a prominent intellectual center of the ancient world, attracting Persian, Greek, Syrian, Alexandrian, and Hindu scholars (Nakosteen, 1964). Jundishapur remained an influential center of scientific, philosophical, and medical studies until A.D. 900.

Islamic Education

The advent of Islam in Iran in A.D. 642 fundamentally altered the society and changed the system of education. Islam became the state religion, and Muslim education replaced Zoroastrian learning.

Among the first educational steps taken by Muslims was the establishment of Qur'anic schools known as *maktabs*—religious schools that provided traditional education, including reading, writing, arithmetic, basic Arabic, and familiarity with the Qur'an and classical Persian texts (Arasteh, 1970). Children of various age and educational level groups were taught by a religious figure, with an emphasis on rote learning and memorization and the use of strict discipline and physical punishment. *Maktabs* provided the only form of elementary education available in Iran before the emergence of state-supported public schooling, and was basically aimed at training the children of merchants, government officials, and shopkeepers. Children of upper class and aristocratic families were educated by private tutors. Although boys were the main recipients of this education, girls were occasionally taught by female educators in the highly gender-segregated Iranian society.

Whereas *maktabs* provided elementary education, the *madraseh* was equivalent to the secondary school system. Attached to a mosque and run by the *ulama* (Islamic scholars), the course of study in the *Madraseh* centered around religious instruction and was based on classical Islamic texts. Thus, rhetoric, syntax, etymology and derivation, logic, jurisprudence, philosophy, Arabic, and the Qur'an comprised the bulk of the *madraseh* courses of study (Fischer, 1980).

The theological centers (*hozeh 'elmiy eh*) as institutes of higher learning have survived until the present time, offering an alternative to public schooling and aimed at training Shi'i religious leaders. The new curriculum includes religious education as well as history, political science, education, mathematics, English language, and computer science (*Kayhan* [Daily Newspaper], May 30, 1990). In 1986 a total of 67,936 men and 7,347 women were studying at theological centers throughout the country (*Statistical Yearbook*, 1990). The theological centers in Iran have always been independent of the state and funded by religious endowments. Historically, they have differed from the famous state-sponsored centers for higher education known as *Nezamiyeh* founded in the eleventh century. In modern times, they have also competed with the faculties of theology in the state-sponsored universities. In fact, the financial independence of Iranian Shi'i *ulama* from state funding and the absence of a government-appointed hierarchy among them are believed to have led to their independence and thus revolutionary potential in recent times (Keddie, 1980).

Modern Education

Given the fact that formal education was exclusively religious, the educated Iranians—with the exception of civil servants—were mostly members of the *ulama* who monopolized the nation's educational and legal institutions. The situation was to be changed in the nineteenth century. Iranian reformers both inside and outside of government began searching for educational solutions to the problems of backwardness, domestic despotism, and foreign domination. Thus began the period of viewing education as a panacea.

The growing threat of Western industrial, technological, and military advancement indicated the inadequacy of religious education in training for modern conditions and needs. Education had to be made more relevant and practical. The products of Islamic education were lawyers, judges, notaries, and educators; Iran also needed specialists in engineering, medicine, and military knowledge. In the latter half of the nineteenth century, both Iranian merchants, who had been exposed to modern schools abroad, and selected members of the ruling power advocated the need for education along modern lines.

It was in response to these needs that the first state-sponsored, nonreligious institution of higher learning, known as Dar al-Fonun (the House of Sciences), was established in 1851 through the efforts of Naser al-Din Shah's reformist prime minister Amir Kabir. Dar al-Fonun was an elitist college attended by the sons of top government officials and prominent landowners at the age of sixteen. The course of study was based on the European model, geared toward Iran's immediate needs in the scientific and military fields, and included physics, mathematics, chemistry, medicine, surgery, engineering, mineralogy, and military tactics. Owing to the lack of Iranian instructors and Persian texts, Amir Kabir initially employed Austrian teachers and used European texts that were later translated into Persian (Arasteh, 1963).

The establishment of Dar al-Fonun was not the first Iranian contact with the West. The early nineteenth century had witnessed both European military missions to Iran in order to train the army and the dispatching of selected Iranian students abroad. Furthermore, foreign missionary schools had been active in Iran in the 1800s, "playing a major role in transferring Western values and educational patterns" (Mohsenpour, 1989: 10). Rather, the importance of Dar al-Fonun lies in two factors: (1) it was a starting point for modern secular education in Iran; and (2) it fit in with the major goal of reform, including educational reform—namely, modernization in an effort to fortify Iran against the West.

Founding a modern school, together with strengthening the army and establishing industrial factories to supply the army, reflected the dominant belief of the time that Iran's inertia and vulnerability to foreign domination were attributable to its technological and military backwardness. Thus, nineteenth-century modernization attempts by reformists were intended solely to improve Iran's conditions and in no way aimed at undermining traditional values and heritage. Modernization was not synonymous with Westernization. Rather, it referred to the adoption of modern technology and science, whereas Westernization meant the acceptance and imitation of Western models and ideas. In fact, one can argue that the intention was to prevent Western ideological penetration by standing firmly against its military and economic pressures. Such clearcut distinction between modernization and Westernization was totally blurred in later years, especially during the reign of the Pahlavis, to be reasserted in the post–1979 period.

Whereas any educational reform effort up to the twentieth century had been geared toward higher education and the schooling of the elite, the constitutional revolution of 1905–1911 turned its attention to basic education for all. For the first time in Iranian history, private donations and religious endowments to support Islamic education in the *maktabs* were complemented by government funding for secular elementary schools. The foundation of the Ministry of Education, Arts, and Endowment in 1911; the declaration of compulsory and free elementary education; centralized teacher selection and training; and the introduction of a secular curriculum in schools led to a complete transformation in Iranian education.

The Pahlavi dynasty (1925–1979) further consolidated the modernization, centralization, Westernization, and secularization of Iranian education. The reign of Reza Pahlavi (1925–1941) witnessed major changes in the educational system. By imitating the French model of educational administration, schooling became highly centralized with standard curricula, textbooks, and national examinations. The University of Tehran was established as the first coeducational center in Iranian history. Religious education was banned, *maktabs* were dissolved, *madrasehs* and theological centers were restricted, and religious studies were eliminated from the school curriculum. Educational change efforts were not only aimed at modernization but were also clearly antireligious (Szyliowicz, 1973).

Reza Shah, like Ataturk in Turkey, believed in the total secularization and de-Islaminization of the society and used the system of education to achieve its goal. Given the public nature of education, schools became the main socialization agents in which government-approved values and beliefs were disseminated. Thus began the dual culture in Iranian society in which the value system of the family is often questioned and challenged by the teachings of the school and vice versa.

The schism continued during the reign of Mohammad Reza Pahlavi (1941–79) during which secular, Westernized education reached its climax. Before the 1979 revolution, the nation's education was pro-Western and nonreligious in approach, being characterized in part by coeducation at the primary school level; abundance of foreign schools, some of which enrolled only non-Iranians; large numbers of students abroad; use of Western instructors at all levels of education and employment of overseas educational consultants; emphasis on the pre-Islamic Aryan, as opposed to the Islamic, identity of Iranians in the curricular content; and presentation of the Western society as an ideal model.

What Amir Kabir had begun in the nineteenth century was therefore completed, and yet the end was totally different from what was originally intended. Amir Kabir modernized to free Iran and to fortify it against the West. However, political, economic, and cultural dependence on the West was the legacy of equating modernization and Westernization during the reign of the Pahlavis.

EDUCATIONAL REFORM IN THE ISLAMIC REPUBLIC

In February 1979 a major social, political, and economic revolution took place, overthrowing a 2,500-year-old monarchy and declaring the Islamic Republic of Iran. The postrevolutionary regime inherited a malfunctioning system of education, characterized by unequal distribution of resources between urban and rural areas; marked inequity between schooling provided for the rich and the poor; a high dropout rate; rote learning and memorization and teacher-centered education; undue emphasis on examinations; limited university capacity despite high demand; emphasis on academic as opposed to vocational education; and irrelevance of curricular content to the needs of the economic and industrial sector (for a review, see Redjali, 1988). Yet the Islamic Republic had its own priorities as far as the most urgent reform efforts were concerned—namely, to Islamize and politicize education in an effort to bring about a cultural revolution.

The authorities of the Islamic Republic refer to the 1979 revolution as first and foremost a cultural revolution, aimed at creating a new moral order and fundamental transformation in the value system of individuals. The major goal of the Iranian cultural revolution has been the revival of Islamic values and the replacement of secular and Western ways by a new religio-political order.

Ever since the establishment of the Islamic Republic, Iranian authorities have attempted to Islamize and politicize the educational system in accordance with the aim of the cultural revolution—namely, to bring about a "revolution in values." Politicization in this context refers to the effort to create individuals with total ideological and political commitment to the Islamic Republic. Islamization, on the other hand, aims at reviving Islamic values and returning to the

Muslim identity. The ultimate aim of the socialization process in Iranian schools is the creation of a model citizen—the New Islamic Person—who is pious, committed, doctrinaire, loyal to the government and obedient to his or her country's religio-political leaders, is proud of the Islamic heritage, hates the prerevolutionary regime, rejects any form of dependence on the West, mistrusts the non-Muslim world, is highly critical of Western ways, and aims at the unity of all Muslims (Mehran, 1989).

This chapter therefore analyzes postrevolutionary educational reform from 1979 to 1989 within the framework of efforts to Islamize and politicize schooling. Six areas of education most affected by the cultural revolution and the transformation of values will be discussed in depth as we look at postrevolutionary reform efforts in general: (1) higher education, (2) curricular content, (3) education of the oppressed, (4) education and war, (5) work and study, and (6) education of women.

(1) HIGHER EDUCATION

Educational transformation in the Islamic Republic has been most abrupt and visible at the university level. Through what is known as the cultural revolution, or *Engelab-e Farhangi*, the Iranian government launched a campaign to "purify" and Islamize the content of higher education, and create *maktabi* (committed and doctrinaire) students as opposed to "mere" experts. Similar to the duality of redness and expertness in the Chinese cultural revolution, Iran has also witnessed a confrontation between commitment (*ta'ahod*) and expertise (*takhassos*) (Sobhe, 1982).

During the Pahlavi rule, Iranian universities were criticized for being centers of propagation for Western values, serving the "foreigners" and failing to produce "committed" individuals with Islamic culture and morality. Universities were thus closed in the summer of 1980 for a period of three years during which the content of instruction, especially in the humanities and social sciences, was changed by emphasizing Islamic ideology and de-emphasizing Western norms and values (Sobhe, 1982).

Yet the closing of the universities was not aimed merely at changing the academic curricula and rewriting the textbooks. The 1980 cultural revolution was also directed at purging dissident students and expelling faculty members labeled as anti-Islamic and counterrevolutionary. Large-scale purging and the establishment of a highly ideological university entrance selection system based on commitment to and support of the Islamic Republic have indeed transformed Iranian universities from bastions of political activism and dissidence to institutes characterized by passivity and quietism.

The 1980 cultural revolution that took place at the university level has brought about a strict selection system. Although elementary and secondary school pupils are at all times subject to intense Islamic and political education both in and out of their classrooms, their level of faith and loyalty are once again checked before entering the university. Entering higher institutes of learning has always been very difficult for high school graduates who have to take a national, unified entrance examination. Iranian universities have continuously faced high demand and limited space. The Islamic Republic's policy has led to the further filtering of applicants by introducing a highly ideological selection procedure. Those aspiring to attend university must pass both the academic aptitude exam and the loyalty-morality checks. The checks were introduced by the Islamic authorities to assess the applicant's degree of loyalty to the government, political activity, and commitment to Islam and belief in the concept of the political rule of the *ulama*—namely, *velayat-e fagih* (governance of the religious jurisprudent). The postrevolutionary quota system, ensuring the entrance of eligible candidates who fought in the 1980s Iran-Iraq War, those maimed or crippled in the war, family members of the martyrs, and students from impoverished regions of the country, has led to further competition for limited space.

The cultural revolution has resulted in the establishment of two important organizations in higher education–namely, the High Council of Cultural Revolution (*Shora-ye 'Ali Engelab-e Farhangi*) and the University Crusade (*Jihad-e Daneshgahi*). Together they are referred to as the engine of the cultural revolution. At the time of its establishment in 1980 through the decree of the Ayatollah Khomeini, the High Council of Cultural Revolution was assigned the task of eliminating "the influence of the anti-Islamic culture of the monarchic regime" and rendering education "more relevant to the needs of the Islamic Society of Iran" (Ministry of Education, 1990: 36). The High Council is composed of the representatives of the legislative, executive, and judiciary powers as well as various ministers, educational authorities, and members of the *ulama*. It is in charge of educational planning, designing the course of study for each specialization, selecting the faculty members, determining the curricular content, and compiling textbooks mainly in the social sciences and humanities.

The University Crusade, on the other hand, is in charge of Islamizing the universities. Together with the students' Islamic Associations (*Anjoman-e Islami*), the University Crusade administers extracurricular activities ranging from student field trips to political meetings and speeches, book exhibitions, lectures, and conferences. A third organization, known as the Center for University Publications (*Markaz-e Nashr-e Daneshgahi*), has also been founded to provide scientific and educational textbooks in Persian and to obtain Western-language books that can be used at the higher education level; it has acted as an "informational bank."

All three organizations work closely with the long-established Ministry of Culture and Higher Education that is responsible for supervising and expanding higher education institutions throughout the country; developing and maintaining university research activities; supervising educational planning in accordance with the nation's socioeconomic development plans; and expanding international academic and scientific relations. The existence of two parallel organizations simultaneously dealing with higher education in the country—namely, the High

Council of Cultural Revolution and the Ministry of Higher Education—is a typical phenomenon of postrevolutionary Iran in which the old and the new coexist in response to the special requirements of the times and in order to supervise and check each other's activities.

Despite the existence of 126 universities and institutes of higher education in the 1988–1989 academic year, attended by 250,709 students specializing in 450 fields of study, taught by 17,447 faculty members (*Statistical Yearbook*, 1990), Iranian universities face major problems in meeting the demand for higher education and absorbing all eligible candidates. In 1979 only 10 percent of 550,000 applicants were admitted (Sobhe, 1982); in 1990, 50,000 out of 790,000 applicants—that is, 6 percent—were expected to be able to attend university (*Kayhan*, May 3, 1990).

One solution to the limited capacity of universities in a society characterized by "diploma disease" has been the establishment of the Free Islamic University (*Daneshgah-e Azad-e Islami*). Despite the nationalization of all universities immediately after the revolution, economic and educational shortcomings have led to a reversal in policy and the creation of the above-mentioned fee-based, private university established in Tehran in 1984 and expanding throughout the country ever since. Despite its original nondegree status, claiming to provide education for the sake of knowledge as opposed to merely obtaining a degree, the Free University at present offers bachelor's, master's, and Ph.D. programs in engineering, pure sciences, mathematics, medicine, social sciences, and humanities (Ministry of Education, 1990). It has a separate entrance examination and yet its grading and examination patterns are similar to those of the other universities. The main difference is that students are charged to attend.

The establishment and growth of the Free University is a vivid example of reversal of policy set in revolutionary times and revised according to postrevolutionary realities. Yet another example is the establishment of nonprofit, private schools known as *Madares-e ghayr-e entefa'i* approved by the *Majles* (Parliament) in 1988 (Berenji, 1988). In spite of the nationalization of all private and foreign schools immediately after the revolution, this has been done in an effort to reduce the gap between public and private schooling and to improve the quality of education provided for their clientele.

Another measure to provide increasing educational opportunity has been the establishment of the Distance Education University known as *Daneshgah-e Payam-e Nur* in 1987. This institution has its headquarters in Tehran with several units across the country. By offering bachelor's degrees in several subjects through correspondence and use of audiovisual learning materials along with weekly meetings with the instructors, the Distance Education University has been able to offer limited opportunities for higher education.

Another major problem faced by Iranian universities has been the shortage of faculty members leading to a high student/instructor ratio. The 1980 expulsion of many faculty members, the migration of a considerable number to the West, along with the increase in the number of students have led to an urgent need for more than 9,000 full- and part-time instructors (Jihad-e Daneshgahi, 1990). Tarbiyat-e Modarres University has been established in response to this need. Offering master's and Ph.D. degrees in various fields of study, the university has assumed the responsibility of training university instructors. Candidates are selected from among the most doctrinaire applicants with a guaranteed position awaiting their graduation. Ph.D. candidates from Tarbiyat-e Modarres University already had teaching and top-level administrative positions in many universities. They provide a short-term alternative and most probably a long-term replacement for Western-educated, less doctrinaire faculty members, especially in the more sensitive fields of social sciences and humanities.

Sending students abroad to continue their higher education represents another attempt by the Islamic Republic to provide specialists. Despite the original condemnation of education in the West, undeniable realities have led to a reversal in policy and the sending of graduate-level students abroad to pursue their education in needed technical and professional fields. Whereas the authorities prefer such nations as India and Japan owing to the "perseverance of tradition" in those countries, Western European countries, Canada, and Australia remain the first choice of many students, especially since education in England and the United States is not allowed.

Thus, we come to two concluding points. First, the higher educational system in Iran, like that of most postrevolutionary societies, is attempting to socialize a new generation of individuals loyal to the regime, believing in its ideals and values, and faithful to its official ideology. What distinguishes the Iranian system of education is its Islamic nature. Similar to other revolutionary societies, higher education reform efforts have served both an educational and a political-ideological function, with the latter being dominant in the earlier phase of the revolution. Second, as in other postrevolutionary nations, economic realities and the need for specialists have gradually led to alterations and accommodations in the initial strict "revolutionary" measures. Although politics and ideology still determine the basic content and direction of higher education in Iran, the need for skill and expertise and for academic and scientific research is regaining part of its rights.

EDUCATIONAL REFORM AT THE ELEMENTARY AND SECONDARY SCHOOL LEVELS

The cultural revolution at the precollegiate level took a less drastic course in Iran. The schools were never closed, and changes in the educational content came about gradually. As opposed to the universities in which changes took place in the name of the cultural revolution, the alterations in the pre-university system are referred to simply as educational transformation. Furthermore, while a new and separate organization, namely, the High Council for Cultural Revolution, assumed direct responsibility for Islamizing the content of higher education, changes in the elementary and secondary school level remained in the hands of the Ministry of Education. It was only in December 1984 that the task of changing precollegiate education was assigned to the Council for the Fundamental Transformation of the Educational System (*Shora-ye Taghyir-e Bonyadi Nezame Amuzesh va Parvaresh*). Reform and innovative measures have been taken in six areas of education in Iran, each reflecting the political, ideological realities, and necessities of its time.

Structure, Organization, and Planning of Iranian Education

The structure, organization, and planning of education in the Islamic Republic are very similar to those of the prerevolutionary period. Education in Iran is highly centralized, with the Ministry of Education in Tehran determining the content and structure of elementary, secondary, vocational, and exceptional education throughout the country. The ministry is also in charge of educational planning, administration, and financing, curriculum and textbook development, literacy campaign and adult education, and extracurricular activities. Teacher training, grading, and examinations are also the responsibility of the ministry. The language of instruction in the entire nation is Persian, and all school books are in the same language.

Such total centralization of education, in existence since 1911, and a strict pyramid of authority with the minister at the top and the principals and teachers at the bottom, has led to a rigid system marked by lack of dynamism. By denying the teachers, parents, and other members of the community the right to participate in the decision-making process, the Iranian educational system has become unresponsive to local needs. Teaching is basically composed of giving lectures with minimum class discussion. Overcrowdedness in the classrooms also leads to poor teacher–student interaction. Rote learning, recitation, and memorization are the dominant forms of learning in Iranian schools, with little laboratory work or use of audiovisual facilities. Despite innovative programs to remedy the above situation, recommended by the Council for the Fundamental Transformation of the Educational System and approved by the *Majles* in 1989 (Council for the Fundamental Transformation of the Educational System, 1988), the Iranian schooling system suffers from the same ills that plagued the system before the 1979 revolution.

Ever since 1970 and continuing today, the educational system still consists of a one-year preschool program or *amadegi* (age five), five-year primary education or *dabestan* (ages six to ten), a three-year guidance cycle or *rahnema'i* (ages eleven to thirteen), and four-year secondary education or *dabirestan* (ages fourteen to seventeen). Whereas primary and guidance cycle education is the same for all school children, secondary education is divided into the theoretical-academic and technical-vocational divisions. The academic division is further divided into the mathematics-physics, experimental sciences, literature-culture, and socioeconomic branches. Technical-vocational education is composed of three subdivisions, namely, agricultural, technical, and business branches. The graduates of academic secondary schools have the option of entering universities or teacher training institutes, while technical-vocational school graduates either join the workforce or continue on to higher institutes of technology or technical-vocational teacher training centers.

During the 1988–1989 academic year, 13,046,358 students were enrolled in various educational centers administered by the Ministry of Education (*Statistical Yearbook*, 1990). Despite the importance of the preschool program in preparing young children for primary studies, only 177,979 children were enrolled in public preschools sponsored by the ministry, although statistics point to a total enrollment of 2,089,710 in that stage. The reason is simply that preschool education is basically handled by the private sector that charges tuition, resulting in the inability of low-income children to attend. In 1988–1989, a total of 8,262,441 children attended elementary schools; 2,724,606 were enrolled in guidance cycle schools; 1,363,310 were in academic secondary schools, while 209,887 were enrolled in technical-vocational schools. According to the Ministry of Education, only 78 percent of the elementary school-age children actually attended school in the 1988–1989 academic year; 41.7 percent of all eleven- to thirteen-year-old pupils were in guidance cycle level schools; and only 18.9 percent of the fourteen- to seventeen-year-old group were enrolled in secondary schools (Ministry of Education, 1990: 14–15). These statistics point to the educational system's inability to provide schooling for the entire school-age population and a high dropout rate at every level. Any effort at educational reform in present-day Iran should assign first priority to remedying this problem. It should be noted, however, that ongoing research points to economic limitations and cultural restrictions (especially where female education is concerned) as the main reasons for limited schooling and illiteracy among the school-age children (Mehran, research in progress).

(2) CURRICULAR CONTENT

Changing the curricular content of the Iranian educational system has been among the major reform efforts of the postrevolutionary period. In an attempt to Islamize the content of education, an ideologically approved curriculum has been introduced, emphasizing religious belief and including more Islamic subjects. Religious studies, the Qur'an, Islamic ethics, and Arabic have now become an important part of precollegiate education in Iran. Religion and ethics is now offered three hours per week in the elementary and guidance level, and two hours per week in the secondary schools. The Qur'an is also studied two hours per week beginning in the third grade and continuing to the end of the guidance cycle, and one hour per week at the secondary school level. Arabic language is taught throughout the three years of the guidance cycle for two hours per week in accordance with Article 16 of the Constitution, which states: ''Since the language of the Qur'an and of Islamic learning and culture is Arabic, and since Persian literature has been thoroughly permeated by this language, it must be taught in all classes ... and in all areas of study" (*Constitution*, 1980: 34). Islamic culture and ideology as well as Arabic are included in the secondary school curriculum. Morning prayers have also been included in the school program in an effort to revive religion. Furthermore, evening courses have been established to familiarize teachers with the teachings of Islam and the recitation of the Qur'an. The three recognized religious minorities in Iran—the Christians, Jews, and Zoroastrians—are allowed to teach the principles of their own religion in schools at the time allotted for religion and ethics (see Shorish, 1988).

Most importantly, the Ministry of Education, under the auspices of the Bureau of Research, Curriculum, and Textbook Development, changed the curricular content by rewriting the textbooks. The aim was to "demonarchize" the content and eradicate the secular, pro-Western, and anti-Islamic messages of the prerevolutionary books. Although some school books remained intact, such as those used in higher grades for physics and mathematics, many textbooks were completely changed to present an exclusively Muslim perspective and the worldview of the present Iranian government. Among these texts are the ones in history, economics, sociology, psychology, religious studies, Persian literature, Arabic, art, and social studies. The present educational authorities believe that social science books were specifically used in prerevolutionary times to "efface or even annihilate Islam and to impoverish the students' religious beliefs" (Ministry of Education, 1984: 23).

Changing the content of textbooks began shortly after the victory of the revolution, following Ayatollah Khomeini's February 20, 1979, demand from education authorities to fundamentally change the primary, secondary, and higher level education books, purifying them from all "colonial and tyrannical" topics and replacing them with Islamic and revolutionary subjects that would awaken the children and render the youth free and independent (Organization of Research and Educational Planning, 1980b). The task of rewriting textbooks was completed two years after the establishment of the Islamic Republic. Since 1981, no major rewriting has taken place except for some minor additions and omissions in accordance with the changing political realities and necessities of the day.

A content analysis of social studies textbooks used in the postrevolutionary schools indicates that education in the Islamic Republic is openly avowedly political, and every topic is used for conscious political ends. Curricular content reflects the official state ideology and indicates the appropriate attitudes, values, and beliefs in the young needed to maintain the status quo. The study points to the educators' deliberate intent to gain a commitment to the Islamic Republic and loyalty to its leadership among school children. More importantly, however, is the intended commitment to Islam for which any hardship, deprivation, and even self-sacrifice is justified (Mehran, forthcoming).

(3) EDUCATION OF THE OPPRESSED

The Islamic Republic has continuously referred to the 1979 revolution as the revolution by and for the oppressed. The disinherited, weak, and downtrodden (*mostaz'afin*) of the society are regarded as the true owners of the revolution, whose martyrdom and self-sacrifice have led to the establishment of the Islamic Republic and its ability to sustain the Iran-Iraq War.

In accordance with the Islamic Republic's policy of elevation of the downtrodden, the Iranian educational system must pay special attention to the schooling of the poor. Yet poverty, economic hardships, rural agricultural tasks, constant nomadic migration, and illegal child labor in cities have led to low educational levels for the poor school-age population. Statistics point to a marked disparity between rural and urban areas. As far as school enrollment is concerned, although the rural population comprises 43.2 percent of the total population of the country, only 39.87 percent of pupils across the country are from rural regions. During the 1988–1989 academic year, only 70 percent of the rural school-age children were enrolled in elementary schools compared to 87 percent of urban children; the percentage dropped to 25.6 percent at the guidance cycle level (58 percent urban) and 10.5 percent at the secondary school level (26.5 urban) (Ministry of Education, 1990: 14–16).

School wastage is also higher among the rural school children who either fail school examinations or leave school before completion at a higher rate than their urban counterparts. During the 1987–1988 academic year, the retention rate at the primary school level was 17.07 percent for the rural population as opposed to 9.7 percent among urban school children. The disparity continued at 23.29 percent rural and 15.66 percent urban at the guidance cycle level, and 20.8 percent rural compared to 18.89 percent urban at the secondary school level (Ministry of Education, 1990: 33). In addition, a shortage of qualified teachers, inadequate and ill-equipped school buildings, and insufficient educational supplies in rural regions and poor urban areas and among nomads have led to a lower standard of education among the poorest sector of the society.

The Ministry of Education's efforts to resolve the above disparities and provide more and better educational opportunities for the "owners of the revolution" is an ongoing process, the most important of which will be discussed. The first six years of the revolution witnessed an unprecedented increase in the number of rural schools built by the Reconstruction Crusade, leading to the establishment of 25,000 schools in remote rural areas (*Kayhan*, February 23, 1985). Among the initial steps taken by the educational authorities are the free distribution of textbooks among rural and nomadic school children; the establishment of rural teacher training centers; recruitment of local teachers; attempts to prevent the transfer of teachers from rural to urban areas by providing extra benefits and facilities for them in villages; the creation of nomadic educational units and training multispecialized teachers able to cover all educational fields during the annual migration; the assignment of newly recruited teachers only to deprived areas; and the determination of a quota for rural applicants and those coming from poor and depressed provinces in the universities.

A more recent program implemented in 1986 includes free meals for school children at the primary and guidance cycle level in the most economically deprived regions of the country—especially at the borders among nomads, in the desert area, and among the scattered population living in remote, mountainous areas. The result has been increased enrollment, a lower dropout rate, and better physical-psychological-intellectual conditions among the 2.5 million pupils who have received free nutrition (Ministry of Education, forthcoming).[1]

The establishment of model schools (*Madares-e Nemunch*) represents yet another effort to provide better educational opportunities for school children from deprived areas. Since 1986, model schools have aimed at identifying and developing the potential capabilities of selected pupils who are assigned to boarding schools and provided with financial aid, highly qualified teachers and academic-vocational counselors, and special instructional materials. The ultimate aim is to train highly needed skilled humanpower for deprived regions among the selected pupils. At present sixty-five guidance cycle and thirty-five secondary level model schools are in operation (Ministry of Education, forthcoming).

One of the most effective measures to meet the problem of teacher shortages in remote rural areas has been the use of military conscripts as teachers. Since 1986, selected conscripts holding a high school diploma have been dispatched to rural primary schools instead of undergoing military service in the armed forces. After receiving military and educational training, conscripts are sent to the most remote areas for the academic year. As of 1990, 90,000 pupils had been educated by 3,200 soldiers (Ministry of Education, forthcoming). The importance of the above plan also lies in the fact that it was put into effect at the peak of the Iran-Iraq War, pointing to the importance attached to education in the deprived regions.

Last, but not least, the most recent attempt to eradicate illiteracy among the deprived population should be mentioned. As part of the worldwide Education for All and 1990 International Literacy Year efforts, the Islamic Republic began the 1990–1991 Mass Mobilization Plan to uproot illiteracy among the six- to thirty-five-year-old population. The postrevolutionary battle against illiteracy began following a decree by the Ayatollah Khomeini on December 28, 1979, emphasizing the need to "turn Iran into a school." Noting that it is shameful to have a high illiteracy rate in an Islamic nation that has historically been the seat of culture and knowledge, and emphasizing that Islam regards education as a form of prayer, he asked all those who could read and write to teach their illiterate brothers and sisters (Organization of Research and Educational Planning, 1980a).

Eleven years after the onset of the literacy campaign and the Ayatollah Khomeini's emphasis on it as a religious duty, the literacy rate in Iran is 61.7 percent; 73.1 percent of the urban population and only 48.4 percent of the rural residents are literate (*Statistical Yearbook*, 1990). Although the above figures reflect relative success compared to the prerevolutionary period—47.5 percent total, 65.4 percent urban, and 30.5 percent rural literacy in 1976—the Islamic Republic has a long way to go to reach total literacy.

The 1990–1991 Mass Mobilization Plan aims at eradicating illiteracy among the 2 million urban and 5 million illiterates in the six- to thirty-five-year-old age group. It should be noted that, despite the traditional religious resistance to the use of obligatory measures to enroll illiterates in literacy classes, Iranian religio-political leaders have determined that class attendance by illiterates is to be mandatory, justifiable on the basis of national welfare. The success of the Iranian literacy campaign in mobilizing and teaching illiterates will be a positive step in providing education for the nation's *mostaz'afin*.

(4) EDUCATION AND WAR

The Iranian educational system is intimately linked to the larger society, reflecting the events that occur at the political level, and no event has affected the schooling system as much as the 1980–1988 Iran-Iraq War. The impact of the war on the educational system was visible both during the war and after the 1988 cease-fire.

The training of young pupils and their participation in the war took various forms after 1980. With the establishment of the Aid and Support Headquarters of the Ministry of Education in 1981, until 1984 a total of 62,285 pupils were trained and sent to the fronts. By 1986, according to government sources, 500,000 pupils were sent to war organized in special groups called volunteers for martyrdom (*davtalabin-e shahadat*). Furthermore, 57 percent of the Mobilization Force (*Basij*), largely comprised of civilian fighters, had been school pupils (*Iran Times*, October 10, 1986). At present, those pupils who participated in the war for six months or more receive a quota in the university entrance examination.

To make up for the academic loss brought about by long periods of absence from school, the Ministry of Education sent more than 30,000 teachers to teach students behind the fronts and in nearby cities. The same number of teachers was sent directly to the battlefield to teach the fighters. A total of 480,000 fighters were educated in sixty-eight educational centers at the fronts (Ministry of Education, forthcoming). Furthermore, 5 percent of the entire teaching force underwent military training, and by 1986, 7,000 teachers had participated in the War (*Iran Times*, August 1, 1986). Although compulsory drafting only includes the male students, girls have also been encouraged to learn the use of arms. The Women's Defense Committee offers six months of intensive training using female instructors. In Tehran alone 1,000 female pupils have been trained.

The above-mentioned forms of military training have basically been out-of-school activities. It was not until the 1986–1987 academic year that military training, referred to as defense education (*amuzesh defa'i*), became part of the formal curriculum. Beginning in the second year of the guidance cycle, that is, at age twelve, pupils are offered both theoretical and practical military education taught by members of the Revolutionary Guards. The aim of this education is to teach the use of arms, tactics of defense against air raids and chemical warfare, and first aid methods to treat the wounded.

The war has led to the death of many Iranians, estimated at 600,000 along with 1.5 million injured and maimed. Yet it was only in 1986 that the educational system paid special attention to the schooling of the martyrs' children. Despite opposition by those who consider it a form of favoritism and discrimination, the Ministry of Education has, since 1986, established special schools known as Martyrs' Schools (*Madares-e Shahed*) to educate the children of the soldiers lost in action, prisoners of war, and those maimed in battle. So far 384 schools have been established, funded by the Martyrs' Foundation (*Bonyad-e Shahid*) in which 40 percent of the pupils are children with the above-mentioned characteristics and the remaining 60 percent are selected through intensive ideological screening. Pupils enrolled at Martyrs' Schools benefit from exceptional teaching staff and educational facilities, expert counselors who deal with the children's special psychological and emotional needs, free transportation, and one free meal per day. Furthermore, the government has determined a quota for the children of the martyrs in the universities.

Whereas academic excellence or exceptional abilities lead to the establishment of elitist schools in various nations, political-ideological commitment and membership in a special group of citizenry—namely, the martyrs—determines the foundation of exclusive schools in the Islamic Republic. It is too early to assess whether these schools offer better education than the rest, yet larger membership in them is a sign of prestige in a country that values martyrdom and refers to war victims as holy people.

(5) WORK AND STUDY

Among the educational innovations introduced by the Islamic Republic has been the KAD project. Referring to the combination of work (*kar*) and knowledge (*danesh*), the KAD project was introduced in 1982 with three aims: to foster the students' skills and talents, to direct them into productive activities, and to familiarize them with the realities of life (Ministry of Education, 1984).

As opposed to the concept of vocational training—aimed at preparing students for a specific vocation—and polytechnical education—directed at eliminating the gap between mental and manual labor and the disdain for the manual—the KAD project in Iran is mostly an attempt to prepare the young pupils for the outside world. To achieve this second goal, secondary level students in non-vocational programs are dismissed from school one day per week to do practical work in various factories and workshops and to engage in agricultural tasks under the supervision of educational authorities.

More recently, in an attempt to combine theoretical and practical knowledge, students undergoing technical-vocational training have been able to study in educational centers attached to factories known as Education Alongside Factories (*Amuzesh Javar Karkhaneh'i*). The aim has been active exchange between scientific centers and industrial settings that leads to the training of highly needed humanpower, with expertise in both the theoretical and technical domain. By September 1989, twenty-five such centers were established through the cooperation of the Ministries of Education and Industry (Ministry of Education, forthcoming). The expansion of such educational activities to the agricultural sector would be a most welcome addition in an effort to bridge the gap between scientific knowledge and technical know-how.

There is a significant difference between the kind of practical work performed by boys as opposed to girls. The Ministry of Education has stated the aim of the KAD project as "familiarizing the male students with industrial, agricultural, reconstructive, and scientific subjects," while the goal for females is to acquaint them with "skills demanded by the Islamic culture and society" (Ministry of Education, 1984: 27). As a result, boys participate in practical workshops to pursue their interests, while girls take additional courses in health, nutrition, childrearing, cooking, sewing and knitting, and handicrafts. The educational authorities in Iran regard the girls' skills as most appropriate and necessary for them in their role as mothers and housewives. They criticize the Westernized notion that men and women are "similar"; they believe them to be both different and complementary, and therefore, needing a different kind of training to prepare them for their traditional roles in society. Their reasoning is that as future mothers and educators of the next generation, girls must be acquainted with the responsibilities assigned to their gender. They further state that the "natural" physiological and psychological differences between men and women dictate different training for them.

Thus, what could have been a remarkable innovation to close the gap between mental and manual labor, eliminate the traditional and elitist disdain for nonintellectual activity, and create a tie between theoretical and practical knowledge has ended up as yet another form of imparting theoretical information and segregating boys and girls in accordance with the Islamic Republic's understanding of the "appropriate" role of men and women in society and the "proper" education of females in a Muslim society. The last section of this study examines the role of women in Iranian society and its impact on their schooling.

(6) EDUCATION OF WOMEN

Much has been written about the changing position of Iranian women since the 1979 revolution which has aimed at transforming a secular society to one in which Islam and politics and thus religion and education are highly intertwined. A close look at the female experience in the postrevolutionary educational system of Iran provides some insight into what has actually taken place.

The first step taken by Islamic authorities shortly after assuming power was the banning of coeducation in May 1979. The government declared that all educational institutions, with the exception of universities, were to be segregated on the basis of Islamic morality. Even before the revolution, Iranian high schools were segregated by gender with the exception of a few private and international schools. There was, however, a higher degree of integration at the elementary school level. Male and female students have not been separated in language schools and university entrance examination preparation classes in the Islamic Republic. At the university level, men and women still attend the same classes, with the women occupying the back seats in the classrooms and the men sitting in the front. In some instances, though uncommon, men and women are separated by drawing a curtain in the middle of the classroom. Since June 1979, married female students are no longer allowed to attend regular high schools for fear of "corrupting" younger unmarried girls (Tabari and Yeganeh, 1982).

In 1980 teaching was also segregated, so that only female teachers can now teach in girls' schools and the teachers in boys' schools are all men. There are some exceptions to this rule, especially in rural areas where the small number of girls and the shortage of teachers has led to the integrated classes taught by male teachers. Female teachers are still used in the first and second years of most boys' elementary schools, and male math, physics, and science teachers still teach in all-girls high schools owing to the lack of female instructors in those subjects.

With the gradual pressure on women to wear the Islamic veil in public in the summer of 1980, female students and teachers were among the first to be affected by the compulsory veiling order. Following the declaration of compulsory veiling for all women in the summer of 1981, girls six years of age and older have to wear dark color (brown, dark blue, black, grey) uniforms and headcovers to school at all times.

Given the Islamic Republic's understanding of the "appropriate" role and position of women in society, female university students have been barred from entering certain male-oriented fields of study. For example, at present specializations that demand extensive fieldwork such as mining and petroleum engineering are closed for women, while male students cannot apply for admissions to obstetrics-gynecology. As early as June 1979, women judges were expelled and female law students can no longer aspire to become judges. This was done in accordance with the Islamic belief that women are not fit to judge because their sentimentality and emotions make them act according to the dictates of their "heart" rather than the ruling of their "head."

In its effort to direct pupils toward "suitable" studies and professions at the guidance cycle level, the Ministry of Education has prepared different sets of the Study of Professions textbooks for girls and boys at that stage. Tailoring, nursing, and teaching are emphasized in girls' books, while boys learn about the various fields of engineering and their future job prospects. In this way, the Islamic Republic hopes to segregate the academic pursuit of individuals as well as their future professions according to the dictates of Islam.

Given the above facts, it is not surprising that it is generally assumed that female education in the Islamic Republic has suffered a major setback since the 1979 revolution. Assumptions about women automatically dropping out of the educational race abound among laypeople and scholars alike. Yet statistics prove that female education has not changed significantly since the Shah and that both the level of enrollment and attainment have remained the same.

Despite various claims about the grand achievements of the Pahlavi period regarding female education, literacy among women above the age of six was 35.5 percent in 1976; only 55.6 percent of the urban and 17.3 percent of the rural women were able to read and write (*Statistical Yearbook*, 1990). Although it has a long way to go, the Islamic Republic has been able to increase the literacy level of women. In 1986 their literacy rate was 53 percent, with 65.4 percent and 36.3 percent literacy rates among urban and rural women, respectively. Such comparative study of pre- and postrevolutionary statistics dismisses the widely held belief that the Islamic Republic shuns any form of education for girls.

The enrollment of girls in formal schools has also increased. Although girls' schooling still lags behind that of boys throughout the nation, the percentage of school enrollment among girls increased from 37.99 percent in 1978 to 43 percent in 1988. Among rural girls, the percentage increased from 31.79 percent to 40 percent in the ten-year period (Ministry of Education, 1989).

Interestingly, a change has also taken place in the specializations elected by female pupils at the secondary school level. Traditionally, girls have chosen the socioeconomic and literature-culture branches of the academic divisions, with 46.71 percent and 15.92 percent enrollment, respectively, in 1978. Ten years later, the female enrollment has been reduced to 22.54 percent in the socioeconomic branch, while literature-culture has witnessed an increase to 24.11 percent. Meanwhile, there has been an increase in the mathematics-physics branch from 4.84 percent in 1978 to 7.87 percent in 1988, and from 32.52 percent to 45.46 percent in the experimental sciences branch (Ministry of Education, 1989).

Statistics show that the total enrollment of girls is behind that of boys at all levels of schooling, yet their success level is higher at every stage. During the 1988–1989 academic year, 83.8 percent of school-age boys attended elementary school compared to 74.2 percent of girls. The percentage of rural girls drops to 61.1 percent. In the same year, 46.5 percent of eleven- to thirteen-year-old boys attended guidance cycle schools as opposed to 36.6 percent girls, with 16.7 percent rural female enrollment. The secondary school level witnessed 20.2 percent male enrollment compared to 17.4 percent female, with a very low percentage of 6.8 percent for rural girls (Ministry of Education, 1990: 14–16). Despite generally low enrollment at technical-vocational schools, the percentage rose from 18.3 percent to 20.5 percent between 1978 and 1988.

As far as completion rates are concerned, girls show high achievement. During the 1978–1988 academic year, 88.8 percent of girls succeeded in completing primary school compared to 85.03 percent among boys. At the guidance cycle level, the gap is widened to 85.11 percent achievement rate among girls as opposed to 78.42 percent among boys. The male pupils' completion rate is reduced systematically as the grades go up, leading to only 73.87 percent completion rate at the secondary school level compared to 90.20 percent for girls. Female pupils at technical-vocational schools also fare better, with an 89.74 percent success rate, while boys lag behind with only 65.97 percent of them passing all examinations (Ministry of Education, 1989).

At the higher education level, there are more male university students—178,887 during the 1988–1989 academic year—than female students—71,882. There are also fewer female faculty members (2,947) than male (14,500). The rank order of female enrollment in the various fields of study is an important indicator of the academic and vocational choices of women. During the 1988–1989 academic year, the highest number of female university students elected medicine and health-related sciences (27,839), followed by education and teacher training (14,636); humanities, literature, and theology (8,907); social and behavioral sciences (5,828); natural and physical sciences (4,531); engineering (2,556); business administration and management (2,185); mathematics and computer science (1,985); fine arts (1,258); communications (679); agriculture and forestry (578); law (458); and architecture and urban planning (355) (*Statistical Yearbook*, 1990).

In sum, despite various legal, economic, social, and professional limitations imposed on women in the Islamic Republic of Iran, little actual change has occurred in the level of women's educational enrollment and attainment since the 1979 revolution. The available data point to the reality that Iranian women have striven to remain active recipients of and contributors to academic, intellectual, and scientific endeavors.

PRIORITIES OF THE POSTREVOLUTIONARY IRANIAN EDUCATIONAL SYSTEM

A study of educational reform in postrevolutionary Iran demonstrates that ideological purification (*tazkiyeh*) and political commitment are deemed more important than mere academic-technical expertise. Educational reform in the Islamic Republic has been basically aimed at meeting short-term, politically significant goals as opposed to long-term plans to correct the various shortcomings of the schooling system. Thus, moral political transformation, leading to a revolution in values, has taken precedence over changes in the structure and organization of schooling.

Attaching greater importance to meeting the political and ideological requirements of the time rather than the training of a skilled labor force has been a common characteristic of schooling in most revolutionary societies. Yet one cannot deny the dire need for expertise, brought about only through a well-equipped, high-quality, efficient, and superbly managed system of education, in the postwar reconstruction of Iran. Given the need to implement the First Five-Year Economic-Social-Cultural Development Plan of the Islamic Republic of Iran (1989–1993), aimed at the growth and advancement of the country in every sphere, it may mean that educational reform efforts will, in the future, shift from being primarily in response to the political requirements of the revolution to an answer to the educational needs of the country.

CONCLUSION

An overview of educational reform throughout Iranian history shows that the ruling power, the reformists, and the revolutionaries have always used the system of education for their own needs and priorities. Reform efforts have basically been made in response to the political requirements of the time, and seldom in reaction to popular needs and demands. Thus, educational decision making has always been a top-down process, with minimum participation by the people.

In fact, educational reform had first and foremost been a tool for the secularization or politicization of the society depending on the ruling ideology of the time, as opposed to a step in the betterment and enrichment of people's lives. It is hoped that one day the ability of education to raise the standard of living, as opposed to its use as a mere political tool, will regain its rightful place and begin acting as an instrument at the service of the people.

NOTE

1. I wish to thank Dr. Gholam 'Ali Haddad 'Adel and Dr. Mahmoud Mehr-Mohammadi for providing me with the most recent and otherwise inaccessible information.

REFERENCES

Arasteh, Reza. 1962. *Education and Social Awakening in Iran*. Leiden, Netherlands: E. J. Brill.
————. 1963. "The Growth of Higher Institutions in Iran." *International Review of Education* 7:327–334.
————. 1970. *Man and Society in Iran*. Leiden, Netherlands: E. J. Brill.
Berenji, Mohammad Reza. 1988. "Madares-e Ghayr-e Entefa'i Komaki beh Tose'eh Amuzesh va Parvaresh" [Non-profit schools aiding the development of education]. *Faslnameh Ta'lim va Tarbiyat* [Quarterly Journal of Education] 4:34–53.
Constitution of the Islamic Republic of Iran. 1980. Trans. Hamid Algar. Berkeley: Mizan Press.
Council for the Fundamental Transformation of the Education System 1988. *Tarh-e Koliyyat-e Nezam-e Amuzesh va Parvaresh Jomhuri-ye Islami Iran* [Plan of the educational system of the Islamic Republic of Iran]. Tehran: Ministry of Education.
Fischer, Michael M. J. 1980. *Iran: From Religious Dispute to Revolution*. Cambridge, Mass.: Harvard University Press.
Jihad-e Daneshgahi [University Crusade]. 1990. *Daneshgah-e Engelab* [The University of Revolution]. Tehran: Ettela'at Foundation.
Keddie, Nikki R. 1980. *Iran: Religion, Politics and Society*. London: Frank Cass.
Mehran, Golnar. 1989. "Cultural Revolution and Value Transformation in Post-Revolutionary Iranian Education." *Muslim Education Quarterly* 7:20–33.

————. Forthcoming. "The Socialization of School Children in the Islamic Republic of Iran." *Iranian Studies*.

————. Research in Progress. "Needs Assessment Among the Illiterate and Semi-literate Population in Iran." Tehran: Al-Zahra University.

Ministry of Education. 1984. *Educational System of the Islamic Republic of Iran*. Tehran: Ministry of Education.

————. 1989. "Amar-e Amuzesh va Parvaresh" [Educational statistics]. *Faslnameh Ta'lim va Tarbiyat* [Quarterly Journal of Education]: 53–57.

————. 1990. *Education in the Islamic Republic of Iran: Now and in the Future*. Tehran: Ministry of Education.

————. Forthcoming. *Educational System of the Islamic Republic of Iran*. Tehran: Ministry of Education.

Mohsenpour, Bahram. 1989. "Education in Iran: Past and Present." *Muslim Education Quarterly* 7:9–19.

Nakosteen, Mehdi. 1964. *History of Islamic Origins of Western Education*. Boulder, Colo.: University of Colorado Press.

Organization of Research and Educational Planning. 1980a. *Engelab-e Farhangi va Taghyir-e Nezam-e Amuzeshi* [Cultural revolution and change in the educational system]. Tehran: Ministry of Education.

————. 1980b. *Piramun-e Engelab-e Farhangi va Engelab-e Amuzeshi* [About cultural and educational revolution]. Tehran: Ministry of Education.

Redjali, S. M. 1988. "Iran." *The Encyclopedia of Comparative Education and National Systems of Education*, ed. T. Neville Postlethwaite. Oxford: Pergamon Press, pp. 364–369.

Salnameh-ye Amari Keshvar [*Statistical Yearbook*]. 1990. Tehran: Statistical Center of Iran.

Shorish, Mobin M. 1988. "The Islamic Revolution and Education in Iran." *Comparative Education Review* 32:58–75.

Sobhe, Khosrow. 1982. "Education in Revolution: Is Iran Duplicating the Chinese Cultural Revolution?" *Comparative Education* 18:271–280.

Szyliowicz, Joseph S. 1973. *Education and Modernization in the Middle East*. London: Cornell University Press.

Tabari, Azar, and Nahid Yeganeh, comps. 1982. *In the Shadow of Islam: The Women's Movement in Iran*. London: Zed Press.

17

ISRAEL

Yitzhak Kashti, Mordecai Arieli, and Rina Shapira

The founders' generation in Israel wished to establish a state in the spirit of democracy, modernity, independence, and equality, primarily for Jews immigrating from various parts of the world. They assumed that one of the ways these values would be actualized would be through the educational process. The founders and subsequent leaders of the state hoped that the educational process would help to build a new society based on these values (Elboim-Dror, 1985b:57).

From the beginning it was understood that for education to help in achieving these goals, its organizational patterns and methods would have to undergo a series of changes and reforms in a process of trial and error. These changes and reforms were directed toward two major goals:

1. To preserve the continuity of the Jewish national tradition while creating, developing, and fostering an infrastructure of shared values appropriate to the emerging heterogeneous society.
2. To reduce the gap between the socioeconomically well-established old-time settlers, most of whom originated from Europe and the Western Hemisphere (the "occidentals") and the still economically unstable immigrants, who came mostly from the Middle East and North Africa (the "orientals") (Chen, 1980).

The educational system would help in this process by enhancing the educational attainments of the weaker groups of students, "absorbing" them in the culture and society that had developed, and ensuring and hastening their social mobility so that they could take their rightful place in the future structure of Israeli society.

Thus, it was assumed that the educational process, following the changes and reforms that would take place in it, would overturn, or at least decrease, the correlation between socioeconomic background and scholastic achievements, and the social reproduction manifested by the continued presence of the second generation in their parents' social position. At the same time, the educational process would help to foster cohesive factors in the Israeli society.

One of the dilemmas facing the Israeli educational system was how to promote cohesion while responding to the pluralistic tendencies that characterized Israeli society. Although most members of this society were Jews, their cultures, customs, and traditions were many and diverse.[1]

In this chapter we will review the changes and reforms that took place in the Israeli educational system in the first forty years after the establishment of the state, focusing on the Jewish majority. In particular, we will consider the contribution of these changes and reforms to the questions of social equality and cultural pluralism, which were among the major goals of the entire educational process.

The state of Israel was established in 1948, but its basis for existence as an autonomous state was being laid down throughout the preceding seventy years, through the gradual immigration of Jews to the region then known as Palestine. This region was ruled first by the Ottomans (until near the end of World War I) and later by the British.

The Jews in Palestine established their own social, economic, and cultural systems, alongside the Arabs. In most of their crucial aspects, these systems were not controlled by the rulers of the region (the Turks and later the British), but by almost totally autonomous mechanisms instituted by the Jewish society. One of the subsystems that was administered in this virtually autonomous manner by the Jewish community was the educational system.

The Jewish community's educational policy, like its policy in all domains where it was granted autonomy, was formulated by the Zionist movement. This movement sought to gather the Jews scattered throughout the world and renew their autonomy in the historical land of Israel. The aims of the Zionist movement, its various streams, power-structuring mechanisms, processes of centralization and decentralization of power through the formation and disintegration of coalitions, and finally the ways of recruiting the national capital and distributing it—all these had considerable influence on the goals, structure, allocation of authority, and allotment of resources in the educational system in the pre-state period (Ackerman, Karmon, and Zukker, 1985; Elboim-Dror, 1985a).

The Zionist movement that generated the establishment of the state of Israel was born mainly in Jewish centers in Europe. This movement arose out of Jewish national aspirations that had developed in the course of generations, as well as in the wake of the emergence of national movements among European nations and of the persecution suffered by the Jews as a minority everywhere in the world. The Zionist movement had parallels in North African and Middle Eastern centers, but it was more dominant and developed in the European centers. Thus, most of the Jewish settlers in the pre-state period came from Eastern and Central

Europe. The European origin of many of the settlers, the European source of the ideology—from liberal nationalism to utopian socialism—that guided them in Israel, and the European model of the organizational and institutional structures they brought with them, led, in the nature of things, to a concentration of power in the hands of European Jews and to the creation of a European orientation in the various systems of the modern society that was being formed.

After 1947, when the survivors from the European holocaust began to arrive in Israel in growing numbers, and particularly after the establishment of the state in May 1948, the demographic structure of the Jewish society began to change. From a society of 600,000 in 1947, Israel's population grew more than threefold in the first five years of the state. Most of those who joined the new state were immigrants from North Africa or the Middle East. Over the years these grew to become the majority, albeit not a large one, in Israeli society.[2]

Correlations between the "ethnic" and the socioeconomic dimension soon appeared. People originating from Europe were higher up on the social ladder, dominating social, financial, cultural, and educational loci. This state of affairs aggravated the eastern immigrants' marginality and sense of difference in society, politics, finance, and education. This marginality was to leave its mark on the class structure of the emerging society, on the social changes that would occur in it, and particularly on the educational reality. The reforms that the political center was to effect in the educational system were influenced by this state of affairs and were introduced largely in order to combat it.

Five reforms of education, of varying scope and influence, characterize the first four decades of the state: in the early years the schools were incorporated into a state system; in the 1950s formal equality was established; in the 1960s differential input was introduced; in the 1970s the reform aimed at social integration; and in the 1980s the school's method of functioning was revised.

THE REFORM OF THE EARLY YEARS—STATE SCHOOLS

The first reform, from which all the other reforms and changes derived (as will be shown below), found expression in the passing of the Law of State Education (1953).

This law aimed to set the common factors above the differences and the unifying above the dividing among elementary school pupils, in terms of curriculum and organization of teaching. The background to this legislation was the pluralistic nature of Zionist ideology and of Jewish society at the time the state was established.

The Zionist movement, as well as its members and representatives in pre-state Israel, were not all of a piece, but were divided into several ideological streams. Each of these streams had created for itself fairly autonomous subsystems which included schools and other educational organizations, welfare and health services, and also employment agencies. These subsystems attempted to expand by dint of constantly recruiting new members and providing increasingly varied services to the "members" who identified with them.

In the years preceding the establishment of the state, three autonomous streams emerged in the Jewish population's educational system: the general stream, which represented the liberal groups in the Zionist movement; the workers stream, representing the socialist groups; and the Mizrachi or religious stream, representing the Zionist groups among the religious population. This third stream sought to bridge the gap between the modern, basically secular Zionist vision and the traditional Jewish religious outlook. The elementary education system, which was partly funded by the British Mandatory government, at that time included 97 percent of the six to fourteen age group, and was administered entirely by the leaders of the above-mentioned streams (Survey of Palestine, 1945–1946).

Upon the establishment of the state, there was a trend to replace the political party centers with a new national center, emphasizing ethnic integration. This unifying trend encompassed the ultimate aims and symbols of the Zionist ideology and Zionist movement, such as ''one people'' and ''a new culture'' shared by all, while seeking to herald the coming of a new era of universalism and equality. Thus, the Knesset decided to cancel the streams in education and replace them with a state educational system established by law.

The State Education Law (1953) was designed to ensure education, provided by the state, not linked to any political, religious or extragovernmental body, and executed under the supervision of ''a Minister or someone authorized by him.'' In the framework of the law, parents were given the freedom to choose between three options: general state schools, religious state schools, or unofficial recognized schools (mainly for children from ultraorthodox groups). Through this law the educational system acquired a centralized structure in place of its previous one. This state education system also undertook responsibility for the education—in conditions of formal equality but in their separate cultural frameworks—of the children of the Arab minorities (Muslims, Christians of various sects, Druse, and Circassians).

The new educational system faced two major dilemmas. The first was between the tendency to inculcate in the younger generation—members of various ''ethnic'' groups—a kind of uniform culture, and the need or the possibility of taking into account the discrete ethnocultural traditions.

The second dilemma was between the preference for equal educational inputs and the aim for high scholastic achievements and excellence through differential inputs. Equal education was seen as compromising the level of scholastic attainments of the more gifted, while opting for high achievements was perceived as widening the gap between the more achieving occidental pupils and the less educated, largely eastern, population.

After the large waves of immigration of the 1950s diminished and Israeli society began to stabilize as an independent society, it became clear that implementation of the State Education Law (1953) was not enough in itself and that further changes in the educational process were required for this society.

THE REFORM OF THE 1950s—THE PRINCIPLE OF FORMAL EQUALITY

As stated, the introduction of state education constituted an educational reform in the reality of the emerging Israeli society, compared with the patterns prevalent in the education of Jewish children in pre-state days. Now, the state was obliged to provide every child with education, following a curriculum that was fairly uniform in terms of its content and guiding ideology.

An elementary school system was established and expanded fourfold in the course of one decade. The educational system exposed many parents to the norm of the importance of schooling for their children and mediated to them the perception of the school as a cultural melting pot for children coming from various parts of the diaspora, and a route of social mobility. However, the scholastic achievements of children of eastern origin did not reach the anticipated levels, particularly in comparison with the achievements of those who came from Europe.

Secondary education, which was mainly academic, still retained the patterns that had characterized it before the state. The schools were selective with regard to attainments and in effect were open only to pupils of relatively high socio-economic background, because of the relation between socioeconomic background and scholastic attainments (Kleinberger, 1969). As stated, this situation did not change substantially during the first decade of the state.

In response, several steps were taken, the major one being a national test of achievement (the *seker*, or review), which was introduced in 1956 and administered to all eighth grade pupils (the last grade of elementary education). The purpose was to obtain general information on the level of education in the system, but it sought mainly to discover those with potential ability for further education at the secondary level. Based on the background data, it was decided that a more lenient norm would be applied to pupils from weak social groups and that they would pass the *seker* tests at norm B. The pupil's score in the test, together with the marks given by the teacher, served as a measure for selecting pupils for secondary educational frameworks and for granting them the graduated school fees that were introduced by the Ministry of Education in 1958. The monthly payment system was supposed to help gifted pupils from low-income families (most of whom, as stated, were of eastern origin) to continue their studies in academic secondary schools. However, the proportion of pupils of eastern origin in secondary education did not increase substantially during this period, mainly because these pupils failed the *seker* test, even at the level of norm B.[3]

This state of affairs was inevitably reflected in higher education, too: in the first decade of the state no more than 5 percent of the secondary school graduates who were admitted to one of the two Israeli universities of those days were of eastern origin, although they formed almost half of the general population (Nahon, 1987).

Students of eastern origin were channeled, when they grew up, into low-level occupations, and found themselves at the bottom of the wage ladder or unemployed. In general, the formal equality in supplying educational inputs—the second significant educational reform—did not in its turn lead to equality in educational outputs. The recognition grew among the makers of educational policy that the educational reform needed could not be based merely on formal equality in inputs (Shmida, 1987; Swirsky, 1990).

THE REFORM OF THE 1960s—FROM FORMAL EQUALITY TO EQUAL OPPORTUNITIES

The second educational reform that was designed to decrease the socioethnic and "cultural" gap among the younger generation was expressed by a move from doctrinaire ideological equality to a policy that sought pragmatic organizational and pedagogic solutions.

Educational inputs began to be applied in a differential manner, mostly on the basis of needs diagnosed in the field. One of the major expressions of this reform related to the division of pupils into two categories: (1) socially disadvantaged or culturally deprived (terms then prevalent in educational literature in the Western world) and (2) mainstream. Pupils were selected individually according to these two categories, based on socioeconomic variables such as parents' income, education, and ethnic origin. These variables were found to be good predictors of success in studies. The "disadvantaged" enjoyed various advancement programs, such as supplementary study frameworks, special textbooks, enrichment programs, the introduction of a longer school day, and extension of the school year. In addition, the practice of making pupils repeat a class was stopped.

The main thrust of the efforts was aimed at improving the "disadvantaged" pupils' chances of receiving secondary education that would be meaningful for them both in terms of education and of helping them to advance in society. These efforts focused on three main points: to ease the transition from elementary to secondary education; to open new secondary educational frameworks of a less academically demanding nature; and to foster the top third of gifted pupils among those of eastern origin, bringing them into educational frameworks such as special residential schools for gifted pupils. These residential schools were expected to help them advance educationally and socially more than the home environment— including the local schools—which was regarded as a depriving environment (Smilansky et al., 1966).

Evaluation of most of the new programs showed their success to be somewhat limited. Many of the initiatives turned into administrative and organizational innovations, devoid of any deep educational significance. Similarly, it emerged that the new educational frameworks that were established—mainly vocational schools—enjoyed much less prestige than the traditional academic secondary schools. The heads of the educational system became increasingly convinced that administrative changes in the existing structure would not bring about the desired result, namely, to decrease or close the educational gap. At this stage, the awareness developed that in order to increase educational and social equality, it was necessary to institute a change in the structure of the educational system, a change that would lead to more effective use of the years of schooling and bring together children from different socioeconomic strata and different cultures into one educational framework. This organizational change would be the next reform of the Israeli educational system.

THE REFORMS OF THE 1970s: THE REFORM AIMED AT INTEGRATION

This reform, which began at the end of the 1960s, strove to advance the scholastic achievements of all the pupils, particularly the twelve to fourteen age group, while helping to integrate children from various social strata. The "integration" of the late 1960s was accompanied by an increasing awareness that educational inputs directed at weak groups of pupils, with all their importance, could not narrow the gap between them and the "mainstream" children. The heads of the educational system began working on public opinion, particularly by political lobbying, to implement an educational reform that would encompass the entire educational system and help to achieve the educational goals of Israeli society.

This integration would, they hoped, bring about two results: it would enhance social and cultural contact between children from various groups in the spirit of the Zionist ideal of "in-gathering of exiles"; and the mainstream children would serve as models for their weaker friends, the "disadvantaged," in the domain of studies and other school achievements.

This was the first time that the planned change in the educational system was called a "reform." This reform was based on two components:

1. Extension of the period of study. The Law of Free Compulsory Education, which until then had encompassed children aged five to fourteen, was now extended to include children aged five to sixteen, and in "disadvantaged" areas, from four to sixteen, with an option given to sixteen year olds to continue studying free of charge up to the age of eighteen.

2. A change in the structure of the educational system. In the years preceding the establishment of the state of Israel, and during the first two decades after the rise of the state, the educational system was based on a European model, consisting of two stages: eight years of broad general elementary education followed by four years of secondary schooling, which was for the most part academic and selective. The reform program sought, within the structure of twelve years of schooling, to maintain three frameworks forming three stages: a six-year elementary stage, a three-year intermediate secondary stage, and a three-year upper secondary stage. The move from stage 1 to stage 2 was intended to be completely nonselective. Pupils would be placed in an intermediate school (junior high school) solely on the basis of zoning.

Thus, it was expected that all the pupils finishing elementary school would move on to the second stage, the intermediate school, ensuring everyone of at least nine years of schooling. The planners of the reform hoped that many areas would adopt this new structure. However, the law permitted the previous organizational structure (eight years of elementary school followed by four years of secondary school) to be retained in those places that chose to do so. Indeed, as we will see below, the organizational aspect of this reform was not adopted in all the educational frameworks. Implementation of the reform plan met with ideological, political, and practical organizational difficulties, as follows.

In moving pupils from the six-year elementary school to the three-year intermediate school, the administrators of the reform did indeed adhere to the principle of nonselection of pupils on the basis of achievement. However, the pupils entering the new school met with a dual selection: on the one hand, they were assigned to homerooms, which in most cases were nonselective or "heterogeneous" as regards level of scholastic achievement, but on the other hand, they were placed in tracks on the basis of their previous achievements in some of the most critical subjects for academic success, such as Hebrew, mathematics, and English. Each track included pupils from several homeroom classes. In this way the pupils underwent selection within the school, instead of the previous selection to separate schools (or separate classes).

Moreover, the tracks based on achievements again paralleled the children's social background, so that the eastern pupils were generally placed in the low tracks and the western pupils in the high ones.

In some places the selection processes in the intermediate school began to affect the educational measures in the elementary school; the sixth grade in the elementary school was devoted to "preparing" for selection. Apparently, all these outcomes were unexpected and unintended.

Implementation of the change in the structure of schooling necessitated far-reaching changes in the curricula (such as "academization" of grades 7 and 8) and in the teaching methods (the shift to scholastically heterogeneous classes). Changes of this nature take place more slowly than changes on the organizational level. In addition, the educational system was not adequately equipped for such changes, and in many places the change did not go beyond the purely organizational level.

The idea of bringing educationally weak and strong children together in the same classroom was greeted with reluctance mainly—but not only—on the part of the parents of the mainstream children. They feared that mixing with children from weak groups would lower the standard of studies and achievements and hinder their children's progress and development. In addition, it seems that some of the representatives of the "weak" groups were rather reluctant to accept the new structure, fearing the failure of their children in the integrated schools and the loss of their community identity, which they wished to preserve.

Another serious difficulty was caused by the demographic structure of urban and rural regional settlements. In some cases, the demographic structure of an area prevented a balanced and feasible mixture of children from different social classes, especially in neighborhoods or settlements where the number of children in one of the groups (the "mainstream" or the "weak") considerably exceeded the number in the other. The "integration potential" was especially low among children whose parents chose for them to study in the state religious schools. Many of these families live in villages whose population is overwhelmingly eastern and which are located in rather remote places, to which it is hard to send religious children of more established, western origin.

In many places parents and community leaders chose not to shift to the new structure (6 + 3 + 3), despite the encouragement they received from the state system, such as promises of new buildings and budgets. These people thought that their local system in its existing pattern (8 + 4) met the challenges facing them. Moreover, in their opinion nobody could know better than the community members themselves what was good for them and for their children.

Some local authorities tried to solve the geographical problem and achieve the required "heterogenization" by bussing children from their homes to regional intermediate schools. In most cases the new intermediate schools functioned in middle-class areas; thus, the bussed children were mostly from the weak groups. In the unknown territory, these children experienced feelings of alienation that apparently detracted from their chances of adjustment and progress. It was found that most of the children from the weak strata studying in intermediate schools in middle-class areas dropped out of school during the three years of study (Kfir and Chen, 1985).

From the beginning it was decided not to apply the reform in the case of two special groups: children whose parents chose to send them to *yeshivot* (religious boarding schools), which operate outside the community, and children in *kibbutzim*, which are collective settlements of an idiosyncratic ideological character. Needless to say, leaving out these two social groups from the reform and integration process had a injurious effect on certain aspects of the program.

The Israel Teachers Union, which included all the elementary teachers in the old-style eight-year school, opposed this reform for several weighty reasons. One argument was the educational perception that viewed grades 7 and 8 as the school "leadership," with the pupils serving as models for imitation in several respects for the younger pupils, so that the school operated as an influential center of social learning. However, there are those who claim that certain power-related organizational motives were behind their opposition: the Teachers Union feared it would lose 25 percent of its members, who would probably join the rival Union of Secondary School Teachers if the reform were implemented.

Turning grades 7 and 8 into secondary school classes called for "academization" of the teachers in these classes. The inclusion of large groups of teachers in frameworks of higher education presented considerable operational difficulties and was not a task that could be accomplished overnight.

From its beginning, in the late 1960s and early 1970s, until 1987, the reform process encompassed only about 65 percent of all the towns and villages in

Israel. The reluctance of the middle-class parents, the opposition of local politicians and educators, added to reasons of social and educational principles, prevented implementation of the reform process in some of the cities with "heterogeneous" populations in the center of the country. (In recent years there has been a certain change in some of these towns, too.) On the other hand, the reform was fully implemented in towns with a more "homogeneous" population, which was socioeconomically weaker. Thus, the reform tended to operate more fully—especially at the beginning—in areas with a low potential for social-educational integration than in areas whose integrative potential was high.

The research accompanying the process of educational reform in Israel tends to show that the new arrangements (1) cause children from weak social groups to remain in school longer; (2) lead to increased social contact between weak and mainstream pupils; and (3) raise the level of achievements of weak pupils in heterogeneous classes. In spite of the new measures, no significant closing of the gap between the weak and strong pupils has yet been proven (Swirsky, 1990).

At this stage, voices began to be increasingly heard in favor of pluralism in the educational system and the right of individuals and communities to determine individual patterns and orientations to suit themselves, and against the uniform central instruction of one national authority. Against this background, and in light of the failure to achieve some of the goals of the integrational reform, new attempts at reform were made in the 1980s.

THE REFORM OF THE 1980s: THE AIM FOR PLURALISM, DECENTRALIZATION, AND AUTONOMOUS APPROACHES

The process of unifying the Israeli educational system began with the centralization of state education on the establishment of the state, and some claim that it reached its peak with the reform of the 1970s. In the mid–1980s an additional educational perception began to form, stressing the rights of communities to individual patterns. This led to growing demands for decentralization of the system, giving schools more pedagogical independence and allowing them to develop their own curricula and apply more varied teaching methods. These approaches, with their focus on the school and their recognition of the community's right to share in determining the curriculum of the school that educates its children, seem to indicate a further step in the sequence of educational reform in Israel.

Among the attempts at variety and educational innovation based on school-oriented approaches, we may find today a broad network of community schools, independent schools, including specialist schools, and schools with specific educational approaches such as open schools.

Some of these attempts were made on the direct initiative of the Ministry of Education, and some stem from initiatives in the field. Among the initiatives of the Education Ministry are the establishment, development, and encouragement of community schools throughout the country, functioning in a manner similar to community schools in the United States. These schools are characterized by their belief in the importance of parental involvement and the aim for autonomy, meaning that decisions regarding the school's goals and ways of functioning are made locally (Pur, 1985; Reshef, 1984). The encouragement and realization of the idea of school autonomy, beginning in elementary schools and spreading recently to intermediate and upper schools, underline the need for change. The school in its present form has difficulty coping with the problems of cultural orientations characteristic of a pluralistic society, with pupils' declining motivation to study, and with the community's growing demand to be involved in its children's education. The idea is to turn the school into a social-pedagogical system that defines its own credo according to which the school staff acts and supplies many of its own pedagogical needs from within as well as from its immediate surroundings, while responding to the community it serves (Reshef, 1984).

In the context of the move toward autonomous school approaches, we may see the appearance of schools with individual educational or ideological shades, such as schools of art, science, Jewish, and labor values.

Some of these are regional schools, like most schools in Israel. Some are supraregional and operate on the principle of "parents' choice," a trend that has developed considerably in recent years in the United States and Britain. These schools tend to be organized around a specific educational credo (Shapira, 1988).

Several factors led to the establishment of the "specialist" schools. Many parents wanted to give their children an education matching their outlooks and beliefs. They wished to be involved in the educational process itself, and the heads of the central educational system understood that the parents' involvement might be a positive factor in the life of the school. The parents' new awareness was also the result of an uneasy feeling concerning the conservative character of the educational system and the uniform character of the subject matter, as well as disappointment in the way in which the school organization responded to their social and cultural aspirations (Shapira, 1988).

Another factor that encouraged the establishment of "specialist" schools is connected with a line of policy that has recently developed in the educational system. This policy advocates focusing on specialized subject matter to meet the needs of pupils with specific tendencies and abilities.

Promoters of these schools believe that their approaches present a further model for the achievement of social integration. The integration, they suggest, is not "statistical integration," but the integration of people from various backgrounds, based on uniting the pupils and their parents around a common interest in a certain subject (Shapira and Goldring, 1990).

Despite the educational reforms, most of which were aimed at equalizing the scholastic achievements of children of different "ethnic" groups and classes, the educational gap between eastern and western pupils in Israel was not lessened.

According to Nahon (1987:31–32), the gap actually widened during the first forty years of the state. Nahon reports that Iraqi Jews came to Israel with an average educational level equal to that of immigrants from some European countries and higher than that of other eastern immigrants. Comparative findings of educational data on the first and second generation of immigrants from Iraq show that in the second generation their education level was lower than that of people of European origin, and approached the level of those coming from the countries with the lowest achievements.

The pupils in the Jewish educational system may be divided into two categories (Swirsky, 1990). One category consists mainly of youth of western origin. It includes the elementary schools in established urban and rural areas, the academic secondary schools, the academic and vocational classes in prestigious trends (electronics, computers) in the comprehensive schools that provide academic and technical education in a shared organizational framework, and the high tracks in subjects considered complicated, such as reading comprehension, mathematics, and English in the intermediate schools.

The second category comprises mainly youth of eastern origin: its pupils are found in peripheral regional elementary schools, in vocational schools, in the vocational classes of comprehensive schools, and in the lower tracks in the intermediate schools. The shared organizational frameworks permit the move from one category to another, but the option most frequently realized is the move from the mainstream to the weak category.

Some analysts attribute the reform programs lack of success to cultural and psychological obstacles in the collective and personal biography of the "disadvantaged" eastern children, obstacles that organizational and pedagogical changes cannot overcome, even less eliminate, within a few decades (Minkowitz, 1969).

Some observers attribute the lack of success, at least partly, to the stigmatization of weak populations, which interferes with the educational and organizational efforts to advance them and lowers the pupils' expectations of themselves (Kashti et al., 1989).

There are still others who see this lack of success primarily as a side effect of the proletarization of the eastern immigrants by the social center and its various establishments, which are populated by the middle-class descendants of the western founders of the pre-state society. According to this latter approach, the attempts of the state educational system to lessen the gap and advance the weaker populations are spurious, and, in fact, the eastern children are educated in a separate system—to prepare them for low-status occupations (Swirsky, 1990).

In our opinion, although none of these three theories (the cultural, the labeling, and the proletarization theories) should be rejected outright, none of them, by itself, can account for the meager achievements of the attempts at change and reform whose aim was to achieve educational and social equality in Israel.

A scrutiny of the macro-social policy of Israel's state educational system, and of the micro-social policy followed by local educational systems and schools, indicates several characteristics that are particularly conducive to failure. First, the educational policy aims that accompanied the reform and change plans were (and often still are) presented in a vague and diffuse manner. No distinction was made between the aims calling for integration that was supposed to be achieved by mixing different social groups together in the same classroom, and the aims behind the structural reform which led to reorganization of the educational system. This combination of different matters leads to confusion (Klein and Eshel, 1979).

Thus, although reforms or changes in the educational system need clear and well-defined goals, among other things in order to create motivation for effecting the change, in many cases the educational goals are stated and formulated in a vague and diffuse manner. This phenomenon is explained by Schmuck and his colleagues (1977) by the lack of consensus concerning the necessity of the new aims and the nature of the required changes. It may be that the vagueness in defining the goals of educational reform in Israel also stems from the absence of full agreement among the policymakers, and reservations on the part of some of them.

Second, the initiators of the integration policy describe it as permitting a response to conflicting demands and sets of expectations. Elboim-Dror argues (1985a): "Thus the Ministry of Education can take decisions at the national level that are appropriate to the principles of equality and closing the gaps, while at the same time responding to the pressures of special interest groups at the level of the local authority, which has powers of decision delegated to it" (ibid.:31).

Another possible cause of failure is that reforms in the Israeli educational system were always presented as an overall ideology, or part of one, that permitted them to be viewed on the national level. The process of change that was instituted for the purpose of implementing the reform included the stage of taking an initiative (such as appointing a parliamentary committee), examining the existing educational system and its problems, forming overall ideas, and allocating resources for implementing changes in the field. But the preparation for reform did not include explaining the ideas to those who were supposed to apply them in practice (teachers, pupils, and parents) and training them for this, nor did it include finding solutions suited to daily life in the classroom.

In other words, the reforms instituted in Israel were based mostly on a "rational strategy" (Benne, 1976), which says that people change when the change seems to them desirable and worthwhile. The "tool" of change is, therefore, theoretical and empirical knowledge used effectively and logically to create attitudes, values, and inclination to act. This strategy of change is the dominant one in the educational system, says Benne, and "it is undoubtedly the most prevalent and popular one among educators and the general public" (ibid.:24).

This strategy was used in implementing the educational reform of the 1970s and worked outstandingly in raising the standard of teachers and their education. On the other hand, it worked less successfully in realizing the aims of social integration in education, since in the implementation of these aims opposition to change is not on the rational level. "The effectiveness of the rational approach is limited," says Babad (1985). "People are more rational when the matter concerns others and less rational when it concerns themselves."

The reforms in education have thus not settled the various dilemmas which the Israeli educational system has been facing since its inception: the problem of bridging educational gaps and the issues of unification versus cultural pluralism.

Some of Israel's current educational problems may have been actually caused by the solutions that have been offered to previous problems, while others are the outcome of recent social, political, and cultural changes such as new waves of immigration.

It doesn't appear that Israel is about to reach a "settled" or "permanent" set of educational procedures and arrangements. The emerging Israeli society undergoes a constant process of "becoming and changing." Educational reforms are a characteristic trait of the Israeli society rather than a passing stage in its development.

NOTES

1. From the start, two educational systems were set up that were separate in culture but united in their legal base and organizational pattern: one for the children of the Jewish majority and another for the Arab minorities who remained within the state after the war of independence in 1948. This arrangement is still considered desirable and preferred by the political and educational establishment of both groups. The percentages of pupils in the Arab educational system are as follows:

1949	1960	1970	1980	1987
7.88%	7.98%	13.40%	14.72%	15.60%
(11,100)	(46,100)	(110,500)	(177,200)	(218,200)

Source: Ministry of Education and Culture, 1987.

2. The percentage of pupils of eastern origin in the Israeli educational system rose gradually from the early 1950s, reaching 60 percent in the late 1980s (Nahon, 1987; Yogev and Shapira, 1987).

3. In the 1960s, 10 percent of the pupils of eastern origin studied in academic streams in secondary schools, compared with 30 percent of western origin (Nahon, 1987).

REFERENCES

Ackerman, W., A. Karmon, and D. Zukker, eds. 1985. *Education in an Emerging Society: The Israeli System*. Tel Aviv: HaKibbutz HaMeuchad (Hebrew).

Babad, E. 1985. "Processes of Psychological Change: Principles and Strategies." In *School and Education*, ed. Z. Lamm. Jerusalem: Magnes (Hebrew).

Benne, K. D. 1976. "The Process of Re-education: An Assessment of Kurt Lewin's Views." *Group and Organization Studies* 1:57–63.

Chen, M. 1980. "Some Outcomes of School Reform in Israel." In *Law and Equity in Education*, ed. S. Goldstein. Jerusalem: Academic Press.

Elboim-Dror, R. 1985a. "Decision Strategies in Treating Conflicts in the Education System." In *School and Education*, ed. Z. Lamm. Jerusalem: Magnes (Hebrew).

———. 1985b. "The Formation of Educational Policy in Israel." In *Education in an Emerging Society: The Israeli System*, ed. W. Ackerman, A. Karmon, and D. Zukker. Tel Aviv: HaKibbutz HaMeuchad (Hebrew).

Kashti, Y., et al. 1989. "Classroom Management in the Intermediate School: Problems and Meanings." In *The Planning of Educational Policy*, ed. Y. Danilow. Jerusalem: Ministry of Education and Culture (Hebrew).

Kfir, D., and M. Chen. 1985. "Interethnic Integration at School and the Personality of the Adolescent." In *Between Childhood and Adulthood*, ed. A. Ziv. Tel Aviv: Papyrus (Hebrew).

Klein, Z., and Y. Eshel. 1979. "Integration and the Fostering of Educational Objectives in Israel." *Megamot* 26(3):271–280 (Hebrew).

Kleinberger, A. F. 1969. *Society, Schools and Progress in Israel*. London: Pergamon Press.

Ministry of Education and Culture. 1987. *Selected Data on Israel's Education System*. Jerusalem (Hebrew).

Minkowitz, A. 1969. *The Disadvantaged Child*. Jerusalem: Hebrew University (Hebrew).

Nahon, Y. 1987. *Patterns of Educational Expansion and the Structure of Occupational Opportunities: The Ethnic Dimension*. Jerusalem: Jerusalem Institute for the Study of Israel (Hebrew).

Pur, D. 1985. "Autonomy in Education." *Hed HaHinuch* (Hebrew).

Reshef, S. 1984. *Autonomy in Education: Meaning and Inspiration*. Tel Aviv: Tel Aviv University (Hebrew).

Schmuck, R. A., P. Runkel, J. Arends, and R. Arends. 1977. *The Second Handbook of Organizational Development in Schools*. Mountain View, Calif.: Mayfield.

Shapira, R. 1988. "Social Educational Uniqueness." In *Planning Educational Policy*, ed. D. Pur. Jerusalem: Ministry of Education and Culture (Hebrew).

———, and E. Goldring. 1990. *Parents' Involvement in Specialized Schools*. Sapir Institute. Tel Aviv University (Hebrew).

Shmida, M. 1987. *Between Equality and Excellence: Educational Reform and the Comprehensive School*. Ramat Gan: Bar-Ilan University (Hebrew).

Smilansky, M., et al. 1966. *Gifted Children from Culturally Disadvantaged Schools: The Identification and Fostering and Secondary Education*. Jerusalem: Szold Institute (Hebrew).

Survey of Palestine (1945–6). Vol. 2. Jerusalem: Government Printer.

Swirsky, S. 1990. *Education in Israel: Schooling for Inequality*. Tel Aviv: Brerot (Hebrew).

Yogev, A., and R. Shapira. 1987. "Ethnicity, Meritocracy and Credentialization in Israel: Elaborating the Credential Society Thesis." Tel Aviv University, Department of Sociology and Anthropology.

18

JAPAN

James J. Shields, Jr.

Several major periods of educational reform have taken place in Japan in the modern era. One of the most important occurred under the Meiji Restoration in the 1880s when a national system of education was created which exists today under the central authority of the Ministry of Education, Science, and Culture (Monbusho).

Another significant period of reform in terms of the existing structure of schooling in Japan took place after World War II when compulsory education was extended from six to nine years and the "6–3–3" system, comprised of six years of elementary school and three years each of lower and upper secondary schooling, was established. These reforms were based on democratic principles aimed at achieving equality of educational opportunity and high academic competency related to economic development.

The postwar history of education in Japan has been primarily one in which educational equality is defined as the comprehensive expansion of schooling on all levels. By 1987, for example, 94.3 percent of the appropriate age group attended upper secondary schools. By 1990 the proportion of eighteen to twenty-one year olds enrolled in higher education reached 36.8 percent on the university and junior college levels and 53.7 percent if attendance rates at special postsecondary training schools are included (Japan. Monbusho, 1989; Takizawa, 1990).

The private sector has played an important role in the expansion of educational opportunity on the kindergarten, upper secondary, university, junior college, and special training school levels. In fact, it is widely believed in Japan that the increase in the number of students in higher education is due to the remarkable expansion of private universities and junior colleges in the postwar period. Throughout this expansion, the government has played a major role in encouraging private sector growth through legislative action, policy, and funding (Japan. Monbusho, 1989; Takizawa, 1990).

A change in the pattern of growth in attendance began to take place in the 1980s when the number of students at both public and private upper secondary schools, junior colleges, and universities began to show signs of stabilizing. In the 1990s the trend lines moved sharply downward. This is due primarily to a rapidly declining decrease in the age group between eighteen and twenty-one years (Takizawa, 1990).

With the ending of the expansion of schooling, and with the acceleration of social changes related to urbanization and industrialization in recent years, the focus of Japanese educational reform is shifting from quantitative to qualitative issues. More fundamental questions related to the meaning and the significance of education are being raised.

In recognition of this important turning point in Japanese educational history, the government established the National Council on Educational Reform as an advisory body to the prime minister in 1984 to define the educational problems and to establish a reform agenda. Before its termination in 1987, the council had submitted four reports to the prime minister. Among the major problems the council identified were (1) excessive competition for university entrance examinations; (2) problem behavior and lack of discipline among young people; and (3) uniform and inflexible structures and methods of formal education that are not responsive to student diversity (Japan. Monbusho, 1989).

The response to these reports in the media, among university scholars, educational leaders, and the public, has been immense. It has led to an outpouring of newspaper and journal articles and letters, books, unpublished papers, and governmental documents on the reports' findings and recommendations.

Through partial support from the Japan–United States Friendship Commission, the author visited Japan in 1987, 1988, and 1990 to interview the leading participants in this national debate on education and to review the large body of literature generated by the reports. In addition, the collateral publications of U.S. and European scholars on these reports were analyzed.

What follows is a summary of the findings of this research study. Overall, a pattern of core assumptions and beliefs that have framed the debate over the findings and recommendations of the National Council on Educational Reform since 1987 became evident in this study. This chapter focuses on a number of these beliefs which were isolated for analysis on the basis of the impact they are projected to have on the future success and failure of Japanese educational reform.

Some of these assumptions and beliefs support, while others significantly depart from, the findings and recommendations of the National Council. Among those discussed here regarding the perceived role of governmental policy and strategy and the existing educational structure are (1) the importance of high academic standards for Japan's economic development; (2) the relationship of early maternal and child care and education to school success; (3) the critical part the private educational sector plays in upgrading academic competency; (4) the continuing decline in equality of educational opportunity; (5) the crisis in moral education which in the words of a Monbusho report (1989:108) has created a pressing need "to cultivate people with rich and strong hearts and minds!"

What has clearly emerged from the national dialogue in Japan on educational reform is the existence of deep conflict over establishing the relative importance of each of a number of very notable educational goals among which are academic excellence, educational equality, parental choice and responsibility, and moral values.

This chapter presents an analysis of these goals and of the tension and contradictions that exist among them, with the objective of finding a way of bringing all the goals into balance with each other. For it is only when this is realized that the fundamental purpose for establishing the National Council of Education Reform, the maximizing of each student's individual strengths as well as enhancing the common good, will be achieved.

EMPHASIS ON EDUCATIONAL ATTAINMENT

Japan is generally considered the second most important economic power after the United States, with a possibility of becoming number one. Whatever its ranking, Japan's economic record is formidable. It has the highest per capita income in the world; it is a major source of long-term capital, the financier of a big part of America's budget and trade deficits; it is a leading direct investor in Western Europe and North America; and it is at the forefront in many areas of technology (Johnson, 1989).

As impressive as these achievements are in the economic sphere, especially in terms of the pace with which Japan was able to achieve them, its achievements in education are even more spectacular. In a broad range of measures of school participation and educational attainment, Japan ranks in the top categories, even though other nations, such as the United States, spend more per pupil on elementary and secondary education.

Japan has an exceptionally high percentage of appropriate age groups not only enrolled, but also in daily attendance at each level of schooling. As for achievement, Japanese students excel in every measured international standard up to the age of seventeen both for the top students and for the 95 percent of students who graduate from high school.

In mathematics and science, for example, Japanese students received the highest scores in a study of children from twenty countries, and at the twelfth grade were second only to Chinese students in Hong Kong. In contrast, poor achievement by American students on tests in mathematics and science has reached the level of a national crisis. In a recent cross-national study of mathematics achievement, American students in eighth and twelfth grades were below the international average in problem-solving, geometry, algebra, calculus, and other areas of mathematics (Stevenson and Lee, 1990).

Recently, a Swiss study carried out by the World Economic Forum and International Institute for Management Development ranked Japan as the most competitive country among the twenty-three major developed nations analyzed in 1990, a position Japan has held since 1988. The study singled out Japan's active domestic investment and well-planned education for workers. The United States came in third and was described as having the poorest quality compulsory educational system of all the nations studied ("Japan Most Competitive Nation," 1990).

Michael Porter in *The Competitive Advantage of Nations* (1990) has pointed out that U.S. economic problems do not lie in the lack of openness of Japanese markets, but in too little investment in the development of skills required by the technological workforce. This, he believes, is as important, if not more so, than harmonious labor-management relations, government investment, and tax policies.

U.S. education deficits are so serious that they have become a matter for discussion among political leaders in U.S.–Japanese policy negotiations. In response to U.S. criticism of Japan's trade policies, a group of sixteen Japanese Liberal Democratic party members led by the transport minister, Shintaro Ishihara, released a report in June 1990 calling on the United States to increase the percentage of its GNP spent on education to 5 percent. The low level of educational achievement in the United States, the report says, is partly responsible for the declining competitiveness of U.S. industry ("Ishihara Group...," 1990).

The Need for Multidimensional Analysis

From past experience in the West and elsewhere, we know that schooling is usually the dependent variable within the context of the broader political, economic, and social forces within which it functions. The prevailing belief today is that educational development alone does not explain economic growth or the movement toward democracy. The utility of any educational proposal, therefore, depends on an understanding of the differences between "macro" and "micro" orientations to research and policy (Foster, 1989).

The severe limitations of one-dimensional thinking apply to all fields of inquiry, not just educational studies. In the past, Japanese studies was dominated by works that attempted to treat Japan as a totality that could be understood in terms of a single concept: "emperor worship," "rice culture," "groupism," "modernization," or "class conflict."

Such theorizing in the grand nineteenth-century style has often been interpreted within the framework of two major conflicting interpretations of Japan: (1) the mainly Anglo-American modernization school and (2) the Japanese Marxist school. The first tended to portray Japan as a model of peaceful transition from feudalism to modernity. In contrast, the Marxist school painted a picture of the persistent failure of opposition groups to oust the ruling oligarchy by exposing the authoritarian nature of the Meiji state (Williams, 1990). By the late 1970s, however, both approaches began to fall into increasing disfavor.

An excellent model of multidimensional analysis can be found in Harold Crouch and James W. Morley's "Dynamics of Political Change" (1990) which deals with the role of economic and social factors in political change. They argue that the economic growth process is mediated through the social and political processes it generates. "Who can doubt," they state, "that in Japan the democratization of its system in the Occupation period has been legitimized at least in part, by the high economic growth it sustained throughout the postwar period. It is not accidental that higher rates of economic growth are associated with democracy" (Crouch and Morley, 1990:7).

Crouch and Morley (1990) believe that the role of education is dependent on economic growth, and that in turn economic growth is dependent on education to improve human resources which an expanding economic system requires.

In their analysis of nine Asian countries, Crouch and Morley (1990) found that countries where the middle class had been most active in the drive for democratization also had the greatest percentage of the population with high levels of education. What seems to happen is that when working, business, farming, and middle classes become well educated, large, politically conscious, and mobilized, they no longer accept the authority of any government that excludes them from real political participation. When this occurs, pressure and movement toward the democratic transformation of the state takes place.

The process of change, of course, is never simple. Political change is not only stimulated by economic, social, and educational change, but has its own dynamic as well. Even when economic and social factors seem to favor democratization, essentially political factors can obstruct change. In Japan, internal, ethnic conflict has not been a large problem. But elsewhere the presence of strong ethnic groups has impeded democratic political reform (Crouch and Morley, 1990). Certainly, for example, ethnic turbulence in the former Soviet republics, some of which are now independent states, was instrumental in the dissolution of the Soviet Union and was an obstacle to liberalization under *perestroika*, it may continue to be so in the new independent republics.

FOSTERING PARENTAL COLLABORATION IN MATERNAL AND CHILD CARE

Among the most critical influences in any individual's life is his or her early childhood experience. Childrearing patterns affect society as a whole and, of necessity, have to be considered whenever such issues as standard of living, political empowerment, and educational reform are explored.

Shortly after World War II, Japan ranked seventeenth in infant mortality rates. Today Japan has the lowest infant mortality rate in the world. This has been attained through governmental strategies to encourage private, parental, and community involvement in maternal and child health care and education.

In contrast, U.S. infant mortality rates moved in the opposite direction, down from fifteenth place in 1968 to twenty-first in 1990. A particularly worrisome component of these data is that the rate for U.S. African-Americans is about twice that for whites. According to a report distributed during the 1990 Education Commission of States National Forum, more than 40,000 U.S. children in any given year suffer preventable learning impediments brought on by low birth weight, substance abuse, lead poisoning, and malnutrition ("Health Problems . . . ," 1990).

Japan's approach to maternal and child care and education could prove instructive to the United States and other nations where infant mortality and preventable child disability rates are high, whereas William Steslicke (1990:31) states "there is death before life."

Under Japan's 1951 Children's Charter, mothers voluntarily register their pregnancy with the municipal government and begin to use a comprehensive range of health examination, assistance, and education programs made available to them. At that time, they are given a copy of the *Maternal and Child Health Handbook* which provides practical health and nutritional information and a record of diagnostic and treatment procedures related to pregnancy, delivery, and child care in the first year of life. This handbook has become the core of Japanese maternal and child health services (Steslicke, 1990) which foster strong parental collaboration with public health programs.

Private individuals and groups play an equal, if not a more important, role in the infant health miracle in Japan. In particular, the work of *Aiiku-han* established in the 1930s provides a good example of an effective voluntary, community-based, and nonprofessional agency that has collaborated in the upgrading of maternal and child care (Steslicke, 1990).

The Japanese government's strategies to forge partnerships with parents and community groups to improve child care function within the context of three factors. The first is the high value placed on childbearing and childrearing in Japan. This is reflected in the high standards and the unrelenting dedication Japanese mothers have for their children (Steslicke, 1990; Stevenson and Lee, 1990).

A second factor is the relatively low rate of births in Japan to women under the age of twenty compared to other nations. A third factor is the comparatively higher rate of induced abortion, notably in the thirty to thirty-four age category which in 1985 was only exceeded by India (Steslicke, 1990).

While all these factors play a role in explaining the low infant mortality rates in Japan, they do not appear to be as important as the progress that has been made in improving the overall health status of the entire population. For instance, Japan has ranked first in life expectancy for the last five years for both males (75.91 years) and females (81.77 years). And this has been achieved in spite of the fact that Japan has the highest percentage of men who smoke (about 61 percent) among developed nations.

Between infancy and death, many other measures of Japanese health are also impressive. Teenagers score relatively high in psychological tests of self-esteem and confidence and rank relatively low in suicides and drug use (White, 1989). Clearly, Japan's achievements in educational attainment, maternal and child health, and longevity are impressive.

PLACING HUMAN RESOURCE DEVELOPMENT BEFORE RAISING LIVING STANDARDS

Although Japan ranks first in the world in terms of per capita GNP, it is far behind other major industrialized nations in many measures of individual afflu-ence and life-style. The Japanese general public has yet to experience a full sense of the wealth that Japan as a nation has attained.

The Japanese Transportation Ministry has introduced an index called the Life GNP which shows per capita GNP after allowing for working hours and individual purchasing power. The Life GNP puts Japan at two-thirds of the U.S. level, even though its GNP is 15 percent higher than that of the United States. The large gap in living standards is due to inadequate infrastructure in such areas as housing and parks and in purchasing power. For example, housing space available for individual Japanese is 40 percent less than that for the average person in the United States, Britain, West Germany, and France. In addition, the Japanese have only one-tenth the park space of the average person in these countries ("Improved Infrastructure . . . ," 1990).

The policy of placing producers' needs before consumers' and human resource development before the distribution of material goods among the general public has a long history in Japan. As E. Sydney Crawcour (Williams, 1990) has pointed out, Japan's success in the nineteenth century depended significantly, and perhaps critically, on the ability of the Meiji government to resist consumption in the interests of industrial and military development. As a result, there is little ex-pectation that there will be a dramatic shift toward consumer interests in the near future.

The extremely large family expenditures for education in Japan demonstrate how the general public places production priorities and human resource devel-opment before immediate, material consumption needs. The expansion of pa-rental funding in Japan for education has not been accompanied by the agonizing debates and resistance found in the United States over the extent to which parents should involve themselves financially in maximizing their children's educational opportunities.

A recent *White Paper on the Nation's Living Standards* points out that family expenditures on education in Japan account for 34 percent of their total spending and reach even higher levels in peak years. In 1989 an Education Ministry study showed that family spending for cram schools had doubled since 1979. Since 1980 alone, there has been an 11.5 percent increase for cram schools and private tutors for primary school students. These expenditures are believed to be a major factor in depressing Japanese family consumption levels for items usually fac-tored into calculations of a nation's living standards (Kaneko, 1989).

Where there is agreement in the West over parental involvement, it exists for strategies related to political control and moral responsibility rather than for financial support. Currently, in the United States there is interest in the work of James P. Comer (1980), Yale University psychiatrist, who has demonstrated in a number of school districts that early and intense parental and community involvement can dramatically improve the learning of poor, urban minority children. As a result, considerable public funding has been generated in the United States to support public programs to actively promote parental involvement in their children's schooling.

PROMOTING PARENTAL CHOICE AND RESPONSIBILITY: THE "DOUBLE-SCHOOLING" PHENOMENON

The Japanese educational system consists of legally authorized public schools and a whole array of other institutions outside the purely public sector. The School Education Act distinguishes between formal schools and nonformal schools. Included in the formal are elementary, junior, and senior high schools and institutions of higher learning.

The private sector is strongly evident in both formal and nonformal education. Private schools account for nearly 29 percent of upper secondary school, 73 percent of university, and 91 percent of junior college students. Also, 77 percent of total kindergarten enrollment is in the private sector (Japan. Monbusho, 1989).

Private schools differ from their public school counterparts in many important ways. Private upper secondary schools, for example, are more often located in urban than in rural areas. In addition, matters such as admissions and curriculum are left to a private school's discretion under the supervision of prefectural governors rather than to prefectural boards of education as is the case in public schools. This probably explains why private secondary schools occupy either the top or the bottom of their community's school hierarchy (Iwaki, 1986–1987).

Private higher education is largely funded by student tuition fees, which relative to per capita GNP have already reached their highest level in the postwar period. In addition, approximately 17 to 20 percent, depending how and when it is calculated, of private university funding comes from the national government. Apart from this, many prefectural and municipal governments also provide financial assistance as they do on the private kindergarten and secondary school levels as well (Ichikawa, 1988–1989; Kaneko, 1989; Kitamura, 1990).

Nonformal schools take many forms, including cram schools (jukus), proprietary technical and vocational schools (kakushu-gakkos), and life-long learning and training programs usually provided by corporations as part of on-the-job training.

The largest out-of-public school sector in Japan is the study institution (juku). It is believed that there are about 100,000, which make jukus the second most important layer of educational institutions in Japan after the regular schools (Yuuki, 1986–1987).

Exercise and sports jukus are also widely used in Japan, especially on the elementary school level. Recent studies have found that 50 percent of all Grade 1 and 80 percent of Grade 4 pupils attend exercise and sport juku, usually twice a week. At about fourth grade when attendance at study jukus increases, many pupils attend both study and exercise juku. Overall, it is estimated that about 71 percent of elementary school and lower secondary pupils receive supplementary instruction of one kind or another after school and away from regular school premises (Yuuki, 1986–1987).

A strong mutually supporting relationship between the formal and nonformal systems has evolved on all levels and has created a "double-schooling" phenomenon. Partly this has happened because Japanese schools produce two extreme groups of pupils: high achievers and low achievers. High achievers usually become dissatisfied with the slow progress of their classes and turn to private preparatory schools or jukus where they receive more advanced and individualized instruction geared to university examinations. The low achievers, unable to keep up with their classmates, attend other types of private cram schools which offer remedial instruction (Kitamura, 1990).

The interrelatedness of the two kinds of supporting systems contributes greatly to the strength of Japanese education in terms of low dropout rates, high academic achievement, and cost-effectiveness. In addition, the privately supported system compensates for the inflexibility and uniformity of the public system in initiating educational reform.

The double schooling phenomenon, as we have seen, requires defining parental responsibility and choice around (1) principles rooted in collaboration between the public and private sectors, and (2) the placement of human resource development before immediate consumption needs.

Furthermore, the movement toward privatizing schooling in Japan is due to deliberate governmental reform strategies and not to Japan's so-called unique culture. The National Council on Educational Reform established in 1984 as an advisory committee to the prime minister has recommended that "in view of the role played by private institutions in the formal educational system, the government needs to expand its subsidies to private educational institutions placing emphasis on assistance for unique and distinctive programs" (Japan, Monbusho, 1989:182).

THE DECLINING ROLE OF TRADITIONAL PATTERNS OF MORAL EDUCATION

There is much that is impressive about the strategies undertaken in Japan to promote private and public collaboration in attaining high student achievement and maternal and child care and in fostering parental choice and responsibility of schooling and supplementary education. However, there is a darker side to Japanese education characterized by serious discontinuities that seem to be embedded in these strategies as well. These are related to the diminishing role of the school in guaranteeing equality of educational opportunity and the declining role of moral education which are thought to be rooted in a brutal examination system.

The issues of equality and moral education are also troublesome outside of Japan in other nations such as the United States where there is less of a commitment to privatizing educational choice and where parents assume a much smaller financial responsibility for their children's education.

Since the Meiji period, the school in Japan has been a major agent of moral and religious socialization. Schools became the institutional nexus linking the family with the polity around a hierarchical ideology that sanctified the relationship among children, their parents, ancestors, and the emperor. By means of school rituals, courses of study, and extracurricular activities, principles in the Shinto and Confucion moral order, such as loyalty, filial piety, the discipline of group life, industry, cleanliness, physical strength, and perseverance, were reinforced (Fujita, 1985).

The role of the school in Japan has been defined so comprehensively and broadly that it has extended to supervisory rights over student behavior outside the school. Almost all elementary and secondary schools still have prescribed codes over such matters as clothing and places students may go by themselves and with adults (Fujita, 1985). The extremely broad custodial role of schools is strengthened by the importance given to *girininjo*, the web of reciprocal obligations in which the social order is enmeshed. In Japan, these obligations are regarded as the guarantors of rights and duties in much the same way that law is in the United States (Smith, 1983).

Officially, strong acceptance continues for the view that schools should keep their broad custodial roles and strong orientation to moral education. But, in fact, the school is becoming increasingly secularized. As University of Tokyo professor Hidenori Fujita (1985) points out, a qualitative change has taken place in the linkages among schools, families, and the polity. As a result, the effectiveness of traditional patterns of moral education has been undermined in Japan (Smith, 1983).

Fellow sociologist and University of Tokyo colleague Ikuo Amano (1986) lends support to Fujita's view that troubled relationships exist between pupils and the educational system which have led to pathological phenomena. Amano sees the changed orientation of young people and the unchanged values and attitudes of the older generation as the reason for the problem.

These views are given support in the *Summary of the Second Report on Educational Reform* in which it is stated, "A general diagnosis must be made of the grave social illness now affecting our educational system, the 'desolation' whose symptoms include bullying, school violence, and excessive competition in entrance examinations" (Japan, Prime Minister's Office, 1986:4).

Japanese children appear to enjoy primary school. Foreign observers generally find that pupils look and sound happy in their environment. The dark side of the system becomes more apparent when pupils reach the second year of junior high school. This is the point at which what they have to do to succeed becomes clear and their feelings and attitudes change.

Kazuhiro Mochizuki (1982), long-time Tokyo high school principal, reports that the whole weight of Japan's competitive society falls on the junior high school. He identifies the highly charged atmosphere of academic competition as the cause of the growing violence and the extreme dysfunction found on the junior high level where 80 percent of the incidents occur.

Specifically, in many schools there has been a buildup of an unhealthy energy that takes the form of what is called *ijime*. Translated, *ijime* means bullying directed at certain individuals, sometimes with the tacit approval or even the complicity of adults. Usually, the victim who is singled out is particularly vulnerable or seems to be different. Some students have died directly from the treatment, while a number of victims have committed suicide.

In addition to academic competition, other reasons cited for *ijime* are the increasingly materialistic culture, which gives more importance to economic success than to the dignity of individuals, and the overly indulgent childrearing practices of this generation of parents. Moreover, the way pupils are used to enforce discipline among their peers in the early years of schooling has been cited as a possible contributing factor to the phenomenon. There is some evidence to support the view that youth, given free rein to do so, often impose more stringent and authoritarian values and attitudes on each other than adults would (Murakami, 1985; Smith, 1983).

PARENTAL CHOICE AND RESPONSIBILITY AND EQUALITY OF EDUCATIONAL OPPORTUNITY

Just as discontinuities have surfaced in the historical role of the school in Japan as a socializing agency for moral development, so too have problems arisen around the role of schooling as a vehicle for economic and social mobility. Today these two dominating purposes of Japanese education, the one moral and the other economic, are being seriously undermined.

Schooling in Japan is a huge sorting machine characterized by meritocracy and competition, a hierarchical and pyramidal structure with elite universities on the top, and prestige differentiation on every level. Individuals are identified and defined by their university credentials, which are absolute yardsticks for measuring the achievement of each individual as well as for determining his position in the social hierarchy (Fujita, 1985).

As stated in the *First Report on Educational Reform*, "in evaluating an individual more importance is attached to 'When and where did he learn?' than to 'What extent did he learn?' and such criteria are applied to judging even an individual's value, ability, and personality" (Japan, Prime Minister's Office, 1985:45).

Ikuo Amano (1986) tells us that a key element to keep in mind when looking at the relationship between the educational system and credentials and the examination system that joins the two is the matter of equality of educational opportunity. He believes that because the prime requirements for examination success are intellectual ability and individual effort, equality of educational opportunity has been achieved and is no longer an issue. This, he feels, explains why there are so few calls for reform on this issue in Japan.

Support for this position can be found in the work of William Cummings (1982) who, on the basis of his work in the early 1970s on elementary schools, concluded that available data reveal an educational system in Japan that is more equitable and democratic in orientation than that of the United States. More recently, however, the prevailing view is more differentiated and negative. Thomas Rohlen (1985–1986) argues that, while up to high school, the system offers a greater basic equality than American reformers have dreamed possible, after that the system is competitive and produces an elaborate hierarchy.

In his research on equality, Hidenori Fujita (1985) found an unchanging pattern of differences in academic achievement by father's occupation, which has persisted throughout the remarkable expansion in secondary and higher education. In effect, he found that the higher the father's educational level, the higher the student's academic achievement.

Thomas Rohlen's (1985–1986) studies also reveal a trend toward a greater role for family factors in educational outcomes. By the mid–1970s, for instance, he found fewer and fewer students from poor families were entering the elite universities. He also found that delinquency rates are closely correlated to the academic rank of high schools and that high schools reflect differences in family background. Japan, like the United States, he concludes, has a school system that partially replicates the status and class system of its society. But the distinct, stratified subcultures are attained through an examination system rather than through segregation as is often the case in the United States.

Privately purchased advantage in the preparation process for the examination system at juku, yobiko, and at private high schools seems to be looming larger and larger in significance in the calculation of life chances for social and economic mobility. Nationally, successful applicants to Tokyo University are now equally divided between free, public schools and fee-based private schools. It is ironic, argues Fujita (1985:129), "that on the one hand, people expect the school to be a total agency of socialization and on the other hand, the most fundamental role of modern education, that of developing basic skills, has been personalized and left to alternate institutions."

Estelle James and Gail Benjamin (1984) provide excellent insight into the impact of private education in Japan on educational opportunity. They found that public education is utilized primarily for basic schooling up through the ninth grade by the whole population, and beyond that by increasingly smaller percentages of the population. At the upper secondary level, the government, through partial funding, has encouraged private enterprise to respond to demands for schooling that exceed the carefully regulated public supply.

The number of academic track places in public high schools is limited. As a result, they are oversubscribed. This situation tends to favor upper-economic strata children whose families consider expenditures for private tutoring and secondary and higher education a good investment for gaining a competitive advantage in examinations.

In metropolitan areas such as Kyoto, Osaka, Tokyo, and Kanagawa, which have the largest and wealthiest populations, we find a pattern of small public enrollments, a large private sector, and large academic track populations. This, as James and Benjamin (1984) tell us, is because the politically influential upper classes in these areas know they have a good chance either of getting their children into high-quality public schools or of paying the fees required by private schools.

Working urban-class families who prefer more public academic high school places do not have the political power in these prefectures to bring this about. One exception is Tokyo, where the metropolitan government reformed the elitist aspects of the system. The result was a massive flight of "better students" to private schools. The public schools, which used to dominate the admissions lists for national public universities, have been replaced by private academic schools in Tokyo. Thus, a reform designed to be egalitarian had the opposite effect and helped push private schools to the top of the status hierarchy.

The results of the reforms in Tokyo are similar to those found in most other nations whenever selectivity is ruled out and attempts are made to homogenize student bodies in open-access public schools. For example, in the United States, as public schools became less selective, so did their reputations as quality institutions. In contrast, Japan, for the most part, has been able to maintain selective and elite public education, with the prestige hierarchy dominated by public institutions. The unanticipated and most troubling effect has been that elite public secondary schools are utilized disproportionately by upper income groups (James and Benjamin, 1984).

SCHOOL PROBLEMS: A MIRROR OF SOCIETAL PROBLEMS

The problem of equality in Japan is not a school problem alone. Actually, the structural relationships among the examination system, the stratified educational institutions, and credentials have changed little over the years. What is different is that there has been a large increase in the number of people attending school without a commensurate increase in the number of good jobs in the marketplace. With over 90 percent of the high school-age group attending secondary school, the occupational rewards promised by academic credentials are no longer what they once were.

For the first time in the 100 years of modernization, as Amano (1986) tells us, Japan has ceased to be a land of opportunities and success stories. Japanese youth recognize this, and this realization has affected their attitudes about schooling. The examination system, which once greatly encouraged the aspirations of parents and their children, has begun to play a role in cooling them down.

On the one hand, the young are aware that earning an academic credential will not necessarily gain them a higher rank in the social order. On the other hand, they are aware that with so many people having diplomas, the lack of one constitutes a serious life-long handicap. Involuntary school attendance by students with diminished ability and interest in academic work has emerged as a serious problem (Kobayashi and Ota, n.d.).

The school has done surprisingly little to respond to these problems. Reforms are needed in the very structure of schooling itself. As Herbert Passin (1984) has argued, there is a real question as to whether the existing university system that was developed in an elitist period is appropriate to an egalitarian age. He speculates that the university structure and curriculum, developed for elite societies, may not be useful beyond attendance by more than 10 percent of the population.

Although the variations in the economic level of the general population appear smaller and class disparities seem to be greater in the United States than in Japan, both nations fit Carnoy and Levin's (1986) definition of democratic capitalistic states. As such, they have egalitarian and inegalitarian features, with equality on the one hand and an ideology of capital on the other. In both nations we find an historical tension between democratic equality and unequal accumulation of capital.

To the degree Carnoy and Levin (1986) are correct, the demand for social mobility through schooling in the face of unequal employment results will continue, and average attendance rates will be pushed higher. Even though students find schooling oppressive and boring, families will continue to take seriously the democratic promise that school is the route to higher income. As a result, the pressure on school systems to raise both academic standards and graduation rates will increase in the 1990s.

Cross-nationally, this appears to be what actually has been happening. In a 1983 study of eleven nations (Iannacone, 1985), it was found that academic quality had moved ahead of educational equity as a policy value in many of these nations, and that national productivity attained fresh prominence in their reports on educational reform. These formulations of educational policy promise to continue the primary goal of schooling as the development of basic skills and academic achievement to enhance national productivity for some years to come. This probably explains why Amano (1986) and others find that the issue of educational equity in Japan and elsewhere is no longer a very prominent one.

SOCIAL EQUALITY AND EDUCATIONAL OPPORTUNITY FOR SPECIAL GROUPS

Society is nowhere nearly as homogeneous in Japan as many would have it, nor is there as much harmony as many believe there is. Vast differences function

around an aristocratic structure in which every greeting and every contact indicates the kind and degree of social distance among individuals. The effect has
been to render the entire system less socially democratic than that of the United
States and other Western nations. As Seymour Martin Lipset (1987) has written,
Japan is a society in which deference and status remain strong. In this respect,
the dominant value orientations regarding equality in the United States and Japan
are very different.

The United States began as a settler society with very egalitarian communities
and was the first country to become democratic. Americans stress quality of
respect as well as equality of opportunity. While recognizing that inequalities
do exist, there is a pervasive belief that, in social relations at least, all people
should be treated with equal respect because they are human beings. By contrast,
in Japan, hierarchy remains important in defining the way people deal with each
other. Each person has an accepted place in the prestige order. As a result, as
Lipset (1987) indicates, a great emphasis on status differentiation in social relations remains.

Article 14 of the Japanese Constitution states, "All of the people are equal
under the law and there shall be no discrimination in political, economic and
social relations because of race, creed, social status or family origin." Although
official policy as reflected in this constitutional statement prohibits discrimination
against any group and although theoretically the system is open to all, statistically
we find it is not. School choice ends up being rationed on the basis of gender;
physical, mental, and emotional handicap; foreign study; and cultural background
as well as on social class position and examination scores.

The Social Darwinism that relegates ninth graders who score low in examination to second-class economic status for life, with virtually no opportunity for
another chance through schooling, also by definition has shut out other special
populations through differentiated treatment which is legitimately organized and
financed. These patterns exist in varying degrees elsewhere, of course. But what
seems to distinguish Japan from many other developed nations is the relatively
limited amount of attention and effort currently being given to finding solutions
to these problems.

Women

Kumiko Fujimura-Fanselow (1985) has done a very comprehensive study of
how schooling for women in Japan functions to perpetuate educational inequality
through its structure and by the nature of its curriculum. In spite of reforms,
which on the surface appear to offer great opportunity to women, sex differences
in education persist. Not only does the overall enrollment of Japanese women
in higher education continue to lag behind that of men, but there is a significant
difference between male and female patterns of participation in various types
and levels of schooling.

A large proportion of women pursue higher education through junior colleges rather than in four-year institutions. Those who do manage to attend four-year institutions tend to limit themselves to majoring in literature, home economics, and education. Junior colleges have become in effect the "women track" in higher education and as such are looked upon as forming the bottom layer of the university pyramid (Fujimura-Fanselow, 1985).

This sex-typed education in schools to a great extent reflects the job discrimination linked with certain employment practices that inhibit women's opportunities for occupational mobility and financial independence. Even women with degrees from prestigious national universities find that the employment options open to them are extremely limited. The acquisition of a university degree is a much surer channel for social mobility for men in Japan than it is for women. The choices women make about courses of study, type of institution attended, and years of schooling mirror the narrow roles defined for women in society at large. As such, they provide us with a classic example of the extent to which schooling is the dependent variable in the school–society relationship (Fujimura-Fanselow, 1985).

Handicapped Pupils

Turning to children with special emotional, physical, and mental needs, the so-called handicapped, we find that in Japan equality for them is defined in terms of education in separate schools. Marilyn Goldberg (1989) points out that scant attention is given to individual differences in the regular Japanese school. Even though many parents prefer that their children be given the opportunity to attend regular schools with special classes, resource rooms, and mainstreaming into regular classrooms, such children mostly are sent to separate schools. This is especially true for adolescents, for whom there is relatively little help on either the junior or senior high school level. As pupils move up through the system, the options tend to become even more separate and restrictive for children with handicapping conditions.

In a good number of industrial nations, considerable attention is given to finding ways to integrate students with special needs into regular schools. However, equality in Japan has not yet been defined in such a way as to bring these pupils into the "least restrictive environment" in regular schools. By and large, special education means "separate but equal," a concept that has been repudiated by national movement mandate in the United States. To date, in Japan there is very little mainstreaming into regular classes. Quality integration for those with special needs continues to be a major piece of unfinished business.

Returning Pupils

Another special class of children who face prejudice are overseas and returning pupils, of whom there has been a great increase in recent years. According to Tetsuya Kobayashi (1987), the returning children often differ in their academic achievement and personal and social behavior from children at home. In class-rooms, it is reported that they often irritate teachers and classmates by their inquisitive attitudes, which are interpreted as disruptive.

Returning pupils create a problem because the Japanese school system has been developed to work with children from identical cultural backgrounds. Inev-itably, children who attend school abroad for a time come back culturally altered. In order to cope with these "problem children," special classes have been established for readjustment education. It is not uncommon in these classes, Kobayashi (1987) reports, for children to be forced to give up what they have learned abroad because it is considered to be an obstruction to good adjustment at home.

Some parents prefer a much different approach, one that would allow inter-national children to enter Japanese schools with the full advantage of their overseas experience. Potentially, this approach holds great promise not only for the returning children, but also for teachers and their fellow classmates, to become more internationally aware. It also fulfills the mandate of recent governmental reports which call for promoting deeper international understanding among pupils (Kobayashi, 1987).

Fundamental to this issue is the conflict that parents of returning children necessarily have between wanting their children to do well in university ex-aminations and their desire to have their children retain their international characteristics.

What ultimately brands schooling abroad as a negative rather than a positive experience is the narrow focus of the entire Japanese educational system on academic preparation for entrance examinations for higher levels of schooling. A school system preoccupied with examinations hinders true progress toward the internationalization of the educational experience. Until this changes, those with different national and cultural experiences will continue to be discriminated against and restricted from fully participating in the teaching and learning process in Japan.

The Burakumin

The Burakumin, termed Japan's "invisible people," have become a discrete subgroup outside the pale of the majority. Although racially and linguistically part of the Japanese majority, their association with occupations involving blood and death (butchers, cremators, leather workers, and the like) was used as a basis for identifying them as a hereditary, ritually impure outcaste group with virtually no chance for upward mobility. As the research of John Hawkins (1983) and others indicates, the exploitative and demeaning discrimination against the Burakumin continues to exist in some ways today.

Eventually, the political organizations and protests of the Burakumin and their supporters forced the government into policy changes under the rubric of "dowa education," which translated means assimilation or liberation education for the

Burakumin. As Hawkins's (1983) studies reveal, their struggles provide a good model of how a disenfranchised group can organize politically to bring about the passage of important government legislation on its behalf.

The government put additional funds into schools to pay for compensatory education. In some instances expenditures for outcaste children were three times as great as those for other children. In the process, dowa education enforced a new definition of educational equality in Japan, one that moved away from the more restrictive definition of equality based on opportunity or input to a broader one based on equality of outcome or results (Hawkins, 1983).

As a result of the political activities of the Burakumin and their allies and an improved economy that increased employment and income nationally, the plight of the Burakumin did improve. Educational attainment did rise. Yet, as Nobuo Shimahara (1984) has reported, there is still a gap in school performance between the Burakumin and majority students. In particular, there is still frustration over entrance examination results for preferred high schools.

Of all the groups that have experienced varying degrees of selective exclusion in Japan, the Burakumin more than any other have demonstrated that subordinate groups can mold education to achieve authentic gains in equality of educational opportunity and other democratic demands. Even though not fully successful, the Burakumin provide an important example of how a social movement can change the way a large bureaucratic institution functions.

As Carnoy and Levin (1986) have argued, the power of individuals to alter conditions and their lives through social movements is shaped by the development of a social consciousness and the ability to come together in an essentially political way.

Meaningful change is less possible when approached individually or in small-group factions. The Burakumin have demonstrated that groups can resist social practices. Their recent history has much to teach other restricted groups in Japan—women, the handicapped, and students who have studied abroad—how to gain more choice and a better voice in schooling and society.

CONCLUSION: MORAL EDUCATION IN CRISIS

The emphasis in this chapter has been on the educational and other human resource development strategies that a defeated and bankrupt Japan used to carve its democracy and economic miracle out of a totalitarian regime since World War II. These are contrasted to the often less successful results found in an older democracy, the United States.

They also related to issues in *perestroika* reforms that were introduced to move the Soviet republics and Eastern Europe from totalitarianism to democracy, especially those related to raising standards of living, and expanding freedom of parental choice and responsibility. In terms of these issues, Japan represents a particularly apt case study for these and other nations to review for possible ideas for their own reform agendas.

Historically and cross-nationally, educational reform moves in two directions: one having to do with jobs and income, and the other with citizenship, patriotism, and morality. The first is in the economic sphere, and the second in the political and moral sphere.

In today's world, these twin goals are deeply complicated by the gap between growing global economic interdependence and the strong rekindling of regional politics and cultural differences. Nowhere is this better demonstrated than in the breakup of the Soviet republics into their polyglot political and ethnic elements just as another superethnic and economic structure, the European Community, is coming into being.

Education has clearly played a very important role in Japan's economic revitalization. But what about education's role in Japan's moral and political development? The answer to this question is left unanswered by the statistics on GNP and academic achievement levels rooted in the discipline of Japanese education prior to the university years.

Before dealing with the question on moral and political socialization, it should be noted that one of the formidable anomalies of Japanese education is the casualness of higher education compared to the rest of the system. For instance, 57.5 percent of U.S. university students claim to spend four hours a day on school work, nearly twice the figure for Japan. Thirty-five percent of Japanese university students may never open a book at all ("Statistics Often Offer . . . ," 1990).

U.S. higher education, while it appears more demanding in these statistics than the Japanese system, has many serious problems of its own, and its prospects for the future do not look promising. In an 1988 study, Fiske (1990) found that only 23 percent of U.S. students spent more than sixteen hours per week studying outside the classroom, down from 33 percent in 1985. College presidents and faculty generally agree that students do only enough work to get by.

Education in Japan prior to the university level has become a highly distorted effort by students to pass entrance examinations for admissions into first-rank universities. As a result, many people view the system as producing compliant workers who focus primarily on building the economic strength of Japan. This has tended to overshadow those educational goals related to preparing students for democratic citizenship.

Youth in Japan appear to acquire very little knowledge of the relationships between ethical principles and their lives. Nor do they appear to acquire much of an understanding of political processes, especially of the connections between the actions of the government and those of citizens on issues that affect the common good.

Moral education is in crisis. "The current younger generation," claims Shigeo Masui (1982a, 1982b), "is failing to develop human personality in terms of individual as well as social integration. The result is shallow uniformity." Surveys report painful and contradictory attitudes among Japanese parents regarding this problem. On the one hand, parents feel compelled to direct their children toward successful examination results. On the other hand, they desire an integrated personality in their children. Ultimately, however, this second desire is stifled by their compulsion to submit to the examination system.

Although not rooted in a highly competitive examination system, U.S. education has experienced real failure in humanistic and democratic political goals as well. A report funded by the Carnegie Foundation, *Campus in Research and Community*, describes a breakdown of civility and the emergence of other disruptive forces that have undermined social values on U.S. campuses. The report's author, Ernest Boyer, wrote, "In our hard-edged competitive world, humane, more integrated purposes must be defined. In the end building a vibrant community is the challenge" (Fiske, 1990:A15).

Going back to its *Central Council for Education Report* in 1971, the Japanese government has made recommendations for school reform emphasizing humanizing over economic and ability-focused aspects to correct earlier reforms stressed during the period of recovery from wartime destruction. However, a balance has yet to be achieved between the new and the old, the foreign and the Japanese, the physical and the moral, and the mechanistic and the humanistic (Masui, 1982a, 1982b).

As always, we need to remind ourselves, as the earlier discussion of parent and community choice and collaboration in Japanese education highlights, that these kinds of improvements cannot come through school reform alone. Change is also required in government and business employment practices and in parent and community attitudes about their responsibility for bettering society—individually and collectively and nationally and internationally.

If there is any one challenge drawn from the histories of capitalism in the United States and Japan that we should emphasize for Eastern European and the Soviet republics, as they move toward democracy and capitalism, it is the need to balance economic imperatives with strong moral and humanistic values.

While it is not inherently opposed to social responsibility, capitalistic growth has resulted in widening economic and social disparities in many developing countries. Often, as the frontiers of freedom are extended, inequality and social alienation result. These kinds of problems are particularly striking in the United States, especially in urban areas. However, they are also surfacing in Japan as the critical problems in school violence, educational inequality, and housing signify.

What is needed is an approach that blends the economic rewards of capitalism with a strong moral conscience. Today, one hope is that as the *perestroika* nations mold their own unique blend of capitalism out of their socialistic foundations, they will generate new models that will prove useful for other capitalistic nations such as the United States and Japan for remedying the deepening cultural lag between material and technological growth and the development of ethical values and humanistic social institutions.

REFERENCES

Amano, Ikuo. 1986. "The Dilemma of Japanese Education Today." *The Japan Foundation Newsletter* 13 (No. 5):1–10.

Carnoy, Martin, and Henry M. Levin. 1986. "But Can It Whistle?" *Educational Studies* 17 (Winter):528–541.

Comer, James P. 1980. *School Power Implications of an Intervention Project*. New York: Free Press.

Crouch, Harold, and James W. Morley. 1990. "The Dynamics of Political Change." Paper presented at the Modern Japan Seminar, East Asian Institute, Columbia University.

Cummings, William K. 1982, February. "The Egalitarian Transformation of Postwar Japanese Education." *Comparative Education Review* 26:16–35.

Fiske, Edward B. 1990, April 3. "Fabric of Campus Life Is in Tatters, A Study Says." *The New York Times*, p. A15.

Foster, Philip. 1989, November. "Why the Issue of 'Relevance' Is Not So Relevant." *Comparative Education Review* 33:519–524.

Fujimura-Fanselow, Kumiko. 1985, November. "Women's Participation in Higher Education in Japan." *Comparative Education Review* 29:471–489.

Fujita, Hidenori. 1985. "A Crisis of Legitimacy in Japanese Education-Meritocracy and Cohesion." *Bulletin of the Faculty of Education, Nagoya University* 32:117–133.

Goldberg, Marilyn P. 1989. "Recent Trends in Special Education in Tokyo." In *Japanese Schooling: Patterns of Socialization, Equality and Political Control*, ed. James J. Shields. University Park: Pennsylvania State University Press.

Hawkins, John. 1983, June. "Educational Demands and Institutional Response: Dowa Education in Japan." *Comparative Education Review* 27:204–226.

"Health Problems Linked to Learning Impairment." 1990, August 9. *San Francisco Chronicle*, p. A14.

Horio, Teruhisa. 1988. *Educational Thought and Ideology in Modern Japan: State Authority and Intellectual Freedom*. Trans. and ed. Steven Platzer. Tokyo: University of Tokyo Press.

Iannacone, Lawrence. 1985. "Excellence: An Emergent Educational Issue." *Politics of Education Bulletin* 12 (Summer-Fall):1–12.

Ichikawa, Shogo. 1988–1989. "Study of Prefectural and Municipal Subsidies to Private Schools." *Research Bulletin of the National Institute for Educational Research (Japan)* 26:1–6.

"Improved Infrastructure Key to Better Lifestyles, Report Says." 1990, July 30–August 5. *The Japan Times Weekly International Edition* 30:14.

"Ishihara Group Unveils 109 Demands for Reform of American Economy." 1990, June 22. *The Japan Times*.

Iwaki, Hideo. 1986–1987. "Current Issues/Problems and Policy Trends About Japanese Upper Secondary Education." *Research Bulletin of the National Institute for Educational Research (Japan)* 25:33–104.

James, Estelle, and Gail Benjamin. 1984. *Public Versus Private Education: The Japanese Experiment*. New Haven, Conn.: Institute for Social and Policy Studies, Yale University.

Japan. Monbusho. 1989. *Outline of Japanese Education 1989*. Tokyo: Monbusho.

"Japan, Most Competitive Nation." 1990, June 20. *Daily Yomimuri*.

Japan. National Institute for Educational Research. 1990. *Basic Facts and Figures About the Educational System in Japan*. Tokyo: NIER.

Japan. Prime Minister's Office, National Council on Educational Reform. 1985. *First Report on Educational Reform*. Tokyo: The Council.

Japan. Prime Minister's Office, National Council on Educational Reform. 1986. *Summary of the Second Report on Educational Reform*. Tokyo: The Council.

Johnson, Chalmers. 1989. "The Problem of Japan in an Era of Structural Change." *IHJ Bulletin* 9 (Autumn):1–7.

Kaneko, Motohisa. 1989. *Financing Higher Education in Japan*. Hiroshima: Research Institute of Higher Education, Hiroshima University.

Kitamura, Kazuyuki. 1990. "The Future of Japanese Higher Education." Chiba, Japan: National Institute of Multimedia Education. (Mimeographed.)

Kobayashi, Tetsuya. 1986. "The Internationalization of Japanese Education." *Comparative Education* 22:65–71.

———. 1987. "Educational Problems of Returning Children." In *Education and Social Concern: Approach to Social Foundations*, ed. Robert F. Lawson, Val D. Rust, and Susanne M. Shafer. Ann Arbor, Mich.: Praaken Publishing, pp. 205–213.

———, and Haruo Ota. n.d. "Secondary Education in Japan." Kyoto: School of Education, Kyoto University. (Mimeographed.)

Lipset, Seymour Martin. 1987. "Tradition and Modernity in Japan and the United States." *IHJ Bulletin* 7 (Winter):1–7.

Masui, Shigeo. 1982a, March. "The Methodology Used in Japan for Reform Curricula." *Research Bulletin of the National Institute for Educational Research (Japan)* 21:76–84.

———. 1982b, March. "Problems and Solution in Education from Comparative Perspective Particularly in Relation to the School Curriculum in Japan. *Research Bulletin of the National Institute for Educational Research (Japan)* 21:85–88.

Mochizuki, Kazuhiro. 1982. "The Present Situation of Japan's Education: A Report from School." Orientation Seminars on Japan, No. 11. Tokyo: Office of Japanese Studies Center, The Japan Foundation, pp. 15–24.

Murakamai, Yoshiro. 1985, October. "Bullies in the Classroom." *Japan Quarterly* 32:407–411.

Passin, Herbert. 1984, November 26. "Common Educational Problems of Advanced Industrial Nations." Keynote Address, Northeast Regional Annual Comparative and International Education Society Meeting. (Unpublished.)

Porter, Michael. 1990. *The Competitive Advantage of Nations*. New York: Free Press.

Rohlen, Thomas. 1985–1986. "Japanese Education: If They Can Do It, Should We?" *American Scholar* 55 (Winter):29–43.

Shields, Jr., James J., ed. 1989. *Japanese Schooling: Patterns of Socialization, Equality and Political Control*. University Park: Pennsylvania State University Press.

Shimahara, Nobuo. 1984. "Toward the Equality of a Japanese Minority." *Comparative Education* 20 (3):350–360.

Smith, Robert J. 1983. *Japanese Society: Tradition, Self and the Social Order*. Cambridge: Cambridge University Press.

"Statistics Often Offer Little Food For Thought." 1990, July 30–August 5. *The Japan Times Weekly International Edition* 30:10.

Steslicke, William E. 1990. "Maternal and Child Health (MCH) Policies in Japan's Rapidly Aging Society." Tampa: College of Public Health, University of South Florida. (Mimeographed.)

Stevenson, Harold W., and Shin-ying Lee. 1990. *Contexts of Achievement: A Study of American, Chinese and Japanese Children*. Monographs of the Society for Research in Child Development. Serial No. 221. Vol. 55, No. 1–2. Chicago: University of Chicago Press.

Takizawa, Hiromitsu. 1990, November. "Back to Basic Issues in Education." *NIER News letter (Japan)* 22:1.

White, Merry. 1989, November 15. "Emerging Adolescence in Japan." Paper presented at a Symposium on Japanese Education: Students, Schools and Reforms. Teachers College, Columbia University. (Unpublished.)

Williams, David. 1990, July 10. "Cambridge History Bridges the Historiological Chasm." *The Japan Times*, p.14.

Yuuki, Makoto. 1986–1987. "Out-of-School Supplementary Education in Japan." *Research Bulletin of the National Institute for Educational Research (Japan)* 25:21–31.

19

KENYA

Reese Hughes

The current educational system in Kenya reflects the influence of the country's unique historical, cultural, political, and economic position. Although at the time of independence in 1963 the Kenyan educational system mirrored that of the British colonizers, reform since that time has gradually, but inexorably, dismantled much of the British legacy. Reform has occurred in the curriculum, in the financing, and in the delivery of education, and it has occurred through both public and private initiative. Reform has responded to issues of equity and employment, as well as the need to fashion a unified nation out of a loose, often competing collection of some forty different tribes.

In all of this, however, there has been one dominant theme—expansion. What was an anemic, poorly supported social service at independence has grown into the dominant national institution. The system of education has reached even the most peripheral regions and touches virtually every family. The number of students in primary education grew from 891,000 students in 1963 to nearly 5 million by the end of the 1980s. Secondary education burgeoned from 30,000 at independence to over 500,000 by the end of the 1980s. University enrollments grew from 565 to over 26,000 in the same period (Republic of Kenya, 1988b). It is an arena of rapid, if not urgent, change.

THE HISTORICAL CONTEXT OF KENYAN REFORM

Education in East Africa clearly predates the arrival of European colonists. Traditional education was interwoven and in many ways inseparable from daily life. It integrated physical training with character building and manual activity with intellectual preparation. Traditional education was neither specialized nor institutionalized; it was intended to foster social cohesiveness and understanding of communal responsibilities.

The coming of Europeans brought a type of education that was alien in form, content, and goals. As articulated by the Phelps-Stokes Report in 1924, Kenyans were provided vocational training following an academic primary education. What evolved over the next several decades was a three-tiered system "with community development for the majority, technical training for a minority, and academic secondary education for a tiny fraction of the African population" (Sheffield, 1973:24). The rural-practical focus gradually gave way to the traditional British literary-humanistic-religious emphasis. This occurred, in part, because efforts to develop vocational or agricultural training programs were perceived as offering second-rate education. Both colonial and independent Kenya have failed to develop and sustain credible alternatives to the tradition of academic education.

At the time of independence, Kenya inherited a system of education segregated on the basis of race.[1] It was very British in design and orientation, and inadequate for the human capital needs of this nascent republic. The British influence was all-pervasive. English served as the language of instruction then as now for all students beginning in Standard IV. Seven years of primary school were followed by four years of O-level secondary school training, two years of A-level secondary school training, and three years of university. Each stage was concluded with a standardized national selection examination that served to identify those students who would continue their education in this tightly controlled meritocracy. Until 1967 secondary school graduates completed examinations for the Cambridge Higher School Certificate which required knowledge of English and European history.

Slowly, many of these vestiges of the colonial past have been eliminated through conscious reform as well as through the less premeditated response of the Kenyan populace. The following sections will briefly discuss three key reforms of the past three decades: the Harambee movement, 8–4–4, and the coming of mass education.

KEY REFORMS: THE HARAMBEE MOVEMENT

Although the Harambee school movement has its roots in the independent school movement of the colonial days, the phenomenon achieved prominence when Kenya's first president, Jomo Kenyatta, advocated a development strategy based on self-help. Following independence, the Harambee spirit, which means "pull together," quickly inspired the creation of hundreds of community secondary schools and even a handful of colleges of science and technology. By 1987 there were over 1,880 Harambee secondary schools which accounted for more than half of Kenya's secondary school enrollment (Mwiria, 1990:355).

Ironically, contrary to Kenyatta's proclamations, the government's early re-

Table 19.1
Harambee and Government-Maintained Secondary Schools: The Paradox of Cost and Performance

Performance KCE* - 1984	Government Maintained	Aided- Harambee	Unaided- Harambee
Division 1 or 2 Passes	30%	13%	8%
Division 3 Passes	33%	26%	26%
Division 4 Passes	26%	32%	34%
Fail	11%	29%	35%
Cost (1979)	1438 KSh	2734 KSh	3228 KSh

*KCE is the Kenya Certificate of Education, the national secondary school selection examination.

Sources - Mwiria (1990, p. 361); Bray and Lillis (1988, p. 91)

action to the Harambee school movement was at best ambivalent (Mwiria, 1990). Governmental concerns existed regarding the quality of these institutions, the ability of the economy to absorb these graduates, and their inability to control such a mobilized peasantry. Frank Holmquist (1984) observed that the government attempted to reassert its control over educational development activities by channeling local projects into planning structures. The *1970–1974 Development Plan* (Republic of Kenya, 1974) announced the government's intent to consolidate Harambee schools and assist in the improvement of their quality. Beginning in 1975, fifty Harambee schools per year were offered limited government support (e.g., some trained and qualified teachers). By 1984, a total of 1,142 schools, accounting for 36 percent of the total secondary enrollment, were receiving partial government support (Mwiria, 1990:355–356).

Unfortunately, disproportionately few Harambee secondary school graduates perform well enough to qualify for postsecondary training (Shiman and Mwiria, 1987). For example, 87 percent of the 1981 intake to the University of Nairobi was comprised of students from government-supported secondary schools, which enrolled 39 percent of all secondary students. Graduates from Harambee schools, which enrolled 61 percent of all secondary school students, accounted for only 7 percent of first-year students at the University of Nairobi. Despite their high cost,[2] Harambee secondary schools are generally of poor quality (see Table 19.1). Yet, in a country where education is virtually the only means of achieving social mobility, the Harambee school movement provides an important alternative to the government secondary education effort. As a result, throughout the 1980s this irrepressible populous movement has continued to blossom in defiance of both economic logic and government directives aimed at diminishing the rate of Harambee school growth.

Table 19.2
Primary and Secondary School Course Requirements—The 8–4–4 System

Subjects	Lower Primary*	Upper Primary**	Secondary***
Agriculture	–	3	Optional
Art	–	3	Optional
Arts and Crafts	3	–	–
Biological Science	–	–	Required
Business Education	–	3	Optional
Crafts	–	4	Optional
English	5	7	Required
Foreign Languages	–	–	Optional
Geography	–	–	Required
Geography/History/Civics	2	4	–
History and Government	–	–	Required
Home Science	–	4	Optional
Industrial Education	–	–	Optional
Kiswahili	5	4	Required
Mathematics	5	6	Required
Mother Tongue	5	–	–
Music	2	2	Optional
Pastoral Program	1	1	–
Physical Education	5	3	–
Physical Science	–	–	Required
Religious Education	4	3	Optional
Science	3	3	–
Social Science and Ethics	–	–	Optional

*Number of 30-minute lessons per week
**Number of 35-minute lessons per week
***Students must take three optional subjects in additional to the seven required subjects.

Source: Republic of Kenya (1988b: 156, 160).

KEY REFORMS: THE 8–4–4 MODEL

In 1985 the 7–4–2–3 system of education was changed to an 8–4–4 model, as recommended by the Presidential Working Party on the Second University (Republic of Kenya, 1981) and strongly advocated by President Daniel arap Moi. Eight years of a vocationally oriented primary school curriculum were to be followed by four years of secondary school and four years of university. University students will complete a compulsory core curriculum (called "common courses") before beginning work in their major area of study.[3] It is a bold and dramatic departure from the British model that has already changed the face of education in Kenya.

However, the 8–4–4 system was rapidly, if not hurriedly, conceived and implemented. As a result, some serious flaws have become apparent in this reform effort. It is anticipated that this system will experience some significant modifications in the 1990s.

First, the curriculum is overloaded (Mulusa, 1990). As evident in Table 19.2, upper primary students (Standards 4–8) are exposed to fifteen different subject

Table 19.3
Looking at the Implications of the 1990s

YEAR	STUDENTS IN FINAL YEAR OF SEC SCHOOL	% OF FORM VI WHO QUALIFY*	% OF FORM VI ADMITTED*	IF 33% QUALIFY	IF 15% ADMITTED
1982	9,865	49.2%	25.0%	--	--
1983	11,637	47.2	23.1	--	--
1984	11,868	55.7	29.5	--	--
1985	18,074	38.7	19.0	--	--
1986	17,513	55.2	29.4	--	--
1987	22,244	62.2	31.8	--	--
1990	172,400	--	--	56,890	25,860
1991	190,300	--	--	62,800	28,550
1992	199,800	--	--	65,930	29,970
1993	206,500	--	--	68,150	30,980

*Includes Private Candidates

-- signifies not relevant or not important.
Note: For the 1982-1987 data, the actual data exists so only columns headed
% of Form VI who qualify and % of Form VI admitted are relevant. For the
1990-1993 data, which did not exist at the time this table was developed, the
more hypothetical columns "If 33% Qualify" and "If 15% Admitted" are
relevant.

Source -- Hughes and Mwiria 1990, p. 217.

areas weekly, and secondary school students must take ten. In an effort to provide practical training for primary school students, there is concern that an inadequate foundation is developed for the level of knowledge expected of secondary school students. This may particularly be the case in science subjects. If the 1989 candidates for the Kenya Certificate of Secondary Education (KCSE) examination are representative, then there may be reason for concern. Of the 104,271 who sat for the physical and biological science examination, only 6 percent passed with a D+ or better (Mulusa, 1990:13). Although it could be argued that these results reflected the lack of laboratory equipment,[4] the results on the math examination were little better. Math does not require expensive laboratory equipment. In sum, it seems that 8–4–4 is faced with the rather impossible task of trying to provide terminal education while concurrently attempting to prepare those students who will proceed with their education.

Second, the advent of 8–4–4 has unleashed an unparalleled expansion at the university level. Until 1990, the A-level barrier effectively screened potential university applicants. Beginning in 1990, unprecedented numbers of students completed their pre-university training. As shown in Table 19.3, the 170,000 secondary school students in their final year in 1990 is eight times the comparable number in 1987. As a result, the university enrollments, which were under 10,000 in 1985, will exceed 35,000 by the end of 1990. Despite frantic efforts to prepare for this growth, insufficient numbers of qualified faculty and an inadequate physical infrastructure have already begun to have a significant deleterious impact on the quality of higher education.

Apart from these difficulties, many of the curricular changes initiated as part of the 8–4–4 system represent a positive effort to respond to Kenya's economic realities. However, because Kenyan society continues to reward the educated, these efforts to vocationalize the curriculum will be resisted (Foster, 1965).[5]

KEY REFORMS: MASS EDUCATION

Since independence, Kenya has gradually eroded the elite system of education inherited from the British. As mentioned above, the 8–4–4 reform represented the most dramatic move in a long series of policies that have improved the access of Kenyans to educational opportunity. However, another dramatic move initiated the coming of mass education. In December 1973 a presidential decree mandated that the first four years of primary school be free. This edict had a staggering effect on primary school enrollments. The Standard I enrollments rose from an anticipated 400,000 to 1 million (Indire, 1982:130); the total primary enrollment increased from 1.8 million to 2.7 million (Republic of Kenya, 1988b:152). The introduction of free school milk in 1979 caused another 23 percent increase in primary school enrollment (Republic of Kenya, 1988b:21). By 1980, Kenya had effectively achieved universal primary education (World Bank, 1988:131).

There has proved to be a steady relationship between the growth of primary school graduates and the intake at the secondary level. The size of the terminal class in primary school contributes to the growth rates of secondary education in Kenya. The secondary school enrollment grew from 30,000 in 1963 to 127,000 in 1970, 399,000 in 1980, and 511,000 by 1984 (Republic of Kenya, 1988b:157). Much of this growth was made possible by the blossoming of Harambee secondary schools.

As noted earlier, this same phenomenon is now occurring at the tertiary level in Kenya. The elimination of the A level has, in effect, brought the rising tide of educational populism to the door of the university system. The late 1980s and early 1990s promise to feature incredible growth at the postsecondary level.

One feature of this expansion is that educational planning and decision making have become highly politicized. In the case of higher education it appears that if universities do not adequately expand opportunity, then outside society appears prepared to compel compliance with this national agenda. Two times in the past two years, President Moi has intervened in the university admissions system to significantly increase the intake ("Something Wrong," 1990). In 1988, for example, 13,832 A-level leavers met the minimum university admission requirements. The initial plans to accept just over one quarter of those applicants caused reverberations that ultimately resulted in a doubling of the initial intake to accept just over 7,000. As was reported in the *Nation* ("President Acts," 1988:28):

President Moi yesterday directed the Minister for Education and the vice-chancellors of the four national universities to work out ways of admitting most of the 13,000 qualified students left out in the recent selection. . . . The President said he had been moved by appeals from the affected parents, students and Kenyans in general during the on-going public discussion about the 13,000 students.

In essence, as Hughes and Mwiria (1990) observed, educational planning in the 1990s promises to be an intensely political endeavor that touches on the very essence of the state's legitimacy. Faced with a seemingly insurmountable range of problems, the increasing politicization of educational planning may reflect the almost desperate hope leaders have that through education solutions will emerge. At a minimum, promotion of educational opportunity offers the promise of buying a little more time.[6] In this context, the expansion agenda has significant political clout.

LESS SIGNIFICANT REFORMS

In addition to these three highly significant reforms, there have been a number of much less consequential reform efforts. Five warrant discussion: adult and distance education, examination reform, the national service scheme, women in education, and efforts to vocationalize the curriculum.

Unlike the formal educational system, the adult education programs have experienced a steady decline since 1978 when the Kenyan government embarked on a campaign to eradicate adult illiteracy. In 1986 participation in adult education programs amounted to less than 5 percent of the enrollment in primary and secondary schools (Republic of Kenya, 1988b:166). There has been some limited use of radio and television in educational delivery. The radio, in particular, could enable more effective linkage with the many remote regions of Kenya. The Kenya Radio Language Arts Project (RLAP), an interactive program of instruction broadcast to primary school children, exemplifies the potential of a medium that remains largely untapped (World Bank, 1988:43). Distance education, extramural courses, and extension training also exist, but the commitment of resources in these areas has largely been token (Davison and Gezi, 1987).

Although the names and content of the examinations have changed, the fundamental role that examinations play in the Kenyan educational system has not changed since colonial times. The Cambridge School Certificate and Cambridge Higher School Certificate have, with several examinations in between, been replaced by the Kenya Certificate of Secondary Education (KCSE) examination. Similarly, the Kenya Primary Education exam has evolved into the Certificate of Primary Education (CPE). Examination content has been revised to make it more applicable to the Kenyan setting, to reduce the rural-urban bias (Makau and Somerset, 1980), and to reflect a changing curriculum such as was necessitated by the conversion to 8–4–4. Despite an attempt to institute a policy of continuous assessment (Republic of Kenya, 1988c), the importance still placed on the examinations as screening devices means that teachers concentrate largely on preparing students to pass these examinations.

In response to the criticism that higher education in Kenya was preparing an educated elite who had "come to think of themselves as a 'chosen' group—if not 'born' to their place, at least 'made' for it" (Koff and von der Muhll, 1967:34), all students admitted to university have been required to complete a six-month stint with the National Youth Service (NYS). This effort to instill a commitment to national development and inculcate a sense of service and discipline has been largely ineffective, if not counterproductive. Indicative of this problem was the riot between students and regular NYS servicemen and women in 1988 ("First-Year Students," 1988). Although a well-intentioned reform, the service requirement has yet to be effectively instituted.

As is the case throughout sub-Saharan Africa, women are dramatically underrepresented in the Kenyan educational system. As Kinyanjui (1978:23) noted, "As girls ascend from one level of education to another, their proportion of the total enrollment decreases by 10 percent." In 1986 women comprised 48 percent of primary students, 41 percent of secondary students, and only 30 percent of university students (Republic of Kenya, 1988a:148–149). In Kenya, as in other African countries, the reasons for poor persistence have been well documented. Women are more likely to attend poorer quality schools in disproportionately high numbers (Kinyanjui, 1987; Smock, 1977) have restricted access to a broad range of curricula, particularly in the sciences (Kinyanjui, 1987; Lewis, 1986; Smock, 1977), and are conditioned by biased learning materials and classroom dynamics (Obura, 1986; Owino, 1987). There have been a paucity of reform efforts specifically aimed at improving women's access to and persistence in the educational system in Kenya. For example, of the 232 recommendations made by the Presidential Working Party on Education and Manpower Training for the Next Decade (Republic of Kenya, 1988b), not one specifically addressed the plight of Kenyan women in the educational system.

No reform effort has consistently received more fiscal and verbal support from donors and government officials than vocational training. However, it has yet to be perceived (somewhat accurately) by students and their parents as a viable alternative to formal, academic training. This was illustrated by a tracer study of technical secondary students (Lauglo, 1988:16), which reported that only 15 percent of those studied actually found employment because of their technical skills training (and usually not in a position specifically related to their trade). Nearly three times as many graduates eventually continued their education in purely academic subjects.

Vocational intervention in Kenya has taken three forms:

1. A parallel structure to the academic system in which technical, agricultural, and industrial schools are established, with the aim of providing intermediate-level skills for the wage economy (e.g., Youth or Village Polytechnics, Harambee Institutes of Technology, National Polytechnics, Technical Training Institutes).

2. Curricular intervention within the formal, academic system (e.g., 8–4–4).

3. Nonformal training programs directed at individuals who are outside of the formal

Table 19.4
Education's Proportion of the Kenyan National Budget, 1972–1988

Year	Total Recurrent Budget (000)	Total Recurrent Education Budget (000)	Proportion of Total
1972/3	2,003,744 KSh	650,998 KSh	32.4%
1975/6	3,800,516	1,291,828	33.9%
1978/9	7,439,620	1,907,470	25.6%
1981/2	11,006,004	3,298,184	29.9%
1984/5	14,825,570	4,429,154	29.8%
1987/8	23,338,193	7,711,678	37.7%

Source: Republic of Kenya (1988b: 169)

educational system (operated by the government as well as nongovernment organizations and private firms).

In 1987 there were four National Polytechnics, seventeen Institutes of Technology, and eighteen Technical Training Institutes which enrolled over 18,100 students (Republic of Kenya, 1988b:36, 161). The 545 Youth Polytechnics (which often offer basic courses in carpentry, masonry, and tailoring) and the Technical Training Institutes both now target primary school leavers. The National Polytechnics and Institutes of Technology cater to secondary school leavers. Despite the obvious government commitment to vocational preparation, Kenyans themselves remain wary of vocational training. There was no outcry when the rapid growth of the university system necessitated usurping polytechnic facilities. Thus far in Kenya, as elsewhere, valiant attempts to effectively integrate vocational preparation into the school system have yet to render dividends. Until the occupational reward structure reflects the priority of vocational training, further initiatives appear destined to fail.

These five areas of reform represent efforts that have yet to significantly impact the educational system in Kenya. Although these encompass critical issues in Kenyan education, they have failed to garner the necessary resources, and the political and/or popular support to play a dominant role in the education agenda. It seems unlikely that they will emerge in the 1990s.

POTENTIALLY IMPORTANT REFORMS IN THE NEXT DECADE

Two areas of educational reform have yet to blossom, but they may capture the education agenda in the next decade. Both are outgrowths of the tremendous expansion that is underway. First is the area of financing education. Second is the return of private initiative, particularly at the postsecondary level.

Although financing education has always been an issue, it has grown in importance because of the tremendous fiscal requirements of the most recent round of expansion. As is evident in Table 19.4, education threatens to consume nearly

40 percent of the national budget. This drain on the national budget necessitates, in a sense, sacrifices in terms of rural development and employment generation efforts.

In an effort to regain control of educational expenditure, the government has actively begun exploring a number of cost-sharing and cost-reduction measures. It has made clear its intention to shift additional financial burdens back to communities, parents, and the students themselves. This promises to be a critical theme in the 1990s.

Several areas of expenditure seem destined to be among the first addressed (Republic of Kenya, 1988c):

1. The willingness of the government to continue to absorb greater responsibility for Harambee schools.
2. The expenditure of over 600 million Kenyan shillings (1987–1988) to support the School Milk Scheme (8 percent of the entire education budget).
3. The allocation of 6 percent of the education budget for allowances to students in training institutions.[7]
4. Increased emphasis on day scholars (as opposed to boarding institutions) in all public educational and training institutions.
5. The requirement that all residential students pay the full cost of boarding.
6. The implementation of a functional loan scheme to minimize the impact on the less advantaged.

Cost-sharing is not a painless intervention, however, and, to some extent, not a reasonable expectation. A taste of the difficult times ahead was illustrated in 1988 when the Voice of Kenya announced the discontinuation of university student allowances, and 5,000 students rioted at Kenyatta University (Muya, 1988). Tensions eased when it was subsequently "clarified" that students would continue to receive their allowances. The political will required to implement cost-sharing measures is not insignificant.

In addition, families in many regions already contribute as much as 80 percent of household incomes to education (Martin, 1982). Steve Orvis (1985) found that the expenditure for education is "especially large relative to any other use of male earnings, including investment in land. A man's investible income is spent, to a large degree, not on agriculture but on education for his children and/or his siblings" (p. 28). In essence, cost-sharing may be limited by the inability of most Kenyans to pay more for education. There simply is not significant untapped disposable family resources in most Kenyan households. To insist on cost-sharing in this context will only diminish access to education.

In sum, it seems clear that some manner of cost containment will occur in the 1990s. The question has become not "if" but "how much" and "what kind" of fiscal reform will be implemented.

The second focus of reform, private initiative at the postsecondary level, may transform higher education like the Harambee school movement secondary education in Kenya. The government's inability to accommodate all qualified secondary school leavers in postsecondary institutions has created the demand for a private sector response. In 1990 over 130,000 form 4 graduates were expected to sit for the KCSE examination with the hope that they would secure a space at the tertiary level (Kariithi, 1990:1). Approximately 25,000 will be placed in teacher training, technical, and university programs. Despite the tremendous university expansion of the late 1980s, the demand appears insatiable.

Overseas training opportunities have been able to alleviate some of the pressure,[8] particularly for those students from more advantaged families (Migot-Adholla, 1985). However, the costs of studying abroad can exceed $11,000 in countries like the United States and Canada (Hughes and Mwiria, 1990:221); this high cost represents a deterrent for all but the most affluent.

As of 1988, private initiative at the university level had been limited to eleven institutions that enrolled a total of 1,146 students (Hughes and Mwiria, 1990:234). Most of these were small, highly specialized religious institutions with limited interest in dramatic growth. Perhaps the most significant difference is not what currently exists but the potential for future proliferation. The government has voiced a new receptivity to "the development of private educational and training institutions at all levels" (Republic of Kenya, 1988b:119). This openness may foster the advent of private higher education as a significant force in Kenyan education. Already by May 1988, fourteen private universities had applied to the government for registration (Osiemo, Onyango, and Kubai, 1988:2).

CONCLUSION

This examination of educational reform in Kenya has highlighted the important role of the Harambee school movement, the adoption of the 8–4–4 system, and the inexorable expansion of educational opportunity. These reforms have served to dismantle the British colonial educational legacy and introduce a more singularly Kenyan approach to addressing problems of national unity, equity, and manpower preparation through education. What has emerged is a populous or mass system of education that is only marginally touched by efforts to vocationalize the curricula, promote distance and adult education, and inculcate a sense of service.

Today, the urgency of Kenya's economic situation has served to heighten the importance of education as the hope for the future. As politicians increasingly place their own futures in the success of the school system, the locus of control is removed from educators. Decisions concerning educational policy are made at the highest level. Sadly, education, the planning process, and national dialogue have become distant cousins.

A COMMENT ON UGANDA AND TANZANIA

Loosely bound together as the East African Community through the late 1960s and early 1970s and strongly influenced by a common colonial heritage and geopolitical situation, Kenya, Tanzania, and Uganda have experienced many parallels in the reform and development of their educational systems. For example, expanding educational opportunity, vocationalizing the curriculum, and inculcating a sense of national identity characterize all three countries. However, there have been important differences too. Tanzanian schools have placed a greater emphasis on the promotion of an egalitarian society and reinforcing socialist attributes and attitudes (Court, 1984). The Ugandan educational system was buffeted by the national turmoil of the 1970s and 1980s. Thousands of outstanding teachers fled Uganda; books, supplies, and governmental support varied between scarce and nonexistent; school children joined the fray. In this context of adversity, survival has been an overriding concern.

NOTES

1. In 1959 the per capita expenditure on education ranged from £4.19 for each African student to £17.06 for each Asian (those whose ancestors came from South Asia) and £83.89 for each European student (Indire, 1982:120).

2. Bray and Lillis (1988:91) found that students attending Harambee secondary schools paid over twice as much in school fees as did students attending government-maintained secondary schools.

3. At the University of Nairobi four common courses are required of all students: Principles of Development and Application, Institutions and Value in Kenya's Development, Science and Technology in Development, and Communication Skills. In addition, students are required to select from several science-based or arts-oriented elective courses. This curriculum is not dissimilar to the general education requirement common in most U.S. universities.

4. In 1988 about 45 percent of the 2,800 secondary schools in Kenya had no science laboratories, even though science subjects were compulsory ("Nearly Half," 1988).

5. As Foster (1965:137) observed: "The causes for . . . such unemployment were normally attributed to the academic curriculums of the schools, and 'vocational and agricultural education' was deemed the solution for the problem. [When, in fact] . . . vocational aspirations were less determined by the educational system than by African perceptions of relative occupation rewards."

6. From the perspective of the government, the expansion of educational opportunity is more attainable than the creation of meaningful new economic opportunities for secondary and tertiary leavers. Apart from an economic renaissance that would provide school leavers with employment, only the exertion of tremendous political will has the potential to curb the rising tide of educational democratization. Neither seems likely.

7. For example, in 1987 each university student received 10,395 KSh (over $600) as an allowance or "boom" that far exceeded the per capita income in Kenya (Republic of Kenya, 1988a:173).

8. Even as early as 1981, it was estimated that 7,000 Kenyans were studying abroad

(Republic of Kenya, 1981). More recent data suggested that 2,700 students were pursuing first degrees in India, 1,446 in the United States, nearly 400 in Britain, and 192 in Canada (Hughes and Mwiria, 1990:221).

REFERENCES

Bray, M., with K. Lillis, 1988. *Community Financing of Education: Issues and Implications in Less Developed Countries*. Oxford: Pergamon Press.

Court, D. 1984. "The Education System as a Response to Inequality." In *Politics and Public Policy in Kenya and Tanzania*, ed. J. D. Barkan. Nairobi: Heinemann Kenya, pp. 265–295.

Davison, J., and K. Gezi. 1987. "The Right to Lifelong Education in Kenya and the United States with Special Reference to Adult Education." In *Human Rights and Education*, ed. N. Tarrow. Elmsford, N.Y.: Pergamon Press.

"First-Year Students Back to Try Again." 1988, October 28. *Weekly Review*, pp. 10–12.

Foster, P. 1965. *Education and Social Change in Ghana*. London: Routledge and Kegan Paul.

Holmquist, F. 1984. "Class Structure, Peasant Participation, and Rural Self-Help." In *Politics and Public Policy in Kenya and Tanzania*, ed. J. D. Barkan. Nairobi: Heinemann Kenya, pp. 171–197.

Hughes, R.; and K. Mwiria. 1990. "An Essay on the Implications of University Expansion in Kenya." *Higher Education* 19:215–237.

Indire, F. 1982. "Education in Kenya." In *Education in Africa: A Comparative Study*, ed. A. B. Fafunwa and J. U. Aisiku. London: George Allen and Unwin, pp. 115–139.

Kariithi, N. 1990, April 11. "Varsity Entry Points Raised." *Kenya Times*, p. 1.

Kinyanjui, K. 1978. "Education and Formal Employment Opportunities for Women in Kenya: Some Preliminary Data." In *The Participation of Women in Kenyan Society*, ed. A. Pala, J. Awori, and A. Krystall. Nairobi: Kenya Literature Bureau, pp. 25–32.

———. 1987. "The Status of Secondary School Education for Girls in Kenya: The Need for a More Science-Based Curriculum to Enhance Women's Greater Participation in Development." Institute for Development Studies Working Paper 459. Nairobi: University of Nairobi.

Koff, D., and G. von der Muhll. 1967. "Political Socialization in East Africa." *Journal of Modern African Studies* (1):33–35.

Lauglo, J. 1988, October. "Technical Secondary Students in Kenya: Origins, Achievement and Destinations." (Mimeograph.)

Lewis, M. 1986. *Girls' Education in Kenya: Performance and Prospects*. Washington, D.C.: Urban Institute.

Makau, B. M., and H.C.A. Somerset. 1980, May. "Primary School Leaving Examinations, Basic Intellectual Skills, and Equity: Some Evidence from Kenya," Institute for Development Studies Discussion Paper 271. Nairobi: University of Nairobi.

Martin, C. J. 1982. "Education and Consumption in Maragoli (Kenya): Households' Educational Strategies." *Comparative Education* 18:139–155.

Migot-Adholla, S. E. 1985. "The Evolution of Higher Education—Kenya." In *The*

   Development of Higher Education in Eastern and Southern Africa, ed. L. Tembo, M. Dilogassa, P. Makhurance, and P. Pitsoin. Nairobi: Hedaya Educational Books, pp. 1–26.

Mulusa, T. 1990, April 27. "Conceptualising, Administering and Evaluating the 8–4–4 System." *The Weekly Review*, pp. 12–16.

Muya, W. 1988, September 21. "Varsity Allowances to Stay." *Nation*.

Mwiria, K. 1990. "Kenya's Harambee Secondary School Movement: The Contradictions of Public Policy." *Comparative Education Review* 34:350–368.

"Nearly Half of Secondary Schools Have No Labs, Yet Science Is a Must." 1988, July 2. *Nation*, p. 10.

Obura, A. 1986. "Learning the Gender Bias Early: Primary School Textbooks." *CERES*, FAO Review 19(3).

Orvis, S. 1985. "Men and Women in a Household Economy: Evidence from Kisii." Institute for Development Studies Working Paper 432. Nairobi: University of Nairobi.

Osiemo, N., E. Onyango, and M. Kubai. 1988, May 12. "More Admissions to Varsities Being Studied." *Standard*, p. 2.

Owino, G. 1987. "Sex-role Stereotyping in Secondary School Textbooks and Its Effects on Women's Attitudes Towards Science and Technology." Kenya Educational Research Awards (KERA) report. (Mimeograph.)

"President Acts on Varsity Applicants." 1988, May 11. *Nation*, p. 28.

Republic of Kenya. 1974. *Development Plan, 1970–1974*. Nairobi: Government Printer.

———. 1981. *Report of the Presidential Working Party on the Second University* (Mackay Report). Nairobi: Government Printer.

———. 1988a. *Economic Survey 1988*. Nairobi: Government Printer.

———. 1988b. *Report of the Presidential Working Party on Education and Manpower Training for the Next Decade and Beyond* (Kamunge Report). Nairobi: Government Printer.

———. 1988c. *Sessional Paper No. 6 of 1988 on Education and Manpower Training for the Next Decade and Beyond*. Nairobi: Government Printer.

Sheffield, James R. 1973. *Education in Kenya: An Historical Study*. New York: Teachers' College Press.

Shiman, D. A., and K. Mwiria. 1987. "Struggling Against the Odds: Harambee Secondary Schools in Kenya." *Phi Delta Kappan* 68:369–372.

Smock, A. C. 1977. "Women's Education and Roles in Kenya." Institute for Development Studies Working Paper 316. Nairobi: University of Nairobi.

"Something Wrong with Admission Systems." 1990, May 18. *The Weekly Review*, pp. 18–20.

World Bank. 1988. *Education in Sub-Saharan Africa*. Washington, D.C.: World Bank.

20

MEXICO

Eduardo Peña de la Mora

THE REFORM CONTEXT

Mexico's economy and social well-being developed rapidly from 1940 to 1970. This development was so remarkable that it was called the Mexican miracle. Several leading indicators demonstrate this development. During the 1940–1970 period, the average annual rate of growth, as measured by gross domestic product (GDP), was above 6 percent, and the per capita GDP rate of growth was above 3 percent (Latapí, 1980: 49–50). Both the generation of electricity and the highway system expanded more than twenty times during the 1940–1977 period (González, 1980). Furthermore, a number of aggregated indicators show that social conditions generally improved. For example, infant mortality decreased significantly, and life expectancy increased twenty years during 1940–1970 (CONAPO, 1982: 60; González, 1980: 23–24). School enrollment increased more than 600 percent from 1935 to 1970 (Solana, Cardiel, and Bolaños, 1981: 596–599) and adult literacy increased from 33 percent in 1930 to 76 percent in 1970 (CONAPO, 1982: 74; González, 1980: 162). These global indicators do not show, however, that development was highly unbalanced and that this imbalance is still growing.

The distribution of family income has been very unequal. In 1950 the incomes of those families in the top 5 percent were thirty times higher than those in the bottom 10 percent (Gollás, 1978: 77; IBRD, 1937); by 1970 the ratio was thirty-nine times higher (González, 1980: 162). In 1950 the wealthiest 10 percent received 49 percent of the national income, and in 1969 it received 51 percent (Gollás, 1978: 75–77).

Another indicator of the unbalanced development within Mexican society is nutrition. Studies conducted during the 1960s and 1970s have shown that about two-thirds of the Mexican population have nutritional deficiencies (Chávez, 1979: 225). These deficiencies mainly affect the poorer sectors of society. In 1974 a national survey showed that 18.4 million people who lived in the most marginal areas of the country consumed between 1,500 and 2,100 calories daily—less than the required minimum of 2,300 for this population (Chávez, 1979: 220). On the other hand, the well-fed consumed processed foods of an equivalent raw food value of 12,000 calories daily. People in the top 15 percent income bracket absorb 60 percent of the agricultural production of grains, while the lowest 25 percent utilize only 10 percent of this production (Chávez, 1979: 227). According to several experts in nutrition, the real cause of malnutrition in Mexico is not the lack of food but its unequal distribution (Chávez, 1979).

The model of economic development followed in Mexico since 1940, called stabilizing development, showed its inability to satisfy the social needs of the majority of the population during the 1960s. This development was initially promoted by the role played by the Mexican economy during World War II and later by state policy geared to protect capitalistic production. The state and the private sector invested in agricultural surplus to create an infrastructure for industrial production. At the same time, agricultural investment dropped, and, consequently, production and productivity in this sector decreased considerably (Gómez and Rivera, 1982: 262–272). Income and standard of living decreased for the great majority of the rural population (Rovzar, 1984: 315). A large percentage of this population migrated to the cities, searching for better life conditions. In 1940, 65 percent of the total population of Mexico lived in rural areas. In 1970 only 41 percent remained in those areas, while 59 percent were living in the cities (CONAPO, 1982: 57).

The expansion of monopolistic industrial production in Mexico began during the 1960s. The most productive sectors raised their level of technology, while the less productive sectors lagged behind in technological development. Workers of the less productive sectors experienced a decrease in incomes. The middle-class workforce was devalued in the labor market, and, as a consequence, its standard of living dropped (Gómez and Rivera 1982: 266–272).

The decline of the standard of living of large sectors of the Mexican population, the absence of real channels for democratic participation in social and political life, and one of the most authoritarian forms of government were, according to many authors, some of the most important factors in the social and political crisis of 1968 (Gómez and Rivera, 1982: 272–275; Latapí, 1980: 49–55; Paoli, 1986). The excessively violent repression unleashed by the government to control protesting groups left a profound mark on large sectors of the population. The state lost legitimacy as a representative of the diverse social groups. A significant number of guerrilla groups appeared in rural and urban areas confronting the government that had emerged from the 1910–1917 Mexican revolution. The crisis had a significant influence on the policies of the following presidential administrations in subsequent years through the 1970s.

In 1970 Luis Echeverría Alvarez became president for the six-year period established by the Mexican Constitution. His government opted for a reconciliation with civil society and initiated a wide reform movement in all areas. In the economic field, policies were oriented toward modernizing the productive sector, increasing state participation in production, increasing productivity, and decreasing technological dependency, as well as opening external markets and promoting a more equitable distribution of income.

In the sociopolitical field, Echeverría's government was characterized by an effort to regain the legitimacy and hegemony lost in the eyes of large segments of society. This administration liberalized the political milieu by opening new channels for democratic participation, considerably expanding the state apparatus and increasing social services. In the educational field, it implemented a wide reform that included a considerable expansion of services.

EDUCATIONAL REFORM, 1970–1976

In a broad reform context, educational policy was directed toward national unity and socioeconomic development. At the same time, the Mexican political system utilized educational reform to regain political legitimacy and to bargain with the diverse social classes, offering educational opportunities to social groups and, as a consequence, increasing the possibility of upward social mobility. The hostility and distrust of students were met by dialogue, openness, and reconciliation.

The Echeverría administration's concept of education, as expressed in public statements, was an optimistic view: education would contribute to the solution of all national and individual problems. As a presidential candidate, Echeverría stated that "all of our problems converge on or are related to the educational problem. . . . No economic improvement or social betterment is possible if education and culture do not benefit the people" (in Latapí, 1980: 65).

Educational reform was initiated during the first days of the administration with a broad consultation of all social sectors. The government's interpretation of this consultation was characterized as follows: Educational reform should be carried out with the participation of all sectors involved in education; it should involve all aspects, modes, and educational levels. This reform should equalize and increase schooling opportunities for all social groups in order to attain a more just social order. The educational system should be transformed to achieve the flexibility to move vertically and horizontally on all levels and to provide the opportunity to successfully enter the labor market for those who drop out of school, regardless of what grade they have completed. Educational reform should be centered on the teacher and on the active role of the student in the learning process.

This educational reform was later expressed in a legal form as the Federal Law of Education (FLE) and the National Education Law for Adults (NELA). The FLE, which was promulgated in 1973 and which took the place of an obsolete law of education passed in 1941, clearly expressed the new educational views that guided the reform.

Education is a fundamental means to acquire, transmit, and increase culture; it is a permanent process that contributes to the development of the individual and to the transformation of society, and is a determinate factor for the acquisition of knowledge and the formation of the individual in a way in which he/she will be in a position to contribute to society (FLE, 1976: Art. 2).

The law sets forth various goals, including the promotion and development of knowledge, art and culture, national and international consciousness, a democratic form of government, social conditions that will lead to the equitable distribution of material and cultural goods, and the attitudes necessary to achieve a just society (FLE, 1976: Art. 5). In accordance with the Constitution, this law states that no religion should be taught in the schools, that all schooling offered by the state should be free, and that a primary education is compulsory for all persons living in Mexico (FLE, 1976: Arts. 8 and 12).

In 1975 the National Education Law for Adults, which outlined the principles for establishing a national system of adult education, was promulgated. This law also expressed the new educational conceptions of the government which guided the reform. The reform was to open and make more flexible the educational system so that it would have the capacity to reach every social group and to overcome the educational disadvantages of these groups (SEP, 1976: 83, 85). Regarding adult education, this law stated the following objectives:

that every person may achieve, as a minimum, a level of knowledge and skills equivalent to a basic general education . . . to raise the cultural level of the marginal population so it will be able to participate in the responsibilities and benefits of shared development . . . the promotion of self-teaching, consciousness raising with reference to social, labor and family life'' (NELA, 1976: Art. 4).

PEDAGOGIC CONCEPTIONS OF THE REFORM

In the two laws mentioned above, education is conceived of as a life-long process in which the active participation of students in their own learning is a necessary condition to develop critical thinking skills, initiative, social responsibility, and creativity (FLE, 1976: Art. 20; NELA, 1976: Arts. 2, 4). It is also considered that education should promote scientific attitudes, rejecting dogmatism and adopting a critical approach to knowledge (FLE, 1976: Art. 8). The educational process will be based on freedom and responsibility to insure an adequate environment for developing self-learning skills and to promote dialogue and academic work in groups (FLE, 1976: Art. 44; NELA, 1976: Arts. 2, 4). Knowledge is seen as something that should be continuously revised and reconstructed. An historical consciousness should be developed in the students so that they may understand the past and present in order to plan for the future.

The Federal Law of Education specifies that "educational programs should state specific objectives; methods and activities should be suggested to achieve those objectives, and steps should be outlined to evaluate if students have fulfilled those objectives" (Art. 46).

Although this reform did not opt for any exclusive theoretical perspective in education, it can be argued that behaviorism had a predominant influence on the educational principles that guided and organized the pedagogic reform. From the methodological standpoint, "educational technology" had a strong influence on the reform. To support these arguments, we list below some of the characteristics of the reform which were generalized in most educational institutions.

1. Curricular plans and programs were organized according to behavioral principles.
2. Curricular contents were methodologically developed in accordance with the principles of educational technology and were expressed in terms of specific behavioral objectives.
3. The techniques for measuring achievement were those promoted by behaviorism.
4. The teacher's role in the educational process was significantly reduced to performing activities previously programmed by curriculum development experts.
5. Specialists appeared for the planning, control, and evaluation of the educational process.
6. Schools, mainly at the higher educational level, were organized in a departmental fashion. Departments of academic disciplines, vocational orientation, student affairs, educational technology, sports, arts, and so on, appeared in the schools.
7. Emphasis was put on planning, control, and evaluation of all educational activities.
8. The use of media for teaching was significantly increased.

ELEMENTARY LEVEL EDUCATION REFORM

The elementary level in Mexico, which is called the primary school, includes school years one to six. Educational reform at this level was the most intense. It was centered, in addition to the changes in organization and conception mentioned above, on the restructuring of study plans and programs. Program contents were regrouped in seven new disciplinary areas. Four of them concerned basic academic areas: mathematics, Spanish, social sciences, and natural sciences; and three concerned complementary areas: arts, technology, and physical education (Latapí, 1980: 73).

Free textbooks and teaching guidebooks were completely reformed.[1] More than 300 million textbooks were distributed free to all primary students during the 1970–1976 administration. Fifty-four different books were developed according to the postulates of the reform: thirty to be used by students and twenty-four as auxiliary texts for teachers (González, 1981: 418; Latapí, 1980: 73).

The reform we are analyzing here was preceded by the Eleven Year Program which started in 1960 and had as its main objectives the improvement and expansion of the primary school level. From 1950 to 1959 only 30 percent of the children who began elementary school finished that level. As a result of the Eleven Year Program, the corresponding percentage rose to 35 (Latapí, 1980: 95) and school enrollment increased significantly at the primary level. Nonetheless, at the end of the program, in 1971, the demand for primary school education of the corresponding age cohort was only satisfied in 83 percent of the cases in urban areas and 62 percent in rural areas (Caballero and Medrano, 1981: 371). Although school enrollment increased by 36 percent during the 1970–1976 reform period, the fulfillment of the constitutionally established minimum schooling of primary level was not very encouraging (Latapí, 1980: 80). Those students over fourteen years of age who had completed this level, or a higher one, went from 30 percent in 1970 to 40 percent in 1980 (COPLAMAR, 1982: 54, 55).

SECONDARY SCHOOL REFORM

Secondary school has two three-year levels: basic and upper. Besides the changes in orientation, organization, and pedagogy, previously described for all school levels, emphasis was placed on attempting to link each school year to the labor market, so that dropouts could join the labor market at any point of the school program (SEP, 1974).

Reforms for the basic level resulted in the implementation of two different curricular designs in 1975. One was organized by subjects and the other, the most diffused, by academic areas. Each area was comprised of several subjects. The main objectives of the reform for this level were to continue primary school education, to stimulate knowledge of the situation in Mexico, to develop artistic, technical, scientific, and humanistic education, and to offer sex education to students oriented toward family planning. The upper level was organized in semesters and course credits, and three different areas of specialization were introduced: engineering–mathematics–physics, biology–medicine, and economics–administration. Two different objectives were established for this level: to function as a vocational program, that is, to prepare students to join the labor market; and to prepare students to continue on to higher education.

TEACHER TRAINING REFORM

Teacher training education, which is called normal education, has two levels: basic and upper. Basic normal education was considered to be at the same level as upper secondary school; however, they were not equivalent. During the reform period, the basic normal educational program was modified so that students would study upper level secondary school and the professional teacher training program simultaneously in eight semesters. Later, study programs were modified to include teacher training courses in each specific discipline (Curiel, 1981: 459; Latapí, 1980: 75).

HIGHER EDUCATION REFORM

Higher education in Mexico was (and still is) a highly heterogeneous educational level. In terms of financing and internal government, the institutions are classified as private, federal, state, and autonomous.[2] The differences between institutions are so great that, for instance, one institution, the National Autonomous University of Mexico (UNAM), had more than 120,000[3] students enrolled, while others had only a few hundred (Castrejón, 1976: 45–47, 151; Salinas, 1990: 353). In 1970 the UNAM received 85 percent of the federal budget for higher education, but produced only 44 percent of the country's undergraduates (Latapí, 1980: 192).

Since the 1960s, it has frequently been said that higher education in Mexico is in "crisis." What is generally understood by crisis is that higher education is detached from the socioeconomic development of the nation, is inefficient educationally and administratively speaking, has low academic quality, and lacks adequate planning (Mendoza, 1981: 7). Several efforts during the succeeding years were aimed at resolving this crisis. However, according to critics, the crisis was not overcome.

Although efforts were made during the reform period to create a higher education system, it was not achieved as originally planned. There exists, however, a large and influential organization that attempts to regulate and organize higher education and also the university-controlled upper secondary level education. This organization, the National Association for Higher Education Institutions (ANUIES), promotes and fosters educational reforms at this level. In general, and according to ANUIES, these reforms attempted to transform higher education to respond to social needs, be closer to scientific and technical progress, and contribute to a more just national development (Vielle 1976: 13). More specifically, reforms were directed toward modernizing higher education, making it efficient and more flexible, and achieving a closer relationship between higher education and national development.

The main reforms proposed by ANUIES were directed toward (1) creating outlets from programs to facilitate the insertion of student dropouts in the labor market; (2) reorienting curricula toward practical skills; (3) searching for a balance between specialized and general education; (4) shortening educational programs; (5) organizing institutions by departments, semesters, and course credits; (6) separating higher education from the upper secondary level; (7) making it mandatory that every student at this level carry out non-remunerative work for approximately 800 hours designed to help satisfy regional social needs; and (8) adhering to behavioral educational technology (ANUIES, 1972, 1974, 1975). Some of the strategic decisions involved in the reform were that each university would decided on the type and depth of the reform; ANUIES would implement a national training program for higher education teachers; and information and teacher training centers would be developed at each university.

The reforms proposed by ANUIES were related to transformations in higher education in industrialized countries, and were influenced by guidelines provided by U.S. universities and international agencies for institutions of higher education in Mexico. (For more details, see Kuri and Follari, 1985: 57–59; Puiggrós, 1983: 126–31, 140–41, 180–81; Rodríguez and Zapata 1985: 18–20).

ADULT EDUCATION

A large number of educational programs for adults were in effect during the 1970–1976 period. Among the most important were the Adult Basic Education Centers which provided literacy training and offered intensive educational programs for adults at the primary level. The Cultural Missions is a program established at the beginning of the century. It is oriented toward the vocational training of adults in rural areas and, less intensively, toward general basic education. Two other important programs for adults are Primary Courses at Night and Basic Secondary for Workers.

Probably the most ambitious adult education effort of the reform was the creation of the National System of Education for Adults (SNEA) in 1976. SNEA developed open educational programs directed toward adult illiterates and those individuals who had not completed their primary and/or secondary educational levels.[4] Students who register in these programs may choose to study either in groups or by themselves. SNEA periodically offers examinations to students enrolled in its programs. When students pass all necessary examinations, which cover the whole content of the chosen educational level, they are awarded a certificate equivalent to those awarded to graduates of the formal system.

Government officials continually alleged that SNEA would significantly alleviate the grave educational deficiencies of the adult Mexican population and that this would, in turn, contribute to bettering the socioeconomic well-being of adults, to increasing national economic growth, and to achieving greater equality (SEP, 1976: 83, 85, 87). These positions, however, were based more on faith in education as a tool for development than on any firm empirical evidence.

Formally, these programs were an option for the 26 million adults who had not completed their basic education in 1982. Nevertheless, only a meager percentage of those potential students were involved in SNEA programs, and only a relatively small number graduated from them. From 1976 to 1982 only 66,000 certificates were awarded for completing these programs (DGAC, 1978: 70; López, 1982: 885).

Regarding the socioeconomic well-being of SNEA graduates, a study conducted in 1983 showed that only a small percentage of them would better their chances of getting a job or obtaining more income. Because of the high unemployment and underemployment rates, many graduates could not get a job and, obviously, did not increase their socioeconomic well-being (Peña, 1983: 141–42, 153–54).

NONFORMAL EDUCATION

During the reform period, many nonformal educational programs were initiated while others were continued. Five different programs aimed at the Indian population were carried out: (1) Boarding houses attached to schools were built in regions where the Indian student population was scattered; these boarding schools were attending by more than 23,000 students. (2) A program of bilingual teachers and promoters was aimed at the development of Indian communities through educational activities. (3) A program of brigades for the social development of Indian communities served 85,000 people in 1976. In this program, a brigade remained for four to five years in the community promoting social, cultural, and economic development. (4) Another program was aimed at encouraging the learning of Spanish without affecting Indian languages and cultures. (5) A program offering legal and social counseling for Indian communities was established (González, 1981: 420–421).

Other programs aimed at the rural population—Brigades for Rural Development, Cultural Missions, Mobile Schools, and Peoples' Reading Rooms—served more than 27,000 people in 1975, attempting to promote the social, economic, and cultural development of rural communities. In marginal urban areas, there were fifty-seven Centers for Educational Action which promoted cultural and industrial labor training programs. In 1976 more than 15,000 students were enrolled in these programs. In 1975 there were almost 9,000 school cooperatives, the purpose of which was to help to provide schools with supplies and services (González, 1981: 421).

EDUCATIONAL REFORM ASSESSMENT

Before 1970, the public education system in Mexico was almost completely centralized. Administrative and pedagogic decisions were made in the central offices of the Public Education Ministry (SEP) in Mexico City. At the beginning of the reform, SEP had nearly 1 million education workers throughout the nation. The ministry represented a huge, slow, and inefficient bureaucratic mass that was an obstacle to the reforms' modernization program.

One important action of the 1970–1976 educational reform was to amend the administrative organization of SEP. It was restructured in a new organization, and a slow decentralization process, still in effect, was initiated. During the reform period, some of SEP's functions heretofore concentrated in Mexico City, were transferred to units established in some of the other important cities of the nation. The functions initially transferred were the accreditation and certification of studies and a minimal control of the budget assigned for public education in the corresponding area. One merit of the reform was to initiate the decentralization process which is still being carried out. However, it has been a prolonged and (still) highly inadequate process. At the end of the 1970–1976 reform, only

Table 20.1
Enrollment by School Level, 1958 to 1976

Educational Level	1958	1964	Growth 1958-64	1970	Growth 1964-70	1976	Growth 1970-76
Preschool	199	314	7.92	440	5.81	550	3.77
Primary	4,570	6,513	6.12	8,948	5.39	12,555	5.81
Secondary	253	608	15.75	1,192	11.89	2,143	10.27
Upper Secondary	95	175	10.75	310	10.01	822	17.62
Higher Education	64	117	10.55	194	8.86	528	18.15
	5,081	7,727	6.91	11,034	6.16	16,598	6.96

Note: Enrollment is expressed in thousands of students.
Growth is expressed in annual geometric rates.
Source: Muñoz and Rodríguez (1977b: 4).

a few functions were decentralized, and most of the decisions were still being made in the central offices in Mexico City.

EDUCATIONAL SYSTEM GROWTH

The most publicized achievement of the educational reform during the 1970–1976 administration was the rapid growth of the school system. School enrollment increased from 11 million to more than 16 million students (see Table 20.1).

Of the total student enrollment in 1976, only 10 percent were in private schools, 23 percent in state public schools, and the remaining 67 percent in federal government public schools (SEP, 1978a: 347). The annual rate of growth of enrollment in the educational system at all levels during this period was close to 7 percent. This rate was well above the 3.4 rate of growth of the population during the 1960s (CONAPO, 1982: 45). Although the rate of growth of school enrollment during the 1970–1976 period was considerably elevated, it was no higher than that of the 1958–1964 presidential administration.

When we analyze enrollment growth by school level, it is interesting to note that rates vary widely. The annual preschool and primary levels growth was only 3.8 and 5.8, respectively, while the upper secondary and higher education levels grew at the annual rates of 17.6 and 18.2, respectively (see Table 20.1). Because of the relatively high satisfaction of the demand for low-level schooling by corresponding age groups, it seems reasonable to assume that rates of growth of enrollment for postprimary educational levels should be larger. However, it

Table 20.2
Expenditures in Education and GDP, 1958 to 1976

Year	GDP	Educational Expenditures	Percentage
1958	135,550	2,168	1.6
1964	199,390	5,807	2.91
1970	296,600	9,780	3.06
1976	397,800	17,361	4.36

Note: GDP and expenditures are expressed in constant pesos of 1960.
Source: Muñoz and Rodríguez 1977b, p. 12.

appears disproportionate that the higher education level had grown 172 percent during the 1970–1976 period, corresponding to an annual rate of growth three times that of primary school (see Table 20.1), when 1.8 million children from ages six to fourteen (that is, 13 percent of the total age cohort) did not have access to primary school in 1976 (COPLAMAR, 1982: 25) and 12 million people over fourteen years of age had not finished primary school which, as already mentioned, is obligatory according to the Constitution. Furthermore, of those 12 million people, 6.2 million had never had access to any kind of schooling (Latapí, 1980: 95).

Expenditures in education had grown considerably in the previous decades (see Table 20.2). During the 1970–1976 reform period, total educational expenditures went from 3.06 percent of GDP to 4.36 percent. The federal government contributed considerably to this growth. From its total direct budget, 28 percent went to the educational sector in 1970 and almost 39 percent in 1976 (see Table 20.3). Distribution of the budget for the different school levels, however, was considerably unbalanced. During the reform period, this imbalance grew, as shown in Table 20.4. In 1971 primary level had 84 percent of the entire school enrollment but only got 52 percent of the budget. Corresponding percentages for higher education were 2.2 and 13.4. At the end of the 1970–1976 presidential administration, the proportion of enrollment at primary level dropped 5 percent, while the budget dropped more than 15 percent. The opposite occurred at the upper secondary and higher education levels: enrollment grew by 2.2 percent for the upper secondary level, while the budget increased 8.3 percent; higher education enrollment grew 3.3 percent, while its budget increased by 5.4 percent. This means that during the reform period, more emphasis was put on the growth of enrollment and budget for higher school levels than for lower levels. This tendency was consistent with the general policy of the state which

Table 20.3
Educational Budget and Federal Government Budget, 1958 to 1976

Year	Direct Federal Budget	Educational Budget	Percentage
1958	8,957	1,229	13.72
1964	13,749	3,501	25.46
1970	19,930	5,630	28.25
1976	33,596	13,007	38.72

Note: Budgets expressed in constant 1960 pesos.
Source: Muñoz and Rodríguez (1977b: 13).

Table 20.4
Percentages of Enrollment and Budget by School Level, 1971 and 1976

School Level	1971		1976	
	Enrollment	Budget	Enrollment	Budget
Primary	83.8	51.9	78.2	36.6
Secondary	11.1	22.8	13.4	24.5
Upper Secondary	2.9	11.9	5.1	20.2
Higher education	2.2	13.4	3.3	18.8

Sources: Latapí 1980, p. 108 for 1971 data and Muñoz and Rodríguez 1977b, pp. 4, 9 for 1976 data.

sought to win over the middle and upper classes after the 1968 social crisis and to regain its legitimacy as a state which mediates between socioeconomic classes.

Expansion of the educational system was determined mainly by social demand (Castrejón, 1976: 39). The government justified this criterion by arguing that any action taken to expand schooling opportunities would result in increased social mobility (see Latapí, 1980: 104–105). Actually, the system expanded according to the power of the demands of each sector of the population. This meant that, even though the educational system expanded considerably at all levels, the sectors of society most benefited were those that already had significant amounts of social bargaining power: in other words, the middle and upper classes.

Educational expansion was not utilized to increase schooling opportunities to compensate for existing social and educational inequalities, or to contribute to the transformation of pervading unjust social relations.[5]

Two studies of public expenditures for higher education in Mexico (conducted in 1977 and 1978) suggest that low-income families subsidize higher education for those who come from higher income families (Quintero, 1978: 85), and that the sector most benefited in society is comprised of the middle classes (Pescador, 1977: 74–76). The proportion of taxes paid in relation to economic benefits received from higher education level studies is the greatest for low-income families (Pescador, 1977: 76). Therefore, contrary to what was frequently alleged, that expansion of educational enrollment would contribute to a more just society, it seems unlikely that public expenditures at the higher education level will contribute to a more equitable distribution of income in society (Pescador, 1977: 76; Quintero, 1978: 85).

Special education programs and actions focused on the rural population were carried out. Two-thirds of all new teachers were sent to rural schools; at the end of the administration, close to 35,000 new teachers had been sent to these schools. A new program of Community Teachers was created to serve primary school-age children from small and isolated communities (Latapí, 1980: 81). Though praiseworthy educational efforts, they reach rural zones only when urban zones have been satisfied regarding their primary education demands and then require postprimary education. In 1970 the demand for primary schooling was 88 percent satisfied in urban zones and in rural zones, only 66 percent. Of those who began their primary level studies, 54 percent finished primary school in urban zones, while only 10 percent did so in rural zones (Latapí, 1980: 110–111).

PEDAGOGIC REFORMS

Educational reform introduced flexibility to a formerly rigid system and attempted to transform old educational practices into new, modern, scientific, and efficient practices. In order to bring about these changes, it was necessary to profoundly modify educational practices, relations, attitudes, and the behavior of administrators, teachers, and students. Short courses were given to teachers and administrators at all school levels on the new conceptions of education and use of educational technology. At the primary level, new textbooks for students and auxiliary books for teachers were given great importance in the changing of educational practices in the classroom. These books have been considered a positive contribution to education; however, they can do little to change teacher and administrator attitudes and behavior, and social relations within the schools. Short courses cannot penetrate the new educational practices proposed by the reform and adequately train teachers in the methodology suggested by educational technology (see Latapí, 1980: 99).

In a study conducted in thirty-five schools at the primary and upper secondary levels in rural areas and in Mexico City, it was found that teachers combined traditional practices and new practices introduced by the educational reform. This was found more frequently in rural schools and in low socioeconomic level schools in urban areas. The authors of the study suggested that teachers were not homogeneously trained and that many needed pedagogic training in the new practices introduced by the reform (Muñoz and Rodríguez, 1976: 132–133).

New educational methodologies introduced by the reform offered teachers modern, scientific, and efficient procedures that allowed them to understand and modify their educational practices. These methodologies presented a scientific and technical rationale similar to that of modern industrialization (see Rodríguez and Zapata, 1985: 21–22).

Following Ibarra (1989: 270), we believe that the changes in teaching practices were mainly nominal. Teachers complied with the demands related to new regulations for achievement evaluation, supplied grades periodically, reported program advances, and so on, but did not significantly change their teaching strategies or their relationships with students and disciplines.[6]

Normal education was reformed in 1975 in accordance with reforms for the primary and basic secondary levels. However, this reform was late and inadequate (see Curiel, 1981: 459; Latapí, 1980: 99–100). Changes introduced at the primary and secondary levels were not put into effect in the training of teachers until 1975. As mentioned before, most of the basic secondary schools modified their programs to introduce academic areas instead of subjects. Before 1975, teachers were trained to teach one particular subject. With the new programs introduced by the reform, they had to take charge of a disciplinary area in which the content of several subjects was included. As a result, many of the teachers were not qualified to teach a disciplinary area. In a survey that included 57 percent of the teachers from the disciplinary area of natural sciences carried out in one state, 89 percent of these teachers disapproved of changes introduced by the reform in which physics, chemistry, and biology were integrated in one area. In addition, 45 percent of the teachers surveyed admitted that they had problems dealing with this new organization (Huerta, 1982: 184, 186).

Another deficiency of normal education during the reform was that no special studies were introduced to prepare teachers for the upper secondary level, in spite of the development of new upper secondary programs, the creation of new institutions for this level, and one of the highest enrollment growths.

STUDENT ACHIEVEMENT AND RETENTION RATES

We are not aware of the existence of any comprehensive studies of student achievement related to educational reform changes. We do know of achievement studies preceding and subsequent to the reform; however, they have diverse scopes and methodological differences that make comparisons difficult. Nevertheless, they all report similar results which suggest that the achievement level did not change significantly.

In a study conducted in 1970 in twenty private middle-low socioeconomic level primary schools in Mexico City, a total of 519 students were examined with standardized tests in mathematics, geometry, and Spanish. Results showed that on a 0 to 100 scale the average achievement was 57 (Muñoz and Guzman, 1971)—an average grade below the minimum necessary to pass an examination.

In 1975 a study was conducted to determine achievement factors in Mexican education as part of an international comparative study. A stratified sample was taken covering public and private schools, different socioeconomic levels, and urban or rural location. Students of fourth, sixth, and twelfth grades were examined in reading comprehension and natural sciences. Exam results were discouraging. Average percentages of items correctly answered by subsample groups went from 27 to 53 in reading comprehension and from 22 to 40 in natural sciences, with rural schools having the lowest percentages and private urban high socioeconomic level schools the highest (Muñoz and Rodríguez, 1976). Although in 1975 educational reform was still being carried out, and achievement comparisons with the 1970 study mentioned above are not totally valid, it is interesting to note that urban private primary schools of both low and high socioeconomic level appeared to have lower achievement levels (37 and 39 percent, respectively) when compared to the results of the private schools of middle-low socioeconomic level of the 1970 study mentioned above (57 percent)[7] (Muñoz and Guzmán, 1971; Muñoz and Rodríguez, 1976).

In the study mentioned previously, conducted at the secondary level in one state of the nation, 287 students were given an examination in natural sciences. Their average achievement level was 63 on a 0 to 100 scale. Surveyed teachers expressed the opinion that student achievement levels were higher before the reforms were introduced in 1975. After an analysis of survey results and study programs, the author of the study concluded that low student achievement was caused by the lack of interdisciplinary training of teachers and deficient integration, sequence, and continuity of the natural science programs introduced during the reform (Huerta, 1982: 191–198).

Although studies on student achievement levels are dispersed and no definite conclusion can be reached about the educational reforms introduced, it appears that the reforms have not had any significant effect on student achievement. The percentage of failing students cannot be considered a good indicator of educational quality, because there is evidence that school administrators frequently demand from teachers that failing grades not exceed a given percentage.[8] Nonetheless, we are including some data related to students who failed the school year and dropped out; these data should, therefore, be considered with caution.

The number of failing students at the primary level decreased slightly during the reform period. In 1970, 13.2 percent of the primary school population failed, while in 1974 this percentage decreased to 12.1 (Latapí, 1980: 95). The percentage of intracurricular school dropouts at the primary school level decreased during the reform period; however, its magnitude was still considerable. Only

35 percent finished sixth grade in the 1966–1971 primary school cohort, while from the 1970–1975 cohort, 42 percent were in a similar case (Latapí, 1980: 95).

The reform was initiated in 1970, but some time had to elapse for changes to occur at the different school levels and yet more time for its effects to become evident. Therefore, we will compare school dropouts for 1970, 1976, and 1980. The percentage of school dropouts from primary school level, considering the enrollment of the age cohort six to fourteen, grew from 14 in 1970 to 31 in 1976. This percentage reached its highest point in 1977 but decreased to 22 in 1980 (COPLAMAR, 1982: 33). The percentage of dropouts considering the basic education enrollment (that is, primary and basic secondary levels) and the age cohort six to seventeen was 28 in 1970 and steadily decreased to 27 in 1976 and 19 in 1980 (COPLAMAR, 1982: 49).

In short, there is not enough evidence to support the assumption that achievement levels improved owing to changes brought about through the reform. The number of students remaining in school, however, seems to have increased slightly.

WOMEN IN THE EDUCATIONAL SYSTEM

Historically, women in Mexico have been relegated to a socially and politically inferior status, partly because of the role women have played in economic production. Of the Economically Active Population (EAP) in 1950, only 13 percent were women. In 1969 women had modestly increased their participation to 19 percent; that is, only 18 percent of all females older than eleven years of age formed part of the EAP, either as employed or unemployed workers (González, 1972: 113–114). During the reform period, the participation of women increased in the labor market and reached a still small percentage of 23 (CONAPO, 1982: 70). Furthermore, most of the women in the EAP occupy lower level positions. In 1970 only 10 percent of women in the EAP occupied positions as technicians or professionals and only 2 percent as high management personnel.

This low participation in economic production and the cultural role that has been assigned to women in Mexico have contributed to the small participation of women in the educational system. Table 20.5 shows the percentages of male and female participation in the educational system in Mexico. Clearly, women participate at all levels in lower percentages than men. The higher the educational level, the lower the participation of women. As the participation of women in the EAP increases, so does their participation in the educational system. During the reform period, women participated more at the upper secondary and higher education levels. Proportionately, however, only a small percentage of women participated at the higher education level in 1976.

Although it may be difficult to appreciate many of the effects of the educational reform, it is clear that during the 1970–1976 administration, schooling expanded considerably at all educational levels and reached population sectors that were

Table 20.5
Percentages of Enrollment by Sex and Educational Level, 1970 and 1976

Educational Level	1970			1976		
	Females	Males		Females	Males	
Primary	48.1	51.9	100	48.3	51.7	100
Secondary	42.2	57.8	100	43.8	56.2	100
Upper Secondary	34.0	66.0	100	41.6	58.4	100
Higher Education	23.2	76.8	100	25.3	74.7	100

Sources: SEP 1978a, pp. 21, 101, 177, 181, 301 for 1976 data.
IX General Population Census for 1970 data.

previously without access. This expansion, however, did not benefit all sectors of Mexican society equitably. The middle classes benefited most by this expansion. During the period analyzed, the international economy was reactivated. This permitted a high rate of expansion of the national product—an annual rate of 5 percent—(Muñoz and Rodríguez, 1977b: 12), which in turn, made available external and internal resources to the government. As a result, public expenditures were increased, and a significant number of jobs were created at all levels. Proportionately, the largest number of new jobs were created at professional and semiprofessional levels. This contributed to the hiring of university and upper secondary graduates. As stated before, university and upper secondary educational levels had the largest expansion of enrollment during the period under consideration. Once again, the middle classes were the most benefited sector of society.

With regard to education, it can be safely stated that traditional school organization and pedagogic practices were shaken. The Mexican educational system became more dynamic, open, and flexible. Teachers were presented with new, modern, and scientific ways of approaching their work. New educational subsystems were created, and new educational programs were developed. Although at this point in time we are not enthusiastic about the benefits of the new pedagogic practices introduced and the transformation of the educational system, and we do not think the changes brought about were spectacular, we are nevertheless convinced that during the reform period, the educational system became more dynamic, open, and tolerant. Education was being debated in Mexican society.

POST-REFORM PERIOD

The most recent wide educational reform in Mexico has been that carried out during the 1970–1976 presidential administration period. The following administrations did not make significant changes in the educational model introduced during that period. As we will briefly discuss in this section, educational conceptions, classroom practices, and techniques were not replaced or significantly changed. Those administrations basically maintained the same educational policies and educational model and continued implementing the programs initiated during the reform. Nonetheless, at the beginning of each sexennial period new educational reforms have been proposed at the speech level.

Toward the end of Echeverría's administration, Mexico's economy plunged into a severe recession.[9] The new administration under José López Portillo inherited that recession. During the first three years of this new administration, restrictive economic measures were put into effect. The growth of workers' salaries was limited, and market prices were freed so that capital returns would increase.[10] During this phase, an attempt was made to make the economy more efficient in order to improve productivity and to increase the competitiveness of Mexican products on the world market. This change in the economy affected the educational sector. Educational planning was introduced as the tool to achieve a better adjustment of the school system to the needs of the productive sector and to raise the quality and efficiency of that system (SEP, 1979a: 19). During this period, educational spending decreased in real terms. Consequently, the rate of expansion of school enrollment diminished, and no important educational programs were created.

López Portillo's administration made the Mexican economy highly dependent on oil exports. Mexico received huge foreign loans that were partially utilized to expand oil production. While international oil prices were high and interest rates low, Mexico strengthened industrial production, and the government increased expenditures and expanded its participation in the productive sector. During this period, the government stated that "Mexicans should learn to administer abundance." Unfortunately, this period was extremely short, and Mexicans lost their opportunity to learn to administer abundance. While it lasted, however, school enrollment rates regained their high levels. Enrollment grew from 16 to 23 million students in those six years—that is, an annual rate of growth of 6.10 (see Table 20.6). As was the case with former administrations, higher education received preferential treatment, and enrollment increased from 528,000 to more than 1 million (see Tables 20.1 and 20.6).

In 1980, still in the "abundance" period, the government introduced a national plan for development. The educational objectives of the plan were very similar to those proposed during the reform period 1970–1976: to offer basic education (ten years of schooling) to the entire population, to raise the quality of education, to establish a stronger tie between the educational and productive sectors, and to improve the efficiency of the educational system (PEF, 1980: 346).

Table 20.6
Enrollment and Annual Growth by School Level, 1976 to 1990

Educational Level	Growth 1970-76	1982	Growth 1976-82	1988	Growth 1982-88	1990
Preschool	3.77	1,691	20.59	2,669	7.90	2,865
Primary	5.81	15,223	3.26	14,656	-.63	14,622
Secondary	10.27	3,991	10.91	4,795	3.11	4,842
Upper Secondary	17.62	1,732	13.26	2,071	3.02	2,210
Higher Education	18.15	1,047	12.09	1,257	3.09	1,357
	6.96	23,684	6.10	25,448	1.21	25,896

Note: Enrollment is expressed in thousands of students. Growth is expressed in annual geometric rates.
Source: Muñoz and Rodríguez (1977b: 4); Salinas (1989: 165; 1990: 341); Lopez (1982: 47-49).

According to the government, its most ambitious and important social program during this administration was Education for All (SEP, 1978b: 9). The program proposed to offer primary education to the entire population and to promote adult education. The views expressed in official documents depict education as a panacea. Education is perceived as the key to improving the quality of life and as a necessary element in allowing individuals to participate in society and to prepare them to improve the possibilities of satisfying their own needs. In addition, increased access to education for the whole population is seen as an element essential to decreasing social inequalities and achieving social justice in a democratic society (SEP, 1976, 1978a, 1978b, 1979a, 1979b; Solana, 1980).

Education for All satisfied 95 percent of first-year demand at the primary level and promoted adult education programs through the National System of Education for Adults (SNEA). As described above, this adult education program, though very ambitious and greatly expanded, had meager results. During this administration, only 66,000 certificates were awarded to adults at primary and basic secondary levels (DGAC, 1978: 70; López, 1982: 885).

Unfortunately, the "abundance" period was ephemeral. International oil prices dropped drastically in 1981 and interest rates climbed. This forced the Mexican government to demand more foreign loans to pay the interest on national and foreign debts. The foreign debt increased from $18 to $94 billion during the 1976–1983 period (Rosenthal, 1989: 241). Mexico's economy, therefore, became increasingly dependent on foreign capital and on the policies determined

378 International Handbook of Educational Reform

Table 20.7
Expenditures in Education and Interest on Public Debts as Percentages of
Corresponding GDP, 1976 to 1990

| Year | Expenditures | | Interests on Debts |
	Federal Government	Total	
1976	3.3	4.4	3.8
1982	3.8	5.3	20.6
1988	2.0	3.6	28.6
1990	2.9	3.4	11.7

Sources: Muñoz and Rodríguez (1977b:12,13);
Guzmán and Vela González (1989: 45);
Diez and Frutos (1988: 225);
Salinas (1989: 187); Prawda (1989: 180);
Campa (1990: 24, 26); Banamex (1991:19-20).

by foreign financial institutions. In 1982 more than 20 percent of Mexico's gross domestic product (GDP) was used to pay interest on debts, while only 3.8 percent was budgeted for education (see Table 20.7). Inflation rates grew to unknown levels in Mexico's modern history,[11] and this contributed to an unstable situation for Mexican currency. As a result, large amounts of capital were taken out of the country. All these factors contributed to leading the Mexican economy into a new recession toward the end of López Portillo's administration in 1982.

During the 1976–1982 administration, the educational system was not reformed. The policies followed did not aspire to change educational practices in the classroom. The educational model introduced during the preceding administration was never questioned, modified, or replaced (see Ibarra, 1989: 308–314). Efforts were aimed mainly at increasing school enrollment, offering educational services to marginal social sectors, adjusting and making more efficient educational services, and decentralizing the Public Educational Ministry.

The following administration, under Miguel de la Madrid Hurtado, was completely immersed in the most severe economic crisis experienced since the Mexican revolution at the beginning of the century. Inflation rates reached the highest levels ever seen in this century, and domestic production stagnated.[12] Government expenditures decreased considerably in real terms. The interest on public debt absorbed a great deal of the GDP. In 1987, 31.7 percent of GDP was used to pay the interest on debts (Guzmán and Vela, 1989: 45). This critical situation resulted in a drastic reduction of production, investment, and expenditures in social development and education. In 1982, 7.4 percent of GDP was budgeted for public expenditures in social development, while during the 1982–1988 administration, this percentage dropped to an average annual level of 5.6 (Guzmán and Vela, 1989: 45). Total expenditures for education were reduced even more drastically. The percentage of the GDP allotted to education in 1982 was 5.5. The corresponding percentage for 1988 was reduced to an all-time low of 3.6 percent (see Table 20.7). This percentage is way below the 8 percent suggested by Unesco for countries with development similar to that of Mexico.[13] It is also below what other countries actually spend. In 1984, on the average, African countries allotted 5.4 percent of their GDP to educational services, while the corresponding percentage for Latin American countries was 4.4 (Diez and Frutos, 1988: 226).

This critical reduction of expenditures diminished rates of school enrollment and the creation of new educational programs. Nevertheless, this administration launched a new educational movement that was called the Educational Revolution. Once again, the main objectives of this movement were to adjust educational resources, raise the quality of education, expand educational services, establish a closer tie between the educational system and national development, and decentralize basic and normal education (PEF, 1984: 47–56).

This so-called Educational Revolution, which rhetorically promised "to solve educational problems from the roots on up" (Reyes, 1983: 2), in reality did not propose to change educational contents or teaching practices and methods in the classroom, nor did it offer a new educational model to substitute the one implemented during the 1970–1976 period.

The approach proposed for increasing educational quality (and considered the most relevant) was to improve teacher qualifications (PEF, 1984: 47; Reyes, 1983: 4). An increase in educational quality cannot depend solely on the goodwill of teachers or on an official mandate. Certain conditions must be created, such as having real access to adequate training and updating, books, auxiliary printed materials, educational techniques, and adequate school areas. Contradictory to the objectives this educational policy proposed, these conditions were actually hampered.

From 1982 to 1987, total educational expenditures decreased at an average annual rate of 11 percent, while educational investment expenditures decreased 15 percent (Prawda, 1989: 195). The government demanded that schools "do more with fewer resources." This drastic reduction of educational resources had unfortunate consequences. The annual rate of enrollment growth for the entire educational system diminished from 6.1 percent during the previous administration to 1.2 percent (see Table 20.6). Furthermore, teachers' real incomes were severely reduced during this administration. For instance, the salaries of elementary school teachers were reduced by 67 percent and those of university professors by 41 percent (Guzmán and Vela, 1989: 48). In 1988 primary school teachers had an approximate monthly salary equivalent to only $115 (calculated from Guzmán and Vela, 1989: 47). These low salaries were probably the main source of teacher unrest and political movements toward the end of the de la Madrid administration. No improvement of teacher qualifications is conceivable with this kind of remuneration. Many teachers have to engage in other activities in order to supplement their meager wages. Obviously, this contributes to lower educational quality, contrary to what was intended.

The new government administration, which began at the end of 1988 under Carlos Salinas, has been carrying out important transformations in Mexico's economy—congruent with present changes in the world economy and dominant trends. These transformations attempt to "modernize" the economy, committing the nation to a market economy, increasing productivity and production, opening the economy to world markets, reducing the direct role of government in the control of the economy by selling public enterprises to private entrepreneures, and encouraging foreign investment.

This modernizing trend has affected the educational system. In 1989 the Program for Modernizing Education, 1989–1994 was introduced. This program seeks to promote the joint participation of civil society and government in satisfying social demands and contributing to national development (PEF, 1989: 17, 18). The new educational model proposes, among other things, to contribute to eliminating social and geographic inequalities, to increase educational quality and efficacy, to develop closer ties between education and economic development, and to expand educational services (PEF, 1989: 18). This educational model is proposing changes in contents, teaching–learning methods, teacher training approaches, and so on. Until now the public has not been informed of the specific changes proposed. However, new programs, methods, and approaches are being tested at some grades at the primary and secondary levels. Many different work teams are currently evaluating these experiences.

Judging by the importance of the transformations being carried out in Mexico's economy and by the changes proposed (and those that are already in effect) in the educational system at this time, it appears that this "modernizing" effort will constitute a true educational reform. However, it is too early to state this with any degree of certainty.

CONCLUSION

The severe and prolonged economic recession that Mexico has suffered has had a profound effect on most sectors of society. During the last fifteen years, salaries have drastically lost their purchasing power. Minimum wages have dropped 63 percent, while elementary school teachers' salaries decreased by 74 percent and those of university professors by 69 percent (Guzmán and Vela, 1989: 45, 48). This general salary reduction is not a result of the stagnation of production, but mainly a product of the inequality in the distribution of wealth. As a result, salaries now represent a reduced portion of the total wealth of what is produced in Mexico. In 1976 salaries accounted for 40 percent of the GDP. This percentage dropped to 26 in 1987 (Guzmán and Vela, 1989: 45, 48).

According to official figures, in Mexico there are 41 million people who cannot satisfy their basic needs. Of these, 17 million people are at extreme poverty levels. Their incomes satisfy only 60 percent of the goods and services needed. Most of them, 10 million, live in rural areas (Reyes, 1900: 6; Rodríguez Castañeda, 1990: 7). Of an estimated population of 30 million people in the rural areas, 10 million do not have access to medical services, 24 million have no potable water, 10 million earn no income, and 15 million earn less than the minimum wage (Reyes, 1990: 6).

Rural and marginal urban sectors have had to decrease food consumption to such a degree that malnutrition has become generalized among the younger population. In a recent study, it was found that 50 percent of rural children suffered some degree of malnutrition. In 1974, 7.5 percent suffered severe malnutrition, while in 1989 this percentage increased to 15 percent. In urban zones it was found that malnutrition rose from 7 to 17 percent among children (Luis Rodríguez 1990: 9).

It is evident that malnutrition will have serious social consequences at present and in the future. From the educational standpoint, severe malnutrition is an important obstacle to any kind of learning. Chávez and Martínez (1979) point out that malnutrition delays the social, psychomotor, and intellectual development of children. Their explanation is that malnourished children suffer from a deficient availability of energy, forcing them to save energy by reducing their activity and, consequently, diminishing their learning capacity.

Efforts to reduce the profound educational gap in Mexican society have been insufficient and therefore exceeded by reality. In 1989 it was estimated that Mexico had 52 million adults. Of those, 4 million were illiterate, 20 million had not concluded their primary education, and 16 million more had not finished their basic secondary level (PEF, 1989: 82). That is, in 1989, 40 million adults (78 percent) had not completed what is considered to be the basic schooling level. Furthermore, these figures have grown in the last decade: 17 million more adults have less than the basic schooling level.

During the last six years, only 450,000 adults finished their primary or basic secondary studies (PEF, 1989: 82). Furthermore, every year an average of 860,000 children drop out of primary school (Rodríguez Reyna, 1990) and will most likely join the adults left behind.[14] If this tendency continues, in 1994 more than 47 million adults will have a schooling level below the basic secondary level (PEF, 1989: 82).

It can be concluded that no educational reform will have any significant consequences as long as the present profound social and economic inequalities persist. Changes in the content of educational programs, methods, perspectives, organizational modes, and so on, will provide negligible contributions to national socioeconomic development and to the development of a more equitable, just, and democratic society.

For an educational reform to be truly transcendental, it must constitute part of an overall reform aimed at reducing the pervading and profound socioeconomic inequalities existing in Mexico. It must allow the marginal sectors to organize so that they may create jobs, become productive, and take part in the political life of the nation. In turn, they could then be able to rise above their present situation and depend less on the dominant sectors of society. Only then will educational reform have an important effect on national socioeconomic development, giving the vast majority of Mexicans the opportunity to find in the educational system a way to better their family life and socioeconomic well-being.

NOTES

1. Since 1960, textbooks for students and auxiliary books for teachers at the primary level have been published and distributed free. A special book is used for each discipline and school year in primary schools (public and private) throughout the nation. Since they first appeared, these textbooks have been severely criticized by the most reactionary groups in Mexico (Caballero and Medrano, 1981: 372–377).

2. Autonomous universities obtain most of their financing from state and federal governments, but they govern themselves with relative autonomy.

3. Not considering upper secondary cycle students enrolled in institutions controlled by UNAM.

4. SNEA educational programs exist until the present time with different name and small changes. A new program was later implemented at the upper secondary level.

5. See Latapí (1980: 104–107) who contributes to these arguments. Other studies, carried out at the beginning of the period analyzed, also support these arguments. In a study of the existing relations between educational development and regional development. Muñoz Izquierdo (1983: 28–35) found that in 1960 and 1970 they were highly related in a positive manner. Similar relationships were found by Barkin (1971: 970–974) in his analysis of the Mexican educational system from 1950 to 1970. These findings indicate that the most highly developed regions had the greatest access to schooling.

6. In a long study about teaching practices in a higher education Technological Institute, Luis Ibarra (1989) found that teaching practices did not significantly change as a consequence of the introduction of educational technology. Professors complied with the remaking of course programs in terms of behavioral objectives and achievement evaluation regulations, but did not change their teaching strategies. Professors continued lecturing as a form of teaching, not encouraging the active participation of students in the teaching–learning process and not giving special consideration to cognitive learning taxonomy. See Olac Fuentes (1979: 235–236) who arrives at similar conclusions.

7. Here we should mention that exams for the 1970 study were developed for the corresponding study programs for Mexican schools, and those for the 1975 study were elaborated for an international comparison.

8. These kinds of demands are, of course, most of the time oral and not formal. Nevertheless, some public statements have been made, demanding that teachers void failing students. The public reacted to this statement, and in 1976 Victor Bravo Ahuja, secretary of public education, explained that "the demand on teachers to avoid failing students at the primary level, does not mean giving away grades" (Bravo, 1976b: 535). Recently, the author has questioned some teachers about this phenomenon, and all of them have assured him that such demands are still made.

9. The following indicators show the severe decline of Mexico's economy: (1) the foreign debt has grown from $3.8 to $18.3 billion (Rosenthal, 1989: 237); (2) the gross domestic product dropped rapidly from its highest level of 7.7 percent in 1973 to its lowest level of 2.0 percent at the end of the administration; (3) the inflation rate went from a stable figure close to 5 percent from 1970 to 1972 up to 22 percent in 1976; and (4) the currency devalued more than 70 percent toward the end of this administration (Banamex, 1980: 617–621).

10. As a result of this economic policy, during the 1970–1976 administration the minimum blue-collar wage—at constant prices—decreased 37 percent and participation of salaries in the gross domestic product dropped from 40 percent in 1976 to 36 percent in 1980 (Guzmán and Vela, 1989: 45, 48). See also Mendoza (1981: 17) for an analysis of Mexico's economy during the first years of this administration.

11. The inflation rate in 1982 reached 99 percent (Prawda, 1989: 181).

12. The inflation rate in 1987 was 159 percent (Prawda, 1989: 181), and the average annual growth during the 1983–1987 period was 1 percent (Yunez, 1989: 678). This percentage is considerably lower than the population rate of growth of 2 percent for 1985 (Expansion, 1990: 60)

13. Federal government expenditures, measured as a percentage of the GDP, decreased even more rapidly. During the 1982–1988 period, this percentage dropped from 3.76 to 2.00 (Diez and Frutos, 1988: 225; Guzmán and Vela, 1989: 45). In 1987 total expenditures for education were as follows: federal government, 78 percent; state governments, 12 percent; and private, the remaining 10 percent (Prawda, 1989: 188).

14. Besides, 300,000 rural children—age six—do not have access to the primary school level each year. From those who initiate this level, 80 percent drop out of primary school (Hernández, 1990: 15).

REFERENCES

ANUIES (Asociación Nacional de Universidades e Institutos de Educación Superior). 1972 October–December. "Declaración de Tepic." *Revista de la Educación Superior* 1 (4): 50–57.

———. 1974, January–March. "Declaración de Veracruz." *Revista de la Educación Superior* 3 (1): 77–86.

———. 1975 April–June. "Declaración de Querétaro." *Revista de la Educación Superior* 4 (2): 40–60.

Banamex (Banco Nacional de México). 1980, December. *Examen de la Situación Económica de México*, 56 (661).

———. 1991, January. "Ingresos y Gasto Públicos." *Examen de la Situación Económica de México* 57 (782): 17–22.

Barkin, David. 1971. "La Educación Superior: ¿Una Barrera al Desarrollo Económico?" *El Trimestre Económico* 23: 951–993.

Bravo Ahúja, V. 1976a. *Diario de una Gestión 1972*. Vol. 3. Mexico: SEP.

———.1976b. *Diario de una Gestión 1976*. Vol. 6. Mexico: SEP.

———, and José A. Carranza. 1976. *La Obra Educativa*. Mexico: SepSetentas.

Caballero, Arquimedes, and Salvador Medrano. 1981. "El Segundo Periodo de Torres Bodet, 1958–1964." In *Historia de la Educación Pública en México*, ed. F. Solana, R. Cardiel, and R. Bolanos. Mexico: Fondo de Cultura Económica-SEP, pp. 360–402.

Campa, Homero. 1990, December. "Escuelas Públicas: Enseñar y Aprender en la Pobreza." *Proceso*, 17 (737): 24–27.

Castrejón Diez, J. 1976. *La Educación Superior en México*. Mexico: SEP.

Chávez, Adolfo. 1979. "Nutrición: Problemas y Alternativas." In *México, Hoy*, ed. C. P. González and E. Florescano, Mexico: Siglo XXI, pp. 220–229.

———, and C. Martínez. 1979. *Nutrición y Desarrollo Infantil*. Mexico: Neuva Editorial Interamericana.

CONAPO (Consejo Nacional de Población). 1982. *México Demográfico. Breviario 1980–81*. Mexico: author.

COPLAMAR (Coordinación General del Plan Nacional de Zonas Deprimidas y Grupos Marginados). 1982. *Necesidades Esenciales en México. Situación Actual y Perspectivas al Año 2000. 2, Educación*. Mexico: Siglo XXI.

Curiel Méndez, M. E. 1981. "La Educación Normal." In *Historia de la Educación Pública en México*, ed. F. Solana, R. Cardiel, and R. Bolaños. Mexico: Fondo de Cultura Económica-SEP, pp. 426–462.

DGAC (Dirección General de Acreditación y Certificación). 1978. Organización y Características de los Educandos del "Sistema Nacional de Educación de Adultos." Mexico: unpublished manuscript.

Didriksson Takayanagui, A. 1985. "Las Falacias de la Revolución Educativa en la Calidad de la Enseñanza." *Foro Universitario*. Mexico: CISE-UNAM.

———. 1987. *De la Planeación a la Evaluación. Los Primeros Pasos de la Revolución Educativa*. Serie Sobre la Universidad. Mexico: CISE-UNAM.

Diez, Ignacio, and Verónica C. Frutos. 1988. "Matrícula escolar 1987–1988 y Gasto Nacional en Educación 1982–1987." *Revista Latinoamericana de Estudios Educativos* 17, (3–4): 185–226.

Expansion. 1990, December. "Avances y Retrocesos. Informe Exclusivo." *Expansión* 22 (556): 60–65.

FLE (Federal Law of Education). 1976. "Ley Federal de Educación." In *Documentos Sobre la Ley Nacional de Educación de Adultos*, ed SEP. Mexico: SEP, pp. 41–49.

Fuentes Molinar, O. 1979. "Educación Pública y Sociedad." In *México, Hoy*, ed. P. González C. and E. Florescano. Mexico: Siglo XXI, pp. 230–265.

Gollás, Manuel. 1978, May–June. "El Desempleo en México: Soluciones Posibles." *Ciencia y Desarrollo* 20: 73–86.

Gómez, Pedro, and Miguel Rivera. 1982. "Acumulación de Capital en México, en la Década del Sesenta." *Génesis y Desarrollo del Capitalismo en México*, ed. Universidad Autónoma de Querétaro. Mexico: editor.

González Casanova, P. 1980. "The Economic Development of Mexico." *Scientific American* 243: 154–163.

González Cosío, A. 1981. "Los Años Recientes. 1964–1976." In *Historia de la Educación Pública en México*, ed. F. Solana, R. Cardiel, and R. Bolaños. Mexico: Fondo de Cultura Económica-SEP, pp. 403–425.

González Salazar, G. 1972. "La Mujer: Condiciones Estructurales y Educación." In *Reforma Educativa y "Apertura Democrática,"* ed. by several authors. Mexico: Editorial Nuestro Tiempo, pp. 106–124.

Guzmán Ortiz, E., and J. H. Vela González, 1989. July–August. "Maestros 1989: Crisis, Democracia y Más Salario." *El Cotidiano* 30: 44–49.

Hernández, Evangelina. 1990, September 14. "Es Deficiente la Educación en el Medio Rural: CNC." *La Jornada*, 15.

Huerta Treviño, M. E. 1982. "Resultados de la Reforma Educativa (1975) a Nivel de Educación Media Básica en el Area de Ciencias Naturales en el Estado de Nuevo León." *Enseñanza + Aprendizaje* 4: 181–198.

Ibarra Rivas, L. 1989. "Los Escenarios de la Práctica Docente en los Tiempos de la Transición." Unpublished master's thesis, Mexico: Universidad Autónoma de Querétaro.

IBRD (International Bank for Reconstruction and Development). 1973. *The Economy of Mexico: A Basic Report*. Washington, D.C.: Author. (Mimeograph.)

Kuri, Alfredo C., and Follari, Roberto A. 1985. "Para Una Crítica de la Tecnología Educativa. Macro Teórico e Historia." In *Tecnología Educativa*, Universidad Autónoma de Querétaro. Mexico: editor, pp. 45–74.

Latapí, Pablo. 1980. *Análisis de un Sexenio de Educación en México, 1970–1976*. Mexico: Nueva Imágen.

López Portillo, J. 1982. *Sexto informe de Gobierno. Sector Educativo*, México: Secretaría de Programación y Presupuesto.

Mendoza Rojas, J. 1981, April–June. "El Proyecto Ideológico Medernizador de las Politicas Universitarias en México." *Perfiles Educativos* 12: 3–21.

Muñoz Izquierdo, C. 1973. "Evaluación del Desarrollo Educativo en México (1958–1970)." *Revista del Centro de Estudios Educativos* 3 (3): 11–46.

———, and José T. Guzmán. 1971. "Una Exploración de los Determinates del Rendimiento Escolar en la Educación Primaria." *Revista del Centro de Estudios Educativos* 1 (2): 7–27.

———, and Pedro G. Rodríguez. 1976. Factores Determinantes de los Niveles de Rendimiento Escolar Asociados con Diferentes Caracteristicas Socioeconómicas de los Educandos. Investigación Integrada al Proyecto "Educación y Desarrollo" del Programa ECIEL. Mexico: Centro de Estudios Educativos. Mimeo.

———. 1977a. "Orígen, Distribución y Eficiencia del Gastro Educativo en México." *Revista del Centro de Estudios Educativos*, 7 (3): 1–54.

———. 1977b. *Costos Financiamiento y Eficiencia de la Educación Formal en México*. Mexico: Centro de Estudios Educativos.

NELA (National Educational Law for Adults). 1976. "Ley Nacional de Educación para Adultos." In *Documentos Sobre la Ley Nacional de Educación de Adultos*. Mexico: SEP, pp. 87–90.

Paoli Bolio, F. J. 1986. *Estado y Sociedad en México, 1917–1984*. Mexico: Océano.

PEF (Poder Ejecutivo Federal). 1980. *Plan Global de Desarrollo 1980–1982*. Mexico: PEF.

———. 1984. *Programa Nacional de Educación, Cultura, Recreación y Deporte 1984–1988*. Mexico: SEP.

———. 1989. *Programa para la Modernización Educativa 1989–1994*. Mexico: SEP.

Peña de la Mora, E. 1983. "Educational Innovation and National Development: a Study of the Mexican Parallel Education System for Adults." Unpublished Ph.D. diss., Florida State University.

Pescador, José A. 1977. "El Efecto Redistributivo del Gasto en Educación Superior en México. Una estimación Preliminar." *Revista del Centro de Estudios Educativos* 7 (3): 55–78.

Prawda, Juan. 1989. *Logros, Inequidades y Retos del Futuro del Sistema Educativo Mexicano*. Mexico: Grijalbo.

Puiggrós, Adriana. 1983. *Imperialismo y Educación en América Latina*. Mexico: Nueva Imagen.

Quintero, José L. 1978. "Metas de Igualdad y Efectos de Subsidio de la Educación Superior Mexicana." *Revista del Centro de Estudios Educativos* 8 (3): 59–92.

Reyes Heroles, J. 1983. *Revolución Educativa*. Mexico: Cuadernos SEP.

Reyes Estrada, J. 1990, July. "Viven en Extrema Pobreza 10 de los 30 Millones de Habitantes en el Campo." *Uno Más Uno*, 1: 6.

Rodríguez, Eufrosina and Oscar Zapata. 1985. "La Docencia de Acuerdo a los Supuestos de la Tecnología Educativa." In *Tecnología Educativa*, ed. Universidad Autónoma de Querétaro. Mexico: editor, pp. 13–27.

Rodríguez, Luis A. 1990, October 23. "Aumentaron 100% los casos de desnutrición en el medio rural." *La Jornada*, p. 9.

Rodríguez Castañeda, R. 1990, October 8. "Mexico, Pobre e Injusto; el Destino de los Pobres, Más Pobreza; la Unica Solución, Politica." *Proceso* 727: 6–11.

Rodríguez Reyna, I. 1990, October 2. "Desertaron de la Educación Primaria Entre 1982 y 1989 Más de Seis Millones de Niños." *El Financiero*, p. 41.

Rosenthal, Gert. 1989, March. "Balance Preliminar de la Economía Latinoamericana en 1988." *Comercio Exterior* 39, (3): 235–247.

Rovzar, Eugenio. 1984. "Análisis de las Tendencias en la Distribución del Ingreso en México (1958–1977)." In *La Desigualdad en México*, ed. R. Cordera and C. Tello. Mexico: Siglo XXI, pp. 233–332.

Salinas de Gortari, Carlos. 1989. *Primer Informe de Gobierno. Anexo*. Mexico: Secretería de Programación y Presupuesto.

———. 1990. *Segundo Informe de Gobierno. Anexo*. Mexico: Secretaría de Programación y Presupuesto.

SEP (Secretariat of Public Education). 1974. *Educación Media Básica, Resolución de Chetumal, Plan de Estudios, Programas Generales de Estudio*. Mexico: SEP.

———. 1976. *Documentos Sobre la Ley Nacional de Educación de Adultos. Mexico: SEP.*

———. 1978a. *Estadística Básica del Sistema Educativo Nacional*. Mexico: SEP.

———. 1978b. *Educación Para Todos/5. Metas Preliminares*. Mexico: SEP.

———. 1979a. *Programas y Metas del Sector Educativo 1979–1982*. Mexico: SEP.

———. 1979b. *Educación Para Todos*. Mexico: SEP.

Solana Morales, F. 1980. *La Política de Educativa México en la UNESCO*. Mexico: SEP.

———, R. Cardiel Reyes, and R. Bolaños Martínez, eds. 1981. *Historia de la Educación Pública en México*. Mexico: Fondo de Cultura Económica-SEP.

Vielle, Jean P. 1976. "Planeación y Reforma de la Educación Superior en México, 1970–1976." *Revista del Centro de Estudios Educativos* 6 (4): 9–31.

Yunez Naude, A. 1989, August. "Factores Determinantes de la Balanza Comercial Agropecuaria de México, 1965–1987." *Comercio Exterior*, 39 (8): 674–687.

21

NICARAGUA

Susan Rippberger, Mark B. Ginsburg, and Rolland G. Paulston

This chapter describes educational reform in Nicaragua from the time of Sandino to the present. Reform is viewed in four historical periods identified by the individual or group assuming a leadership role: (1) Augusto Cesar Sandino, the inspirational and ideological forefather of the Sandinistas, who in 1926–1934 fought the U.S. military occupation of Nicaragua; (2) the Somoza family dynasty, which ruled Nicaragua from 1936 to 1979, in accord with the U.S. government and business interests; (3) the Frente Sandinista de Liberacion Nacional (FSLN), which initiated widespread, profound revolutionary reforms from 1979 to 1989; and (4) the Violeta Chamorro government, elected in February 1990 on a neo-liberal platform.

While these reform periods are not equivalent in time frame or scope of reform, they represent fundamental ideological positions on education and the groups whose interests should be served through education.

THE HISTORICAL AND GEOGRAPHICAL SETTING

Much of Nicaragua's history of foreign intervention and domestic exploitation can be traced to its strategic geographic location. Nicaragua, with both Pacific and Atlantic coastlines, is one of the largest countries in Central America (120,254 square kilometers), yet it contains only 27 people per square kilometer (compared to neighboring El Salvador, with nearly 300 people per square kilometer) (Hull, 1990). The land is attractive and rich in agricultural lands, timber, and mineral resources.

Its location and system of rivers and lakes make it an ideal location for an interoceanic canal. During Spanish colonization (1522–1822), Nicaragua was used regularly as an overland transcontinental commercial route for all of Central America, then known as the Kingdom of Guatemala. Richard J. Kraft (1983:80) describes how the possibility of a transcontinental canal has affected U.S.-Nicaraguan relations: "since first seeking a canal route to the North American west coast during the gold rush of the mid–19th century," the U.S. government "has involved itself in setting up and controlling successive Nicaraguan governments."

The western coast of Nicaragua has good agricultural lands and a relatively comfortable climate. This region includes the nation's most fertile croplands, the capital, Managua, most of the important economic and political centers, and almost all the nation's industry. Mestizos and those of European heritage live predominantly on the populated western coast of Nicaragua. In the 1500s the Spanish explorers occupied and colonized the Indian lands in this area. They took over the indigenous population's centralized governmental structure and either eliminated or assimilated those Indians who survived slavery and European diseases. Today the west coast population is Spanish speaking and culturally integrated.

Nicaragua's west and east coast areas are divided by a thinly populated central mountainous region that has acted as a geographic and cultural barrier between the two coasts. The Atlantic coast region, with hot and humid rain forests, swamps, and savannahs, is less able to support a large population. It has only 8 percent of the population and most of the minorities (black and Amerindian). The Spanish, never able to dominate the east coast, eventually abandoned their efforts at colonization. Neither the Spanish language, the Catholic religion, the Spanish patterns of administration, nor Spanish town formation developed there, leaving the Indian and Caribbean black way of life for the most part intact.

The Atlantic coast population later came under the British sphere of influence. From England's Caribbean administrative seat in Jamaica, the British established their presence through trading contacts. The United States also had an economic and cultural impact on the Atlantic coast, creating a market for many of the natural resources of the area such as mahogany, pine, resin, gold, silver, bananas, and ocean turtles. This trade reinforced the use of the English language and strengthened east coast economic ties outside of Nicaragua.

The Spanish explorers and later the Hispanic government of Nicaragua largely ignored the Atlantic coast. It was not until 1860 that this area became a state of Nicaragua as a result of the Treaty of Managua between Nicaragua and the United States. A separatist tendency persists in the Atlantic coastal region; for example, in 1986 the FSLN-led Nicaraguan National Assembly approved an "autonomy" statute that recognizes and guarantees the right of self-government and other specific rights of the indigenous peoples of the country's Atlantic coast.

THE ECONOMIC SETTING

Although Nicaragua is rich in resources, the nation as a whole has not benefited materially. With the notable exception of the 1979–1989 period, the country and its resources have been controlled by Nicaraguan and international elites who have accumulated Nicaragua's wealth for their own benefit. Since the sixteenth century, the economy has been oriented toward external markets. The first Spanish government in Nicaragua used the indigenous population as an inexpensive labor source rather than a consumer market (Walker, 1986).

Because of its policy of dependency and domestic exploitation, and its coveted geographic location, Nicaragua has been a focal point for interventions. Spain, England, and the United States have all actively pursued control of the area. Military interventions were considered justifiable because they were usually at the request of a Nicaraguan government figure.

THE EDUCATIONAL SETTING

Nicaraguan education developed along the lines of most Latin American countries colonized by Spain. Spanish Catholic priests began formal school efforts in the 1500s, but only Spaniards were given access to education beyond the primary level. Female children learned domestic technology and arts through nonformal education at home. Male children of wealthy Nicaraguans frequently returned to Europe for continued formal education.

Along the Atlantic coast the first schools were opened by German Moravian missionaries in the 1840s. Moravian schools were primarily seminars for training the natives to become priests, but they also provided general education for many people. Moravian missionaries taught the indigenous people to read in their own language using Miskito and Sumo translations of the Bible and the Moravian Hymnal.

By the early 1900s, public and private education was highly centralized, under the secretary of public instruction. Primary school subjects were Spanish, arithmetic, geography, history, morals, civic instruction, home economics, music, religion, physical training, gardening, and industrial work. The secondary school curriculum was geared toward the urban middle and upper classes to prepare male children for a university education and/or leadership in business or government.

MAJOR REFORM PERIODS

Education in each reform period is used as an instrument to promote the ideology and politics of the individual or group associated with that period. We have characterized each reform period in Figure 21.1 by its goals and achievements, its opponents, and the short- and long-term effects. Each of the four periods, represented by Sandino, Somoza, the FSLN, and Chamorro, will be discussed in turn.

Figure 21.1
Education Reform Efforts in Nicaragua, 1926–1990

Major Reform Periods	Educational Reform Advocates	Educational Reform Goals	Educational Reform Opponents	Short Term Effects	Long Term Effects
SANDINO	Sandino, peasants, workers	National autonomy, empowerment and liberation through education	U.S. government, Somoza, National Guard	Elimination of literacy training of Sandino's troops, maintenance of elitist education	Influence on Sandinistas for liberation through universal education
SOMOZA	Somoza, U.S. Government, national and international political and business elites	Modernization, efficiency, technical development, expansion in urban areas	FSLN, peasants, workers	Modernization of education in a limited context	Alienation of students, intellectuals
SANDINISTA	FSLN revolutionary government, grassroots organizations, churches, middle class, working class, peasants, women	National sovereignty, the "new person", empowerment, universal education, redistribution of resources, participatory learning methods, ideological orientation to education	Ex-elite, ex-National Guard, U.S. government	Dramatic increase in literacy, doubling of enrollment rates on all levels, new schools built, U.S.-funded Contra war, U.S.-funded opposition party	Constitutional guarantees of educational opportunity, consciousness raising in peasants and working classes
CHAMORRO	U.S. government UNO	Efficiency, elimination of revolutionary ideology	Sandinista party, autonomous universities, teachers	Reduction in adult education programs, reduced funding for education, reintegration into U.S. context and international funding agencies, e.g. USAID	

The Sandino Reform Period

Augusto Cesar Sandino is characterized as a radical humanist; that is, he struggled to overcome man-made inequities and dominance. He led a seven-year guerrilla war against the U.S. Marine occupation of Nicaragua between 1926 and 1933. U.S. troops had previously intervened in Nicaragua in 1894, 1896, 1898, and twice in 1899, and U.S. Marines occupied Nicaragua from 1912 to 1925. Ostensibly, the U.S. military intervened to monitor elections, to protect presidents, and to help the Nicaraguans maintain an orderly system. A field commander in Nicaragua in 1928 (Macaulay, 1967:126–127) illustrates the attitude of U.S. military and government leaders toward the Nicaraguans:

If, as a people, the Nicaraguans had any sense of law, order, honesty and common ordinary decency, there would be no occasion for the United States to lend its assistance to them to straighten out the pathetic mess they have made of their efforts to negotiate the complicated machinery of modern civilization. . . . This is a sorry country and a sorry people and the better Nicaraguan knows that when it becomes a better land, it will be because of the United States and you Marines.

It was also clear that the U.S. military occupation was designed "to protect the interests of the United States" (which should be understood to mean the interests of economic elites in the United States) and to engage in "activity against the outlaw Sandino" (Anon., PACCA, 1984:19).

Sandino's message was patriotic, based on a spiritual sense of brotherhood: "Our cause will triumph because it is the cause of justice, because it is the cause of love" (Fonseca, 1981:35; our translation). He fought for the autonomy of all Nicaraguan citizens, but primarily to expel the U.S. Marines. From his stronghold in the mountains of northern Nicaragua, Sandino declared: "I will not abandon my mountains while one gringo remains in Nicaragua; I will not abandon my fight while my people lack even one right to be rectified. My cause is the cause of my people, the cause of America, the cause of all oppressed peoples" (Fonseca, 1981:17; our translation). Sandino fought for a more equitable distribution of resources, an economic and political balance, and a Nicaraguan people-oriented economy and politics, rather than an export economy that benefited only the wealthy. He condemned his country's subordination to U.S. interests as being in the interest of neither country.

Sandino's program of educational reform was for the purpose of empowerment and liberation. His troops, workers and peasants from rural areas, had little, if any, opportunity for formal education. Sandino established an educational unit in his troops, taught his generals to read, and encouraged literacy for all his fighters. He advocated education as a foundation of government and as the right of all Nicaraguans, female and male, rural and urban (Roman, 1979).

Sandino, like the Sandinistas almost fifty years later, was driven by pragmatism and ideological flexibility and by a desire for radical change based on an ethical and political critique of the status quo. Donald Clark Hodges (1986:20, 23) argues that "Sandino's ideology was fundamentally eclectic. . . . In Sandino's pragmatic approach to belief systems may be found the basis of his ideological pluralism. The more ideologies the better, as long as they served the purpose for which they were intended—mobilizing the people toward a specific goal."

In opposition to Sandino were the U.S. Marines and later their proxy, the U.S.–trained and funded National Guard. This so-called apolitical police force, headed by Anastasio Somoza Garcia, was designed to keep order and maintain stability, as defined by U.S. government and business interests. In 1934, under Somoza's command, the National Guard abducted and assassinated Sandino and destroyed his troops. In 1936 Somoza led a military coup against the elected president, had himself nominated as the Liberal party's candidate for the office in the upcoming elections, and without political opposition took the presidency. The presidency retained strong U.S. government support and remained in the family or among close associates until 1979.

The Somoza Reform Period

Anastasio Somoza Garcia, and later his two sons, Luis and Anastasio, Jr., ruled Nicaragua as faithful (and well-rewarded) supporters of U.S. policy. Because of continued U.S. backing and through their own deviant means, the Somozas were able to amass a fortune, estimated to be over one-half billion dollars (Kraft, 1983:81). By 1979 the Somoza family's land and other economic holdings (in radio and television, banks, construction firms, coffee, cattle, dairy, shipping, airline, mining, cement, textile, fishing, and paper industries, casinos, and drug and blood trafficking) constituted approximately 25 percent of Nicaragua's assets (NACLA, 1976).

The educational system under the Somozas was one of modest expansion and modernization for limited urban areas. "During the Somoza era, education was seen as a tool to train a technical cadre to run the family enterprises and state bureaucracies" (Kraft, 1983:85). Thus, the Somozas took a personal interest in education. In their efforts (or lack thereof) in education, the Somoza regime received considerable support from the United Nations Educational, Scientific, and Cultural Organization (Unesco) and the U.S. government. Loans and grants from the U.S. Agency for International Development (AID) went to expand the number of schools and improve the technical quality of textbooks. These reforms can be seen, however, as oriented more toward preserving existing power relations in Nicaragua and internationally than substantially improving the lives of the Nicaraguan people, particularly those living in rural areas.

While education was free, compulsory, and constitutionally mandated, it remained undeveloped, particularly in the rural areas where illiteracy exceeded 80 percent. Although the rural peasant or "campesino" population comprised 65 percent of the total population, it received only 30 percent of educational funding.

Educational services were heavily concentrated in urban centers of the Pacific coast where literacy averaged about 50 percent (Ramirez, 1987).

The low literacy rate has been attributed to a feudal social system associated with lack of schools, electricity, running water, transportation, communication, and basic health care for the rural population. Cardenal and Miller (1981:4) provide a critical explanation of educational underdevelopment:

The development model of export agriculture depended upon a large pool of unskilled workers, and therefore it neither required nor encouraged an educated labor force. Politically, it was unwise for Somoza to undertake a genuine nationwide literacy program. Basic education would have provided the poor and disenfranchised with the potential tools to analyze and question the unequal power relationships and economic conditions under which they had lived.

While 65 percent of the school-age children attended school, only some 20 percent completed sixth grade. For the peasant population, only 5 percent finished primary school. Fifteen percent of the population attended high school, leaving very few prepared for higher education. In 1978 only 7.4 percent of students enrolled at the university were children of working class, while approximately 75 percent came from the upper class (Lopez, 1979:138). Higher education had traditionally focused on the humanities, philosophy, and law, rather than on the country's technical or social development needs.

It was against this calculated, structured inequity that the FSLN began to gather support from all levels of society in the 1970s. Opposition continued to grow as U.S. dependency tightened and Somoza's self-serving policies (e.g., pocketing much of the international aid received and tricking central Managua property owners out of their holdings following the 1972 earthquake) alienated virtually all sectors of Nicaraguan society. The FSLN, through a tolerance for diversity, incorporated all social sectors into their revolutionary movement for the eventual overthrow of Somoza.

The Sandinista Reform Period

The insurrection and revolution of the FSLN began in 1961 as a university-based organization, the Frente de Estudiantes Revolucionarios, but later attracted mass support from campesinos, the working class, and many segments of the capitalist and middle classes. The FSLN took its name and a major part of its ideology from Sandino. Sandinismo is a unique combination of revolutionary theories and practices. Bayardo Arce, when asked, ''In Nicaragua there are fighting units that affirm that the revolution is socialist, others say it's Marxist, or Leninist, etc. Could you define the character of the revolution?'' he answered: ''It's Sandinista'' (Lopez, 1979:63, our translation). Like Sandino, the FSLN articulated the desire for an autonomous nation working for the good of all its citizens and used education as a means to empower those previously marginalized or ignored under dependency.

The Sandinistas led a campaign of ideological pluralism. In contrast to Somoza's fear of public organization and opposition, the FSLN organized drives to raise union membership. They passed laws abolishing capital punishment and guaranteeing freedom of speech and association, the right to join unions, freedom of religion, equal rights for women, and the rights of blacks and Indians to their own languages, traditions, and cultures. Christian grass-roots communities organized and thrived (Cardenal, 1983).

For the Sandinistas, pragmatism was more important than ideological purity. Hodges (1986:291) observes: "What counts in practice is the mutual reinforcement of Sandinismo, Marxism, and Christianity, despite their inconsistency on selected issues. The ideological pluralism of the FSLN has had a strategical objective–the forging of a broad alliance for revolution unobstructed by ideological differences."

Since 1979, the Sandinistas have involved many Nicaraguans in all stages of educational planning and implementation. The new government surveyed 50,000 representatives from 30 grass-roots community organizations with differment social, political, and religious orientations. From this survey, they developed the basic principles of the new educational system. The Sandinistas considered the concerns and aspirations of the people in determining the skills and values education should promote (Arrien, 1985). From the national survey four major goals for educational policy resulted: (1) a structural transformation of the society, (2) a productive way of life for the development of the new society, (3) an incorporation of the basic principles of the Sandinista revolution (populist, democratic, nationalistic, and anti-imperialist, for the self-determination and independence of Nicaragua), and (4) an understanding of the ideology and example of the heroes and martyrs of the revolution (Arrien, 1985).

The educational objectives derived from these four fundamental policy goals include strengthening national identity; associating teaching and research with the lives of the people; promoting respect for individual rights; stimulating a liberating conscience and an analytical, critical, and participatory capacity in students; offering humanistic, political training; strengthening national identity; and preparing human resources for the development of the country (Arrien, 1985). Specific curricular changes involved more technical training, a greater amount and variety of instructional materials, and varied teaching methods. New pedagogical methods included group discussion, bibliographic and field research, and active participation in work projects in conjunction with academic learning. The Ministry of Education developed and evaluated new educational materials to reflect the society's new image (Arrien, 1985). In contrast to the former regime, the Sandinista government encouraged the development of a literate and informed populace capable of participation in the work and politics of the nation. Nationwide literacy was one of the highest priorities in the National Development Plan for Nicaragua.

Two weeks after the Sandinista-led Government of National Reconstruction took power in 1979, it launched a literacy crusade. Embracing widespread enthusiasm of the Sandinista triumph, approximately 225,000 (out of a population of 2.4 million) volunteers worked for the literacy campaign. They brought educational materials and supplies to develop reading and writing abilities among the rural and urban poor. The experience built solidarity between urban elite and middle classes and the rural poor, where all obtained first-hand exposure to the gaping economic and educational differences of their society (Sanders, 1983). R. Arnove (1986:245) reports on the perspective of the Ministry of Education:

to carry out a literacy project and consolidate it with a level of education equivalent to the first grades of primary school, is to democratize a society. It gives the popular masses the first instruments needed to develop awareness of their exploitation and to fight for liberation. Therefore, literacy training was something that the dictatorship would not accept without contradicting itself.

Functional literacy (defined as reading at a third grade level) for 50 percent or more of the population was a primary educational goal of the literacy campaign. Within six months the national literacy rate increased from 48 to 87 percent, meaning that approximately 500,000 previously illiterate youth and adults were able to pass the designated examinations and write simple sentences (Rudolph, 1982). In recognition of progress made, Unesco awarded Nicaragua the Literacy Prize for 1980.

The Ministry of Education offered a bilingual, bicultural educational program in an attempt to integrate the Atlantic coast groups into the political and social mainstream of the country, and to nurture a respect for their cultural individuality. They taught literacy skills in Spanish, English, Miskito, and Sumo. They revised materials for the literacy campaign to reflect the language, lifestyle, and locale of the Indians, and they trained members of the local population to work as instructors for their own indigenous groups, using the native languages (Arnove, 1986).

The national literacy crusade continued throughout the era of FSLN political dominance with special programs and classes to maintain literacy for adults. The Ministry of Education created the Peasant's Agricultural School, providing basic training in agriculture and animal husbandry techniques. For urban areas, the Accelerated Elementary School served laborers in urban areas with intensive night courses (Arrien, 1985).

The Sandinista government tried to create a new society by instilling pride in Nicaraguan history and culture. It promoted the values of collectivism, austerity, and hard work to facilitate national reconstruction and development following centuries of feudalism and underdevelopment and a decade of civil war. The government extended education to the majority, offering the means of advancement to all Nicaraguans. In seeking to create the "new person," the government combined productive labor with academic studies, recreational activities, political socialization, and cultural awareness.

Beginning with the literacy campaign, the FSLN, albeit sometimes hesitantly, promoted equal status for women. People learned to identify and discuss gender oppression and exploitation as a consequence of structural domination and subordination. Women began to participate on all levels of the campaign. Their visibility in participating equally with men was important as a concrete example of the "new person." Mass organizations drew women into the mainstream of political activity in reconstructing the nation. These organizations created a forum that encouraged women to participate in shaping social change and helped to remove impediments to equality. Some of their achievements were equal pay for equal work and the legal right to hold land titles. While progress has been made in the male-oriented society, the rhetoric of gender equality remains an ideal that has not yet been fully realized.

In order to promote a more democratic educational system that would reach students from all social and economic levels, the Sandinista government hired and trained thousands of new teachers, and built nearly 4,000 new classrooms, 95 percent of which were constructed in rural areas (Ramirez, 1987). Between 1979 and 1982, the Sandinista government built eight additional normal schools, increasing the number of teachers from approximately 12,000 to 42,000. School attendance increased correspondingly, almost doubling on every level, preschool through university (Valenta and Duran, 1987).

With the rapid increase in students, a teacher shortage arose. In many ways the government encouraged people to teach, but the number of teachers did not keep pace with expanding education. The government increased the social recognition and status of teachers, and raised salaries to that of comparable professionals. It decentralized training for teachers in an effort to find local teachers for local schools. The Ministry of Education implemented alternative methods of teacher training such as Saturday classes, mobile teacher education units that traveled to distant, inaccessible areas, and group correspondence courses.

The government expanded and refocused the program offerings in higher education. Through a policy of open enrollment and reduced tuition costs, the size of the student body doubled. Enrollment in science and technology programs increased by 15 to 18 percent, while enrollment in the humanities declined by 35 percent (Paulston and Rippberger, 1991).

Opposition from the U.S. government interrupted this period of educational growth. In seeking to overthrow the Sandinista government through counterrevolutionary forces and an economic embargo, the United States slowed and eventually reversed many of the Sandinistas' achievements in education. The decade-long trade embargo and the Contra war ravaged the nation's infrastructure and subverted funds and resources to defense.

By 1987, defense consumed 50 percent of the national budget, severely limiting the material achievements of reconstruction and development. The literacy rate of 88 percent attained immediately after the revolution fell to approximately 78 percent (*Barricada Internacional*, April 7, 1990). The dropout rate rose to 50 percent, and construction stopped on 25 percent of the rural schools (Ramirez, 1987). This situation was exacerbated as the Contras singled out and sought to kill teachers, health workers, and agricultural cooperative members as models of Sandinista success. The Contras seriously damaged or destroyed over 50 schools and killed 400 literacy teachers. Inflation rose from 200 percent into the thousands between 1985 and 1987, eroding the substantial wage gains teachers (and other workers) had made after the revolution.

The Chamorro Reform Period

In this context, the Sandinistas won against six opposition parties in 1984. By the March 1990 national elections, the economic situation had deteriorated much further, and the Sandinistas were defeated by a coalition of leftist and rightist parties, the United Nicaraguan Opposition (UNO), dominated by the right and led at least symbolically by Violeta Chamorro. Americans living in Nicaragua commented on the elections:

"Elections 1990" took place on the tail end of eight years of contra aggression waged against Nicaraguan people by the United States. In both the city and the countryside it appears that many Nicaraguans voted against the FSLN in the believe that only an UNO victory could bring peace and prosperity (*Nicaragua Through Our Eyes*, March/April 1990:1).

Many also feel the Sandinistas lost the election because they were out of touch with grass-roots levels, overly authoritarian, and too self-assured.

Chamorro's campaign cry, "No los aguantamos!" ("We're not going to take it anymore!"(Cruz and Falcoff, 1990:30) voices the desire for a break with the past, that is, an end to the radical changes implemented by the Sandinistas and an end to the war, the draft, inflation, the U.S. trade embargo, and the growing arrogance of the FSLN.

The emerging Chamorro administration is marked by renewed compliance with the economic authority of the United States and may include a partial reinstatement of dependency. It is noted in *Nicaragua Through Our Eyes* (1990, 4 [5/6]:1) that UNO "has tendered to the voters a program of change which would reverse many of the Sandinistas' accomplishments while reestablishing Nicaragua's pre-1979 dependence on the U.S." The U.S. government participated in the presidential election through funding for the opposition party and through promises to end the war, lift the embargo, and renew economic aid.

Cruz and Falcoff (1990:36) explain the influence of the U.S. dollar:

that Mrs. Chamorro was identified as "the candidate of the United States," far from being a disability, was perhaps her greatest asset. . . . Most Nicaraguans . . . actually like and admire the United States, and wish to intensify the relationships as much as possible. . . . Ortega even found it necessary (in a somewhat twisted fashion) to compete with Mrs. Chamorro for the role of the leader who could "deliver" Washington's resources and support.

While the new government has been in operation less than six months, it has cut educational funding and reduced adult education programs. The universities, which traditionally supported the Sandinistas, fear cuts in funding for scholarships and educational programs. They also fear that degrees earned after 1979 may be declared invalid. Private university subsidies from the government, if cut, would once again make higher education accessibly only to the wealthy (*Barricada Internacional*, March 24, 1990).

Sandinista education has been described by the Chamorro government as "totalitarian indoctrination, aimed at destroying the family and religious values" (Hackel, 1990:A39). Accordingly, in May the Ministry of Education announced that Nicaragua's elementary and secondary textbooks would be exchanged for others written abroad and that this effort would be funded by USAID. However, because of opposition from teachers, the Chamorro administration eventually decided not to substitute the books. Instead the Ministry of Education decided to revise current textbooks to promote UNO's neoliberal values (*Barricada Internacional*, June 16, 1990).

The Chamorro government plans to orient education toward a more peaceful, stable, and settled process, while removing the revolutionary ideological content. UNO opponents see this move as promoting a more passive, less participatory education, which may generate less active, assertive attitudes among the Nicaraguan populace. The FSLN party sees the textbook change as related to UNO's larger neoliberal political and economic objectives to introduce a free market economy and privatization:

The FSLN sees their educational reform dissolving: In import, then, UNO's vision of the future is perfectly clear–it is to erode and finally erase the essential features of the Revolution's mixed economy system, reintroducing a variant of the market capitalism that generated Nicaragua's historic social inequities. This can only be a prelude to reversing the rest of the Nicaraguan Revolution, in particular the organization of the popular sectors that represents the backbone of the revolutionary process (*Barricada Internacional*, June 16, 1990:9).

CONCLUSION

Struggle between opposing currents of ideology in Nicaragua and the intervention of the U.S. government have formed the basis for much of Nicaragua's educational reform during this century. The struggle is characterized by a conflict between the preservation of structured inequality on the political right and radical structural change on the left.

The conservative or functionalist viewpoint, the ideological basis of Somoza and Chamorro, is accompanied by the economic and political cooperation of the U.S. government. Their ideological position is manifested in a preoccupation with order and maintenance of an efficient system. Reform is defined in terms of modest, technical, incremental change. Therefore, for Somoza and Chamorro educational reform is seen not so much as a need for a change in structure, but as a need for order, stability, and a protection of privilege.

Sandino and the Sandinistas represented an opposition to the status quo, seeing in it inequity and indignity for the majority of Nicaraguan people. They sought popular support based on national autonomy, a more democratic basis of power, and a more equitable distribution of national resources. This is evidenced by their support for consciousness-raising where those habitually without power were encouraged to find a voice. Grass-roots organizations, volunteer organizations, and liberation theology sectors within the Catholic Church, all supported the Sandinista goals.

As a transitional government, the Chamorro administration appears to be seeking a synthesis, a new ideological pluralism, where Nicaragua can approach independence and autonomy, yet return to a more structured class system and maintain strong U.S. economic, political, and military ties. While some rolling back of Sandinista policy and reform is taking place, a complete reversal is unlikely. The UNO party has a sense of pragmatism and some tolerance for diversity (Quest for Peace, 1990).

Many of the changes instituted by the FSLN to democratize the nation have been made constitutional. The desire for personal and national autonomy, cultivated by the Sandinista-led government, cannot be taken away. Susanne Jonas (1990:11–12) summarizes the enduring nature of Sandinista reform:

Following two decades of upheaval before the Sandinista triumph in 1979, the struggles of the last ten years have seen advances and setbacks. But above all, these revolutionary processes have permanently transformed the region and its people, and they can be expected to continue into the future, albeit in new forms. . . . The material achievements of the Revolution were limited from the start, and some were reversed, by the U.S. determination to turn a positive example into a negative example; but other aspects of the Revolution have been institutionalized (primarily in the Constitution) to the point that they can be rolled back only by further violence. The Sandinistas laid the bases for a profound democratization of Nicaraguan society, and undertook a unique experiment in revolutionary pluralism, based on the integration of representatives with the popular/ participatory democracy.

Such an analysis may be overly optimistic or pessimistic (depending on one's perspective on the Sandinista revolution), but we should also recall that many aspects of the educational reform were retarded, deflected, and aborted in the face of U.S. government military intervention (by proxy) and economic sanctions. Thus, in some ways what the Chamorro-led government inherits also resembles the educational system put in place during the early Somoza era. In any case, we assume that education and attempts to reform it will continue to occupy a central place in the local, national, and global political and economic struggles within Nicaragua.

REFERENCES

Anonymous. 1984. "Policy Alternatives for the Caribbean and Central America (PACCA)." Changing Course: Blueprint for Peace in Central America and the Caribbean. Washington, D.C.: Institute for Policy Studies.
———. 1990. "20–20 Hindsight: Anatomy of the FSLN Defeat." *Nicaragua Through Our Eyes* 5(1):1–7.
———. 1990, April 7. "Constitution Sets the Limits of Change." *Barricada Internacional* 7:6–7.
———. 1990. "Elections 1990: Process, Positions and Possibilities." *Nicaragua Through Our Eyes* 4(5 & 6):1–7.
———. 1990, July. "In Search of an Answer: The Polemic among the Sandinista Grassroots Membership." *Barricada Internacional* 14(8).
———. 1990, June. "Neoliberalism in the Classroom." *Barricada Internacional* 16:8.
———. 1990, May. "Nicaragua." Quixote Center/Quest for Peace.
———. 1990. "The Opposition: 'UNO'—What Sort of Change?" *Nicaragua Through Our Eyes* 6(5 & 6):8–10.
———. 1990, July. "The Revolution and the Electoral Defeat." *Barricada Internacional* 14:1–7.
———. 1990, March. "Universities Waiting to See." *Barricada Internacional* 24:7.
Arnove, R. 1986. *Education and Revolution in Nicaragua.* New York: Praeger Publishers.
———. 1988. "Education and Revolutionary Transformation in Nicaragua." Paper presented at the annual meeting of the Midwest Association of the Latin American Studies Association, Bloomington, Ind.
———, and A. Dewees. 1990. "Teacher Education in Revolutionary Nicaragua." In *Fit to Teach: Teacher Education in International Perspective*, ed. E. Gumbert. Atlanta, Georgia: Center for Cross-Cultural Education.
Arrien J. 1985. "Nicaragua: System of Education." In *The International Encyclopedia of Education*, vol. 6, ed. T. Husen and T. Postlethwaite. New York: Pergamon Press.
Aulestia, J. 1983. "Nicaragua." *Integrated Education* 20:29–31.
Belausteguigoitia, R. 1981. *Con Sandino en Nicaragua.* Nicaragua: Editorial Nueva Nicaragua.
Cardenal, E. 1983. "Toward a New Democracy of Culture." In *The Nicaraguan Reader: Documents of a Revolution Under Fire*, ed. P. Rosset and J. Vandermeer. New York: Grove Press.
Cardenal, F., and V. Miller. 1981. "Nicaragua 1980: The Battle of the ABCs." *Harvard Educational Review* 51 (1):1–16.
Carnoy, M., and J. Samoff. 1990. *Education and Social Transition in the Third World.* Princeton, N.J.: Princeton University Press.
Cruz, A., and M. Falcoff. 1990. "Who Won Nicaragua?" *Commentary* 89(5):31–38.
Docherty, F. 1988. "Educational Provision for Ethnic Minority Groups in Nicaragua." *Comparative Education* 24(2):193–201.
Escobar, J. 1980. *Ideario Sandinista.* Managua: Secretaria Nacional de Propaganda y Educacion Politica del FSLN.
Fonseca, C. 1980. *Sandino Guerrillero Proletario.* Managua: Secretaria Nacional de Propaganda y Educacion Politica del FSLN.

————. 1981. *Ideario Politico del General Augusto Cesar Sandino*. Managua: Secretaria Nacional de Propaganda y Educacion Politica del FSLN.

Hackel, J. 1990, March. "Nicaragua's Universities Prepare for a New Wave of Conservatism in Wake of Chamorro Victory." *Chronicle of Higher Education* 21:39,A42.

Hodges, D. 1986. *Intellectual Foundations of the Nicaraguan Revolution*. Austin: University of Texas Press.

Hull, J. 1990, August. "Nicaragua Land Battles Challenge Chamorro." *The Christian Science Monitor* 21:7.

Hurtado, A. 1984. *Sandino Desconocido*. Costa Rica: Ediciones Populares Nicaraguenses.

Jonas, S. 1990, June. "Central America in the Balance: Prospects for the 1990s." *Monthly Review*:11–24.

Kraft, R. 1983. "Nicaragua's Educational Opportunity Under Pre- and Post-Revolutionary Conditions." In *Politics and Education*, ed. R. M. Thomas. New York: Pergamon Press.

LaFeber, W. 1983. *Inevitable Revolutions*. New York: W. W. Norton.

Lopez, A. 1979. "La UCA ante el processo revolucionario Nicaraguense." *Encuentro*, Special Edition.

Lozano, L. 1985. *De Sandino al Triunfo de la Revolucion*. México: Siglo Veintiuno editores, S.A. de C.V.

Macaulay, N. 1967. *The Sandino Affair*. Durham, N.C.: Duke University Press.

Macruc, B., ed. 1985. *Nicaragua: The Sandinista People's Revolution*. New York: Pathfinder Press.

NACLA. 1976. "Nicaragua." *Latin America and Empire Report* 1(2):2–40.

Paulston, R., and S. Rippberger. 1991. "Ideological Pluralism in Nicaraguan University Reform." *Understanding Reform in Global Context*, ed. Mark Ginsburg. New York: Garland Publishing, pp. 179–200.

Ramirez, S. 1987. "The Political-Educational Plan of the Sandinista Popular Revolution." Inaugural Report to the Fourth National Congress of the National Association of Nicaraguan Educators, Managua.

Roman, J. 1979. *Maldito Pais*. Nicaragua: Ediciones INPRHU.

Rosset, P., and J. Vandermeer. 1983. *The Nicaragua Reader: Documents of a Revolution under Fire*. New York: Grove Press.

Ruccio, D. 1988. "State, Class, and Transition in Nicaragua." *Latin American Perspectives* 15(2):50–71.

Rudolph, J., ed. 1982. *Nicaragua: A Country Study*. Washington, D.C.: American University.

Sanders, W. 1983. "Literacy Crusades and Revolutionary Governments: The Cases of Cuba, 1961 and Nicaragua, 1980." Washington, D.C.: Department of Education.

Sandino, A. 1980. *Escritos Literarios y Documentos Desconocidos*. Managua: Ministerio de Cultura.

Selsor, G. 1984. *Nicaragua de Walker a Somoza*. Méxio: Mex Sur Editorial S.A.

Somoza, A. 1936. *El Verdadero Sandino o El Calvario de Las Segovias*. Managua: Tipografia Robelo.

Urbina, M. 1972. *Educacion para la modernizacion en Nicaragua*. Argentina: Editorial Paidos.

Valenta, J., and E. Duran, eds. 1987. *Conflict in Nicaragua*. London: Allen and Unwin.

Walker, T. 1986. *Nicaragua: The Land of Sandino*. Boulder, Colo.: Westview Press.

————, ed. 1985. *Nicaragua: The First Five Years*. New York: Praeger Publishers.

22

NORWAY

Val D. Rust

For the past two centuries Norwegian education has been in a state of continual transition, because educational reform has been a characteristic of the system since the country gained independence from Denmark in 1914. Throughout Norway's modern history, a number of reform cycles have been initiated and brought to successful conclusion; however, each reform cycle has typically barely begun to be implemented before another reform cycle has been set into motion. Until the early 1970s all reform cycles had focused on a single major issue: structural reform. Norway had inherited a dualistic school structure characterizing education throughout Europe. Such a structure reflected the socially stratified societies of the major nation-states and tended to reinforce social stratification, even in those countries, such as Norway, where social stratification was not so pronounced.

Even though it has taken more than a century for Norwegian reformers to accomplish their structural reform objectives, when compared with most Western European countries, the Norwegians have been eminently successful. Norway is one of the few countries that can claim that the comprehensive school reform era is behind it, that it has entered into a "postcomprehensive era" in educational reform (Marklund, 1981). Popular myth suggests that a primary reason Norway has been so successful in school reform has been that the Labor party has been in power for almost half a century. Without question, the Labor party was instrumental in establishing Norway's welfare state, but it did not come to dominate politics until the 1930s, almost half a century after Norway had adopted a five-year national common school and over a decade after it had instituted a seven-year common school. Even after the Labor party came into power, subsequent structural reform in education was largely a bipartisan enterprise.

A more reasonable explanation for Norway's success could undoubtedly be traced to the tasks it faced. Whereas most European countries have attempted to use common school reform to help break down social class differences, the Norwegians have turned to school reform in order to align their schools with the social conditions that already exist. Norwegian society is relatively homogeneous and has possessed neither significant ethnic minorities nor sharply divided social classes. Norway was able to escape a feudal phase in its historical development; it has not had an aristocracy; and its underprivileged cotter class quickly disappeared after it gained the right to own land and become part of the electorate. Over time the social classes have become even more integrated, until today the social structure is relatively flat. This is well reflected in the salary scales, which are relatively undifferentiated. In fact, the average income of the highest professional classes is only about 60 percent higher than the average income of unskilled workers (Central Bureau of Statistics of Norway, 1988).

Norwegians have not intended their educational reforms to alter Norway's basic social fabric but to help their schools better reflect existing social conditions (Rust, 1989). The aims of past Norwegian school reform have been defined in such a way that it would reinforce a sense of social unity (*enhet*), helping all members of society to feel comfortable living, associating, and working with all other members.

A second explanation for Norway's success has to do with its policy formation process. Politically speaking, Norwegians have been able to resolve political conflicts and work harmoniously more easily than has been the case in most European countries (Elder, Thomas, and Arter, 1982). Such an observation is not intended to imply that controversy and conflict do not exist in the political arena, as illustrated by the teacher strikes of 1987–1988 over wage disputes. In fact, from an internal perspective Norwegians see their society as being very conflictual; from an outsider's perspective, however, the conflicts appear to be relatively tempered and to fall within a rather narrow spectrum. In addition, Norway's mode of policy formation, known generally as corporatism, has not been so susceptible to the whims of wide-open interest group politics but has reserved a special role to teachers, school administrators, and university professors to dictate what would occur in educational reform (Rust, 1990). In certain respects, such a practice has tempered the reform process, but it has also not made it vulnerable to popular issues portrayed in the media and broader public, so that reform has held a steady and incremental course over the past century.

HISTORICAL TRENDS IN EDUCATIONAL REFORM

In order to accomplish the unifying aims of education, Norway adopted an orientation that would be considered radical by most external observers. Administratively, the country moved from a decentralized administrative structure in the nineteenth century to a highly centralized structure in the twentieth century.

This shift was particularly stressed when the Labor party gained control of politics in the 1930s, so that by the 1970s almost all elements of education in Norway, including its curriculum and examination system, were centrally defined and determined.

In terms of the sponsorship of schooling, even though private schooling played a major role in nineteenth-century Norway, the press toward uniformity eventually led to the decline of private schooling to the point that, by 1970, less than 1 percent of all primary school and less than 2 percent of all secondary school youth were attending private schools (Rust, 1984).

In terms of attendance regulations, Norway has the distinction of having instituted universal schooling at a very early date in Western history. By the mid–1700s, all children appear to have participated in some form of schooling. Reading literacy was universal by the beginning of the nineteenth century (Tveit, undated). Compulsory attendance laws have been extended until currently all young people must attend through the end of the nine-year basic school. In addition, all young people now possess a statutory right to education for at least three years of upper secondary education (Ministry of Church and Education, 1974, Art. 8). Approximately 90 percent of all youth remain in some form of education or training; upper secondary school has become a universal reality for almost all youth in Norway. The most important educational shift that has occurred in Norway, however, came with the abolishment of the dualistic school structure and the adoption of a comprehensive school structure.

THE BASIC SCHOOL

The major educational reform symbol intending to reflect a culturally integrated society has been some form of comprehensive school structure that would provide a common schooling experience for all. Norway was one of the few countries that developed a common primary school tradition prior to the turn of the twentieth century. We recall that countries such as England, France, Denmark, and Germany would not adopt such a plan until the 1930s and 1940s. In spite of delays attributable to the terrible events of World War II, Norway was able to adopt a nine-year common school policy by 1959 and actually mandate such schools on a universal basis in 1969. Of course, structural unity was necessary to achieve an objective of unity, but important internal elements were also imperative. Unity in the curriculum was generally defined as "sameness." Everyone in the nine-year basic school was to be exposed to essentially the same program of studies having the same content. The ideal was that all children, throughout the country, would have a genuinely common school experience, regardless of geographic location, social background, or intellectual capacity.

THE UPPER SECONDARY SCHOOL

Historical reform issues surrounding the upper secondary school have also been guided by cultural integration imperatives. However, "sameness" could not be the guiding rule to curricular programs, because the Norwegians recognized the necessity to address various career interests; consequently, cultural integration took on a different dimension at the upper secondary level. In Norway, as elsewhere in Europe, the practical vocations have traditionally been relegated to a second-class status, while academic, liberal arts programs have maintained higher value. The comprehensive school reforms initiated mainly by the Labor-dominated governments since the early 1930s have attempted to break down this status difference. The secondary school act of 1974 aimed to join the two forms of education under a single roof at the upper secondary level and to give equal status to practical and theoretical education. In addition, the 1974 law was structured in such a way that the choice students would make in terms of course of upper secondary study would no longer have such permanent consequences, because all branches of study would allow students, at least in theory, to proceed to higher education studies. Eight branches of study were designed: general education, manual and industrial studies, arts and crafts, fishing and maritime studies, sports, clerical and commercial studies, domestic arts and sciences, social and health studies.

All branches had the same structure, consisting of one- or two-year foundation courses and continuation studies (I and II) each lasting one year. The two-year foundation course combined the one-year vocational course with another year of general education. The programs were flexible in that they allowed pupils to finish a program after one, two, or three years of study.

The Norwegian upper secondary school model represents a middle ground between the two major vocational education models in Europe. Whereas the West German model requires young people to attend formal school one full day and to be under supervision in the work environment for the rest of each week, and the French model places young people full time in formal schooling at least to the end of compulsory attendance before they become full-time vocational students, the Norwegians have structured their system so that a full range of options between the French and German models are available. However, three full years of upper secondary schooling are necessary for a student to become eligible for higher education study.

In many respects, the struggle for structural reform, which has given focus and meaning to educational reforms for the past century, has come to a successful conclusion. And yet, during the 1980s Norway has been engaged in a reform discussion as lively and volatile as at any time in its history (e.g., Bergersen et al., 1988; Riksaasen, 1988). On the surface, the educational reform debates sound very familiar in that they focus on rather common international trends, including declining government revenues that can be directed to education, growing unrest among teachers, and claims that standards have fallen and that edu-

cational "quality" must be restored. However, Norway is charting a response
to these demands that deviate from countries such as the United States and Great
Britain (e.g, Rust and Blakemore, 1990). The above summary is intended to
provide some context for the current reform debate taking place in Norway. We
will begin by suggesting a number of general environmental elements that come
into play. We will then look at the educational innovations and debates
themselves.

CONTEMPORARY FORCES FOR EDUCATIONAL CHANGE

We have already noted that the major historical forces determining school
policy have been cultural integration forces. In spite of the fact that other forces
are now entering the picture, cultural integration forces remain paramount. The
values of cultural integration have long been toward equity and unity, and in
the past two decades a good deal of evidence has emerged showing that structural
reforms have fallen short in bringing about the kind of educational unity and
equity envisioned in earlier educational reform endeavors. Social classes remain
separated in educational programs to some degree, and educational differences
continue in spite of heroic efforts to abolish them. These differences manifest
themselves on several fronts. There remain clear differences in educational
achievement across social class groups. Great educational achievement differences between various geographic regions also persist, even when controlling
for social class. Fortunately, however, these differences have been reduced over
time. For example, from 1951 until 1978 the number of children of fishermen
passing the secondary school-leaving examination increased by a factor of 8.4,
while the number of children of professionals and teachers increased only by a
factor of 1.3 (Aamodt, 1982: 81).

Differences between the sexes also continue. Whereas differences in achievement between boys and girls through upper secondary school have been eliminated, great differences remain with regard to advanced educational
accomplishments and in the occupations boys and girls choose to engage in.

Those committed to cultural integration recognize that structural and curricular integration efforts have achieved about all they are able to achieve.
Consequently, during the past two decades those interest groups have begun
to explore other means of further reducing differences created by social and
sexual backgrounds.

At the same time, a new voice has emerged in the cultural integration debate,
arising mainly from two sources. First, Norway has been sensitized to international discourse and action against a highly nationalistic orientation of unity and
sameness. This plays itself out in two directions. On the one hand, there is
movement toward greater recognition of local cultural variance. Norway, as a
party to the international community, has not been insensitive to this movement,
even though less than 1 percent of Norway's indigenous population belongs to
a conventional minority group, known internationally as the Lapps and internally

as the Samer. This group, living generally in the far north of the country, has never had a voice in politics, and the major orientation of Norway toward the Lapps has long been to integrate them into the mainstream society by instilling in them a sense of devotion to Christianity and the Lutheran Church and by requiring them to learn the Norwegian language. In addition, in the past two decades an immigrant group entered into the picture as a small number of refugees, approximately 10,000, from Pakistan entered the country. At first, the Norwegians also attempted to impose their policy of integration on the Pakistanis, but the Pakistanis resisted those attempts (Awan, 1987). The Pakistani presence, along with international cries for recognition of cultural differences, have led Norwegian policymakers to become more sensitive to variance and to see that their policies toward *enhet* were somewhat naive.

On the other hand, Norway has been very sensitive to the internationalizing forces taking place around it. Of particular importance is the decision on the part of Economic Community countries to create a free market system without national boundaries and to allow people to move freely within that system for occupational and educational purposes. The so-called Single European Act, which goes into effect in 1992, forms the basis for this development. The Norwegians recognize that, if the country is to remain competitive and viable, it too must work to instill a sense of "European citizenship" as much as Norwegian citizenship in the youth and ensure that the academic and vocational standards of its youth are integrated with European standards (Bjorndal, 1990).

Even though contemporary reform impulses continue to center on cultural integration issues, a somewhat new voice has arisen in the name of outspoken, vigorous, and generally conservative economic interests. Certainly, economic interests have been served in the past, but they have rarely dominated cultural integration interests. Norway finds itself in the middle of a debate somewhat similar to that taking place throughout the industrialized world, where governments are seeking effective policies for enhancing economic productivity through education and employing economic incentives to promote the productivity of schooling. The focus is not only reflected in shifts in political parties, but economic-oriented interest groups have been able to gain control of aspects of the educational discussion and have begun to formulate economically based policies. These policies promise to make schools more effective while receiving less money, and ultimately to help enhance the national economy. Economically oriented critics of the schools claim that educational costs have skyrocketed while achievement standards have fallen. They state that Norway has entered a period of fiscal austerity, which means there is a shrinking amount of money available for education. The solution is that the school system must operate more efficiently while at the same time reversing the trend toward slipping standards. It must be pointed out that the economically driven Norwegian debate is much more tempered than in countries such as Great Britain, and as yet there is almost no discourse on the "evils" of social welfare and the need to dismantle the welfare state. Curiously, cultural integration and economic interests have coalesced in terms of certain specific proposals that are under discussion.

SPECIFIC FORMS OF CONTEMPORARY EDUCATIONAL REFORM

System Integration

One of the curious historical aspects of Norwegian education is that the government has always dealt with it in a piecemeal fashion, which has never allowed the educational system to be treated as a unified whole. Commissions and laws have emerged that deal separately with such aspects as the primary school curriculum, vocational education, private schooling, upper secondary schooling, teacher training, and special education. Legislation regarding one aspect of education has historically set off a series of commissions and laws that have attempted to adjust other aspects of the system to the earlier changes; these adjustments would usually ricochet back on the other parts of the system. The Norwegian response to educational reform has never quite allowed it to deal with education as an integrated system. In addition, the educational enterprise has been under different ministerial jurisdictions. It was not until 1939 that vocational education was considered to be a part of the educational system and finally received appropriate legislation coming out of the Ministry of Church and Education, which is responsible for primary and secondary education. Even today kindergartens are considered to be social welfare institutions, and they fall under the jurisdiction of the Ministry of Consumer Affairs and Government Administration. Tertiary education has fallen under the jurisdiction of the Ministry of Culture and Science.

In 1989 two major innovations came about that promise to change all of this. These innovations appear not to have been ideologically charged but were technocratic in nature. That is, it has long been apparent that the system was too fragmented and disjointed to operate smoothly.

The first innovation is represented by a new Ministry of Education, called the Ministry of Education and Research (*Utdannings- og forskningsdepartementet*), which brings together all educational aspects of the old ministries devoted to primary, secondary, and higher education. The only important element of the entire educational enterprise that now remains outside a single ministerial body is the kindergarten. While, in some respects, such an arrangement complicates the administrative structure, it also sorts out many religious and cultural elements that have not been directly related to the educational enterprise, and it does provide a better base for allocating resources to the various segments of the educational system and for improving relations between them. Innovations and reforms can also be introduced in a more coordinated and planned manner.

Coinciding with administrative streamlining has come the first comprehensive education act in the history of the country (Ministry of Church and Education,

1988–1989). The bill states the overall goal of education, including developing
the Norwegian culture, preserving the environment, furthering equality and democracy, contributing to international coexistence, and creating new economic
growth and occupational opportunities for everyone. The bill addresses new
innovations at all levels of schooling, spelling out curricular innovations, relations between schools and outside agencies, and the connections of educational
activities from one level to another in an attempt to conceptualize a fully integrated and functioning system. Consequently, Norway has a mechanism for
dealing with anomalies such as pushing the age of entrance into the system from
seven down to the more conventional six years, extending the age of compulsory
attendance to ten years, and implementing curricular programs that span across
the entire spectrum of the system.

Decentralization

We have noted that in the past century Norway moved gradually and even
reluctantly to a highly centralized system. In the past two decades forces for
change have reversed that condition until now it is almost axiomatic that as much
of the educational enterprise as is possible ought to be given over to the local
level. Decentralization appeals have come from both the right and the left,
focusing on issues such as funding provisions, school development, curriculum,
and assessment.

Cultural integration advocates generally view local control as a possible mechanism to further equity aims. Recognizing that structural integration and curriculum uniformity have been insufficient, cultural integration advocates claim that
the individual teacher may be critical. The teacher receives a diverse group of
children in the classroom, and he or she must deal with their unique personalities
and different backgrounds in such a way that each child receives the kind of
assistance necessary to fulfill his or her potential. In this context, individualized
instruction ought not to result in greater diversity, but it should ensure that
children, regardless of social level or geographic location, reflect standards
roughly equivalent to children of other social and geographic backgrounds.

Such an orientation has important institutional and curriculum implications,
and has resulted in an attempt to decentralize control to the local school level.
Authorities claimed that centralized mandates and provisions could only assist
the school in creating the creative, innovative, vital development of each child.
The schools themselves must define courses of study and time arrangements;
much of the content and working arrangements, particularly the inclusion of
local subject matter and the use of the local milieu as a resource in instruction;
and flexibility in managing organizing and allocating teacher resources (Dalin
and Rust, 1983).

The new thrust has presented a genuine dilemma for the school, which had
become habituated to direction from the central authorities. Local innovation,
institutional creativity, and individual school development posed as much a threat

as it did an opportunity. School leaders and teachers were now being told they must take individual initiative, and they were trying desperately to comply with such a central mandate, but without much guidance or experience as to how to accomplish such a task.

A number of initiatives have ultimately been undertaken by the Council for Innovation in Education, the councils for Basic Education and Upper Secondary Education, and groups such as the Work Research Institute. These agencies are seeking to provide schools with assistance in engaging in a self-assessment process to identify their strengths and weaknesses and begin defining what kind of institution they must be to satisfy the needs of the children in the community where the school is located.

The drive for decentralization has not been advanced just by cultural integration advocates. We have noted that another impulse for local control began to emerge out of the growing awareness that a policy for equality was detrimental to minority group interests. Norway possesses two major minority groups: the Lapps in the far north who constitute an indigenous population, and the Pakistanis who represent a recent immigrant group in the major urban centers of the country. Throughout its modern history, Norway has maintained a policy of assimilation with regard to its Lapp population, but in the 1960s, academic research studies began indicating that great injustice was being done to the population in schools, in that the Lapp children were not only performing poorly in public schools, but also were resisting the imposition of what they considered to be a foreign culture. The arrival of a small but visible Pakistani ''guest-worker'' population reinforced the notion that not all people could be treated in the same manner in schools. For example, Norwegians stress equality between the sexes, while equity between boys and girls contradicts some of the basic values of Pakistani culture. Reformers claimed that programs of study must be developed that would help minority groups work productively in Norwegian society while retaining their unique character. They declared that this could be accomplished only by allowing local communities to participate in defining the educational process.

More conservative, economics-oriented forces have also advocated decentralization of the educational programs, but for quite different reasons than the above noted reasons. They recognize that government funds have been shrinking, and they have argued that local schools are in a better position to know how to become more efficient, so that they are able to maintain a high standard while receiving less revenue. Schools are, therefore, being given much greater control over their budgets under the assumption that local school personnel know better than anyone else what is useful and what is essential and that they will cut the elements of the program that are unproductive and of little value. These positions have solidified the notion that local schools must be given greater assistance in defining what they are about and how they will define their curricula.

A second educational funding issue has also entered the picture, which has been a law to abolish state subsidies earmarked for schooling and other local services. In 1986 Norwegian law created a block grant policy, which eliminates earmarking where central funds are to be channeled at the local level. Rather, these funds are now given in a block grant, and the local authorities themselves must decide what the best use of the funds will be (Ot. prp. nr. 48 1984–85).

Distribution of educational funds to the local level is perceived as a radical change in Norway, especially by teachers and educational administrators, who had never expected that they would have to compete with other local agencies for funds. Consequently, both the Secondary Teachers Association and the Basic School Teachers Association initially opposed the reforms; their major criticisms centered on issues on equity, between localities and between education and other social services. They claimed that the reforms would spell the end of Norwegian education as a nationally oriented service (St. meld. nr. 26 1983–84). Such fears appear to have been unwarranted, at least in the first years, because the local governments have, by and large, continued to support school budgets at or above the level that the central government was giving support.

In Norway the central government has also endeavored to shift the assessment process to the local level. Local schools have struggled to come to terms with the central mandate to experiment with different kinds of assessment, with teachers often finding it difficult to break away from the traditional evaluation scheme based on standard marks. In Norway, contrary to developments in places such as the United Kingdom, but as in the other Nordic countries, there has been a significant reduction in the number of assessments made during the compulsory or comprehensive phase of schooling. There have also been experiments with "relative marking," and discussion of the principle that student assessment should be sensitive to individual developmental differences and of the question of whether all subjects should be formally assessed.

Sponsorship of Schooling

As we have noted, the Norwegian state has become a monolithic agent of education in Norway, intent on ensuring that every child, regardless of home background or geographic locality, shall be rescued from whatever accident of birth it came from and given a common Norwegian identity. Whereas private schooling played a major role in the earlier stages of modern Norwegian education, during this century national unity took on overwhelming significance. By the 1950s and 1960s the general consensus was that private schooling was almost undemocratic, an outmoded carryover from a period when private schools were the exclusive enclaves of the wealthy. Defenders of Norwegian democracy, dominated by cultural integration interests, maintained that all schools must be under public control authority. Otherwise, the self-interest choices of parents in terms of schooling would divide youth along social class lines and subvert democratic life.

In recent years a new, more conservative orientation has begun to permeate society, which recognizes the value of diversity and suggests that schools ought to be an extension of family values and cultural uniqueness. Such an orientation has found expression throughout the developed world, claiming the label of parental choice. In Norway, parental choice is also at issue, but in a more restricted sense than in most other countries. Whereas in most countries parental choice has come to mean options both within and outside the public school sector (Glenn, 1989), parental choice in Norway is almost entirely channeled toward private schooling. Public schools have attained such a uniformity of program and standard, at least with given communities, that no one is demanding greater choice within the public sector beyond the extensive provisions already available.

Another way in which parental choice has a restricted meaning in Norway is that religion is a relatively minor issue, because public schools already have a religious, Lutheran, basis and most private schools do not have religious sponsorship. Consequently, the issue of choice surfaces in Norway in terms of demands that government approve and support groups that wish to sponsor mainly secular private schools that deviate in some meaningful way from the public sector schools. In the past a small number of private schools have existed, and they have usually received substantial public funds, amounting to 85 percent of running costs. However, Norwegian law only allowed private schools to exist if they were run in accordance with basic school and upper secondary school state regulations. This meant that private schools must fit into the plans and regulations of public school authorities.

In 1984 the law on private schools was changed so that they were no longer dependent on the requirements of public school authorities, allowing them to deviate markedly from the educational norms. Such a decision was the culmination of a movement set in motion in the early 1960s, when a small Seventh Day Adventist school applied to the government for support, claiming that it was only fair that the school be treated as others that were receiving assistance. This request led to the establishment of parliamentary committees during the next decade charged with the responsibility of recommending some general private school policy. By 1970 the political climate had shifted sufficiently toward the conservative end of the continuum, so that politicians began to allow enough flexibility in the system for a generous private school law to be passed, which provided up to 85 percent of running costs to all private schools.

One consequence of this provision was a jump in the number of private schools, which increased in the next decade from 117 to approximately 180 schools. This represents a definite tendency, but the actual numbers have remained inconsequential. In the 1980s, as Conservatives gained full control of Parliament, "privatization" began to take on great significance, as parents demanded the right to enroll their children in private schools. It led to some of the most stressful partisan debates in the country. The debates were fueled by a growing sense of disenchantment with public schooling. The public media had begun to portray the school curriculum, which was being decentralized and defined by local communities, as becoming "watered down," and the public perception was that students were being allowed to choose programs of studies that failed to provide the academic foundation that would help them make sound choices as adults. A rash of applications for private schools began to pile up in the Private School Section of the Ministry of Church and Education, and the trend has not abated yet.

Curriculum Reform

Three major plans have been adopted for the basic school in the past two decades, and they have been the product of radical and liberal elements in Norwegian politics, as well as of conservative opposition to centralization. The first model plan was adopted in 1974, the second in 1985, and the third in 1987 (Grunnskoleradet, 1985, 1987). The general direction of the first two plans was toward provisions for ever greater local control. In 1974 the Norwegian Parliament passed a so-called Model Plan for its basic school curriculum, which represented a significant step in Norway because it reversed the centralized principle set by the Labor government in 1939 that mandated a national curriculum (Harbo, Myhre, and Solberg, 1982). The new plan stipulated that local school boards, schools, and individual teachers be given considerable authority to emphasize local imperatives and deal with individual pupil needs by integrating subjects of study, introducing more flexible and localized assessment procedures than before, and introducing thematic topics into the curriculum, even though the emphasis during the first nine years of Norwegian education remained on providing all children similar instruction throughout all their years of compulsory education. The plan also provided for a separate Lapp program, including instruction in the Lapp language.

The 1985 plan placed even greater responsibility on the local schools and classroom teachers to individualize both content and methods of instruction as teachers were expected to consider individual abilities and capacities as well as interests in deciding how to communicate the contents of courses. Reflecting the greater voice of economics-oriented Conservatives, the plan also advanced a program, particularly for the lower secondary school that would allow each child to be introduced to "practical, social, and cultural work" that provided for general work experience and professional guidance that would introduce each child to the problems and opportunities in the local environment.

The most recent plan, adopted in 1987, reflects a shift toward cultural integration forces, for it has included some directives for a return to uniformity in curriculum reform. For example, because of alarmist claims that the core learnings have declined, the number of hours devoted to Norwegian and mathematics in all basic schools has been increased. In fact, the 1987 plan, presented by the Labor party, mandates an increase of four hours of Norwegian each week through primary school, and two hours a week through lower secondary school. In deference to demands for local variance, however, children will be able to use phonetic spelling in their first year of schooling, which means they will be able to write in their local dialect before moving on to the more formal Norwegian-language studies.

In recent years, curricular considerations have focused on international perspectives. Although Norway is not a member of the European Economic Community, the coming unification efforts of EC countries, as spelled out in the Single European Act scheduled to take effect in 1992, is having a dramatic impact on those who are attempting to anticipate the consequences of unification on the country. This impact has been particularly evident at the upper secondary level, where those involved in designing curriculum in each of the subject fields have been forced to ask themselves what factors would require revision of the course content, textbooks, and other teaching materials so that the educational and professional accomplishments and certificates of Norwegian adults and their children will be internationally recognized and honored (Bjorndal, 1990). The task is formidable, but adjustments are already being made to enhance the role of student exchange programs and see that worker credentials are acceptable throughout Europe.

CONCLUSION

In this chapter we have examined educational reform in Norway, giving attention not only to the types of reform undertaken but also to the types of political and ideological interests that have pushed for these reforms. Without question, the major reforms in the past century have been inspired by cultural integration interests, although in recent years more conservative economic interests have posed a major challenge. In the contemporary world, however, these interests have at times come together to redirect the reform trends of the past century. In the past the major reforms have focused on structural integration of education symbolized mainly in the comprehensive school. That reform process has come to a successful conclusion, and all interests have come to recognize that such reforms are not enough. In the postcomprehensive era, a number of innovations have been undertaken both to counteract the effects of comprehensivization and to further comprehensive aims. These innovations have centered on system integration, decentralization, privatization, and curriculum reform. The Danish sage, Robert Storm Petersen, once remarked that "nothing is harder to predict than the future," and if history has any value as a teacher, we can expect that Norway will continue to devote itself to fundamental reform even after this era is past.

REFERENCES

Aamodt, Per O. 1982. *Education and Social Background*. Oslo: Central Bureau of Statistics of Norway, Samfunnsokonomiskestudier 51.

Awan, Mohammed D. 1987, July 6–10. "Socialization of Pakistani Children in Norway." Paper delivered to the Sixth World Congress of Comparative Education in Rio de Janeiro.

Bergerson, Arne, et al. 1988. *Skolen i Krise?* [Schools in crisis?] Oslo: Gyldendal Norsk Forlag.

Bjorndal, Ivar. 1990, February 5. "1992–Et Skjebnear for Norsk skole?" [1992—A Year of Destiny for Norwegian Schools?] Mimeographed paper produced at the National Council for Upper Secondary Schooling, Oslo.

Central Bureau of Statistics of Norway. 1988. *Statistical Yearbook 1988*. Oslo: Statistisk Sentralbyra.

Dalin, Per, and Val D. Rust. 1983. *Can Schools Learn?* London: NFER–Nelson.

Elder, Neil, Alastair H. Thomas, and David Arter. 1982. *The Consensual Democracies? The Government and Politics of the Scandinavian States*. Oxford: Martin Robertson.

Glenn, Charles L. 1989. *Choice of Schools in Six Nations*. Washington, D.C.: U.S. Department of Education, Office of Educational Research and Improvement.

Grunnskoleradet [Primary Schools Council]. *Horingsutkast til Monsterplan for Grunnskolen* [Hearings report on the Model Plan for primary schools] Oslo: Universitetsforlaget, 1985, 1987.

Harbo, Torstein, Reidar Myhre, and Per Solberg. 1982. *Kampen om Monsterplanen [Fight concerning the Model Plan]*. Oslo: Universitetsforlaget.

Marklund, Sixten. 1981. "The Post-Comprehensive Era of Swedish Education." *Compare* 11:185–190.

Ministry of Church and Education. 1974. *Act of 21 June 1974 Concerning the Upper Secondary School* (English translation). Oslo: Fellestrykk A/S.

————. 1988–1989. *Mer kunnskap til flere* [More knowledge for more]. Storting meldingen nr. 43/1988/89.

Ot. prp. nr. 48. 1984–1985. (Lower House Government Bill Number 48) "Om endringer i lover vedrorende inntektssystemet for kommunene og fylkeskommunene" [Concerning changes in laws related to the revenue system for communities and counties].

Riksaasen, Steinar. 1988. *Grunnskolen-Et System i Krise* [Primary schools—A system in crisis]. Oslo: Gyldendal Norsk Forlag.

Rokkan, Stein. 1967. "Geography, Religion, and Social Class: Crosscutting Cleavages in Norwegian Politics." In *Party Systems and Voter Alignments: Cross-National Perspectives*, ed. Seymour M. Lipset and Stein Rokkan. New York: Free Press.

Rust, Val D. 1984. "Private Schooling Arrangements in Europe." *Private School Quarterly* 1:1–30.

————. 1989. *The Democratic Tradition and the Evolution of Schooling in Norway*. Westport, Conn.: Greenwood Press.

————. 1990. "The Policy Formation Process and Educational Reform in Norway." *Comparative Education* 26:13–25.

————, and Kenneth Blakemore. 1990. "Educational Reform in Norway and England and Wales: A Corporatist Interpretation." *Comparative Education Review* 34.

St. meld. nr. 26. 1983–1984. (Parliamentary Report Number 26). "Om et nytt inntektssystem for kommunene og fylkeskommunene" [Concerning a new revenue system for communities and counties].

Tveit, Knut. Undated. "School and Literacy. Introduction of the Elementary School in Norway in the 1730s and 1740s." Unpublished manuscript from the University of Oslo.

23

PERU

Sydney R. Grant

Educational reform in Peru has closely followed that nation's political currents. By the term *reform* we mean major attempts to improve education through quantitative and qualitative measures. Peruvian education was codified in 1941 in the Public Education Law of 1941 (Ley Organica de Educación Pública No. 9359), and that law marked the first major comprehensive attempt to organize Peru's education enterprise into a meaningful whole.

More recently, in the 1960s, 1970s, and 1980s, the reform efforts in Peru have gathered greater momentum, following the emphases given to education for development worldwide (Coombs, 1968). In Peru, as elsewhere in Latin America, many of the reform efforts depended in part on external inputs from such international agencies as Unesco and the World Bank, and from such donor countries as the United States, the German Federal Republic, France, and Hungary.

In this chapter we examine the sequential array of reform efforts over a twenty-five-year period. We will draw some general conclusions that may be helpful to those who undertake national reform, now and in the future, in other countries.

In addition, because education as an enterprise is one of the financially significant sectors of a developing nation's economy, and because education, dealing as it does with culture and national identity, is a "sensitive" area of national life, educational reforms have to be reviewed within the context of national political life. Therefore, the natural organizing framework will be the political one. Finally, in Peru as in many countries, reforms are expressed in law, and so education law is a good indicator of what is intended and what may be permissible.

THE FIRST ERA: THE PRE-BELAUNDE JUNTA, 1961–1963

The 1962 Peruvian national elections were annulled by a military junta under General Ricardo Perez Godoy (Dobyns and Doughty, 1976). This regime lasted only a year until elections were held again, assuring the presidency for Fernando Belaunde Terry, leader of the reformist liberal party, Acción Popular.

During the Perez Godoy era, no new initiatives were taken in educational reform, but this era did mark the final phase of the earlier reform effort begun under the Public Education Law of 1941 (Ley Organica de Educación Pública No. 9359). That reform was heavily oriented toward improving rural education and developing vocational and technical education. A strong thrust aimed at increasing school enrollments also characterized the post–World War II years. The educational reforms in the decade prior to 1962 received strong influence from U.S. technical assistance under the *servicio* programs.

In Peru, the *servicio* was called SECPANE (Servicio Cooperativo Peruano-Norteamericano de Educacion) (the Cooperative Peruvian-North American Educational Service). Under the SECPANE arrangement, U.S. educators worked as advisers to Peruvian educational leaders to shape and stimulate Peruvian education. SECPANE lasted more than seventeen years. More than a dozen North American educators were permanently employed in SECPANE along with scores of Peruvians, and the SECPANE group was the spearhead of Peruvian educational reform from 1944 to 1962.

The reform efforts that culminated in the pre-Belaunde era resulted not only in dramatic growth in enrollments and in national budget allocation to education, but also "in the new skills and attitudes taught through scholarships for training abroad, through workshops; and through a wide variety of other training courses" (Paulston, 1971). Nevertheless, curricular reform had been minimal, and with the demise of SECPANE, many of its reform initiatives died on the vine.

THE SECOND ERA: THE FIRST BELAUNDE GOVERNMENT, 1963–1968

President Fernando Belaunde Terry was elected in 1963 and served an almost complete presidential term until he was ousted in a military coup in October 1968. Belaunde was a middle-of-the-road reformer, dedicated to free enterprise and to bringing a broad range of reforms to the Peruvian people (Paulston, 1971).

In education, Belaunde's regime aimed at reforms to decentralize the administrative structure, to consolidate and improve teacher education, to modernize vocational and technical education, to improve rural education, and to develop a research and planning unit in education. These initiatives were to be supported by loans or grants from the World Bank and from U.S. sources, as well as from the Peruvian government. To this end, there was a new U.S. presence in the Ministry of Education in the form of a United States Agency for International

Development/University Contract Team. This team, supported in part by U.S. funds and under the coordination of Teachers College, Columbia University, consisted of ten persons who served as advisers in the specialties of educational administration, vocational and technical education, teacher education, and elementary and secondary curriculum development. An economist, an anthropologist, and a researcher were also members of the team. The writer was one of the team members from 1964 to 1968. Implicit in the team's presence was the possibility of developing a large loan for educational reform to be funded by U.S./AID.

Because of poor relations at the time between the United States and Peru over Peru's threatened nationalization of the Talara holdings of the International Petroleum Company, no loan was forthcoming. Therefore, Peru sought funding from other sources, especially from the World Bank. Furthermore, Peruvian educators concentrated on parts of a reform effort that could be carried out without funding. (The World Bank loan was granted after Belaunde's ouster.)

The nonfunded reforms consisted of administrative changes to decentralize and increase regional autonomy, and the development and partial implementation of various curricular changes. In administration, for example, the creation of eight and later eleven regional offices of education permitted more localized school supervision, planning, and budget-making. In the area of curriculum, materials and ideas aimed at making instruction more relevant to the everyday world of work were developed. More active teaching–learning methods were emphasized. The sciences and mathematics received special attention in the curriculum development effort at the secondary school level.

The process was slow and painstaking. Much of the input in terms of value and philosophy emanated from the developed world. The implicit assumption was, "If we want to achieve modernization and development, we must do as the developing countries do, and have done." Opposed to this thinking was a contrary current that questioned the ability of the teaching force to accept, absorb, and practice the new approaches. The argument was that the values of Peruvian teachers were different, their level of education and training was insufficient, and the circumstances of their work were so different and so challenging that transplanted reform ideas would not take and, if they did, would not hold for long.

In the Peruvian congress, Luis Alberto Sánchez, the Aprista ideologue senator and then rector of San Marcos University, led the legislative Education Committee and developed his own new General Education Law to replace the old 1941 General Law. The "Sánchez Law" was never presented, but it was reformist in nature and had as one of its chief features the creation of regional postsecondary technical institutes.

During this first Belaunde era, relationships between the executive and the legislative branches were poor, and the legislature, under control of the rival APRA party, was seen as a barrier to reform. Therefore, most of the reform initiatives in education were carried out by administrative and executive decree. Although the Sánchez Law was known to the ministry officials, it was never officially recognized.

As the Belaunde regime began to falter in 1967 and 1968, ministers of education were changed more frequently, causing uncertainty and paralysis in educational reform operations. Finally, in October 1968, the Velasco military junta seized power, ending the more than five years of slow, uneven, and intangible educational reform efforts by the Acción Popular regime.

THE THIRD ERA: THE VELASCO AND MORALES MILITARY JUNTAS, 1968–1980

General Juan Velasco Alvarado and his junta surprised Peru and the world by their determination not to be a conservative caretaker government until the civilians could reorganize and pull things together again. From the very start of his regime, Velasco, a man of humble background, declared his intention to remake Peru and to carry out sweeping reforms in all sectors in order to change the structures of society and promote social justice. His government was to be a nonaligned one—dealing with both East and West—but with clear preference for the planning, controls, and ideals of socialist nations. There was a genuine attempt to make the "revolution" deeply Peruvian and to eschew non-Peruvian labels, that is, "Marxist," "Cuban," "Soviet," or "communist" tags. The aim was to transform Peruvian society in the social, economic and cultural realms, and to create "the new Peruvian man" (Delgado, 1973; Dobyns and Doughty, 1976).

Education was to be one of the main means for changing the social order. Using the power available to it, with minimal concern for public opinion in the early days and with no worry about the opposition of a nonexistent congress, Velasco appointed General Alfredo Arrisueno Cornejo as minister of education. Arrisueno vigorously moved to reorganize the Ministry of Education and to set up an Education Reform Commission. "It was made up of individuals who came from *outside* the Ministry of Education. Most were left-wing intellectuals" (Churchill, 1976).

The Education Reform Commission, led by philosopher Dr. Augusto Salazar Bondy and two educators, Dr. Emilio Barrantes and Dr. Walter Penalosa, produced one of the most remarkable, creative, and original national reform laws of modern times. This was the General Education Law No. 19326, promulgated by decree in March 1972 and commonly known as La Reforma. Members of the reform commission later stayed on in a new group known as El Consejo Superior de Educacion (Higher Educational Council), serving as the advisers on policy to the minister and as the watchdogs of the law's implementation.

The law was notable for its attempt to express educational problems as symptoms and to address the causes of the symptoms. It was also notable in its attempt to integrate indigenous Peruvian culture into a mystique of economic and social developmentalism and Peruvianism, expressed as an educational program. The law expressed holistic reform and avoided patchwork. It envisioned formal and nonformal education, education for useful life and work, and it placed the individual as an end rather than as a means (Ministry of Education, 1972).

In order to implement the reform, a special training institute, the Instituto Nacional de Investigación y Desarrollo de la Educación or INIDE (the National Institute for Research and Development in Education), was set up in a building physically removed from the ministry itself. INIDE's purpose was to create materials for the reform, train supervisors and teacher trainers, and serve as the ideological spearhead of the reform. INIDE's staff members were selected from the universities and public schools, commanded higher pay than their Ministry of Education counterparts, and in general were younger and better educated than the usual Ministry of Education personnel.

During the reform of the Velasco era, outside assistance was much more seriously and carefully assessed than before. Where past programs in bygone eras could be bent to fit in with the lending guidelines of the donor agencies, now the ministry was more adamant about maintaining its own goals and ideals. Nevertheless, there were instances of outside support, but this support dealt only with what the Peruvians saw as implementation and not with the content of the reform. For example, there was a multimillion dollar loan from Hungary for the purchase of Hungarian equipment for technical and vocational education. Technical assistance was obtained from the United States in the area of instructional design and educational technology to assist in the design of more effective materials to implement the reform.

INIDE's work was done both on INIDE premises and out in the field. Teachers and teacher trainers came into INIDE to attend workshops in specific fields such as science teaching. But INIDE also trained and sent out *entrendadores* (trainers) to the outlying regions of the whole nation to make the teaching staff nationwide more conscious of the reform and to win support for it.

During this era, the ideas of Ivan Illich, Paulo Freire, and Edgar Faure (Faure, 1972) were much in vogue. "Raising consciousness" among Peru's teachers was a major goal of INIDE. Indeed, many of INIDE's training campaigns were oriented toward political socialization as a support of the reform and the general governmental program. The message involved very little that dealt with specific classroom teaching practice, but a great deal that expressed Peru's self-affirmation. The emphasis was on creating the new Peruvian man who would be patriotic, scientific, and humanist, and who would break the bonds of dependency forged during the colonial era and during the more recent neocolonialism of the developed capitalist world (Delgado, 1973).

In specific educational terms, the reform called for extending education downward into preschool education and basic education upward to nine years instead of six, doing away with the academic—vocational dichotomy by making all education in both elementary and secondary school "vocational," by emphasizing the teaching of science and mathematics, by developing further literacy and basic work education for adults, and by bringing the autonomous universities into the national education picture, tying them more firmly to public education and the development process.

No evaluation of this reform was carried out, but it was obvious that Velasco's reform was quite ambitious. The reform was pervasive and global, but it slowly tapered off in vigor and into inactivity as the government ran short of money. The regime experienced a run of bad luck: the fishing sector was struck by several annual precipitous shortfalls; a major earthquake devastated the northern region near Chimbote; the price of copper fell on the world market; and the oil from the newly discovered field in the Amazon region near Iquitos did not flow in the expected abundance. Moreover, there was a shortage of capital as the have-nations avoided investments in Peru, fearing intervention and excessive control. Without money to print books, hire specialists, and continue the training programs, the reform fell back on its rhetoric. Furthermore, feeling the economic pinch, the teachers became more concerned about their own welfare than about reform. If the reform demanded more of them (and it definitely did), they wanted more remuneration, and it turned out that with inflation they were getting less.

The death knell of the Velasco reform in education came with an internal military coup against Velasco in 1975. General Francisco Morales Bermudez, representing a centrist military group, ousted the ailing Velasco and placed a de facto cessation on the entire reformist operations of the Velasco regime.

The education reform itself was not repudiated, nor did Morales repeal the law, but the rhetoric of the reform disappeared. Moreover, the more radical elements of the reform were phased out, and their implementing leaders were transferred or their contracts were not renewed. "Reform" in education returned to the usual professional language without the socioeconomic and nationalistic thrusts.

THE FOURTH ERA: THE SECOND BELAUNDE REGIME, 1980–1985

In 1980, Fernando Belaunde Terry after an absence in the United States for twelve years, was reelected president of Peru. His regime ignored the previous twelve years, and he resumed where he had left off when ousted in 1968. He proposed a new General Education Law (El Peruano, December 1, 1980) and declared that there had been a "deterioration in education since 1968." The new law, he said, must address the needs created by a rapidly growing population and by the demands of an ever-evolving economic and technical and commercial sector. At the same time, the new proposed law reiterated much of the national diagnosis of the Velasco law, but without the socialist coloration.

The New General Education Law was finally promulgated as Law No. 23384 in May 1982, under education minister Jose Benavides Muñoz. The new law was a rollback of the Velasco Reform and was similar to the earlier 1941 law in force during the 1960s.

The Belaunde General Education Law (Law No. 23384) of 1982 was a straight-forward law that described education in the traditional sense of reading, writing, and arithmetic, and the usual subjects appropriate for primary, secondary, and adult education. In contrast to the previous Velasco reform law, it did not call for social transformation. It was explicit, however, in setting forth nondiscriminatory features that guaranteed education to all persons regardless of race, religion, political affiliation, gender, language, or socioeconomic condition (Art. 4-e—Law 23384). The "New Law" was a reform that stepped backward into the status quo ante. This law remained even into the presidency of Allan Garcia Perez, Peru's first Aprista president who was elected in 1985 (Crabtree, 1987).

THE FIFTH AND PRESENT ERA: NONREFORM, 1985–1990

The Alianza Popular Revolucionaria Americana (APRA) party was founded by Haya de la Torre in 1924 as a native socialist party originating in Peruvian traditions. It had great appeal among the masses, but because of the enmity of the military, it was never permitted to assume power until the elections of 1985, when the threat of the Izquierda Unida (IU) (United Left) made the APRA seem like a centrist compromise. The first two years of Alan García's presidency were promising from an economic point of view, and his personal charismatic style enhanced his popularity. By 1988, however, an attempt to nationalize the banks backfired, and along with other internal and external economic pressures, the APRA bubble burst and plunged Peru into an economic and social abyss. Plagued by problems and the increasing prevalence of the Sendero Luminoso (Shining Path) guerrilla movement, the García government was beleaguered.

With so much on its mind, and with a general education law of recent vintage (1982), it was little wonder that the García regime was not able to promote its own major education reform, but limited itself to initiatives such as printing and distributing pupil textbooks, establishing new postsecondary technical institutes, and setting up child day-care centers for children of employed mothers. But all of this was within the context of the previous 1982 Belaunde reform.

As of 1989, the Belaunde counter-reform remained the national education program for the García presidency, despite the strong populist philosophy that has undergirded the APRA political platforms since its beginnings early in this century.

FOUR REFORMS AND FIVE ERAS: OBSERVATIONS TO BE MADE AND LESSONS TO BE LEARNED

The purpose of this general review of educational reform in Peru over a twenty-five-year period has not been to review in detail each reform, but rather to set these reforms side by side and in sequence in order to discern overall patterns and to determine if there are lessons to be learned for the sake of national educational reform movements in general. In considering these questions, two groupings of general statements come to the fore. The first deals with some propositions about the Peruvian reforms themselves. The second deals with the processes at work in general educational reform at the national level.

Observations about Educational Reform Statements

One of the most interesting observations from the point of view of planning and policymaking is that *reforms have been symbolic statements rather than plans for action*. In four of the reforms considered, it is clear that the reform statements both in law and in the general supporting documents served the function more of ideological reference rather than programmatic plan. Reform statements serve as beacons, guidelines, and intentions, but not as programmatic mandates.

Following reform situations elsewhere, in Peru *reforms are political statements as much as they are educational ones*. Either implicitly, as in the pre– and post–Velasco eras, or explicitly as in the Velasco era, educational reform closely reflected the national social, economic, and cultural goals as expressed in the overall politics of the regime. Even the nonreform of the García regime reflected its stymied performance across the board.

From an evolutional point of view, it is clear that in Peru *reforms have been spiral in their content*. This regime's reform law inevitably reflects and picks up on elements expressed in the previous era. What was new then is taken for granted now, and unless they are controverted politically, reform elements will be cumulatively recapitulated. In this sense, there is progression in the long run.

Following the nineteenth-century French thought that had such great influence in Latin America, in Peru *reforms are deductive, comprehensive, and encyclopedic*. Reformers, when writing reform statements, go from A to Z, following a real or imaginary analytic outline that leads them to make statements about everything they can think of. Even though reform writers intend to touch on only two or three important areas, there seems to be a compulsion to reach holistic closure regarding all features of the system. This is certainly true of code law, also in the French style, which is strongly reflected in Peruvian law.

Closely related to law and to the comprehensive approach to speeches, presentations, and expositions, in Peru *reforms tend to be high on statement and low on performance*. Reforms and the language of reform cover everything, but, of course, it is impossible to do everything at once. So, a great deal is never done. Moreover, the reform writers are rare indeed who think their job involves any responsibility for carrying out their reform. As the expression goes, "After all is said and done, more is said than done."

Related to this penchant for rhetoric, *reforms are enabling rather than stipulative*. As guidelines, reform statements present the allowable limits, but there are few imperatives. Furthermore, the specific procedures are left for the particular regulations (*reglamentos*), which are drawn up at a later time. Often, the regulations are *not* drawn up, or they are not agreed upon by the drafting parties, with the result that no further action is taken. Reforms embedded in law suffer the fate of all law: enforcement or nonenforcement.

Another very clear observation from a review of the history of Peruvian educational reform is that *reforms are affected by the educational world milieu in vogue at the time they are drafted*. World educational themes (Faure, 1972) such as nonformal education, consciousness-raising, adult basic education and literacy, life-long learning, educational television, and others which are stressed by Unesco and by the developed world will find their echo in the warp and woof of the reform laws, even if these slogans do not always respond to specific national education needs. If "distance learning" is in vogue, you will find it mentioned in the reform.

Regarding assessments of the Peruvian reforms, *"evaluations" of reforms have been informal and impressionistic*. During the writer's experience in Peru throughout the 1964–1989 period, no comprehensive evaluations were carried out of previous or current reform efforts. Nevertheless, judgments *were* made. These were based on informal interviews by technical assistance donors who gathered word-of-mouth impressions from central ministry directors and their technical staffs, as well as from regional office personnel. Such informal evaluations did not extend to the teacher level, nor was an attempt made to measure student gains, or learning outcomes.

Observations about the Process of Educational Reform

When considering who were involved in the reform process in Peru, it is clear that *reforms are shaped by the intellectual and technical elites*. In each of the reforms examined, the reform commissions whose members wrote the reform were drawn from two major institutions: the universities and the "normative" offices of the Ministry of Education. Included in these commissions were particular individuals who had distinguished themselves in some facet of education, and a representative or two of classroom teachers. But these teachers were not representatives of teacher associations or unions. Foreign experts were also attached to the reform commissions as advisers, except for the reform commission during the Velasco regime, which tended to exclude outside advisers.

As in many countries, *undertaking educational reforms is time-intensive*, and Peru is no exception. Committee meetings, the drafting of documents, the clearances that are needed, and the actual reproduction of the reform document or law take from one to two years or more. Even the noncomprehensive reforms, that is, those aimed at a specific target, such as the development of a new biology program, take at least a year. Even under the best of circumstances, there are no fast reforms.

In most cases in Peru, *the reform writing effort is a part-time effort for those who are involved in it*. As the commission members have other work to do, they do not normally work full time on the reform effort. Consequently, reform efforts do not receive exclusive attention or dedication from the reform actors.

426 International Handbook of Educational Reform

As would be expected in a situation that is politically charged, and *in addition to the political content in educational reform laws, the reform commission members are selected on the basis of political acceptability as much as for their professional education expertise.* National political party membership, or neutrality, are major factors in the selection of members for a reform commission.

In recent development work, we almost always tie planning statements with outcomes and with enabling budgeting resources, but, in Peru, in the past, we note that *reform laws, as guiding statements, did not have action-performance plans or cost estimates.* How the reform was to be achieved, and how much it was to cost, were not concerns of the reform commission when it was writing and setting forth its ideas. As mentioned previously, it was expected that *reglamentos* would take care of specific details and that implementing projects would be worked out, costed, and funded later.

Not surprisingly in situations where effort is equated with result as it sometimes has been in the past in Peru, *no evaluation guidelines are considered for a reform.* Evaluation, if considered at all, has usually been an ex post facto activity after a reform has been implemented.

Lessons to Be Learned

We must pose the most important question: "What can be learned from this rapid overview of twenty-five years of Peruvian educational reform?"

Five "lessons" stand out. First is the weakness of the situation created by allowing reform writers to have their head of steam without being responsible for at least thinking about implementation and cost.

Second is the weakness inherent in having the elites solely responsible for the reform, and not getting broader participation, especially from the "grass-roots" classroom teaching staff and from local communities. It would seem suicidal not to have involved early and often a range of representation from teachers who were actually on the "front lines" in the classroom, and who in the long run would have been the ones who would make or break a reform. (Despite the dynamic egalitarianism of the Velasco reform, much of its implementation seemed coercive to the teaching staff who considered it more work for less pay.)

Third is the weakness in conceiving the implementation as a process of rapid imposition of ideas and materials on the teaching force, rather than by slower, participatory means. In this, the old adage, "Make haste slowly," seems to apply.

Fourth is the absence of child development, psychological, and anthropological field studies to serve as the human, orienting factor and as an additional reality research base in formulating reform ideas. If development of the nation is one element in the equation, surely the individual clients are part of that equation.

Fifth is the very human weakness of not realizing what an important factor time is. Things take time to write, to consider, to get agreement on, and to carry out. In human affairs, short of military or autocratic procedures, time must be a factor in any equation. Although time is invisible, it is very real, and people interested in reform simply have to understand that the period of time available can present serious problems in terms of one's ability to get things done within the mandate that one has. Here, we face the need to plan for periods that may extend beyond the tenure of the incumbent regime. Is this possible, given the political nature of educational reform?

As a final word, readers in other countries will judge if these observations and lessons are applicable to their own educational reform situations. One must ponder: why have reforms at all? Perhaps it is because *renewal* is very much a part of human development, symbolizing our strivings for personal self-actualization and social development. On the other hand, from an anthropological perspective, reforms may be part of the ritual inherent in the political process, giving political leaders another way of expressing their programs to gain support.

REFERENCES

Churchill, Stacy. 1976. *The Peruvian Model of Innovation: The Reform of Basic Education*. Experiments and Innovations in Education No. 22. Paris: Unesco Press.

Coombs, Philips H. 1968. *The World Educational Crisis: A Systems Analysis*. New York: Oxford University Press.

Crabtree, John. 1987, July. "The Consolidation of Alan García's Government in Peru." *Third World Quarterly* 9 (3): 804–824.

Cuban, Larry. 1990, January–February. "Reforming Again, Again, and Again." *Educational Researcher* 19 (1): 3–13.

Delgado, Carlos. 1973. *Problemas sociales en el Peru contemporaneo*. Instituto de Estudios Peruanos, LIMA: Compodonico Ediciones.

Dobyns, H., and P. Doughty. 1976. *Peru: A Cultural History*. New York: Oxford University Press.

Fagerlind, I., and L. Saha. 1989. *Education and National Development: A Comparative Perspective*. 2nd ed. Oxford: Pergamon Press.

Faure, Edgar. 1972. *Learning to Be*. Paris: Unesco.

Grant, Sydney. 1966. "Twenty-five Friday Reports Representing the Period 11 September 1965–4 March 1966." Typescript, Teachers College Columbia University Contract Team U.S./AID, LIMA.

Matos Mar, José, ed. 1969. *La crisis del desarrollismo y la nueva dependencia*. Lima: Instituto de Estudios Peruanos.

———, et al. 1971. *Peru: Hoy*. Mexico: SigloVeintiuno, Editores, S.A.

Ministry of Education. 1970. *Reforma de la educación peruana: informal general*. Lima.

———. 1972. *Ley general de educación: Decreto Ley No. 19326*. Lima: Editorial Universo.

———. 1989. *Nueva Ley General de Educación (Ley No. 23384) y sus Modificatorias, Leyes 23626–24194*. Editorial El Carmen, Lima, Peru.

Paulston, Rolland. 1971. *Society, Schools and Progress in Peru*. New York: Pergamon Press.

24

SOUTH AFRICA

Harold D. Herman

The 1980s was a decade of conflict and strife in South African schools. Significant events have taken place in education which have shaken the pillars of the apartheid system devised to perpetuate white minority rule within this divided country.

This chapter explores some of the significant changes that have taken place in education in South Africa over the past decade. Since the 1960s, the international experience has shown that education is seldom an agent for dynamic social change. In fact, it more often reinforces the status quo. In South Africa with its unique system of racial capitalism, education has for many decades been the handmaiden of racial capital and white minority rule. Its capacity for social transformation of South African society has been decidedly limited, and social analysts have often seen educational change as no more than a restructuring to adjust to the changing needs of capital and as a powerful agent for social, racial, and economic reproduction.

Over the past decade, resistance within schools has been a powerful counter-hegemonic force challenging the apartheid state as progressive forces within the country pursue the struggle for a just, nonracial democracy. This chapter highlights some of the crucial aspects of the educational struggle and the education's potential role in shaping a new post-apartheid society.

HISTORY OF RESISTANCE TO APARTHEID EDUCATION

Racially separate, discriminatory, and unequal education in South Africa evolved from its roots in the second half of the seventeenth century, its infancy in the eighteenth century, a well-defined institutional growth in the nineteenth century to its notorious heights, and close links with the state policy of apartheid in the middle of the twentieth century.

Table 24.1
Estimated Population of South Africa, 1988

	NUMBERS	PROPORTION
AFRICAN	29,974,284	74.9%
ASIAN	928,000	2.6%
COLOURED	3,127,000	8.7%
WHITE	4,949,000	13.8%
TOTAL	35,978,284	100.0%

After the Afrikaner-dominated Nationalist party came to power in 1948, a series of laws were passed to entrench the white population group's political and economic power. White domination of the disenfranchised black majority population intensified in the 1950s and 1960s, supported by an expanding economy exploiting the country's enormous mineral wealth and cheap, unskilled black labor.

All citizens were racially classified as White, Coloured, Asian, or African. Bantustans or black homelands were established to marginalize the rural African population and provide a labor reserve for the rapidly expanding industrial state. These ten geographically scattered areas were to become the future independent black states in which urban blacks were to be resettled and exercise their rights of citizenship in terms of entrenched ethnic and language differences of groups such as the Zulus, Xhosas, and North and South Sothos.

The pass laws and influx control mechanisms curbed black migration to metropolitan areas, and separate residential areas were enforced. Marriages across color lines were forbidden by legislation. The iniquitous and long-term disastrous consequences of such policies in a modern world need not be explained to enlightened scholars in international education if the South African demographic patterns are understood. Table 24.1 presents the estimated population of South Africa (Survey of Race Relations, 1989: 149) in 1988. The white population decreased proportionately to 13.8 percent of the total population in 1988. The implication of this decrease for continued White minority domination of the vast black majority is self-evident.

As the forces implementing apartheid have expanded, so have those opposing it with increasing intensity to establish a just, democratic, nonracial society. The anti-apartheid struggle intensified significantly in the late 1970s and over the past decade—so much so that the South African government has had to seriously reassess its policies of racial segregation and economic exploitation. On February 2, 1990, the state president, F. W. de Klerk, made a crucial policy speech at the opening of Parliament in which he admitted the wrongs of the apartheid system, the need to move toward a nonracial democracy, the need for a universal franchise, but also the need for protecting individual and group rights. The ban has been lifted on political organizations such as the African National Congress (ANC), the Pan Africanist Congress (PAC), and the South African Communist Party (SACP), and some political prisoners, notably Dr. Nelson Mandela, have been released. The government recognizes the need for a negotiated settlement of the constitutional crisis with representatives of all people of the country, and the long road toward a nonracial, nondiscriminatory society with justice and democratic values as its cornerstones lies ahead. An era of political, social, and educational reconstruction is at hand.

Education and politics are inseparable in South Africa. A rigidly controlled centralized system of schooling with elements of decentralization to follow the apartheid contours had been foisted on the black majority since 1948, with the late former Prime Minister, Dr. H. F. Voerwoerd as the architect-in-chief of the separate-but-never-equal subsystems of Bantu, Coloured, and Indian Education in the 1950s and 1960s. Black education was to be separate even at university level after the passing of the Universities Education Extension Act of 1959. White primary and secondary schooling is controlled by the White provincial governments of the four provinces of South Africa, Coloured and Indian (Asian) education by two or more separate education departments, urban African education outside the Bantustans by the Department of Bantu Education (now the Department of Education and Training, DET), and rural African education by the quasi-independent "homelands," four of the ten having opted for "independence." There is also a Department of National Education, a central government department controlling important segments of White tertiary education, core curricula for schools, rules for certification at school-leaving age, and university entrance requirements. There are, in fact, eighteen education departments at present in a country with 36 million people.

Despite great resistance from the black people, the powerful state legislature and educational bureaucracy implemented the educational policy after passage of the Bantu Education Act of 1952 and other acts that followed. In 1988 there were 9,029,715 pupils enrolled at primary and secondary schools in South Africa, 7,027,573 of whom were classified African, 935,903 White, 832,329 Coloured, and 233,910 Asian.

Over many decades many brilliant intellectuals, political analysts, and social scientists have been wrong in their predictions of rapid social transformation in South Africa. It is not a country to be easily caught up in civil war or classical revolution. At the start of the 1990s it does appear that the violent revolution scenario is still unlikely and that a negotiated political settlement between the present government and the liberation movements is probable.

EDUCATIONAL CHANGE IN THE 1980s

Up to the mid–1970s, the policy of separate and unequal schooling for blacks in South Africa was never seriously at risk in spite of much opposition on the part of the black community, liberation movements, and progressive organizations to Bantu Education, Coloured Education, and the enforced policies of Christian National Education. Among the reasons why were the immense power of the regime, the strength of the economy, effective control by the educational bureaucracy, the relative security and prosperity of civil servants and teachers, the effectiveness of divide-and-rule policies, the repressive state security apparatus, and the resulting limitations placed on mass mobilization and trade union power. The experience in many countries has shown that education has limited power to advance the cause for changing the status quo. In varying degree this has also been done in respect to state schooling in South Africa.

In the mid–1970s a social crisis was increasingly confronting the South African state. The most salient features of this crisis are economic stagnation, the resurgence of black labor militancy, the Soweto's students' uprising of 1986, intensified international pressure on the regime to abandon apartheid, and the detrimental shifts in the balance of power in the subcontinent following the collapse of the Portuguese Empire.

The increasing challenge of black radical politics since 1976 has been accompanied by a surge in resistance to Bantu Education. Educational reform and transformation were now key aspects of the agenda of change for radical students, parents, nationalists, populists, socialists, and trade unions, with the state being forced to impose its own version of reform from above.

A number of important state reform initiatives were taken after the Soweto riots of 1976. The reports of the Wiehahn and Riekert commissions on trade unions and influx control, respectively, were seen in liberal circles as significant breakthroughs in the reform process. Some space was created for black trade unionism and migration to the cities after the pass laws were scrapped.

The massive student protest and boycotts in 1980, particularly in secondary schools, precipitated an educational crisis that led to the appointment of the Human Sciences Research Council (De Lange) Commission of Inquiry into educational provision by the state. The De Lange Report recognized the need for a more comprehensive policy of mass schooling, the large-scale pre- and in-service training of teachers, one national education department, and a break from the traditional formal schooling patterns toward a new structure in which academic and vocational streams would run parallel. It proposed the principle of equality of educational opportunity for all. Reformists and the liberal press hailed the report as a major breakthrough, giving new direction to South African education. Its distinction between academic and vocational secondary school tracks was controversial and was criticized as leading to the reproduction of class differences and racial capitalism. The report recommended increased emphasis on technical and vocational education. Some regarded its emphasis on personnel planning and remedying of skills shortages as playing into the hands of oppressive, exploitive, capitalist forces.

The government accepted some of the recommendations and eventually announced a ten-year plan for the "equalization" of educational provision across color lines. However, in a white paper published in 1983 it rejected the idea of one education department and racially integrated state schools. It became clear that it was not prepared to consider the fundamental question of a nonracial system of schooling within an undivided South Africa.

As the anti-apartheid and pro-democracy struggles intensified, the education crisis deepened. The government came under increasing pressure from the business community to liberalize education policies. Gradually, the apartheid structures in education were adapted to suit the slowly changing policies of the ruling Nationalist party. Private schools were allowed to enroll black pupils, and universities were given the freedom to decide whom they wished to enroll. The emphasis was increasingly on technical vocational and management skills training for blacks, training for "Free enterprise." Technical colleges and technikons for blacks were expanded, with industry and commerce playing a larger role in industrial and management training programs.

After 1982, the education struggles intensified even more. Despite harassment of pupils, university students, parents, and teachers organized and mobilized against Bantu and "gutter" education. Student protests centered around issues such as control over schools, opposition to the DET, the right to have democratically elected Student Representative Councils (SRCs), and lack of physical facilities and school books. Between 1982 and 1986 widespread protests and boycotts occurred in African schools, particularly in the Eastern Cape and Transvaal. In 1986 the DET stated that the number of schools involved in boycott actions varied from 210 to 450 at any one time out of a total of about 7,500 schools. Yet, according to Bot (1986) there were only 328 DET secondary schools in urban areas, and as the boycotts occurred mainly at secondary level and in urban areas, they had a significant disruptive impact on DET schools. In addition, 400,000 African pupils did not re-register in July/August 1986, and thirty-three schools were then closed for the year.

The township unrest intensified further from 1984 to 1986, and the demand for equal, free and compulsory education in 1980 was replaced in 1985 by the slogan "Liberation Now, Education Later." After the establishment of the National Education Crisis Committee (NECC) by concerned black leaders and parents in 1986, the rallying cry changed to "people's education for people's power," a shift from the strategy of educational protest to one of educational empowerment of black pupils and teachers.

The DET was unable to solve the education crisis. It responded by stating that it remained committed to separate education, while striving for parity. In 1986 it announced a ten-year plan for African education according to which all the country's educational institutions would fall under one umbrella, with the same standard for all. The measures to be included were

1. Increased finance. (Despite the considerable increases, DET's 1985–1986 budget was R1158 million compared to R3222 million spent on White education.)
2. Teacher training. The DET hoped to have trained another 69,000 qualified black teachers by the end of the century.

3. The improvement of teacher qualifications through various in-service training programs. (94.6 percent of the teachers did not have matriculation and at least three years
   of teacher training.)

4. An improved teacher-pupil ratio of 1:30.

5. Improved facilities such as laboratories, libraries, workshops, and playing fields and
   an improved pupil:classroom ratio.

6. Guidance counselors and a system of career-oriented education.

7. The establishment of a preschool orientation year.

8. The availability of technikons and technical colleges, of which there were forty countrywide at the time.

The NECC responded by rejecting the ten-year plan because the content of
education and the structure in which it was taught remained intact. It had completely different criteria for legitimacy, viz., community acceptability in the form
of parent, teacher, and student participation and the contribution by progressive
intellectuals. They proposed to work on an alternative education program suitable
to all the country's inhabitants which will harmonize relations between mental
labor and intellectual labor by merging theory with practice (Bot, 1986: 48).

The slate clamped down in June 1986. Additional security measures became
applicable in African schools, and a large number of NECC members were
detained. Thus, the educational impasse continued.

PEOPLE'S EDUCATION FOR PEOPLE'S POWER

During the period 1976 to 1980 the demands of black pupils shifted from an
initial rejection of Afrikaans and Bantu Education to a demand for equal, free,
and compulsory education. The continued intransigence and persistence of the
government and its educational bureaucracy with discriminatory education policies, and the refusal to meet black aspirations for democratic rule, evoked
extreme anger in the minds and hearts of young black people. As noted earlier,
between 1980 and 1985 the black pupils' cries of anger and protest changed to
the slogan "Liberation Now, Education Later." Although understandable in its
context, this view was impractical, ill founded as a strategy, and unhelpful to
the struggles of the mass democratic movement. Revolutionary rage was also
fueled by the declaration of the state of emergency in 1985 and the banning of
the Congress of South African Students (COSAS). Student calls went out for a
total boycott of classes and examinations in 1986. There was a widely held
attitude, described by some as immediatism, that the imminent collapse of apartheid was at hand and there were calls for 1986 to become the "year of no
schooling."

It was in this context that the Soweto Parents' Crisis Committee (SPCC) was
formed in 1985 and a decision was taken to call a national consultative conference
to devise a strategy to consolidate the gains made up to that point and to advance

the education struggle. The conference led to the formation of the NECC in March 1986. The general feeling among teachers was that while the school boycott was important, the political role of the student was to prepare through education for a useful role in society and this positive contribution could not be made by sacrificing education (Kruss, 1988: 7). The African National Congress in Lusaka was consulted, and it concurred that it was essential for young people to continue their education without giving up the struggle to end apartheid.

It was in this context that the call for People's Education for People's Power was formulated, with pupils and teachers returning to school to use the schools as the basis for People's Education. It would be a deliberate attempt to move away from reactive protests around education to develop a counter-hegemonic strategy and to contribute by laying a basis for a future, post-apartheid South Africa.

People's Education attempts to make explicit the links between education and political, economic, and cultural reproduction. It represents a shift from reactive responses to a more serious questioning about the nature of education itself. Kruss (1988: 19) sums up the key feature of People's Education as follows:

1. Based on decades of education resistance, People's Education (PE) is a rejection of Apartheid Education, which is education for domination.

2. PE's underlying assumption is that education and politics are linked and, consequently, that the struggle for an alternative education system cannot be separated from the struggle for a nonracial democratic South Africa.

3. People's Education for People's Power is thus at the same time an educational strategy and a political strategy. Through PE, people will be mobilized and organized toward the goal of a nonracial democratic South Africa, but at the same time, through PE people are beginning to develop a future education system.

4. Central to the success of PE is the organization of all sectors of the people, to take control of education and their lives. Students, teachers, and parents need to build democratic organization in their own sectors, as well as establish strong working alliances and mutual understanding.

5. PE as an education system must be controlled by and advance the interests of the mass of the people.

6. Arising out of the education crisis, PE initially addressed itself to formal, school-based education. It is intended to educate and empower all, and not just school students.

7. PE must instill democratic values such as cooperative work and active participation, in opposition to current authoritarian and individualistic values dominant in schools.

8. PE must stimulate creativity and critical thinking to equip students for the future.

9. Educational practices implementing the principles have to be developed, particularly by teachers.

10. PE is in process; it can only be fully achieved when apartheid is abolished. In the meantime, it will be shaped and developed according to these guidelines. Thus, it is constantly changing and dynamic.

The arenas in which PE hopes to be meaningful are diverse. One of its aims is to formulate an alternative, school-based education, in order to extend community control over education. It seeks to do so by establishing a people's authority alongside the existing state authority, with parents and teachers leaving statutory bodies in favor of these new structures.

English, Mathematics and People's History commissions have been set up to work on developing alternative curricular material and resources. These will help students and teachers present the syllabus in a different way and run alternative programs with parents and teachers outside of school boundaries. The role of teachers is crucial for the implementation of PE. This is a difficult task, however, for teachers are often criticized from all sides and are treated by the educational bureaucracy as instruments of policy. The teachers often find that their own training in the apartheid system of education has not equipped them well for progressive, critical thinking and learning. In many areas the teachers' morale, confidence, and self-image are at low ebb.

Many questions yet remain to be answered about PE. In a recent paper, C. Soudien et al. (1986) raise serious questions as to how PE will be able to face problems relating to certification of pupils and the inevitable links between certification and employment. N. Alexander (1986), in a paper delivered at the National Consultation of Education for Affirmation, points out that it would be naive to believe that an "alternative education system" can be set up as long as the apartheid state lasts. At most, he states, we can encroach on the control, content, and methodology of education within the schools. The Teachers League of South Africa in its *Teachers Journal* of January–February 1988 expresses reservations about the concept of People's Education. It states in an editorial that the ideas thus far generated by the notion of People's Education for People's Power have proved almost wholly inadequate and off the mark.

At the Research on Education in South Africa (RESA) conference held at Grantham, England, in March 1989, some reservations were expressed about PE on the grounds of

1. Lack of clarity over precisely what it means, from the theoretical imprecision over the concepts of the people and the community.
2. Lack of consensus over the precise trajectory and content of PE.
3. The fact that not only state repression will block the move toward PE, but also headmasters, teachers, and school inspectors. Repression is experienced not only through the ideological character of education and state intervention, but also through the undemocratic character and organization of capitalist schools, a factor that many teachers and educators perceive to be to their advantage.
4. If PE is to contribute to a more just society, it will have to move beyond the common formula for mass education to an understanding of how reform in education is related to a fundamental redistribution of power, wealth, and privilege in society.

Despite these criticisms, People's Education is to be taken seriously as an alternative to state schooling. Academic debates at universities and the literature

Table 24.2
Number of Students in South Africa by Year and School Phase, 1960, 1980, 1987, and 2000

Year and school phase	Africans	Whites	Asians IN THOUSANDS	Coloured	Total
1960					
Primary	1452	462	111	276	2301
Secondary	48	246	17	29	340
Total	1500	708	128	305	2641
1980					
Primary	4067	608	150	618	5443
Secondary	774	348	67	141	1330
Total	4841	956	217	759	6773
1987					
Primary	5171	547	143	597	6458
Secondary	1474	407	91	216	2188
Total	6645	945	234	813	8646
2000					
Primary	6226	521	134	527	7408
Secondary	2453	338	89	320	3200
Total	8679	859	223	847	10608

From: Dostal, E. The long-term future of education in South Africa, June 1989, p. 7.

in South Africa and in overseas academic forums (see Levin, 1989; Unserhalter and Wolpe, 1989) have generally been supportive of PE. The future will tell to what extent it will succeed as a strategy for alternative education and in the transformation of South African schooling.

THE QUANTITATIVE CHALLENGE TO EDUCATION IN THE 1980s

Despite the inequalities and neglect of Bantu education since the implementation of Bantu education in 1953, there have been substantial increases in school enrollments, particularly in the past decade. Table 24.2 presents the number of pupils in South Africa according to school phase and population group for 1960, 1980, and 1987, and gives projections for the year 2000.

In 1988 there were 9.03 million pupils enrolled in primary and secondary schools in South Africa, and of these 77.8 percent were African. Forty-two percent of the African pupils were enrolled in the "independent" homelands (Transkei, Ciskei, Venda, and Bophuthatswana), 28 percent in the "nonindependent" homelands (Gazankulu, Kangwane, Kwandabele, Kwazulu, Lebowa, and Qwaqwa), and 30 percent in schools in the Department of Education and Training (Du Plessis et al., 1989: 4).

Table 24.3
Per Capita Expenditure, 1987–1988 (Including Capital Expenditure)

	RANDS
AFRICAN	595 39
COLOURED	1507 55
INDIAN	2014 88
WHITE	2722 00

(from Race Relations Survey, SAIRR, 1989)

Table 24.4
Number of Matriculation Certificates Obtained in South Africa, 1980, 1987, and 2000

Popula-tion Group	1980		1987		2000	
	Number in thousands	% of total	Number in thousands	% of total	Number in thousands	% of total
Africans	22,7	27	85,0	50	198,0	68
Whites	48,2	59	62,0	36	51,0	17
Coloureds	7,0	8	12,4	7	31,0	11
Asians	4,8	6	11,8	7	13,0	4
Total	82,7	100	171,2	100	293,0	100

From: Dostal, E.   The long-term future of Education in South America, June 1989, p. 10.

Table 24.3 gives the per pupil expenditure of the state during 1987–1988 for the various racial groups (excluding the homelands).

Despite the unfavorable per capita expenditure on African pupils (22 percent of the figure for a White child), there was a massive increase in enrollment from 1.5 million in 1960 to 6.7 million in 1987. This is largely because of parents' concern for the education of their children, often at great personal cost. The preponderance of enrollment at the primary level reflects the great difficulties of parents in keeping their children at school when every extra wage earned even by young children is essential for household survival. In the 1960s and 1970s there was an increasing demand for more highly skilled African labor. After 1976 attempts were made to create a larger skilled, professional, and managerial class of Africans both inside and outside the Bantustans with a stake in the apartheid system, a class which, it was believed, would be more politically compliant and which would assist in imposing political order (RESA, 1989).

Table 24.4 gives the actual number of matriculation or equivalent certificates obtained in South Africa during the years 1980 and 1987, with projected figures

Table 24.5
Number of University Students per 1,000 Population, 1985 and 2010 Projection

	AFRICAN	COLOURED	INDIAN	WHITE	TOTAL
Total Population in millions	25.4	4.4	1.2	5.7	36.7
Students at university in thousands:					
-projected 2010	231.1	40.4	10.9	51.9	33.4
-actual 1985	39.7	12.9	17.5	141.9	21.2
-% change	482.1	213.2	-37.7	-63.4	57.5

From: Booysen, (1990).

for the year 2000. Despite the unrest in the black townships, student protests and boycotts, and a pupil–teacher ratio of 42:1 (1985), the increases in black pupils passing the senior certificate examination have been dramatic. The number of African matriculants as a percentage of the total number obtaining certificates nearly doubled from 27 to 50 percent between 1980 and 1987. This has led to an increased shortage in the provision of teachers. The number of teachers to be trained will have to double to 302,000 by the year 2000 to bring African schools on a par with the 19:1 pupil–teacher ratio of White schools (Dostal, 1989: 18).

A recent paper delivered by the chairperson to the Committee of University Principals in South Africa (Booysen, 1990) discusses the number of university students per 1,000 of the total population in the year 2010 for South Africa, assuming 9.1 students per 1,000 head of population for each race group (see Table 24.5).

Here again the increase in African enrollment will be phenomenal, showing that the black advancement to the university level is irreversible. This huge increase in enrollment could, however, lead to large numbers of educated unemployed young people. In 1981 the National Manpower Commission indicated that 59 percent of the Africans and 66 percent of the Coloureds under the age of thirty were unemployed. Unemployment has had a radicalizing effect on black youth, and the above figures suggest that the problem can get much worse if the economy does not grow at a much faster pace. In an article entitled ''School and Revolution'' in *New Society* (January 10, 1986), C. Bundy mentions four factors that underlie the youth component of the confrontations of 1985.

1. The glaring defects of black education.
2. The very substantial expansion of black schooling over the past few decades.

3. The issue of unemployment among black school leavers.

4. The way in which organizational capacity and experience has transformed consciousness.

The militancy of black youth has caused great concern over the past few years. In a paper at the RESA conference at Grantham in March 1989, O'Connell discussed various aspects of youth power in schools and colleges. More recently, the call went out to the school-going children from within the mass democratic movement to return to school at the beginning of 1990. Both Walter Sisulu and Nelson Mandela appealed to black pupils to return to school. However, during 1990 the majority of the urban black schools were not yet functioning normally since pupils were not returning to classes. This is a very disturbing aspect of the struggle for democracy in the schools. One can only hope that the present mood of optimism about a negotiated settlement for the political future of South Africa will save a generation of young people from alienation and despair.

Some significant changes have taken place in government thinking on education by the middle of 1991. It has accepted the principle of one educational system in an undivided South Africa. Parents of pupils at White schools have been informed of the opening of schools to children of all race groups. Some schools that have closed down as a result of decreasing enrollments in White areas have been made available to education departments of other racial groups and there seems to be some commitment by government to the normalization of education. The government released a controversial educational policy document titled the Educational Renewal Strategy (ERS) which outlines its views on how to de-racialize and equalize education. It has not been well received by the Mass Democratic Movement, which has instituted its own educational policy initiative called the National Educational Policy Investigation (NEPI). Crucial to the settlement of the controversies in education is a political settlement, the negotiation of a new constitution for the country, and a political dispensation acceptable to the majority of South Africans.

REFERENCES

Alexander, N. 1986. "Ten Years of Educational Crisis: The Resonance of 1976." Paper presented at conference Education for Affirmation, Broederstroom.

Azapo Education Policy, Azapo Centre Committee. 1984. Unpublished paper.

Booysen, P. de V. 1990. "The Challenge of Numbers." Paper, Committee of University Principals. University Principal, University of Nakl.

Bot, M. 1986. "The Future of African Education." *Indicator S.A.*, No. 2.

———. 1989, May 7. "Facing the Challenge of Equal Education." *Sunday Times*.

Buckland, P. 1982. "The Education Crisis in S.A.: Restructuring the Policy Discourse." *Social Dynamics* 8 (1).

"Building a People's University." 1988. Proceedings of Conference, University of Western Cape.

Bundy, C. 1986, January 10. "Schools and Revolutions." *New Society*.

Christie, P., and M. Gaganakis. 1989. "Farm Schools in South Africa: The Face of Rural Apartheid." *Comparative Education Review* 33 (1).

Daniels, N. J. 1987. "The Struggle for People's Education." Unpublished Master's dissertation, University of California at Berkeley.

Dostal, E. 1989. *The Long-term Future of Education in South Africa.* Institute for Future Research, University of Stellenbosch.

Du Plessis, A., et al. 1989. *Education and Manpower Development.* Research Institute for Education Planning, Bloemfontein.

Education Journal. 1988, January-February. Teacher's League of S.A., 58 (1).

Erwin, A. 1987. "People's Education from a Worker's Perspective." Address, Conference, Faculty of Education, University of Western Cape.

Hartshorne, K. 1983. *White or Black Education.* Energos.

———. 1989. *Education in the Homelands.* RETPESA, University of Western Cape.

Kallaway, P. 1988. "From Bantu Education to People's Education in South Africa." Unpublished paper.

Kruss, S. 1988. *People's Education—an Examination of the Concept.* CACE, University of Western Cape.

Levin, R. 1989, March. "People's Education and the Struggle for Democracy in South Africa." Paper delivered at RESA conference, Grantham.

Mkatshwa, S. 1985. Keynote address. NECC, Johannesburg.

O'Connell, B. 1989. "Education and Transformation—A View from the Ground." Paper delivered at RESA Conference, Grantham.

Research on Education in South Africa (RESA). 1989. Papers 1, 2, & 3 delivered at RESA Conference, Grantham.

Sisulu, Z. 1986. *People's Education for People's Power.* Transformation 1.

Soudien, C., et al. 1986. *The Problems of Certification and People's Power.* Transformation 1.

Suckling, J., et al. *After Apartheid.* Centre for Southern African Studies, York.

Survey of Race Relations. 1989. South African Institute of Race Relations.

Task Force on Education of the Signatory Association. *Black Education in South Africa.* Johannesburg.

Unterhalter, E., and H. Wolpe. 1989. "The Politics of South African Education." Paper delivered at RESA Conference, Grantham.

25

UNITED STATES

Susan F. Semel, Peter W. Cookson, Jr., and Alan R. Sadovnik

The 1980s were years of significant debate and reform in U.S. education. Beginning in 1983, with the National Commission on Excellence's report *A Nation at Risk*, government leaders, educational reformers, teacher organizations, administrators, and various other interest groups attempted to improve the quality of U.S. schools. Although the decade included two specific waves of reform, the first beginning in 1983 and the second in 1985, the period as a whole must be understood as a conservative response to the progressive reforms of the 1960s and 1970s, if not to the entire progressive agenda of the twentieth century. This chapter outlines the reforms of the 1980s by placing them within the broader social and historical context of which they were a part. In order to do so, we first provide a general overview of the structure of U.S. education. We also present a brief outline of the history of U.S. education from 1945 to 1980, for the postwar years marked significant reforms in U.S. education and are necessary to understand the reforms of the 1980s. Next, we present an overview of the most important educational reforms of the 1980s and relate them to some of the decade's major educational problems. Finally, we conclude the chapter with a thematic discussion of the educational reforms of the period.

THE STRUCTURE OF AMERICAN EDUCATION

Education in the United States is organized primarily on the local, state, and federal level. Unlike the national or highly centralized systems of education found in the Soviet Union, France, or Japan, education in the United States is considered to be a function of the states. Since fifty states comprise the nation, many variations can be found, even among local school systems within a particular state. The precedent for delegating education to the states can be found in the Tenth Amendment to the U.S. Constitution, which reserves all powers not specifically delegated to the federal government to the states.

Although the states are responsible for public education, the daily operation of school systems has been delegated by the states to local school districts. A local school district usually consists of a relatively small geographic area and operates schools for children within a particular community. It represents a channel of communication for citizens at the grass-roots level, allowing them to have a voice in shaping their schools. Nevertheless, because education is a state and not a local function, the policies established on the local board level must be in accord with those established at the state level.

Public schools are funded by revenues generated through taxes. On the local level, revenues are generated through property taxes, and, on the state level, through sales and income taxes. Traditionally, the federal government has not assumed fiscal responsibility for education. However, after the Soviets launched Sputnik in 1957, national policy became increasingly linked to education, and federal funding began in earnest. This trend continued until the Reagan and Bush presidencies. As will be discussed in greater length, during the 1980s federal funding to education was cut drastically and in its place politicians are encouraging funding from the private sector.

Although nonpublic schools are privately funded, they are also subject to education laws passed by state legislatures—laws regulating building codes, child welfare, and health standards. Currently, over 11 percent of the school-age population are enrolled in nonpublic schools. Although Catholic schools account for the majority of private school students, the percentage of students in Catholic schools declined from 87 percent in 1966 to 60 percent in 1986 (National Catholic Education Association, 1987). Independent or private, nondiocesan schools increased their enrollments from 5 percent in 1965 to 16 percent in 1986. Evangelical and fundamentalist schools have grown in number, thus reflecting an interesting trend toward a particular type of Christian-based school which has its roots in the evangelical Protestant movements of the nineteenth century.

Since the beginning of the twentieth century, school enrollment has increased dramatically. In 1940 enrollment in schools from kindergarten through twelfth grade, private and public, was estimated at 29,751,000. By 1980, enrollment had almost doubled (U.S. Department of Commerce, 1983). Projected enrollment of students in public elementary and secondary schools for 1991 (in thousands) is 41,306 (NCES, 1989). Projected enrollment for 1991 of students in private elementary and secondary schools (in thousands) is 5,412 (NCES, 1989). Although there is no national compulsory school law, each state has its own school attendance requirements, generally requiring attendance from age six through age sixteen.

Schools are organized as elementary, junior high or middle school, and high school. Elementary school usually encompasses grades K–5 or 6; junior high, 7–9; middle school, 6–8; and high school, 9–12. Children usually enter kindergarten at age five and graduate from high school at age eighteen.

The elementary school program usually consists of mastery of the "basics," such as reading, writing, and mathematics. In addition, socialization and/or citizenship skills are emphasized. Recently, several school districts throughout the country have introduced "values education." The secondary or high school program usually contains four particular tracks: college preparatory; business or commercial; industrial or vocational; and, finally, a modified academic program for noncollege-bound students. While elementary schools tend to be small and possess a familial ambiance, high schools are usually large, especially in urban and suburban locations, and can have enrollments of 4,000 to 5,000 students. They often serve diverse populations with a variety of educational goals. Currently, their size and purpose are being hotly debated, and alternatives, such as schools within schools, magnet or special interest schools, are being created as alternatives to serve the needs of those adolescents who are not currently being addressed.

Although the American educational system attempts, at least ideologically, to be committed to equality of opportunity and does provide access free of charge to all students in public elementary and secondary schools, there are significant differences in the types of schools, and their quality, available to students from different social and economic backgrounds. This stratification system continues and is perhaps more pronounced in the U.S. system of higher education. Colleges and universities charge tuition and tend to be socially stratified, based on the amount of tuition charged. Indeed, there is a significant difference between tuition rates in public and private institutions.

Many public institutions of higher learning, such as state colleges and universities, were founded in the nineteenth century, under the Morrill Act of 1862. This federal act provided each state with land to establish institutions for the study of mechanical and agricultural instruction. The effect of the Morrill Act was to bring higher education within the grasp of students seeking a more utilitarian education, as opposed to the liberal arts curriculum offered by private institutions, as well as to make higher education affordable to a wider range of people. Although many state universities remain highly specialized and technical, many are devoted to the liberal arts as well.

The greatest growth in higher education occurred after World War II. From 1950 to 1965, college enrollments doubled in size from 2.4 million to 4.9 million. Ten years later, by 1975, the number had practically doubled again to 9 million. By 1980, 12 million students were enrolled in institutions of higher learning, and by the late 1980s the figure had reached 12.5 million (NCES, 1989).

THE HISTORY OF EDUCATION, 1945–1980

During the post–World War II period, the patterns that emerged during the Progressive Era (1890–1945) were continued. First, the debate about the goals of education (i.e., academic, social, or both) and whether all children should receive the same education remained an important one. Second, the demand for the expansion of educational opportunity became perhaps the most prominent feature of educational reform. Whereas the Common School era (nineteenth century) opened access to elementary education and the Progressive Era to secondary education, the post–World War II years were concerned with expanding opportunities to the postsecondary level. They were also directed at finding ways to translate these expanded opportunities into more equal educational outcomes at all levels of education. As in the first half of the twentieth century, so too, in the second half, the compatibility of expanded educational opportunity with the maintenance of educational standards would create serious significant problems. Thus, the tensions between equity and excellence became crucial in the debates of this period.

Cycles of Reform: Progressive and Traditional

The post–World War II years witnessed the continuation of the processes that defined the development of the comprehensive high school. The debates over academic issues, begun at the turn of the century, may be defined as the movement between pedagogical progressivism and pedagogical traditionalism. This movement continues a pattern that originated at the turn of the century and focuses not only on the process of education, but also on its goals. At the center of these debates are the questions regarding the type of education children should receive and whether all children should receive the same education. Although many of these debates were over curriculum and method, they ultimately were associated with the question of equity versus excellence.

Perhaps these debates can be best understood by examining reform cycles of the twentieth century which revolved between progressive and traditional visions of schooling. On the one hand, traditionalists believed in knowledge-centered education, a traditional subject-centered curriculum, teacher-centered education, discipline and authority, and the defense of academic standards in the name of excellence. On the other hand, progressives believed in experiential education, a curriculum that responded to both the needs of students and the times, child-centered education, freedom and individualism, and the relativism of academic standards in the name of equity. Although these poles and educational practices were rarely in only one direction, the conflicts over educational policies and practices seemed to move back and forth between these two extremes. From 1945 to 1955, the progressive education of the previous decades was critically attacked.

These critics, including Mortimer Smith, Robert Hutchins, and Arthur Bestor, assailed progressive education for its sacrificing of intellectual to social goals. They argued that the life adjustment education of the period combined with an increasingly anti-intellectual curriculum destroyed the traditional academic functions of schooling. Arthur Bestor, a respected historian and a graduate of the Lincoln School, one of the early progressive schools in New York City, argued that it was "regressive education," not progressive education, that had eliminated the school's primary role in teaching children to think (Ravitch, 1983:76). Bestor, like the other critics, assailed the schools for destroying the democratic vision that all students should receive an education that was once reserved for the elite. He suggested that the social and vocational emphasis of the schools indicated a belief that all students could not learn academic material. In an ironic sense, many of the conservative critics were agreeing with the radical critique that the Progressive Era distorted the ideals of democratic education by tracking poor and working-class children into nonacademic vocational programs.

Throughout the 1950s, the debate between progressives who defended the social basis of the curriculum and critics who demanded a more academic curriculum raged on. What was often referred to as "the great debate" (Ravitch, 1983:79) ended with the Soviet launching of the space satellite Sputnik. The idea that the Soviets might win the race for space resulted in a national commitment to improve educational standards in general and to increase mathematical and scientific literacy in particular. From 1957 through the mid–1960s, the emphasis shifted to the pursuit of excellence, and curriculum reformers attempted to redesign the curricula in ways that would lead to the return of academic standards (although many doubted that such a romantic age ever existed).

By the mid–1960s, however, the shift in educational priorities moved again toward the progressive side. This occurred in two distinct but overlapping ways. First, the civil rights movement, as we will discuss, led to an emphasis on equity issues. Thus, federal legislation, such as the Elementary and Secondary Education Act of 1965, emphasized the education of disadvantaged children. Second, in the context of the antiwar movement of the times, the general criticism of American society, and the persistent failure of the schools to ameliorate problems of poverty and of racial minorities, a "new progressivism" developed that linked the failure of the schools to the problems in society. Ushered in by the publication of A. S. Neill's *Summerhill* in 1960, a book about an English boarding school with few, if any, rules and dedicated to the happiness of the child, the new progressivism provided an intellectual and pedagogical assault on the putative sins of traditional education, its authoritarianism, its racism, its misplaced values of intellectualism, and its failure to meet the emotional and psychological needs of children.

Throughout the 1960s and early 1970s, a variety of books provided scathing criticism of American education, including Jonathan Kozol's *Death at an Early Age* (1967), which assailed the racist practices of the Boston public schools; Herbert Kohl's *36 Children* (1967) which demonstrated the pedagogical possibilities of "open education"; and Charles S. Silberman's *Crisis in the Classroom* (1970) which attacked the bureaucratic, stultifying mindlessness of American education. These books, along with a series of articles by Joseph Featherstone and Beatrice and Ronald Gross on British progressive or open education, resulted in significant experimentation in some American schools. Emphasis on individualism and relevant education, along with the challenge to the unquestioned authority of the teacher, resulted in "alternative," "free," or "open" education:

schooling that once again shifted attention away from knowledge (product) to process. There is little evidence to suggest that the open classroom was a national phenomenon, and as the historian Larry Cuban notes in his history of teaching, *How Teachers Taught* (1984), there has been surprisingly little variation in the twentieth century in teacher methods. (That is, despite the cycles of debate and reform, most secondary teachers still lecture more than they involve students.) Nonetheless, the period from the mid–1960s to the mid–1970s was a time of great turmoil in the educational arena: a time marked by two simultaneous processes: (1) the challenge to traditional schooling and (2) the attempt to provide educational opportunity for the disadvantaged. In order to understand the second process, we must look back to the origins of the concerns for equity.

Equality of Opportunity

The demand for equality of opportunity has been a central feature of U.S. history. From the Jeffersonian belief in a meritocratic elite, to Horace Mann's vision of schooling as a "great equalizer," to John Dewey's notion that the schools would be a "lever of social progress," U.S. reformers have pointed to the schools as capable of solving problems of inequality. More importantly, as Lawrence Cremin points out, Americans have expected their schools to solve social, political, and economic problems and have placed on the schools "all kinds of millennial hopes and expectations" (1990:92). While this has been true throughout our history, the translation of this view into concrete policy has defined the postwar years and also helps explain the increasing politicization of the educational conflicts.

Immediately following World War II, the issue of access to educational opportunity became an important one. The GI Bill of Rights offered 16 million servicemen and women the opportunity to pursue higher education. As Diane Ravitch (1983:12–13) points out, the GI Bill was the subject of considerable controversy over the question of access and excellence. On the one hand, veterans groups, Congress, and other supporters believed that the bill provided both a just reward for national service and a way to avoid massive unemployment in the postwar economy. Furthermore, although aimed at veterans, it was part of the growing policy to provide access to higher education to those who, because of economic disadvantage and/or poor elementary and secondary preparation, had heretofore been denied the opportunity to attend college. On the other hand, critics such as Robert Maynard Hutchins, chancellor at the University of Chicago, and James Conant, president of Harvard University, feared that the policy would threaten the traditional meritocratic selection process and result in the lowering of academic standards (Ravitch, 1983:13). Despite these criticisms, the GI Bill was, according to Ravitch, "the most ambitious venture in mass higher education that had ever been attempted by any society" (1983:14). Furthermore, she notes that the evidence does not suggest a decline in academic standards, but rather a refreshing opening of the elite postsecondary education system. While historians and policymakers may disagree about the success of the GI Bill, it is clear that it represented a building block in the post–World War II educational expansion. This expansion was similar to the previous expansions, first in the Common School Era to compulsory elementary education, second in the Progressive Era to the high school, and in the post–World War II years to postsecondary education. The same types of questions left unresolved, especially from the Progressive Era, as to whether mass public education was possible, would become central points of controversy in the coming years.

Although the GI Bill set an important precedent, the issue of educational inequality for the poor and disadvantaged, in general, and for black Americans in particular, became the focus of national attention and debate during this period. From the years immediately following World War II to the present, the questions of equality of opportunity at all levels have been significant areas of concern. In the late 1940s and 1950s, the relationships between race and education and the question of school segregation were at the forefront of political, educational, and moral conflicts.

Race, as much as any other single issue in American history, has challenged the democratic ethos of the American dream. The ideals of equality of opportunity and justice have been contradicted by the actual practices concerning black Americans and other minorities. Although legally guaranteed equal protection by the Fourteenth Amendment, blacks continued to experience vast inequities. Nowhere was this more evident than in education.

The post–Civil War Reconstruction period, despite the constitutional amendments enacted to guarantee equality of treatment before the law, had little positive effect on blacks, especially in the South. During the latter years of the nineteenth century, the Supreme Court successfully blocked civil rights legislation. In the famous 1896 decision relating to education, *Plessy* v. *Ferguson*, the Court upheld a Louisiana law that segregated railway passengers by race. In what is commonly referred to as its "separate but equal" doctrine, the Court upheld the constitutionality of segregated facilities. In his famous dissenting opinion Justice John Marshall Harlan stated:

in view of the Constitution, in the eye of the law, there is in this country no superior, dominant, ruling class of citizens. There is no caste here. Our constitution is color blind, and neither knows nor tolerates classes among citizens. In respect of civil rights, all citizens are equal before the law. The humblest is the peer of the most powerful. The law regards man as man, and takes no account of his surroundings or of his color when his civil rights guaranteed by the supreme law of the land are involved (cited in Ravitch, 1983:120).

Despite Justice Harlan's interpretation that the Constitution guaranteed a color-blind treatment of all citizens, the *Plessy* v. *Ferguson* decision remained the precedent through the first half of the twentieth century. In the 1930s and 1940s, the National Association for the Advancement of Colored People (NAACP) initiated a campaign to overthrow the law, with school segregation a major component of its strategy.

The unequal and separate education of blacks in the South became a focal point of the civil rights movements of the 1930s, 1940s, and 1950s. While the *Plessy* decision supported separate and equal, it was apparent to civil rights advocates that the schools for blacks were anything but equal. Furthermore, in terms of both educational opportunities and results, black Americans in both the North and South received nothing approximating equal treatment.

After a series of minor victories, the advocates of civil rights won their major victory when on May 17, 1954, in its landmark decision in the *Brown* v. *Topeka Board of Education* case, the Supreme Court ruled that state-imposed segregation of schools was unconstitutional. Chief Justice Earl Warren wrote: "it is doubtful that any child may reasonably be expected to succeed in life if he is denied the opportunity of education. Such an opportunity, where the state has undertaken to provide it, is a right that must be made available to all on equal terms" (cited in Ravitch, 1983:127). Thus, the Supreme Court reversed the "separate but equal" doctrine enshrined in the *Plessy* case and stated that separate educational institutions were unequal in and of themselves.

Although there would be considerable conflict in the implementation of this ruling, and although many legal scholars criticized both the basis and scope of the decision, the *Brown* decision marked both a symbolic and concrete affirmation of the ethos of democratic schooling. Although a compelling victory, *Brown* served to underscore the vast discrepancies between what Gunnar Myrdal pointed to as the American belief in equality and the American reality of inequality. In the coming years, the fight for equality of opportunity for blacks and other minorities would be a salient feature of educational reform. The *Brown* decision may have provided the legal foundation for equality, but the unequal results of American schooling did not magically change in response to the law.

In the years following the *Brown* decision, the battle for equality of opportunity was fought on a number of fronts with considerable conflict and resistance. The attempt to desegregate schools first in the South, and later in the North, resulted in confrontation and, at times, violence. For example, in Little Rock, Arkansas, in 1957, President Eisenhower sent federal troops to enforce desegregation. When Arkansas Governor Orval Faubus responded to the Supreme Court's refusal to delay desegregation by closing Little Rock's high schools, the federal courts declared the Arkansas school closing laws unconstitutional. Thus, events in Little Rock made it clear that the federal government would not tolerate continued school segregation. Although protests continued in the South into the 1960s, it was apparent that the segregationists would lose their battle to defend a Southern tradition.

The issue of school segregation, however, was not an exclusively Southern matter. In the Northern cities and metropolitan area suburbs, where housing patterns resulted in segregated schools, the issue of de jure (segregation by law) segregation was often less clear. Where de facto segregation existed (that is, the schools were not segregated intentionally by law, but by neighborhood housing patterns), the constitutional precedent for desegregation under *Brown* was shaky. Nonetheless, the evidence in the North of unequal educational opportunities based on race was clear. Thus, civil rights advocates pressed for the improvement of urban schools and for their desegregation.

The desegregation conflicts in Boston, which were every bit as embittered as those in the South, demonstrated the degree to which the issue divided its citizens. As recently as the 1970s and early 1980s, the Boston School Committee was under judicial mandate to desegregate its schools. Judge Arthur Garitty ruled that the School Committee knowingly, over a long period of time, conspired to keep schools segregated and thus limited the educational opportunity of black children. For a period of over five years, the citizens of Boston were torn apart by the Garitty desegregation order. Groups of white parents opposed, sometimes violently, the forced busing that was imposed. As J. Anthony Lukas, in his Pulitzer Prize–winning account *Common Ground* (1986) notes, the Boston situation became a symbol of frustration as it signified how a group of families, all committed to the best education for their children, could have such significantly different visions of what that meant. Judge Garitty stood resolute in his interpretation of the Constitution. Over time, the violence subsided, and many white Bostonians who could afford to do so either sent their children to private schools or moved to the suburbs. Thus, the Boston school system moved into an uneasy "ceasefire" committed, at least publicly, to the improvement of education for all.

The Boston desegregation wars, like the conflicts a decade earlier in the South, revealed that American society, though moving to ameliorate problems of racial inequality, was nonetheless a society in which racist attitudes changed slowly. Moreover, the Boston schools were a microcosm of the American educational system, a system in which inequalities of race and class were salient features. Educational reforms of the 1960s and 1970s were directed at their elimination.

An important concurrent theme was the question of unequal educational outcomes based on socioeconomic position. From the late 1950s, the findings of social scientists, including James Coleman, author of the 1966 report *Equality of Educational Opportunity*, focused national attention on the relationship between socioeconomic position and unequal educational outcomes. Furthermore, as part of Presidents John F. Kennedy's and Lyndon Baines Johnson's social programs, Americans were sensitized to the idea of ameliorating poverty. Since schools were, in Horace Mann's vision, the lever of social reform, it was only natural that schools once again became the focal point.

During the 1960s and 1970s, a series of reform efforts were directed at providing equality of opportunity and increased access at all levels of education. Based on the Coleman report findings that the unequal educational achievement of minority students was caused more by family background than by differences in quality of schools attended, federally funded programs, such as Project Headstart, were aimed at providing early preschool educational opportunities for the disadvantaged. While many radicals criticized the assumption of cultural deprivation implicit in these efforts, many reform efforts were aimed at the family and the school, rather than the school itself.

Nowhere was the conflict over these liberal reforms more clearly demonstrated than in the area of higher education. During the 1960s, educational reformers placed significant emphasis on the need to open access to postsecondary education to students who were traditionally underrepresented at colleges and universities, namely, minority groups and the disadvantaged. Arguing that college was a key to social mobility and success, reformers concluded that college was a right rather than a privilege for all (see Lavin, Alba, and Silberstein, 1981). Defenders of the traditional admissions standards argued that postsecondary education would be destroyed if admissions standards were relaxed (see Sadovnik, forthcoming).

By the late 1960s, many colleges and universities adopted the policy of open enrollment. The City University of New York, long a symbol of quality education for the working class and poor, guaranteed a place for all graduating New York City high school students in either its four-year colleges (for students with high school averages of 80 and above) or its community college system (for students below 80). Similar open admissions systems were introduced in other public university systems. Furthermore, federal financial aid monies were appropriated for students from low-income families. The results were a dramatic increase in the numbers of students participating in American higher education and a growing debate over the efficacy of such liberal reforms.

Conservatives bemoaned the decline of standards and warned of the collapse of the intellectual foundations of Western civilization. Radicals suggested that more often than not students were given "false hopes and shattered dreams" as they were sometimes underprepared, given their unequal educational backgrounds, for the rigors of college education. Liberals, while agreeing that the new students were often underprepared, suggested that it was now the role of the college to provide remedial services to turn access into success (see Sadovnik, forthcoming).

During the 1970s, colleges took on the task, however reluctantly, of providing remediation for the vast number of underprepared students, many of whom were first-generation college students. The City University of New York became perhaps the largest experiment in compensatory higher education. Its efforts symbolized both the hopes and frustrations of ameliorating unequal educational achievement. While there is significant disagreement as to the success of these higher education reforms (which we will examine more closely in Part II), it is important to recognize that this period did result in the significant expansion of higher education.

We have looked at two related processes that define the post–World War II history of education. The first is the continued debate between progressives and traditionalists about the proper aims, content, and methods of schooling. The second is the struggle for equality of opportunity and the opening of access to higher education. The educational history of the 1980s, as we will see, was characterized by the perceived failure of the reforms of this period, most particularly those of the 1960s and 1970s.

EDUCATIONAL REACTION AND REFORM: 1980s–1990s

By the late 1970s, conservative critics began to react to the educational reforms of the 1960s–1970s. They argued that liberal reforms in pedagogy and curriculum and in the arena of educational opportunity had resulted in the decline of authority and standards. Furthermore, the critics argued, the preoccupation with using the schools to ameliorate social problems, however well intended, not only failed to do so, but also was part of an overall process that resulted in mass mediocrity. What was needed was nothing less than a complete overhaul of the American educational system. Although radical critics also pointed to the failure of the schools to ameliorate problems of poverty, they located the problem not so much in the schools, but in the society at large. Liberals defended the reforms of the period by suggesting that social improvement takes a long time, and a decade and a half was scarcely sufficient to turn things around.

In 1983 the National Commission on Excellence, founded by President Reagan's secretary of education, Terrence Bell, issued its now famous report, *A Nation at Risk*. This report provided a serious indictment of American education and cited high rates of adult illiteracy, declining SAT scores, and low scores on international comparisons of knowledge by American students as examples of the decline of literacy and standards. The committee stated that "the educational foundations of our society are presently being eroded by a rising tide of mediocrity that threatens our very future as a Nation and a people" (1983:5). As solutions, the commission offered five recommendations: (1) that all students graduating from high school complete what was termed the "new basics"—four years of English, three years of mathematics, three years of science, three years of social studies, and a half year of computer science; (2) that schools at all levels expect higher achievement from their students and that four-year colleges and universities raise their admissions requirements; (3) that more time be devoted to teaching the new basics; (4) that the preparation of teachers be strengthened and that teaching be made a more respected and rewarded profession; and (5) that citizens require their elected representatives to support and fund these reforms (cited in Cremin, 1990:31).

In starkly pessimistic and action-oriented language, the commission placed educational reform at the forefront of the political agenda of the 1980s:

Our Nation is at risk. Our once unchallenged preeminence in commerce, industry, science, and technological innovation is being overtaken by competitors throughout the world . . . the educational foundations of our society are presently being eroded by a rising tide of mediocrity that threatens our very future as a nation as a people . . . we must dedicate ourselves to the reform of our educational system for the benefit of all. . . .

Our concern, however, goes well beyond matters such as industry and commerce. It

454   International Handbook of Educational Reform

also includes the intellectual, moral, and spiritual strengths of our people which knit together the very fabric of our society (National Commission on Excellence in Education, 1983:1).

This battle cry was echoed by a series of other groups including the Education Commission of the United States (1983), the Business/Higher Education Forum (1983), the Carnegie Foundation for the Advancement of Teaching (Boyer, 1983), the Twentieth Century Fund (1983), the College Board (1983), the National Governor's Association (1986), and leading educational scholars such as Mortimer Adler (1982), John Goodlad (1984), and Theodore Sizer (1984). By the mid–1980s a wave of educational reform swept the nation (Bacharach, 1990).

Dougherty (1990) suggests that the reforms of the 1980s were dominated by what he terms "centrist conservatism." In contrast to the new right's call for a complete reversal of the liberal reforms of the 1960s and 1970s, and the left's belief that educational problems reflect the inherent dilemmas of capitalism, centrist conservatives believed that "education is crucial to the basic interests of society, whether economic competitiveness, military preparedness, or cultural transmission" (Dougherty, 1990:3). In addition, a common theme in the major reports was that the American schools were beset by significant problems, with the decline in academic standards and preparation resulting in a threat to national economic and intellectual competitiveness.

The educational reforms of the 1980s consisted of two waves of reform (Bacharach, 1990; Passow, 1989). The first wave, marched by the reports of the early and mid–1980s and the educational initiatives directly responding to them, was concerned primarily with the issues of accountability and achievement (Bacharach, 1990:3). Responding to the call for increased academic achievement, many states increased graduation requirements, toughened curriculum mandates, and increased the use of standardized test scores to measure student achievement.

By the mid- to late 1980s, however, it became increasingly clear that such top-down reform would be ineffective in dealing with the schools' myriad problems. Although raising achievement standards for students and implementing accountability measures for evaluating teachers had some positive effects, many, including the National Governors Association (which took a leading role in reform), believed that educational reform had to do more than provide changes in evaluation procedures. The second wave of reform, then, was targeted at the structure and processes of the schools themselves, placing far more control in the hands of local schools, teachers, and communities. Whereas the first wave was highly centralized at the state level, the second wave was more decentralized to the local and school levels. What they had in common, however, was what the Governors Conference emphasized as the "triple theme of achievement, assessment, and accountability" (Bacharach, 1990:8).

Despite the second wave's insistence that locally based reforms were central to success, many critics, including teacher organizations and unions, argued that the reforms were highly bureaucratic and aimed primarily at assessment procedures. Significant reforms, they suggested, had to emphasize both changes within schools and changes that involved teachers, students, and parents, as part of the reform process, not merely as objects of it. Toward the latter part of the 1980s, reforms that emphasized teacher empowerment, school-based management, and school choice became the most important ones under consideration.

To summarize, the first wave of reform reports stressed the need for increased educational excellence though increased educational standards and a reversal of the rising tide of mediocrity. Passow (1989:16) states the following themes as essential to the first wave of educational reform.

1. The need to attain the twin goals of excellence and equity.
2. The need to clarify educational goals, unburdening schools from responsibilities they cannot or should not fill.
3. The need to develop a common core curriculum (not unlike the standard college-bound curriculum) with few or no electives, little or no curricular differentiation, but only pedagogical differentiation.
4. The need to eliminate tracking programs so that students could tackle the common core courses in a common curriculum in different ways.
5. The need for major changes in vocational education: in the student populations served, the curricula provided, and the sites of such education it offered.
6. The need for education to teach about technology, including computer literacy, and to become involved in the technological revolution.
7. The need to "increase both the duration and intensity of academic learning," lengthening the school day and the school year.
8. The need to recruit, train, and retain more academically able teachers, to improve the quality of teaching, and to upgrade the professional working life of teachers.
9. The need to redefine the principal's role and put the "principal squarely in charge of educational quality in each school."
10. The need to forge new partnerships between corporations, business, and the schools (Passow, 1989:16).

Typifying the second wave of educational reform were the recommendations of the State Governor's Conference. Governor Lamar Alexander in *Time for Results: The Governor's 1991 Report on Education* (1986) summarized the Governor's Association's year-long analysis of a variety of issues, including teaching, leadership and management, parental involvement and choice, readiness, technology, school facilities, and college quality, with (among others) the following recommendations:

1. Now is the time to work out a fair, affordable Career Ladder salary system that recognizes real differences in function, competence, and performance of teachers.
2. States should create leadership programs for school leaders.
3. Parents should have more choice in the public schools their children attend.

4. The nation—and the states and local districts—need report cards about results, and about what students know and can do.

5. School districts and schools that do not make the grade should be declared bankrupt, taken over by the state, and reorganized.

6. It makes no sense to keep closed half a year the school buildings in which America has invested a quarter of a trillion dollars while we are undereducated and overcrowded.

7. States should work with four and five year olds from poor families to help them get ready for school and decrease the chances that they will drop out later.

8. Better use of technologies through proper planning and training for use of video disks, computers, and robotics is an important way to give teachers more time to teach.

9. States should insist that colleges assess what students actually learn while in college (Passow, 1989:23).

During both waves of educational reform, a number of programs and initiatives received considerable attention. Among these are school choice, school-based management, school-business partnerships, the effective school movement, and reform of teacher education. The following sections discuss these in more detail.

School Choice

During the 1980s, many educational researchers and policy analysts indicated that most public schools were failing in terms of student achievement, discipline, and morality. In the same period, some researchers were investigating private schools and concluding that they were more effective learning environments than public schools. Private schools were reputed to be accountable, efficient, and safe. Moreover, the work of Coleman, Hoffer, and Kilgore (1982) seemed to prove that private school students learned more than their public school counterparts. Other research on "magnet" schools (schools with special curricula and student bodies) seemed to indicate that public schools that operated independently of the public school bureaucracy were happier, healthier, and more academically productive than zone schools where students were required to attend based on their residence.

As the decade came to a close, some researchers reasoned that magnet schools and private schools were superior to neighborhood public schools because schools of choice reflected the desires and needs of their constituents and were, thus, sensitive to change. For several decades, the idea of school choice had been on the fringes of the educational policy world in the form of voucher proposals. Essentially, voucher proponents argued that funding families, rather than schools, would allow for greater parental choice and participation. Moreover, by voting with their dollars, parents would reward good schools and punish bad schools. A voucher system, in effect, would deregulate the public school system. That a voucher system might also privatize the public school system was a muted issue.

By the late 1980s, however, school choice was at the forefront of the educational reform movement. Presidents Reagan and Bush supported choice, and one influential White House report enumerated a number of reasons why choice was the right reform for the times (Paulu, 1989). In essence, choice was a panacea that was nonbureaucratic, inexpensive, and fundamentally egalitarian because it allowed market forces to shape school policy, rather than subjecting educators to the heavy hand of the educational bureaucracy. A very influential book by John E. Chubb and Terry M. Moe, *Politics, Markets and America's Schools* (1990), seemed to provide empirical evidence that unregulated school choice policies, in and of themselves, would produce a structural reform in American education. Congressional support for greater school choice has been expressed in a bill that was passed by the House of Representatives in the summer of 1990 that, among other things, provides direct federal support for open enrollment experiments. Needless to say, all this political activity has stirred up a great deal of controversy and confusion. Choice is controversial because it is deeply political and rests on a set of assumptions about educational marketplaces and private schools that are questionable. It is confusing because choice is a rubric that covers a wide variety of policies that are quite different, except that they include an element of student and parental choice. Below we briefly touch on some of the major types of school choice plans that have been recently implemented in the United States.

Intersectional choice plans include public and private schools. Very recently, for example, the city of Milwaukee, Wisconsin, provided grants of $2,500 to students who attended private neighborhood academies. The inclusion of private schools in choice plans has stirred a great deal of debate among policymakers because fundamental issues of constitutionality and equity are inherent in any public policy that transfers funds from the public sector to the private sector. In the United States, there is a constitutionally protected division between church and state which forbids the establishment of any state religion and, thus, prohibits state support of any particular religion. Because the overwhelming number of private schools in the United States are religiously affiliated, this issue is critical. In addition, equity issues arise from the fact that some private schools are believed to contribute to the maintenance of social inequalities. The most elite secondary schools in the United States, for instance, are private. A public policy that would transfer funds to these schools would clearly raise issues of equal educational opportunity.

Intrasectional school choice policies include only public schools. States, such as Minnesota, permit students to attend school in any public school district in the state, as long as the nonresident school district is willing and has space and the transfer does not upset the racial balance. Statewide choice plans, such as Minnesota's, have been considered by a number of other states. Most choice plans, however, are more limited geographically. The most common form of intrasectional choice plans permits students to attend schools outside of their community school district. These interdistrict choice plans commonly allow urban students to cross district lines and attend suburban schools and vice versa. In St. Louis, for example, minority students from the inner city are able to attend suburban schools which are located in relatively affluent white neighborhoods. In theory, students from the suburbs are supposed to be drawn into the inner city by some outstanding magnet schools, but, in fact, only a handful of white students have traveled into the inner city to attend school.

Intradistrict choice plans refer to any option available to students within a given public school district. These options range from a choice of curriculum within a particular school to allowing students to attend any school in the district. One particular intradistrict choice plan that has gained a great deal of recognition is "controlled choice." In this type of plan, students choose a school either anywhere in a district or within some zones within a district. The key to this policy is that student choices are not allowed to upset racial balances. In effect, some students may not be able to enroll in their first-choice schools, if it means increased districtwide racial segregation. Often, other factors are also taken into consideration, such as whether or not an applicant already has a sibling in his or her school of choice. There are several successful controlled-choice districts in the United States including Cambridge, Massachusetts, Montclair, New Jersey, and District 4 located in the Borough of Manhattan in New York City. District 4 also allows students outside its boundaries to attend schools within the district, thus combining intradistrict and interdistrict features.

The city of Boston recently initiated a controlled-choice plan that may serve as a test of whether or not these types of plans can be successfully implemented on a citywide basis. According to Charles L. Glenn, executive director of the Office of Educational Equity in the Massachusetts Department of Education, the choice plan in Boston appears to be operationally successful, although "vulnerable schools" (i.e., those with declining student populations) need extra assistance to remain open and to provide services to the students who attend them. According to Glenn (1991:43), "Public school choice will not produce overnight miracles, and the Boston experience—like that of Soviet-bloc economies—shows how very difficult it can be to reform an entrenched institution with a monopoly position and a tradition of top-down decision making."

Clearly, it is too early to tell whether or not school choice will lead to the revitalization of public education in the United States. It may well be that choice is a method of school improvement, but cannot by itself resolve many of the fundamental problems associated with public education. Moreover, choice plans usually involve complex and volatile issues of constitutionality, equity, and feasibility. How, for instance, will already impoverished school districts pay for the increased transportation costs required by many choice plans? In sum, there is evidence that school choice can lead to improvement in individual schools, but there is little convincing evidence that choice will result in the overall improvement of American education.

School–Business Partnerships

During the 1980s, business leaders became increasingly concerned that the nation's schools were not producing the kinds of graduates necessary for revitalizing the American economy. Several school–business partnerships were formed, the most notable of which was the Boston Compact begun in 1982. These partnerships have been formed in other cities, too; for instance, in 1991 the Committee to Support Philadelphia Public Schools pledged management assistance and training to the Philadelphia School District to restructure and implement a site-based management plan. In return, the city promised that by 1995 it would raise the test scores of its graduates and improve grade promotion rates. Other school–business partnerships include scholarships for poor students to attend college and programs where businesses "adopt" a school.

Despite the considerable publicity that surrounds these partnerships, the fact is that in the 1980s only 1.5 percent of corporate giving was to public primary and secondary public schools (Reich, 1991:43). In fact, corporate and business support for public schools has fallen dramatically since the 1970s. School–business partnerships have attracted considerable media attention, but there is little convincing evidence that they have significantly improved schools or that, as a means of reform, school–business partnerships will address the fundamental problems facing American education.

School-Based Management and Teacher Empowerment

In part, the history of education in the United States can be characterized as a struggle between the rival traditions of decentralization and centralization. Generally, the educational system, as a whole, is decentralized, because the ultimate authority for educational policy rests with the individual states and not with the federal government. Yet, within states and school districts, there has been a long-term tendency to centralize decision making in state agencies, elected and appointed school boards, and superintendents' offices. Throughout the 1980s there were repeated calls for the exercise of local and community authority in educational decision making. After all, the argument runs, who knows best what the children in any one particular school need—administrators and teachers or state and local bureaucrats? School-based management is a decentralizing policy that has captured the imagination of many American educators and much of the public at large. Joseph Fernandez, New York City's schools chancellor, for instance, is a powerful advocate for school-based management because it enables those who interact with students every day to oversee budgets and set curricula most relevant to the needs of students.

Major school-based management reforms have been instituted in such places as New York City; Dade County, Florida; San Diego, California; Rochester, New York; Louisville, Kentucky; and Chicago. Perhaps the most dramatic of these reforms has been in Chicago, where locally elected councils—composed of six parents, two community residents, two teachers, and the principal—have been put in charge of each of the city's 541 public schools. While all the legal issues surrounding this reform have not been settled, there is little doubt that school-based management reforms will continue to enjoy support among many policymakers, some teachers, and in local communities.

The notion that local decision making, however, will automatically make schools better learning environments and more collegial may ignore some of the problems implicit in extreme decentralization. For example, how can the tension between providing teachers with more decision-making authority, while simultaneously providing for administrative action and initiative be resolved? There is considerable research that suggests that principals play a key role in creating effective schools. Moreover, some actions that may be required to make schools more effective may run counter to teachers' desires and self-interests. If teachers and parents are to successfully formulate and implement policy, they need to be given training and related technical assistance and unless teachers are given substantial amounts of time to plan, implement, monitor, and change their initiatives, there is little reason to expect that school-based reforms will be successful. This issue is becoming more acute in states where budgetary shortfalls have resulted in teacher layoffs and increased teaching workloads. Finally, school-based management requires that some rules and regulations be waived by federal, state, and local authorities as well as teachers' unions. To some extent, these negotiations may mean that school-based reforms may be slowly and partially implemented, and, thus, their effectiveness may be diminished.

Clearly, school-based management implies teacher empowerment. Without providing teachers the professional opportunities and responsibilities that come with decision making, many school-level reforms will wither. Yet, what does the phrase "teacher empowerment" really mean? How much power should teachers have in policymaking, and how much power do teachers want? It is becoming increasingly common for principals to establish faculty councils or committees that, in effect, administer the school. These committees and councils may have actual power, or they may be regarded more as advisory bodies. It is far too early to tell if the teacher empowerment movement will reshape the authority systems within elementary and secondary schools in the United States. In particular, if there is no basic redefinition of teachers' roles within schools, there is little likelihood that teachers will have the opportunity, time, or support to implement change. It is not entirely clear that all teachers want to be policymakers. Definitions of professional responsibilities are not universally agreed upon. Undoubtedly, each school and school district will arrive at a definition of what constitutes teachers' roles and responsibilities in the coming decade. In some schools and school districts, teachers may gain real authority, while in others, principals and superintendents may retain most of the decision-making power. If, however, the movement toward school-based management continues, it is likely that teachers will be increasingly empowered and be given authority to make professional decisions regarding school management, school curriculum, and pedagogy.

The Effective School Movement

In response to *A Nation at Risk* and other reports criticizing the effectiveness of American public schools, the school effectiveness movement emerged and suggested that certain characteristics in good schools could be used as models for improving educational effectiveness. The late Ron Edmunds, one of the early leaders of this movement, argued that educational reform and improvement must consider problems of both equity and quality. The school effectiveness research points out five key factors that define successful schools: (1) high expectations for all students and staff acceptance of responsibility for student learning; (2) instructional leadership on the part of the principal; (3) a safe and orderly environment conducive to learning; (4) a clear and focused mission concerning instructional goals shared by the staff; and (5) frequent monitoring of student progress (Gartner and Lipsky, 1987:389).

Based on these principles, school effectiveness researchers and reformers focused their attention on both the content and process of education. First, some critics of present educational practices argued that American schools paid too little attention to the traditional curriculum and that students learned very little subject matter. From Powell, Cohen, and Ferrar's *Shopping Mall High School* (1987) to Ravitch and Finn's *What Do Our Seventeen Year Olds Know?* (1987), the American schools were portrayed as having lost their sense of what knowledge is important and, therefore, left students with very little sense of the value of knowledge. Recent popular critiques, including E. D. Hirsch's *Cultural Literacy* (1987) and Allan Bloom's *The Closing of the American Mind* (1987), although the subject of passionate criticism, also portrayed a school system that, in their view, had failed to teach a systematic common body of culturally valuable knowledge. The debate over the usefulness of such knowledge, the Eurocentric and Western bias of the authors, and other criticisms, though important, is not central to this chapter. What is important, however, is that such criticisms have resulted in an increasing emphasis both on what should be taught and how it should be taught. Thus, much of the school effectiveness movement places a primary emphasis on teaching, teacher effectiveness, and learning, not in terms of the process of learning, but in terms of the outcomes of learning.

According to Larry Cuban (1984), the school effectiveness movement's recommendations on teaching, teacher effectiveness, and learning are based on research findings concerning the factors that positively affect student achievement. For example, the following teacher factors, according to the effective school research, correlative favorably with student test scores on standardized tests in reading and math:

1. Teacher focuses clearly on academic goals.
2. Teacher concentrates on allotting the instructional period to instructional tasks (Time on Task).

3. Teacher presents information clearly, organizing by explaining, outlining, and reviewing, and covers subject matter extensively.

4. Teacher monitors student progress toward instructional objectives, selecting materials and arranging methods to increase student success.

5. Teacher feedback is quick and targeted on content of instructional tasks (Cuban, 1984:266).

Based on these research findings, the school effectiveness movement sought to develop scientific models for insuring better teaching (defined as behaviors responding to the above correlations) and the supervision of teachers to insure increased student achievement. The best example of the attempt to create a rational-scientific pedagogy is the work of Madeline Hunter, who at present is one of the most popular figures in school administrative circles. According to Hunter (1982), while teaching is both an art and a science, the scientific model is essential to effective schools and teaching is a manifestation of science because

1. Identifiable cause-effect relationships exist between teaching and learning.

2. Those relationships hold for all teaching and learning regardless of content, age, and socioeconomic and ethnic characteristics of the learner.

3. While many of these relationships were identified in the static purity and potential sterility of the research laboratory, those relationships seem to hold in the dynamics inherent in the vitality of a functioning classroom.

4. Those relationships are stated in terms of probability and not certainty.

5. The deliberate, intuitive, or inadvertent use of those cause-effect relationships can be observed and documented in the process of teaching.

6. The principles derived from those relationships should also be incorporated in the process of planning and evaluating before and after teaching.

7. The science of teaching can be taught and predictably learned by most professionals who are willing to expend the required effort.

Although Hunter concedes that ''effective teaching also can be an art that goes beyond proficiency,'' the core of her work emphasizes a science of teaching that revolves around content decisions, learner behavior decisions, teacher behaviors, and the design of effective lessons. Thus, Hunter's model, much like B. F. Skinner's call for a technology of behavior (1971), proposes a technology of teaching, one that reduces the art of teaching to a series of categories, decisions, steps, and types.

While there is some merit to the attempt to rationalize educational practice based on research findings, the bureaucratic-rational model that underlies this science of teaching is often misguided and distorted by its becoming an end, rather than a means to an end. Most importantly, it ignores important realities of teaching and learning and the relationship between schools and other external institutional and societal forces.

Teacher Education

The emergence and development of teacher education as a social problem was a response to the initial debates concerning the failure of the schools. If the schools were not working properly, then teachers and teaching, perhaps the most important piece in the puzzle, had to be looked at critically. In addition, teacher organizations such as the National Education Association (NEA) and the American Federation of Teachers (AFT), fearing the scapegoating of their members, took an active role in raising the debate as the opportunity to both recognize and improve the problematic conditions under which, from their perspective, most of their members work. Finally, if teachers and teaching were indeed part of the problem, then perhaps the education and training of teachers was a good starting point for analysis. Thus, teacher education and schools and colleges of education, long the object of critical scrutiny within universities, became the subject of intensive national investigation. By 1986 at least five major reports (by the National Commission on Excellence in Teacher Education, the California Commission on the Teaching Profession, the Holmes Group, the Southern Regional Education Board, and the Carnegie Report of the Task Force on Teaching as a Profession) all outlined major problems in teacher education and the professional lives of teachers and proposed a large-scale overhaul of the system that prepares teachers. Although the reports differed in some respects, there was widespread agreement about the nature of the problem.

The debate revolved around three major points:

1. The perceived lack of rigor and intellectual demands in teacher education programs.
2. The need to attract and retain competent teacher candidates.
3. The necessity of reorganizing the academic and professional components of teacher education programs at both the baccalaureate and postbaccalaureate levels (Teacher Education Project, 1986).

While all five reports contributed to the ongoing discussions, the Carnegie and Holmes reports, perhaps because they represented two of the major interest groups in teacher education (in the case of Carnegie, major political and educational leaders and for Holmes, the deans of education from the major research universities), have attracted the most public response and have become symbolic of the teacher education reform movement. The next section, therefore, will analyze the Carnegie and Holmes reports as representative of the current attempts to improve the training of teachers.

The Carnegie Report, entitled *A Nation Prepared: Teachers for the 21st Century* (1986) and prepared by its Task Force on Teaching as a Profession (including representatives from corporations, the NEA and AFT, school writers and administrators, legislators, the governor of New Jersey, and a dean of education of a major research university), focused on the necessity of educational quality for a competitive U.S. economy, and the value of education in a democratic political system. Building on the critique offered by *A Nation at Risk*, the Carnegie Report suggested that improvements in teacher education were necessary preconditions for improvements in education. Finally, in addition to this underlying democratic-liberal model of education, the report argued that the decline in traditional low-wage jobs in the U.S. economy and the corresponding increase in high-technology and service positions would require the schools to better prepare students for this "new" economic reality. In this regard, too, the Carnegie Report stressed the centrality of better prepared teachers to meet the challenges of the twenty-first century. Echoing this political-economic perspective, the report states

If our standard of living is to be maintained, if the growth of a permanent underclass is to be averted, if democracy is to function effectively into the next century, our schools must graduate the vast majority of their students with achievement levels long thought possible for only the privileged few. The American mass education system, designed in the early part of the century for a mass production economy, will not succeed unless it not only raises but redefines the essential standards of excellence and strives to make quality and equality of opportunity compatible with each other (p. 3).

In order to accomplish these democratic-liberal goals, the Carnegie Report (1986:3) calls for "sweeping changes in educational policy." These changes would include restructuring the schools and the teaching profession, eliminating the undergraduate education major, recruiting minorities into the teaching profession, and increasing standards in teacher education and in teaching.

The Holmes Group, on the other hand, avoids explicit political-economic goals, but also focuses on the relationship between university-based teacher education, the professional lives of teachers, and the structure of the schools themselves. Arguing that their role as teacher educators gives a unique as well as perhaps a subjective perception of these issues, the Holmes Report, entitled *Tomorrow's Teachers* (1986), outlines a set of five goals and proposals for the improvement of teacher education. Michael Sedlak, one of the original coauthors of the report, introduces his brief summary of the document by stressing that "the Holmes Group is dedicated not just to the improvement of teacher education but to the construction of a genuine profession of teaching" (1987:315). The goals of the report included raising the intellectual soundness of teacher education, creating career ladders for teachers, developing entry-level requirements into the profession, linking schools of education at the university level to elementary schools, and improving schools for students and teachers.

Despite differences in tone and some minor differences in emphasis, both the Carnegie and Holmes reports focus on the same general concerns. First, they agree that overall problems in education cannot be solved without corresponding changes in teacher education. Second, teacher education programs must be upgraded in terms of their intellectual rigor and focus, their need to emphasize the liberal arts and to eliminate undergraduate teacher education programs, and, like other professions (i.e., psychology, social work, law, medicine) must move professional training and certification to the graduate level. Third, rigorous standards of entry into the profession must be implemented, and systematic examinations to monitor such entry must be developed. Fourth, university teacher education programs and schools must be connected in a more systematic and cooperative manner. Fifth, career ladders that recognize differences in knowledge, skill, and commitment must be created for teachers. Sixth, necessary changes must be made in the schools and the professional lives of teachers in order to attract and retain the most competent candidates for the profession.

Representative of the second wave of educational reforms, both the effective school movement's recommendations and those of the Carnegie and Holmes reports emphasized the processes of teaching and learning, the school environment, and especially the need to improve the professional lives and status of teachers.

EDUCATIONAL REFORM IN THE 1980s: MAJOR THEMES

Bacharach (1990:415–430) suggests that U.S. educational reform in the 1980s may be understood in terms of five central themes or questions:

1. The reform actors and their roles.
2. Excellence or equity?
3. Redefining good education for a new century.
4. Toward an education marketplace: choice or greater inequality?
5. Reconceptualizing the role of the teacher.

Reform Actors and Their Roles

In the 1980s the major reform actors shifted from the federal to the state to the local levels. From the outset, the federal government through the Department of Education attempted to balance its ideological belief that education is not a federal governmental matter with its commitment to provide the impetus for change. First, through its influential report *A Nation at Risk* written during the tenure of Secretary Terrance Bell, and, second, through his successor William Bennett's use of his office as a "bully pulpit," the U.S. Department of Education played a significant role in keeping the pressure on states and localities to improve educational results, which for Secretary Bennett defined the goals of educational reform.

The first wave of reforms involved the states becoming the primary level of educational reform. By setting tougher standards and implementing new standardized testing procedures, educational reform became centralized to the state level (Honig, 1990; Passow, 1990). As many critics began to point out the problematic and, at times, contradictory nature of these rational-bureaucratic processes, the second wave of reforms began to target the local and school levels as the appropriate venues for improvement, and administrators, teachers, and parents as the appropriate actors.

Bacharach (1990:418) points out that many discussions of school reform refer to top-down or bottom-up reforms as either-ors, as if these are mutually exclusive options. He cautions that the lessons of the 1980s portend that only through an overall reform process that integrates the many levels of reform (federal, state, local, school) and the diverse actors (governors, legislators, administrators, teachers, parents, and students) will meaningful reform have the opportunity to succeed.

Excellence and Equity

From the outset of the reforms of the 1980s, the tensions between excellence and equity have been a central concern. Although, as Passow points out (1989:16), "excellence became a shibboleth of the reform movement," many writers were equally concerned with how the new tougher standards would affect students already disadvantaged because of unequal educational opportunities (Apple, 1990; Boyer, 1990; Cuban, 1990). Whereas the first wave of reforms was explicitly tied to the excellence side of the equation, the second wave was more often concerned with the need to balance the objectives of equity as well. Many of the reform proposals of this period, including magnet schools, the effective school movement, public school choice, and school restructuring, all, at least in part, addressed the need to create schools that work for all students. Although many critics of proposals such as school choice asserted that they would increase, not decrease, inequality, nonetheless during the second wave equity issues began to emerge as vitally important.

At the core of the discussion about these issues are fundamentally differing views of the goals of education. On the one hand, the conservatives, as exemplified by the Heritage Foundation (see Pincus, 1985) stressed the role of schools from a functionalist perspective. From this perspective, the role of the schools is to provide a sorting mechanism to select and educate the "best and the brightest" to fill the functionally essential positions in our society. To do this effectively requires that educational funding be geared to programs that ensure high standards. On the other hand, liberals and others on the political left stress the importance of serving the educational needs of all students, and have warned of the deleterious effects on the already disadvantaged of raising standards. Although there have been no easy answers to these complicated questions, it is safe to say that the reforms of the 1980s, at least ideologically, were concerned with balancing excellence and equity. In practice, however, this balance has been far from a reality.

Redefining Good Education

As in previous periods of U.S. educational reform, the 1980s were concerned with defining what constitutes a good education. Just as in the progressive era of the first part of the twentieth century, educational reformers debated the question of whether all children should receive the same education, or whether the schools should provide different types of education for different students? In addition, the question of what constitutes the type of education necessary for the increasing technological demands of the twenty-first century became a critical issue of the decade.

Interestingly, it was centrist conservatives such as E. D. Hirsch (1987) and Ravitch and Finn (1987) who seized the offensive in these debates. Arguing that the progressive reforms of the twentieth century had resulted in the decline of traditional knowledge (defined as Western), they called for a return to a liberal arts curriculum for all students. By inserting the concern for equity into the call for action, they seized the left's own platform; in addition, by criticizing progressive education, they sought to combine the dual demands for excellence and equity. Although the left would criticize this centrist conservative position for its ethnocentric Western bias (and call for a more multicultural curriculum), the centrist conservatives effectively dominated the curriculum discourse by taking what they saw as the "moral high ground."

Whereas these curriculum debates were essentially about what should be taught to students within the liberal arts tradition, another aspect of the debates concerned the role of education in preparing students for life and the world of work. Although a major theme of many of the reports concerned the relationship between education and economic competitiveness, it was not clear throughout the decade exactly what constituted the proper role of the school toward the end. Many business leaders, including David Kearns of Xerox Corporation, called for closer linkages between school and corporations. Others, such as Robert Reich (1990), pointed out that fundamental changes in the global economy would necessitate workers who could be creative, imaginative, and flexible and that schools would have to change accordingly. Still others, such as Michael Apple (1990), suggested that the new global economy would reduce the number of jobs requiring such intellectual and analytical dispositions, and that the contradiction of the reforms of the 1980s was the increased emphasis on critical and analytical thinking in a world where the largest number of new jobs would not require them. Finally, others, such as Futrell (1990) and Ravitch (1985), returned to the notion that education had to prepare students for civic responsibility and, in Futrell's words, (1990:423) for "[an education] that prepares them not only for a life of work but for a life of worth."

Clearly, the debate about what constitutes a good education for the twenty-first century, although a central philosophical concern of the 1980s, is nowhere close to resolution. Perhaps, as Diane Ravitch (1985) pointed out, because

Americans have had little consensus about the goals of education, they have been unable to create an educational system with a unified set of objectives.

Toward an Educational Marketplace

The question of school choice became the burning issue of the late 1980s. Supported by both conservatives and some liberals, given national exposure by Chubb and Moe's (1990) controversial book, *Politics, Markets, and America's Schools*, and supported by elected officials as diverse as President Bush and Milwaukee black city councilwoman Polly Williams, school choice programs have been seen by many as the most effective mechanism for school improvement. Although many agree that reforms that are aimed at the schools themselves, and, at the school bureaucracy in particular, are likely to be more effective than those that simply make top-down mandates, critics such as Cookson (1991) point out that the free market strategy is not likely to produce the educational panacea forecasted. Given the vicissitudes of the free market and the ways in which it will likely be more advantageous to the economically advantaged, Cookson cautions against unrealistic optimism.

By the close of the 1980s, the question of whether school choice programs would improve education for all students or increase educational inequality was left unanswered. As the choice programs become the popular reform of the 1990s, however, educational researchers will have the opportunity to assess empirically the important answer to this question.

Reconceptualizing the Role of the Teacher

The first wave of reform in the 1980s attempted to reduce uncertainty in the classroom and thus sought to increase bureaucratic controls on teacher behavior. The standardization of teaching through tightened bureaucratic control, it was thought, would result in increased student achievement. As it became increasingly clear that these efforts were often counterproductive, and as they led to the deskilling of the teaching profession and teachers mindlessly teaching to tests, the second wave of reforms sought to redefine the role of teachers as professionals. Both the Holmes (1986) and Carnegie (1986) reports proposed radical reforms in teacher education and the professional lives of teachers. Stressing career ladders, a national board for professional standards, and cooperation between universities and schools, among other things, these reports sought to professionalize rather than deskill teachers. Other reforms of this period, including teacher empowerment and school-based management, sought to make teachers essential actors in the reform process.

As the decade drew to a close, the conflict between two differing models of school administration, the bureaucratic and the professional (Bacharach, 1990:427), was still unresolved. The bureaucratic dominated the first wave of reformers, and the professional, the second wave. As the 1990s unfold, this conflict will surely remain central to ongoing reform efforts.

CONCLUSION

The 1980s was a decade of momentous debate on education and considerable efforts at school improvement. As Passow (1989:37) points out, the fact that educational issues became so fundamental to the nation, and that the emphasis in the second wave was on pedagogy, curriculum, teachers as professionals, school organization, and school improvement, is reason for continuous optimism. However, as many of the best criticisms of American education such as Boyer's (1983) on high schools, Sizer's (1984) on school structure and process, and McNeil's (1988) on the contradictions of reform point out, educational improvement will require far more than ideological rhetoric; it will require fundamental school restructuring. So far, despite some efforts such as Sizer's imaginative Coalition of Essential Schools, a nationally implemented school restructuring effort, the nation's schools appear resistant to structural change. This should not come as a surprise. As Seymour Sarason (1982) has suggested, the culture of the school has always been difficult to alter. Nonetheless, at the very least the 1980s represented a period of national soul searching about complex educational problems. Hopefully, the 1990s will begin to produce some of the improvements only discussed so far. Whether or not these reforms can actually balance the dual goals of excellence and equity is perhaps the nation's greatest challenge. To date, the goals have remained only a dream.

REFERENCES

Adler, Mortimer. 1982. *The Paideia Proposal*. New York: Macmillan.

Alexander, Lamar. 1986. "Chairman's Summary." In *Time for Results: The Governor's 1991 Report on Education*. National Governor's Association Center for Policy Research and Analysis. Washington, D.C.: National Governor's Association.

Apple, Michael. 1990. "What Reform Talk Does: Creating New Inequalities." In *Education Reform: Making Sense of It All*, ed. Samuel Bacharach. Needham Heights, Mass.: Allyn and Bacon, pp. 155–164.

Bacharach, Samuel. 1990. *Education Reform: Making Sense of It All*. Needham Heights, Mass.: Allyn and Bacon.

Bloom, Allan. 1987. *The Closing of the American Mind*. New York: Simon and Schuster.

Boyer, Ernest. 1983. *High School*. New York: Harper and Row.

———. 1990. "The New Agenda for the Nation's Schools." In *Education Reform: Making Sense of It all*, ed. Samuel Bacharach. Needham Heights, Mass.: Allyn and Bacon, pp. 30–38.

Business/Higher Education Forum. 1983. *America's Competitive Challenge*. Washington, D.C.: American Council on Education.

Carnegie Task Force on Teaching as a Profession. 1986. *A Nation Prepared: Teachers for the 21st Century*. Washington, D.C.: Carnegie Forum on Education and the Economy.

Chubb, John E., and Terry M. Moe. 1990. *Politics, Markets, and America's Schools.* Washington, D.C.: Brookings Institution.

Coleman, James S., et al. 1966. *Equality of Educational Opportunity.* Washington, D.C.: U.S. Government Printing Office.

————, Thomas Hoffer, and Sally Kilgore. 1982. *High School Achievement: Public, Catholic and Private Schools Compared.* New York: Basic Books.

College Board. 1983. *Academic Preparation for College.* New York: College Board.

Cookson, Peter W., Jr. 1991. "Politics, Markets, and America's Schools: A Review." *Teacher College Record* 93:156–160.

Cremin, Lawrence. 1990. *Popular Education and Its Discontents.* New York: Harper and Row.

Cuban, Larry. 1984. *How Teachers Taught: Constancy and Change in American Classrooms, 1890–1980.* New York: Longman.

————. 1990. "Why Do Some Reforms Persist." In *Education Reform: Making Sense of It All,* ed. Samuel Bacharach. Needham Heights, Mass.: Allyn and Bacon.

Dougherty, Kevin. 1990. "Quality, Equality, and Politics: The Political Sources of the Current School Reform Wave." Paper presented at the Annual Meeting of the American Sociological Association.

Education Commission of the United States. 1983. *Action for Excellence.* Boulder, Colo.: Education Commission of the States.

Futrell, Mary Hatwood. 1990. "Redefining National Security: New Directions for Education Reform." In *Education Reform:* Making Sense of It All, ed. Samuel Bacharach. Needham Heights, Mass.: Allyn and Bacon, pp. 259–268.

Gartner, Alan, and Dorothy Kerzner Lipsky. 1987. "Beyond Special Education: Toward a Quality System for All Students." *Harvard Educational Review* 57:367–395.

Glenn, Charles L. 1991. "Will Boston Be the Proof of the Choice Pudding." *Educational Leadership* 48:41–43.

Goodlad, John. 1984. *A Place Called School.* New York: McGraw-Hill.

Hirsch, E. D. 1987. *Cultural Literacy.* Boston: Houghton Mifflin.

Holmes Group. 1986. *Tomorrow's Teachers.* East Lansing, Mich.: Holmes Group.

Honig, Bill. 1990. "The Key to Reform: Sustaining and Expanding Upon Initial Success." In *Education Reform: Making Sense of It All,* ed. Samuel Bacharach. Needham Heights, Mass.: Allyn and Bacon, pp. 52–56.

Hunter, Madeline. 1982. *Mastery Teaching.* El Segundo, Calif.: TIP Publications.

Kohl, Herbert. 1967. *36 Children.* New York: New American Library.

Kozol, Jonathan. 1967. *Death at an Early Age.* New York: Houghton Mifflin.

Lavin, David, Richard Alba, and Richard Silberstein. 1981. *Right Versus Privilege: The Open Admissions Experiment at City University of New York.* New York: Free Press.

Lukas, J. Anthony. 1986. *Common Ground.* New York: Vintage.

McNeil, Linda M. 1988. *Contradictions of Control: School Structure and School Knowledge.* New York: Routledge, Chapman and Hall.

National Center for Education Statistics (NCES). 1989. *Digest of Education Statistics.* Washington, D.C.: U.S. Government Printing Office.

National Commission on Excellence in Education. 1983. *A Nation at Risk.* Washington, D.C.: U.S. Government Printing Office.

National Governor's Association. 1986. *A Time for Results.* Washington, D.C.: National Governor's Association.

Neill, A. S. 1960. *Summerhill*. New York: Holt.

Passow, A. Harry. 1989. "Present and Future Directions in School Reform." In *Schooling for Tomorrow*, ed. Thomas Sergiovanni and John Moore. Needham Heights, Mass.: Allyn and Bacon, pp. 13–39.

———. 1990. "Whither (or Wither?) School Reform?" In *Education Reform: Making Sense of It All*, ed. Samuel Bacharach. Needham Heights, Mass.: Allyn and Bacon, pp. 10–19.

Paulu, Nancy. 1989. "Improving Schools and Empowering Parents: Choice in American Education." Washington, D.C.: U.S. Government Printing Office.

Pincus, Fred L. 1985. "From Equity to Excellence: The Rebirth of Educational Conservatism." In *The Great School Debate*, ed. Beatrice and Ronald Gross. New York: Simon and Schuster, pp. 329–344.

Powell, Arthur, David Cohen, and Elizabeth Ferrar. 1987. *The Shopping Mall High School*. Boston: Houghton Mifflin.

Ravitch, Diane. 1983. *The Troubled Crusade*. New York: Basic Books.

———. 1985. *The Schools We Deserve*. New York: Basic Books.

———, and Chester Finn. 1987. *What Do Our Seventeen Year Olds Know*. New York: Basic Books.

Reich, Robert B. 1991, January 20. "Succession of the Successful." *The New York Times Magazine*, pp. 42–45.

———. 1990. "Education and the Next Economy." In *Education Reform: Making Sense of It All*, ed. Samuel Bacharach. Needham Heights, Mass.: Allyn and Bacon, pp. 194–212.

Sadovnik, Alan R. Forthcoming. *Equity and Excellence in Higher Education*. New York: Peter Lang Publishers.

Sarason, Seymour B. 1982. *The Culture of the School and the Problem of Change*. Boston: Allyn and Bacon.

Sedlak, Michael. 1987. "Tomorrow's Teachers: The Essential Arguments of the Holmes Group Report." *Teachers College Record* 88 (3):314–325.

Silberman, Charles S. 1970. *Crisis in the Classroom*. New York: Random House.

Sizer, Theodore. 1984. *Horace's Compromise*. Boston: Houghton Mifflin.

Skinner, B. F. 1971. *Beyond Freedom and Dignity*. New York: Bantam.

Teacher Education Project. 1986. "A Compilation of the Major Recommendations of Teacher Education."

Twentieth Century Fund, Task Force on Elementary and Secondary Education Policy. 1983. *Making the Grade*. New York: Twentieth Century Fund.

26

USSR

Stephen T. Kerr

As the 1980s came to a close, television audiences around the world watched in incredulous fascination as the Eastern bloc came apart at the seams. Not only the satellite countries of Eastern Europe, but also the Soviet Union itself seemed convulsed by social and economic changes that would have been unimaginable only a few months before. The Western press reportage on the USSR concentrated on shifts in the political and economic arenas. But changes were also underway in other parts of Soviet society, notably also in education.

The attempts Soviet educators and policymakers have made to reform their system of education over the past five years have had uneven results; nonetheless, the attempts have been both serious and varied. They provide useful lessons in several domains—about the difficulties of moving away from a highly centralized approach to educational decision making; about the importance of bringing teachers, students, parents, intellectuals, and others concerned with the state of education into discussions about reform; about the need for explicit links between educational research and practice; about the relationship between educational change and economic development; and about the connections between education and the formation of a civil state grounded on democratic principles and the rule of law.

Surveying these developments in Soviet educational reform, their current status and possible future paths, will be our task here. We will start by reviewing some salient features of Soviet history and social life which have influenced the educational system. Then we will examine what "reform" has meant in three recent (but very different) periods of Soviet history: the pre-Gorbachev period (prior to 1985) of tinkering with the status quo, the early Gorbachev era (1985 to 1989) of increasing demands for "radical reform," and, following 1989, a time of uneasy equilibrium between conservative and reformist pressures. We will conclude by considering the interrelationships between the changes now underway in Soviet educational institutions and those taking place in society more generally, and what those connections imply about the future of education in the USSR.

THE SOVIET CONTEXT: SALIENT FEATURES

Those not familiar with the USSR often find it difficult to develop a coherent picture of the country's system of education. Impressions vary considerably: there were fears of a superior system and accompanying demands for change at home characterized in such titles as "Why Ivan can read and Johnny can't" of the 1950s and 1960s; there were calls for careful study and possibly emulation of Soviet childrearing practices in works such as Urie Bronfenbrenner's *Two Worlds of Childhood* (1970); there were popular accounts of what went on in ordinary Soviet schools that suggested a very traditional view of instruction (Jacoby, 1974; Smith, 1976). And more recent writings have indicated larger stresses in the system from such problems as the need to handle numbers of students from working-class, rural, or minority backgrounds (Szekely, 1985). These differing visions are hard to reconcile: should we think of the Soviet educational system as dominated by ruthless trainers, gentle nurturers, mindless caretakers, or worried jailers? In fact, all these images are probably correct for some parts of the system at certain times. The difficult part is discerning which parts of the system are functional, which have problems, and what the interests are of the various groups seeking to solve those problems.

The Origins of the USSR in Russian History

The USSR is both immense and diverse. With over 8 million square miles of territory in a variety of climatic conditions and 200,000 individual schools, the educational system would be a challenge for any country to administer. Add to this the difficulty of accommodating speakers of more than 100 different languages, an equally large number of varied ethnic groups, and cultural and socioeconomic diversity ranging from preliterate northern nomadic tribes to civilizations with distinctive literary traditions (predating by centuries that of the current ruling power), and the problem becomes daunting indeed.

Historically, it is also important for Western readers to recall that, unlike most Western European states, Russia never experienced the intellectual excitement and social upwelling that attended the Renaissance, Reformation, and Enlightenment during the fourteenth through the eighteenth centuries. While Italian humanists were creating ideals of what a well-educated person should be and know, Russia was oppressed and isolated under the harsh occupation of the "Tartar Yoke"; while the American colonies were drafting a Declaration of Independence and the French Republic issued a Declaration of the Rights of Man, the Russian czars strengthened press censorship and the secret police network; while European countries created parliaments and participatory forms of government, the Russian czar retained, until the end of the Russian Empire in 1917, the official title of "autocrat." Western concepts of individual liberty and responsibility were not widespread in Russia; the power of a strong central state was widely seen as legitimate and necessary.

The Ideological Content of Soviet Schooling

This lack of a liberal heritage may explain in a general way the unique and perplexing role of the Communist party in the era of Soviet power. Until early in 1990, the Soviet Constitution specifically identified the Communist party as society's "leading organ," the embodiment by definition of the will of the people and therefore the supreme authority in all matters, large and small. What this meant in practice for education was that all matters of policy and management were handled de jure by the administrative structure of schools and universities, but these decisions were in all cases de facto examined and approved (and in many cases originally suggested) by an organization's party committee. Since the individuals who occupied party positions often had been trained only in party work and lacked basic educational credentials, it can be imagined that they showed little enthusiasm for educational diversity and experimentation.

Also contributing to this set of problems was the centrality and continual teaching of Marxist-Leninist ideology, an amalgam of nineteenth-century historical determinism and economic theory that continued to hold sway in the schools long after individual citizens began to question its usefulness as a guide to action in the contemporary world. The result of this gap between espoused theory and observed practice was a gradual distancing of ordinary citizens from social life and civic participation. While the Marxist vision of a utopian society had many positive elements, and while many Soviet citizens would probably continue today to applaud the vision of an equitable, socialist society that the ideology suggests, Soviet citizens outside of the party came to have less and less use for the unwavering principles of party omnicompetence and a "correct" Marxist-Leninist interpretation of all aspects of social and political life. The "Moral Code of the Builder of Communism," a high-sounding communist credo that would not sound out of place at a gathering of Boy or Girl Scouts, came to seem less and less relevant at a time when corruption and political careerism were increasingly identified with the Communist party in the public mind.

State Control and Centralization

Soviet schools, like their predecessors in Czarist Russia, have always been highly centralized. This has meant that control over educational decisions, from policy on "channeling" into academic or vocational tracks to the structure of curriculum to particular teaching methods, has rested at the top of the administrative pyramid in the educational ministries and state committees in Moscow.

The pattern was present before the start of Soviet power in 1917, and it was regularly reinforced from that time until the 1980s (Matthews, 1982; Whittaker, 1984). In practice, this meant that educational administrators and directors (principals) at the school level had to cope with an unending stream of directives and commands from on high, demands that were often reinterpreted and restated by several layers of bureaucracy.

The structure for educational research and development was similarly centralized. In the United States, such work is partly directed by federal and state agencies, and there are a few federally funded centers for research and dissemination, but there are also a myriad of private foundations, university-funded centers, private think-tanks, and groups affiliated with private corporations and individual school districts, to say nothing of the agendas of thousands of individual researchers and designers of curricular materials. In the USSR, virtually all these activities have been planned and conducted by a single Academy of Pedagogical Sciences (APS) through a group of fifteen research institutes. Decisions about what directions to pursue, and perhaps more importantly, what directions should *not* be pursued, were made centrally.

The Split Between Academic and Vocational Preparation

As in many European countries, Soviet education had a dual purpose: to prepare a small number of students to continue with higher education, and to prepare the rest to take productive jobs as manual or skilled laborers in the economy. The educational structure that sorted the students and provided the training varied over time, with different degrees of emphasis put on practical labor training versus intellectual preparation. By the mid–1970s, the question came to have more than academic significance as Soviet industry, long less developed and thus more labor-dependent than Western counterparts, found itself facing serious shortages of qualified workers (Kerr, 1982a).

The Soviet tradition of openly recognizing the differences between vocational and academic preparation led to a more stratified and differentiated system than has been the case in the United States. While Americans' democratic and egalitarian sentiments have militated against the establishment of special programs or schools for the highly advantaged, Soviet educators have always accepted the desirability of such an approach. Thus, the Soviet system of schools includes a number of "special schools," officially public institutions that have actually served the intellectual (or politically well-connected) elite (Riordan, 1988). Since these are the schools (especially those that offer specialized training in English or another foreign language) that Westerners often see, the impression of Soviet schools that has been featured in the Western press has long been somewhat idealized. With the advent of more open access by the press in the 1980s, however, the poor conditions in rural and working-class schools have become more widely known, and Soviet leaders have begun to discuss their problems openly (Jones, 1990).

Institutional Decay During the "Period of Stagnation"

After Mikhail Gorbachev came to power in 1985, a number of changes were proposed to cope with the lack of basic economic and social change in the country during the preceding twenty years. The Brezhnev era came to be referred to as the "Period of Stagnation," and new terms quickly entered the language of Soviet citizens: *perestroika* (reconstruction or rebuilding of the economy and social institutions), *glasnost'* (openness in admitting problems and discussing possible solutions), *demokratizatsiia* (democratization of social and political life), and *uskorenie* (acceleration of the economy, principally through rationalization of production and introduction of new technologies). All these were generally summed up by a general rubric, *novoe myshlenie* ("new thinking"; Gorbachev, 1987).

The problems that these remedies were to address did not appear for the first time between 1965 and 1985, but by the 1980s, their presence had become more problematic for Soviet society. Among these problems several stand out as paramount: *declining economic productivity*, produced by wasteful central planning, the collapse of local initiative, an inefficient system of rewards and penalties, lack of investment in needed technology and other infrastructure, and the continuing drain of heavy expenses for nonproductive military activities; *civic malaise and cynicism*, encouraged by lack of basic consumer goods, knowledge of corruption in high circles, favoritism, open flouting of communist ideals, and lack of adherence to legal and constitutional principles; *absence or collapse of regulatory mechanisms*, such as open press coverage to expose wrongdoers, and legal checks and balances to encourage growth of a "civil society"; and the *growth of negative social phenomena*, including such previously unmentionable aberrations as crime, prostitution, use of drugs, youth alienation, alcoholism, and child abuse (Riordan, 1989). Two further rubrics of *perestroika* describe well the old and the new: eschewed was the old-style "command-and-administer" system of Stalinism; encouraged was a new approach based on "the human factor"—a recognition that individuals are important, and that their development cannot be dictated or controlled in the rigorous way Stalin and his immediate successors had assumed.

In education, the agenda of *perestroika* rapidly came to have special significance and application. The new openness permitted critics of the schools to point out discrepancies that had long existed but had been hidden. In place of the vaunted image of the Soviet school as the preparer of cosmonauts came a new picture of decrepit buildings lacking basic amenities such as electricity, running water, and sewer connections, and where principals had to send teachers hundreds of miles on expeditions to find supplies of blackboard chalk (Gershunskii, 1990; Ligachev, 1988). Instead of praise for a new campaign of computer literacy, there were horror stories of malfunctioning machines and cartoons of teachers telling students, "Today, class, we'll learn about computers by modeling them out of clay." In place of the picture of the Soviet teacher as a caring nurturer of individual spirits, there came repeated accounts of soulless taskmasters who browbeat first-graders for getting a wrong answer, who thrived only on bureaucratic proceduralism, and who ruthlessly crushed any attempt at initiative on the parts of their colleagues. Parents, once portrayed as the loyal supporters of teachers and schools, now sent angry letters to editors describing how they had to spend hard-earned money on psychiatric care to help their children overcome the negative effects of schooling. Intellectuals and scholars affiliated with the prestigious Academy of Sciences began to criticize the work of their "colleagues" in the Academy of Pedagogical Sciences and called for its abolishment or radical restructuring (Postnikov, 1987).

Educators were caught off guard by this new attention. Indeed, while some savored the opportunity to speak out, many appeared to be frightened by the prospect of significant change in the institution in which they had chosen to make their careers. This is not surprising if we consider that education had long been a quiet backwater of Soviet society and thus rarely seemed to attract those with intellectual curiosity or vigor. Nonetheless, by the mid–1980s an identifiable group of "teacher-innovators" and others concerned about the state of the schools had appeared in the USSR (Amonashvili et al., 1988). What changes they have proposed, how successful they have been in pushing those changes through the system, what kinds of official support they have had (and have not had)—these are the subjects we turn to next.

THREE RECENT WAVES OF REFORM IN SOVIET EDUCATION

The Soviet system has long styled itself as both revolutionary and meliorist, so it should come as no surprise that there has been a long history of reforms in how schools were to be organized and run (including major shifts in 1931, 1958, 1966, and 1977). The history of the changes that have taken place over the past seventy-five years is available elsewhere (Dunstan, 1987; Matthews, 1982; Muckle, 1988; Shturman, 1988; Tomiak, 1986). Instead, here we will focus only on reforms that have been proposed and discussed since 1980, and organize that discussion on the basis of what "reform" meant during each of three periods: the pre-Gorbachev era from 1980 to 1985; the early Gorbachev period of optimistic strategies and ambitious plans for change (1986–1988); and the most recent period of increasing pessimism and uncertainty over the prospects for real reform of education (1989 to date).

Tinkering with the System: Educational Reform, 1980–1985

The largest reform effort of the early 1980s came just before Mikhail Gorbachev assumed the chairmanship of the CPSU in March 1985. Proposed and debated throughout 1984, the General Education Reform called for a number of changes in how schools were organized and what their tasks were to be (Kaser,

1986; Szekely, 1986; Zajda, 1984). Among the changes were a shift downward in the age at which children were to start first grade from seven to six years; an increased emphasis on the importance of vocational education and a demand that all schools conclude agreements with some local industrial, agricultural, or service institution to provide hands-on work practice for students at all ages; a slightly improved salary scale for teachers; and a new course in "Fundamentals of Informatics and Computing Technology" that was to be taken by all secondary school students in the country (Judy and Lommel, 1986; Kerr, 1987). The last item was reportedly Gorbachev's own suggestion (he headed the commission that drafted the reform document), designed to introduce parents to the importance of computers and to encourage the shift in industry from dependence on vast pools of semiskilled labor to focused use of highly skilled workers.

During this time, there was considerable discussion in the educational press about the need for more variety in teaching methods and wider use of new pedagogical materials and approaches. Readers of *Sovetskaia pedagogika* (*Soviet Pedagogy*) and *Narodnoe obrazovanie* (*Public Education*), the two main educational journals, were constantly assailed with exhortations to "use educational technology more widely!" (Kerr, 1982b, 1985). Discussions of pedagogical technique focused on such new ideas as "problem-centered instruction," "practical games," and classroom "laboratories" (*kabinety*). The prominence given these ideas in the press suggested that their application was widespread, but occasional critical notes suggested otherwise. In fact, most instruction continued to be immensely traditional, with teachers managing rote recitations by students even in the early grades, teaching from a single (often outdated) textbook, and examining students orally or via long essay exams.

Teachers themselves were to be rewarded more concretely for their work. Salary increases of 124 to 153 percent were proposed, and these actually took effect, but changes elsewhere in the economy left teachers no better off than they were previously (Balzer, 1987, November). There were concerns that an increasingly rural and agricultural (and hence, by implication, less well-educated) population was being attracted to teacher training institutes (Pugach, 1985, 1986).

The fate of these reform efforts is interesting and indicative of how Soviet reforms went in the pre-Gorbachev era (and even somewhat into his ascendancy). As one wag characterized the process, "You say that 'The changes have been made!' and that's all that's needed" (Grekova and Myshkis, 1988). Schools did indeed start to admit six year olds, but given the authoritarian attitudes of many teachers, it is perhaps not surprising that many parents rebelled, and this part of the reform did not progress as rapidly as was hoped. Many schools delayed adding the extra grade, and the schedule to be met for making the change in various parts of the country was adjusted several times. In the vocational-academic sphere, there was an increased emphasis on vocational training, and many more students were channeled into pre-vocational tracks. (The mix changed from 53.4 percent academic/46.6 percent vocational in 1980 to 40.3 percent academic/59.7 percent vocational in 1987; *Narodnoe*, 1987.) The course on computer literacy became something of a standing joke among teachers, and the analogy was frequently made to "learning how to ride a bicycle without a bicycle." The attempt to introduce teachers to the new subject during the summer of 1985 was an unmitigated disaster, with no texts or training materials available in many cases. The promised machines arrived much more slowly than had been anticipated, and uncertainties about the course continued (e.g., whether it was to train programmers or to prepare students more generally for the "information age"; Kerr, in press-a).

Throughout this process, there were minimal real changes either in how Soviet schools went about their tasks or in how educators thought about their work. Directors, often political appointees with minimal understanding of educational matters, continued to hold power over activities within a school. Curricular decisions continued to be made centrally. The ideological loading of the educational system, both in terms of curriculum and in terms of practical administration, remained strongly in place. This was how reform was done.

Visions of "Radical Perestroika": Educational Reform, 1986–1988

After Gorbachev's accession to power in 1985, there was considerable uncertainty about his interest in undertaking truly radical change of the Soviet social system. Many Western commentators described him early on as an administrator interested merely in evolutionary development. As matters progressed in education during the period from 1986 through 1988, however, it became clear that the new leader and his advisers had something larger in view for the educational system (Kerr, 1989). While changes in curriculum and instructional approaches were indeed proposed, these went beyond what had been suggested before and in some cases seemed to strike at the heart of the malaise pervading Soviet schools and universities. In addition, certain new shifts were proposed that would affect the role of education as a social institution. Perhaps most interestingly, new structural arrangements were encouraged that indicated the possibility of some transfer of real power from the center down to the educational institutions themselves.

Teaching, and more specifically how teachers and students related to one another in classrooms, became a subject of powerful debate during this period. Soviet educators suddenly came to celebrate diversity, as a corps of "teacher-innovators" from around the country were identified and their work publicly discussed in the press. Shalva Amonashvili, an educational researcher and director of a laboratory school in the Georgian Republic, described the need for what he labeled a "pedagogy of cooperation" between teachers and students, a classroom approach in which teachers would not seek to appear to their charges as infallible experts, but rather would work with them as collaborators and co-investigators. The term "pedagogy of cooperation" was widely adopted as a rallying cry for those seriously concerned about the sorry state of instruction in

Soviet schools (*Pedagogika sotrudnichestva*, 1988; Petrovskii, 1989a; "Reformulating," 1989).

Other innovators created other, different methods, some of which applied to specific subject areas. V. F. Shatalov, for example, a teacher in the Ukrainian city of Donetsk, devised a system for teaching mathematics which he called "supporting signals" based on a kind of verbal-graphic outlining procedure. The approach was widely imitated in other disciplines as well, and new teacher-developed curriculum materials were circulated, illustrated, and discussed in the press ("Povedem itogi," 1988). (To appreciate the novelty of this approach, one must remember that single texts for each subject had formerly been centrally developed and distributed; other materials were seen as unnecessary, and hence were either discouraged or actively forbidden.) Other teachers developed methods based on trying to increase intercultural understanding, on intensive role-playing and simulation, and on interdisciplinary study ("Evrika," 1988).

Several leading journalists raised powerful voices to push for public acknowledgment and acceptance of these new approaches. V. F. Matveev, the editor of the thrice-weekly educators' newspaper, *Uchitel'skaia gazeta* (*Teachers Gazette*), proved to be a formidable proponent of the new and a foe of the establishment (Matveev, 1988a, 1988b). His crusading efforts during this period led to public recognition of the innovators, and more generally to a growing sense among teachers that they had a voice and that it counted. Another journalist and former teacher, Simon Soloveichik, wrote several books describing alternative and more humane pedagogical approaches (Soloveichik, 1986, 1989a, 1989b). And Vitalii Korotich, whose weekly newsmagazine *Ogonek* became a kind of unofficial journal of *perestroika*, championed the cause of school reform and helped to make it a national issue.

By 1988 some official notice of these new approaches apparently seemed necessary, and so a special ad hoc committee was formed to examine the curriculum of the general secondary schools and to suggest changes in both teaching methods and curriculum for the country as a whole (*O sozdanii*, 1988). With representatives from the Academy of Pedagogical Sciences, but also many non-educator intelligentsia from the artistic and scientific communities, the so-called VNIK-Shkola (Temporary Scientific-Research Collective–"School") quickly indicated that it would interpret its charge broadly, and began to publish working papers, results of sociological studies, and conceptual overviews of its activities (e.g., *Konsteptsiia khudozhestvennogo*, 1989; *Kontseptsiia razvitiia*, 1989; Sobkin et al., 1988). When the committee's principal product, the Conception of General Secondary Education, was released in August 1988, there was a good deal of emotionally charged discussion in the press. The image of the Soviet school that emerged was radically different from what existed or had ever been posited before. Indeed, many Western teachers would probably find much of the language inspiring. There were positive comments about the need for a "pedagogy of cooperation," about the role to be played by parents and communities in the life of schools, and about the ways subject matter ought to be taught so as to make it more accessible, more immediately socially relevant, more attractive, and more able to provide the basis for life-long learning ("Konsteptsiia obshchego," 1988a).

Many hailed the VNIK document as the first new vision of what Soviet schools should be since the advent of Soviet power; but other, more conservative educators (including most members of the still-powerful Academy of Pedagogical Sciences—APS) saw it as a direct threat to their authority and to the image and values of socialist education that they had worked to establish. A competing document, prepared by a team representing exclusively the views of those in the APS, was published only days after the VNIK proposal appeared ("Kontseptsiia obshchego," 1988b). While there was some comparative discussion of the two versions in the press, the reactions of teachers suggested that the VNIK approach was notably more popular.

Another ad hoc group was formed at about the same time, the VNTK-Shkola–1 (Temporary Scientific-Technical Collective–"School 1"). The similarity in names was not coincidental; in fact, membership in the two groups overlapped, and they otherwise had much in common. The VNTK focused on technology in the schools, but rather than trying merely to elaborate on the earlier notion of informatics-as-programming, this group sought to consider how technology might affect the curriculum and education more generally. Several projects were started, including some with American and European collaboration using telecommunications to link students internationally. Part of this group's activity involved building cross-disciplinary curricula so as to permit, for example, use of mathematical modeling techniques in examining environmental problems (Bim-bad, 1987, 1988). With thirteen schools involved and with participation by some notable researchers from Moscow State University, as well as many talented educators, the VNTK represented a powerful and focused working group, but it too experienced routine difficulties in acquiring needed computer hardware to carry out its intended plans.

Other curricular shifts during this time were caused partly by the broader changes under way in Soviet society. The teaching of history and social studies, for example, was strongly and immediately affected by Gorbachev's new policy of *glasnost'*, which extended to uncovering the horrors of the Soviet past, especially the mass deportations and executions of the Stalin era. Even educational bureaucrats realized that, in such a climate, continuing to teach the rosy-hued picture of Soviet history that had been offered for years would be disastrous. Consequently, in 1988 the required history exams at the end of secondary school were canceled, and classroom discussions substituted in their stead (Fein, 1988). Textbooks were also thrown out, and teachers were instructed to use clippings from recent newspapers and magazines as the basis for treating history and current topics.

New texts for history and social studies are being developed, but their content is a matter of spirited debate at the moment (Gribov, 1988; Zhuravlev and Lerner, 1989). How to represent the role of the Communist party, for example, now

that its long dominion as sole political arbiter for the country has ended? Or
how to discuss the crimes of the 1930s and the terror inflicted during that time
on households throughout the land? Perhaps most important of all, how to instill
in individuals from their earliest experience in school those qualities that most
adults (and thus most teachers) themselves lack—an appreciation for democratic
principles in government and management; a willingness to take risks and responsibility for one's actions (and a feeling of relative assurance that one will
not be punished for doing so); a vision of a "civil society" founded not on
"command-and-administer," but on consensual agreement among its members;
a willingness to live in tolerance and mutual support with those different from
oneself in culture and background?

In addition to these changes in the what and how of teaching, there were other
proposals that pushed the idea of educational reform during this period beyond
merely tinkering with the status quo and toward serious structural change. A
1987 proposal, for example, called for thoroughgoing reform of the Soviet system
of higher education. (For further details on the plan and the public debate around
it, see Dobson, 1987, and Kerr, 1988.) Improvement of the economy was the
primary reason for undertaking the reform. The relationship among institutions
of higher education, planning agencies, and firms and factories was to be significantly altered, with institutes and universities encouraged to enter into collaborative research and development activities through joint scientific-
instructional-production combines. Faculty were to gain new skills by working
in industry on "practical sabbaticals." The reform also proposed tighter standards
for admitting students and more leeway for administrators to dismiss those unable
to make progress. Substantial changes were to be made in the organization and
administration of higher education. Paradoxically, one such shift was to a *more*
centralized form of planning in the hope of ultimately creating a less bureaucratic,
less centrally directed system. Coordination and control of general policies were
to be taken out of the hands of individual ministries (which had formerly determined the content of education in the institutes under their control) and were
to be centrally determined by the Ministry of Higher and Specialized Secondary
Education. Faculty were to receive new powers of self-government, extending
to the power to elect rectors. Improvements were to be made in evaluation at
all levels, including a rector's right to establish annual "qualification" competitions for faculty positions—the equivalent of abolishing tenure and requiring
a kind of annual probationary trial for faculty.

Some of these changes were accomplished rapidly. The former confusion, for
example, caused by the existence of three separate ministerial bodies (the Ministry of Education, responsible for general education through secondary school;
the Ministry of Higher and Specialized Secondary Education, responsible for
higher education at both universities and specialized higher education institutes,
as well as for some specialized vocational training at the secondary level; and
the State Committee on Professional Education, responsible for lower level
vocational training) was resolved by combining these bodies in March 1988 into

a single State Committee on Public Education. It was hoped that this change would lead to new coordination among the formerly independent agencies, but in fact most of their functions seem simply to have been combined, with little real integration to date.

The educational research and development establishment, one of the most conservative bodies dealing with the Soviet schools, itself came under increasing criticism during this period, and there were serious calls from respected scientists and intellectuals that it simply be abolished. No work of value to teachers was being done, it was claimed, and the projects that were undertaken were assigned to cronies of those in control of the APS without any competitive peer review of proposals. Projects dragged on for years with little discernible result. The internal structure of the Academy itself had not been changed for years, and there were virtually no provisions for conducting research in a practical, empirical fashion that would involve teachers as participants (and thus hopefully make the results of such work more significant; see Dneprov, 1989, and Petrovskii, 1989b). A commission to reform the academy was formed in 1988, and its members included several of the teacher-innovators, along with a number of noted intellectuals, artists, and scientists. The commission made a set of recommendations that stopped short of abolishment, but did call for radical change ("Pedagogicheskoi," 1988). Vacant seats in the Academy were to be filled via open competitions; a new, open procedure for awarding grants and contracts was to be implemented (and there were copious references in this regard to the procedures used by the U.S. National Science Foundation); a new program of studies was to be defined, with emphasis on such previously neglected fields as testing and measurement and multicultural education; and new, practical-oriented institutes were to be created to carry out the new work proposed (Volkov, 1989). Among the pedagogical innovators, many called for the establishment of new experimental sites where educational research and development could go forward in a less fettered way (Tubel'skii et al., 1988).

In a move to connect the work of schools more directly to the concerns of local regions and communities, educational councils were to be established on city, regional, and national levels ("Polozhenie o raionnom," 1988). These groups were to unite educators with parents and community leaders in order to allow the schools to reflect community needs more directly. Some responsibility for determining a portion of the school curriculum was even to be given to local groups. While the bulk of curricular content was still to be decided nationally, the recognition of a local interest—especially for content in such fields as social studies and regional culture—was a first for Soviet education. One of these groups, a National Council on Public Education, was created following a long-awaited nationwide conference of education workers in December 1988.

Beyond these structural changes, there were other developments, perhaps not as strongly determined from above as those noted already, but equally (and perhaps, ultimately, more) significant. One such development was the appearance

of a variety of independent, "informal" interest groups among educators. The
first of these to appear was a nationwide network of some 450 independent
teachers' clubs, many using the name "Evrika" ("Eureka"). The activities of
the Eureka clubs varied, but there was a common interest in engaging teachers
in serious discussion of new pedagogical forms. The clubs held local and then
regional conferences in various parts of the USSR to present and compare new
approaches to teaching, new models of curriculum organization, and new concepts for schools. In Krasnoiarsk in April 1988, a kind of mass elimination trial
was conducted for the most promising alternative models for new approaches to
schooling. Forty proposals were discussed, and six were chosen for "modeling"
("Vmesto retsenzii," 1988). The creators of these six proposals were invited to
"operate" their schools at Asanovo, near Izhevsk in the Udmurt ASSR during
September 1988 ("Evrika," 1988).

By summer 1988 the *Teachers Gazette* was publishing letters from teachers
suggesting that the clubs band together in new organization. That autumn, the
paper polled readers regarding who should serve on the organizing committee
of what had now become the Creative Union of Teachers. That committee
eventually included most of the country's now well-known "teacher innovators,"
as well as other leading social activists. It published and revised a draft charter,
and issued a general invitation for other teachers' groups to affiliate with it
("Ustav," 1988, 1989). To differentiate itself from (and eliminate the suggestion
of competition with) the officially sponsored state Education Workers Trade
Union, the Creative Union portrayed itself as concerned solely with questions
of educational method and philosophy, rather than "bread-and-butter" issues.
There was an initial discussion of the Union and its purposes at the Congress
of Education Workers in December 1988.

The Union's first general Congress was held in May 1989 in Sochi. Eschewing
the stiff formality common to Soviet official meetings, the organizers and delegates purposely avoided general sessions and broke up into smaller discussion
groups (Kolesnikova and Miledina, 1989; Loginova, 1989; Marinicheva, 1989).
Soon after the conference, the Union's new Central Council began to make
strong public statements on matters affecting teachers' work: living conditions
for rural teachers, salaries, pensions, nationality issues, and so on. There were
also demands that state prizes for teaching go to thoughtful and creative teachers
rather than mere supporters of the bureaucracy (Miledina, 1989; "Rezoliutsii,"
1989).

While the Creative Union was the most interesting of these new groups, there
were others (some perhaps formed with semi-official sanction by the APS and
State Committee as a way of diluting the influence of the new Creative Union):
a Soviet Association of Educational Researchers, formed in late 1988 ostensibly
to improve international contacts among Soviet researchers; an association of
vocational educators that made its first appearance in early 1989; a Union of
Professors, perhaps modeled on the Creative Union of Teachers, that also first
appeared in early 1989; and an organization calling itself Education and the

Future, concerned with long-term planning to extract Soviet schools from the morass of current problems.

Several of these groups began publishing their own newsletters, papers, and journals: the Creative Union of Teachers issued *Peremena* (*Break*, in a sense of an interval between classes, but also connoting a shift from past practice); and the Academy of Sciences and the State Committee finally acceded to a thirty-year-old request from the higher education community and allowed publication of *Poisk* (*Search*), a paper for professors and researchers in universities and institutes. Local groups have also issued their own broadsides and newsletters, leading to a flowering of local *glasnost'* in education. Many of these publications, however, have been hampered by lack of access to printing plants and by paper shortages.

There was a further development probably not foreseen by Gorbachev and others who proposed the creation of new, nationally elected representative bodies—the Congress of National Deputies and its smaller subset, the new Supreme Soviet. As these groups were elected in the spring of 1989, many educators were among those chosen (partly because a certain number of positions were reserved for delegates from specific social institutions, including education, but partly also because teachers and higher education faculty have been involved participants in the events of *perestroika*). The education delegates quickly formed themselves into an identifiable interest group and lobbying block ("A istina," 1990; "Biudzhet," 1989; "Obrashchenie," 1990). While their voice has not been heard strongly to date (the competing national priorities of the economy and political instability seeming to require closer attention), their existence and natural affinity suggest that changes may ultimately originate more from the legislature than from older central organs such as the party and State Committee.

Malaise Recrudescent: Educational Reform, 1989–Present

While many educational reform proposals were advanced during the three years from 1986 to 1988, the realization of these proposals has been very slow. Partly this has been due to the extreme severity of the other problems the country faces. The economic tensions long held in check by a strong central government finally found their expression in extreme consumer shortages of the late 1980s; similarly, national discontent among inhabitants of the Soviet Union's fifteen constituent republics and dozens of ethnic groups also boiled to the surface during this time. Freedom of expression meant not only that reformers could state their positions more forcefully and more openly, but also that their opponents could mobilize, and so there was a frightening growth in the number of such "new right" groups as "Pamiat' " ("Memory"), expressing a fiercely nationalistic and xenophobic vision for the nation's future. Political maneuverings as the Communist party began to lose its monopolistic hold on power provided other distractions for policymakers, as did uncertainties over what role the new, increasingly powerful elected legislative bodies would play. All these problems affected schools and the educational establishment, as they did other parts of Soviet society.

Western observers frequently find it difficult to understand why there should be opposition to reforms that on the surface appear so reasonable. The answer lies in the continuing power and position of the middle bureaucracy, the managers and administrators who made their way under the old system and whose prestige, authority, and perquisites are now being threatened by the demands for change. Coupled with this is a continuing reticence on the part of those further down the ladder to "make waves" owing to their uncertainty over which way the political winds will blow tomorrow. Moreover, the fact remains that even if Gorbachev (and others at the top of the education hierarchy, such as G. A. Iagodin, chairman of the State Committee on Public Education, V. D. Shadrikov, president of the APS during 1988–1990 and a ministerial-level functionary in education, and E. P. Velikhov, vice-president of the Academy of Sciences) wanted to replace these individuals on a wholesale basis, it would be virtually impossible to do so—they are in many cases the only ones who know how the system works and the scope of what needs to be done. Even a radical reform, the official view seems to be, would require retaining much of the existing educational structure, and so keeping individuals from that structure appears reasonable.

Whether this approach is in fact reasonable is what the coming years will determine. It can be said with fair certainty at the moment that changes have not come easily or rapidly to Soviet schools over the period of *perestroika*. For example, the proposals for radical curricular change made by VNIK in the summer of 1988 have made their way slowly through the educational and government bureaucracies, with many complaints by their original authors that along the way the really significant aspects of those proposed changes have effectively been vitiated (Dneprov, 1990; Shpeko, 1989). VNIK itself continues to exist, but with a much reduced budget (*O prodlenii*, 1989; *Programma rabot*, 1989).

The higher education reform of 1987 also seems to have foundered, to the chagrin of many rectors and concerned faculty, largely because promised new resources have been unavailable and the intended new relationships with industry have been impossible to develop (because they are so threatening to industrial leaders, most of whom operate what in effect are monopolies and therefore have little interest in fostering change; Kerr, in press-b). In addition, the hoped-for restructuring of the Academy of Pedagogical Sciences has stalled. While a number of reformers have been elected to its ranks, the body as a whole remains cautiously conservative, and the changes in grant-making procedures have not yet produced results that can be evaluated (Davydov, 1989; Matveev, 1989).

Teachers, too, must share some of the blame for the lack of change. The mind-sets of many teachers, formed during the years of "stagnation," or earlier, under Stalinist oppression, are not conducive to radically new visions of what education might be. While the Eureka clubs have gathered a following, there are many more teachers who remain silent or who prefer to continue the status quo, with its many knowns and well-understood structure of power and rewards.

The Creative Union of Teachers, seen as a hopeful beacon of change by many, encountered numerous difficulties and delays in its seeking official approval for status as a legal organization and has been unable to arrange for regular publication of its newspaper. The new National Council on Public Education has emerged as a very conservative voice. And the untimely replacement of V. F. Matveev as editor of *Uchitel'skaia gazeta* in early 1989 (and his death in October of that year) left the reformers without one of their principal champions.

The picture is not entirely bleak. By mid–1990 the Creative Union of Teachers at last was granted official status. And Eduard Dneprov, principal author of the VNIK proposal, was made minister of education for the Russian Republic, a post that could provide considerable visibility for his progressive views. But to many observers, these changes appeared as the exceptions rather than the rule.

The result has been a reappearance of malaise among teachers and others concerned about the state of education that parallels and extends what was felt in the early 1980s. There are a number of private cooperative and religious schools now operating semilegally in the USSR, for example, which may suggest the beginnings of abandonment of hope by parents for the public schools. Other teachers talk more openly about their despair for the current system, a sense that nothing can be done and that it is futile to try. Overturning this sense of impending doom and rekindling a feeling that something can be done will be the major challenge for Soviet educators, planners, and policymakers over the coming decade. Whether it can in fact be accomplished remains to be seen.

CONCLUSION: THE SEARCH FOR A NEW SYSTEM

Even the most conservative of Soviet educators would likely maintain that the current system is in a sad state of disrepair. While conservatives and reformers would disagree about the extent and causes of the chaos, several facts stand out clearly: students are poorly prepared by Soviet schools and universities to enter a technological age in which flexible, creative thinking becomes ever more important; those attracted to work as teachers are in many cases far from imaginative in their approach to their work; the values that students are to imbibe are often modeled in reverse by the system itself; trust among teachers, administrators, parents, and future employers is at its lowest ebb in years. The Soviet system of education is near the point of collapse, and without significant change of some sort seems unable to survive the further social shifts that Gorbachev and his successors feel required to make.

This search for a new system is consuming Soviet educators at the moment. The appearance of interest groups countervailing the old structure of government ministries, the APS, and the Communist party is a hopeful sign of spreading pluralism, but these groups have so far accrued little real power, nor are there traditions of political debate, compromise, and action that allow the new groups to reach balanced agreements with their existing, traditional counterparts. The continuing restrictions on access to public media of communication (some of which, such as paper shortages, are economic rather than ideological in nature) make it difficult for the new groups even to chart each other's positions accurately, much less speak with any kind of unified voice.

And there are continuing difficulties implied by the absence of a liberal, democratic tradition on the Soviet scene. Many progressive educators, for example, seem to find difficult the prospect of a system in which ultimate control is not wielded from the center. In demands for change, there is often a kind of plaintive request that central power be exerted "just once more," so as to assure that a new, more responsive and "more democratic" system is installed. Here again, as in the official communist ideology of the past, the ends are thought to justify the means. It is a "chicken-and-egg" problem that will bedevil for years to come all those in the USSR seriously concerned about fostering change.

A further brake on serious change in education is the perilous state of the Soviet economy. While educational problems may be significant over the long haul, they pale in decision-makers' minds before the immediacy of stores without food, apartments without heat, or armed insurrection by feuding national minorities. Educators might rightly argue that treating only these immediate difficulties would be "penny wise and pound foolish" over the long term; indeed, the immediate problems can be resolved only by creating new institutions and new habits of mind, and these require people who have been educated in a new way. As in the United States, however, Soviet educators have not yet managed to present in a sufficiently sophisticated political fashion the need to raise the place of education on the national agenda. Their task for the coming decade is to discover how to do that, and then to construct a worthy educational system that embodies the ideas and embryonic institutional forms that they have created over the past several years. Doing so will not be easy and may require the support of educators from other parts of the world if changes are to come to fruition. When such support is requested, and when it encourages the new forms now being born, educators from abroad should participate in the effort.

REFERENCES

"... A istina dorozhe" ["... But truth is dearer"]. 1990, January 4–10. *Poisk* 1(36): 1.

Amonashvili, Sh., V. Shatalov, I. Volkov, I. Ivanov, E. Il'in, E. Kurkin, S. Lysenkova, L. Nikitina, B. Nikitin, and M. Shchetinin. 1988, March 19. "Metodika obnovleniia" [The method of renewal]. *Uchitel'skaia gazeta* [*Teachers Gazette*], pp. 2–3.

Balzer, H. 1987, November. "Soviet Secondary Education Reform: A Report Card." Paper presented at the Annual Meeting of the American Association for the Advancement of Slavic Studies, Boston, November 5–8.

Bim-bad, B. 1987, December 22. "Shkola novykh informatsionnykh tekhnologii" [The new information technologies school]. *Uchitel'skaia gazeta* [*Teachers Gazette*], p. 2.

————. 1988. "Operezhaiushchee obrazovanie: Teoriia i praktika" [Surpassing education: theory and practice]. *Sovetskaia pedagogika* [*Soviet Pedagogy*] 6: 51–55.

"Biudzhet–90: Chto dostalos' shkole" [The '90 budget: What the school got]. 1989, November 7. *Uchitel'skaia gazeta* [*Teachers Gazette*], p. 4.

Bronfenbrenner, U. 1970. *Two Worlds of Childhood: US and USSR.* New York: Basic Books.

Davydov, V. V. 1989, October 7. "Chto izmenit Akademiiu" [What is changing the Academy]. *Uchitel'skaia gazeta* [*Teachers Gazette*], p. 2.

Dneprov, E. D. 1989. *Komu i kak perestraivat' Akademiiu pedagogicheskikh nauk.* [For whom and how to reconstruct the Academy of Pedagogical Sciences.] Moscow: State Committee on Public Education, VNIK-Shkola.

————. 1990, June. "Chetvertaia reforma" [The fourth reform]. *Uchitel'skaia gazeta* [*Teachers Gazette*], No. 25, p. 3.

Dobson, Richard B. 1987, July-August. "Objectives of the Current Restructuring of Soviet Higher and Specialized Secondary Education." *Soviet Education* 29(9–10): 5–25.

Dunstan, John., ed. 1987. *Soviet Education under Scrutiny.* Glasgow: Jordanhill College Publications.

"Evrika—avtorskaia shkola–3" [Eureka—Model School–3]. 1988, September 29. *Uchitel'skaia gazeta* [*Teachers Gazette*], pp. 2–3.

Fein, Esther B. 1988, May 31. "Soviet pupils spared exams while history is rewritten." *New York Times*, pp. 1, 14.

Gershunskii, B. S. 1990. "Perestroika v SSSR i problemy pazvitiia sistemy obrazovaniia." [Reconstruction in the USSR and problems of development of the system of education.] Unpublished ms., available from the Laboratory of Pedagogical Forecasting, USSR Academy of Pedagogical Sciences.

Gorbachev, M. S. 1987. *Perestroika: New Thinking for Our Country and the World.* New York: Harper and Row.

Grekova, I., and A. D. Myshkis. 1988. "Ot imitatsii deiatel'nosti—k zhivomu delu" [From imitation of reality to a real thing.] *Vestnik vysshei shkoly* 10: 11–14.

Gribov, V. S., ed. 1988. *Uglublennoe izuchenie istorii.* [A deepened study of history]. Moscow: Institute on Content and Methods of Education, Academy of Pedagogical Sciences of the USSR, Laboratory on History Instruction.

Jacoby, S. 1974. *Inside Soviet schools.* New York: Schocken.

Jones, A., ed. 1990. "Education and the Village." *Soviet Education* 32(2).

Judy, Richard W. and Jane M. Lommel. 1986. "The New Soviet Computer Literacy Campaign." *Educational Communication and Technology Journal*, 34: 108–123.

Kaser, M. 1986. "The Economic Imperatives in the Soviet Education Reform of 1984." *Oxford Review of Education* 12(2): 181–185.

Kerr, S. T. 1982a. "Soviet Interest Groups and Policy Making in Higher Education." *Slavic and European Education Review* 1: 1–12.

————. 1982b. "Innovation on Command: Instructional Development and Educational Technology in the Soviet Union." *Educational Communication and Technology Journal* 30(2): 98–116.

————. 1985. "Instructional Computing in the USSR: A New Vision of interactivity." *Educational Media International* 3: 17–21.

————. 1987. "Soviet Applications of Microcomputers in Education: Developments in

Research and Practice during the Gorbachev Era." *Journal of Educational Computing Research* 3(1): 1–17.

———. 1988. "The Soviet Reform of Higher Education." *Review of Higher Education* 11(3): 215–246.

———. 1989, September. "Reform in Soviet and American Education: Parallels and Contrasts." *Phi Delta Kappan* 71(1): 19–28.

———. 1990. "The Soviet 'Conception of the Informatization of Education'." *Journal of Computer-Based Instruction* 17(1): 1–7.

———. In press-a. "Educational Reform and Technological Change: Computer Literacy in the Soviet Union." *Comparative Education Review.*

———. In press-b. "Debate and Controversy in Soviet Higher Education Reform: Reinventing a System." In *Recent and Current Policy and Change in Soviet Education*, ed. J. Dunstan. Proceedings of the Fourth World Congress on Soviet and East European Studies, Harrogate, UK, July 1990. London: Routledge.

Kolesnikova, I., and T. Miledina. 1989, May 13. "S'ezd—eto tol'ko nachalo" [The Congress is only the beginning]. *Uchitel'skaia gazeta* [*Teachers Gazette*], p. 1.

Kontseptsiia khudozhestvennogo obrazovaniia [*Concept of art education.*] Moscow: State Committee on Public Education, VNIK-Shkola.

"Kontseptsiia obshchego srednego obrazovaniia" [The concept of general secondary education]. 1988a, 23 August. *Uchitel'skaia gazeta* [*Teachers Gazette*], pp. 2–3.

"Kontseptsiia obshchego srednego obrazovaniia kak bazovogo v edinoi sisteme nepreryvnogo obrazovaniia (tezisy)" [The concept of general secondary education as basic in a unified system of uninterrupted education (Theses)]. 1988b, August 25. *Uchitel'skaia gazeta* [*Teachers Gazette*], p. 2.

Kontseptsiia razvitiia shkol'nogo matematicheskogo obrazovaniia [Concept of the development of school mathematics education.] 1989. Moscow: State Committee on Public Education, VNIK-Shkola.

Ligachev, E. P. 1988, 18 February. "O khode perestroiki srednei i vysshei shkoly i zadachakh partii po ee osushestvleniiu" [On the pace of restructuring secondary and higher education and the party's tasks in its realization]. *Uchitel'skaia gazeta* [*Teachers Gazette*], pp. 1–4.

Loginova, N. 1989, June 21. "Uchitel' XXI veka" [Teacher of the 21st century]. *Literaturnaia gazeta* [*Literary Gazette*], p. 12.

Marinicheva, O. 1989, May 24. "Nashe delo!" [Our affair!] *Komsomol'skaia pravda*, p. 1.

Matthews, Mervyn. 1982. *Education in the Soviet Union.* Winchester, Mass.: Allen and Unwin.

Matveev, V. F. 1988, September 8. "Pis'mo v tri adresa" [Letter to three addresses]. *Uchitel'skaia gazeta* [*Teachers Gazette*], p. 4.

———. 1988b, November. "Shkola: Put' k vozrozhdeniiu" [The school: Path to rebirth]. *Kommunist* [*Communist*] 17: 75–82.

———. 1989, February 7. "Na chasakh APN—novoe vremia" [A new time on the clocks of the APS]. *Uchitel'skaia gazeta* [*Teachers Gazette*], p. 1.

Miledina, T. 1989, September 9. "Spiral' tvorcheskogo razvitiia" [The spiral of creative development]. *Uchitel'skaia gazeta* [*Teachers Gazette*], p. 2.

Muckle, James. 1988. *A Guide to the Soviet Curriculum: What the Russian Child Is Taught in School.* New York: Croom Helm/Methuen.

Narodnoe khoziaistvo SSSR v 1987 g. [National economy of the USSR in 1987]. 1988. Moscow: Statistika.

O prodlenii finansirovaniia rabot po obespecheniiu realizatsii reshenii Vsesoiuznogo s"ezda rabotnikov narodnogo obrazovaniia, vypolniaemykh Vremennym nauchno-issledovatel'skim kollektivom "Shkola" [On the continuation of financing the work to fulfill the decisions of the All-Union Congress of Education Workers, carried out by the Temporary Scientific-Research Collective "School"]. 1989, January 2. Order No. 2. Moscow: State Committee on Public Education.

O sozdanii Vremennogo nauchno-issledovatel'skogo kollektiva "Shkola" [On the creation of the Temporary Scientific-Research Collective "School"] 1988, May 31. Order No. 99. Moscow: State Committee on Public Education.

"Obrashchenie narodnykh deputatov SSSR—rabotnikov sistemy obrazovaniia i chlenov Komiteta Verkhovnogo Soveta SSSR po nauke, narodnomu obrazovaniiu, kul'ture i vospiutaniiu k S"ezdu i pravitel'stvu" [Communique of the USSR Peoples Deputies—Workers of the education system and members of the Committee of the USSR Supreme Soviet on Science, Public Education, Culture and Upbringing to the Congress and the government]. 1990, January, No. 2. *Uchitel'skaia gazeta* [*Teachers Gazette*], p. 5.

"Pedagogicheskoi nauke—idiologiiu obnovleniia" [An ideology of renewal for educational science]. 1988, October 22. *Uchitel'skaia gazeta* [*Teachers Gazette*], p. 3.

Pedagogika sotrudnishestva. Otchety vstrech pedagogov-eksperimentatorov. [The pedagogy of collaboration. Accounts of the meetings of teacher-experimentors]. 1988. Tbilisi: Ministry of Public Education, Georgian SSP, Scientific-Production Pedagogical Combine.

Petrovskii, A. V., ed. 1989a. *Novoe pedagogicheskoe myshlenie* [New pedagogical thinking]. Moscow: Pedagogika.

———. 1989b. *Zadachi i napravleniia perestroiki pedagogicheskoi nauki* [Tasks and directions for the reconstruction of pedagogical science]. Moscow: State Committee on Public Education, VNIK-Shkola.

"Polozhenie o raionnom (gorodskom) sovete po narodnomu obrazovaniiu" [Position paper on the local (city) Council on National Education]. 1988, 18 August. *Uchitel'skaia gazeta* [*Teachers Gazette*], p. 2.

Postnikov, M. 1987, November 19. "Kak postroit' shkolu budushchego?" [How should we build the school of the future?] *Uchitelśkaia gazeta* [*Teachers Gazette*], p. 2.

"Povedem itogi." [Let's add things up]. 1988, April 16. *Uchitelśkaia gazeta* [*Teachers Gazette*], p. 2.

Programma rabot vremennogo nauchno-issledovatel'skogo kollektiva "Shkola" na 1989 god [Plan of work for the Temporary Scientific-Research Collective "School" for 1989]. 1989. Moscow: State Committee on Public Education, VNIK-Shkola.

Pugach, V. F. 1985. "O komplektovanii pedagogicheskikh vuzov" [On filling up the teachers colleges]. *Sotsiologicheskie issledovaniia* [*Sociological Research*] 2: 109–111.

———. 1986. "Kolichestvennaia otsenka zakrepliaemosti uchitel'skikh kadrov" [Quantitative assessment of the strengthening of the teacher corps]. *Sotsiologicheskie issledovaniia* [*Sociological Research*] 2:129–131.

"Reformulating the educational reform: Glasnost' " [Special issues]. 1989, May-August. *Soviet Education* 31(5–8).

"Rezoliutsii uchreditel'nogo s"ezda tvorcheskogo Soiuza uchitelei SSSR, sostoiavshegosia v Sochi 18–20 maia'' [Resolutions of the Founding Congress of the Creative Union of Teachers of the USSR, held in Sochi, May 18–20]. 1989, May 27. *Uchitel'skaia gazeta [Teachers Gazette]*, p. 4.

Riordan, Jim, ed. 1988. *Soviet Education: The Gifted and the Handicapped.* New York: Routledge.

———. 1989. *Soviet Youth Culture.* Bloomington: Indiana University Press.

Shpeko, A. 1989, October. ''Khronika odnogo otstupleniia'' [The chronicle of one retreat]. *Peremena 1*: 6.

Shturman, Dora. 1988. *The Soviet Secondary School.* New York: Routledge.

Smith, H. 1976. *The Russians.* New York: Ballantine.

Sobkin, V. S., A. G. Levinson, A. I. Grazhdankin, R. M. Sel'tser, and V. V. Vetrova. 1988. *Shkola—1988. Problemy. Protivorechiia. Perspektivy [The school—1988. Problems. Contradictions. Perspectives].* Moscow: State Committee on Public Education, VNIK-Shkola.

Soloveichik, S. L. 1986. *Vechnaia radost': Ocherki zhizny i shkoly [Eternal joy: Excerpts from life and school].* Moscow: Pedagogika.

———. 1989a. *Vospitanie po Ivanovu* [Upbringing, Ivanovstyle]. Moscow: Pedagogika.

———. 1989b. *Pedagogika dlia vsekh: Kniga dlia budushchikh roditelei [Pedagogy for everyone: A book for future parents].* Moscow: Detskaia Literatura.

Szekely, B., ed. 1985. ''The Adoption of New Soviet School Reforms.'' *Soviet Education* 27(5): 1–102.

———. 1986. ''The New Soviet Educational Reform.'' *Comparative Education Review* 30(3): 321–343.

Tomiak, J. J., ed. 1986. *Western Perspectives on Soviet Education in the 1980s.* New York: St. Martin's.

Tubel'skii, A. N., O. I. Glazunova, D. B. Dmitriev, L. E. Kurneshova, L. A. Perlov, and M. A. Fedotov. 1988. Polozhenie ob eksperimental'noi pedagogicheskoi ploshchadke v sisteme narodnogo obrazovanii [Proposal for an experimental pedagogical test site in the public education system]. Draft. Moscow: State Committee on Public Education, VNIK-Shkola.

''Ustav tvorcheskogo soiuza uchitelei SSSR: Proekt'' [Charter of the USSR Creative Teachers' Union: Draft]. 1988, November 15. *Uchitel'skaia gazeta [Teachers Gazette]*, p. 3.

''Ustav tvorcheskogo soiuza uchitelei SSSR: Proekt'' [Charter of the USSR Creative Teachers' Union: Draft]. 1989, May 13. *Uchitel'skaia gazeta [Teachers Gazette]*, p. 3.

''Vmesto retsenzii kazhdomu obshchii portret'' [In place of a review for everyone a general portrait]. 1988, June 18. *Uchitel'skaia gazeta [Teachers Gazette]*, p. 3.

Volkov, B. 1989b, January 10. ''Potentsial nauchnyi i nravstvennyi'' [Scientific and moral potential]. *Uchitel'skaia gazeta [Teachers Gazette]*, p. 1.

Whittaker, C. H. 1984. *The Origins of Modern Russian Education.* De Kalb: Northern Illinois University Press.

Zajda, J. 1984. ''Recent Educational Reforms in the USSR: Their Significance for Policy Development.'' *Comparative Education* 20(3): 405–420.

Zhuravlev, I. K., and I. N. Lerner. 1989. *Kontseptsiia istoricheskogo obrazovaniia v srednei shkole* [Conception of history education in the secondary school]. Moscow: State Committee on Public Education, VNIK-Shkola.

27

YUGOSLAVIA

Nikša Nikola Šoljan

THE YUGOSLAV CONTEXT

Although the link between educational policies and reforms on the one hand and the social, political, and economic context in which they are formulated and implemented on the other hand is not immediately obvious, a more detailed analysis reveals strong links between them. This is true of Yugoslavia as much as of any other country. That is why we will start with some characteristic attributes that have shaped Yugoslavia's educational policies and reforms over the last few decades.

Federalism

Although the historical roots of the Yugoslav peoples go back many centuries, the history of Yugoslavia as a state is relatively short (see Stančić, 1985). It was first established at the end of World War I in 1918, as a result of an agreement of the great powers of that time and the wish of the representatives of the bourgeoisie of the individual South Slav nations to live in a single country. That "first" Yugoslavia disintegrated in 1941. The "second" or "new" Yugoslavia was formed during World War II, in 1943, as a federal state made up of six constituent units—independent republics/states: Bosnia-Herzegovina, Croatia, Macedonia, Montenegro, Serbia, and Slovenia. The Republic of Serbia included the Autonomous Province of Voivodina and the Autonomous Region of Kosovo-Metchija (which was later upgraded to the status of an autonomous province, and its name was changed to Kosovo).

The federal constitution of the country was intended to safeguard the independence and sovereignty of the individual republics/states. However, in the years immediately following World War II, Yugoslavia functioned as a strictly centralized state. The federal system was more faithfully respected with the adoption of the new Constitution in 1974 (see *The Constitution*, 1974). This was the time when the independence of the constituent units—six republics and two autonomous provinces—began increasingly to assert itself. Some authors are inclined to view this strengthening of their independence and autonomy in a positive light, while others see it as a wholly negative development and the first step toward the country's disintegration.

Multinationality (Multiethnicity)

The "first" Yugoslavia was originally established under the name of the Kingdom of the Serbs, Croats, and Slovenes. The name itself favored certain nations at the expense of others. The existence of other nations and ethnic minorities was simply not recognized. The "second" Yugoslavia made an attempt to solve the problem of equality of all the nations and ethnic minorities in a manner acceptable to all—under the slogan of "brotherhood and unity" of all the Yugoslav peoples. However, the attempt was only partly successful, as shown by the occurrence of national and ethnic conflicts and tensions throughout the postwar period. The conflicts escalated in particular during the 1980s and the early 1990s.

Socialism and Self-Management

Prewar Yugoslavia was an underdeveloped capitalist country. "New," postwar Yugoslavia opted for socialism (Rusinow, 1977). The development of socialist socioeconomic and political relations was intended to pave the way toward a communist society, which the country was supposed to get closer to with every passing day. The collapse of socialism in Central and Eastern Europe in 1989 helped to bring the fate of socialism/communism in Yugoslavia, too, into sharper focus. The country now seeks its future in a return to capitalism. The parts of the country in which transition to parliamentary democracy has been completed are undertaking a critical evaluation of the achievements of socialism. The short historical distance does not allow analysts to make objective judgments free of emotional coloring. But one thing is certain: less and less is being said about socialism in the country, and the socialist/communist project for society has no attraction for anybody but orthodox communists.

Socialism brought a major change in property relations in Yugoslavia. In the immediate aftermath of the war, the state eliminated private property—resorting to a variety of mostly violent means—and transformed it into state property. At the time, private landholdings were drastically reduced in size, even "small businesses" were curtailed, and private entrepreneurship was stopped. The administration and management of the state property was centralized in the hands of the state and party bureaucracy.

Centralized management and the state-planned economy did not, however, make for economic efficiency and industrial democracy. That is why, in the early 1950s, the authorities inaugurated the process of transformation of state property into social property, accompanied by the introduction of workers' self-management (Kardelj, 1977). The process gained particular momentum in the 1960s and 1970s, spreading to all areas of material and nonmaterial production, as well as to the service sector. Self-management, based on socially owned means of production, was a specific feature of the Yugoslav idea of socialist development. However, in the mid–1980s, self-management ceased to be the guiding idea for the development of Yugoslav society. The economic and political crisis reversed the direction of social development toward *non*-self-management options. Privatization, mixed ownership patterns, entrepreneurship, and managerial skills have been climbing on the list of priorities in the early 1990s.

Marxism and Political Monism

Opting for socialism also meant adopting Marxism and political monism in "new," postwar Yugoslavia. Marxism remained the state philosophy throughout the postwar period until the early 1990s. The only thing that had changed in the meantime were its attributes: it was dogmatic at one time, and original and/or authentic at another. But the official ideology never accepted any other view of the world, branding their advocates as enemies of the state who created confusion and corrupted young people. Religion was regarded as the "opium of the masses."

Just as Marxism was the only state philosophy, so also only political monism was permitted in political theory and practice. In other words, the only political system enjoying legitimacy was the single-party system, with the Communist party as the ruling and only allowed party. The Communist party of Yugoslavia (renamed the League of Communists of Yugoslavia in the mid–1950s, and the party of Democratic Change, Socialist party, or Social Democratic party in 1990) regarded itself as the "vanguard" of the working class. The working class imposed the "dictatorship of the proletariat," while the Communist party, as the most "highly conscious" part of the working class, guaranteed the construction of communism in the country. Opponents of political monism and/or advocates of pluralistic parliamentary democracy were considered political enemies, enemies of socialism, and destroyers of the existing constitutional order. In such circumstances, political opponents were not hard to come by. And there has always been uncertainty in one-party communist regimes.

Nonalignment

Nonalignment was the fundamental attribute of Yugoslavia's international political orientation from the early 1960s onward (see *Documents*, 1990). Yugoslavia was one of the founders of the nonaligned movement and an active proponent of nonaligned policies. In the period of the cold war and confrontations between the two blocs, the nonaligned option secured for Yugoslavia a rather special international position. For the West, it was interesting because it managed to extricate himself from the Soviet stronghold as far back as 1948. (The other East European countries succeeded in doing so only in 1989.) For the East, on the other hand, it remained interesting for its potential return under Big Brother's umbrella and into the fold of the monolithic family of communist countries. The Soviet influence continued to be felt in the country even during the 1960s and 1970s, as seen in the forceful ending of the so-called Croatian Spring in 1971 under the influence of the Brezhnev Doctrine of limited sovereignty. (The leaders of the Croatian Spring advocated parliamentary democracy and economic liberalism.)

The international situation changed significantly in the 1980s. Detente, disarmament talks, and cooperation replaced the earlier confrontation between the superpowers. Changes in Central and Eastern Europe led to the disintegration of the Warsaw Pact. Conflicts among the nonaligned nations have tarnished their image of the "conscience of humankind." The total failure of the New International Economic Order and the New International Information Order projects brought into question the attractiveness of the movement and the efficacy of the policy of nonalignment. This has led also to the questioning of nonalignment as Yugoslavia's dominant foreign policy commitment. Adjustment to the new situation in the world is a challenge that the country is facing at the moment.

IMPACT ON EDUCATIONAL POLICIES AND REFORMS

This section considers the impact of Yugoslavia's past political and economic options on the country's educational policies and reforms. The analysis focuses on the post–World War II period.

During that period, as already noted, the country was run on the *federal* principle. Still, the central government retained control over various areas of life well into the 1950s and 1960s. The countrywide literacy campaigns in the early postwar years were the responsibility of the federal bodies. The major reform of primary education in 1958 resulted in the introduction of uniform and compulsory eight-year elementary education. This reform, too, was carried out by the federal educational authorities (Tomich, 1963). When the influence of the federal government in education weakened in the early 1970s, the League of Communists of Yugoslavia appeared on the scene as the motive force and chief agent of the last comprehensive educational reform in 1974 (*The Tasks*, 1974). Changes in education in the 1970s and 1980s were spearheaded by the Socialist Alliance of the Working People and the Confederation of Yugoslav Trade Unions.

As the role of the federal government in education declined during that period, an attempt was made to secure the all-Yugoslav element by strengthening the role of the League of Communists of Yugoslavia, which preserved the ideological monopoly in the sphere of intellectual work and creativity, while the Socialist Alliance and the Trade Unions were given the task of executors of the organizational changes in this sphere. The influence of these political parties/organizations was greater in the 1970s and 1980s than the influence of the education ministries in the individual republics/states and autonomous provinces. It should be noted in this connection that the ministries, too, were under the direct influence and control of the party establishment.

With the introduction of the new federal system in the early 1970s, responsibility for education passed from the central government on to the republic/state government. Identical responsibilities for the formulation of educational policies and conduct of educational reforms were given to the education ministries in the two autonomous provinces. Thus, over the past twenty years, Yugoslavia has had no federal Ministry of Education, but it has had six republic and two provincial ministries. The leading officials of these eight bodies together made up the all-Yugoslav Commission for Educational Reform. The commission's brief was to coordinate educational changes in the different republics and provinces and to ensure that the so-called common core curriculum was introduced in all schools in the country. During the last few years the commission's significance declined appreciably, and its decisions commanded less and less respect. An essential change in the conduct of educational policies and reforms was signaled by the cancellation of the authority of the education ministries in the autonomous provinces of Voivodina and Kosovo (1989) and its transfer under the jurisdiction of Serbia. The new Serbian Constitution of 1990 effectively ends the provincial autonomy, with the provinces losing practically all authority in the sphere of education which they enjoyed during the past twenty years.

Without doubt, the federal organization of the country had a powerful effect on the design of educational policies and the implementation of educational reforms. Advocates of the concept of Yugoslavia as a strictly centralized country never quite accepted the idea of transfer of responsibilities from the federal to the republic, let alone provincial, educational authorities (Bezdanov, 1986). This is understandable, as the formal school systems in communist-ruled countries were always potent instruments of communication of the dominant ideology of the ruling classes, or of securing the interests of the privileged nations within multinational states. Examples are easily found in the Soviet Union and Czechoslovakia.

At this point it is instructive to examine how multinationality (multiethnicity), as one of the key characteristics of the Yugoslav society, affected the country's educational policies and reforms. The analysis that follows is closely connected with the preceding discussion of federalism. Yugoslavia's federal organization is the product of a desire to equip all Yugoslav nations with their sovereign republics/states. Thus, for instance, Slovenia is the republic/state of the Slovene nation, Macedonia the republic/state of the Macedonian nation, and montenegro the sovereign republic/state of the Montenegrin nation and of other nations and ethnic minorities living there.

Residents of Yugoslavia born outside of the country have the status of ethnic minorities. Thus, the Italians, Hungarians, Bulgarians, and Turks are ethnic minorities in Yugoslavia, because the sovereign national states of these nations are Italy, Hungary, Bulgaria, and Turkey, respectively. The same applies to ethnic Albanians in Yugoslavia, with the only difference being that their number is quite large (about 2 million) and that they make an absolute majority (about 90 percent) in the autonomous province of Kosovo. This explains their persistent attempts over a number of years to change their status from that of ethnic minority to that of Yugoslav nation, and, consequently, to turn the autonomous province of Kosovo into the Republic of Kosovo as the sovereign republic/state of ethnic Albanians living in Yugoslavia. Kosovo was, in fact, proclaimed a republic by the provincial Parliament in 1990, but that Parliament was dissolved before that move by the Parliament of Serbia, which rejected the proclamation of the Republic of Kosovo as a legally void and anticonstitutional act.

In order to complete the picture of Yugoslavia as a multinational (multiethnic) country, it should also be said that Bosnia-Herzegovina is the Republic/State of Croats, Muslims, and Serbs. The Muslims have had the status of a nation for the past two decades. It is a rare example of religion serving as the criterion for the recognition of national status. In Croatia there are about 11 percent Serbs in the population, while Voivodina is a veritable mosaic of people (nations) and especially ethnic minorities.

This complex national structure has necessitated an appropriate educational policy in Yugoslavia, while the educational reforms could not ignore the need to respect national and cultural identities. Since there is *no* Yugoslav language, the choice of the language of instruction proved a serious problem (Mikes, 1984). Schools use a variety of languages according to local conditions—Croatian, Serbian, Slovene, Macedonian, and different variants of Croatian and Serbian spoken in Bosnia-Herzegovina and Montenegro. The language of instruction in the Kosovo schools is Albanian and/or Serbian. A particular problem is to provide instruction in the mother tongue in nationally mixed communities with several ethnic groups living together.

A related problem concerns the provision of textbooks, since not only numerous languages but also different scripts are involved. The Roman script predominates in the western parts of the country—in Slovenia, Croatia, and parts of Bosnia-Herzegovina, whereas the Cyrillic script is more prevalent in the east—in Serbia and Macedonia. The problem of textbooks and the language of instruction also appears important for the many thousands of children of Yugoslav migrant workers from all parts of the country who attend schools in Western Europe and additional classes in the so-called homeland subjects. These extra classes are organized by Yugoslav educational authorities. Experience shows that not enough attention has been paid in these classes to the children's native language and script. There is widespread feeling among the parents that national and cultural identities have not infrequently been suppressed in the name of an artificial "general Yugoslav education."

It follows from everything said here that multinationality (multiethnicity) is an essential characteristic of Yugoslav society and its educational policies (see Georgeoff, 1988). All the educational reforms took into account in their documents the multinational structure of the country. Still, it remains an open question whether, in reality, all the conditions were provided for the full assertion of the national and cultural identities of all people within the educational system. The ultimate question is whether past approaches to the solution of the "national question" could have produced more results than they actually did, or whether, perhaps, new paradigms should be sought which will be better attuned to the spirit of the times. Regardless of what answers can be given to such questions, the fact remains that multinationality (multiethnicity), like federalism, has had a powerful impact on educational policies and educational reforms in Yugoslavia. The same can also be said of socialism and self-management as particular attributes of Yugoslav society.

The first thing that socialism brought to "new" Yugoslavia was state control of education. The Federal Ministry of Education and the republic education ministries were the responsible bodies until the mid–1960s for all matters regarding educational policy and changes in education (*General Law*, 1958). Educational reforms were centrally planned (by the federal bureaucracy), while the peripheral (republic) authorities were charged with their implementation. Educational planning was harmonized with economic and social development planning for the country as a whole and for its constituent units. Schools were funded from the state budget. All key decisions were made by the educational authorities and their bureaucracies.

The state's "takeover" of education was the consequence of the type of socialism for which Yugoslavia opted at the end of World War II. It was the so-called state socialism based on state ownership, known as real existing socialism and administrative socialism, which was characterized by the dominance of the state and party apparatus over all areas and aspects of social and economic life. This type of socialism began gradually to be abandoned in Yugoslavia in the early 1950s, when it was replaced by a new type known as self-managing socialism, based on workers' self-management and social self-government. The essence of self-management consists in giving workers and citizens an opportunity to decide themselves on all vital issues of social and economic development. In order to do so, workers and citizens associate themselves in appropriate work organizations and communities of interest. The phrases "associated labor" and "self-managing communities of interest" became synonymous with socialist self-management in Yugoslavia in the 1970s and 1980s (*The Associated*, 1977). The shift from state control to self-management was accompanied by a transformation of state property into socially owned property. The state thus ceased to be the owner of the means of production. The new owner was society as a whole.

The introduction of social self-government in education began in the mid–1950s, when social councils were formed in all schools (Farmerie, 1974). For the following three decades, self-management experiments in schools continued *in vivo*. During that time, schools became self-managed organizations, and teachers and students became self-managers. State planning in education was replaced by self-managing planning, while all educational decisions were made through a process of self-managing decision making stemming from self-managing negotiation and self-managing agreement. The last comprehensive educational reform of 1974 was labeled the "socialist self-managing transformation of education." Educational theory continued to develop only as self-managing socialist pedagogy. The administrative budgetary financing of education was replaced by self-managing financing, first through educational funds and then, starting in the early 1970s, through the self-managing communities of interest for education. In short, new administrative, organizational, and financial structures based on self-management were put into place with the purpose of reducing the role of the state and the party and strengthening the role of workers, citizens, teachers, pupils, and students (OECD, 1981a, 1981b; see also Nikolić and Bogavac, 1980).

As already noted, self-managing socialism relied primarily on social ownership. However, like the centrally planned economies, self-managing socialism, too, neglected the role of the market. Economic subjects were encouraged to communicate with one another without the market as a mediator. For this purpose, tens of thousands of self-managing communities of interest were established, as bodies through which economic subjects were supposed to effect an exchange of labor (Kardelj, 1978). The elimination of market mechanisms, or competition, and the downplaying of profit as a motive in economic behavior, made the Yugoslav self-managing socialist economy inefficient. Healthy economic development was impeded by an overcomplicated self-managing organization of society. Besides, the state never really relinquished its dominant influence in the running of economic and social, including educational, organizations. The influence was most effectively exerted through various parastatal bodies, the party, and other political organizations, all of which were in its service. As a result, self-managing socialism—and its application in education—stood little chance of success. In the mid–1980s, the effectiveness of the self-management road to socialism began to be increasingly questioned, as did socialism itself as a fundamental option for Yugoslav society. Critical debates could not bypass the sphere of education. In the early 1990s, education is being discussed without reference to socialism or self-management.

Just as socialism and self-management are being questioned, so too are *political monism and Marxist philosophy*, particularly from the point of view of their effects on education. In the Yugoslav context, political monism meant the domination of a single-party system from the end of World War II to the spring of 1990, when the first free, multiparty elections were held in two westernmost Yugoslav republics—Slovenia and Croatia. The communists lost the elections and were removed from power, and the multiparty system and parliamentary democracy was established in both republics. This marked the beginning of a transformation from political monism to political pluralism in Yugoslavia. During almost half a century of political monism, education was seen to have an instrumental function: it was an instrument with which to condition people in the spirit of the political monopoly of the ruling party and Marxism as the state ideology (see Bennett, 1972). In the last analysis, education was reduced to ideological conditioning and communication of the views of the ruling communist regime. Other views of the world were proscribed. This is perhaps most visible in the ideals and goals of socialist (self-management) pedagogy. Socialist pedagogy propounded the idea of a "fully developed personality" and "conscious builder of socialist society." All educational reforms and all changes in education were made under the motto of developing—through education—fully formed persons and conscious future self-managers (Bezdanov, 1980).

School curricula were designed to facilitate the realization of precisely such ideals and goals in education. That is why only the subject matter that did not conflict with the ruling ideology was allowed in the curriculum. Special subjects were taught in schools and universities to inculcate the desired ideology into young people. (The subjects had titles such as Marxism and Theory and Practice of Socialist Self-Management.) The same role was played by certain co-curricular activities, especially those carried out in the educational institutions by the Yugoslav Pioneers Organization, Yugoslav Youth Union, and the League of Communists of Yugoslavia.

Obviously, the role of teachers is especially important in monistic communist systems. They are expected to interpret the subject matter they teach in an ideologically plausible way, that is, from a Marxist perspective and in the spirit of atheism. The "political suitability" of teachers was not as rigorously applied in Yugoslavia as it was in the East European communist countries and in the Soviet Union. Still, every teacher needed to be judged "morally and politically suitable" for work school. The state party declared education an area of special social concern, thus reserving for itself the right to influence teaching appointments. This is not to say that all teachers had to be members of the Communist party or League of Communists of Yugoslavia, but it did mean that teachers who were party members had greater scope of authority, greater political influence, and better prospects both within and outside the school.

Under the influence of political monism and ruling ideology, Marxist pedagogy advocated a predominance of work-oriented education defined in categories of manual skill development and the Soviet concept of polytechnical education. The educational reforms consistently favored average education for all, preparing young people for work and self-management, as against quality in general education and emphasis on excellence. Training for work in material production was always more highly valued in Yugoslav Marxist pedagogy than education for intellectual occupations. This is explained by the fact that, in Marxist interpretations, the material basis carries the entire superstructure of society. And the material basis is created by the working class, which, the argument goes, should therefore have greater say in education—hence, the heightened impact of workers from material production on educational policies and, especially, the 1974 educational reform (Šuvar, 1977). When workers themselves were not in a position to influence educational development, this was done through the party and the trade unions. The party presented itself as the vanguard of the working class, its "most highly conscious" part, and one that would secure its power through the dictatorship of the proletariat. The unions, on the other hand, played the role of political "transmitters" throughout the postwar period, and were engaged in implementing party decisions.

Again under the influence of political monism and the acceptance of the Bolshevik version of Marxist philosophy, Yugoslav pedagogy stressed the role of the collective and minimized that the individual and the family. Education through and for the collective was the ideal taken over from Makarenko and copied faithfully for many years from Soviet textbooks (See Šimleša, 1978). The primacy of the collective in education was achieved through the suppression of the individual and the family. The collective, and the school as such, were supposed to replace family education and correct its defects, particularly when it came to the formation of the ideological and religious views of individuals. The collective and the school were meant to help their individual members to form a "scientific view of the world."

Theories of education that came from pluralist democracies and countries with non-Marxist thinking were, of course, deemed unsuitable for application in the Yugoslav situation. Such theories were regarded as potentially dangerous in that they might cause deformations in the ideologically pure and "correct" education. More than that, through education they might threaten the social system of socialist self-management. This is where we must look for an explanation of the relative closeness of the Yugoslav educational environment to theoretical approaches originating in countries with different social and political systems and political orientations.

Any scholar or educational theorist who displayed an enhanced sensibility for non-Yugoslav educational options was in danger of being accused of subversive activity. This attitude to educational science and international education practices was responsible for the paucity of research in international and comparative education. All the educational reforms carried out during the last few decades largely ignored the experience of other countries. (The only exception was the sweeping reform of the educational system at the end of World War II, which followed the Soviet model.) The results of educational research were ignored, and the reforms were planned, instead relying on the country's own monistic political system and its derivative, socialist self-managing pedagogy, a faithful maidservant of single-track thinking.

The consideration of educational influences and interdependencies raises the question of the effects Yugoslavia's foreign policy options have had on the country's educational policy and reforms.

In this connection it should be mentioned that prior to their unification in the "first" Yugoslavia (Kingdom of the Serbs, Croats, and Slovenes), the individual countries that entered into the new state had developed different educational systems. In the case of Slovenia and Croatia, they were formed under the influence of the Central European (particularly Austro-Hungarian) and Mediterranean educational tradition and culture. In the eastern parts of the country (Serbia and Montenegro), the formative influences had come from Eastern Europe. Between the two world wars, various, mostly European, schools of educational thinking made themselves felt in Yugoslavia, with the strongest influences coming from Germany.

As the war ended, Yugoslavia opted for Soviet-style socialism. The clash between Stalin and Tito in 1948 led to a break in relations between Yugoslavia and the Soviet Union and the other Soviet-dominated East European countries. This break only seemingly signified a break with Soviet-style pedagogy. A pedagogy rooted in Bolshevik thought was found to be most convenient for a socialist system organized as a single-party communist regime. For many years Soviet pedagogical literature continued to occupy the pride of place in pedagogical textbooks, especially those intended for future specialists in military education. The orientation to self-management and the development of self-management socialist pedagogy succeeded only partly in softening the rigor of Yugoslav pedagogy derived from the orthodox version of Soviet pedagogy.

The break with the Soviet Union did not mean "turning to the West." Yugoslavia needed the West as a source of economic aid, but continued to view the West as a decadent, declining bourgeois society and, in the last analysis, an ideological opponent. It was in this context that experiences of Western pedagogy, organization of the educational system, and fruits of educational reforms were rejected. Yugoslavia opened itself to Western influences only to the extent that it was inescapable. This remained the constant of its educational policy until the most recent events.

In an attempt to remain equidistant between the (European) communist East and the capitalist West, Yugoslavia—in the early 1960s—opted for a policy of nonalignment (*Documents*, 1990). This option remained the cornerstone of the nation's foreign policy for the following three decades. In the domain of education, the nonaligned orientation involved the training of large numbers of civilian and military personnel from the developing countries at Yugoslav institutions of higher learning. The bulk of the students actually came from several Arab countries (Algeria, Iraq, Iran, Lebanon, Libya, and Syria) (see Unesco, 1989). Yugoslavia geared its activity in international educational organizations (such as Unesco) to a large extent toward the objectives of the nonaligned movement. And yet, despite its sincere commitment to nonaligned policies, Yugoslavia never had a significant educational and scientific cooperation with the movement's member countries. These countries did not reject Yugoslavia's educational, scientific, and technical assistance, but they preferred to have educational cooperation with more developed countries.

Yugoslavia's one-sided political orientation to the nonaligned countries had as its consequence a relative neglect of the countries that did not belong to the movement. This is best seen in an opposition, lasting a number of years, to the European orientation. It was only in the late 1980s that increased interest began to be expressed in the European integrational processes and their possible implications for educational policies and free movement of people throughout the European space (Šoljan, 1988, 1989). However, these were no more than isolated attempts to draw attention to developments that will decisively determine the future place and role of the Yugoslav people in the common European home.

Yugoslavia missed a unique opportunity to participate actively in the work of the Council of Europe's Council for Cultural Cooperation starting as early as the mid-1970s. For reasons of ideological prejudice, it failed to join the joint European educational development project undertaken by the member countries (Šoljan, 1983). It can now also be said that Yugoslavia's participation in the work of the Organization for Economic Cooperation and Development's (OECD's) educational bodies (Education Committee and Centre for Educational Research and Innovation) had only a very slight impact on its own national educational policies and reforms (Šoljan, 1985). Cooperation with the OECD was not stigmatized by ideological prejudice as was cooperation with the Council of Europe. Still, the political, economic, and ideological incompatibility of the two systems—the Yugoslav self-managing, socialist, one-party, Marxist system and the OECD countries' market-oriented, multiparty system based on the respect for human rights and fundamental freedom—was sufficient to simply disregard the OECD's experiences in the development of human resources, design of educational policies, and planning and implementation of educational reforms.

The conclusion that follows from everything said here is that Yugoslavia's foreign policy orientation has decisively influenced its educational policies and reforms throughout the postwar period. Unfortunately, the nature of the conclusion is not encouraging: there can be no doubt that the country's educational orientation has been quite one-sided. Owing to ideological differences and incompatibilities of the social systems, international experiences in the development of educational systems and educational reforms were systematically ignored and the results of educational research in the scientifically more developed parts of the world were simply not taken into account in national educational policy design. All of this led to Yugoslavia's self-imposed isolation as regards international, especially European, educational cooperation. On the other hand, an understanding attitude to the experiences of the socialist countries resulted in an uncritical transplantation of surrogate models (as was the case with the transfer of the Soviet educational model and postwar Soviet pedagogy). This produced long-term negative consequences for the national educational development, which are still acutely felt.

YUGOSLAVIA AT THE START OF THE 1990s: TIME OF CHANGE

This section describes the Yugoslav educational context at the start of the 1990s. This is an important period in view of both the changes affecting the domestic situation and the external developments. Among the external developments, mention ought to be made of the collapse of the communist regimes in Central and Eastern Europe and of the intensive preparations for post–1992 Europe. The changes now taking place will decisively influence the future of education.

Between Federalism and Confederalism

As the 1990s approached, the attention of the Yugoslav public focused on the constitutional crisis and the possible re-design of the country. While the "first" Yugoslavia was a monarchy, the "second" was born as a federal republic, whose chief characteristic until the adoption of the 1974 Constitution was centralist federalism. The new Constitution established a federation consisting of six republics and two autonomous provinces, whose position in the federation is on a par with that of the republics. The Constitution enabled the transfer of power from the central government in Belgrade to the republic and provincial governments (*The Constitution*, 1974). This led to polycentric statism, with state powers distributed over eight republic-privincial centers.

The province of Kosovo, with a predominantly ethnic Albanian population, made several attempts during the 1980s to change its status to that of a republic. This was resolutely opposed by the Republic of Serbia, which felt anyway that a grave mistake had been made in the 1974 Constitution in putting the provinces (Kosovo and Voivodina) on a par with the other constituent federal units. Such reactions provoked ethnic conflicts in Kosovo, and the new Serbian Constitution, adopted in 1990, put an end to the political (and all other) autonomy of the provinces. Nevertheless, the Parliament of the province of Kosovo—that is, its ethnic Albanian parliamentarians—met to adopt a new Constitution and declare Kosovo a republic.

The constitutional crisis came to a head following the first free postwar elections held in Slovenia and Croatia in the spring of 1990. The communists failed to win the voters' confidence in these elections. Efforts to resolve the constitutional and political crisis have led to two proposals for a possible solution: the first advocates a "modernized federation" and the second a confederal state (Petković, 1991). The first option comes from Serbia and Montenegro and enjoys the support of those forces that see Yugoslavia as a unitary structure with the leading role of the central government in Belgrade. The second option is a joint proposal of the western republics of Slovenia and Croatia. According to that proposal, Yugoslavia would be constituted on the model of the European Community. The original legitimacy and sovereignty would rest exclusively with the republics/states, just as originally intended when the "second" Yugoslavia was formed in 1943. Only competences agreed to by the republics, as sovereign and equal states, would be transferred to the common bodies.

If the confederal solution is not accepted, the next step might be the secession of individual republics and the disintegration of Yugoslavia. Such a decomposition of the country could be prevented only by the army, in which the Serbs make the greater part of the officer guard and preserve socialism in the country. Such a course of events would turn the wheel of history seventy years back. This would be a new beginning, but a beginning without hope for all those who have experienced oppression and inequality of people, nations, and ethnic groups in what was euphemistically called the communist community. Regardless of which of the two options wins in a democratic dialogue, each will require new educational policies and inaugurate new educational reforms. Some possible changes that will be needed are discussed further below.

Towards Multinationality in a Multicultural and Civil Society

The root cause of Yugoslavia's constitutional crisis lasting for several years now are in fact the interethnic relations in the country. The current attempts at a re-design of the Yugoslav state are intended to remove this sore point which plagued both "first" and "second" Yugoslavia. Stated in somewhat simplified terms, the problem boils down to a feeling of inequality and lack of sovereignty of the Yugoslav nations and ethnic minorities. Everybody seems to feel unequal, nonsovereign, and threatened. The prewar Yugoslav monarchy was called the "prison-house of the peoples"; the postwar communist regime, for its part, prevented the expression of national sentiments and cultural identity, hectoring people with slogans of brotherhood and unity among the Yugoslav nations and ethnic minorities. The main plank of this policy was the doctrine of the nation as a temporally, strictly limited historical category. It was assumed that one day, in a not very distant future, all people would become Yugoslavs who would not care at all about their national identities.

However, the surge of national awareness paralleled the decline of authority of the communist regimes everywhere. As in the Soviet Union, in Yugoslavia, too, international and interethnic conflicts flared in 1989 and 1990. In some cases (as in Kosovo in 1981), they had the proportions of a civil war. In other cases, the animosities are so great that they might easily lead to conflicts and confrontations (for instance, in Croatia and Bosnia-Herzegovina in 1990 and 1991). National conflicts generate nationalism and strengthen national homogeneity. In debates about the future organization of the country, both nationalism and national homogeneity are exploited in certain constituent federal units as a means of winning better negotiating positions in the forthcoming talks on the future of Yugoslavia or its partitioning. The churches are also involved in national disputes, doing their best to revive the religious spirit among the members of different nations. (There are three dominant religions in Yugoslavia—Catholic, Orthodox, and Muslim.) All such developments have made relations among the people quite complex in recent years.

Regardless of what the future of Yugoslavia may be, the period immediately ahead can be expected to be one of the surge of hidden national feelings stemming from the national past, national myths and heroes, and national iconography.

This must be seen as a consequence of the suppression of national identities during the communist rule. Going hand in hand with this will be attempts to constitute the present republics as independent and sovereign national states. Since the populations in most of the Yugoslav republics are nationally mixed, it can be assumed that sooner or later a shift will have to be made from the national state toward the state of all citizens, regardless of their national backgrounds. The problem of coexistence of people in the Yugoslav multinational (multiethnic) society cannot be resolved in the national states. The best chances probably lie in the adoption of the policy of multiculturalism in civil society and a civil state. This is the path, after all, that the European countries took much earlier.

It does not require much imagination to see how vitally important the future developments in the sphere of national relations will be for educational policies and reforms. A little more is said about this issue later in this chapter in the section New Challenges and Possible Educational Implications. At this point, we will consider the problem of transition from socialism to nonsocialism and the abandonment of self-management.

Beyond Socialism and Self-Management

Until recently, socialism and self-management were the fundamental attributes of Yugoslav society (see *The Associated*, 1977). But self-management began to be abandoned in the mid–1980s, to be followed by socialism itself in the late part of the decade (to a certain extent under the influence of changes in Central and Eastern Europe). The main problem in the early 1990s is how to transform social into *non*social property and how to establish private, mixed, and/or state (public) ownership patterns. A general formula of privatization or state ownership is not easy to devise. Nevertheless, the process of transformation of major socially owned enterprises into public or state enterprises has already started, with the idea that some of them should be privatized in the foreseeable future. The transformation of socially owned enterprises into private firms is accompanied by a variety of problems, including, *inter alia*, the problem of realistic market evaluation of the socially owned companies to be put up for sale, or the problem of mass dismissals of surplus labor at a time when adequate social programs for the unemployed are not available. The operations of privatization and state takeover of socially owned industries coincide with the need to undertake a restructuring of the economy and modernization of production. Fresh capital will be needed for these purposes, but it is not readily available, especially given the rather confused political situation in the country and the absence of sufficient legal guarantees for the security of foreign investments. The process of privatization and transformation of social property into public property is spreading not only in industry but also in the service sector.

The market economy and nonsocial ownership are incompatible not only with socialism, but also with self-management, which thus loses the base on which it was built. Self-management is now being replaced by forms of management that are practiced in market-economy capitalist societies. However, many institutions of civil society and capitalist economy remain to be built in Yugoslavia. For instance, the capital and labor markets are only in their infancy. Problems of industrial democracy and worker participation in management will come to the fore once the trade unions are formed whose main job will be to protect and promote the interests of the employees, while recognizing and respecting the interests of the employers. The passage of education from the social to the public/ state and/or private sector will mean the demise of self-management in education and thus also of self-management socialist pedagogy as a theoretical orientation of the last thirty years or so.

Toward Theoretical and Political Pluralism

From the end of World War II to the early 1990s, Marxism and political monism were promulgated by the communist authorities to the exclusion of all other views. Marxism was supposed to provide a "scientific view of the world," while political monism would guarantee the rule of the working class (dictatorship of the proletariat) through its "most highly conscious" part—namely, the Yugoslav Communist party, or the League of Communists of Yugoslavia. Any political association outside the umbrella of the ruling, and only legally allowed, party was viewed as a subversive act designed to destroy the state. Political monism was justified by the rulers with the need, among other things, to have a strong, monolithic party to avert the civil war that the existence of more parties would inevitably provoke in Yugoslavia's multinational (multiethnic) context.

Under the pressure of events in Central and Eastern Europe, in 1989 and 1990 the authorities finally allowed other political parties in addition to the League of Communists. In a relatively short time, dozens of parties of different persuasions were formed, with the nationally oriented parties attracting most members and acquiring all the characteristics of national movements. Two such parties won the first multiparty elections since the war in Slovenia and Croatia, and then in Bosnia-Herzegovina and Macedonia. It already seems certain that the first multiparty elections in the constituent republics will result in the splitting of the electorate along national lines, the defeat of both orthodox and reformed communists (excluding in Serbia and Montenegro), the victory of parties with national platforms, and the formation of republic parliaments with weak oppositions.

The shift from political monism to multiparty parliamentary democracy, and the abandonment of Marxism as the official state philosophy, will inevitably bring about significant changes in educational policies. The direction of future educational reforms can only be guessed at this point, but how thorough and radical they will be remains unknown. The same holds true, to a certain degree, of the changes that will be brought about by future shifts in Yugoslavia's foreign policy orientation.

Toward a Policy of "Alignment"

In recent years, the nonaligned policy has lost a great deal of its relevance and credibility. Few people in the world today have illusions about the nonaligned movement being the conscience of humankind. Solidarity in the interdependent world is more effectively practiced, it seems, outside the circle of nonaligned countries. This does not at all mean, of course, that there is no longer any need for a collective action of all countries geared toward improving conditions of human life, especially in the least developed countries. The only thing that appears questionable is the effectiveness of a movement and policy that holds itself in such a high esteem. It was precisely this policy that Yugoslavia insisted on for so many years, ignoring the real circumstances in the world. But some new foreign interests and shifts of emphasis can be discerned at the start of the 1990s (Petković, 1989). These are influenced equally by domestic developments and by conditions in the rapidly changing world.

If a "third" Yugoslavia were to be reconstructed on the lines of modernized federalism—roughly in the form that it had before the adoption of the 1974 Constitution—a greater centralization of foreign policy could be expected. Any other version, recognizing the genuine sovereignty of the republics (as in the confederal proposal), would give greater autonomy to the republics/states. Should any of the present constituent units of Yugoslavia actually secede, then it would obviously conduct its own foreign policy in the new situation. Regardless of how the state will be re-designed as a result of the "new historic compact" of Yugoslavia's peoples (barring the outbreak of a civil war or the army's involvement in the solution of political issues), the policy of nonalignment does not promise to enjoy such high priority in the country's future foreign policy. Particularly in view of the crisis in the postwar Persian Gulf period, interest in foreign policy and economic cooperation with the Arab countries in the region is bound to decline. Such cooperation enjoyed a fairly high priority prior to the outbreak of the Gulf crisis, which caused massive losses for the Yugoslav economy in 1990 and 1991.

The greatest challenge for Yugoslavia in the sphere of international political and economic relations is very complex. One of the problems involves the Central and Eastern European countries which have recently abandoned (or are abandoning) socialism and centrally planned economies. Relations with these countries need to be reassessed, bearing in mind also the unification of the two Germanies and the disintegration of the Soviet Union. Another line of development is the integrational effort within the European Community. Remaining outside the reach of the Common Market and the areas of free movement of the people will prove a serious handicap for any country. Access to the European Community will probably be sought in an indirect way—through the various international and regional organizations and associations, such as the OECD or European Free Trade Association (EFTA). While the European Community stresses an economically powerful Europe, the Council of Europe seeks to cultivate the European spirit and to spread Europeanism throughout the continent. To take part in the building of a common European home is an opportunity not to be missed by any country, especially not a Balkan one—and all the more so in this part of the world which has never been known for its respect for authentic democracy, individual and collective human rights, and fundamental freedoms.

Responding to the integration processes in Europe—in the political, economic, or cultural sphere—Yugoslavia will have to "align itself" with its new foreign, particularly European, policy. This new policy will probably mark the country's greatest reorientation in the 1990s. It will be less East European, and more Central European, Mediterranean, Western, and Far Eastern. It will also be less global and world-embracing, and more regional and horizontal. Special features of this policy will be a focus on the neighbors, on expatriates, and on migrants. Greater attention will have to be paid to cooperation with and through international organizations, associations, and groupings and to multilateral relations. Such shifts in the country's international political and economic orientation will necessitate new measures in cultural, scientific, and educational policy. Specific changes that will need to be made in the educational sphere are discussed in the next section.

NEW CHALLENGES AND POSSIBLE EDUCATIONAL IMPLICATIONS

The new picture of Yugoslavia emerging at the start of the 1990s will lead to important changes in a number of aspects of its educational policy. In addition, new issues and new orientations will come within the focus of educational reforms. Since the process of transition from one political and socioeconomic system into another is just under way, the following analysis will rely less on the accumulated and systematized experience and more on prognosis and forecast.

Toward Greater Autonomy in Educational Policy

The resolution of the Yugoslav constitutional crisis will lead to the emergence of a "third" Yugoslavia. It may become constituted as a modernized federation or as a confederation (Petković, 1991). (Again, I do *not* analyze the possible situation following a disintegration of Yugoslavia, or one that might come in the event of a general civil war or an attempt to involve the military in the solution of political problems.) The modernized federation proposal advocates a recentralization of state affairs and greater competence for the federal government in every domain. One such domain is education, where many of the federal functions were transferred to the republic and provincial education authorities in the 1970s and 1980s. Thus, Yugoslavia was one of the few countries in the world that did not have a federal Ministry of Education. This does not mean that there were not several republic-provincial coordinating bodies at the federal level to harmonize domestic and/or foreign educational policies for the country as a whole. At the end of 1989, the educational competences of the autonomous provinces (Kosovo and Voivodina) were transferred de facto and de jure to the Socialist Republic of Serbia.

A confederal resolution of the constitutional crisis would mean a further strengthening of the autonomy and sovereignty of the constituent republics in all matters pertaining to education, so that they would be fully autonomous in the design and conduct of their educational policies. As sovereign states, they would enter into cooperative agreements with other countries and/or international governmental and nongovernmental organizations. This model would certainly require the establishment of new relations among the members of the confederation, all the more so as they would continue to share many educational problems. It is not at all unlikely that in the new constitutional framework they would cooperate among themselves much more actively than they did in the past, when their cooperation was mainly passive and defensive.

The key question of future educational policy, in view of the reconstitution of the country, is that of autonomous and sovereign decision making, that is, whether it will be (and to what degree) in the hands of the federal government or in the hands of the sovereign states—members of the confederation. The answer to this question will determine not only the policy of education but also the nature of future educational reforms.

Toward a Full Respect for National and Cultural Identities and Human Rights

The key to solving Yugoslavia's crisis is the solution of the national crisis—provided that it is a solution acceptable to all. Such a solution, it is now clear, can no longer be sought in the worn-out wartime and postwar slogan of brotherhood and unity, or in the newly coined ideologized phrases invoking Yugoslav unity and togetherness or Yugoslav synthesis. It is also still an open question how far some current advocacy of national states involving the re-drawing of the boundaries of some of the republics serves to aggravate the already difficult interethnic communication. Finally, isn't it something of wishful thinking to expect that the multiparty elections will resolve the long-lasting ethnic animosities now that they have been let out of Pandora's box?

In spite of the many elements pointing to a pessimistic outlook, I prefer the optimistic version of possible future developments—one that is based on the full respect of national and cultural identities and human rights. As a practical educational policy, this means enabling every individual citizen of the civil state, regardless of his or her national and/or cultural identity, to develop himself or herself fully within the school and educational system. Providing such opportunities would be the duty of all the federal or confederal constituent units. Their educational policies would stem from the concept of multiculturalism. This concept is not at all at variance with the right to education in accordance with the national and cultural identity of every individual, which would thus be upheld as a fundamental right.

This is the direction that practical changes in education should follow, for instance, regarding the language of instruction, textbook preparation, use of different scripts, teaching of national subjects, education of migrants' children, and so on. Practical educational policies should ensure full equality for every individual, avoiding any educational and cultural hegemony or assimilation. The same would apply to distinctly underprivileged groups such as the Gypsies.

In order to create favorable conditions for such educational reforms, it is necessary to stem the tide of hatred dividing people of different nations, to develop tolerance, cultivate dialogue, and respect differences. This is not a panacea for education in the Yugoslav multinational (multiethnic) context, but it can take us democratically to the desired end. Any other way would be violent, for it would impose solutions on those who are weaker against their will. Historical experience in this part of the world teaches us that imposition of the will of the majority on the minority population has never brought peace and happiness to either group.

Education Between the Public and the Private Sector

We have already noted Yugoslavia's transition from socialism to *non*socialism and its abandonment of self-management. This transition involves the transformation of ownership patterns. The development of new patterns of ownership is somewhat more complex in a country with self-managing socialism than in the countries of "real existing socialism." The difference is in the fact that in the latter countries most of the means of production is in the hands of the state, while in self-managing socialism the *whole of society* (not the state) is the nominal owner of property. That is why the process of transformation of ownership will proceed along two tracks—state takeover and privatization.

As far as education is concerned, until recently it functioned as an activity "of special social concern." That is why various self-managing mechanisms and bodies were involved in its operation. Now we are witnessing the process of transformation of education from the social to the public sector, with the state assuming competences and responsibilities for education. State bodies are replacing self-managing bodies and displaying the already visible tendency to decide on all the more and less important questions of education and behavior of people working in that sector (*The Elementary*, 1991).

Paralleling the strengthened role of the state in education is another new development—provision of legal possibilities for the operation of private schools. This is not to say that we should expect a rapid growth of the private educational sector, but private initiative will probably make itself felt primarily in the nonformal and continuing professional education of adults. The financing of education out of the students' private pockets has already become a fairly widespread practice in higher education. In 1990 institutions of higher learning started to charge quite high fees for some forms of tuition. Completely free of any tuition charges until very recently, higher education is now becoming the most expensive level of education.

The spread of the private sector, greater entrepreneurship, and sharper competition among the economic subjects will give new dynamics to the behavior of the educational institutions. It can be assumed that the market will better evaluate the human resources and make education more relevant. The hitherto sluggish educational sector may become much more dynamic, flexible, and readier to respond to the challenges of an active society pursuing greater economic liberalism. However, in the absence of appropriate student welfare programs (scholarships, student loans, grants, etc.), shifting the burden of educational expenditure on to private sources will, in the coming years, lead to greater social inequalities in the availability of educational opportunities. This will be particularly the case in higher education.

With the transition from the social to the public and/or private sector, education will cease to be governed by the rules of self-management. Decisions on the development of education will no longer be made as before—by delegates representing educational institutions and those representing other, different areas of material and nonmaterial production. Self-management will be replaced by management, and self-managing financing by public funding (from funds located in education ministries) and private payments (*The Elementary*, 1991). Teachers will no longer debate their salaries among themselves, since these will be fixed by ministerial decisions. At present the teachers' trade unions have no influence over the legal position of teachers and their collective agreements with their employers.

Self-management in schools is being replaced by management, with headmasters receiving fairly wide competences. Self-management by pupils and students, always an innocent game rather than serious business, has been practically eliminated. Self-management pedagogy, developed over the past thirty years as a theoretical basis of the Yugoslav educational practice, is today only part of the Yugoslav historical experience. Viewed from the present perspective, numerous studies into the workings of the self-managed schools appear to be a waste of research money and researchers' energies. The educational reforms motivated by a desire to promote the idea and practice of self-management—especially the 1974 educational reform—are now being rejected in all their aspects, and their results and consequences are seen as wholly negative. All of this means that self-management (such as it was practiced in Yugoslav schools) is now being abandoned as an ideological, political, and social construct. In fact, self-management stood no chance in a country in which absolute priority was given to political monism, a party-run state, and ideological intransigence (Šoljan, 1989, 1991). The question that remains—and one that is not easily answered—is how, under the new conditions, to enlarge the scope for the participation of all people in affairs of interest for the individual and the community, regardless of whether these affairs concern education, the "world of work," or leisure.

Toward a Democratic Education in Pluralist Society

The effects of Marxism and political monism on education have already been reviewed. What now remains to be examined are some of the implications of the abandonment of the one-party system and Marxism as an official (state, party) philosophy.

With the transition from the one-party political system to the multiparty parliamentary system, the League of Communists of Yugoslavia has disappeared as an absolute holder of power in all spheres of political, social, and economic life in the country. The electoral results in the individual republics/states strongly favored those noncommunist parties whose programs emphasize national independence, sovereignty, and the glorious past. Such programs oppose one nation to another, with mutual accusations of monarchic terror (in the "first" Yugoslavia), genocidal behavior (during World War II), or communist dictatorship (in the "second" Yugoslavia). Suitably oriented national programs have produced national homogenization, and leading political parties have turned into mass political movements with characteristically populist patterns of behavior. The parties that have won recent elections have almost absolute power and face very weak parliamentary oppositions.

In this situation, a single-party political system and communist ideology are being replaced by the authority of the ruling party and its philosophy as dominant in education, too. Early experiences allow us to examine certain priority moves taken by the new educational authorities in the wake of the first multiparty elections in some of the republics.

De-ideologization is probably one of the most comprehensive reform measures in education. Its purpose is to cleanse the school ecology and curriculum of ideological rituals and content. Thus, for instance, the sociopolitical organizations of young people—such as the Young Pioneers' Organization and Youth Union—have been abolished. The League of Communists has also left the school. As for textbooks, they are being "pruned" of materials in which the communist regime had shown a keen interest. New elements are being introduced into the curriculum, and historical events are being interpreted in the light of the political changes that have taken place. More emphasis is being placed on aspects of national history and culture. The subjects intended to inculcate a scientific view of the world into young people (Marxism and Theory and Practice of Socialist Self-Management) have been removed from the syllabus, while the preparation of young people for wartime conditions (Popular Defense and Social Self-Protection) has been suspended (Šoljan, 1990). Understandably, the changes are not proceeding at the same pace in all parts of the country. While much of the work along these lines has already been completed in the western republics

(Slovenia and Croatia), in the easternmost republics/states it has barely begun. If socialism is preserved in these parts, the question is whether it will ever begin at all.

Another major debating point is the position of religious education. For instance, should religious education be introduced into schools as a compulsory subject? Or an optional one? Or should religious topics be integrated into other school subjects as part of the general cultural and civilizational knowledge? Hinging on answers to these questions is also the question of who should provide this instruction—priests or regular teachers? Interestingly enough, many church representatives do not insist on the introduction of religious education in schools as a compulsory subject (Pranjić, 1991). On the contrary, they see the separation of the church and state as a valuable civilizational achievement and as an important element for the development of their mutual relations. The problem of religious education is further complicated by the existence of different churches in the multidenominational context of the country.

As for teachers and managers of educational institutions, the new authorities cannot hide their heightened interest in the personnel policy for education. The previous communist regime relied on the clause of "moral and political suitability" in the selection of teachers and headmasters in schools; a similar situation held at institutions of higher learning. The new regime, for its part, tries to place the people it trusts in the leading positions. Although professionalism is often invoked in the current discussions concerning teachers, there are few serious signs that professional behavior has indeed come in the place of "enthusiasm" and "love for children."

The shift to political pluralism, pluralism in thinking, and the freedom of religion in schools points toward a different kind of pedagogy—one that should be rooted in humanism instead of the dogmatically accepted Marxist philosophy. Democratic education and the fostering of critical thought should replace the "pedagogy of violence" and indoctrination. For there can be no doubt that the worst legacy of the former (in some places even present) communist regimes is that left in the minds of people. It is therefore to be hoped that one pedagogy of indoctrination will not be replaced by another pedagogy of indoctrination. The interference of the state and government in education is permissible only to a certain point. Once that point is passed, education loses its autonomy and becomes an instrument of day-to-day politics and of the ruling ideology. The question is whether the new authorities, faced with difficult political conflicts, will be able to resist the temptation to use education for pragmatic ends—in the name of defense of the new and still struggling democracy.

Into Europe and the World—Through Education

With the growing climate of confidence in Europe, it is difficult to imagine a European country that would remain insensitive to the need for greater educational cooperation. This is the rationale on which one can base the inescapability of a reorientation of the country (or its individual parts if they decide to stay together) toward Europe.

The European orientation in educational policy means a coherent set of measures designed to ensure the European quality levels in education and compatibility of the educational systems. Neither of these aims will be easy to achieve. They should be regarded as long-term objectives, and future reforms should be planned accordingly. One of the preconditions of getting closer to Europe is an effective teaching and mastery of foreign languages. For "small" nations, this is a *condition sine qua non* of international communication within Europe and the rest of the world. The already high interest in learning English will be sustained, interest in German will probably grow now that Germany is united, while interest in Russian will decline.

Another important aspect of the European educational orientation will be an active participation in student and academic exchange programs. Remaining outside major projects, such as the European Community's COMMETT, ERASMUS, and TEMPUS, would keep the quality of the human resources and the country's technological capability below the European standards (Neave, 1988). A particularly valuable input for the formulation of a European-style educational policy can come through participation in the Council of Europe's Council for Cultural Cooperation programs (Council of Europe, 1990, 1991). These programs are important for the individual states/republics because, among other things, they stress the importance of democratic education in civil society, human rights, and fundamental freedoms. They contribute to an understanding of different cultures in multinational settings and help to develop an awareness of an integrated Europe and interdependent world. As part of the European educational policy, cooperation among the regions will be a particularly fruitful field. A good example of such cooperation is the Alps-Adria program, which brings together regions from a number of Mediterranean and Central European countries.

An important change and rethinking of educational policies for migrants, expatriates, and national minorities in the neighboring countries will be needed in the 1990s. The policy for migrant children in the past was to make them fully conscious little Yugoslavs. On the other hand, expatriates and their children were for the most part treated as political emigrants. The education of ethnic minorities in the neighboring countries was a taboo topic. Minorities were sources of contention instead of bridges for cooperation.

Another interesting shift could result from the abandonment of the policy of nonalignment as the key foreign policy option. Interest in receiving students from the Arab countries will decline. At the same time, there will be more interest in receiving students from European and overseas countries, particularly those with strong expatriate groups willing to invest in the study of the languages, literatures, and cultures of the different Yugoslav peoples (especially the United States, Canada, and Australia).

As regards the competences in the planning and implementation of international educational cooperation, these will depend on the constitutional makeup of the "third" Yugoslavia. The present trend is toward greater autonomy in the behavior of the individual republics/states, not in regional cooperation but also in relations with international governmental organizations. Still, neither the international organizations nor the European countries favor forms of cooperation that bypass the federal authorities. This is because the developed countries do not have a desire to understand the complex relations in this country and to provide the help it needs in the spirit of solidarity.

CONCLUSION

The above analysis of trends in educational policies and reforms in Yugoslavia has shown their direct dependence on the political, ideological, and economic situation within the country and outside. Over practically the whole of the postwar period, the country's educational policies and the nature of its educational reforms were crucially influenced by federalism, multinationality (multiethnicity), socialism and self-management, political monism, ideological exclusivity, and nonaligned foreign policy orientation. Stated in somewhat simplified terms, the educational reforms were intended to promote the realization of educational policies that would contribute to the development of comprehensively formed persons, educated to live in a federal community, in the spirit of the brotherhood and unity of the Yugoslav peoples, and practicing socialist self-management. This educational policy accepted exclusively the philosophy of Marxism as a scientific world-view, a single-party political system to guarantee the power of the working class, and a policy of nonalignment.

In the 1980s and at the start of the 1990s, however, the fundamental attributes of Yugoslav society began to be radically questioned. The pendulum of the constitutional system moved back and forth between centralist federalism, loose confederalism, and the country's total disintegration. National relations were increasingly characterized by intolerance, conflicts, violence, and elements of the civil war. Socialism and self-management were replaced by a return to undeveloped capitalism, with the dominant role of the state and with the still small but aggressive private capital. An alternative to this would be a well-worn-out model of state socialism and government-planned economy imposed on the country by nonpolitical means. The pluralism of ownership is accompanied by a transition to political pluralism, which is always suspect for political power-holders in a single-party system. An ideological value system of the communist society is now being replaced by the ideas and moral values close to neoconservatism. The policy of nonalignment has definitively lost its appeal. Its place will be taken by alignment—in the first place toward Europe. The alternative would be a new self-isolation.

All these are already influencing and will continue to influence the shape of the new educational policy and the direction of future changes in education. They will, it seems, move between increased centralization and radical decentralization, with the legitimation of complete educational sovereignty; between nationally colored educational policies and multiculturalism in civil society and state based on the rule of law; between a more or less decisive role of the state and the role of private capital in education; between ideological one-sidedness and pluralism of thought, entrepreneurship, and the labor market; finally, between effective European and wider educational cooperation and educational isolationism.

The formulation of new educational policies and the implementation of future educational reforms will not be a historically easy process. A whole decade will be required to build even the basic elements of the new, democratic social order and educational system, regardless of whether the building will take place within a "third" Yugoslavia or within its fully independent constituents. Interethnic and religious conflicts, economic and technological underdevelopment, political and cultural illiteracy cannot be eliminated over a short term. But if the Yugoslav peoples opt (or if the world democratic public opinion forces them to opt) for the path of development chosen by today's Europe and free world, then—in a long-term perspective—the educational reforms themselves may help to strengthen the cause of democratic change in the part of the world still inclined to autocratic forms of irrational behavior.

REFERENCES

The Associated Labour Act. 1977. Ljubljana: Dopisna delavska univerza.

Bennett, William S. 1972, February. "Elitism and Socialist Goals in Yugoslav Education." *Notre Dame Journal of Education* 3:267–277.

Bezdanov, Stevan. 1986. *Jedinstvo i zajedništvo u vaspitanju i obrazovanju u SFRJ* [Unity and togetherness in education in Yugoslavia]. Belgrade: Nova prosveta.

———. 1980. *Udruženi rad i obrazovanje* [Associated Labor and education]. Belgrade: Mladost.

The Constitution of the Socialist Federal Republic of Yugoslavia. 1974. Ljubljana: Dopisna delavski univerza.

Council of Europe. 1990. *Council for Cultural Cooperation (CDCC): Draft Minutes. CDCC–ED (90)5.* Strasburg: Author.

———. 1991. *Council for Cultural Cooperation: Preliminary Draft Programe of the CDCC for 1992. CDCC (91) 2.* Strasbourg: Author.

Documents of the Gathering of the Non-Aligned Countries 1956–1989. 1990. Belgrade: Review of International Affairs.

"The Elementary Schooling Law" [Zakon o osnovnam školstvu]. 1991. *Glasnik* (Ministarstva prosvjete i kulture Republike Hrvatske) 1(1–2):1–6.

Farmerie, Samuel A. 1974, November. "Educational Organization in Yugoslavia." *Educational Forum* 29:71–75.

General Law on Education. 1958. Belgrade: Službeni list.

Georgeoff, John. 1988. "Yugoslavia." *World Education Encyclopedia*, ed. G. T. Kurian. New York: Facts on File Publications, pp. 1404–1426.

Kardelj, Edvard. 1977. "Sistem socijalističkog samoupravljanja u Jugoslaviji" [Socialist self-management system in Yugoslavia]. In *Samoupravlljanje u Jugoslaviji 1950–*

1976 [Self-management in Yugoslavia, 1950–1976]. Belgrade: Privredni pregled, pp. 9–39.

———. 1978. *Slobodni udruženi rad* [Free associated labour]. Belgrade: Radnička štampa.

Mikes, Melanie. 1984. "Instruction in the Mother Togue in Yugoslavia." *Prospects, Quarterly Review of Education* 14(1):121–131.

Neave, Guy. 1988. "Cross-national Collaboration in Higher Education: New Initiatives in European Community Policy." *Compare* 18:53–61.

Nikolić, Milenko, and Tomislav Bogavac. 1980. *Educational Policy in Yugoslavia*. Belgrade: Jugoslovenski pregled.

OECD. 1981a. *Reviews of National Policies for Education: Yugoslavia*. Paris: Author.

———. 1981b. *Conditions, Problems and Policy of Education in Yugoslavia*. Paris: Author.

Petković, Ranko. 1989. "Where Does Yugoslavia Go?" *Review of International Affairs* 40(953):1–4.

———. 1991. "Will Yugoslavia Survive?" *Review of International Affairs* 42(981):1–4.

Pranjić, Marko. 1991. "Nema neutralne škole" [There is no neutral school]. *Školske novine* 42(8):5.

Rusinow, Dennison. 1977. *The Yugoslav Experiment, 1948–1974*. London and Berkeley: University of California Press.

Šimleša Pero. 1978. *Pedagogija* [Pedagogy]. Belgrade: Pedagoško-književni zbor.

Šoljan, Nikša Nikola. 1983. "Obrazovanje i Evropski Savjet" [Education and Council of Europe]. *Pedagogija* 38:151–166.

———. 1985. "Yugoslavia's International Cooperation in the Sphere of Adult Education: Policy and Practice." In *Adult Education in Yugoslav Society*, ed. N. N. Šoljan. Zagreb: Andragogical Center, pp. 259–286.

———. 1988. *Yugoslav Education under Examination*. Zagreb: University of Zagreb Institute for Educational Research.

———. 1989. "Yugoslavia." In *Student Political Activism: An International Reference Handbook*, ed. P. G. Altbach. Westport, Conn.: Greenwood Press, pp. 298–312.

———. 1990. "Higher Education Policy in Yugoslavia: Development, Change, Tendencies." Paper presented at the International Network of Philosophers of Education Conference on "Democracy and Education" held in London, August 20–23, 1990.

———. 1991, February. "Beyond the Myths of a Self-Management Socialist Society: Higher Education in Yugoslavia." *Comparative Education Review* 34.

Stančić, Nikša. 1985. "History of Yugoslavia: A Brief Survey." In *Adult Education in Yugoslav Society*, ed. N. N. Šoljan. Zagreb: Andragogical Centre, pp. 19–30.

Šuvar, Stipe. 1977. *Škola i tvornica* [School and factory]. Zagreb: Školska knjiga.

The Tasks of the League of Communists of Yugoslavia in the Socialist Transformation of Education Along Self-Management Lines. 1974. Belgrade: Komunist.

Tomich, Vera. 1963. *Education in Yugoslavia and the New Reform*. Washington, D.C.: U.S. Office of Education.

Unesco. 1989. *Unesco Statistical Yearbook 1989*. Paris: Unesco.

28

ZIMBABWE

Betty Jo Dorsey

THE COLONIAL-SETTLER ERA, 1890–1980

Zimbabwe achieved independence under a Black majority government in 1980. It inherited an educational system based on inequality of opportunity for the four racial groups, Blacks, Coloureds, Asians, and Whites, which comprise the society. The most disadvantaged group was the Blacks who constituted 96 percent of the population. Race was the main criterion for social stratification in colonial-settler society and the basis for ordering nearly all social relations. The four racial groups had different degrees of control over production and different degrees of access to the rewards that flowed from it. The Whites exercised most control and enjoyed the highest rewards, and the Blacks at the other end of the scale had the least control and the lowest rewards.

From the beginning of White rule in 1890, Blacks were prevented from competing with Whites on equal terms. Segregation was instituted in an early act by the British South Africa Company which governed the colony until 1923, and was incorporated in the Constitution of the self-governing colony of Southern Rhodesia which provided for a Native Affairs Department headed by a chief native commissioner.

Nonetheless, some Blacks, through mission schools, acquired education and skills and were drawn into the modern economic sector. They thus began to be potential economic competitors to Whites. As the threat of Black competition increased, the pattern of segregation became more explicit and separate agencies were established to handle the affairs of each race encompassing all aspects of life, including agriculture, education, housing, taxes, and medical facilities.

In 1931 this segregation culminated in the passage of the Land Apportionment

Act which formally divided the country into discrete racial areas. The segregation of all land into White and Black areas dispossessed the Blacks of most of the more fertile land and undermined their economic self-sufficiency. Their areas were poorer in terms of welfare services as well as productive capacity but had to support higher densities of population, with 63 percent of the Black population living in black areas which constituted only half the country (Kay, 1972: 23).

National resources allocated by an all-White legislature channeled funds into the development of White areas at the expense of the development of Black areas. In addition, labor legislation secured a high wage for White workers by eliminating Black competition for skilled jobs. The artificial scarcity of skilled labor which was created was then recruited from outside the country. The low wages of unskilled Black workers were maintained largely through a policy of importing Black migrant labor from neighboring countries.

The incomes of White farmers were also protected from Black competition through government-controlled marketing arrangements that discriminated against Black farmers. Whenever necessary, legislation was enacted which ensured that Black development did not pose a serious threat to White development and interests. In 1934 Godfrey Huggins, the prime minister, maintained,

If I am allowed to protect my own race and find a niche in this country for every grade of white civilization, then I will dip into the pockets of the Hon. Minister of Finance and see that the native gets more money; but until I know that, I am not moving. That is why you find a standstill in the Native Development Vote (Gray, 1960: 144).

White-dominated governments thus made decisions that limited and restricted Black acquisition of power while at the same time strengthening the position of Whites. Continued manipulation of the economic, political, and educational structures was particularly important in maintaining White dominance, which resulted in the Black majority essentially occupying a dependent and subordinate position in society (Dorsey, 1981: 213).

THE DUAL EDUCATIONAL SYSTEM

The educational system that developed mirrored the structure of colonial-settler society in that separate systems of education evolved to serve the racially defined communities. Although the "European" and "African" Education departments were administered by a single Ministry of Education, each department developed as a separate and distinct system. Asian and Coloured pupils were administered by the European department; however, they attended different schools from those of White pupils. There was very little social mixing.

More significant for Blacks were the differences apparent in the quantity and quality of education that resulted from different regulations and budgetary provisions for the two parallel systems. The Rhodesian Front government, which took office in 1962, attempted to control an expanding Black educational system by instituting a new fiscal policy relating expenditure for Black (but not White) education to the economy of the country. The budget for Black education was pegged at 2 percent of the gross national product, and various economic measures were implemented in order to keep government expenditure within the allotted budget. The government spent twelve times more per primary school pupil in the European system that in the African system and nearly three times more per pupil at the secondary school level (Dorsey, 1975: 47).

The Black system produced a broadly based educational pyramid in which pupils in secondary schools represented only 4 percent of pupils in the system, while in the White system the corresponding figure was 43 percent. Education for Whites was compulsory to the age of fifteen. White pupils proceeded automatically to a comprehensive secondary school and, if sufficiently bright, were assured of going on to Form 6 (advanced high school). The Black pupils, on the other hand, entered a system that was voluntary and highly selective. Whether they continued at various levels depended on their ability to pass examinations with high marks and on their parents' ability to pay school fees. In 1975 only 55 percent of the Grade 1 cohort completed the seven-year primary school course, 10 percent went on to secondary school, 4 percent completed Form 4 (ordinary-level high school), and the number in Form 6 qualifying for university entrance was 0.3 percent (Dorsey, 1981: 214).

The content of secondary education was largely academic. It was narrowly determined by the school-leaving certificate examinations that were set and marked in England. The curriculum in Black secondary schools was similar to that offered in the White system, but the range of subjects was more limited. The government's attempt in 1968 to establish a vocational secondary school for Blacks was rejected by most Blacks on the grounds that it was inferior to an academic curriculum and inferior to the type of education provided for Whites.

The limited provision of secondary education for Blacks and its highly selective nature based on academic merit and to some degree on economic status produced an educational and social elite even more clearly than did its White analogue. The status of these elites in Black society tended to structure their aspirations and expectations in life. Their educational attainment also gave them the potential for competing for the same jobs as their White counterparts (Dorsey, 1975: 165). However, when employment opportunities for Black secondary school graduates were compared with their high aspirations and academic achievement, it was obvious that a serious discrepancy existed in colonial-settler society which contributed to the frustrations of Black youth. They perceived racial segregation as the significant factor frustrating the attainment of their aspirations. Initially, they saw this operating at the educational level, with Blacks being provided with inferior schools and limited access to further education. Ultimately, however, they saw this discrimination extended to their preclusion from many of the best jobs that were reserved for Whites (Dorsey, 1975: 165).

Under such circumstances, it is not surprising that tensions and antagonisms between these youths and the established social order arose. In the years 1972–

1979, thousands of Black youths, both male and female, left the country to join the armed struggle. Many left in the middle of their secondary school careers, relinquishing coveted places in these schools. As Shibutani and Kwan (1971: 135) have noted,

Systems of ethnic stratification begin to break down when minority peoples demand new self-conceptions and refuse to accept subordinate roles. As they become more aware of their worth in comparison to members of the dominant group, what they had once accepted as natural becomes unbearable. What had once appeared to be special privileges for superior persons, is redefined as the right of all human beings.

Although the racial structure of the society was the most important factor in the inequality of educational opportunity, other factors operated which contributed to differential access to education among various groups within the Black population. These factors included gender, rural residence, type of school attended, and socioeconomic status. The second part of this chapter considers the extent to which reforms instituted at independence in 1980 have been able to eliminate these inequalities.

EDUCATIONAL REFORM: POSTINDEPENDENCE, 1980–1990

The vast expansion in the educational system in Zimbabwe at all levels since independence has had the express purpose of eliminating educational and social inequalities that prevailed during the colonial-settler era. Important educational reforms involve a political process and have implications for the redistribution of the power and material resources of the society (Paulston, 1976: 1). For Zimbabwe, the reforms in education involved a fundamental change in national educational policies which sought to initiate major reforms in the following: (1) the national allocation of resources to education, (2) the allocation of resources within the existing educational system, (3) the percentage of students completing different levels of the educational system, (4) the percentage of pupils from different social and racial backgrounds that complete different levels of the educational system, (5) the percentage of female students that complete different levels of the educational system, and (6) changes in the aims of the curricula and their content.

Educational Expansion

At independence the most immediate educational policy reform was the change from an elite racially based system to one of mass education. The imperative to provide mass education had both an ideological and a political rationale. It was not only a response by the newly elected leaders to the popular demand for education from the electorate, but was also perceived by them to be the main instrument for creating a more egalitarian society, for expanding and modernizing the economy, and as an essential element in the process of nation building.[1]

Individual demand for greater provision of education was conditioned by the unequal provision based on race which existed during the colonial-settler era and an instrumental perception of the value of education developed during that period in which education was seen to be the only route to salaried employment in the modern sector of the economy, providing security, affluence, prestige, and a modern style of life. Although other countries in Africa experienced rapid expansion of their educational systems at independence, none has attempted universal access to primary and secondary education to the same degree or as rapidly as Zimbabwe has done.[2]

In September 1980 the government announced free primary schooling for all, with the result that enrollments soared from 819,586 in 1979 to 2,212,103 nine years later, an index increase of 2.7. The government estimates that this represents approximately 97 percent of children of primary school age in school. Although education at the secondary level is not free, an even greater enrollment explosion has occurred, with an increase from 66,215 in 1979 to 641,005 in 1988, or an index increase of 9.7. The percentage of Grade 7 school leavers entering Form 1 had risen from 20 percent in 1979 to 65 percent in 1988. (See Table 28.1.)

NATIONAL ALLOCATION OF RESOURCES TO EDUCATION

The Expansion of Primary and Secondary Schools

To accommodate the increased enrollment, schools were rapidly built at both primary and secondary levels. The number of primary schools nearly doubled from 2,401 in 1979 to 4,471 in 1988, while the number of secondary schools increased from 177 to 1,484 during the same period (Zimbabwe Government, Annual Report, 1988: 35). However, the majority of new secondary schools were built in the rural areas as day schools under the management of district councils. Many of these schools began as "upper tops" attached to existing primary schools until their own buildings could be built. The central government gave specified building grants and per pupil grants to district councils that, together with the help of local communities, have built and managed the schools. There were and still are a number of problems in the operation and management of these schools. Because of the lack of amenities and poor housing conditions in rural areas, it has been difficult to attract trained teachers, and many of the schools are staffed largely with primary-trained teachers and untrained teachers. In some areas, according to the secretary for education, responsible authorities (district councils) failed to use their per capita grants judiciously by spending more on administration than on books and stationery. The quality of learning was adversely affected by the consequential shortage of basic texts. Although with management training for district councils provided by the Ministry of

Table 28.1
Government and Nongovernment School Enrollments, 1979–1988

	1979	1988
Primary:		
Grade 1	170,090	389,019
Grade 2	139,968	331,347
Grade 3	130,106	302,798
Grade 4	109,552	289,265
Grade 5	96,649	291,062
Grade 6	88,287	300,088
Grade 7	82,210	305,136
Special	724	3,388
Subtotal	817,586	2,212,103
Secondary:		
Form 1	18,352	211,816
Form 2	16,031	173,533
Form 3	13,614	128,322
Form 4	12,201	112,865
Form 5	2,141	0
Form 6 lower	2,141	7,946
Form 6 upper	1,067	6,186
Special	416	337
Subtotal	65,963	641,005
Total	883,549	2,853,108

Source: Abstracted from Zimbabwe Government, <u>Annual Report of the Secretary for Primary and Secondary Education, 1988</u>. Harare: Government Printer, 1990, p. 4.

Education the situation improved in some districts, it was still a cause for concern, as noted in the secretary's report for 1984.

Enrollment expanded so rapidly in some areas that pupils arrived before any buildings were constructed, and classes were held in hastily built pole and "dagga" (mud) huts with thatched roofs. In some cases they were held under the open sky. Pupils in rural "day" secondary schools often come from widely scattered communities and have to make their own arrangements for "boarding," either staying with friends and relatives or frequently using classrooms as dormitories at night and classrooms during the day and cooking their food over open fires in the traditional manner. In addition to these problems, there has been the difficulty of providing adequate support services and equipment, particularly in science and technical subjects. Despite all these problems, the expansion of secondary education to the remotest areas of Zimbabwe in such a short time is a remarkable achievement and would not have been possible without the enthusiasm of local communities and their cooperation with the Ministry of Education and district councils. In addition to paying building fees, the local people also contributed their labor in the actual building process.

STAFFING THE SCHOOLS

One of the major problems that the government faced with the introduction of mass education was staffing the schools. In 1981 the pool of qualified teaching staff quickly dried up, especially since it also had to cater for expansion in the secondary sector. Faced with the possibility of having no teachers at all, the teaching service was opened to experienced untrained teachers with a basic standard 6 (Grade 8) qualification (Zimbabwe Government, Annual Report, 1981: 6). It was also opened to unqualified persons who had two to four years of secondary schooling. Table 28.2 shows that by 1988 primary schools were staffed with 49.0 percent untrained teachers.

In the rapidly expanding secondary school sector, the staffing situation was also critical. In 1980 graduate-trained secondary school teachers constituted only 10.5 percent of the teachers in this sector, whereas 66.3 percent of the staff in secondary schools consisted of primary-trained teachers, nongraduate student teachers trainees, and untrained teachers. It has also thought that the use of the best trained primary school teachers to staff rural secondary schools has probably had an adverse effect on the quality of primary education in some cases. However, by 1988 this situation had improved somewhat, through the increased output of locally trained teachers and the recruitment of teachers from other countries, largely from Britain and Canada.

FINANCING EDUCATIONAL EXPANSION

The financing of the new educational policy, aimed at a more equitable distribution of educational opportunities, has involved a massive increase in public

Table 28.2
Percentage of Trained Teachers in Primary and Secondary Schools, 1988

Sector	Trained %	Untrained %	Total Numbers
Primary	51.0	49.0	57,762
Secondary	50.5	49.5	23,598
Total	51.0	49.0	81,360

Source: Abstracted from Zimbabwe Government, Annual Report of the Secretary for Primary and Secondary Education, 1988. Harare: Government Printer, 1990, p. 5.

expenditure for education. Prior to independence, in 1979 the education vote totaled Z$118,705,000, which represented 11.6 percent of the total budget. In the first year of independence, it doubled to 22.1 percent. In every budget since then it has had the largest vote of any government ministry. In 1983 the Minister of Finance, when presenting the budget to Parliament, warned that the strain on national resources had reached its limit and that responsibility for educational expansion must increasingly devolve on citizens through local authorities and community-based organizations.

The Ministry of Education's policies have been affected in a number of ways. First of all, they have sought to rationalize the role of the state in the provision of education so that urban and rural communities have equal access to government financial support. The government had been providing one-third of the cost of building rural primary and secondary schools, with the local communities providing two-thirds, while in urban areas it financed the entire cost. It has now been decided that new urban primary schools must be built and financed by urban councils. Presumably a similar policy with regard to urban secondary school expansion will follow. Second, the government instituted a policy whereby parent-teacher associations could establish management committees, charge school levies per pupil, and with these funds hire additional teachers to improve the pupil-teacher ratio. Many urban government schools in higher socioeconomic areas accepted the management committee concept and have been able to maintain higher standards than they would otherwise have been able to do. This has had the effect of enabling wealthier communities that can afford a better standard of education for their children to have the opportunity of providing it. In addition, the government has not discouraged new, private, high fee-paying schools from being established or the expansion of existing ones, but it has insisted that they be fully racially integrated with a substantial intake of black pupils.

The greatest proportion of the education budget is spent on teachers' salaries. The government pays teachers' salaries in all schools, including private schools. Thus, Zimbabwe faces the problem that has bedeviled other independent countries in Africa—an extremely high expenditure for education in proportion to the total state budget, thereby using up resources that might have been used to further the growth of the economy in order to generate employment for the products of the educational system.

Curriculum Reforms and Achievement Levels

Government policy in Zimbabwe aspires to both quantity and quality in education. Statements from the Ministry of Education and government officials have affirmed the need to maintain high standards in education while at the same time expanding education for all. Until 1988 the policy had been to provide a common curriculum to O level for all pupils regardless of ability or location, responding to a social demand that is consistent with the government's socialist ideology but one that has produced declining examination success for the vast majority of pupils. (See Chung and Ngara, 1985: 98–106.)

The first nonselective group of students wrote O levels in 1984 with a national pass rate of 20.6 percent. This was a decline of 30 percent from the previous year. However, Table 28.3 indicates that, as the number of candidates increased over the eight-year period 1980–1988, the percentage achieving an O-level certificate declined from 66.6 percent in 1980 to 12.4 percent in 1988.

A study by Ncube and Neilson (1985) showed that pass rates were related to the type of school that pupils attended. The older established schools, particularly mission and private (high fee-paying) schools, with long experience in preparing pupils for O levels, with more qualified teachers and better learning resources, had a much higher pass rate than the recently built rural secondary schools with less qualified staff, poorer learning resources, and pupils with lower pass rates in the primary school-leaving examination (Table 28.4).

However, the pattern that has emerged even in the long-established, better resourced schools is that, where enrollments increased rapidly and the number of qualified teachers declined, the result was a declining pass rate in the O-level examinations. Many of the schools, particularly the district council schools, had neither the experience nor the resources that the O-level examination requires. They lacked textbooks, libraries, audiovisual materials, and teachers with an adequate command of English. According to the Minister of Primary and Secondary Education, "We have to confess that of the 1502 secondary schools only 800 are good, which means that we have a stiff challenge in improving the other 700" (Chung, 1989: 11).

532   International Handbook of Educational Reform

Table 28.3
Percentage and Number of Pupils Achieving Passes in Five or More Subjects in the O-level Examinations, 1980–1988

Year	Total Number of Candidates	Percentage Achieving Five or More Passes	Total Number of Pupils Passed
1980	6,012	66,6	4,008
1981	10,396	57,1	5,932
1982	13,733	59,2	8,134
1983	21,733	54,6	11,872
1984	73,724	20,6	15,159
1985	112,881	13,0	14,760
1986	127,265	11,4	14,566
1987	152,181	11,9	18,124
1988	183,753	12,4	22,786

Source: Zimbabwe Government, Annual Reports of the Secretary for Education. Harare: Government Printer, 1980-1988.

Equity and Excellence

Despite the government's attempt to eradicate inequalities in education, a number of inequities still remain. One of the most important of these is the urban/rural inequality of access to schooling and particularly access to quality education in good schools as described in the previous section. One factor thought to contribute to this problem is population density. It is easier to build and staff schools to cater for a concentrated urban population than a scattered rural one. In some rural areas children must walk up to ten miles a day to attend the nearest school. This undoubtedly has an adverse effect on academic performance as well as contributing to a higher wastage rate in rural areas.

To some extent, urban/rural enrollment inequalities reflect economic inequalities between these areas. Farming parents are on the whole poorer and require their children's labor more than urban parents. This is particularly true in the case of girls and may be one factor in the higher dropout rate for girls and slightly lower enrollment figures for girls in rural areas. The labor of young girls is more essential for a family than that of young boys both in domestic chores such as cooking, babyminding, water and firewood carrying, and often

Table 28.4
Comparison of O-level Passes by Type of School, 1982–1984, by Percentage of Pupils Gaining Five or More O-levels

Type of School	1982		1983		1984	
	%	N	%	N	%	N
Government Group A (urban)	44	1,065	39	1,164	30	1,783
Government Group B (urban)	42	582	38	998	22	2,482
District council schools	n.a.			n.a.		141,120
Mission schools	58	714	52	1,345	45	1,995
Private schools	52	166	67	180	57	279
Rural government schools	22	225	31	216	18	387

Sources: Percentages based on selected sample from three regions: Harare, Mashonaland and Manicaland, from Examinations Branch Statistics, 1982-1984; Zimbabwe Government, Ministry of Education "National English Survey Conference Secondary Education 1985" (Ministry of Education, Harare, 1985, mimeographed), p. 104.

Notes:

n.a. = not available

Group A = former urban schools for Whites

Group B = urban schools for Blacks

in agriculture. Poorer parents sometimes cannot afford to educate all their children, and when a choice has to be made, it is usually in favor of educating a boy rather than a girl. Nevertheless, at the primary school level, Zimbabwe has achieved near gender equality in enrollment, with only a 2 percent difference in the proportion of girls to boys enrolled. This difference occurs in the rural primary schools only (Zimbabwe Government, Annual Report, 1987: 45).

GENDER INEQUALITIES AT THE POSTPRIMARY LEVEL

Since independence, the transition of pupils from the primary to the secondary level of education has had an overall increase from 20 percent in 1979 to 65 percent in 1988. In urban areas the transition is approximately 88 percent. However, a higher percentage of girls drop out at the end of primary school— 33 percent versus 27 percent for boys. Although the actual number of girls having access to secondary education has increased, the *proportion* of girls to boys has actually decreased at the senior secondary school level since independence as Tables 28.5 and 28.6 show. The proportion of girls at Form 4 decreased from 43 percent in 1979 to 39 percent in 1988. At Upper Sixth Form (advanced high school), the proportion of girls decreased from 35 percent in 1979 to 26.0 percent in 1988.

Tables 28.5 and 28.6 clearly show that girls have been disadvantaged in access to the higher educational rewards of the society after independence, even with a definite government policy to eliminate gender inequalities in education. Girls began to drop out in greater numbers than boys as early as primary school, fewer proceed to secondary school, and again they drop out in greater numbers than boys. Therefore, the ratio of boys to girls in the Upper Sixth Form is 3:1. The minister of primary and secondary education, addressing this issue, said, "This is a phenomenal waste of valuable human resources and there is little doubt that the development of Zimbabwe will be seriously hampered if we do not educate our girls" (Chung, 1988: 3). Similar gender inequalities are reported in other countries in sub-Saharan Africa. Cooksey and Ishumi (1986: 25) note with regard to Tanzania, "Over a twenty year period the proportion of girls in total secondary school enrollments increased only modestly." (See also Hyde, 1989: 1.)

Girls are not only underrepresented in secondary schools, but on the whole they underachieve compared with boys. Fewer girls than boys study mathematics and the hard sciences, and their performance is considerably poorer, particularly at the O level. In 1987, 7.4 percent of girls passed five or more subjects and thus earned a Cambridge School Certificate versus 15.5 percent for boys (Table 28.7).

At A level the performance of girls is more comparable to that of boys (Table 28.8), but the percentage passes by subject is lower for girls, except for English and the vernacular languages (Dorsey, Gaidzanwa, and Mupawenda, 1989: 107– 113). While the causes for this underachievement of girls are complex and probably cumulative, the transmission of cultural values and beliefs about the

Zimbabwe 535

Table 28.5
Form 4 Enrollment Trends by Gender, 1979–1988

Year	Boys %	Girls %	Total Enrolment N
1979	57.0	43.0	12,201
1980	57.0	43.0	12,811
1981	56.5	43.5	15,323
1982	58.7	41.3	15,772
1983	57.4	42.6	24,509
1984	62.0	38.0	71,014
1985	62.0	38.0	89,517
1986	62.0	38.0	97,820
1987	61.0	39.0	113,915
1988	61.0	39.0	112,865

Sources: Zimbabwe Government, Annual Reports of the Secretary for Education, 1979-1988. Harare: Government Printer.

sexes through early socialization and secondary socialization in the school seems to be a significant contributing factor to the continued underachievement of girls in secondary schools in Zimbabwe.

Gender Inequalities in Access to University Education

Because of the rapidly expanding secondary school system since independence, enrollments at the university have more than trebled in the past ten years. The output of qualified students from A-level secondary schools now exceeds the intake capacity of the university. The number of female students increased from 508 in 1979 to 1,930 in 1988. However, the proportion of female to male students remains unchanged at 3:1. Female students are unequally distributed among the university's ten faculties owing to the subjects they studied at A level. As we noted previously, fewer girls take mathematics and science at A level; therefore, they are underrepresented in the science faculties at the university. (See Table 28.9.) Engineering has the lowest proportion of female students (1.5 percent),

Table 28.6
Form 6 Enrollment Trends by Gender, 1979–1988

Year	Boys %	Girls %	Total Enrolment N
1979	65.0	35,0	1,067
1980	71.0	29.0	1,413
1981	70.0	30.0	1,673
1982	70.0	30.0	1,729
1983	67.7	32.4	2,890
1984	73.6	26.4	2,911
1985	72.8	27.2	3,281
1986	75.8	24.2	5.258
1987	69.0	31.0	5,966
1988	74.0	26.0	6,186

Sources: Zimbabwe Government, Annual Reports of the Secretary for Education,

1979-1988.   Harare: Government Printer.

followed by veterinary science (13.0 percent), agriculture (16.3 percent), and science (17.8 percent). The medical faculty has a higher proportion of female students than the other science faculties (25.4 percent). As is common elsewhere, the arts faculties have the highest proportion of female students.

At the postgraduate level, the proportion of female students is approximately the same as at the undergraduate level (24 percent). Within this range, a slightly lower percentage are pursuing master's and doctoral degrees, while a higher percentage are pursuing less demanding diplomas and certificates.

It has been found that there is no significant difference in achievement between male and female undergraduates. A slightly higher percentage of females achieved a 2.1 or better (18.7 versus 18.1 percent), and a slightly higher percentage of male students failed (10.8 versus 8.4 percent).

Consequences of Gender Inequalities

One fact emerges when examining national policies with regard to the education of girls and the status of women, and that is the inability of political

Table 28.7
Cambridge School Certificate O-level Results: Number of Subjects Passed by Gender, 1987

Number of Subjects Passed	Boys %	Girls %	Total %	N
5 or more	15.5	7.4	12.3	(18,070)
4 or less	84.5	92.6	87.7	(129,292)
Total	100.0	100.0	100.0	(147,362)

Note: Five or more subject passes necessary to achieve an O-level Certificate.

Chi-square = 215,338 df 1C = .12.

Table 28.8
Cambridge School Certificate A-level Academic Achievement, 1987

Number of Subjects Passed	Boys N	%	Girls N	%	Total N	%
2 or more	2,367	44.2	758	44.8	3,125	44.3
1 or less	2,991	55,8	935	55.2	3,926	55.7
Total	5,358	100,0	1,693	100,0	7,051	100,0

Chi-square = 0.185 df 1 N.S.

N.B. Two or more subject passes are necessary to achieve an A-level certificate.

reform to change the entire structure of roles and activities based on gender in this strongly patriarchal society. Despite the government's stated policy at independence to eliminate inequalities in education based on gender, inequalities persist.

The consequences for economic development may be far-reaching. A cross-national study by Benavot (1989: 84) involving ninety-six countries looked at education, gender, and economic development over a twenty-five year period, 1960–1985. Previous studies utilizing modernization theories assumed that the

Table 28.9
University Undergraduate Student Enrollment by Faculty and Gender (Full Time), 1988

	Males %	Females %	Total Number N
Agriculture	83.7	16.3	307
Arts	59.5	40.5	1,028
Commerce	75.7	24.3	800
Education	72.0	28.0	270
Engineering	98.5	1.5	583
Law	68.8	31.2	234
Medicine	74.6	25.4	489
Science	82.2	17.8	674
Social Studies	76.0	24.0	1,207
Veterinary Science	87.0	13.0	108
Total	76.0	24.0	5,700

Source: University of Zimbabwe, Student Numbers 1988.

AC/182/88 Amended.

effect of education would not differ qualitatively by gender. Human capital theorists predicted that women's education would have stronger long-term effects than men's but that these effects would decline significantly when appropriate controls for labor force participation and fertility rates were included. From his study Benavot concluded that in less developed countries, education expansion among school-age girls has a stronger effect on long-term economic prosperity than does educational expansion among school-age boys, particularly at the primary school level. According to Benavot (1989: 19), these findings provide qualified support for institutional theories of education's impact on society which maintain that the expansion of formal schooling alters important institutional arrangements in society. Formal schooling, with its emphasis on citizenship, middle-class values, and national progress, will construct new rights and duties for women as potentially productive citizens in the national economy and will begin to erode the role of women in the traditional family economy. As females gain equal treatment with males, the collective resources of society for dealing with disease, poverty, technology, and economic development will be substantially increased.

In Zimbabwe the need for greater equity in educational access is at the senior secondary school level and higher educational institutions. It is significant that girls who succeed in reaching the Sixth Form and university perform as well academically as their male counterparts. A developing country cannot afford to waste the talent of half its population.

Educational Reform and Economic Development

It can be argued that education is essential to economic development, because it creates productive resources by improving the economically useful qualities of men and women. However, the educational process also uses up economic resources in the form of money and personnel, and the experience of most of the developing countries of Africa has been that economic development has not kept up with the massive expansion in education. Zimbabwe's experience since independence is no exception to this. (See Zvobgo, 1986: 55.) As a service sector of the economy, education has expanded at an average 13 percent since 1980 while the economy as a whole has grown at an average of 3.8 percent (Sibanda, 1989: 1). An estimated 80,000 youths enter the job market every year while only a few thousand new jobs are created. According to the Minister of Finance, economic planning, and development (Chidzero, 1989: 5), Zimbabwe spends 10 percent of its gross domestic product on education, the highest ratio in the world. He suggests that resources be shifted to material-producing sectors in order to stimulate sustained economic growth. The difficult lesson to be learned is that if substantial investments in education are not accompanied by equally substantial investments in the economy, education will not further economic development.

In order to make education "more productive," the Ministry of Education introduced a new educational reform in 1987. Instead of all pupils following a common curriculum at secondary school, some schools are being developed to teach technical subjects at a higher level. Technical high schools are being planned for each district in the country. However, because of the high cost of equipment and the lack of trained technical teachers, it will be a long time before this side of the educational system is fully developed. In 1988 thirteen pilot schools introduced the Zimbabwe National Craft Certificate (ZNCC), with subjects covering bricklaying, carpentry, machine shop engineering and motor mechanics. Another nineteen schools joined the program in 1989 (Zimbabwe Government, Annual Report, 1988: 4).

Since the new vocational curriculum has only recently been introduced, it is too early to evaluate its acceptance by parents and pupils and its effectiveness in contributing to economic development. The experience of other countries has not been very positive. (See Foster, 1965; Kahane and Starr, 1976.) However, there is some evidence that the new vocational emphasis in secondary education

is being accepted by pupils and parents who view the acquired skills as a means
of self-employment if it is not possible to find a job in the formal economic
sector.

CONCLUSION

In Zimbabwe at independence, the government that came to power sought to
redress the inequalities in education which had prevailed during the colonial-
settler era. Consequently, a vast expansion in the educational system took place
at all levels but particularly at the secondary school and higher educational levels.

The reforms sought to eliminate racial, gender, and regional differences in
educational opportunity. While it has succeeded in abolishing racial inequalities,
gender and regional differences persist.

Educational expansion has provided greater access to education for the masses
but owing to a lack of economic resources, personnel, and infrastructure, the
quality of education has declined in nearly all schools. The increased expenditure
on education has affected investment in the economy. The result is that with a
stagnant economy, unemployment of the products of the schools has risen dramatically. Recent vocationalization of the curriculum in selected secondary
schools has been introduced in an attempt to eliminate the problem.

NOTES

1. See B. Teala and A. G. Lanford, "Educational Ideology and the World Educational
Revolution, 1950–1970." *Comparative Education Review* 31, no. 3 (1987): 315–332,
for a more complete discussion of the rationale for educational expansion.

2. For a comparative analysis of educational development in sub-Saharan Africa, see
also D. Court and K. Kinyanjui, "Education and Development in Sub-Saharan Africa:
The Operation and Impact of Education Systems," Working Paper No. 421 (Nairobi:
Institute for Development Studies, 1985), pp. 1–59; K. Kinyanjui, "Education and Inequality in Kenya: Some Research Experience and Issues," Working Paper No. 373
(Nairobi: Institute for Development Studies), pp. 1–27; E. Keller, *Education, Manpower
and Development* (Nairobi: Kenya Literature Bureau, 1980); R. Carr-Hill, *Primary Education in Tanzania* (Stockholm: Swedish International Development Authority, Education Division, 1984); B. Cooksey and A. Ishumi, "A Critical Review of Policy and
Practice in Tanzanian Secondary Education since 1967" (Afro-Aid Development Consultants, Dar Es Salaam, 1986, mimeographed), pp. 1–77.

REFERENCES

Benavot, Aaron. 1989. "Education, Gender and Economic Development: A Cross-
National Study." *Sociology of Education* 62(1):14–32.
Chidzero, Bernard. 1989, April 25. "Funds Hamper Development." *The Herald*, p. 5.
Chung, F. 1988, October 28. "20,000 Girls Drop Out of School Every Year." Quoted
in *The Herald*.

———. 1989, September 29. *The Herald*, p. 11.

Chung, Fay, and Emmanuel Ngara. 1985. *Socialism, Education and Development*. Harare: Zimbabwe Publishing.

Cooksey, Brian, and Abel Ishumi. 1986. *A Critical Review of Policy and Practice in Secondary Education in Tanzania*. Dar Es Salaam: Afro-Aid Consultants.

Dorsey, Betty Jo. 1975. "The African Secondary School Leaver." In *Education, Race and Employment in Rhodesia*, ed. M. W. Murphree. Salisbury: ARTCA, pp. 15–174.

———. 1981. "Equality of Educational Opportunity in Zimbabwe: Past and Future," In *World Yearbook of Education*, ed. J. Megarry, S. Nisbet and E. Hoyle. London: Kogan Page, pp. 211–225.

———, Rudo Gaidzanwa, and Anna Mupawenda. 1989. *Factors Affecting Academic Careers for Women at the University of Zimbabwe*. Harare: HRRC, University of Zimbabwe.

Foster, Phillip. 1965. "The Vocational School Fallacy in Development Planning." In *Education and Economic Development*, ed. C. Anderson and M. J. Bowman. Chicago: Aldine, pp. 25–55.

Gray, Robert. 1960. *The Two Nations*. London: Oxford University Press.

Hyde, Karin. 1989. *Improving Women's Education in Sub-Saharan Africa: A Review of the Literature*. Education and Employment Division. Washington, D.C.: World Bank.

Kahane, Robert, and Leonard Starr. 1976. "The Impact of Rapid Social Change on Technological Education: An Israeli Example." *Comparative Education Review* 20(2):165–178.

Kay, George. 1972. *Distribution and Density of the African Population in Rhodesia*. Hull: Miscellaneous Series 12, University of Hull.

Ncube, T., and R. Neilson. 1985. "Indications from Data Based on a Survey of Sampled Secondary Schools in Harare, Mashonaland and Manicaland." *Proceedings of the National English Survey Conference Secondary Education*. Harare: Ministry of Education, mimeographed, pp. 1–46.

Paulston, R. 1976. *Conflicting Theories of Social and Educational Change: A Typological Review*. Pittsburgh: University Center for International Studies.

Shibutani, T., and K. Kwan. 1971. "Changes in Life Conditions Conducive to Interracial Conflict." In *Racial Conflict: Tension and Change in American Society*, ed. G. May. Boston: Little, Brown, pp. 150–175.

Sibanda, Isaiah. 1989, October 9. "New Education Strategy to Focus on Jobs." *The Herald*, p. 1.

Zimbabwe Government. 1979–1988. *Annual Reports of the Secretary for Education*. Harare: Government Printer.

Zvobgo, Rugano Jonas. 1986. *Transforming Education: The Zimbabwean Experience*. Harare: College Press.

Part II

Comparative Issues in Stratification

29

WOMEN AND HIGHER EDUCATION REFORMS: EXPANSION WITHOUT EQUALITY

Gail P. Kelly

This chapter focuses on reform in higher education since World War II. It asks how these reforms, which sought to democratize higher education and link it more closely to national economic development needs, affected female enrollment patterns, the fields of study women pursue, and the role of women as academics and administrators. The chapter will show that, for the most part, female enrollments in higher education have soared, even to the point that in some countries women outnumber males. However, this change has not meant that equality in higher education has been achieved. Why this is the case will be explored in the final section of the chapter.

TRENDS IN HIGHER EDUCATION IN THE POSTWAR PERIOD

Since World War II, higher education worldwide has undergone massive change. In most of Africa and Asia higher education was virtually nonexistent. In sub-Saharan Africa, several "colleges" had been formed which later formed the basis of higher education (Ashby, 1966). Many were secondary-level teacher training institutions, and all served exclusively male populations. In Asia universities had formed in India, Indochina, and China. These were small institutions, and most were not comprehensive. The Indochinese University in Hanoi, for example, offered degrees in law, pedagogy, medicine, bridges and posts, and "Indochinese" humanities in the 1930s, and its student body numbered 300 at most at any given time (Kelly, 1980). Chinese universities tended to specialize in medicine or education. Many were missionary institutions. Women were a small minority, if present at all, in higher education (Mak, 1990). In Latin

America, unlike most of Asia and Africa, universities predated World War II; indeed they had a long tradition. Based on European models, they focused on providing liberal arts and limited professional training. The universities served a small, mostly male elite.

Higher education was far more developed in North America and Europe than in the Third World, but it was every bit as elitist, serving a fraction of the population. In the United States, higher education tended to bring in a wider, more diverse population than was the case elsewhere. In the United States the concept of higher education related to the economy—as well as to the development of a political and social elite—was well entrenched. American higher education included greater numbers of women than elsewhere in large part because teacher education, home economics, and "female-appropriate" occupational training were included in the large land grant universities established in the nineteenth century (Graham, 1978).

After World War II, higher education expanded greatly worldwide as part of a conscious effort to strengthen national economies. In countries where higher education was well established, new universities formed to take in everbroadening segments of the population. University education became associated with entry into technical and skilled midlevel occupations and not solely with the professions and the conferral of political and social elite status. Democratization characterized higher education reform as did national economic priorities.

In the Third World, higher education became institutionalized, and it expanded greatly. In 1945 Nigeria had no universities; by the 1980s it had in excess of thirty universities (Okeke, 1989). While the expansion of higher education in Nigeria is perhaps most dramatic, most Third World countries experienced spectacular expansion of higher education at great costs. These universities, modeled on European institutions, were built as part of national government policies designed to promote economic development and prepare a bureaucratic elite. Democratization, which impelled university reform in industrialized countries, was not the guiding principle of university reform or expansion in most of the Third World (Altbach, 1991).

A second trend in the postwar period has been diversification. As higher education has expanded, the number and type of institutions providing tertiary education have proliferated, and a status hierarchy among institutions has emerged. Higher education is no longer confined to university settings; teacher training colleges, technical and vocational institutions, junior colleges, and so on, have increasingly been incorporated into the tertiary section. This is as much the case in Western industrialized nations as in developing countries like Nigeria, Botswana, India, and Indonesia.

Diversification within as well as between institutions has also come to characterize higher education as it has sought to respond to national economic priorities. The number of fields of study has proliferated within institutions of higher education. Universities have come to offer courses in new and more specialized fields of study. Liberal arts and professional studies no longer dominate as universities have extended their programs to include specialized studies in engineering, computer science, business, nursing, and a variety of medical-related fields (Altbach, 1991).

The relationships between higher education and the state have also changed over the postwar period. The reliance on state funding has grown as higher education has expanded, as has the government's role in the university. In many countries, the government has come to control university admissions, the types of programs universities offer, and research conducted in universities. This is the case in countries as diverse as India, Nigeria, Great Britain, China, and the Soviet Union. In the United States, both federal and state governments have controlled in part the flow of students into higher education through direct funding to higher education and direct grants and loans to students. Government control in some countries has also meant that some fields of study have been left to languish and have disappeared from a good many tertiary institutions. In Vietnam, sociology as a field of study is virtually nonexistent as a result of deliberate policies favoring other fields. In England, the Thatcher government successfully sought to undermine sociology in that country's universities, teacher training colleges, and polytechnics (Walford, 1990).

While expansion, institutionalization, diversification and stratification, and increasing government control are features of postwar higher education worldwide, so also is the convergence of national systems of higher education. Higher education in the past had its distinctive national forms. In Third World countries where institutions were initially based on the systems of European colonial powers, universities tended to take on particular national characteristics. In some Third World countries, indigenous forms of tertiary education remained despite years of European colonial rule and the imposition of European educational forms. Increasingly, national differences in higher education have eroded, and while there are differences in quality, extensiveness, and linguistic media among countries, increasingly institutional forms across nations have merged, leading to international student as well as faculty migration, usually from Third World countries to the universities of North America and Western Europe (Ramirez and Boli-Bennett, 1982).

Concentration of resources and of research and knowledge production in the postindustrial societies of North America and Europe has also increased over the past decades. Higher education in the United States has placed a great premium on research and publication, greater than in most other nations. The United States and Great Britain publish the vast majority of academic journals and books. American and European academics, as Altbach and others have demonstrated, increasingly produce knowledge that it taught worldwide in universities as Third World universities have focused, for lack of resources, on teaching rather than research (Altbach, 1982). Thus, American and European academics have come to have a profound influence on what knowledge is taught worldwide. Social movements in these countries, like the women's movement, have led to the rise of knowledge for and about women which has tended to proliferate to other countries.

Many of the changes in higher education which have just been reviewed were not specifically intended to end the very deep gender-based inequalities in higher education. Other reforms, which will be discussed next, did focus on increasing women's access to higher education.

REFORMING WOMEN'S ACCESS TO HIGHER EDUCATION

Most of the postwar reforms in higher education were motivated by national policies aimed at reconstructing or developing national economies or at democratizing society by widening access to higher education to previously underserved populations, in the hopes of producing social stability. The underserved populations targeted by socialist and nonsocialist and industrialized and developing countries alike tended to be defined in class and ethnic terms. In China, as in most socialist societies, the concern was with workers and peasants; in Western Europe the focus was on the working class and low-income groups. In many Third World nations, ethnic imbalance in higher education was the paramount concern, while in India the absence of unscheduled castes at all levels of education became the focus of government activities. In the aftermath of the civil rights movement of the 1960s, the United States directed its efforts to providing African-Americans and Hispanics as well as low-income whites an opportunity to enter higher education. It was not until the 1970s, when the women's movement re-emerged, that the United States and other countries initiated reforms designed to redress gender-based inequalities in education. Particularly important in this movement internationally has been the United Nations which in 1975 declared the International Decade for Women and sought to encourage its member states to open education at all levels to women.

The strategies adopted by countries to increase female participation in higher education vary among countries. Some have taken no initiatives whatsoever; others, like the United States, introduced programs of affirmative action, which were legally binding. Universities, if they did not produce plans to equalize access to women and minorities or hire women and minorities as faculty, were liable to have all federal funding withdrawn (Klein, 1985; Seller, 1989). In addition, the Office of Civil Rights was made available to litigate class-action suits on the part of women and minorities against tertiary institutions that systematically discriminated in admissions to degree programs and in hiring and firing faculty. The U.S. government insisted particularly that professional schools, especially graduate-level law, medical, and business programs, admit women and minorities.

Other national governments, while not always adopting American-style affirmative action plans, have sought to encourage female enrollments in higher education by developing programs designed to tailor higher education to women's lives in the family. In Great Britain, the Open University was founded in the 1970s to provide higher education by correspondence to women who could not attend full-time residential programs (Blair, 1989). The Indian government's Commission on Women has put pressure on universities to open their doors to women, particularly in the sciences and traditionally male-dominated subjects (Chitnis, 1990). It has also sponsored research on women and the development of women's studies. The Australian government has sought to increase female enrollment in higher education via programs of affirmative action, by removing age-specific requirements for attending higher education, providing day care for students' children, and making curricular reforms in primary and secondary education to encourage girls to enter scientific and technical fields and to pursue higher education (Yates, 1989).

It is difficult to gauge how successful government programs to encourage female participation in higher education have been, since many were initiated just recently. In addition, it is difficult to assess the impact of specific policies meant to encourage women's enrollment as distinct from the impact of policies meant to expand and democratize higher education as a whole or women's increasing demand for higher education resulting from changed family and economic circumstances. In the pages that follow, we will look at changing patterns of female enrollment in higher education and ask whether they are different in countries that have specifically sought to encourage female participation in the tertiary sector.

WOMEN'S ENROLLMENT PATTERNS

Charting the changes in women's enrollment in higher education is no easy task. For the most part statistics are incomplete, and, when available, they may be quite inaccurate. Unesco, which provides compilations of such statistics, reprints data provided by national governments. Until the United Nations Decade for Women (1975–1985), most countries neglected to provide gender breakdowns of students enrolled at the tertiary level. (This was the case for primary and secondary enrollments in most countries as well.) Unesco collects the most reliable statistics on educational enrollments worldwide, and the data it reports are not always timely or accurate. Nonetheless, they provide a rough idea of the changes in higher education enrollments that have occurred since 1965. The discussion that follows is based on Unesco data.

The number of females enrolled in institutions of higher education has grown massively since 1965.[1] This is the case in developing Third World nations as well as in the industrialized countries of North America and Europe. For example, in Ethiopia the number of women students in the tertiary sector in 1965 numbered 152; it rose to 4,881 by 1986. Similarly, in 1965 in Ghana 346 women attended university versus 3,326 in 1981. Throughout sub-Saharan Africa the number of females in the tertiary sector grew about tenfold, and sometimes more. In Asia the increases were every bit as dramatic—in India 200,480 women were enrolled in higher education in 1965, rising to 1,396,466 by 1986; in the Philippines the increase was from 282,266 in 1965 to 1,074,045 in 1985. Similar increases can be charted for most Latin American, Caribbean, and Middle Eastern countries.

The rise in female enrollments in the industrialized nations of Europe and North America is equally dramatic in most countries—notably Belgium where female enrollments went from 27,523 in 1965 to 118,491 in 1986; France where the corresponding increase was from 167,810 to 653,330; the Federal Republic of Germany which went from 88,243 in 1965 to 646,631 in 1986; Norway from 4,775 in 1965 to 45,742; Portugal from 12,912 to 59,763; and the United Kingdom from 113,015 to 451,258. In the United States the number of females enrolled in higher education tripled from 2,151,722 to 6,558,000 between 1965 and 1985; in Canada the rise was fivefold, from 110,625 to 543,888.

The increases in female enrollment are not as dramatic in most of the former Soviet bloc nations of Eastern Europe. The most notable exception is the German Democratic Republic where female enrollment rose from 24,186 in 1965 to 232,383 in 1986. More typical is Bulgaria where the number of women students went from 43,427 in 1965 to 69,498 in 1985; Czechoslovakia where the corresponding figures were 54,049 in 1965 and 71,664 in 1986; and Romania where 51,360 women were enrolled in higher education in 1965 versus 71,658 in 1986.

While the number of females entering higher education grew dramatically, so did the proportion of female students, except in a few countries, namely, Angola, Congo (Brazzaville), Togo, Mozambique, Afghanistan, Hong Kong, and Fiji. Elsewhere females' share of higher education enrollments rose, more than doubling in Ethiopia where it went from 7 to 29 percent between 1965 and 1985. In Ghana the share rose from 8 to 21 percent; in Rwanda it went from 1 to 14 percent. In Indonesia the percentage of females in higher education went from 16 to 32. The female share of higher education enrollments doubled in Mexico (from 17 to 36 percent), Nicaragua (from 26 to 57 percent), Colombia (from 23 to 49 percent), and Guyana (from 15 to 48 percent). Similar, if not greater, gains are evident in Tunisia where the percentage of students who are female increased from 17 to 37; in Bahrain where the gain was from 37 to 60; in Lebanon where it rose from 18 to 39; and Syria where it went from 17 to 34. The most impressive increase in the Middle East was in Saudi Arabia where females went from 6 to 39 percent of all enrollments.

In most of the world, the gains in female representation in higher education were less dramatic but nonetheless substantial. In most of Europe, women accounted for over 40 percent of all students in higher education. In Finland, although the number of female students in higher education tripled, female share of higher education enrollments remained stagnant. Finland, is the exception, however. In most of the world, female representation in higher education rose between 10 and 20 percentage points; in most Asian countries, while the numbers of females enrolled soared, the proportion of students in higher education who were female registered small gains. For example, in India the number of women enrolled at the tertiary level increased from 200,480 in 1965 to 1,396,466 in 1986, while the proportion of female students went from 20 to 26 percent in the same period. Similarly, in South Korea the number of females went from 35,361 to 458,602, while their proportion increased from 25 to 30 percent. In industrialized nations of Western Europe and North America, while the numerical gains were smaller, women's share of enrollments grew more rapidly between 1965 and 1986—for example, from 24 to 45 percent in Austria; from 30 to 51 percent in France; from 32 to 48 percent in Greece; from 30 to 45 percent in Great Britain; and from 39 to 53 percent in the United States.

In developing countries, higher education for women expanded dramatically— almost no women attended in the 1940s. The baseline was so low that the increases were greater both numerically and proportionately than in Europe and North America. However, the countries of Europe and North America initially had more women students, and their enrollment share relative to that of Third World countries remains higher. The gains in the developed world, though less dramatic, tended to bring women closer to parity with men in access to tertiary-level education.

Although the increases in women's enrollment in higher education are impressive, in most countries women form a minority of students. A recent study of enrollment in higher education in 135 nations (Kelly, 1991) indicated that in 1986 in only twenty-four countries did female enrollments equal or exceed those of males. Of these, thirteen were in the Third World, and the rest were in North America and Europe. A number of these countries were in the communist bloc— for example, Cuba, Bulgaria, the German Democratic Republic, Hungary, Poland, and the USSR. A number were not—for example, Lesotho, Finland, France, Iceland, Norway, Argentina, Brazil, and the United States. By contrast, in sixteen countries women made up less than 20 percent of students in higher education, and in another sixteen their enrollment share ranged from between 20 and 29 percent. In twenty-three more countries between 30 and 39 percent of all students were female. There are a number of countries in which the proportion of female students is approaching that of males. This is the case in most of Western Europe and Latin America.

Without question, then, women today have more access to higher education than ever before. In this sense, the reforms in higher education aimed at democratizing education and promoting the national economic well-being have benefited women. But they have not resulted in equality. This becomes clearer when we consider the types of tertiary-level institutions women versus men attend and the sex segregation of fields of study.

WOMEN'S HIGHER EDUCATION: UNIVERSITIES VERSUS "OTHER" INSTITUTIONS

As pointed out earlier, over the past years higher education has diversified, including not only university-based higher education, but also tertiary-level teacher training, business, computer, agricultural, and technical education provided in some countries outside of the university setting. In addition, in some countries the two-year junior or community college has expanded greatly, as has "distance" or correspondence higher education. Data on female attendance in university versus nonuniversity-based higher education are sparse, but the fragmentary data we do have suggest that as of 1986 women tend disproportionately to enroll in nonuniversity higher education, where in some countries they form 85 percent of all enrollments (Unesco, 1988). In many countries, namely, Lesotho, Mongolia, the Philippines, the German Democratic Republic, Norway, Portugal, Barbados, Belgium, Jordan, the United Kingdom, Trinidad and Tobago, Singapore, Hong Kong, Mauritius, Iraq, Kenya, Ghana, Bangladesh, Pakistan, Guinea, and the Congo, female enrollments in nonuniversity settings exceed their enrollments within the university. In some cases the number of females attending nonuniversity-based tertiary-level institutions is four times the number of females enrolled at university.

More common is the pattern where a third to a half of all women in higher education are enrolled in nonuniversity tertiary-level institutions. This is the case in Poland, Nicaragua, Hungary, Argentina, the United States, Greece, New Zealand, Sweden, Israel, Ireland, the Republic of Germany, Sri Lanka, Japan, Haiti, Syria, Switzerland, Gabon, Uganda, Ethiopia, and Afghanistan.

That women are disproportionately enrolled in nonuniversity higher education is best illustrated by data from Japan. In 1986 approximately 300,000 women entered higher education. Of these, 60 percent went to junior colleges. In the same year 340,000 males began higher education, and 95 percent of them went to university (Fujimura-Fanselow, 1989).

It is impossible, given the fragmentary data available, to ascertain whether the tendency for females to be relegated to nonuniversity-based higher education is a growing phenomenon. As women become a majority of students in higher education, there is a tendency for them to be segregated into nonuniversity-based programs, but this is only a tendency since a number of countries that have very few women in higher education (e.g., Uganda where in 1986 women accounted for 23 percent of all students and Ghana where in 1986 women constituted 21 percent of higher education enrollments) also have segregated them off into nonuniversity tertiary institutions. Diversification of higher education, coupled with expansion of the tertiary sector, has meant that, while women have greater access to higher education, they do not have access to the same institutions as do men. Neither, as the next section will show, do they have access to the same fields of study even when they enter universities.

SEX SEGREGATION WITHIN THE UNIVERSITY

Women who attend universities tend to specialize in fields of study that already have large numbers of women enrolled in them. Worldwide a number of specializations have become "female"—namely, education, the humanities, and, to a lesser extent, the social and behavioral sciences. For example, 78 percent of all women in universities in Lesotho in 1985 studied education, 50 percent in Israel and Ethiopia, respectively, and 44 percent in the Philippines. The proportion of women in these countries studying business administration, engineering, or mathematics and computers was quite low. In Lesotho, 8 percent of women in universities studied business, and less than 0.33 percent studied mathematics and computers. In Israel 3.3 percent specialized in mathematics and computers, while 9 percent were in engineering. In the Philippines 4 percent of all women were in engineering, and 3 percent were in mathematics and computers. In countries like the United Kingdom, Finland, and the German Democratic Republic, only a small percentage of women in universities study education (11, 14, and 18 percent, respectively) simply because most teacher training lies outside the universities. In these countries women are clustered in the humanities and social and behavioral sciences.

In most countries education, the humanities, and the social and behavioral sciences account for specialization at the university pursued by 40 percent or more of all female students. In Lesotho 83 percent of all women were enrolled in these fields in 1985; the corresponding figure for Nepal was 72 percent; Israel, 68 percent; Sudan, 62 percent; Iran, 49 percent; Turkey, 48 percent; the Federal Republic of Germany, 47 percent; Italy, 46 percent; Spain, 45 percent; the United Kingdom, 44 percent; and Nicaragua, 42 percent. In no country are women evenly distributed across fields of study, although there is some variation by country as to which fields women study. In the Philippines, 44 percent of all women study business administration, while in most of the world female enrollments in that field are quite low, ranging from under 1 percent in Italy and 2 percent in the Federal Republic of Germany to 10 percent in Finland, 12 percent in Nepal, and 18 percent in Burundi.

While there may be some national variation in fields in which women cluster, very little difference exists among countries as to fields that exclude women almost entirely. Worldwide, women are noticeably absent from engineering or mathematics and computer science. In only three countries as of 1985—the German Democratic Republic, Israel, and Turkey—did as many as 10 percent of all female students specialize in engineering. In most countries, fewer than 5 percent of all women enter that field. Less than 3 percent of all female students worldwide study mathematics and computer science. Women tend also not to study the natural sciences; in most nations fewer than 10 percent of all women students are enrolled in this field.

The extent of sex segregation in higher education becomes clearer when we consider the proportion of students in any given field who are female. The proportion of students who are female in education ranges from 92 percent in Argentina (in 1985) to 2 percent in Chad (in 1986). Women universally are overrepresented in that field. In over 106 countries studied (Kelly, 1991), in only 10 was the proportion of students who were female in education equal to the proportion of female students enrolled in higher education as a whole. In countries like Poland, where women constituted 56 percent of higher education enrollments in 1985, 80 percent of all students specializing in education were female.

Not only is education a predominantly female field, but so too is the humanities, where in most countries over 50 percent of all students are female. The few countries in which women are not disproportionately enrolled in the humanities are very poor Third World nations like Rwanda and the Central African Republic, which have a very small tertiary sector and very low female enrollments.

As of 1985 women have become increasingly large proportions of students in medical sciences and health-related professions. In over twenty-two countries they account for 50 to 88 percent of all students in these fields. In a number of other countries, female enrollments in these fields tend to be proportionate to their overall enrollment in higher education.

Women's enrollments are disproportionately low in a number of fields. With the exception of Finland and Czechoslovakia, engineering has systematically excluded women. In most countries women constitute less than 25 percent of all engineering students; in fifty-one countries they are less than 15 percent (Kelly, 1991: Table 4).

Several fields of study admit to great national variation in terms of the proportion of female students enrolled. Women form a disproportionately high proportion of students studying law in fifteen countries, a disproportionately low proportion in that field in thirty countries, and in another twenty-one, women's representation in law equals their share of enrollment in university-level education (Kelly, 1991). Women's share of enrollments in the social and behavioral sciences follows a pattern similar to that of law.

Very real changes have occurred in the degree and type of sex segregation by field of study between 1965 and 1985. Generally, as higher education over time has taken in more women, fields that already have sizable female enrollments have taken in more and more females so that they have become female dominated. Female enrollments in the humanities and education, always quite strong, grew so much that by the 1980s they became female ghettos in the higher education systems of most countries (see Unesco, 1988). Some fields previously closed to women—namely, law and the social and behavioral sciences—did take in increasing numbers of women, and females' share of enrollments rose markedly. However, the "hard sciences"—mathematics, computer science, and engineering—remained firmly entrenched as "male" fields, and female representation in them remained stagnant despite rising female enrollment in universities.

Expansion of higher education has not only meant increasing sex segregation by fields of study in most of the world, but also increasing segregation by level of study. The data reported thus far made little distinction between undergraduate, master's or doctoral programs. This is the case because little cross-national data exist making such distinctions. The scarce data available suggest that the greatest gains in female enrollment have been at the undergraduate level. In Sweden, for example, in the mid–1980s women represented 60 percent of all undergraduates and only 31 percent of all graduate students (Elqvist-Saltzman, 1988). Margaret Sutherland (1988) in her study of women's higher education worldwide found that women were a small minority of graduate students even in countries where over 50 percent of all higher education enrollments were female. In Australia women received about a third of all graduate degrees (Yates, 1989). Only in the United States did women represent 50 percent of students receiving master's degrees. Most were in education (Seller, 1989). In Norway, of 6,632 female students enrolled in the humanities in the 1983–1984 academic year, only 168 were pursuing graduate studies (Ve and Fjelde, 1990). Of the 5,766 women studying education, only 61 were graduate students (Ve and Fjelde, 1990). Kay Moore's remark that in higher education the more advanced the degree, the fewer the number and proportion of women enrolled is borne out by the evidence currently available (Moore, 1987).

This survey of women's enrollments in higher education underscores the fact that, while women's access to higher education has opened considerably, women have by no means achieved equality in higher education. Their entry to the tertiary sector has been paralleled by increasing institutional differentiation which has tended to segregate women into nonuniversity higher education settings. Women, when they are enrolled in universities, are segregated into undergraduate studies and into increasingly female-dominated fields, receiving a different education from their male peers and one that has less value in an increasingly technically oriented job market.

The gains women have made as students in higher education have not been replicated among female academics, where, as the following section indicates, women remain marginal, clustered in female-dominated fields.

WOMEN ACADEMICS

In almost every country, regardless of field of specialization, women constitute a very small minority of professors according to figures issued by Unesco in 1988 (pp. 3–169–3–305). In only 5 countries of the 106 countries for which Unesco reported data do women constitute 40 percent or more of university faculty: in the Philippines 53 percent of all university faculty were female; in Argentina and Brazil women were 47 and 43 percent, respectively, of all faculty, and they represented 43 percent of all faculty in Cuba and 40 percent in Switzerland. In another 19 countries women accounted for between 30 and 39 percent of faculty, while in 34 nations they made up between 20 and 29 percent of the faculty and in another 41 they were between 3 and 19 percent of the faculty.

The proportion of female academics bears little relation to the proportion of females enrolled in higher education. In Poland where 56 percent of the students were female in 1986, 35 percent of the faculty were female; in the United States where 51 percent of all students were female, only 26 percent of the faculty were female.

Not only are women a minority among faculty, but they are for the most part part-time and junior faculty, clustered in fields where the vast majority of students are female. In Greece, for example, in 1980 there were in all 46 female full professors out of the over 3,400 women faculty members (Eliou, 1988). Women represented 3.4 percent of all full professors, 7.6 percent of associate professors, and 9.1 percent of assistant professors. On the other hand, they did comprise 42.9 percent of all teaching assistants. Women faculty were segregated into a few fields. While 3.4 percent of all full professors were female, 8.6 percent of full professors in the humanities were women versus 2.6 percent of full professors in engineering, architecture, and natural sciences. In Israel in the 1982–1983 academic year, 40 women were full professors out of the 3,275 female faculty members (Toren, 1988). Only 413 women held tenured or tenure track appointments. Of these 10 percent were full professors, 15 percent associate professors, 42 percent senior lecturers, and 33 percent lecturers (Toren, 1988: 527). In Peru in 1982 half of the women teaching in higher education were temporary employees. Of the 1,036 full-time women faculty, 16 percent were full professors, 27 percent associate professors, 36 percent assistant professors, and 21 percent teaching assistants. In contrast, of the 9,195 male faculty, 29 percent were full professors, 29 percent associate professors, 32 percent assistant professors, and 9 percent teaching assistants (Stromqvist, 1988: 587). This pattern of segregating women faculty into the lowest academic ranks, into part-time work, and according to fields dominated by female students is replicated elsewhere in the world (Moore, 1987).

The underrepresentation of women as faculty and their marginal positions in higher education is explained in part by female enrollment patterns in higher education. Women tend not to continue their studies beyond the baccalaureate. They are clustered in a few fields, and a number of studies have documented high dropout rates among women in graduate degree programs (see, for example, Eliou, 1988; Moore, 1987; Sutherland, 1988). Discrimination against women in hiring, promotion, and tenure persists. Women do not get sponsored into the academic profession the same way as do men. Finally, many women, faced with a dual career in academia and in the home, tend to accept marginal, part-time work (see, for example, Elqvist-Saltzman, 1988).

Women are a minority among higher education teaching staffs, but they are an even smaller minority among academic administrators. Women tend not to become department chairs, deans, or university presidents except in sex-segregated systems of higher education.

WHY INEQUALITY PERSISTS

The reforms in higher education over the past few decades were not, for the most part, intended to benefit women. Rather, they were meant to stimulate national economic growth or to provide greater educational opportunity for working-class and, in some countries, racial and cultural minority youth. Women benefited from the expansion of education, even though in many countries they were not the intended beneficiaries of reform. This was particularly the case in many nations where female enrollments rose dramatically but no particular reforms aimed at redressing gender-based inequalities of access in higher education occurred. Among those twenty-four countries where women's enrollments in higher education exceeded or equaled males, few had initiated affirmative action reforms, had sought to open institutions like open universities to draw women into the higher education mainstream, had initiated programs for returning women, had developed secondary school programs to encourage females to enter the tertiary sector, or had developed women's studies as a course of study in higher education. The gains in female enrollment seem also to be the same in countries with reforms aimed at incorporating women into higher education (the United States, Canada, France, and the United Kingdom, for example) as in countries that had no specific reforms intended to bring women into higher education (for example, Ghana, Lesotho, Mongolia, the Philippines, Panama, Bahrain, Kuwait, and Brazil). Most, with the exception of the United States, France, and possibly Finland, simply enrolled more women without consciously seeking to do so.

While women entered higher education in larger numbers than ever before, they entered male-dominated institutions that were scarcely friendly to educating women. Women were shunted off into "female" fields of study, often educated outside university settings, and confined to undergraduate study that prepared them for female occupations, particularly teaching, or for unemployment in fields like the humanities. Women have enrolled in a number of nontraditional fields, but, for the most part, their numbers in these fields are small and have remained small for decades. Women have been given access to some sorts of "male knowledge," taught by men. This has, however, been confined to fields which men consider appropriate for women or which in the postwar period have become increasingly devalued in increasingly technological workplaces. Women remain noticeably absent from fields like computer science, mathematics, business administration, or the hard sciences. The only change that has occurred in the past few decades is that women have managed to gain access to law, social and behavioral sciences, and medical and health-related professional preparation in some countries.

The persistence of gender-based inequalities in higher education, while attributable in part to discrimination, relates to the absence of any strategies in most countries to deal with the problem. In countries like the United States, Australia, France, and the United Kingdom which have tried to reform higher education to provide gender-based equality, most reforms have been piecemeal and ineffective. They have not dealt systematically with primary and secondary school practices that deny girls the opportunity to learn mathematics, the sciences, or computer technology or with in-school and out-of-school socialization patterns that lead girls to "choose" not to enter fields of study that do not already have appreciable numbers of females enrolled. Lack of scholarship aid or work/study opportunities for females has barely been addressed, nor has higher education tried to accommodate women by providing child care facilities or services to married women with children. Many universities still insist on full-time residential studies, which preclude married women. Nor have any universities systematically dealt with sexual harassment which many female students experience, or with the male bias embedded in traditional academic disciplines. Unless reform deals with some of these issues, inequality between males and females in higher education will likely persist, even if women emerge as the majority of students, as they have in a number of countries.

NOTE

1. Statistic provided by Unesco (1988).

REFERENCES

Altbach, Philip G. 1982. "Servitude of the Mind? Education, Dependency, and Neo-colonialism." In *Comparative Education*, ed. Philip Altbach, Robert Arnove, and Gail Kelly. New York: Macmillan, pp. 453–468.
————. 1991. "Trends in Higher Education." In *Emergent Issues in Comparative Education*, ed. Robert Arnove, Philip Altbach, and Gail Kelly. Albany, N.Y.: SUNY Press.
Ashby, Eric. 1966. *Universities: British, Indian, African.* Cambridge, Mass.: Harvard University Press.
Blair, Gage. 1989. "Great Britain." In *International Handbook of Women's Education*, ed. Gail P. Kelly. Westport, Conn.: Greenwood Press, pp. 285–322.
Chitnis, Suma. 1990. "Women's Studies in India." In *Women's Higher Education in Comparative Perspective*, ed. Gail P. Kelly and Sheila S. Slaughter. Amsterdam: Kluwer Academic Publishers, pp. 315–327.
Eliou, Marie. 1988. "Women in the Academic Profession: Evolution or Stagnation?" *Higher Education* 17:505–524.
Elqvist-Saltzman, Inga. 1988. "Educational Reforms—Women's Life Patterns: A Swedish Case." *Higher Education* 17:491–504.
Fujimura-Fanselow, Kumiko. 1989. "Japan." In *International Handbook of Women's Education*, ed. Gail P. Kelly. Westport, Conn.: Greenwood Press, pp. 163–186.
Graham, Patricia A. 1978. "Expansion and Exclusion: A History of Women in American Higher Education." *Signs* 4(Summer):759–774.
Kelly, Gail P. 1980. "The Myth of Educational Planning: The Case of the Indochinese University." In *Education and the New International Order*. New York: Praeger, pp. 93–108.
————. 1991. "Women and Higher Education." In *International Encyclopedia of Higher Education*, ed. Philip G. Altbach. New York: Garland.
Klein, Susan S., ed. 1985. *Handbook for Achieving Sex Equity in Education.* Baltimore: Johns Hopkins University Press.
Mak, Grace. 1990. "Continuity and Change in Women's Access to Higher Education in the People's Republic of China, 1930–1980." In *Women's Higher Education in Comparative Perspective*, ed. Gail P. Kelly and Sheila S. Slaughter. Amsterdam: Kluwer Academic Publishers, pp. 31–46.
Moore, Kathryn M. 1987. "Women's Access and Opportunity in Higher Education Toward the Twenty-First Century." *Comparative Education* 23:23–34.

Okeke, Eunice A. C. 1989. "Nigeria." In *International Handbook of Women's Education*, ed. Gail P. Kelly. Westport, Conn.: Greenwood Press, pp. 43–64.

Ramirez, Francisco, and John Boli-Bennett. 1982. "Global Patterns of Educational Institutionalization." In *Comparative Education* ed. Philip Altbach, Robert Arnove, and Gail Kelly. New York: Macmillan, pp. 15–38.

Seller, Maxine S. 1989. "The United States." In *International Handbook of Women's Education*, ed. Gail P. Kelly. Westport, Conn.: Greenwood Press, pp. 515–546.

Stromqvist, Nelly P. 1988. "Feminist Reflection on the Peruvian University Politics." *Higher Education* 17:581–601.

Sutherland, Margaret. 1988. "Women in Higher Education: Effects of Crises and Change." *Higher Education* 17:479–490.

Toren, Nina. 1988. "Women at the Top: Female Full Professors in Higher Education in Israel." *Higher Education* 17:525–544.

Unesco. 1988. *Statistical Yearbook*. Paris: Unesco.

Ve, Hilde, and Nina Fjelde. 1990. "Public-Private Tendencies Within Higher Education in Norway from a Woman's Perspective." In *Women's Higher Education in Comparative Perspective*. Amsterdam: Kluwer Academic Publishers, pp. 117–130.

Walford, Geoffrey. 1990. "The 1988 Education Reform Act for England and Wales: Paths to Privatization." *Educational Policy* 4 (2):127–144.

Yates, Lyn. 1989. "Australia." In *International Handbook of Women's Education*, ed. Gail P. Kelly. Westport, Conn.: Greenwood Press, pp. 213–242.

30

ISSUES OF CLASS AND EDUCATIONAL REFORM IN COMPARATIVE PERSPECTIVE

Irving Epstein

Few would argue with the contention that over the past twenty years, discussions of class and class consciousness have had a significant influence on formal Western educational discourse and scholarship. A fundamental dissatisfaction with those functionalist and positivist assumptions that marked educational research of the 1950s and 1960s led to the New Sociology of Education of the 1970s, whose tenets were first articulated in the United Kingdom and then exported to the United States. More recently, numerous American scholars have embraced the principles of critical pedagogy, arguing in favor of the proposition that educational practice can and should produce personal empowerment and social transformation, if one is able to accurately analyze the power relationships that are fundamental to curricular and instructional practice. In making these arguments, educational scholars and researchers have necessarily drawn on the work of the most important social theorists: Marx and Engels, of course, Weber, Durkheim, Gramsci, Althusser, Poulantzas, Offe, Habermas, Foucault, Derridas, Bakhtin and others. A few—Bernstein, Bourdieu, Freire—have gained international notoriety in their own right as their focus on education has expanded our understanding of social interaction in other realms as well.

One positive outcome of this scholarship has been to position education at the forefront of all discussion that involves fundamental questions of social behavior and thought. One cannot conceive of ''the state,'' for example, without making reference to those specific institutions such as schools, of which it is comprised and give it its legitimacy. Similarly, if one is to comprehend the basic nature of social class formation, class consciousness, and reproduction, the contributions schools make to these processes cannot be ignored and deserve intensive scrutiny. More than alluding to the importance of educational activity as a fundamental component of all social interaction, critical theorists have argued that basic questions of social interaction—the contestation for power and authority, the relationship between personal agency and social structure, and the very nature of social and cultural reproduction—must be addressed and answered within educational contexts, if they are to be adequately addressed at all.

One might therefore conclude that the use of comparative analysis would necessarily contribute to these aims, for comparative research inherently demands an appreciation for contextual diversity as the researcher strives to justify the general nature of specific claims. However, with some notable exceptions, cross-national contributions to critical social theory as applied to educational activity and process have been limited, both by topic and source of authorship, to those writing from Western perspectives. Not only has the applicability of critical pedagogy to the practical concerns of the comparative educator been only intermittently explored, but also investigations of class and class conflict in educational arenas have rarely been pursued.

This chapter summarizes some of the more influential critiques of Western educational practice during the past two decades. It discusses the application of a "conflict perspective" to comparative educational concerns, and finally proposes future agendas that would incorporate class analysis as a fundamental component of comparative inquiry with reference to educational change and educational reform.

THE GROWTH OF CRITICAL PEDAGOGY

Within the United States, the work of Samuel Bowles and Herbert Gintis (1976) must be considered as a foundational, if flawed, attempt to explain the roles schools play in reproducing social class divisions. The authors' correspondence theory postulated that social class affiliations and divisions, determined by the nature of one's work, were mechanically played out within school borders, as working-class children were socialized into accepting the inevitability of securing working-class jobs, after being tracked into vocational streams. The school was viewed as producing a hierarchically skilled labor force, fulfilling the economic exigencies of modern capitalism, with its increasingly stratified and specialized workforce. In arriving at their conclusions, Bowles and Gintis borrowed from a structuralist orientation that has been criticized for its determinism and negation of human agency as a crucial factor in promoting praxis and, ultimately, revolutionary change. The educational implications of the correspondence theory included a denial of the transformatory character of classroom interaction, or the power of teachers, students, and/or parents to consciously reshape the culture of the school in their own terms. Nonetheless, the work of Bowles and Gintis was important for its realization that schooling processes were contextually significant, related to external forms of division of labor and capital accumulation.

The writings of Basil Bernstein and Pierre Bourdieu represented substantive attempts to examine the ways in which social, economic, and political influences are mediated within school walls. Bernstein (1971), a British sociolinguist, hypothesized that the use of restricted or elaborated linguistic codes by working- or middle-class children influenced their school performance. He argued that working-class children, in possession of restricted linguistic codes, perpetually faced severe disadvantages when placed within school environments that naturally favored those middle-class values respectful of competition, independence, autonomy, and the desirability of demonstrating elaborate self-expression so as to guarantee that one's meaning is understood—in short, possession of an elaborated linguistic code. Bernstein's later work (1975) drew from Durkheimian concepts of mechanical and organic solidarity, as he sought to explain the existence of instrumental and expressive classroom rituals, with curricula based on loose or tightly constructed collection codes and pedagogical techniques expressing strong or weak classification schemes, in terms of the changing notions of appropriate forms of work among the British middle class.

Bourdieu's notions of *habitus*, cultural capital, and cultural arbitrariness, initially explored with Jean-Claude Passeron in *Reproduction in Education and Society* (1977) and expanded in *Distinction* (1984) and *Homo Academicus* (1988), can be viewed as explanatory devices that directly addressed the means through which schools contribute to social and cultural reproduction. The concept of habitus, or the internalization of external environmental conditions so as to affect the personal choices and preferences one makes throughout life, is of key importance throughout Bourdieu's writing. One's habitus influences the desire to acquire and invest forms of cultural capital. Educational institutions are assigned the task of preserving the highest forms of cultural capital, possessed by members of upper and upper middle classes. They legitimize these forms by excluding from school curricula that cultural capital judged to be inferior. Thus, educational systems participate in a process that inherently is culturally arbitrary, a process that uses the symbolic violence of exclusivity to reproduce that cultural capital that is most highly valued by those with predominant social influence and power.

From a social reproduction perspective, Bourdieu argues that schools are forced into playing dual roles. They must insure that upper class students obtain the necessary cultural capital so as to contribute to the social reproduction of their class. At the same time, educational institutions must be in a position where they can preserve their own authority as gatekeepers of cultural capital. In order to fulfill this role, they must train those future educators who will possess the expertise and knowledge to pass on valued cultural capital to future generations.

Educational institutions draw on upper class and middle-class elements in order to train future scholars. In pursuing this aim, they systematically discriminate against middle and lower middle-class students who desire to enter the academy, since these students are less likely than their privileged counterparts to already possess the cultural capital institutions most highly value. Nonetheless, the educational system will selectively admit certain members from among its ranks in spite of prevailing class and gender bias, if only to guarantee the preservation of its own social authority. For lower middle-class students, an academic life represents one of the few available opportunities for upward social mobility. It is therefore an attractive career choice in spite of their unequal chances of success.

Certainly, the work of Bernstein and Bourdieu can be characterized by a muted, if ever present, form of determinism. The linguistic (and presumably cultural) deficits that Bernstein alleges are experienced by working-class students in possession of restricted linguistic codes, the mechanistic internalization of environmental realities as depicted in Bourdieu's notion of habitus, are concepts that do not support broad claims of human agency. One could also question the precision with which these scholars define class composition and class relations. However, their contributions lie in their willingness to directly explore the contexts in which educational institutions reflect and mediate social and cultural forces.

One of the first American scholars to apply critical thought directly, as conceived by the above-mentioned authors, to basic classroom practices and procedures was Michael Apple. In his early work (1979), one of Apple's primary concerns was to trace the use of formal and hidden curricula to train students in those technocratic and managerial skills that are of use in the bureaucratized corporate world of modern capitalism. The proliferation of programmed individualized instructional modules and kits during the 1960s and 1970s created an omnipresent structure that standardized the teaching process and emphasized product. Students were given some responsibility to work according to their own pace, but they were never allowed to question an impersonal curricular structure, to which they were forced to submit. As a result, they assimilate the ethos of the modern technocratic manager, the position they will likely attain in the working world. Teacher work is affected too, through the marketing of supposedly "teacher-proof" curricular materials that force teachers to assume the role of practitioner rather than curricular innovator. This "deskilling" of teacher work occurs in an age of popular mistrust of the profession and of the teacher's role. Apple (1983) borrows from Erik Olin Wright's concept of contradictory location within a social class (1978) to explain how teachers, as members of the middle class, can find themselves as subjects of overt domination, having lost control of curricular decision making, which is traditionally an essential form of teacher work.

Apple views his own analysis of repressive curricular structures as a necessary first step to acquiring teacher empowerment. The writings of Freire and Willis, however, have directly addressed issues of resistance and agency among educators and students. Paulo Freire (1970) was one of the first scholars to associate illiteracy with social marginality and literacy with consciousness-raising and enrollment empowerment. His methods, originally created for an impoverished peasantry living under repressive conditions in the developing world, have had popular appeal in the industrialized world too.

Willis (1977), in writing about working-class students in the United Kingdom, discovered that their opposition to the structure and values of schooling represented significant class resistance to an orientation they realized was antithetical to their own value claims. By embracing the working-class culture of their fathers, with its emphasis on peer comradeship, loyalty, and group spontaneity, masculinity, sexism, and racism, Willis' "lads" consciously chose to resist their school authorities and the achievement ideology they embraced. However, their resistance was only partially formed and represented an inherently unsuccessful alternative to the dominant middle-class values propagated by the school. The "lads' " acceptance of sexist and racist attitudes, and their glorification of violence, gave evidence of their inability to form a reasonable ideological alternative to the predominant framework that governed their schooling.

In Jay MacLeod's study of an American working-class inner city gang (1987), the Hallway Hangers, the author similarly concluded that these youth consciously rejected the relevance of schooling, displaying an affinity for group solidarity, promiscuity, sexism, racism, and repeated drug use. In this case, their awareness of the lack of a basic economic opportunity structure, and the unlikely possibility that they would ever be able to leave the housing projects where they resided, along with a recognition that physical survival depended on acquiring a street-wiseness not valued in schools, led the Hallway Hangers to reject the importance of schooling altogether. Their resistance to schooling was not due to their lack of self-esteem or lack of faith in their ability to succeed academically if they had wished to do so. They simply made the determination that academic success was not a worthy investment of their time or effort, for it was irrelevant to their ability to survive on the streets.

Willis and MacLeod, as well as Freire, represent varying ends of the spectrum in their analyses of resistance and empowerment. For both Willis and MacLeod, student resistance to school structure does not lead to permanent personal empowerment, or pressure for educational and social reform. Freire's faith in the power of consciousness-raising to effect change in popular education settings, on the other hand, is almost unconditional. The logical results of Freire's methods must categorically include personal and social liberation.

One important author who has further explored the nature of class consciousness within formal educational settings is Henry Giroux (1981, 1983, 1988a) who relies on Gramsci's concepts of hegemony and theory of organic intellectuals to map out the role of teacher as intellectual and potential change agent.

Ideological hegemony, as conceived by Gramsci, included all attempts by ruling elites to justify their positions of power ideologically, "with the aim of securing general popular acceptance of their dominant position as something 'natural,' part of an eternal social order, and thus unchallengeable" (Boggs, 1984: 161).

It was through the institutions of the state that ideological hegemony was transmitted to society in general. Yet Gramsci believed that the process of such transmission was not passive but was continually subject to contestation on the part of dominant and subordinate groups. Rather than viewing institutions of the state as serving only as the mechanical apparatuses through which dominated classes imposed their view of the world on the masses, state institutions were conceived of as places where hegemony could be directly contested. The unmasking of values that are claimed to be commonsensical, but can be shown to serve the specific interests of the dominant class, would be a first step toward depriving the ruling class of its legitimacy, setting the stage for the development of working-class consciousness and its successful struggle for power. The development of class consciousness thus depended on the efforts of organic working-class intellectuals, who, Gramsci argued, would play an instrumental role in bridging theory and practice (Boggs, 1984: 199–242). For Giroux (1988a), teachers can and should play a corresponding role in schools.

Questions of educational reform and the role of teachers in effecting systematic change speak to larger issues concerning the state and the relative autonomy of the state, with reference to its relationship to dominant social classes. Poulantzas (1978) and others have argued that the existence of such autonomy is necessary for the survival of capitalism, for the state not only serves to legitimize dominant-subordinate class relations, but it must also guarantee that capital will be continually accumulated. Without the state playing an interventionist role so as to guarantee continued capital accumulation and production, and left to the pursuit of short-term economic gain, dominant classes within advanced capitalist economies would create economic catastrophe through their myopic pursuit of class interests. Thus, the growth of the welfare state is viewed historically as a necessary step whereby state intervention masks the conditions of contradiction and exploitation within the market and, so doing, guarantees its own existence as protector of the status quo.

The conditions under which the autonomous role of the state manifests itself may be in dispute (perpetual evolutionary growth, enhanced visibility only under circumstances of economic crisis), but the implications of the role force one to conclude that control of the institutions that comprise the state is subject to frequent contestation by dominant and subordinate classes. This places employees of state institutions in the position of taking sides, or pursuing their own interests that may be at variance with those of other groups (Sorj, 1983, as cited in Foley and Yambert, 1989: 46).

For educators, the implication is that they need not be so constricted so as only to play the role of pawn to the interests of dominant classes. A more general conclusion is that, as the illegitimacy of specific power relations is unmasked, class conflict is expressed precisely in ideological terms, making the role of educator/intellectual as ideological critic crucial to the pursuit of class struggle.

For Giroux and others, critical pedagogy is a means of contributing to this struggle, through debunking the mainstreamed assumptions that have governed curriculum formation and decision making, and pedagogical practice. Apple's efforts to expose the technical-functionalist assumptions behind the curricular innovations of the 1960s and 1970s have been noted. Peter McLaren (1986) has looked at classroom knowledge as ritualized performance, while others, in attempting to contextualize the curricular assumptions that have so heavily influenced classroom practice, have borrowed principles from literary criticism and post-modernism (Cherryholmes, 1988). Mikhail Bakhtin's notion of dialogue (1981), for example, has been mentioned in this context (Quantz and O'Connor, 1988) as a powerful indictment against the presumption that language can be monopolized and its meanings isolated or unified into a single truth. The vocabulary of deconstructionism has also been employed in arguing for the abolition of traditional curricular authority and the creation of alternative curricular content that is representative of popular culture, with its mass appeal and constantly changing rules of expression (Giroux, 1988b; Giroux and Simon, 1989). Kathleen Weiler (1988) and Mary O'Brien (1987) have argued that issues of gender cannot be separated from this discussion, and that the development of a feminist critical pedagogy is crucial if patriarchal hegemony is to be contested. As Weiler conceives of the term, feminist pedagogy does not preclude critical analyses of the influences of class or race on teaching, but extends these analyses into areas that touch the core sensibilities of both students and teachers. Given the role the teaching profession has traditionally played and continues to play in perpetuating an unequal sexual division of labor, the development of a feminist critical pedagogy appears to be particularly salient.

The fact that critical pedagogy has not been directly applied to educational cases in the developing world is in part due to its focus on education in advanced capitalist societies. It may be easier for certain authors to offer sophisticated cultural critiques of nativistic processes with which they are most familiar. However, conflict theory in its entirety has had an important influence on comparative education, explicitly expressed through efforts to apply dependency theory, neocolonialism, and various theories of the state to the field. It is to these efforts that we now turn.

CONFLICT THEORY AND COMPARATIVE EDUCATION

In its earliest formations, dependency theory, as articulated by scholars such as Gunder-Frank, Amin, and Wallerstein, borrowed from Rosa Luxembourg's theory of capitalist accumulation in chronicling patterns of economic dependency between core and peripheral countries. The artificial creation of metropolises inside and/or external to developing regions, for the specific purpose of creating and then reproducing their economic dependency, was first applied to Latin America and then generalized to other developing areas. The concept of neocolonialism, which assumed a willingness on the part of former colonizer and colonized countries to continue their historic relationship, redefined in economic and cultural terms after the granting of political independence, further broadened the scope of the discussion (Altbach, 1977).

For comparative educators, dependency theory and neocolonialism presented creative opportunities to pursue new forms of analysis. By examining educational patterns from a world systems perspective, one need not rely only on the nation-state as an a priori unit of analysis, a determination of obvious advantage to those comparativists who had grown disillusioned with the arbitrary political boundaries that were superimposed on discussions of comparative issues (Arnove, 1980). At the same time, discussions of world systems, dependency theory, and neocolonialism extended the debate beyond problems affecting formal education systems in the direct sense. The policies of international public and private donor agencies (Berman, 1979), textbook publishing and practice and technology transfer patterns (Altbach, 1982), and brain drain issues (Weiler, 1984) became newly recognized areas subject to serious scholarly study.

More recently, attempts have been made to examine theories of the state and to apply them to comparative analysis. Martin Carnoy (1990a: 19–21), for example, has argued that developing countries in transition to capitalism continue to be plagued with weak state institutions that lack popular support. Unlike their advanced capitalist counterparts, "conditioned capitalist states" never develop institutional legitimacy as they fail to promote mass participation in the democratic election of their state officials. State bureaucracies are believed to perform self-serving roles, offering little accountability to the citizenry. When disillusioned political actors operating within conditioned capitalist states seek revolutionary alternatives in their efforts to transform the political status quo into socialist states, however, they are forced into developing and imposing a new state bureaucracy, intent on accumulating capital, and then redistributing it on a collective rather than an individual basis. However, in attempting to implement this objective, they must rely on many of the predecessor state bureaucratic institutions that lacked the popular legitimacy the new leaders need to create. They must also confront the possibilities of foreign military intervention on the part of advanced capitalist states while surviving in a capitalist-dominated world economy (Carnoy, 1990a: 26–27).

Education plays a crucial role in the transitional process. Carnoy and Levin (1985) have argued that in capitalist states education serves as a democratizing force as its expansion simultaneously fulfills both political and economic mandates while symbolizing the possibility of achieving increased social mobility and equality. At the same time, educational systems continue to produce the social inequalities inherent in capitalism, as access to select institutions, particularly at higher levels, is denied while strong private interests maintain control over important sectors. In conditioned socialist states, the mandate for political inclusivity, now defined in collectivist terms, influences the expansion of mass education in formal and popular education sectors. However, these states have had less success in reforming their education bureaucracies, as their character remains centralized and hierarchical, and as alternative pedagogies and curricular forms are rarely reproduced with vigor (Carnoy, 1990b: 81–96). The growth of new conflicts, between rural and urban, and popular and formal education sectors becomes evident.

It is clear that Carnoy's discussion of the relationship between education and conditioned-capitalist states experiencing revolutionary activity, and then becoming conditioned-socialist, extends previous discussions of educational dependency to include those cases that have resisted some of the traditional dependency pressures (Cuba, Nicaragua, Mozambique, China, Tanzania), while utilizing a theoretical analysis of the state to support his claims. To that end, he is indebted to the writings of Claus Offe (1975), who argued that the modern capitalist state finds itself in the unique situation of guaranteeing capital accumulation on a class basis, while also acting as its own producer of capital when the survival of the state is in doubt. Education, in the form of mass compulsory schooling, is one of the social services that the state provides in order to produce capital, although when the production of capital is mandated in bureaucratic rather than consensual terms, policy conflicts inevitably arise.

One can fault Carnoy for a view of educational change that is in its own way elegantly functional, but fails to elaborate in specific terms the relationship between political activism and pedagogical innovation, or the dynamic interplay between cultural and structural reproduction forces as defined within educational systems. Certainly, a more lengthy comparative analysis of the conditions under which social inequalities are reproduced within advanced capitalist, conditioned capitalist, and conditioned socialist states, as defined by the various characteristics of their respective educational bureaucracies, is called for. However, Carnoy's analysis is particularly useful to the extent that it places issues of the state at the forefront of comparative educational concerns.

In a similar vein, Hans Weiler has applied Habermas's concept of legitimation crisis to explain the formation and implementation of educational policy in West Germany (1983) and France (1988). In these cases, it is argued that policy arises from the need of the state to legitimize class inequality, made apparent during periods of economic crisis, without jeopardizing existing class relations. Educational reform is invariably viewed as a top-down rather than a grass-roots affair.

In an insightful overview of conflict and functional paradigms, as they have been applied to the comparative education field, Mark Ginsburg et al. (1990) argue that a theoretical approach to the study of comparative education that appreciates the dynamics of political contestation within every educational sector is useful, regardless of whether the results imply conservative reformism or include the possibilities for revolutionary activity.

Yet it appears that a number of the conceptual tools that have been summarized to this point, be they Bowles and Gintis's correspondence theory, Bernstein's theory of linguistic codes and the accompanying cultural deficits they are presumed to inflict, Bourdieu's notion of habitus, Willis's concept of working-class resistance, Freirean consciousness-raising, the assumptions of dependency theory, postmodernist critiques of curriculum, and discussions of the role of the state and class conflict—all fail to adequately address basic questions involving the relationship between cultural and social reproduction, or, in Margaret Archer's (1988) terms, culture and agency. They either assume a determinism between external social-cultural forces and the cultural systems of schools, or view school culture as containing significant autonomy, with its practitioners able to directly promote social change.

For Archer, both views fall victim to the fallacy of conflation. She asserts that an appropriate alternative perspective would view the relationship between cultural systems and social-cultural interaction through the perspective of analytic dualism. To be sure, we interact with linguistic and cultural systems whose symbols and values we naturally assimilate at birth, and those systems influence behavioral and cognitive patterns. But all cultural systems, including those of the school, contain logical contradictions in meaning that, under various circumstances, we accept or reject. If cultural systems influence the nature of our social interactions, those interactions can equally heighten our awareness of the logical contradictions within cultural systems, and the impossibility of their resolution without rejecting fundamental assumptions governing their formation and continued presence. It is under these circumstances that social change occurs. Similarly, Raymond Williams (1980), writing within a more traditional Marxist frame of reference, argues that the relationship between base (the economic means of production, or control over what and how one produces) and super-structure (ideological, cultural, and political beliefs and values) must be seen as dialectical, with each sector operating with a considerable degree of mutual interdependence.

Returning to the discussion of education, an expansive view of issues of social class would necessarily include discussions of both the social and cultural reproductive forces within schools. It would ground analyses of pedagogy and curriculum to the economic, political, and environmental factors that influence school cultures but would give equal weight to an examination of the impact of schooling on local environments. Neither the unilateral autonomy nor the dependency of educational structures and those who work within those structures would be assumed, and when evidence of these tendencies was discovered, it would be contextualized. Discussions of student resistance to the formalized rituals of schools, or teacher empowerment and activism, would be grounded in economic and political realities.

COMPARATIVE INVESTIGATIONS OF SOCIAL CLASS

It is unfortunate that cross-national analyses of social class formation and reproduction are few in number, although the paucity of work in the area is somewhat understandable given issues of cost and access that typically plague cross-national and cross-cultural studies. Investigations of social class issues are especially difficult because class is a relational rather than a fixed concept, possessing a fluidity that complicates attempts to compare empirical data. In addition, the existence of radically different economies where mechanisms governing income distribution, ownership of land and property, and the determination of occupational status are varied and can hinder comparative efforts.

Finally, the comparativist must confront the existence of dual economies in rural and urban areas, and/or underground economies that are more powerful than their formal counterparts, all of which serve to impede the completion of her or his task.

Nonetheless, significant preliminary work in this area has progressed under the direction of Erik Olin Wright and his associates, who in their Comparative Project on Class Structure and Class Consciousness have used quantitative methods to compare class structures, class definition, class boundaries, and class consciousness in eleven countries. In one of the group's most interesting findings (Wright et al., 1989), where class relationships in Sweden and the United States are compared, it is argued that three distinct ideological coalitions exist in Sweden, but only two exist in the United States. The authors attribute this difference to the ability of the Swedish middle classes to distinguish themselves from the bourgeoisie, and the ability of the Swedish working class to carve out its own distinctive niche. In the United States, however, the ethos of the bourgeoisie permeates further into middle-class contradictory class locations, while working-class consciousness is absorbed by prevailing middle-class ideological orientations. The authors conclude that expansive state employment in Sweden has allowed that country's middle class to articulate a distinctive class boundary, while the existence of strong trade unionism and a deep division between blue- and white-collar labor has similarly influenced the Swedish working class. These structural factors are not present in the U.S. case. One would hope that comparative educators would attempt to conduct similar studies with reference to the impact of educational structures on class formation. However, interest in these lines has not been overwhelming.

COMPARATIVE EDUCATION AND ANALYSES OF CLASS

Comparative educators, in their efforts to investigate foreign educational systems and policies, often place themselves in the role of outsider looking in. That stance creates a presumption of objectivity, derived from the physical and affective distance implicit in the role. As a result, the personal dimension of educational policy and practice is often lost. By hiding behind the presumed objectivity of positivist language, or remaining content to describe broad trends and policies rather than seeking to discover their multilayered influences and conflicts, the basic humanity of educational experience can easily be denied.

When anthropological methods of inquiry are employed, they tend to revert to relativistic descriptions of specific cases without attention being paid to larger and more complicated reference points. The theories used to contextualize the cases are often based on accepted Western premises, themselves derived from context-specific situations that are conveniently forgotten when application to the foreign case is made. This author, for example, has in previous work (Epstein, 1983) attempted to define Chinese curricular and pedagogical change in Bernstein's and Bourdieu's terms, without deference to the "Britishness" or "Frenchness'' of these authors' respective writings. The diversity with which various cultural groups, particularly those living in the developing world, conceive of basic concepts of time, space, and distance, as well as their divergent patterns of thinking and knowing, remain underappreciated (Masemann, 1990). Even native researchers, who analyze educational issues within their own countries for a comparative audience, are forced into accepting predominant Western social science methodologies, and the assumptions that accompany their use, in order to gain acceptance from the comparative education community for the legitimacy of their work. To the extent that one cannot investigate issues of class without demonstrating some degree of social concern with respect to the nature of repression and domination, how class affiliation occurs, the power of ideological belief-systems, and so on, these tendencies can be considered impediments to a serious investigation of class issues.

For many who study and practice comparative education, the field is thought to be useful for the policymaking implications that naturally generate from the research. Reform-minded practitioners look to foreign contexts to make the case for policy change domestically, but they often fail to address or overcome their own class biases in the process. The American fascination with Japanese student achievement, for example, must be viewed in terms of the economic productivity that country's educational system is assumed to promote, and the accompanying fear of long-term U.S. economic decline. But the comparison between Japanese and American educational systems becomes insidious as soon as one realizes what must be compromised in order to conduct the comparison in the first place. The heterogeneity of the U.S. school population with particular reference to its ethnicity, class, and religious diversity, the degree of geographical mobility within our society, distinctive family socialization patterns, and so on, are all factors that must be necessarily underplayed, if not ignored, for the comparative analysis to proceed.

It is equally instructive to note what we fail to compare. We are aware, for example, of the fact that mortality rates and life expectancy figures for those aged five to sixty-five living in Harlem are worse than those for natives living in Bangladesh (McCord and Freeman, 1990), yet comparative analyses of New York and Bangladeshi schooling, or even more appropriately, inner city and Third World schooling in the general sense, have not been forthcoming. Nor have American researchers sought to view the discrepancies between suburban and urban educational realities as our own version of educational apartheid, deserving of comparison with the South African counterpart, although such a comparative study might prove interesting, especially with changing demographic trends that have contributed to increasing minority student enrollments and shrinking property tax bases in inner city schools. Although ethnicity and education and gender and education themes have been topics of serious comparative inquiry, rarely do such studies include class analyses. In the former case particularly, minority-ethnic relations are usually described in interest group politics rather than class conflict terms (La Belle and White, 1980; Wirt, 1979).

John Ogbu (1978, 1983) has described ethnic relations in the United States as being caste-like in the generic sense. The perspective is provocative and probably deserves further comparative study.

The lack of attention that comparative educators have paid to issues of class should not imply that serious themes have not been pursued over the past decade or that the research agendas of comparative educators lack purpose. Insightful discussions of the politics of centralization and decentralization efforts (McGinn and Street, 1986), the nature of bureaucratic networking through cultivation of personal relations (Plank, 1990), the impact of examination reform (Eckstein and Noah, 1989), socialization and civic education patterns in developing countries (Torney-Purta and Schwille, 1986), and attempts at teacher empowerment through school-based management reform (Hansen, 1990) are a few of the important themes that have been intelligently discussed over the past few years. Void of a class perspective, however, the research is limited in its portrayal of the dynamism of social conflict, or its larger implications.

A FUTURE RESEARCH AGENDA

A prospective research agenda for the future would build on many of the themes enumerated in this chapter but with a specific focus in mind. As has been noted, comparative educators have recognized the importance of examining theories of the state, as a means of understanding the political context under which policymaking occurs. Further research in this area would concentrate on the specific conditions under which state bureaucracies are controlled or remain independent from dominant class interests. At what point and under what circumstances do they compromise popular mandates to serve specific class interests? How are teacher roles affected by recruitment schemes, entry qualifications, unionism, and professional status considerations? And how does their class background mesh with that of their students, students' parents, and/or members of the state educational bureaucracy? Before one can assume that the teacher can play an active role in agitating for positive social change, it seems important to address these types of questions in detail.

Archer (1979, 1989) has argued, for example, that the structure of an educational system with respect to its centralized or decentralized nature will influence how internal and external interest groups will seek to bring about change, influencing their abilities to use political manipulation, internal initiation, or external transaction strategies in order to negotiate their interests. Decentralized educational systems allow for the latter two strategies to occur; centralized bureaucracies are more likely to be immune to the latter strategies and can only be influenced through political manipulation. Remembering Wright et al.'s analysis of the influence of state bureaucracy on class position in Sweden and the United States, it would be interesting for the comparative educator to extend Archer's analysis by looking at how teachers define their own class affiliations, examining issues of ideological and professional cohesiveness and teacher–civil servant, teacher–community relations in centralized and decentralized educational systems.

If we are going to seriously examine issues of the state and educational reform, it seems crucial to examine the educational provisions for the stateless, or refugees. Focusing on issues of class also implies investigating the education of the underclass, or street children and the homeless, on a comparative basis.

An investigation of class formation and cohesiveness would dictate that the comparative researcher look at the implications of educational attainment and credentialism, not only on occupational mobility and professional status, but on marriage and friendship ties, as well as leisure and recreational pursuits. Schools must be analyzed as institutions that not only reproduce class affiliation, but also help define class boundaries and class distances.

Above all, class analysis demands that issues of class consciousness be rethought or examined more carefully, with specific regard to school processes. Although it may be overly simplistic to make a direct association with the expansion of schooling and democratic inclusiveness, given the conditions under which such expansion typically occurs in the developing world—inadequate teacher training, poor materials and facilities, exorbitant student-teaching ratios, teaching strategies that rely on traditional forms of rote memorization and irrelevant curricula—it would be equally fallacious to deny the possibilities of educational empowerment categorically, or to assume that all educational reform must be inherently hegemonic. One could use some of the tools of analysis employed by advocates of critical pedagogy to examine comparative school cultures and their impact on cultural reproduction, without necessarily succumbing to the fallacies of cultural or social determinism that have been previously discussed.

Serious investigations of class consciousness must reexamine issues of educational socialization and resistance. Under what conditions is withdrawal from school indicative of resistance to the dominant values schools attempt to reinforce? Under what conditions does school withdrawal indicate subservience to market forces or dominant class interests? To what extent do alternative forms to traditional educational practices such as popular and nonformal educational initiatives represent examples of class resistance or class consciousness? Carlos Torres (1990) has begun to explore these issues with reference to Latin America. Much more work can and should be pursued. Given the degree of linguistic and cultural diversity that exists within the developing world, critical pedagogues need not rely on the incorporation of popular culture forms alone, to find evidence of curricular and pedagogical democratization or, conversely, authoritarianism and cultural imperialism. Comparativists can make a substantial contribution in this area by chronicling the ways in which indigenous cultural forms are used, abused, or ignored within school settings. Eisemon, Hallett, and Maundu's (1986) study of African folk tales and their use within the formal Kenyan school curriculum is one example of such a focus, although the authors do not use the theoretical frameworks of critical pedagogy to arrive at their conclusions.

CONCLUSION

Comparative educators and cultural theorists have for some time argued that the use of critical ethnography to study comparative issues could prove to be enlightening (Masemann, 1982; Quantz and O'Connor, 1988). Cultural anthropologists have made similar claims with reference to the methods that can be employed to extend our knowledge of the state in the developing world (Foley and Yambert, 1989). This chapter has echoed these sentiments in calling for a class analysis of educational policies, practices, and reform efforts. It has assumed that any discussion of educational reform must address fundamental issues of power: the degree and extent of social inclusivity, and the terms under which domination, repression, and conflict are expressed with respect to the decision-making process and forms of implementation. It has argued that the use of social class as an analytical tool in its widest sense can play a useful role in extending our knowledge of important educational processes, particularly those that occur within school settings. Although these issues continue to influence American educational scholarship, they have only been intermittently explored in the comparative education field. The rectification of this omission remains a worthy goal for those who are seriously concerned about the ramifications of educational change on a comparative basis.

REFERENCES

Altbach, Philip G. 1977, May. "Servitude of the Mind: Education, Dependency and Neo-colonialism." *Teachers College Record* 79:188–204.
———. 1982. "The Distribution of Knowledge in the Third World." In *Higher Education in the Third World: Themes and Variations*, ed. Philip G. Altbach. Singapore: Maruzen.
Apple, Michael W. 1979. *Ideology and Curriculum*. Boston: Routledge and Kegan Paul.
———. 1983. "Curricular Form and the Logic of Technical Control." In *Ideology and Practice in Schooling*, ed. Michael W. Apple and Lois Weis. Philadelphia: Temple University, pp. 143–165.
Archer, Margaret S. 1979. *Social Origins of Educational Systems*. London: Sage.
———. 1988. *Culture and Agency: The Place of Culture in Social Theory*. Cambridge: Cambridge University Press.
———. 1989. "Cross-National Research and the Analysis of Educational Systems." In *Cross-National Research in Sociology*, ed. Melvin L. Kohn. Newbury Park, Calif.: Sage, pp. 242–262.
Arnove. Robert F. 1980, February. "Comparative Education and World Systems Analysis." *Comparative Education Review* 24:48–62.
Bakhtin, M. M. 1981. *The Dialogic Imagination*, ed. Cayl Emerson and Michael Holquist. Austin: University of Texas.
Berman, Edward. 1979, May. "Foundations, United States Foreign Policy and African Education." *Harvard Educational Review* 49:145–179.
Bernstein, Basil. 1971. *Class, Codes and Control, Vol. 1: Theoretical Studies Towards a Sociology of Language*. London: Routledge and Kegan Paul.

———. 1975. *Class, Codes and Control, Vol. 3: Toward a Theory of Educational Transmission*. London: Routledge and Kegan Paul.

Boggs, Carl. 1984. *The Two Revolutions: Gramsci and the Dilemmas of Western Marxism*. Boston: South End Press.

Bourdieu, Pierre. 1984. *Distinction*. Cambridge, Mass.: Harvard University Press.

———. 1988. *Homo Academicus*. Stanford, Calif.: Stanford University.

———, and Jean-Claude Passeron. 1977. *Education, Society and Culture*. Beverly Hills, Calif.: Sage.

Bowles, Samuel, and Herbert Gintis. 1976. *Schooling in Capitalist America*. New York: Basic Books.

Carnoy, Martin. 1990a. "The State and Social Transformation." In *Education and Social Transition in the Third World*, ed. Martin Carnoy and Joel Samoff with Mary Ann Burris, Anton Johnston, and Carlos Torres. Princeton, N.J.: Princeton University, pp. 15–61.

———. 1990b. "Education and the Transition State." In *Education and Social Transition in the Third World*, ed. Martin Carnoy and Joel Samoff with Mary Ann Burris, Anton Johnston, and Carlos Torres. Princeton, N.J.: Princeton University, pp. 63–96.

———, and Henry Levin. 1985. *Schooling and Work in the Democratic State*. Stanford, Calif.: Stanford University.

Cherryholmes, Cleo H. 1988. *Power and Criticism: Poststructural Investigations in Education*. New York: Teachers College Press.

Eckstein, Max A., and Harold J. Noah. 1989, August. "Forms and Functions of Secondary-School Leaving Examinations." *Comparative Education Review* 33:295–316.

Eisemon, Thomas Owen, Martin Hallett, and John Maundu. 1986, May. "Primary School Literature and Folktales in Kenya: What Makes a Children's Story African?" *Comparative Education Review* 30:232–246.

Epstein, Irving. 1983. "The Politics of Curricular Change." In *Education and Social Change in the People's Republic of China*, ed. John N. Hawkins. New York: Praeger, pp. 77–96.

Foley, Michael W., and Karl Yambert. 1989. "Anthropology and Theories of the State." In *State, Capital and Rural Society: Anthropological Perspectives on Political Economy in Mexico and the Andes*, ed. Benjamin S. Orlove, Michael W. Foley, and Thomas F. Love. Boulder, Colo.: Westview, pp. 39–67.

Freire, Paulo. 1970. *Pedagogy of the Oppressed*. New York: Seabury.

Ginsburg, Mark, and Susan Cooper, Rajeshwari Raghu, and Hugo Zegarra. 1990, November. "National and World-System Explanations of Educational Reform." *Comparative Education Review* 34:474–499.

Giroux, Henry. 1981. *Ideology, Culture and the Process of Schooling*. Philadelphia: Temple University.

———. 1983. *Theory and Resistance in Education*. London: Heinemann Education Books.

———. 1988a. *Teachers as Intellectuals*. Granby, Mass.: Bergin and Garvey.

———. 1988b. *Schooling and the Struggle for Public Life: Critical Pedagogy in the Modern Age*. Minneapolis: University of Minnesota Press.

———, and Roger Simon. 1989. "Popular Culture and Critical Pedagogy: Everyday Life as a Basis for Curriculum Knowledge." In *Critical Pedagogy, the State and*

Cultural Struggle, ed. Henry Giroux and Peter McLaren. Albany: State University of New York Press, pp. 236–252.

Hanson, E. Mark. 1990, November. "School Based Management and Educational Reform in the United States and Spain." *Comparative Education Review* 34: 523–537.

LaBelle, Thomas J., and Peter S. White. 1980, May. "Education and Multiethnic Integration: An Intergroup-Relations Typology." *Comparative Education Review* 24:155–173.

McCord, Colin, and Harold P. Freeman. 1990, January 18. "Excess Mortality in Harlem." *New England Journal of Medicine* 322:173–177.

McGinn, Noel and Susan Street. 1986, November. "Educational Decentralization: Weak State or Strong State?" *Comparative Education Review* 30:471–490.

McLaren, Peter. 1986. *Schooling as a Ritual Performance*. Boston: Routledge and Kegan Paul.

MacLeod, Jay. 1987. *Ain't No Makin' It: Leveled Aspirations in a Low-Income Neighborhood*. Boulder, Colo.: Westview.

Masemann, Vandra Lea. 1982, February. "Critical Ethnography in the Study of Comparative Education." *Comparative Education Review* 26:1–15.

———. 1990, November. "Ways of Knowing: Implications for Comparative Education." *Comparative Education Review* 34:465–473.

O'Brien, Mary. 1987. "Education and Patriarchy." In *Critical Pedagogy and Cultural Power*, ed. David Livingstone et al. South Hadley, Mass.: Bergin and Garvey, pp. 41–54.

Offe, Claus. 1975. "The Theory of the Capitalist State and the Problem of Policy Formation." In *Stress and Contradiction in Modern Capitalism*, ed. Leon N. Lindberg, Robert Alford, Colin Crouch and Claus Offe. Lexington, Mass.: D. C. Heath, pp. 125–144.

Ogbu, John. 1978. *Minority Education and Caste: The American System in Cross-cultural Perspective*. New York: Academic Press.

———. 1983, June. "Minority Status and Schooling in Plural Societies." *Comparative Education Review* 27:168–190.

Plank, David N. 1990, November. "The Politics of Basic Educational Reform in Brazil." *Comparative Education Review* 34:538–559.

Poulantzas, Nicos. 1978. *State, Power, Socialism*. London: New Left Books.

Quantz, Richard A., and Terrence O'Connor. 1988. "Writing Critical Ethnography: Dialogue, Multivoicedness, and Carnival in Cultural Contexts." *Educational Theory* 38 (Winter):95–109.

Sorj, Bernardo. 1983. "The State, the Bourgeoisie and Imperialism in the Light of the Peruvian Experience." In *Military Reformism and Social Class*, ed. David Booth and Bernardo Sorj. London: Macmillan, pp. 185–204.

Torney-Purta, Judith, and John Schwille. 1986, February. "Civic Values Learned in School: Policy and Practice in Industrialized Nations." *Comparative Education Review* 30:30–49.

Torres, Carlos Alberto. 1990. *The Politics of Nonformal Education in Latin America*. New York: Praeger.

Weiler, Hans N. 1983. "West Germany: Educational Policy as Compensatory Legitimation." In *Politics and Education*, ed. R. Murray Thomas. New York: Pergamon Press, pp. 34–54.

―――. 1984, May. "The Political Dilemmas of Foreign Study." *Comparative Education Review* 28:168–179.

―――. 1988, August. "The Politics of Reform and Nonreform in French Education." *Comparative Education Review* 32:251–265.

Weiler, Kathleen. 1988. *Women Teaching for Change: Gender, Class and Power*. South Hadley, Mass.: Bergin and Garvey.

Williams, Raymond. 1980. "Base and Superstructure in Marxist Cultural Theory." In *Problems in Materialism and Culture*. London: Verso, pp. 31–49.

Willis, Paul. 1977. *Learning to Labour*. New York: Columbia University Press.

Wirt, Frederick M. 1979, February. "The Stranger Within My Gate: Ethnic Minorities and School Policy in Europe." *Comparative Education Review* 23:17–40.

Wright, Erik Olin. 1978. *Crisis and the State*. London: New Left Books.

―――, Carolyn Howe, and Donmoon Cho. 1989. "Class Structure and Class Formation: A Comparative Analysis of the United States and Sweden." In *Cross-National Research in Sociology*, ed. Melvin Kohn. Newbury, Calif.: Sage, pp. 185–217.

SELECTED BIBLIOGRAPHY

Altbach, Philip G., Robert F. Armour, and Gail P. Kelly, eds. 1982. *Comparative Education.* New York: Macmillan.

Andreski, Stanislav. 1965. *The Uses of Comparative Sociology.* Berkeley: University of California Press.

Archer, Margaret. 1979. *Social Origins of Educational Systems.* London: Sage Publications.

Archer, Margaret, and Edmund J. King. 1980, June. "Macro-Sociology and Comparative Education: Two Points of View." In *Comparative Education* 16(2):179–195.

Armer, Michael. 1973. "Methodological Problems and Possibilities in Comparative Research." In *Comparative Social Research*, ed. Michael Armer and Allen Grimshaw. New York: John Wiley, pp. 49–70.

Bendix, Reinhard. 1977. *Nation-Building and Citizenship: Studies of Our Changing Social Order.* Berkeley: University of California Press.

Broadfoot, Patricia, and Margaret B. Sutherland eds. 1987. "Sex Differences in Education." *Comparative Education* 23(1): whole issue—special issue (10).

Cárceles, Gabriel. 1990, February. "Word Literacy Prospects at the Turn of the Century: Is the Objective of Literacy for All by the Year 2000 Statistically Plausible." *Comparative Education Review* 34:4–20.

Chapman, David W., and Roger A. Boothroyd. 1988, November. "Threats to Data-Quality in Developing Country Settings." *Comparative Education Review* 32:416–425.

Cheng, Kai Ming. 1986. "China's Recent Education Reform: The Beginning of an Overhaul." *Comparative Education* 22(3):255–269.

Collins, Randall. 1979. *The Credential Society.* Orlando, Fla.: Academic Press.

Comparative Education Review—Cumulative Index Volumes 1–33, 1957–1989. Edited by Philip G. Altbach, Harold J. Noah, and Gail P. Kelly.

Comparative Education Review. 1990, August. "Colloquy on Comparative Theory." 34:369–404.

Comparative Education Review. 1991, May. "Survey of Events 1990." 35:383–398.

Coombs, Philip H. 1985. *The World Crisis in Education: The View from the Eighties*. New York: Oxford University Press.

Crossley, Michael, and Graham Vulliamy. 1984. "Case-Study Research Methods and Comparative Education." *Comparative Education* 20(2): 193–207.

Curtis, Bruce. 1988, August. "Patterns of Resistance to Public Education: England, Ireland and Canada West, 1830–1890." *Comparative Education Review* 32:318–333.

Delacroix, Jacques, and Charles Ragin. 1978. "Modernizing Institutions, Mobilization, and Third World Development: A Cross-National Study." *American Journal of Sociology* 84:123–150.

Eckstein, Max A. 1983, October. "The Comparative Mind (Presidential Address)." *Comparative Education Review* 27:311–322.

Evans, Peter. 1979. *Dependent Development: The Alliance of Multinational, State, and Local Capital in Brazil*. Princeton, N.J.: Princeton University Press.

Fafunwa, A., and J. Aisuku, eds. 1982. *Education in Africa*. London: George Allen and Unwin.

Geertz, Clifford. 1963. *Old Societies and New States: The Quest for Modernity in Asia and Africa*. New York: Free Press.

Ginsburg, Mark B., Susan Cooper, Rajeshwari Raghu, and Hugo Zegarra. 1990, November. "National and World-System Explanations of Educational Reform." *Comparative Education Review* 34:474–499.

Hackett, Peter. 1988, November. "Aesthetics as a Dimension for Comparative Study (Presidential Address)." *Comparative Education Review* 32:389–399.

Holmes, Brian. 1984, November. "Paradigm Shifts in Comparative Education." *Comparative Education Review* 28:584–604.

Hopkins, Terence, and Immanuel Wallerstein. 1970. "The Comparative Study of National Societies." In *Comparative Perspectives: Theories and Methods*, eds. Amitai Etzioni and Fredric Dubow. Boston: Little, Brown, pp. 183–204.

Husen, Torsten. 1989. "The Swedish School Reform—Exemplary Both Ways." *Comparative Education* 25(3):345–355.

Ignas, Edward, and Raymond J. Corsini. 1981. *Comparative Educational Systems*. Itasca, Ill.: F. E. Peacock.

Inkeles, Alex, and David Smith. 1974. *Becoming Modern: Individual Change in Six Developing Countries*. Cambridge, Mass.: Harvard University Press.

Judge, Harry G. 1988, May. "Cross-National Perceptions of Teachers." *Comparative Education Review* 32:143–158.

Kelly, Gail P. 1987. "Setting State Policy on Women's Education in the Third World: Perspectives from Comparative Research." *Comparative Education* 23 (1):95–102.

Kelly, Gail P., and Philip G. Altbach. 1986, February. "Comparative Education: Challenge and Response." *Comparative Education Review* 30:89–107.

La Belle, Thomas J., and Christopher R. Ward. 1990. "Educating Reform: When Nations Undergo Radical Political and Social Radical Transformation." *Comparative Education* 26 (1):95–106.

McGinn, Noel, and Susan Street. 1986, November. "Educational Decentralization: Weak State or Strong State." *Comparative Education Review* 30:471–490.

Masemann, Vandra L. 1990, November. "Ways of Knowing: Implications for Comparative Education." (Presidential Address). *Comparative Education Review* 34:465–473.

Massialas, B. G., and S. A. Jarrar. 1983. *Education in the Arab World*. New York: Praeger.

Maynes, Mary Jo. 1985. *Schooling in Western Europe: A Social History*. Albany: State University of New York Press.

Meyer, John W., Francisco O. Ramirez, Richard Rubinson, and John Boli-Bennett. 1977. "The World Educational Revolution, 1950–1970." *Sociology of Education* 50:242–258.

Meyer, John W., David Tyack, Joane Nagel, and Audri Gordon. 1979. "Public Education as Nation-Building in America: Enrollments and Bureaucratization in the American States, 1870–1930." *American Journal of Sociology* 85:591–613.

Moore, Barrington, Jr. 1966. *The Social Origins of Dictatorship and Democracy: Lord and Peasant in the Making of the Modern World*. Boston: Beacon.

Nikandrov, Nikolai D. 1989. "What to Compare, When and Why: A Soviet Perspective." *Comparative Education* 25(3):275–282.

Paulson, Rolland G. 1990, May. "Toward a Reflective Comparative Education—An Essay Review." *Comparative Education Review* 34:248–255.

Ragin, Charles. 1987. *The Comparative Method*. Berkeley: University of California Press.

Ragin, Charles, and David Zaret. 1983. "Theory and Method in Comparative Research: Two Strategies." *Social Forces* 61:731–754.

Ramirez, Francisco O., and John Boli. 1987. "The Political Construction of Mass Schooling: European Origins and Worldwide Institutionalization." *Sociology of Education* 60:2–18.

Skocpol, Theda. 1979. *States and Social Revolutions: A Comparative Analysis of France, Russia, and China*. Cambridge: Cambridge University Press.

Spaulding, Seth. 1988. "Prescriptions for Educational Reform: Dilemmas of the Real World." *Comparative Education* 24(1):5–17.

Thomas, George, John W. Meyer, Francisco O. Ramirez, and John Boli. 1987. *Institutional Structure: Constituting State, Society, and the Individual*. Beverly Hills, Calif.: Sage Publications.

Wallerstein, Immanuel. 1974. *The Modern World System: Capitalist Agriculture and the Origins of the European World Economy in the Sixteenth Century*. New York: Academic Press.

———. 1980. *The Modern World-System II: Mercantilism and the Consolidation of the European World-Economy 1600–1750*. New York: Academic Press.

———. 1984. *The Politics of the World-Economy: The States, the Movements and the Civilizations*. Cambridge: Cambridge University Press.

Welch, Anthony R. 1985. "The Functionalist Tradition and Comparative Education." *Comparative Education* 21(1):5–19.

INDEX

Abortion, 326
Academic career: in Colombia, 123–25; women academics, 555–56
Academic freedom in Brazil, 64, 65
Academic success. *See* Achievement level
Academy of Pedagogical Sciences (APS) in USSR, 476, 478, 481, 482, 484, 487
Academy of Sciences (USSR), 478, 486, 487
Accelerated Elementary School (Nicaragua), 395
Accessibility, Canadian reforms of 1980s and, 75, 76–77
Acción Popular (Peru), 418
Accountability, U.S. reforms of 1980s and, 454
Achievement level: family background and, 246, 332; in Mexico, 372–74; U.S. reforms of 1980s and, 454; in Zimbabwe, 531–32, 534–35

Achievement tests in Israel, 309. *See also* Examinations
Adler, Mortimer, 454
Administration, school: in China, reform of, 100–102, 109; models of, 468–69
Adult Basic Education Centers (Mexico), 366
Adult education: in Argentina, 30; in Brazil, 64; in Egypt, 164; in Kenya, 351; in Mexico, 362, 366, 377; in Yugoslavia, 514–15
Advanced Supplementary Examination (AS level), 244
Affirmative action, 548
African National Congress (ANC), 431, 435
Aiiku-han, 326
Ain Shams University, 159
Al-Azhar Mosque (Cairo), 149
Al-Azhar University, 159, 161
Alexander, Lamar, 455
Alfonsín, Raúl, 20, 34, 35

Benavides Muñoz, Jose, 422
Bennett, William, 465
Bernstein, Basil, 562–64
Bestor, Arthur, 446–47
Betancourt, President, 120
Bilingualism in Canada, 73–74
Blackburn, Jean, 41, 44
Blackburn review of postcompulsory
schooling in Australia, 41–44
Blacks, education of: in Cuba, 135, 136;
in U.S., 449–51, 452. *See also*
Minority groups, education of; South
Africa, education in; Zimbabwe,
education in
Bloch Commission (1984, France), 179–
80
Block grants, 412
Bloom, Allan, 461
Bosnia-Herzegovina, 495, 500, 510
Boston: controlled-choice plan in, 458;
desegregation conflicts in, 451
Boston Compact (1982), 459
Bought Places Scheme (Hong Kong), 246
Bourdieu, Pierre, 562–64
Bowles, Samuel, 562
Brazil, education in, 51–67; adult, 64;
during coup of 1964 and military
regime, 56–58, 59; long-term historical
forces and factors framing, 51–54;
national development and, 57; from
1920–1963, 54–56; from 1964–1978,
56–58; from 1979–1989, 58–65;
preschool, 64; primary, 55, 59, 60;
private, 55; secondary, 54–55, 59–60;
teacher training, 62; technical, 55, 56;
tertiary, 57, 59–61; U.S. and, 56, 57;
women academics in, 555
Brazilian Democratic Movement Party,
61
Brazilian Society of Researchers and
Scientists (SBPC), 64
Brezhnev Doctrine of limited sovereignty,
498
Brezhnev era, 477
Brigades for Rural Development
(Mexico), 367
Britain. *See* Great Britain
British Foreign School Society, 210

British North America Act of 1867, 71
British South Africa Company, 523
Brizola, Leonel, 61, 62
Bronfenbrenner, Urie, 474
Brown v. *Topeka Board of Education*,
450, 451
Budget, education. *See* Financing of
education
Buildings. *See* Facilities, school
Bulgaria, women's enrollment in tertiary
education in, 550
Burakumin, 337–38
Burundi, sex segregation within
universities in, 553
Bury, J. B., 2
Bush, G., 444, 456, 468
Business, partnerships between education
and: in France, 179–80; in U.S., 458–
59, 467. *See also* Industry, education
and
Business/Higher Education Forum (U.S.),
454
Busing: in Israel, 313; in U.S., 451

Cairo University, 159
California Commission on the Teaching
Profession, 463
Callaghan, James, 212
Calmon Amendment (1984), 60
Cambridge Higher School Certificate,
346, 351
Cambridge School Certificate, 351
Campaign Against Illiteracy (Cuba), 139–
41
Canada, education in, 69–96; anticipating
1990s and, 84–87; diversity and, 72,
73–74, 75, 77, 86–87; educational
reformers and, 80–84; geography and,
72, 73, 75, 76–77, 86; national trends
in 1980s in, 74–77; pervading themes
in society and, 72–74; power and, 72–
73, 74–76, 85–86, 87; primary, 72; as
provincial system, 71–72; secondary,
72; sources on, 70–71; teachers' place
in reform of, 69–70, 77–84, 85, 87–
88; tertiary, women's enrollment in,
550
Cantonese (Guangdonghua), 211, 243

ABOUT THE CONTRIBUTORS

MORDECAI ARIELI is a lecturer at the Tel Aviv University School of Education and the chairman of the Educational Administration Program. Among his publications is "Cultural Transition Through Total Education: Actor's Perspectives," in M. Gottesman, ed., *Cultural Transition of Youth: The Israeli Case* (Jerusalem).

PETER W. COOKSON, JR., is the associate dean of the School of Education at Adelphi University. He is coauthor, with Caroline Hodges Persell, of *Preparing for Power: America's Elite Boarding Schools* (1985) and *Making Sense of Society* (forthcoming), and with Alan R. Sadovnik and Susan F. Semel, of *Exploring Education* (forthcoming). He has written numerous scholarly and popular articles and is currently at work on a book about school choice.

ROBERT COWEN is chairperson of the Department of International and Comparative Education in the University of London Institute of Education. His most recent work has been on cross-cultural comparisons of the evaluation and management of higher education systems, with special reference to quality control.

BETTY JO DORSEY is associate professor of sociology of education at the University of Zimbabwe. Her recent research focuses on gender inequalities in higher education in Zimbabwe. An ongoing research project is a panel longitudinal study of high school graduates, "The Class of 1971," which looks at aspirations, academic achievement, and employment.

IRVING EPSTEIN is an assistant professor of education and head of the Education Department at Lafayette College. He is an associate editor of the *Com-*

parative Education Review and serves on the editorial advisory committee of *Chinese Education*. His edited volume, *Chinese Education: Problems, Policies and Prospects*, has recently been published.

MARIA FIGUEIREDO is the Brazilian Lektor in the University of London Institute of Education where she concentrates on maintaining liaison between Brazilian universities and the London Institute. Her publications have included articles on curriculum reform in Brazil, higher education and academic freedom, and the social construction of educational excellence in Brazil.

MARK B. GINSBURG is director of the Institute for International Studies in Education and professor in the Administrative and Policy Studies Department, School of Education, and the Department of Sociology at the University of Pittsburgh. His research interests focus on the ideology and practice of educators as workers and political actors and the connections between education and unequal class, race, gender, and international relations. Recent publications include *Educational Reform in Global Context: Economy and Ideology* (1991) and *Contradictions in Teacher Education and Society: A Critical Analysis* (1988).

SYDNEY R. GRANT is a professor at the Florida State University's College of Education where he teaches in the Deparment of Educational Foundations and Policy Studies, specializing in international-intercultural development education. Dr. Grant received his Ed.D. from Teachers College, Columbia University. He teaches courses in education and development, anthropology applied to education, comparative education, and the role of the consultant.

JOHN N. HAWKINS is professor of comparative and international education at UCLA. He has served as director of UCLA's International Studies and Overseas Programs (ISOP) since 1987 and has recently been named dean of ISOP. After receiving his Ph.D. from Vanderbilt University, he joined the faculty of the UCLA Graduate School of Education in 1973. His current research focuses on the transformation of rural educaton in Asia. He has written or edited fourteen books and fifty articles on education, health, and political issues, including *Education and Intergroup Relations: An International Perspective*, which was named "one of the most outstanding books in recent years" by the American Educational Studies Association.

HAROLD D. HERMAN is professor and dean of education at the University of the Western Cape in Bellville, South Africa.

REESE HUGHES has done graduate and postgraduate research on education in Kenya at Humboldt State University, Arcata, California. He has specialized on issues related to Kenyan higher education and has published articles in the *Comparative Education Review*, *NASPA Journal*, *Kenya Journal of Education*, and *World Development*. He is currently examining the implications of the tremendous expansion of postsecondary education in sub-Saharan Africa.

SAMIR A. JARRAR is the chief executive officer of the Educational Development Group, International. Besides serving on the faculties of Florida State, University of South Florida, and Kuwait University, he has held visiting professorial appointments at Georgetown and George Washington universities. He co-authored *Education in the Arab World* (Praeger, 1983), and *Arab Education in Transition* (1991), and contributed chapters on education in different Arab countries.

YITZHAK KASHTI is an associate professor at the Tel Aviv University School of Education and chairman of its Sociology of Education Program. Among his publications is *The Socializing Community* (1979).

CATHY C. KAUFMAN is an assistant professor at Indiana University of Pennsylvania in the Department of Professional Studies in Education. She has conducted both ethnographic and policy evaluation research in Eastern Europe.

GAIL P. KELLY was professor and chair of the Department of Educational Organization, Administration, and Policy at the State University of New York at Buffalo. She wrote extensively on education in colonial Vietnam, with articles appearing in the *British Journal of Sociology of Education*, *Comparative Education Review*, *Comparative Education*, and *Comparative Studies in Society and History*. She also wrote extensively on women and was coauthor of *Women's Education in the Third World: Comparative Perspectives* and *Feminist Scholarship: Kindling in the Groves of Academe*.

STEPHEN T. KERR is associate dean for Professional Programs and Professor of Education in the College of Education at the University of Washington. He holds a Ph.D. from the University of Washington (Educational Technology). His work on the Soviet Union has dealt with reforms of the educational system on various levels, attempts to make students in the USSR "computer literate," and the emergence of nonformal organizations of educators under conditions of *perestroika*. His research on technology in education focuses on the ways in which new technologies affect patterns of social organization within educational organizations.

MARY ANN LARSEN-PUSEY is professor of education at Fresno Pacific College in Fresno, California, and received her Ph.D. in education in 1988 from the joint program offered through San Diego State University and the Claremont Graduate School. Her dissertation was based on a national survey of full-time professors in Colombian public universities funded by the Organization of American States. She has studied, taught, and conducted research in Colombia since 1966.

GEORGE A. MALE, a past president of the Comparative and International Education Society, is director of the Comparative Education Center, University of Maryland, and professor of comparative education. His publications include *Issues in the Education of Minorities: Education in France*; *Teacher Training in Belgium, Luxembourg and the Netherlands*; and *The Struggle for Power: Who Controls the Schools in England and the United States*. He coedited *Religion, Education and Government: A Worldwide View of Policy Issues*.

BYRON G. MASSIALAS is professor of education and multicultural studies at Florida State University, Tallahassee. He has conducted research in the Arab countries of the Eastern Mediterranean region. He is author or coauthor of several books, including *Education and the Political System, Teaching Creatively, Education in the Arab World*, and *Arab Education in Transition*. He is currently working on a study in the region to examine the influence of the hidden curriculum on student learning.

GOLNAR MEHRAN is assistant professor of education at Al-Zahra University, Tehran, Iran. She specializes in comparative and international education, with emphasis on education in the Middle East and issues of literacy and female education. She is a member of the planning committee and editorial board of the International Institute for Adult Literacy Methods. She is author of several publications on education in postrevolutionary Iran, ideology, and education in the Islamic Republic, and female schooling and training in Iran.

WOLFGANG MITTER holds a Ph.D. from the Free University of Berlin and is director of the Research Board of the German Institute for International Educational Research at Frankfurt/Main, and holds a teaching commission at Frankfurt University. He is past president of the Comparative Education Society in Europe (1981–1985), and since July 1990 has been co-president of the World Council of Comparative Education Societies. His publications include numerous books, research reports, essays, and other publications in the area of general and comparative education, with special regard to the educational systems of the Soviet Union and Eastern Europe and to comparisons between the educational systems of Western and Eastern Europe.

ANA MUÑOZ-SANDOVAL has a B.A. in anthropology and an M.A. in higher education from the State University, College at Buffalo. She is presently a doctoral candidate in intercultural education at the University of Southern California.

ILA PATEL has a Ph.D. degree in education from Stanford University. She specializes in policy studies in education and communication in developing countries, media in education, and nonformal education for development and social change. Currently, she is a consultant in the Development and Educational Communication Unit of the Indian Space Research Organization, Ahmedabad (India), for the Project in Radio Education for Adult Literacy. She has contributed to several journals and conferences.

EDUARDO PEÑA DE LA MORA is a tenured professor at the Interdisciplinary Center of Research and Teaching in Technical Education and received his Ph.D. in Foundations of Education, specializing in International/Intercultural Development Studies in Education at Florida State University. He has published several books including *Mechanisms in Engineering*, and *Adult Education in Mexico*, and coauthored *Social Prejudices and Education in Mexico*. He has also published several journal articles on measurement and evaluation in schools, social determinations of evaluation and social compromises in higher education.

ROLLAND G. PAULSTON is a professor of international and development education at the University of Pittsburgh. His teaching and research addresses problems in change theory (*Conflicting Theories of Social and Educational Change*), change policy (*Educational Change in Sweden*), and change practice (*Changing Educational Systems*, and *Other Dreams, Other School*). His current research includes studies of education in social movements, epistemological politics in reform explanation, and the phenomenographic method.

GERARD A. POSTIGLIONE is lecturer and director of Advanced Studies in Education and National Development at the University of Hong Kong and earned his Ph.D. from the State University of New York at Albany. His books include *Ethnicity and American Social Theory: Toward Critical Pluralism*, and *Education and Society in Hong Kong: Toward One Country and Two Systems*. He has published works on education in China, including education of national minorities, and has been guest editor for several issues of *Chinese Education*.

SUSAN RIPPBERGER is a doctoral student in the International and Development Education Program at the University of Pittsburgh. Her research interests include bilingual indigenous education in Mexico and Central America, and educational reform in Nicaragua. With Rolland Paulston, she recently coauthored "Ideological Pluralism in Nicaraguan University Reform," a chapter in *Educational Reform in Global Context*, edited by Mark Ginsburg (1991).

VAL D. RUST is a professor of education at UCLA and served as the president of the Comparative and International Education Society in 1990–1991. He has published widely about educational conditions in Norway, in journals such as *Comparative Education Review*, *Comparative Education*, and *Teaching and*

Teacher Education, and in his book *The Democratic Tradition and the Evolution of Schooling in Norway* (Greenwood Press).

ALAN R. SADOVNIK is an associate professor of education at Adelphi University and received his Ph.D. in sociology from New York University. He is the coeditor of *Exploring Society* (1987), the author of *Equity and Excellence in Higher Education* (forthcoming), and coauthor of *Exploring Education* (forthcoming) as well as the author of numerous articles in professional journals.

SUSAN F. SEMEL is an assistant professor of education at Adelphi University. She received her M.A., Ed.M., and Ed.D. in the history and philosophy of education from Teachers College, Columbia University. She taught history at the Dalton School from 1965 to 1988 and was a recipient of a Klingenstein Fellowship at Columbia University. She is the author of *Dalton School: The History of a Progressive School* (forthcoming), the guest editor of the February 1991 issue of *Pathways*, and coauthor of *Exploring Education* (forthcoming).

RINA SHAPIRA is a professor at the Tel Aviv University Department of Sociology and Anthropology and School of Education. Among her publications is "Understanding Youth Culture Through Autograph Books: The Israeli Case," *American Journal of Folklore* 97/386 (1984), coauthored with H. Herzog.

JAMES J. SHIELDS, JR. is professor and former chair of the Department of Social and Psychological Foundations, City College, City University of New York. He is also chair of the Japanese Initiative Committee and has been visiting research professor at Tokyo Metropolitan University. He is the author of numerous articles and books, including *Japanese Schooling: Patterns of Socialization, Equality and Political Control*; *Problems and Prospects in International Education and Community Development*; and *Foundations of Education: Dissenting Views*.

NIKŠA NIKOLA ŠOLJAN is professor of educational policy studies and international problems of education at the Department of Educational Studies, Faculty of Philosophy, University of Zagreb, in Croatia, Yugoslavia. His most recent publications include *Higher Education in Yugoslavia* and *Higher Education and the World of Work* (coeditor with Hans Georg Schutze). He is editor of *Andragogy* and a member of the Council of the International Bureau of Education, in Geneva.

RICHARD TEESE is a senior lecturer in education in the University of Melbourne. He is currently project director, Data Information and Research Unit in the Ministry of Education in Victoria. He has published papers on urban differences in school completion rates, curriculum placement, and examinations success. In 1984 and 1987 he was *maitre assistant associe* and visiting scholar in the Centre de Sociologie Européenne in Paris. He has written on Catholic education in France and produced a comparative monograph on education and training in France and Australia.

DENNIS THIESSEN is the associate dean of the School of Education at the University of Toronto. His research interests include curriculum change orientations, school-based and classroom-based teacher development, and the experiences of students in educational reform. He is currently writing a book that examines the role of students as junior partners in the collaborative classroom.

GEOFFREY WALFORD is senior lecturer in sociology and education policy at Aston Business School, Aston University, where he is course organizer for the university's Society and Government course. He is the author of *Life in Public Schools* (1985), *Restructuring Universities: Politics and Power in the Management of Change* (1987), and *Privatization and Privilege in Education* (1990). His edited books include *Doing Sociology of Education* (1987), and *Doing Educational Research* (1991). His recent research, *City Technology College* (1991), was coauthored with Henry Miller.